CENSORSHIP OF HISTORICAL THOUGHT

A World Guide, 1945–2000

Antoon De Baets

Foreword by John David Smith

GREENWOOD PRESS
Westport, Connecticut • London

Library of Congress Cataloging-in-Publication Data

Baets, Antoon De, 1955–
   Censorship of historical thought : a world guide, 1945–2000 / by Antoon De Baets ;
foreword by John David Smith.
      p.   cm.
   "Information on the censorship of historical thought and the fate of persecuted
historians in over a hundred and thirty countries since 1945"—Introd.
   Includes bibliographical references and index.
   ISBN 0–313–31193–5 (alk. paper)
      1. Censorship—History—20th century.   2. Freedom of the press—History—20th century.
I. Title.
Z657.B135   2002
363.3'1'0904—dc21   2001023309

British Library Cataloguing in Publication Data is available.

Library of Congress Catalog Card Number: 2001023309
ISBN: 0–313–31193–5

First published in 2002

Greenwood Press, 88 Post Road West, Westport, CT 06881
An imprint of Greenwood Publishing Group, Inc.
www.greenwood.com

Printed in the United States of America

The paper used in this book complies with the
Permanent Paper Standard issued by the National
Information Standards Organization (Z39.48–1984).

10 9 8 7 6 5 4 3 2 1

To the memory of those historians and citizens
concerned with the past who have defended the right to
history, sometimes at the risk of their lives

Contents

Foreword

Though today it is not fashionable for historians to explain what in fact they do, historians worldwide do at least three things. They ask questions, they conduct research to answer them, and they draw conclusions based on their findings. Implicit in their day-to-day work is the assumption that historians will be free to pursue their research critically and honestly and disseminate their conclusions without interruption by authorities. Freedom of inquiry, freedom of information, and freedom of expression always have been at the heart of the historian's craft.

Despite this ideal, the Belgian scholar Dr. Antoon De Baets has written, "From time immemorial, rulers have tried to manipulate the past, discipline historians, and control collective memory." Once they censor historians, governments next construct historical propaganda to replace the excised history. "The aim of censoring regimes," De Baets maintains, "is to purge historiography in order to make it a tool of the ideology justifying the rulers' position of power." Confronted with political censorship, historians must decide whether to collaborate with their government, impose self-censorship (and thus circumscribe their own critical powers), or resist, thereby opening themselves to persecution—physically or professionally, or both.

The prevalence, power, and pathos of historical censorship are captured in De Baets's encyclopedic and carefully organized and executed *Censorship of Historical Thought: A World Guide, 1945–2000*. This is the first systematic and authoritative reference work of its kind and it documents numerous cases of censorship and persecution of historians in more than 130 countries. For years De Baets has monitored instances where historians were persecuted—first from his post with Amnesty International in Costa Rica—and now from his academic appointment at the University of Groningen, the Netherlands, where he regularly circulates his findings globally through the Internet. De Baets ranks among the leading authorities on historical censorship.

Though, as De Baets notes correctly, historians long have recognized the existence of censorship and the persecution of historians, the topic nevertheless has remained shrouded in obscurity and confined to the margins of historiography. Much like the practice of writing history itself, historians have chosen not to document the process of censoring the work of historians—how the fruits of their labors repeatedly have been "erased." Indeed, threats of retaliation or worse have kept many persecuted historians silent. De Baets, however, gives example after example of governments interrupting historians at work—destroying documents, banning their publications, slandering scholars, arresting and imprisoning researchers, even murdering those historians considered to be dissidents, subversives, or traitors.

De Baets organizes the case studies in *Censorship of Historical Thought: A World Guide, 1945–2000* alphabetically by country—from Afghanistan to Zimbabwe. He arranges entries for each country chronologically and provides detailed examples of states expurgating or simply banishing the work of historical scholars. To assist researchers, short introductory statements precede many of the entries. These assess the nature of the persecution in the respective countries over time. Every entry lists the sources De Baets unearthed, thus providing avenues for further inquiry. Cross-references and subject and name indexes provide easy access to the wealth of material De Baets has chronicled.

Historians and others interested in the open and free dissemination of ideas will welcome and value De Baets's work, marveling at the painstaking detail that he has amassed, digested, and organized. They will learn, for example, of the vast banning of books in Malawi from 1968 to 1994, including works on the Russian Revolution, the revolt of Ghana's first president, Kwame Nkrumah, and works that documented the growing pains of postindependence Africa. De Baets documents how, during Brazil's military dictatorship (1964–85), many left-wing historians lost their academic jobs, were persecuted, or were exiled. And to cite another example, numerous Chinese historians were repressed after the 1949 communist takeover, the Anti-Rightist Campaign of 1957–58, and the Great Proletarian Cultural Revolution of 1965–76 and its aftermath. Inclusive of all genres of history, not just printed books, articles, and journals, *Censorship of Historical Thought: A World Guide, 1945–2000* records the suppression of historical poems, films, museums, sites, and cultural relics and properties as well.

In sum, De Baets has compiled an invaluable guide, one that conceptualizes and details the methods and targets of historical censorship over the last five decades of the twentieth century. To an important degree he has discovered many historians who, paradoxically, have been lost to history. In addition to documenting censorship and ideological persecution, his work raises vital questions about who controls memory and how history is constructed and disseminated. De Baets's important book thus reminds us of the central place that the study of the past plays in every society. By practicing their craft, historians repeatedly have become victims. By persevering in their quest for historical truth, they have become in no small measure heroes as well.

John David Smith
North Carolina State University

Acknowledgments

While working from 1980 to 1982 at Amnesty International's former publication office in San José, Costa Rica, I regularly came across cases of persecuted historians. A historian myself, I eagerly read about the fate of Hasan Kakar (Afghanistan), Ernest Wamba-dia-Wamba (Zaire/Congo), Walter Rodney (Guyana), Maina wa Kinyatti (Kenya), and Raúl Cariboni (Uruguay) in those years. I noticed that, in every corner of the globe, historians were among those suffering from political persecution because of either their work, other activities, or both. I also realized that human-rights reports contained a great deal of useful information about these historians that was possibly unknown to their colleagues around the world, although organizations such as Amnesty International emphasized that campaigns waged by victims' colleagues were the most effective. In addition, comparative analysis of the cases of persecuted and censored historians constituted a largely unexplored empirical base for interesting and important research into the relations between history, power, and freedom. During my last year in San José, I began collecting the material that caught my eye. Due to several factors, however—the most important being a doctorate on the influence of history textbooks on public opinion at the University of Ghent—I interrupted the project for five years. It was always at the back of my mind, and in September 1988 I took it up again, more systematically this time. After two years I began lecturing on the topic before an audience of history students at the University of Groningen. This resulted in a first publication in Dutch in 1991, entitled *Palimpsest,* for which the students and I collaborated with a local human-rights center.[1] Other time-consuming tasks caused new delays, but the 1993 announcement that the 18th International Congress of Historical Sciences in Montréal intended to organize a special theme on "Power, Liberty, and the Work of the Historian" provided a new and lasting impetus. At the congress in 1995, I presented a paper, *The Organization of Oblivion: Censorship and Persecution of Historians in Africa, Asia and Latin America.* After the congress, I attempted to unite the colleagues I had met at Montréal who were willing to campaign for their persecuted colleagues in a Network of Concerned Historians (established October 1995). The paper itself—a report of 118 pages, in fact—provided the starting point for the present Guide. The problems of censorship of historical thought are well known in the historical profession but judged all too often as "obvious"[2] and therefore, paradoxically, seldom studied. When in 1994 I proposed to my Canadian colleague Daniel Woolf that I outline the problem as an entry in his *Global Encyclopedia of Historical Writing*, he immediately agreed. When the encyclopedia was published in 1998, it became the first international historiographical work of reference to cover the topic. I was truly astonished when I saw the encyclopedia index; "censorship and persecution of historians or historical works" had more references than the term "capitalism" on the same page! Perhaps this was a sign of the times, but it also implied that, aside from my explicit coverage, many other contributions had referred to it in their own entries, a fact brought to light now.[3]

I am deeply indebted to many people who encouraged or supported my work. I want to thank the following human-rights organizations for their encouragement and information: American Association for the Advancement of Science—especially its senior program associate, Sage Russell (Washington); Amnesty International (London)—especially its urgent action coordinator, Scott Harrison; Article 19 International Centre on Censorship—especially its head of law programme, Toby Mendel (London); Human Rights Watch (Washington/New York)—especially its former academic freedom coordinator, Joe Saunders; Index on Censorship (London)—especially its news editors Adam Newey and Michael Griffin; International PEN Writers in Prison Committee (London); UNESCO Office of International Standards and Legal Affairs (Paris); and World University Service (formerly Geneva and Amsterdam)—especially Frederiek de Vlaming. When in 1996–97 I approached the Bureau 1995–2000 of the International Committee of Historical Sciences (CISH) for support, President Ivan Berend, Secretary-General François Bédarida, and bureau members Natalie Zemon Davis, Eva Österberg, and Jürgen Kocka reacted with a mixture of principled distance (which I understood well) and sympathy (for which I felt gratified) to the project. A similar reaction came from the CISH International Commission for the History and Theory of Historiography. Although no formal cooperation with the CISH Bureau or its Historiography Commission came about, I must nonetheless warmly thank all its members for their attention to the project, particularly the commission president at the time, Georg Iggers, whose moral support was invaluable. I remember with much affection the inspiring conversations with Derek Jones, editor of *Censorship: A World Encyclopedia*, during his March 1997 visit to Groningen, and our almost weekly correspondence. At the faculty of arts of the University of Groningen, I want to thank Doeko Bosscher, professor of contemporary history and rector, and the history department board in facilitating a much-needed sabbatical leave in the academic year 1998–99. My task would have been excruciatingly difficult without it. In addition, I am indebted to my students in the various editions of my seminars on censorship of history and related topics, which I have regularly directed between 1990 and 1997. They provided interesting bibliographical clues and, above all, their critical remarks sharpened my thoughts. I want to express my deep appreciation for their enthusiasm. I should also mention the excellent Groningen University Library, where I found most of my information. The following colleagues from all over the world have provided me with useful suggestions, additions, or corrections: Floribert Baudet (Yugoslavia, USSR), Thom Benjamin (Mexico), Jean Biskup (Poland), Flip Bosscher (the Netherlands), Inge Brinkman (Kenya), Hans Brinks (Germany), Robert Cribb (Australia, Indonesia), Lieve De Mey (Congo), Marc De Tollenaere (Mozambique, Brazil), Raymond Detrez (Bulgaria, Yugoslavia), Bruno De Wever (Belgium), Ewa Domańska (Poland), Toyin Falola (Nigeria), Ulrike Freitag (Middle East), Adolfo Gilly (Mexico), Erik de Graaf (GDR), Tony Griffith (Australia), Eric Hobsbawm (United Kingdom), Hero Hokwerda (Greece), Jozef Jablonický (Czechoslovakia), Harvey Kaye (UK, USA), Peter Kerkhof (Egypt), Hugo Klooster (Indonesia), Ernst Kossmann and Johanna Kossmann-Putto (the Netherlands), Kees Kuiken (China, Hong Kong), Nanci Leonzo (Brazil), Marion Marshrons (Cuba), Álvaro Matute (Mexico), Stevan Pavlowitch (Yugoslavia), Vilém Prečan (Czechoslovakia), Hans Renner (Czechoslovakia), Marc Reynebeau (Czechoslovakia, Poland), Zbigniew Romek (Poland), Edward Saveth (USA), Ingrid Sennema (Ghana), Walter Simons (USA), Jean Stengers (Belgium), Arturo Taracena Arriola (Guatemala), Tracy Ulltveit-Moe (Guatemala), Jan Vansina (Africa, Belgium), Francesca Verheest (Portugal), Jules Verhelst and Griet Maréchal (Archives), Romke Visser (Germany, Italy), Ingrid Wittebroodt (Chile), Sacha Zala (Switzerland), and Erik-Jan Zürcher (Turkey). There were many others, some of whom are mentioned in the source lists. A few of my informants, however, preferred to remain anonymous. To all the above I express my profound gratitude. While many whom I approached to discuss the project had critical remarks (especially about the Guide's inclusion of historians persecuted for nonprofessional reasons), only one or two explicitly dismissed the work as "too political" and refused cooperation. A few others were perhaps too skeptical to reply to a request of mine. I hope that the present Guide convinces them of the scholarly nature of my work. John David Smith, Graduate Alumni Distinguished Professor of History at North Carolina State University, who supervised the project for Greenwood Publishing Group, Cynthia Harris, who served as its acquisitions editor, Frank Saunders, production editor, Geoffrey Garvey, copyeditor, and Jan Jamilkowski, proofreader, were beacons during the book's design and production process. Despite their overburdened schedules, they were always prepared to offer their wise advice. Without their unswerving aid, the Guide would have contained a great many more errors, omissions, and inconsistencies. Those that remain are entirely my own responsibility. The last word of warm affection is for Elly, my wife, and Hopi, Seppo, and Mafalda, my children: in the course of seven intense years, I told them many of the dramatic stories I had come across. Perhaps I am not too wrong in saying that each time those stories became a living part of our conversations, their power directed our attention to questions that really mattered and made our life richer. They are in our memory forever.

Antoon De Baets, 1 May 2001

NOTES

1. A. De Baets, J.B. Meyer, & W. Mik, eds., *Palimpsest: De Geschiedenis geschrapt* [*Palimpsest: The Erasure of History*] (Groningen 1991).

2. The following quotes by two eminent historians, who are keenly aware of the problem, seem to "overrecognize" it, as it were. François Bédarida: "J'en vois [d'une série de pièges pour la liberté de l'historien] quatre, du plus simple au plus compliqué, ou du plus évident au plus subtil, donc au plus dangereux. Le premier est terrible, mais si évident que l'on peut résister: c'est la menace contre la liberté par le pouvoir, et notamment le pouvoir d'État. Chacun de nous est assez averti pour en être immédiatement conscient. Pourtant cet état de chose est assez répandu à travers le monde." (I see four [traps for the historian's liberty], from the simplest to the most complicated or from the most obvious to the subtlest—that is, to the most dangerous. The first trap is terrible but so obvious that it can be resisted: the threat against liberty emanating from power, and state power in particular. Each of us is sufficiently aware of it to detect it immediately. Nevertheless, this state of affairs is rather widespread in the world.) From "Le Métier d'historien aujourd'hui", in: R. Rémond ed., *Être historien aujourd'hui* (Paris 1988) 342; Peter Burke, "Official censorship of the past is all too well-known, and there is little need to talk about the various revisions of the *Soviet Encyclopaedia*," from "History As Social Memory," in: T. Butler ed., *Memory: History, Culture and the Mind* (Oxford 1989) 108.

3. A. De Baets, "Censorship and Historical Writing", in: D.R. Woolf, ed., *A Global Encyclopedia of Historical Writing* (New York 1998) 149–50. See also index, pages 1000–1001.

Abbreviations

Abbreviations used in the Guide in more than one chronological item are listed below. Abbreviations for states in the United States are not included.

AAA	Argentinian Anticommunist Alliance
AdW	Academy of Sciences (from 1969; GDR)
AHA	American Historical Association
ANC	African National Congress (South Africa)
ANSP	Agency for National Security Planning (South Korea)
AVČR	Academy of Sciences of the Czech Republic
BAN	Bulgarian Academy of Sciences
BBC	British Broadcasting Corporation
BCE	Before Common Era
BKP	Bulgarian Communist Party
CAS	Chinese Academy of Sciences
CASS	Chinese Academy of Social Sciences
CC	Central Committee
CCP	Chinese Communist Party
CCPDH	Cuban Human Rights Committee
CE	Common Era
CIA	Central Intelligence Agency (successor to OSS from 1947; United States)
CNRS	National Scientific Research Agency (France)
CP	Communist Party
CP-ČSSR	Communist Party of Czechoslovakia
CPGB	Communist Party of Great Britain
CPSA	Communist Party of South Africa

CPSU	Communist Party of the Soviet Union
CPUSA	Communist Party of the United States of America
CPV	Communist Party of Vietnam
ČSAV	Czechoslovak Academy of Sciences
DAW	German Academy of Sciences (until 1969; GDR)
DINA	National Intelligence Directorate (Chile)
DK	Democratic Kampuchea
ETA	Basque Nation and Liberty (Basque separatist movement; Spain)
EU	European Union
EZLN	Zapatista Army of National Liberation (Mexico)
FBI	Federal Bureau of Investigation (United States)
FOIA	Freedom of Information Act (United States)
FRG	Federal Republic of Germany
FRUS	Foreign Relations of the United States
FSLN	Sandinista Front of National Liberation (Nicaragua)
G30S	September 30th Movement (Indonesia)
GDR	German Democratic Republic
Gestapo	Secret State Police (Nazi Germany)
HSWP	Hungarian Socialist Workers' Party (Communist Party)
HUAC	House Un-American Activities Committee (United States)
ICHR	Indian Council of Historical Research
IHC	Indian History Congress
INAH	National Institute of Anthropology and History (Mexico)
INS	Immigration and Naturalization Service (United States)
IUPPS	International Union of Prehistoric and Protohistoric Sciences
KGB	Committee of State Security (Soviet secret police 1953–91)
KKE	Communist Party of Greece
KOR	Committee for the Defense of the Workers (Poland)
KPD	Communist Party of Germany
LCY	League of Communists of Yugoslavia (Communist Party)
MfS	State Security Ministry (or: Stasi; GDR)
MGH	*Monumenta Germaniae Historica*
MI5	Domestic security service (United Kingdom)
MI6	Secret intelligence service (United Kingdom)
MIR	Revolutionary Left Movement (Chile)
MPRP	Mongolian People's Revolutionary Party (Communist Party)
NAACP	National Association for the Advancement of Colored People (United States)

NDH	Ustasha Independent State of Croatia (1941–45)
NKVD	People's Commissariat of Internal Affairs (Soviet secret police 1934–43)
NOWa	Independent Publishers (Poland)
NSC	National Security Council (United States)
NSDAP	National Socialist German Workers' Party (Nazi Party; Nazi Germany)
NSL	National Security Law (South Korea)
NSR	National Salvation Revolution (Sudan)
OAH	Organization of American Historians (United States)
OSA	Official Secrets Act (United Kingdom)
OSS	Office of Strategic Services (intelligence service 1942–45; United States)
OUN	Organization of Ukrainian Nationalists
PAN	Polish Academy of Sciences
PCB	Brazilian Communist Party
PCF	French Communist Party
PEN	Poets, Playwrights, Essayists, Editors, Novelists (international writers' association)
PIDE	Secret police (Portugal)
PKI	Indonesian Communist Party
PLO	Palestine Liberation Organization
PNM	Peoples' National Movement (Trinidad & Tobago)
PPR	Polish People's Republic
PRI	Institutional Revolutionary Party (Mexico)
PRO	Public Records Office (United Kingdom)
PUWP	Polish United Workers' Party (Communist Party)
RCP	Romanian Communist Party
RIOD	Netherlands State Institute for War Documentation
SANU	Serbian Academy of Sciences and Arts
SAV	Slovak Academy of Sciences
SAVAK	Iranian secret police
SBZ	Soviet Zone of Occupation in Germany (later the GDR)
SCAP	Supreme Commander for the Allied Powers (Japan)
SED	Socialist Unity Party (Communist Party; GDR)
SS	Defense Corps (special NSDAP security force; Nazi Germany)
SSR	Soviet Socialist Republic
TFA	Texans for America
TKN	Society for Academic Courses (or: Flying University, Poland)
TRC	Truth and Reconciliation Commission (South Africa)
UBCV	Unified Buddhist Church of Vietnam

UCR	Radical Civic Union (Argentina)
UNAM	National Autonomous University of Mexico
UNESCO	United Nations Educational, Scientific and Cultural Organization
US[A]	United States [of America]
USAC	University of San Carlos (Guatemala)
USSR	Union of Soviet Socialist Republics
WWW	World Wide Web

Introduction

"Y tan sólo con nuestra memoria escondida fuimos exiliados."
[We only had our hidden memory when we lived in exile.]
Dennis Mesén, *Ceremonial Desconocido* (San José, Costa Rica, 1996), 59

GUIDE TO THE GUIDE

This Guide supplies information on the censorship of historical thought and the fate of persecuted historians in more than a hundred and thirty countries since 1945. Its aim is to encompass all countries where such censorship and persecution have taken place. The presentation of information under certain countries should not be taken as indicating any view on the status of disputed territory. In addition, notwithstanding sustained efforts to unearth relevant information, some countries or regions that should have been treated are not included in the Guide. The absence of an entry on a particular country in this work does not imply, however, that no censorship of history has occurred there. Although censorship of history is a phenomenon of many times and places, this Guide is limited to the period from 1 January 1945 to 31 December 2000. Information prior to this period is included in three cases only: when historical works published before 1945 were (also) censored after 1945, when historians were victims of censorship or persecution both before and after 1945, and, finally, when censorship or persecution suffered before 1945 could reasonably be assumed to have substantially influenced the historian's fate after 1945. An obvious example of this last possibility is the (political) exile of historians. For reasons of space, however, cases of prewar exile continuing after 1945 are mentioned only briefly at the beginning of an entry. These cases will be covered more extensively in a planned companion volume to this Guide.[1]

The Guide covers three types of cases:

1. Historians persecuted/censored for reasons related to the field of history.
2. Nonhistorians persecuted/censored for reasons related to the field of history.
3. Historians persecuted/censored for reasons outside the field of history.

This introduction is divided into four parts.

- *A practical part* describing the editorial policy. This is recommended reading for anyone who wants to understand the organization of the work.

- *A conceptual and methodological part* devoted to an extensive discussion of the author's research procedure. First, the boundaries of the work are clarified by defining the key concepts "historians" and "censorship", and by indicating problems of inclusion of (a) nonhistorians, (b) extraprofessional persecution and censorship, and (c) restrictions different from but similar to censorship. In addition to the definition of the Guide's framework, epistemological questions are tackled: How can we know censorship when we realize that it is usually surrounded by secrecy? What are the strengths and weaknesses of the three types of sources utilized in the Guide: (a) the works of censors and censored, (b) historical and biographical dictionaries and historiographical surveys, and (c) reports from international human-rights organizations? What is "the principle of explicit information"? What problems inhere to the observer of worldwide censorship? What is "the principle of distance"? Why are certain problematic categories of historians excluded? Which types of information are omitted from cases in the Guide?

- *A theoretical part* offering a framework for data analysis. How is censorship justified? What is the relationship between censorship and propaganda? Which methods do censors use? Which historians are their targets? What problems do historians confront when dictatorships tumble and censorship is abolished? What are the intended and unintended effects of censorship? This part concludes with some ideas for utilizing the Guide in comparative analyses.

- *An ethical part* containing a list of questions which indicate the multiple ethical implications of the censorship of historical thought.

The *conclusion* discusses the fourfold value of the Guide as perceived by this author: as an indicator of the universal presence of the censorship of historical thought; as a heuristic compass; as a tool of awareness of the risks run in the historical profession; and, finally, as a tribute to victimized historians and an appeal to memory and responsibility.

EDITORIAL POLICY

The following principles of description, developed over time, have guided the author's research. The main division is by countries, listed alphabetically. The information in the Guide is cataloged under the country responsible for the persecution, not the historian's country of origin or the country where the historian suffers from the consequences of the persecution.[2] Cases of censorship occurring in colonies are classified under a special subheading of the independent country (e.g., "Algeria" has a subheading "French Algeria"). Very exceptionally did doubt persist over which country was actually persecuting.[3] Entries for the larger and better-covered countries are prefaced by short panoramic overviews (of unequal lengths) indicating the climate of freedom of expression or patterns and trends (if any) affecting the entire community of historians.

Within each country cases are listed chronologically, according to the date of the crucial persecuting event or the date of the first in a series of persecuting events. This chronological arrangement has three clear advantages: it clarifies connections between ostensibly separate cases, suggests peaks of repression,[4] and facilitates comparisons between countries at one specified moment. There is also one important disadvantage: items of minor censorship may be somewhat deceptively juxtaposed with major ones, only because they occurred around the same time. Unfortunately, chronological indications were often poor. Events with general time indicators (e.g., "In the early 1950s") usually precede those with exact ones (e.g., "In 1952"). Events for which a month but no year is indicated happened in the year last mentioned, but the year is omitted only when no confusion is possible. The relatively new BCE/CE chronographic notation (Before Common Era/Common Era) has been preferred to the usual BC/AD. For epistemological and other reasons explained below, the chronological gaps between the various cases often remain huge.

The description of individual cases is governed by a style as accurate and concise as possible. With regard to archival access, not only was lack of access considered but also its opposite, privileged access. *Reasons* for the censorship or persecution obviously attracted my special attention, but their mention, if any is made, was often scarce or contradictory and their formulation vague. Frequently, our sources "translated" official reasons and charges (e.g., "sedition") into the supposedly real reasons, with various degrees of plausibility.

For the sake of clarity and elegance, abbreviations are avoided as much as possible. Country-specific institutions with well-known abbreviations are mentioned the first time in full with the abbreviation following in parentheses. In addition, a complete list of abbreviations used in more than one chronological item is provided at the beginning of the book. *For easy reference, names of persons who are the subject of an item are in bold, regardless of whether they were censors or censored.* Middle initials have been omitted everywhere, except where this caused confusion or where the middle initial was known to be part of the spoken form of the name.

When a name is mentioned in another case in the same country entry, it is followed by [q.v. + date], thus alerting the reader that it is treated elsewhere in the entry. As a rule, victims who encountered trouble in several countries are listed under the country that was most important in this respect and cross-referenced under the other(s). Uncertain names or dates (such as birth dates derived from mentions of age) are put in brackets or preceded by a question mark. Titles of book-length publications (either original or translated) are in italics, translated titles of untranslated publications are in italics and between quotation marks (to avoid misleading a reader into thinking that an English edition of the work exists). Some well-known universities have not been identified by city in the text; some well-known cities not by their country. Universities containing the name of a city have usually been given their short form (e.g., "Kabul University" instead of "the University of Kabul"). Diacritical marks were omitted from non-Western words. With regard to the spelling of names and terms, to original and translated book titles, and to transcription, consistency could unfortunately not always be achieved due to the bewildering variety of sources. The reader is asked to excuse any inconsistencies and oversights.

I keenly realize that no style, certainly not the factual and dry style of this Guide, is able to render accurately the historians' individual and collective suffering. To that end, testimonies, diary extracts, or autobiographical accounts from historians should be consulted. Only a bare outline of the cases is presented, although many merit more extensive coverage. The source list at the end of each country entry, whose primary function is verifiability, partially meets this need. Taken together, the source lists should form a solid bibliography on the subject.[5] Every effort has been made to provide appropriate sources. The author welcomes any suggested references. He also hopes that readers will help him put right any errors of omission, fact, formulation, or judgment, which he is bound to have made (please send any comments to me via the Greenwood Publishing Group).

TERMS OF REFERENCE

Scope and Principal Definitions

As I mentioned, the Guide covers three types of cases:

1. Historians persecuted or censored for reasons related to the field of history.
2. Nonhistorians persecuted or censored for reasons related to the field of history.
3. Historians persecuted or censored for reasons outside the field of history.

Two questions arising from this categorization will be discussed: Why include nonhistorians? Why include extraprofessional persecution or censorship?

Nonhistorians are included to avoid a double myopia. First, the further one moves away from the present age and from countries with firm historiographical traditions, the less obvious is the classical definition of the historian as a professional who methodically studies the past. Second, as the censors' aim is to control the past, they do not necessarily distinguish between professional historians and others dealing with the past. They deal with a perceived danger irrespective of the qualifications of those behind it. Censors actually attach importance to both professional and nonprofessional producers of expressions of historical thought and to interpretations of the past in either written, spoken, or visual form. Indeed, popular history is as much a target of censorship as is academic history, probably even more so.[6] In addition, nonprofessional historians are often the first to explode taboos or break the silence. Therefore, a flexible definition of historians includes two categories. On the one hand, there are the professionals and trainees in the historical sector in the broad sense, in other words, historians *appellation contrôlée*, archivists, archeologists, art historians, literary historians, egyptologists, assyriologists etc., but also students of history.[7] On the other hand, there are the nonhistorians who write popular or academic historical works such as novelists, scholars of related disciplines, journalists, and politicians.[8] An attempt has been made to cover this ambitious field of endangered historical works as exhaustively as possible, but some genres— particularly (historical) photographs[9] and theater—are covered far from completely.[10] Comprehensive as this definition may seem, it excludes producers of such historical sources as memoirs or testimonies and journalists in their daily business, although it is naturally clear that censorship of such writers and the press will affect the volume and quality of sources at the disposal of future historians.[11] There is a logical exception to this exception: when those who encountered difficulties for writing or editing memoirs, diaries, or press articles were historians, they were included.

In this Guide, our definition of censorship is broader than the usual legal definition: censorship of history must be taken as the systematic *control* of the content or exchange of information and ideas concerning the past imposed by, or with the connivance of, the authorities.[12] This form of censorship can be directed against a historical work in all its stages or against its producers or consumers. As is clear from the definition, censorship may be either official or unofficial, formal or informal. Special attention is given to the multiple guises of censorship and the varieties of indirect and de facto censorship. The range of persecution of historians includes pressure, harassment, dismissal, imprisonment, torture, and death.

The second question, asked by several colleagues who were consulted for this Guide, has yet to be tackled: Why are historians persecuted or censored for reasons *outside* the field of history included? Almost forty years ago, Edward Carr formulated the famous maxims: "Study the historian before you begin to study the facts", and "Before you study the historian, study his historical and social environment."[13] When applying these maxims to the Guide, one could say that this particular category of information provides a glimpse of the nonprofessional activities of historians and often reveals their prominent roles on the public scene. Thus, its inclusion is, first of all, a modest contribution to intellectual and cultural history. However, the main reason for this category's inclusion is different. Academic freedom in the broad sense, argues the late Edward Shils—perhaps the world's foremost authority on academic freedom— "includes the political freedom of academics" which "extends to political activities outside the university." One of the main reasons for including political freedom in the definition of academic freedom becomes clear when Shils discusses the infringements on academic freedom: "by far most of the actions for which sanctions were taken," he continues, "were for expressions or activities in the public sphere. The reasons why there have been very few instances of academics who have suffered sanctions for their teaching or research and publications are not far to seek. For one thing, teaching and research are not easily visible."[14] Although the present Guide does not support the contention of the "very few instances",[15] from Shils's words it should be clear that to omit the political dimension of the historian's life is to miss important aspects of the problem.

Another essential reason for inclusion is epistemological. The historical work and other activities of historians may be intertwined to such an extent that it frequently becomes almost impossible to distinguish between them.[16] The interconnection may adopt four different forms. First, their professional work may lead historians to positions outside the historical field for which they are persecuted. As historians reflect on their work and the world they live in, their commitments outside the historical field—for example, in politics, journalism, or human rights—may very well be inspired by their historical work. Our data strongly suggest that this is frequently the case, although the influence of particular historical views is generally hard to verify.[17] Second, persecution for reasons outside the historical field may influence the historical work. In the first place, it nearly always causes delays in the work's progress and completion. In addition, the persecution itself may trigger a process of reflection in which all sorts of viewpoints, including historical ones, are tested or changed. Imprisonment and exile, for example, constituting as they do a total breach with the life the historian previously led, make suddenly available a large amount of time which, if conditions permit, leads to fresh views on history. It is truly remarkable how frequently this has been the case.[18] Likewise, persecuted politicians and journalists may conclude that they need a firmer historical basis for their work and become amateur historians. Third, persecution for reasons outside the historical field may hide persecution for reasons inside the historical field, and vice versa. Resistance on the historical front is often part of broader resistance movements. Consequently, historians may ostensibly be persecuted for their historical work but actually for their political views and nonhistorians ostensibly for political reasons but actually for their interpretations of the past. Fourth, some persons are multifaceted characters and known as much for their historical as for their other work; he or she being a historian is but one aspect of their personality.[19] For all these reasons the third category, although analytically different from the other two, is included in the Guide.

Borderline Cases and Gray Areas

What is the past and when does it begin? The only adequate answer to this question, "everything and now", is untenable as a practical criterion. From which moment can we see the policing or repression of commemorations of recent massacres or anniversaries of recent rebellions as expressions of censorship of history? With no methical answer to this question, the inclusion of cases was weighed individually. Not only the concept of the past, but also the concept of censorship, provides similar difficulties. The natural habitat of censorship of history is a nondemocratic climate, but its traces are sometimes recognizable in the restrictions put upon historians living in democracies. These borderline cases and gray areas of censorship can be mapped on six levels.

It is clear that restrictions upon the activities of the historian emanate, first of all, from the general context. Conditions such as war, colonization, poverty, and violence affect all people to some degree and may have the same net effect as censorship. The vicissitudes of international and civil war may cause the loss of manuscripts or the destruction of archives or lead to dangerous working conditions.[20] Archives destroyed or badly damaged through natural causes or accidents as a rule do not appear in the Guide; willful actions designed to damage archives do. Similar is the theft, by colonizers and occupiers, of items from the archival and monumental heritage of occupied lands, a worldwide problem receiving increasing attention.[21] The third condition, widespread illiteracy and poverty restricting access to many forms and channels of history and excluding large groups from pursuing historical studies, does not figure in the Guide. The final general condition, the expulsion of indigenous peoples from their ancestral lands (which is instrumental in destroying their telluric memory and can therefore be seen as a form of de facto censorship), was excluded.[22] Sometimes, however, tensions and conflicts between indigenous peoples and archeologists were reported.[23]

Second, every government imposes constraints on historical research. Freedom of Information Acts and Archival Laws regulating the selection of, and access to, records vary by country, especially in the domains of foreign policy, national security, public order, and privacy.[24] Whenever official information policies are arbitrary and secrecy areas too broadly formulated, governments are on the brink of practicing indirect censorship. At that moment, governments arrogantly identify their interests with the lasting interests of the state, of which they are but caretakers. Secrecy is used to conceal sensitive information, avoid criticism, and reduce accountability.[25] Like archives, public libraries might restrict the acquisition and consultation of historical information or monitor a suspected reader's profile on ideological grounds. The risks also appear in other areas, such as the relatively normal governmental quasi-monopolies on historical museums or certain large source editions. Long ago, Herbert Butterfield formulated two maxims on the uneasy marriage between governmental secrecy and official history: "First, that governments try to press upon the historian the key to all the drawers but one, and, secondly, that if the historian can only find out the thing which government does not want him to know, he will lay his hand upon something that is likely to be significant."[26]

Another domain is the relationship between governments and truth commissions. These commissions usually investigate human-rights abuses committed under a past dictatorship but are frequently hampered in their work when they are unofficial. Even officially installed commissions may encounter many obstacles. Those who investigate the abuses of past regimes or organize exhumations of clandestine cemeteries must reckon with more than the usual hardships to uncover the historical truth.[27] Some examples of their ill fortune may be found in the Guide.

Of a different order is the official ban on controversial acts. This includes the suppression of traditions and commemorations. As stated already, commemorations and anniversaries are problematic for inclusion, but not only because they may occur soon after the event to be commemorated. In many countries and epochs, commemorations—or even the mere vicinity of a sacred site—are often but a pretext for immediate political action because they constitute a rare possibility for, and a major moment of, political opposition. Is their prevention or disturbance censorship or not? Their nature is often transformed to such an extent as to make it difficult to judge the importance of the historical aspect.[28] A similar example is seen in dissidents who demanded independence for their country or region or, alternatively, its (re)unification with another territory. When they had been arrested because they claimed independence or (re)unification, they were not included in the Guide; when arrested because they maintained that their country had been independent or united during large parts of its history, the principle was inclusion.

The executive branch of government is the main censor, but other branches are not immune from the practice. Parliaments may adopt laws mandating the teaching of history in the language of the majority.[29] Judges may check too eagerly whether the historians carried out their research honestly and prudently in accordance with the accepted professional methods; they may consequently interpret normal historical practice as defamation of the dead.[30] This, of course, does not imply at all that lawsuits against historians always imply censorship. Some historians have been fairly tried and penalized or sentenced. But lawsuits, whether their outcome is favorable for the defendant or not, are attempts, successful or not, to restrict the liberty of the historian, whether desirable or not. These restrictions, while often not the same as censorship, amount to the same effect. *Therefore, lawsuits against historians were, as a rule, included in the Guide.* As I shall explain later (under "the principle of distance"), this does not mean that I approve of nor that I reject the statements of the defendants.[31]

Third, educational authorities implement certain types of restrictions. The general policies governing university entrance, funding of research and teaching, personnel recruitment, and infrastructure management all influence working conditions. As a result, academics in most countries are heavily dependent on government budgets. In times of political crisis, entire universities are liable to be closed.[32] Hence, when university autonomy is restricted, it indirectly infringes on academic freedom. In the specific field of history, censorship may be further disguised as pressure from the historical establishment, corporatism, political correctness on the campus, or rejection of theses and manuscripts for supposed incompetence. It often takes the form of "minor" harassments or career restrictions. Professional and economic types of repression such as loss of salary,

refusal of promotion, demotion, revocation of academic degrees and responsibilities, restrictions on travel abroad and contacts with foreign scholars, and
finally, loss of employment, are sometimes insidious forms of censorship and
not always recognizable as such. A not uncommon form of hidden censorship
occurs when historians advise publishers to refuse manuscripts because their
contents do not conform to their viewpoint or signify competition for their own
work. According to Shils, "the most frequently employed sanctions by authorities are dismissal from academic posts; variants include the withdrawal of the
right to teach while retaining title, salary, etc.; the withholding of promotion;
censure, oral or written; withholding of research funds, income, honors, opportunity for publication; refusal of perquisites such as leaves of absence; restrictions on travel within or outside the country; etc."[33] For this reason, discussions
on academic freedom are inextricably linked with questions of permanence of
tenure. Large parts of the Guide are filled with examples of these common and
uncommon forms of censorship. Cases where censorship was clearly *attempted*,
without actually succeeding, are also included. Conversely, it is equally true that
legitimate dismissal for incompetence is sometimes presented by the victim as
a case of censorship. In countries where illiteracy and weak academic structures
make (written) history an affair conducted by the elite, censorship attempts may
either be stronger (the domain to supervise is smaller) or weaker (the reach of
historians is generally less influential). A peculiar variant of the action undertaken by educational authorities are boycotts by the international community of
historians. The boycott may be triggered by the obvious lack of professional
ethics displayed by the targeted group of scholars, but it may be much less
justified when individual scholars challenge the orthodoxies of the trade, thereby
occasioning a major controversy.

Fourth, individuals and unofficial groups outside academe may threaten unwelcome manifestations of the past: they loot archives or museums, destroy or
desecrate historical monuments and statues,[34] boycott books, and sue historians
on religious, political, or ethnic grounds. Other acts with a possible historical
dimension include the slander of former heads of state, the possession of banned
flags, and flag desecration. In many countries, unofficial groups are—sometimes
in alliance with, sometimes in opposition to, the government—involved in censorship activity.[35]

Fifth, there are general cultural traits such as nationalism and ethnocentrism,[36]
leading to the misrepresentation, negligence, or denial of large parts of the history of others. These instances are not included in the Guide. Nor is the frequent
discriminating exclusion of entire categories, women and nonwhites primarily,
from the historical profession. Only some particular consequences, such as destruction of historical traces as the result of nationalism or censorship of a historical work because of the sexual or racial origin of its author,[37] are
incorporated in the Guide. Furthermore, each society has its taboos (subjects
surrounded by silence) and its amnesia (subjects surrounded by oblivion). These
taboos and amnesia range from a few selected topics to whole fields in the

history of the country concerned.[38] When centrally planned or officially enforced through a policy of secrecy and suppression, these taboos and amnesia amount to censorship. It is essential, however, to keep in mind the crucially different levels of consciousness in censorship and amnesia. Taboos not accompanied by censorship are not included in the Guide.

Sixth and last, as Carr's maxims remind us, it is a well-known fact that historians themselves are "prisoners" of a score of factors: their own biographies, their epoch and time, their culture, and the knowability of the past through the historical work and its sources. Together, these factors constitute historians' subjectivity and selectivity. At a certain point, however, the inherent bias affecting all stages of historical scholarship (definition, collection, analysis, and interpretation of data), hence the level of distortion, becomes intentional falsification and deception and threatens the historian's intellectual integrity. If the seduction of deception is a possible danger, self-censorship is a more likely reaction. Self-censorship is the most efficient, widespread, but least visible form of censorship. It is often difficult to distinguish the cautious historian who prefers to remain discreet from the intimidated historian who engages in self-censorship, avoids controversial topics and interpretations, and seeks refuge in "safe" topics. Personal conduct as well may have ambiguous meanings: the destruction of personal research notes may be more than a cleaning, a stay abroad or a voluntary emigration may be involuntary exile, a retirement compulsory, a suicide due to political pressure. Sometimes, self-restraint and conformity are violently imposed upon the historian. This occurs when official propaganda (which we discuss later) sweepingly transcends its usual borders and fills almost entirely the available space in which historians are permitted to work. Indeed, the propagation of the tyrant's own version of history can be accompanied by tremendous pressure upon historians, even when no direct attempts at censoring their views are taking place. One needs only to think of the virulent public denunciation of historians in former communist countries; there, the borderline between legitimate scholarly criticism on the one hand and vile attacks combined with "confessions" and ostracism of deviating historians on the other was transgressed. The campaigns resulted in intimidation, self-censorship and self-criticism, broken careers, and a climate of fear. In such cases, the violent process of submission to propaganda amounted to censorship.[39] This gray area between censorship and propaganda sometimes caused interpretive difficulties during our research. The Guide's inclusion of these cases was decided ad hoc, but it is clear that, in principle, *the Guide includes not only censorship but also closely related phenomena.*

Data Collection and Description: Sources and Problems of Evidence

As can be seen from these six "twilight zones" of censorship, the bewildering potential of empirical material defies any clear-cut definition of censorship or rules of inclusion. But problems of evidence arise not only from borderline cases and gray areas. The Dubnov case illustrates some of the difficulties: Simon Dubnov (1860–1941) was a prominent Jewish historian and a double exile from the USSR (1922) and Nazi Germany (1933). In the weeks before his death in December 1941, while he was living in the ghetto of Riga, Latvia, his library was seized and he was obliged to hide his manuscripts. Cut off from his daily work, he began chronicling life in the ghetto. His notebooks were smuggled out to some friends in the city. During one of the roundups in the ghetto, a Gestapo officer (a former student of Dubnov, some assert) murdered him. Later his daughter heard the rumor that Dubnov repeatedly exclaimed in the minutes before his death: "People, do not forget. Speak of this, people; record it all."[40] Dubnov was able to take some posthumous revenge: the Nazis believed they had destroyed the entire run of his autobiography's third volume. But one surviving copy, rediscovered in 1956, served as the basis for a new edition the following year. In this tragic case, many forms of censorship—censorship stricto sensu, book confiscation and destruction, exile, murder—come together. At the same time, Dubnov's "revenge" clearly shows how imperfect censorship is. Moreover, his call to document the situation is an appeal to memory, and, therefore, to the responsibility of historians. The evidence regarding his case is, however, shallow in two respects. First, only some sources mention that his murderer was one of his former students. Second, Dubnov's daughter Sophie wrote that her father's alleged last words had passed from mouth to mouth. From his biography it is abundantly clear that he could have said them, but whether he really uttered them in the dark and tragic hours just before his death is uncertain.

The risk of untraceability, and hence of oblivion, is even greater for the words and deeds of lesser-known historians writing and teaching in similar repressive conditions. As early as 1963, Czech historian Jan Křen (1930–) had launched an appeal for more autonomy in historiography. Dismissed during the "normalization", he became active on the *samizdat* (self-publishing) circuit. In the mid-1980s, he received a visit from a clever history student who had researched a subject that Křen had worked on before his persecution. He did not know any of Křen's works written on the topic in the 1960s and had heard about him only vaguely. "I thought you were dead", the student confessed.[41] To give another example, many sources reported on the persecution and death of historian Wu Han because he was the famous first victim of the Chinese Cultural Revolution, but only a single source alleges that the entire senior staff of the history department at Zhongshan University, Guangzhou (Canton), was hanged during these very same years.[42]

There was no perfect heuristic strategy to resolve these questions of evidence. The historian observing other historians is confronted with many problems of epistemology rooted in the nature of the phenomenon studied, in the sources and their authors, or in the observer himself. Let us look closer into each of these three factors. A general difficulty underlying the absence of information is the fact that many forms of censorship are invisible and difficult to trace, since censorship normally takes place in an atmosphere of secrecy. Michael Scammell wrote that censorship hides itself: "One of the first words to be censored by the censors is the word 'censorship' ".[43] Clive Ponting made a similar remark: "In a secretive country, the extent of secrecy is itself a well-kept secret".[44] Censorship is characterized by two intertwined epistemological paradoxes. First, the more effective censorship is, the less visible it is, and the fewer facts it generates.[45] Second, in a repressive society there is less information about more censorship, whereas in a democratic society there is more information about less censorship.

In addition to general epistemological problems, data origin entails questions of reliability. Data from the victimized historians, their families, or the institutions with which they are affiliated may suffer, first of all, from underreporting. First, some historians prefer that their cases not be highlighted as those of censorship or persecution: in these cases I have tried to strike an appropriate balance between considerations of privacy and reputation, on the one hand, and the evidence, on the other. Second, collecting data about the censorship of history inside a persecuting country is obviously dangerous. More than anything else, research into current censorship runs the risk of being censored. Even when it is undertaken, or when certain facts on specific cases are generally known, little of this type of research seems to have been written down systematically.[46] Third, if it is, another risk lurks around the corner—that sympathy for the victims blinds one to possible biases in their reporting. Fourth, at the other end of the spectrum, data from censors should be handled as carefully as those from victims; these, however, are generally lacking.[47]

Despite this information gap, the names of censors were sometimes known. With regard to naming these censors and their accomplices, utmost reticence was observed; this Guide is not meant as a tribunal. Quantitatively, the works and autobiographies of censors and censored, where available and accessible, were secondary sources for our work. The same applied to historical and biographical dictionaries and information from historiographical surveys. The main trait of the information stemming from this set of sources was its fragmentary character. Obituaries, commemorative addresses, and Festschriften constitute a genre notorious for its absence of critical detachment from the subject. Even critical historiographical surveys yield a disappointing harvest; indispensable for this Guide, most did not address the problem of the political context of historiography, even in cases in which it was clearly the main determinant of the historical profession at a given moment. The reasons were probably diverse: authors slipped into thinking that the power of the political context was obvious and well known, or they considered that mentioning the cases of persecution created an air of controversy and scandal, usually avoided in scholarly publications; some underestimated the problem; others avoided it out of fear for research or career troubles, especially when they worked in the country under consideration or were still allowed to visit there. When these surveys are taken as authoritative descriptions of the state of the art, they may be very misleading. The authors who did mention the subject typically did so in passing (at the top or end of their piece, or cached in footnotes). Sometimes they treated it more extensively, as they wrote under the vivid impression of a recent famous case. Reports from recognized international human-rights organizations, reputed for the quality of their research departments' output and anxious to preserve that quality, were our main sources.[48] They possess a major advantage over the other sources: their data are not compiled with the historians specifically in mind, and therefore it may be safely assumed that petty professional interests did not interfere in their research. Generally, however, they did not begin collecting relevant human-rights data systematically until the 1970s, and with more of them providing more data these days, an undeniable bias toward the present is clearly visible in the Guide. Accelerating Internet access to newspapers and human-rights databases in the 1990s contributed to this bias.

One heuristic problem applies to all the sources: the same phenomenon may be unequally studied in different places. Take the exile of historians: there is abundant information on the exile of historians from Germany and Austria in the 1930s, less (but still substantial) information on the exile of historians under Italian Fascism, or after the Russian Revolution or Spanish Civil War and, to my knowledge, very little systematic information on the exile of historians from Argentina in 1946, Eastern Europe in 1948 (and later), China in 1948–49, Paraguay in 1954, Cuba in 1959–60, or other waves of exile. Much to my regret, as a researcher and lecturer interested primarily in non-Western history and sensitive to the representation of usually "forgotten" countries, I found that information on non-Western countries is generally less readily available than that on Western ones. Scarce information on usually forgotten countries was included, however, if it passed the quality test, even if that meant some very incomplete country entries. This implies that the space devoted to a particular country, or the number of the cases listed, should not necessarily be considered an index of persecution. Likewise, Guide data on a particular historian do not necessarily indicate his/her importance, but rather reflect the amount of available information. Given the lacunae and biases in the information and the great variety in the forms of censorship and persecution, calculating totals of victims for the whole Guide would be senseless and misleading. But it is clear that hundreds of historians and others concerned with the past have been victimized during the second half of the twentieth century.

Smaller lacunae make it difficult to verify chronological details or whether, for example, a given intellectual or academic was a historian or whether the declared motive for persecution was also the actual one. The risk of loss of focus constituted a related problem when delving into the wealth of information. An important tool to avoid this risk was the *principle of explicit information*: as a rule, only explicit information on the censorship of history was considered, and inclusive evidence was avoided. This means that information about the censorship of broader categories than historians (e.g., academics, intellectuals) that may include historians but do not necessarily do so was not judged as sufficient evidence to justify an item. Particularly in large-scale operations like genocides or book burnings, historians and their work were almost certainly among the victims, but precisely this scale often made detailed individual information unavailable. The principle had its price—loss of relevant information—but also its gains—avoidance of untenable deductions and sharper focus. The inclusion or exclusion of cases, and the weighing of contradictory information in a particular case, was approached with the usual critical method. Still, dozens of cases from many countries were eliminated from the Guide because I judged the supporting evidence not to be strong enough. The adoption of the principle of explicit information means that this Guide understates rather than exaggerates the overall situation.

To problems emanating from the phenomenon itself or its sources, those emanating from the researcher should be added. My language mastery is limited,[49] sources and cases may have escaped my attention, my descriptions may be mistaken or flawed. To avoid excessive dependence on the authority of others, I used as many sources as possible and allowed for verifiability via the list of sources at the end of each country entry. I hope that credibility also stems from the international approach and the attention paid to very different ideologies and historiographical traditions. Some Brazilian colleagues told me how important it was that an outsider, untouched by local rivalries, did this work. Gathering information on the repression of historians is a risky task for insiders and their informants, not only when that repression is still occurring, but also afterward. In many situations of transition to democracy, it proves to be potentially dangerous and politically suspect. Even in the quiet circumstances of Costa Rica, Belgium, and the Netherlands, where I worked on this project, I did not entirely escape similar reproaches and fears of colleagues. Such occasional comments helped me to stay alert.

A general principle that I called the *principle of distance* served to shield me from exaggerated personal bias generated by the solidarity that the case of a suffering historian was able to provoke. *This important principle makes clear that I did not (and do not) necessarily share or support the views that have been censored. It also implies that I do not necessarily find censorship unjustified in all cases.* This principle of distance applies to *all* cases but is most obvious in the following five special categories of censorship or persecution of historians: those who illegally gained access to archives and smuggled out information;[50] those who defended the historical truths of official propaganda;[51] those who had previously engaged in some form of hate speech;[52] those who had previously denounced or persecuted their own colleagues;[53] and, finally, those who became persecutors after their own persecution. The Guide contains a few examples of each of these relatively small categories. The persecution of historians who formerly engaged in propaganda for the regime, for example, is telling: their fate often proves the capriciousness to which they are subjected. Likewise, cases of persecuted historians who had previously denounced their colleagues themselves often reveal the cruel pressure put upon them. Aleksandr Nekrich's memoirs reveal the extremely complex, and often thin, line between offender and victim.[54] In general, it is difficult to ascribe unequivocal motives to the position that historians take in times of repression, or for the shift in their position at given moments. Therefore, moral judgments from outsiders on their freedom to act and their collaboration, silence, or resistance are seldom relevant, especially because it remains to be seen how these outsiders would behave themselves in similar circumstances. The outsider's contribution can be valuable only if carried out with humility. The urge to describe and understand was bigger than the urge to praise or condemn. The principle of distance also implies that the Guide is not necessarily a list of morally inspiring examples. Formerly censored historians, amazed to find certain names on the same list as theirs, should not interpret this as indulgence or as moral indifference on the part of this author, or as lack of respect for the profession and for those who have unambiguously suffered for it. Nor should it be considered an attack on their reputation. Conversely, some of these formerly censored historians may find it surprising that a few of their former rivals or enemies were also hit by censorship.

Notwithstanding our principle of distance, two categories of historians were excluded from the Guide: those accused of genocide or war crimes and those accused of Holocaust denial. We found only two examples of the first category.[55] For the second, there were more instances. Although, as stated above, some examples of censorship of hate speech were included in the Guide (however reluctantly), Holocaust denial as a particular type of hate speech was wholly excluded, for two reasons: those who deny the Holocaust are pseudo-historians from the start. In addition, to my knowledge, no government supports their views; Holocaust denial is an affair of unofficial groups.[56] In other cases, official denial of certified genocide or massacres did indeed take place. For half a century, Soviet responsibility for the 1940 Katyń massacre was denied in the USSR. In Turkey, the official historiography does not acknowledge the 1915 Armenian genocide. These cases of official denial were generally accompanied by censorship on the part of the deniers and are therefore incorporated in the Guide.

The reader of the Guide should have an understanding of not only the categories of historians excluded, but also of the information left out for those included. Apart from the "implicit information" discussed above, much context-related information was excluded. First, the Guide describes only one aspect of the historians' lives and does not give complete biographies nor a complete picture of the historical writing in each country. Historians never affected by the powers of repression were excluded. For those listed, censorship was often but one moment in their professional (and private) lives, and generalizing from there would give a wrong impression of their overall performance. Not all the interesting connections among the persons included in the Guide could be indicated. For instance, historians belonging to the same wave of exile may have been acquaintances before exile, or may have been students of the same master, without this being clear from the Guide. Second, there is no systematic description of the network of governmental and other institutions that develop and implement official guidelines of control, nor of the structure and institutions of censorship, nor of the forms of censorship that did not affect the historians. Third, and most important, reverse trends were generally omitted: the Guide does *not* reflect the story of all the positive trends toward openness and tolerance: the rescue of sources; the opening of archives and libraries; the disclosure of formerly secret documents; the reissue of banned works; the exhumation of clandestine cemeteries; the rehabilitation of formerly sentenced historians.

No doubt, some scholars will question the unavoidable element of arbitrariness in our criteria, and our selection will not be to every taste. Others will inspect first (or only) their own country's entry and experience the well-known but perhaps unavoidable disappointment as when one reads a foreign newspaper or travel guide on one's own country. Moreover, although the aim was to be exhaustive, the Guide has a fragmentary character. It contains the traces of the geography of historiographical oblivion and attempts to document this one important dimension. These traces are comparable to archeological discoveries: mostly, they are scattered remnants from various objects and times, but occasionally they can be structured into meaningful sequences and patterns. Several items in the country entry for Belgium, for example, in their accumulated form suggest that King Leopold II's Congo Free State was a very sensitive subject in Belgium until at least the 1980s. Mexico provides another example: the massacre of at least three hundred students at Tlatelolco on 2 October 1968. The dissolution of the state newsprint company in 1968–70, the anger of the army after the 1992 history textbook revision, the refusal to admit an unofficial 1993 truth commission into the archives—all prove how painful a subject Tlatelolco was. These facts form a pattern, but the interpretation of that pattern is also dependent on factors outside our scope supporting the conclusion that, however painful, Tlatelolco was never a taboo subject. The most famous book about the massacre, Elena Poniatowska's *La Noche de Tlatelolco* (1971), had thirty-two editions in seven years and won a prestigious official prize. An attempt to remove the description of Tlatelolco from the 1993 history textbook revision was heavily criticized. Finally, an official truth commission, with promised access to the archives, was installed in October 1997. Thus, provided that the approach is cautious, patterns may be discovered indicating something of the larger picture.

A FRAMEWORK FOR DATA ANALYSIS

Justification of Censorship

From time immemorial, rulers have restricted and suspended the right to freedom of information and expression. When confronted in May 1956 with a French delegation requesting historical research into the political persecutions under Stalin, his successor Nikita Khrushchev declared (in the words of the delegation): "Mais les historiens aussi ont besoin d'être dirigés" ("Historians too must be directed").[57] Many rulers have demonstrated their special interest in history in some way. A superficial count of the heads of state and government between 1945 and 2000 who either had a degree in history, wrote a historical work, held important speeches with historical content, or showed their active interest in history in other demonstrable ways, totals sixty-two leaders in forty-five countries. The eagerness of some rulers to censor history was often proof a contrario for their historical awareness.

Systematic censorship is the characteristic of a tyrannical society. "Not all tyrants torture, but all tyrants censor", observed Article 19's former chairman William Shawcross.[58] The absolute power in such a society does not receive sufficient legitimacy from elections and laws and therefore must seek it elsewhere, often in the past. That power, embodied in an official ideology, attempts to convincingly clarify two major questions: Which historical path did the collectivity follow hitherto? Why is the ruler particularly suited to guide it with a firm hand into the future? Each community (and segment thereof) looks for its roots, needs experiences of continuity with its ancestors, and yearns for uniqueness and pride. At the same time, no ruler whose task it is to give the community that desired background can do without an acceptable biography and a venerable genealogy. The past, as a huge stock of usable examples, is able to satisfy and lend authority to both demands. The problem, however, is that the official selection of historical examples, chosen to give body to the ideology, can be challenged at any given moment. Therefore, the ruler is forced not only to make use of the past, but also to optimize that use. As Bernard Lewis aptly put it, "The problem is to justify a successful revolution without at the same time justifying further revolutions against the first one—or to justify an existing authority without at the same time justifying a restoration of that which it has just overthrown. . . . Probably the only solution to it is . . . complete state control of the means of production, distribution, and exchange of historical knowledge and writing."[59] In a tyrannical system, in short, the official ideology must make history its instrument. In such a system, the present commands the past, but it is highly doubtful whether the tyrant who loses the keys to history is still able to rule.

In contrast to democracies that also partially draw legitimacy from the past, tyrannical regimes do not tolerate alternative historical versions. They use propaganda and censorship as twin cornerstones—the former to promote the official vision, the latter to eradicate the rest. They falsify the past to root their power, the present to glorify it, the future to immortalize it. None of the stages of historical scholarship is safe from propaganda and censorship. Ideally, they do not blatantly falsify the historical record but leave intact as much of the past as possible and only alter key passages. They attempt to distort history gently so as to arouse unanimity, not suspicion and dissent.[60] Reality, however, does not always match the ideal: history, then, is often crudely mutilated and falsified. As Bertram Wolfe wrote: "Shall the Dictator . . . be less harsh with facts and

records than with men? Should he be more tender with the traditions and men
of other lands and other times than he is with the men of his own land and
time?"[61] Historical propaganda—defined as the systematic *manipulation* of information concerning the past by, or with the connivance of, the authorities—
may be of three types: by comission, when it falsifies, embellishes, or invents;
by omission, when it omits and forgets to the degree that there is no chance to
realize that something ever happened; and by a mixture of both when it denies.[62]
The second and third types are close to censorship.

Propaganda is clearly a much broader phenomenon than censorship, but there
are two crucial differences between them. First, historical propaganda is not
absent from democratic societies, while systematic censorship of history generally is. Second, censorship tries to suppress alternative views through control
and coercion, and ultimately through violence, whereas propaganda tries to impose one view through manipulation, and ultimately through lies (including lies
about violence). In other words, propaganda does not necessarily imply censorship, but censorship is always accompanied by propaganda. The union of propaganda and censorship creates an official historiography with monopolistic
pretensions and absolute truths and discourages or blocks inquiry challenging
it. Historical truth, when decreed and absolute, is the companion of oblivion.
Preferred topics for propaganda are those that illustrate the official ideology.
Cherished antecedents and historical parallels favorable to tyrannical power are
praised, enemies and heresies deemphasized or diabolized as subversive. To this
end, key episodes of history need reassessment or recovery. Topics viewed as
controversial and subject to censorship are those that question the official ideology: crimes and victims of the regime, rivalry among its leaders, discord
among the population, allusions to the illegitimate or mystified origins of power,
frictions with other countries, military defeat, periods of humiliation and weak-
ness, and the history of successful rivals, dominated minorities, and classes. A
more detailed analysis of historical propaganda would disclose some interesting
questions: How does the official patronage of cultural and historical activities
work? How understandable and justifiable are the uses of historical propaganda?
What are the differences between propaganda and official history?[63]

The dynamics of making historiography servile have their stages (usually
from "Gleichschaltung" [equalization] to "normality", and finally to "glasnost"
[openness]) and are dependent on many factors: history's place in society; the
traditions of integrity among historians before tyranny and their standing as
public figures; the consistency, elaboration, and monopolization of the degree
of the tyrannical ideology; the centrality of history therein; and the strength of
the repressive apparatus. The manipulated interpretations of the past are adapted
to the needs of the moment; firm and lenient control alternate. Censorship fluc-
tuates with it—at one moment, it is a legal activity, at another an illegal one;
at one moment it differs regionally, at other moments it has, as in the case of
the communist countries, international dimensions. In swiftly changing circumstances, "each earlier version had to disappear, lest, rising from oblivion, it might

bear witness against its successor", as Walter Laqueur stated.[64] In his novel *1984*, George Orwell described the position of history in the model repressive state: "All history was a palimpsest, scraped clean and re-inscribed, exactly as often as was necessary."[65]

Methods and Targets of Censorship

In the film *Schindler's List*, there is a telling scene: a Jew lines up to get a "blue card", a permit stating that one is an "essential worker". Asked for his profession, he tells the German soldier behind the desk that he is a teacher of history and literature. He is promptly refused the card and almost sent off to the concentration camp. After some enervating consultations, Schindler's assistant is able to save the man by having him lined up in another queue with a forged document "proving" that he is a metalworker. Despite the lament of the history teacher, his profession was declared "not essential" and he was destined to be censored away in one stroke.[66] Not only does the teaching of history suffer this fate, censorship affects all modes and genres of history. In many countries, contemporary history is certainly the most dangerous field of study.[67] But in some countries, earlier periods of history constitute the focus of official attention.[68] In yet other countries, the nation's origins and, concomitantly, archeological findings are sensitive topics.[69] Restricted access, negligence, and destruction of archives are sometimes vital expressions of the government's strategy. No genre is really a safe area, not even the most "system-independent" one (such as the edition of sources). Everywhere, official taboos or sensitive analogies can be touched on. Three domains are usually watched very closely: contemporary history (because the witnesses are still alive), popular history with its multiple channels (because of its reach), and all media feeding or reflecting collective memory (such as songs, wall paintings, commemorations, films, and television). "Precensorship" attempts to regulate research. This is the classical form of censorship. Sources are destroyed or inaccessible, manuscripts and data confiscated, rewritten, or rejected. Publishers and printers can be forced to align with official policy. Whereas precensorship is often invisible to the public, postcensorship, aimed at the consumption of the research products, is not: lectures may be boycotted or publications blacklisted, banned, pulped, or burned.

In such a context, the historians are forced to take a position. Schematically, they opt for either *collaboration, silence,* or *resistance.* In the first category (collaboration), *propaganda historians* cooperate with the tyrant. They actively agree with the principle that history serves the reigning ideology and that the ideology controls history. They write a history in which the rulers are glorified such as to be fully justified in controlling history. Among them, the *court historians* write the official history, lead the new history departments and journals, enjoy the privileges and favors of power, and are perhaps engaged as censors. Others, the *bureaucratic historians*, carry out smaller tasks and disseminate the official views. In both groups, some suffer from the moral dilemma engendered by the manipulation of history while others revolt and become dissident or persecuted historians themselves. To the second category belong the *silent historians*, who may follow very different paths. *Accommodating historians* yield to the pressure, tacitly accept propaganda, and employ self-censorship out of fear or for opportunistic or idealistic reasons. It is a position in which ethics can conflict with self-preservation. *Safe-area historians* avoid controversy, switch to relatively safe areas of research and teaching, and enjoy small margins of freedom. Forms of accumulated erudition such as annotated source editions and research into early historical periods are often mentioned as preferred safe areas, in which problems of controversial interpretation are circumvented.[70] *Inner-exile historians* tacitly refuse to endorse the regime, leave their manuscripts in the drawer, or discontinue their historical work. The spectrum of options makes the silent historian the most common, and surely the most enigmatic, type, whose motives are often difficult to guess. To the third category (resistance) belong the *protesting historians*.[71] They differ from the inner-exile historians in that the latter try just to preserve their conscience, while the former aim at an additional social effect. This type has four basic positions.[72] *Aesopian historians* use tricks to evade censorship (historical analogies, an ornate style, omission of the index, original research between obedient introduction and conclusion). *Opposition historians* openly challenge the attempts to curb freedom: they attack falsification, reorient their field of study *toward* prohibited areas, or organize petitions and manifestos. They usually become the object of scathing attacks. *Underground historians* continue their research in clandestinity, often (but certainly not always) to refute official views, and publish their manuscripts in samizdat (self-publishing) style. Theirs is a dangerous and mostly isolated situation, cut off from an audience, barely surviving. They and their readers are torn by the near-impossibility of a freer exchange of ideas. They take extensive personal security measures and their work is characterized by methodological approaches that compensate for the scarcity of historical sources at their disposal. *Refugee historians* try to adapt to a new environment and must overcome financial difficulties and obstacles of language and age. As most have written national history, they confront the painful problem of being cut off from their natural biotope and unportable sources. Some change careers, some keep alive and enrich the critical traditions of historiography. Nonhistorians in exile may turn to historical research.[73] It is not easy to determine why some historians choose clandestinity and others exile. Clandestinity is unnecessary when the regime allows enough freedom and impossible when it allows none. Occasionally, underground and refugee historians have cooperated or been in conflict. Confronting tyranny unites them; mutually incompatible historiographies divide them. When their historical work is polemical, its quality may be affected.

The arsenal of repressive measures is huge. Professional repression ranges from the loss of privilege and promotion, over demotion, to dismissal and unemployment. Measures may be individual or collective. When the historian becomes persona non grata and suspicion is all-pervasive, the terror may transform from professional into physical repression. Mail control, telephone tapping, intimidation, blackmail, smear campaigns, threats (even to those living abroad), house search, interrogation, house arrest, purges, trial, and detention are part of its panoply. The ultimate shapes of censorship are torture, death penalty, political murder, and disappearance. Long before such a point is reached, the peer community of historians ceases to act as an honest check on the scholarly character of historical works, scores of historians are obliged to destroy their own writings; the whole climate is infected and the border between truth and lies almost irreparably blurred. Like a cancer, the censorship of history affects and poisons the professional climate: qualifications become unimportant and judgments twisted; surviving historians are terrorized and begin to neglect sources and research. Ultimately, the once-stuffed drawers stand empty. Censored historians may wrongly claim superiority for their work by the mere fact that it was censored. All this leaves its imprint on the present and future generations of historians as a social group. The main overall effect of censorship on the profession is sterility. But, despite all control, the professionals are seldom a willing tool of some prescribed line; they always retain some bargaining power, represented by their training and knowledge, because they must apply the general guidelines to many different historical problems and contexts or translate them into detailed curricula and textbooks. In doing so, they are able to create margins that increase as one moves further from the kernel of ideology.[74] It implies that a purely instrumental theory of historiography is too poor to be true.

At the wider societal level, the tyrant's aim is a unanimously obedient people, but the effect of censorship may be doubt about dogma and room for dissidence. This has two consequences. First, censorship engenders a credibility gap between the official history taught at school and the unrestricted history told at home, often followed by a feeling of disillusion, especially among the younger generation in the face of a culture of lies.[75] Second, it generates the emergence of substitutes: Whenever the silenced and silent historians are not able to refute the heralded truths of official historical propaganda, novelists, playwrights, journalists, storytellers, singers, and others take care of the historical truth and keep it alive. The example most abundantly documented is the USSR during glasnost.[76] Even in the darkest hours, the distorted past may be challenged by the versions whispered at home or written down by those who replace the silenced historian. The alternative versions may be equally distorting, but they are alternative and, through them, the flame of plurality survives.[77] Therefore, whether the general historical awareness increases or diminishes in times of censorship is difficult to say. Either option is possible (at least in theory). The trauma left by tyranny may crush or arouse memory and stimulate or counter oblivion. In the first instance, the erasure of history leads to a decreasing historical awareness, to amnesia, and to the loss of the vital source of identification that is the past. In the second, it leads to an upsurge of historical awareness whenever the unofficial past is eagerly consulted as a source of consolation and power to counterbalance contemporary terror.

When tyrants are toppled, the windows of the past are thrown open. With a truly Rankean rage,[78] people want to know history "as it actually happened". The transition to democracy and the abolition of systematic censorship go hand in hand and enable the development of an independent historiography. It is an epoch of uncertainty and disorientation, as intimidation and suspicion feverishly change into hope but, at the same time, old habits may suddenly return (under another guise) and prevent the new freedom from rooting. The past plays a key role in this transition process, for the exposure of historical falsifications, the juridical and political rehabilitation of political adversaries formerly fallen into disgrace, the predilection for new historical symbols, all contribute to the de-legitimation of the ancien régime. Rehabilitation, for example, if publicized, contributes to the revival of certain genres, such as biographies and memoirs.[79] Two or more warring pasts may coexist. The task is difficult, especially where the credibility gap appears to engender persistent distrust of the historical profession. It includes the partial replacement—avoiding both purges and impunity—of compromised historians, the rehabilitation and reemployment (if still feasible) of persecuted historians, and the training of a new generation of responsible history students. Archives need a new policy of openness. In terms of personnel and infrastructure, the precarious solution to this problem in most countries leaves room only for a certain degree of generational continuity and, therefore, compromise.[80] Some historical genres—those most abused (chronicles, biographies, genealogies)—could be discredited for a long time to come. In short, tyranny haunts the lands of history long after its own burial. However, also in the new era, official histories will continue to exist and be put at the service of ideology and power. But the difference between tyranny and democracy is crucial: the new historiography, aspiring to be free and independent, will tirelessly open archives, fill in blank spots and black holes, demystify propagandist versions of the past, and further develop its critical method at all stages of scholarship, so as to be less amenable to abuse. Perhaps the hardest task of all is to solidify the transitional fever to learn the truth about the traumas of history and to keep alive a decent memory of past atrocities. This is probably a necessary precondition for political democracy. For historians, the most troubling part of their vocation is to be chroniclers of such painful memory.[81] When novelist Aleksandr Solzhenitsyn tried to be such a chronicler in the face of persecutors who did not want the past to be dug up, he cited an old proverb: "Dwell on the past and you'll lose an eye; forget the past and you'll lose both."[82]

In a paradoxical sense, censorship may have unintended positive effects. While pondering these, South African historian N.G. Garson had in mind the incentive it provides for creativity when he provokingly wrote: "In certain circumstances the non-availability of banned material through censorship might serve as a healthy challenge to academic endeavor or ingenuity. On the other hand, if allowed to reach too formidable proportions, the challenge could weaken the creative and scholarly impulse to probe whole areas of our own history at all."[83] Garson's remark is undoubtedly true for some historians, but not for others. We think of another unintended effect, "the paradoxical ability of censorship that, in its efforts to suppress, it highlights that which it wishes to condemn."[84] Stephen Jones saw this unexpected but logical effect in "the Soviet Union, [where] the system [of politicized history] itself, in its interaction with traditional structures in Georgian society, *did* reinforce the channels, both informal and formal, that created and preserved Georgian national history. To paraphrase Marx, the peddlers of the official Soviet past produced their own grave diggers. These grave diggers are now busily burying what is left of the old past."[85] Hermann Weber recognized the same effect after the dictatorship had withered away: "Die seit Jahrzehnten angeordnete Aussperrung der 'weißen Flekken' . . . hat nun ein verstärktes, ja zur Zeit fast ausschließliches Interesse für diese Fragen provoziert" (For decades the exclusion of "blank spots" had been ordered . . . only to provoke a stronger and almost obsessive interest in these issues nowadays).[86] Taboos always attract curiosity. When history as the classical vehicle of the past is silenced and compromised and has lost its credibility, every utterance—graffiti, literature, theater, film—becomes its potential vehicle. Thus, censorship may not suppress alternative views but rather generate them and, by doing so, undermine its own aims.[87]

A Comparative Research Agenda

We have already argued that patterns may be discovered from the Guide and give some indication of the larger picture. In addition, the data permit many avenues for comparative reflection and analysis. For example, it is truly remarkable how frequently censorship and taboos in Western countries revolve around their colonial role. The cross-references at the bottom of each country entry and the person and subject index provide the key for such comparative attempts. Elsewhere, I myself have tried to make small surveys of censorship, based on this Guide's data, in the following areas: rewriting of history, archeology, archives, history textbooks, and military history.[88] Similar comparative analyses could be attempted for the fate of historians of antiquity (up to 500 C.E.), medievalists (500–1500), historians of modern times (1500–1900), and contemporary historians (1900–2000). The corpus also allows one to compare the problems of other categories, for example, female historians, art historians, literary historians, historical anthropologists, authors of historical novels, makers of historical films, or history students. The fates of refugee historians and to a lesser degree underground historians are already fields in full exploration.[89] The Guide also permits substantiation of obvious correlations between censorship and certain variables, such as coups d'état or mass murder. More difficult but perhaps still feasible would be a comparative analysis of the taboos and blank spots over different countries, or, to a certain extent, the uses of historical propaganda by rulers. The Guide also constitutes an empirical base to study certain aspects of academic freedom and university autonomy, such as, for example, defamation trials against historians, the resistance of historians to censorship and tyranny, or the campaigns of solidarity with the victimized historians.[90]

CENSORSHIP AND THE RIGHTS AND OBLIGATIONS OF HISTORIANS: A LIST OF QUESTIONS

This brings us to the problem of ethics within the historical profession, a wide, complicated, and largely unexplored field of study. Only the relationship between historians' ethics and the problem of censorship are briefly discussed here under the guise of a list of questions. But first, one needs at least a summary understanding of what constitutes the historian's core rights and obligations. The core professional right is Article 19 of the Universal Declaration of Human Rights:[91] freedom of expression for teaching and publishing, and freedom of information for conducting research. The core professional obligation is the search for historical truth(s), based on a critical method and a moral attitude of intellectual integrity. The classic formulation of this obligation was Cicero's. It was repeated by generations of historians, to the point that one may almost speak of a Ciceronian Oath: "The first law for the historian is that he shall never dare utter an untruth; the second is that he suppress nothing that is true."[92] Adapting a general statement by Karl Popper, this professional obligation is created by historians' potential access to knowledge about the past; or, in Popper's words, "sagesse oblige" ("wisdom obligates").[93] Apart from the professional obligations, one could distinguish at least five other types that historians are compelled to discharge: their moral, legal, social, political, and cultural obligations. For example, social obligations are those with regard to past, present, and future generations.

Within this general framework plenty of questions arise, only some of which are related to the censorship debate and presented here. This is not the place for a full discussion of these interrelationships; the questions are meant to be kept in the back of the mind.[94] First on the list are some general questions. Does something like a right to historical truth exist?[95] Is the abuse of history by historians worse than that by laypersons? Are historians allowed to assert their rights when they do not discharge their obligations (when they consciously lie and falsify the past), and to what extent? Does the community of historians in a given country have an obligation to study the entire past rather than its officially preferred episodes[96] and attack monopolies, taboos, and blank spots? Should historians strive for maximal political and intellectual independence in their work, and to what extent should they tolerate commitment to certain causes (when designing their research) and moral judgments (when concluding their research)? Do they still have obligations when they are unable to exercise their rights? Second on the list are some questions in the realm of freedom of information. Should historians actively see to it that archival selection criteria give due weight to historical considerations, and that public and equal access to archives is the rule, and politically inspired selection, privileged access, and secrecy the exception? Third on the list are questions in the realm of freedom of expression. Should historians always denounce historical lies? Are they obliged to react when others abuse their work? Should they always tell the truth, as the "Ciceronian Oath" states, even when they have doubts about their version of the past, despite the risk of being treated as destroyers of reputations or traitors and of being threatened with judicial or physical reprisal by governments, individuals, or radical social and ethnic groups?[97] And when they have decided to remain silent but their expert opinion is explicitly solicited, what should they do? Do they have a right to silence?[98] With regard to historians living in democratic societies: If the freedom of expression of their colleagues living under a tyrannical regime is in danger, is theirs as well (in both the concrete sense that the curtailed freedoms of others literally decrease theirs through the lessened possibilities of exchange, and the philosophical sense that human rights should be universal)? Is it their primary task to defend the core rights of the profession, and, by implication, the rights of their endangered colleagues? How should they express solidarity with these colleagues?[99]

CONCLUSION: VALUE OF THE GUIDE

I believe that the present Guide has a value in four domains.

- *As an indicator of the universal presence of the censorship of historical thought*:
  The Guide demonstrates that history is an important, dangerous, and fragile subject. It attempts to sketch a world map of repression of the historical profession that goes beyond the well-known and well-studied cases. Its geography indicates that censorship of history is widespread and multifaceted and occurs in widely diverging political and historiographical contexts. It shows both the universality of the censorship of historical thought and its infinite variety in amount and degree. As such it is a basis for comparative research.

- *As a heuristic compass*:
  The Guide provides an index of the taboos and fiercely debated historical topics and names them. It is a list, albeit incomplete, of key issues and interpretations of history. Ironically, the list of taboo and falsified subjects is proof a contrario of sharp historical awareness and, as such, a source for the history of mentalities. As Jacques Le Goff put it with regard to forgeries: "Un document 'faux' est aussi un document historique et . . . il peut être un témoignage précieux sur l'époque où il a été forgé et sur la période pendant laquelle il a été tenu pour authentique et utilisé" (A "false" document is also a historical source . . . and it may constitute a precious witness of the period in which it was forged and of the period during which it was believed to be authentic and used).[100] Both the ruler who censors and the historian who resists it are aware of the importance of the censored topics. An analysis of these topics sharpens the critical sense. It contributes to the development of the tools of historical

criticism. It uncovers the mechanisms of oblivion and the abuses of history. It gives insight into the political manipulation of history in its multiple forms as part of the legitimation of power and the construction of collective identities.

• *As a tool of awareness of the risks run in the historical profession*:
Not only does the Guide uncover the mechanisms of oblivion and the abuses of history, it also warns against them. Censorship of history is a well-known and obvious area of interest, but it is also an underestimated and neglected topic of research. In 1985 the Slovak Miroslav Kusý, a dismissed philosopher-turned-unskilled worker under "normalization", complained that famous historians like Marc Bloch and Edward Carr did not pay any attention to the difficulties and risks of the historical profession and the historian's vulnerability in their highly acclaimed works on the methodology of history.[101] Both were, however, very vulnerable themselves and became victims of censorship and repression. Carr's multivolume *History of Soviet Russia* was banned in the USSR for four decades, and Bloch died at the hands of the Gestapo near Lyons in 1944. Historians should always be on the alert for the official and unofficial attempts to silence their colleagues and others concerned with the past.

• *As a tribute to victimized historians and as an appeal to memory and responsibility*:
It is difficult to reconcile the principle of distance, discussed earlier, with a tribute to victimized historians. However, while studying the cases I often admired the historians' courage, the quality of their historical work, and their resistance to the censorship of historical thought. Even when I did not, I caught glimpses of the dilemmas and sad circumstances inflicted upon all those fallen victim to repression. This work is an appeal to remember them, the well-known and the forgotten, and to commemorate them as a part of the history of man's dealings with the past. I believe that this remembrance stimulates our responsibility—professionally, by constituting a powerful incentive for independent and truthful history; morally, by providing the insight that we should utilize our academic freedom on behalf of those to whom it is denied. Neither the past nor the historians who have been prevented from uncovering it should fall into oblivion. When our colleagues' right to history is in danger, ours is too. Therefore, this Guide is dedicated to the memory of those historians and citizens concerned with the past who have defended the right to history, sometimes at the risk of their lives.

NOTES

1. The list of exiles includes not only those persons who were already historians before their exile but also those who became historians or began writing historical works *during* their exile. Historians who were born in exile or who went into exile at a young

age, and before they made the choice of studying history, are mentioned separately for reasons of clarity. This does not rule out, of course, that at least some of these (so to speak) second-generation refugee historians chose to study history in order to understand their roots and migration history. But even then, it remained to be seen whether they specialized in the history of their country or region of origin. Also see H. Lehmann & J.J. Sheehan eds., *An Interrupted Past: German-Speaking Refugee Historians in the United States* (Cambridge 1991) viii–ix, 2, 113, and P. Alter ed., *Out of the Third Reich: Refugee Historians in Post-War Britain* (London/New York 1998) xvii–xx.

2. E.g., the Iranian Ali Shariati, who died in London under mysterious circumstances, and the British citizen Salman Rushdie, against whom Ayatollah Khomeini issued a fatwa, are both cataloged under "Iran" (1957 and 1989, respectively).

3. See the Holden case, listed tentatively under "Saudi Arabia" (1977).

4. Yet one should interpret these peaks carefully so as not to fall victim to epistemological myopia; for example, a major wave of repression in a given country may result in minor persecutions of historians when an earlier wave of repression has already curtailed the profession.

5. In the source list, specific page indications follow the references for works because retrieval of information would otherwise be difficult or confusing. I realize that a system of notes would have greater verifiability—e.g., to identify the origin of small scraps of information incorporated quasi-unaltered in the Guide—but the present format does not allow this. Due to space restrictions, I omitted authors and articles in the abundant references to *Index on Censorship*—a first-rate source—to some other journals, and to all newspapers, book reviews, and obituaries. When I used information from conversations or letters, I generally sought the permission of my interlocutors. Although this was not always possible, most of them generously agreed when I did. This last type of information is always identified as "personal communication".

6. For example, the Guide contains abundant examples of censored films. Many historical films, however, were not censored for their historical content but for other reasons. The historical settings in such censored films as *Il Decameron, I Racconti di Canterbury, Il Fiore delle 1001 notte*, and *Salò o le 120 giornate di Sodoma* (all by Pier Paolo Pasolini, 1971–75) or *Caligula* (Bob Guccione, Franco Rossellini) were apparently not very relevant, or at least not essential, to the censor.

7. See, e.g., the work of Yurasov (USSR 1987–91).

8. In this introduction, I sometimes use the term *historians* as shorthand for all these categories.

9. For examples of photograph manipulation in the USSR, Fascist Italy, Nazi Germany, China, Czechoslovakia, Vietnam, North Korea, Cambodia, the Balkans, Cuba, and France, see A. Jaubert, *Le Commissariat aux archives: Les Photos qui falsifient l'histoire* (Paris 1986).

10. In addition, no attempt has been made to cover censorship of such famous books as the Bible, the Koran, *Das Kapital*, or *Mein Kampf*. With regard to religion in particular, the main problem with which censorship is concerned is blasphemy. Despite the importance of the historical context of all religions, accusations of blasphemy to, e.g., Jesus or Mohammed were excluded from the present Guide. Censorship as a result of unwelcome historical interpretations of holy books, however, was included.

11. Likewise, whereas the ransacking of historical archives is included in the Guide, the ransacking of archives of newspapers—a frequent governmental practice—is not.

12. This definition is derived from general definitions of censorship as discussed by

S. Hampshire & L. Blom-Cooper, "Censorship?" *Index on Censorship* (further abbreviated as *IOC*) 4/77: 55, and M. Scammell, "Censorship and Its History: A Personal View", in: Article 19, *Information, Freedom and Censorship: World Report 1988* (London 1988) 10.

13. E.H. Carr, *What Is History?* (Houndmills, 1961) 23, 44.

14. E. Shils, "Academic Freedom", in: P.G. Altbach ed., *International Higher Education: An Encyclopedia*, vol. 1 (New York/London 1991) 4, 12.

15. Shils's position on the historical profession is ambiguous indeed. He writes: "The traditional humanistic disciplines—classics, philology, oriental studies, modern languages, literature, and history—have generally been spared any restrictions of academic freedom." But only two phrases later he adds: "Historically, the most common victims of sanctions have been teachers of law, history, philosophy, and social science." (Shils 1991: 12).

16. See, e.g., Brazil (pre-1947–: Prado), Ghana (1977–93: Boahen), and Guyana (1974–96: Rodney).

17. See, e.g., China (1989–: Wang Dan) and Nigeria (1989–90: Bala Usman).

18. For the writing, teaching, or telling of history in prison or under house arrest, see A. De Baets, "Resistance to the Censorship of Historical Thought in the Twentieth Century," in: S. Sogner ed., *Making Sense of Global History: The 19th International Congress of Historical Sciences, Oslo 2000, Commemorative Volume* (Oslo 2001) 389–409 (also unannotated as "Resistance to the Censorship of Historical Thought", in: D. Jones ed., *Censorship: A World Encyclopedia* [London/Chicago 2001] 1056–59). Many writers have pointed out the acute awareness of time and the power of memory and memory training as survival tools in prison. Prison reflections on history and time acquire special importance in view of the fact that prisoners generally call the loss of the sense of time one of the greatest dangers of prison life (see, e.g., Nicaragua [1975–77: Benavides]). Indeed, in prison, the present is grim and the future often inconceivable; only the past gives some comfort. For the power of memory while in prison, see S. Zweig, *Schachnovelle* (originally 1942; Frankfurt am Main 1959); P. Levi, *I Sommersi e i salvati* (Torino 1986) 112–13; D. Paillard, "Figures de la mémoire: *Mémorial* et *Pamiat*", in: A. Brossat, S. Combe, J.-Y. Potel, & J.-C. Szurek eds., *A l'Est, la mémoire retrouvée* (Paris 1990) 370. The Russian historian Mikhail Gefter called prison "the land of memory".

19. See, e.g., Argentina (1945: Perón), Romania (1945–: Eliade).

20. See, e.g., Bosnia-Herzegovina (1993–97: Memisević). Also see the remarks of K.K. Aziz on the effects of the partition of British India (1947) and Pakistan (1971) on historical writing in Pakistan, in: *The Pakistani Historian: Pride and Prejudice in the Writing of History* (Lahore 1993) 22–23. Also see A. De Baets, "Archives", in: Jones ed. 2001: 76–82, and De Baets, "The Dictator's Secret Archives: Rationales for Their Creation, Destruction, and Disclosure" (manuscript for the International Conference *Knowledge, Learning and Cultural Change*; Groningen 2001).

21. See A. De Baets, "Archaeology", in: Jones ed. 2001: 73–76.

22. Oral traditionist and historian Amadou Hampâté Bâ used to say: "Any old man who dies is a burning library" (Quoted in: E. de Sousa Ferreira, *Portuguese Colonialism in Africa: The End of an Era; The Effects of Portuguese Colonialism on Education, Science, Culture and Information* (Paris 1974) 117. In this vein, an astute observer of political life in Latin America suggested to me that in some situations of grave repression, as with the Mayas in Guatemala in the 1980s, elderly people were killed in order to prevent the oral transmission of historical knowledge to the youth (personal communi-

cation by Eduardo Mariño, 1988, 1997, 1998). Also see: Comité pro Justicia y Paz de Guatemala, *Human Rights in Guatemala* ([Geneva] 1984) 18: "(. . .) the elders of the community are murdered with exceptional cruelty in order to destroy the people's links with their past. . . . [T]he elders are the trustees of the people's history, culture and beliefs, and responsible for transmitting them to coming generations." This idea is also expressed (not as a policy, however, but as a result) in: *Guatemala: Nunca Más* (special bulletin with summary of REMHI report, 6 June 1998) 13: "Muchas comunidades que sufrieron la pérdida de sus ancianos y autoridades tradicionales, perdieron con ellos la memoria de sus ancestros y las experiencias de resolver los problemas comunitarios según el sistema tradicional maya."("Many communities suffered the loss of their elderly and traditional authorities and with them the memory of their ancestors and the experience of solving the problems of their community according to Mayan custom") Also: *Guatemala: Memory of Silence/Tzinil Na Tabal: Report of the Commission for Historical Clarification—Conclusions and Recommendations* (Washington 1999) 30.

23. See, e.g., Australia (1980s).

24. For privacy, see, e.g., United States (1963–71: Russell).

25. The International Centre Against Censorship Article 19 recommended the following rule of thumb for information policies: "While interference with the holding of opinions is never justified, limits may be placed on freedom of expression and the availability of information in certain circumstances. The general guiding principle is that freedom is the rule and its limitation the exception, with the onus of justification resting with those wishing to impose restrictions. It should be possible to contest any restriction through a procedure independent of the executive branch, such as a judicial hearing or the opportunity for judicial review." Article 19, *Information, Freedom and Censorship: World Report 1991* (London 1991) 411–12. Also see Article 19, *The Public's Right to Know: Principles of Freedom of Information Legislation* (London 1999).

26. H. Butterfield, "Official History: Its Pitfalls and Criteria" (originally 1949), in: Butterfield, *History and Human Relations* (London 1951) 186.

27. See A. De Baets, "Truth Commissions", in: Jones ed. 2001, and De Baets, "Waarheidscommissies als Protohistorici" [Truth Commissions as Protohistorians], *Nieuwste Tijd*, 2001, no. 3 (November).

28. Examples include the annuled celebrations of important anniversaries in Poland (N. Davies, *God's Playground: A History of Poland I* [Oxford 1981] 20); disturbances during annual pilgrimages between Najaf and Kerbala, two holy Shia towns in Iraq (*Amnesty International Report 1977* [further abbreviated as *AIR*] [London 1977] 301–2; *AIR 1978* [London 1978] 158; Human Rights Watch, *World Report 1998* [Washington 1997] 334); violence at the Golden Temple of Amritsar, the main Sikh shrine, in India (*AIR 1985* [London 1985] 210); detention of members of the Shia Muslim community to prevent their presence at the annual Ashoura procession in Bahrain (*AIR 1989* [London 1989] 251); the arrest of persons placing a wreath at a monument to José Martí and reading out loud a declaration in Cuba (*AIR 1989* [London 1989] 118); and the arrest of a tribal leader to prevent him from attending a Buddhist ceremony to commemorate the dead in recent killings in Bangladesh (*AIR 1990* [London 1990] 41).

29. See Romania (1980–96), Yugoslavia (1989–).

30. Compare: ". . . [A] Right to sue in defamation for the reputation of deceased persons could easily be abused and might prevent free and open debate about historical events", in: Article 19, *Defining Defamation: Principles on Freedom of Expression and Protection of Reputation* (WWW-text; London 2000).

31. For the value of the comparison between the judge and the historian, see J. Gilissen, "La Responsabilité civile et pénale de l'historien", *Revue belge de philologie et d'histoire*, 1960: 295–329, 1005–39; "Histoire et droit", *Le Débat*, November 1984: 92–125, "Vérité judiciaire et vérité historique", *Le Débat*, November–December 1988: 3–51; M. Rebérioux, "Le Génocide, le juge et l'historien", *L'Histoire*, November 1990: 92–94; C. Ginzburg, *Il Giudice e lo storico: Considerazioni in margine al processo Sofri* (Torino 1991); J.-N. Jeanneney, *Le Passé dans le prétoire: L'Historien, le juge et le journaliste* (Paris 1998); and N. Frei, D. van Laak, & M. Stolleis eds., *Geschichte vor Gericht: Historiker, Richter und die Suche nach Gerechtigkeit* (Munich 2000).

32. Not included in the Guide are historians who became unemployed after the 1945 closure of universities such as Breslau (now: Wrocław) and Posen (now: Poznań).

33. Shils 1991: 10.

34. In 1966 the Irish Republican Army blew up Nelson's pillar; in 1991 the tomb of Sandinista Front founder Carlos Fonseca was bombed.

35. See, e.g., Egypt (1992: Foda), India ([1981]: Habib; 1992: Hasan; 1994: Hussain; 1989: Kalburgi), Israel/Lebanon (1981: Kayyali), Japan (1963–: Ienaga), South Africa (1979: Van Jaarsveld), Sri Lanka (1994: Sabalingham), Sudan (pre-1989–: Shuqayr), Turkey (1976–: Tanilli), United Arab Emirates ([1979]: Aqil), Zambia (1980–: Papstein).

36. For a presentation of the five layers of eurocentrism, see A. De Baets, "Eurocentrism in the Writing and Teaching of History", in: D.R. Woolf ed., *A Global Encyclopedia of Historical Writing* (New York 1998) 303–5.

37. See, e.g., Iran (1991–92: female archeologists), Uganda (1971–79: Heddle), United States (1966: Franklin).

38. For typologies of taboo topics that are potentially subject to censorship, see *IOC* 4/78: 28; and M. Ferro, *L'Histoire sous surveillance: Science et conscience de l'histoire* (Paris 1985) 52–60. A frequently used term to indicate taboos is *blank spots*. According to Thomas Szayna ("Addressing 'Blank Spots' in Polish-Soviet Relations", *Problems of Communism*, 1988: 37–38), blank spots originally indicated the unexplored territories which left white spaces on nineteenth-century maps of interior Africa. In Poland the concept was first used by Solidarity to indicate the topics too embarrassing to discuss openly and honestly. They were either ignored (such as the deportations of 1939) or falsified (such as the Katyń massacre), but they did not necessarily imply that the scholars or the public had no knowledge of them. Also see V. Tolz, " 'Blank Spots' in Soviet History", *Radio Liberty Research*, 21 March 1988: 1–3. For the synonymous term *black holes*, see M. Simecka, "Black Holes", *IOC* 5/88: 52–54 (he defines them as "segments of history cloaked in total darkness, devoid of life, of persons, of ideas"). Another synonymous term, *memory holes*, was invented by George Orwell, in: *Nineteen Eighty-Four* (London 1949) 40.

39. Stephen Spender called propaganda "positive censorship"; see "Thoughts on Censorship in the World of 1984", in: *Censorship: 500 Years of Conflict* (Oxford 1984) 120.

40. S. Dubnov-Erlich, *The Life and Work of S.M. Dubnov: Diaspora Nationalism and Jewish History* (originally 1950; Bloomington/Indianapolis 1991) 247.

41. B. Unfried, "Tchécoslovaquie: L'Historiographie indépendante depuis 1968", in: Brossat et al. eds. 1990: 484–85.

42. A.F. Thurston, *Enemies of the People* (New York 1987) 133.

43. Scammell 1988: 8.

44. C. Ponting, *Secrecy in Britain* (Oxford 1990) 67. Also see Tzvetan Todorov's

remark that in the USSR they reportedly shot the gulls on the Solovki Islands to prevent them from carrying messages from the detainees (T. Todorov, "The Abuses of Memory", *Common Knowledge*, 1996, no. 1: 7). This characteristic of censors is similar to that of falsifiers; see P. Vidal-Naquet, *Assassins of Memory: Essays on the Denial of the Holocaust* (originally in French 1987; New York 1992) 51: "It is the distinguishing feature of a lie to want to pass itself off as the truth."

45. Also see P. Novick, *That Noble Dream: The "Objectivity Question" and the American Historical Profession* (Cambridge 1988) 331: "With respect to the consequences of repression, one confronts the paradox that the measure of its effectiveness is the scarcity of overt instances".

46. See the preface of one of the rare examples, *Acta Persecutionis: A Document from Czechoslovakia* (San Francisco 1975).

47. See Poland (1977: *Black Book of Censorship*). Also see R. Darnton, "The Viewpoint of the Censor", in: Darnton, *Berlin Journal 1989–1990* (New York/London 1991) 202–17.

48. In particular the American Association for the Advancement of Science (and its Human Rights Action Network), Amnesty International, Article 19, Human Rights Watch (and its Academic Freedom Program), Index on Censorship, International PEN Writers in Prison Committee, and World University Service. The files of one potentially major source, the UNESCO Committee on Conventions and Recommendations (established in 1978 after the mandate of an earlier committee was enlarged), which include cases of persecuted historians, were strictly confidential. See letter of historian and former committee chairman Georges-Henri Dumont to author, October 1990. Also see G.-H. Dumont, "A Behind-the-Scenes Struggle for Human Rights", *UNESCO Courier*, June 1990: 43–44; and letters of the UNESCO Office of International Standards and Legal Affairs to author, February and March 1995, November 1996.

49. Whereas I did the reading of English, Spanish, French, German, and Dutch sources myself, I received some assistance for Portuguese and Italian sources.

50. See, e.g., USSR (1981–: Roginsky, 1987–91: Yurasov).

51. See, e.g., China (1966–: Guo Moruo).

52. See, e.g., Austria (1966: Borodajkewycz).

53. See, e.g., China (1967–: Lin Jie, 1967–: Qi Benyu), Austria and Germany (1945–: purge of historians who collaborated with Nazism).

54. A. Nekrich, *Forsake Fear: Memoirs of an Historian* (originally in Russian 1979; Boston 1991).

55. The first was the Austrian Edmund Glaise von Horstenau (1882–1946), a military historian and archivist, who, imprisoned and summoned at the International Military Tribunal in Nuremberg to testify about his wartime activities as a general in Ustasha Croatia, committed suicide (M. Bernath & F. von Schroeder eds., *Biographisches Lexicon zur Geschichte Südeuropas*, vol. 2 [Munich 1976] 55–56). The second was historian Ferdinand Nahimana (1950–), one of the suspected leaders of the 1994 genocide in Rwanda awaiting trial at the International Tribunal in Arusha, Tanzania. An ideologue of the Mouvement Révolutionnaire National pour le Développement and former history professor and dean at the Faculty of Letters, Université Nationale du Rwanda (1977–94), Nahimana was the cofounder and program director of the extremist Radio-Télévision Libre des Mille Collines (RTLM; Thousand Hills Television and Radio; nicknamed "Radio Machette"). In 1993 his doctoral thesis on the history of northern Rwanda (1500–1931), defended at the University of Paris–VII in 1986, was published as *Le Rwanda,*

Emergence d'un état (Paris). Colette Braeckman ("Où se trouvent les criminels?" *Le Monde diplomatique*, March 1995: 8) asserts that this book had already announced the crimes.

56. See A. De Baets, "Holocaust Denial", in: Jones ed. 2001: 1079–80, and De Baets, "Holocaustontkenning, Censuur en de Waardigheid van de Doden" ["Holocaust Denial, Censorship and the Dignity of the Dead"], in: *Publications of the Rudolf Agricola Institute (University of Groningen)* (forthcoming; Groningen [2002]).

57. M. Pivert, "Problèmes du socialisme: Quelques aspects théoriques des entretiens du Kremlin", in: *La Revue socialiste*, 1956: 289. The Guide contains many examples of direct interventions by heads of state and government against historians and others concerned with the past (some thirty in twenty-one countries). For examples of parliamentary debates on history, see Chile, Egypt, France, India, Jamaica, United Arab Eminates United States.

58. Article 19, *Information, Freedom and Censorship*, 1988: vii.

59. B. Lewis, *History Remembered, Recovered, Invented* (originally 1975; New York 1987) 69.

60. Compare A. Grafton, *Forgers and Critics: Creativity and Duplicity in Western Scholarship* (Princeton 1990) 61–62.

61. B.D. Wolfe, "Totalitarianism and History", in: C.J. Friedrich ed., *Totalitarianism* (New York 1964) 265.

62. When we compare Szayna's remarks with what has been said about propaganda, blank spots may represent any of the three main categories of propaganda (comission, omission, denial), and may or may not be accompanied by censorship.

63. See the discussion on the excusability of the use of historical myths in B. Lewis & P.M. Holt eds., *Historians of the Middle East* (London 1962) 451–502; J. Vansina, R. Mauny, & L.V. Thomas, *The Historian in Tropical Africa* (London 1964) 80; D.C. Gordon, *Self-determination and History in the Third World* (Princeton 1971) 177–92; and Lewis 1987, passim. Also see the important remarks of Butterfield 1951: 182–224; J.H. Plumb, *The Death of the Past* (London 1969) 19–61; J. Vansina, *Oral Tradition As History* (London 1985) 91–108; W.H. McNeill, "Mythistory, or Truth, Myth, History, and Historians", *American Historical Review*, 1986, no. 1: 6–7.

64. W.Z. Laqueur, *The Fate of the Revolution: Interpretations of Soviet History* (London 1967) 142.

65. Orwell 1949: 42.

66. This is not mere fiction. Something very similar happened to the Spanish writer Jorge Semprún at Buchenwald; see his *L'Écriture ou la vie* (Paris 1994) 287–319, especially 307.

67. See, e.g., Brazil, Chile, Congo, Czechoslovakia, Ghana, Japan, Malawi, Mexico, Morocco, Nigeria, Poland, Portugal, South Africa, Spain, Syria, Tajikistan, Tunisia, USSR, Yugoslavia; see also Laqueur 1967: 134ff.; and F. Luna, "Oficio y Responsabilidad del Historiador en la Argentina de Hoy", *Todo es historia*, 1985, 224: 89–90.

68. See, e.g., China (1965–69: Wu Han et al.); India (1977–78: textbook controversy).

69. For the origins of the nation, see, e.g., China (1952–59: Gu Jiegang); for archeology, see A. De Baets, "Archaeology", in: Jones ed. 2001: 73–76. Also Darwin's evolution theory (as opposed to the creationist theory) has been the object of censorship attempts: see Saudi Arabia (1995), Sudan (1989: el-Nur).

70. See, e.g., Egypt (1952–: Zaki, 1954–: Sabri) and many communist countries.

Also Plumb 1969: 14. For different reasons, source editions were frequently undertaken by refugee historians as well; see C. Epstein, *A Past Renewed: A Catalog of German-Speaking Refugee Historians in the United States after 1933* (Cambridge 1993) 18–19.

71. See, for examples of the different types of protesting historians, De Baets, "Resistance to the Censorship of Historical Thought", in: Sogner ed. 2001 and Jones ed. 2001.

72. For an alternative typology, see V. Prečan ed., *Acta Creationis: Independent Historiography in Czechoslovakia 1969–1980* (Hannover 1980) xlvii–li.

73. For some interesting remarks on the positive effects of exile, see C. Hoffmann, "The Contribution of German-speaking Jewish Immigrants to British Historiography", in: W.E. Mosse ed., *Second Chance: Two Centuries of German-Speaking Jews in the United Kingdom* (Tübingen 1991) 153–55, 172–73.

74. See C.E. Black ed., *Rewriting Russian History* (Princeton 1962) 3, 20–21, 27; H. Weber, *Die DDR 1945–1986* (Munich 1988) 108. However, direct intervention in controversial issues is not eschewed, as is proven (to cite but one of many examples) by the SED Politbüro in the German Democratic Republic (GDR), which in 1957 determined the correct interpretation of the 1918 November Revolution. See A. Dorpalen, "Die Geschichtswissenschaft der DDR", in: B. Faulenbach ed., *Geschichtswissenschaft in Deutschland: Traditionelle Positionen und gegenwärtige Aufgaben* (Munich 1974) 123–24.

75. See L. Kolakowski, "Totalitarianism and the Virtue of the Lie", in I. Howe ed., *1984 Revisited: Totalitarianism in Our Century* (New York 1983) 135; and Y. Afanasev, "Return History to the People", *IOC* 3/95: 56–58. Also see Marc Bloch's remarks on the wary reception of propaganda and censorship in the trenches of World War I, which resulted in a revival of oral tradition: M. Bloch, *Apologie pour l'histoire ou métier d'historien* (written 1941, originally published 1949; Paris 1967) 50–51.

76. See USSR entry. Among the many authors signaling the phenomenon of substitutes in the USSR, see, e.g., L. Passerini, "Introduction", in idem, *International Yearbook of Oral History and Life Stories I, Memory and Totalitarianism* (Oxford 1992) 8. Examples outside the USSR include philosophers and journalists in 1956 Poland, poets in Iran under the shah (see *IOC* 4/74: 9–10 and M. Ferro, *Comment on raconte l'histoire aux enfants à travers le monde entier* [Paris 1981] 119–21), novelists in Paraguay (*IOC* 4/83: 15–17; 6/85: 50–51), theater and poetry in South Africa (M. Cornevin, *L'Apartheid: Pouvoir et falsification historique* [Paris 1979] 142). Reasons for the relatively late reactions of USSR historians to glasnost include their nasty experiences with previous attempts at rewriting history and the long delays in the publication of their writings; see V. Tolz, " 'Glasnost' and the Rewriting of Soviet History", *Radio Liberty Research*, 18 May 1987: 9–10. Reasons for the substitutive power of literature are that it is a channel for historical views in any context, that it is a solitary act requiring little institutional support, and that, frequently, its fictional genres are not taken seriously by the authorities and hence escape their attention. See A. Brink, "The Failure of Censorship", *IOC* 6/81: 9–11.

77. R.S. Watson ed., *Memory, History, and Opposition under State Socialism* (Santa Fe 1994), is a book on memory as a corrective to official history.

78. Robert Darnton's term in "Poland Rewrites History", *New York Review of Books*, 16 July 1981: 8.

79. A. Nekrich, "Rewriting History", *IOC* 4/80: 6.

80. See the postunification discussion in Germany on the question of which historians

were entitled to write the history of the GDR. For a description of the transition in Eastern Europe, see K. Pomian, "Logique de la mémoire, logique de l'histoire", in: A. Marès ed., *Histoire et pouvoir en Europe médiane* (Paris 1996) 309–19.

81. P. Burke, "History As Social Memory", in: T. Butler ed., *Memory: History, Culture and the Mind* (Oxford 1989) 110.

82. A. Solzhenitsyn, *The Gulag Archipelago 1918–1956* (originally in Russian 1973; Glasgow 1974) x.

83. N.G. Garson, "Censorship and the Historian", *South African Historical Journal*, 1973, no. 5: 9.

84. Alberto Manguel, "Daring to Speak One's Name", *IOC* 1/95: 29. Manguel refers to Jorge Luis Borges's story *El Jardín de senderos que se bifurcan*; in a riddle whose subject is chess, the only word that cannot be mentioned is precisely the word *chess*: "To *always* omit a word, to make use of inept metaphors and self-evident paraphrases is perhaps the most emphatic way of pointing it out." Also see F. Schauer, *Free Speech: A Philosophical Enquiry* (Cambridge 1982) 75–78.

85. S.F. Jones, "Old Ghosts and New Chains: Ethnicity and Memory in the Georgian Republic", in: R.S. Watson ed. 1994: 164.

86. H. Weber, " 'Weisse Flecken' in der DDR-Geschichtsschreibung" (originally 1990), in: R. Eckert, W. Küttler, & G. Seeber eds., *Krise-Umbruch-Neubeginn: Eine kritische und selbstkritische Dokumentation der DDR-Geschichtswissenschaft 1989/90* (Stuttgart 1992) 372.

87. For examples, see Dominican Republic (pre-1956–: Galíndez), France (1976: Guillebord), Japan (1963–: Ienaga), Malawi (Chirwa trial).

88. All except the last to appear in Jones ed. 2001. Some parts of this introduction owe much to my "Rewriting of History" entry there (pages 1062–67 and 1067–73). For military history, see my entries "Censorship of Military History I: Non-Democratic Regimes"; "II: Democratic Regimes (1945–2000)", in: N. Tobias ed., *The International Military Encyclopedia* (Gulf Breeze, FL, forthcoming).

89. See A. De Baets, "Een vermomde zegen? Gevluchte historici in de twintigste Eeuw" ("A Blessing in Disguise? Refugee Historians in the Twentieth Century"), in: A. Huussen, J. de Jong, & G. Prince eds., *Cultuurcontacten: Ontmoetingen tussen culturen in historisch perspectief* (Groningen, 2001) 177–189.

90. See A. De Baets, "Smaadprocessen Tegen Historici" ("Defamation Trials of Historians"), *Groniek: Historisch Tijdschrift*, 2001: 427–50; De Baets, "Resistance to the Censorship of Historical Thought", in: Sogner ed. 2001; also in Jones ed. 2001.

91. Article 19 of the Universal Declaration of Human Rights (1948) reads: "Everyone has the right to freedom of opinion and expression; this right includes freedom to hold opinions without interference and to seek, receive and impart information and ideas through any media and regardless of frontiers."

92. "Nam quis nescit priman esse historiae legem, ne quid falsi dicere audeat? Deinde ne quid veri non audeat?" (Cicero, *De Oratore* II, 15).

93. K.R. Popper, "The Moral Responsibility of the Scientist", *Encounter*, March 1969: 56. Originally, the expression is André Mercier's.

94. The following considerations are based, among many other sources, on: Gilissen 1960; A. Pork, "History, Lying and Moral Responsibility", *History and Theory*, 1990: 321–30; F. Bédarida ed., "The Social Responsibility of the Historian", *Diogenes*, 1994, no.168: 1–104; A. De Baets, "Human Rights, History of", in: N.J. Smelser & P.B. Baltes eds., *International Encyclopedia of the Social and Behavioral Sciences* (Oxford 2001).

95. An exciting development for historians has occurred recently, in the wake of the success achieved by several truth commissions established in countries in transition from dictatorship to democracy. Official and unofficial truth commissions are so successful that the underlying principle, the right to know the truth about past abuses (and hence the right to history), is increasingly recognized in international law. This principle of obligatory investigation of abuses, *even after a change of regime*, was rapidly taken up by human rights observers. In 1995 Leandro Despouy, the United Nations Special Rapporteur on States of Emergency, called this principle "the right to truth" and "a rule of customary international law", and made a plea to recognize it as nonderogable (see *Eighth Annual Report and List of States Which, since 1 January 1985, Have Proclaimed, Extended or Terminated a State of Emergency, Presented by Mr. Leandro Despouy, Special Rapporteur Appointed Pursuant to Economic and Social Council Resolution 1985/37* (New York, E/CN.4/Sub.2/1995/20, 26 June 1995) 54. In 1997 the International Council on Archives published a report for UNESCO on the archives of the security services of former repressive regimes, in which this body formulated three rights crucial to the profession: the right to historical truth, the right of the people to the integrity of their written memory, and the right to historical research (see A. González Quintana, "Les Archives des services de sécurité des anciens régimes répressifs: Rapport préparé pour l'UNESCO à la demande du Conseil International des Archives", *Janus*, 1999, no.1: 13–31, esp. 20–21). Also see: Article 19, *'Who Wants to Forget?' Truth and Access to Information about Past Human Rights Violations* (WWW-text; London 2000) 4–5.

96. The GDR prior to the 1970s favored an exceptionally selective approach to history; the GDR was considered the successor of revolutionary and progressive traditions in German history, while the official antifascism prevented the black episodes of history, including the Third Reich, from being seen as part of the GDR's historical precedents. When this changed after the Ostpolitik, the Zwei-Linien-Konzeption gave way to the Erbe-Tradition-Konzeption; GDR historians shrewdly continued distinguishing between the tradition of their country, on the one hand, and her (cherished) legacy, on the other. See Dorpalen 1974: 123; and A. Fischer & G. Heydemann, "Weg und Wandel der Geschichtswissenschaft und des Geschichtsverständnisses in der SBZ/DDR seit 1945" (originally 1989), in: Eckert, Küttler, & Seeber eds. 1992: 125, 136–40.

97. C.A. Bayly, for example, asks: "Should the historian point to pre-colonial religious conflict if this might indirectly feed into the armoury of the Hindu and Sikh right-wing or Muslim fundamentalists?" From "Modern Indian Historiography", in: M. Bentley ed., *Companion to Historiography* (London/New York 1997) 689.

98. As advocated by Gilissen (1960: 1006–2, 1021–30, 1039). Also see: E. Barendt, *Freedom of Speech* (Oxford 1985) 63–67 (A right of silence).

99. See also *The Lima Declaration on Academic Freedom and Autonomy of Institutions of Higher Education*, Article 16: "All institutions of higher education shall provide solidarity to other such institutions and individual members of their academic communities when they are subject to persecution. Such solidarity may be moral or material, and should include refuge and employment or education for victims of persecution." In: World University Service, *Academic Freedom 1990* (London 1990) 189–90. The discussion of the *implementation* of the professional responsibility, i.e., the imposition and (un)desirability of imperative and prohibitive measures to be imposed on historians, has serious implications for the censorship debate. Regardless of whether it concerns imperative measures such as the establishment of an International Order of Historians or a code of ethics, or prohibitive measures such as legislation criminalizing

falsified history, and boycotts or trials of historians who do not comply with their professional obligations, the prevailing opinion of the (few) historians who reflected upon the issue seems to be *against* such imperative and prohibitive measures, for the fundamental reason that the historical truth is searched for, not imposed. I support this opinion, with three reservations: there might arise a need to have some regulation in the field of archeology (especially when the scholarly right of archeologists must be weighed against the concerns of the living people whose ancestors' lives are under investigation, such as indigenous peoples), the field of privacy and the fair use of confidential sources, and the field of archives. For archeology, see P.G. Bahn, *The Cambridge Illustrated History of Archaeology* (Cambridge 1996) 358–61, and B.M. Fagan ed., *The Oxford Companion to Archaeology* (New York and Oxford 1996) 172–73, 206–7, 487–88, 573; World Archeological Congress, *First Code of Ethics* (including the 1989 *Vermillion Accord on Human Remains*) [1990]. For the use of confidential sources, see K.J. Winkler, "A Question of 'Historical Malpractice' ", *Chronicle of Higher Education*, 14 January 1980: 3; D.H. Flaherty, "Privacy and Confidentiality: The Responsibilities of Historians", *Reviews in American History*, 1980: 419–29; J. Hoff-Wilson, "Access to Restricted Collections: The Responsibility of Professional Historical Organizations", *American Archivist*, 1983: 441–47; M.L. Benedict, "Historians and the Continuing Controversy over Fair Use of Unpublished Manuscript Materials", *American Historical Review*, 1986: 859–81. For the archives, see International Council on Archives, *Code of Ethics* (adopted by the General Assembly in its thirteenth session in Beijing, China, September 1996).

100. J. Le Goff, *Histoire et mémoire* (Paris 1988) 303.

101. Bloch 1967 and Carr 1961 were commented upon in M. Kusý, "On the Purity of the Historian's Craft", *Kosmas*, 1984–85, III/no.2 & IV/no.1: v, 29–31, 38, as part of an essay on the Jozef Jablonický case.

THE GUIDE

A

AFGHANISTAN

1979–89   During the armed conflict (1979–89), many archives were destroyed.

1982   In March 1982 **Ralph Pinder-Wilson** (?1919–), a British archeologist and head of the British Institute for Afghan Studies, Kabul, was detained and charged with smuggling archeological finds out of Afghanistan and with helping Afghan nationals to emigrate. In addition he was accused of criticizing the government and spreading propaganda against it. Between March and July, he was first sentenced to death, then given ten years' imprisonment, and, finally, granted pardon. In July he was released.

1982–87   In April or May 1982, **Hasan Kakar** (1932–), leading Marxist historian and head of the Kabul University history department, was arrested, together with other intellectuals, by the Khad (state security police), and beaten. He was held in solitary confinement for over a year and allowed only one visit from his family. Charged with distributing "antistate literature", he was tried in camera for "counter-revolutionary offenses" and possibly for "founding an illegal association" and sentenced to eight years' imprisonment in July 1983. He had participated in a discussion group at Kabul University, founded early in 1982, which tried to suggest peaceful solutions to the armed conflict and protested the arbitrary arrest of a number of teachers and students. Kakar had also refused to affiliate with the ruling People's Democratic Party of Afghanistan (PDPA) and protected persecuted PDPA members of the Parcham faction in his house. During the trial he pointed out that his actions had not been unconstitutional. He was denied access to a lawyer during his detention and trial and after the verdict was denied right of appeal. Apparently, pressure was put on him to sign a written "confession" admitting his guilt in having fanned opposition to the PDPA and being a tool of "imperialist and counterrevolutionary elements", but he refused. He was held in Pul-e Charkhi prison, Kabul. He was offered release by a Khad official if he agreed to speak on television in support of the government, but he refused to do so, after which his conditions of imprisonment worsened. Although he was in bad health, his requests for a medical checkup were rejected. In March 1987 he was released and restored to his former post. He went to Pakistan, and from there he emigrated to the United States.

1983   In May 1983 **Mohammed Nader Wardag** (?1956–), archivist in Kabul, was arrested and accused of being a member of the illegal Afghan Mellat (Social Democratic Party).

1998   The public library of Pol-i-Khomri, which contained 55,000 books and old manuscripts, was burned to the ground by Taliban militia.

Also see Moldova (1999), USSR (1989: report; 1986–Tajikistan: Denisov).

SOURCES

Adamec, L.W., *A Biographical Dictionary of Contemporary Afghanistan* (Graz 1987) 79.
Albada, J. van, " 'Memory of the World': Report on Destroyed and Damaged Archives", *Archivum*, 1996, no.42: 19.
Amnesty International, *Report* (London) 1983: 184; 1984: 205–6; 1985: 196; 1986: 206; 1987: 215–16; 1988: 147–48.
Auer, L., "Archival Losses and Their Impact on the Work of Archivists and Historians", *Archivum*, 1996, no.42: 4.
Human Rights Watch, *World Report 2000* (Washington 1999) 503.
Index on Censorship, 4/82: 42; 5/82: 33; 2/84: 43.
Keesings historisch archief, 1987: 112.

ALBANIA

1975–83   Illustrated Albanian history books had to be reedited four or five times, in order to erase several leading political figures who had fallen in disgrace, including **Mehmet Shehu**, a former prime minister officially said to have committed suicide in December 1981.

[1981–]   One of the victims of the purge of the group around Shehu [q.v. 1975–83] was **Ndreçi Plasari**, historian of the Albanian Party of Labor and chairman of the National Organization of the War Veterans of the Albanian People (1974–82).

1995–96   In September 1995 historian **Elvira Shapllo**, archeologist **Vladimir Qiriaqi** and two others were briefly detained on charges of "distributing anticonstitutional writings", an offense punishable by up to three years' imprisonment. They were the authors of a guidebook to Gjirokastër which apparently contained a photograph of former communist ruler Enver Hoxha, a native of Gjirokastër. In February 1996 their trial was adjourned. The court was due to reconvene in March. It appeared that the four defendants were not in detention.

1995   In November 1995 police in Vlora and Durrës arrested and briefly detained some fifty people who tried to lay wreaths on the graves of World War II partisans.

SOURCES

Amnesty International, *Report 1996* (London 1996) 70.
————, *Urgent Action 50/96* (11 March 1996).
Index on Censorship, 3/96: 98.
Jaubert, A., *Le Commissariat aux archives: Les Photos qui falsifient l'histoire* (Paris 1986) 151.
Schmidt-Neke, M., "Politisches System", in: K-D. Grothusen ed., *Albanien* (Südosteuropa-Handbuch VII; Göttingen 1993) 198.

ALGERIA

French Algeria

1962   When Algeria became independent, the French government exported many official documents to France, thus taking with them vital sources of Algerian history.

Algeria

1965–   In August 1965 nationalist and journalist **Mohammed Harbi** (1933–), member of the Front de Libération Nationale, consultant to the Évian negotiations (1961), secretary-general of the Foreign Ministry (1961–62), political adviser to Prime Minister (from 1963 President) Ahmed Ben Bella (1962–65), and editor of *Révolution africaine* (1963–64), was arrested and sentenced without trial to five years' imprisonment because he had opposed Colonel Houari Boumedienne's June 1965 coup. Between the coup and his arrest he had lived in clandestinity. He was held in isolation from August 1965 to November 1969, when he was released and placed under house arrest, first in the south, later in the northeast of Algeria. In the spring of 1973, he escaped to France, where he studied history, wrote works on Algerian history and nationalism, and edited *Les*

Archives de la révolution algérienne (1981), a book of documents on the Algerian Revolution (1954–62). All his works were banned in Algeria. He was a lecturer in sociology at several universities in Paris (1975–80, 1985–89). From 1989 he has been a senior lecturer at the Political Sciences Department of the University of Paris–VIII.

1980   In March **Mouloud Mammeri** (1917–), Berber poet, professor of literature at Algiers University, and director at the Centre de Recherches Anthropologiques, Préhistoriques et Ethnographiques (until 1980), author of *Poèmes kabyles anciens* (Paris 1980), was barred from addressing a conference on the history of Berber poetry at Tizi-Ouzou University in the Kabyle region. It sparked a rising of Berber students, who claimed that the government was suppressing Berber culture. Problems began in 1962, when Ben Bella chose Arabic as the national language and rejected the Berber elements in Algeria's past. In January and February 1980, the government had decided to establish a precise timetable for the "Arabization" of public administration, the economic sector, and higher education.

1986–87   Among the persons placed under town arrest restrictions from November 1986 to March 1987 was archivist **Abdelkarim Badjadja** (1945–). In March 1987 the restrictions, for which no official reasons were given, were lifted.

pre-1996–   In February 1996 **Benjamin Stora** (1950–), history professor at the University of Paris–VIII and author of *Histoire de l'Algérie depuis l'indépendance* (1994), born in a Jewish family and living in France since 1962, announced that he would go into exile in an Asian country because of persistent anti-Semitic attacks in the Algerian press and anonymous threats after his film *Les Années algériennes* had been shown on television in September 1991.

1996   In January **Khaled Aboulkacem**, archivist at *L'Indépendant* newspaper, was killed, and a colleague of his was wounded, in an attack by suspected Islamist gunmen as they left their offices.

Also see France (1952: Julien; 1956: Marrou; 1960: Massignon, Vidal-Naquet; 1962–68: Soustelle; 1996–99: Einaudi), United States (1970–72: Ahmed), Uruguay (1968: Pontecorvo).

SOURCES

Amnesty International, *Report* (London) 1968–69: 25; 1969–70: 28; 1980: 322; 1981: 351; 1982: 316; 1983: 297; 1988: 229.

Article 19, *Information, Freedom and Censorship: World Report 1991* (London 1991) 353.

Bonnaud, R., "Mohammed Harbi: Un Historien Matérialiste", *Le Quinzaine littéraire*, 1993, no.617: 23–24.

Déjeux, J., *Dictionnaire des auteurs maghrébins de langue française* (Paris 1984) 157–59.

————, *La Littérature algérienne contemporaine* (Paris 1975) 66–68, 78.

Gordon, D.C., *Self-determination and History in the Third World* (Princeton 1971) 159.

Index on Censorship, 4/80: 67; 5/80: 37–42; 4–5/94: 151–53, 254–55; 2/96: 80; 2/97: 79; 5/98: 15.

Naylor, P.C., & A.A. Heggoy, *Historical Dictionary of Algeria* (Metuchen 1994) 213–14.

Stora, B., "Deuxième exil", *L'Histoire*, February 1996: 102.

ANGOLA

See South Africa (1953–: Davidson).

ARGENTINA

Among the historians most targeted under successive military governments were those with Marxist and other left-wing approaches to the past.

1945   On 9 October, after a seizure of power by General Eduardo Avalos, Vice President **Juan Domingo Perón** (1895–1974), a former professor of military history at the Escuela Superior de Guerra (1930–36), was forced to resign all his positions and was arrested and placed on the prison island Martín García. On the night of 17 October, he was brought back after large-scale demonstrations. He became president of Argentina (1946–55, 1973–74) but he also lived in exile (1955–73).

1946–   Among the historians who went into exile during Perón's presidency (1946–55) were the following:

Historian **Ricardo Caillet-Bois** (1903–77) had to give up his teaching positions, which he resumed after 1955. In exile he published two books on the Falkland/Malvinas Islands.

Emilio Ravignani (1886–1954), historian of the Argentinian constitution, director of the Instituto de Investigaciones Históricas at Buenos Aires University (1921–51), author of its bulletin, and prominent politician and member of Parliament (1936–43, 1946–47, 1952–53) for the Unión Cívica Radical (UCR; Radical Civic Union), temporarily went into exile in Uruguay. There he organized the Instituto de Investigaciones Históricas at Montevideo University in 1950.

Ricardo Rojas (1882–1957), literary historian, journalist, writer, professor of literature (1913–46), and rector (1926–30) at Buenos Aires University, author of *Historia de la literatura Argentina* (1917–21) and prominent UCR leader, was dismissed and went into exile. He had been imprisoned and internally exiled before, in 1934.

José Luis Romero (1909–77), Marxist professor of medieval history and philosophy of history at La Plata National University (1937–46), was dismissed because of his membership in the Socialist Party. He went to Uruguay to work at the University of the Republic, Montevideo, and continued his research into the medieval bourgeoisie at Harvard University in the United States. In 1955 he returned to Argentina and became intervenor (director of reorganization) at Buenos Aires University in September, but in May 1956 he resigned from that position after a wave of student agitation. Meanwhile he had founded the Buenos Aires University Press. In 1966 he was on the target list of "communist infiltrators in the government" drafted by the Federación Argentina de Entidades Democráticas Anticomunistas.

Mariano de Vedia y Mitre (1880–1958), judge and historian, professor of Argentinian history at Buenos Aires University, left the university and possibly went into exile.

1946–   **Enrique Barba** (1909–88), history professor at La Plata National University (1934–), could not teach during the Perón years. During the dictatorship of General Juan Carlos Onganía (1966–69), Barba reportedly expelled the police from the university.

pre-1948   Other history lectures who left the university before 1948 include **Juan Cánter, Juan Mantovani**, and **Raúl de Orgaz**.

1950–   In [October] 1950 Congress declared the work of U.S. citizen and historian **George Blanksten** (1917–), a former, U.S. State Department collaborator (1945–46) and at the time an Area Research Training Fellow of the Social Science Research Council who had arrived three months earlier in Argentina to do research in political science, to be "espionage" and outlawed his mission. Blanksten claimed that he had a few encounters with the Federal Police in the ensuing months and that he was offered 20,000 pesos to write a pro-Perón volume. He smuggled his notes out of Argentina. Later he became a professor of political science at Northwestern University, Evanston, Ill. He also wrote about Ecuador.

1953   In January the Academia Nacional de la Historia was put under government control.

1966–   **Tulio Halperín Donghi** (1926–), history professor at the universities of Rosario (1955–61) and Buenos Aires (1959–66), resigned after Onganía's military coup. He went into exile and worked at Harvard University (1967–70), Oxford University (1970–71), and the University of California at Berkeley (1971–94). He has written profusely on Latin American history.

1967–   Among the foreign books seized by the Argentinian postal services and burned in [September] 1967 for their alleged communist contents was *Historia del socialismo y las luchas sociales*, by journalist and historian **Max Beer** (1864–1949). In March 1975, for similar reasons, the postal services banned the circulation of several books, including *Los Congresos obreros internacionales en el siglo XX, 1900–1950*, by **Amaro del Rosal** (1904–), a Spanish exile from the civil war, journalist, and leader of the Unión General de Trabajadores (socialist trade union).

1973–80   In October 1973 **Rodolfo Puiggrós** (1906–80), historian, author of a six-volume political and social history of Argentina in the nineteenth and twentieth centuries, and former communist leader, resigned as the left-wing rector of Buenos Aires University (which he had renamed "The National and Popular University"). In September 1974 he was threatened with assassination by the extreme right-wing organization Alianza Anticomunista Argentina (AAA). He sought sanctuary in the Mexican embassy and was flown to Mexico. In exile until his death, he was a leading Montonero (the armed organization of the Peronist left).

1974   **Silvio Frondizi** (1907–74), Marxist professor of history and political science at Buenos Aires University, brother of former president of Argentina Arturo Frondizi (1958–62), and founder of the Movimiento Izquierda Revolucionaria (Movement of the Revolutionary Left), was assassinated by the AAA after denouncing the military's murder and torture practices in Catamarca Province.

1974–   In June the Ministry of Defense opposed the screening of *La Patagonia rebelde* (Rebel Patagonia), a 1973 film by **Hector Olivera** about a rebellion in Patagonia suppressed by the army in 1922–23; it started with an image of a member of the military being assaulted. In June 1975 the film was voluntarily withdrawn from circulation. In 1976 Olivera and Aries Films claimed that the film did not exist; they did not include it in their catalogs.

1976–83   The military governments which ruled from 1976 to 1983 banned the export of [the Spanish version] of *Portrait du colonisé précédé de portrait du colonisateur* (Paris 1957; *The Colonizer and the Colonized*) by Tunisian sociologist and anthropologist **Albert Memmi** (1920–), professor at the University of Paris-X.

1976   All the lecturers at the history faculty of Córdoba University were dismissed.

1976–80   From 1976 to December 1980, *The Great Dictator* (1940), a film by **Charlie Chaplin** (1889–1977), was banned. The unbanned version had several cuts. During the ban, many Argentinians went to see the film in Colonia, Uruguay. In 1976 all the material and the negative of an unfinished semidocumentary by **Jorge Cedrón** (?1942–80) on the history of Argentina from the 1930s until 1976 disappeared. In 1977 Cedrón went into exile.

1976–   In April Brazilian citizen **Jorge Alberto Basso**, militant of the Partido Operario Comunista, was imprisoned in a hotel in Buenos Aires and "disappeared". In 1971 he had traveled to Chile, where he had been a history student at the University of Chile but, after the 1973 coup there, he had moved to Argentina.

           In May cinema director **Raymundo Gleyzer** (?1942–) was picked up by the military as he was about to leave for the United States; he "disappeared". He was considered dangerous because he had made films about trade unions (inter alia *Los Traidores* [The Traitors]) and the Mexican Revolution.

           In November professor of art history **Claudio César Adur** (?1950/52–) "disappeared" in Buenos Aires.

1977–   In April 1977 **Adolfo Pérez Esquivel** (1931–), lecturer in fine arts, secondary-school teacher of philosophy, history, and literature, former university lecturer in architecture, and general coordinator for Latin America of the Servicio Paz y Justicia (Service for Justice and Peace) since 1974, was arrested when he collected his passport in order to travel to Colombia. He was kept in a cell of the Federal Security's Head Office for two months and then transferred to La Plata Prison, where he was tortured for five days and held for fourteen months. He was never formally charged or tried, but the government let it be known that he was a "subversive" and later (in 1980) that he had "contributed to the cause of those who promote terrorism in the nation". In June 1978 he was released into restricted liberty for a further fourteen months. After this period he was not given a passport. While in prison, he was a candidate for the Nobel Peace Prize, which he received in 1980. In 1972 he had already carried out a hunger strike to protest the violence perpetrated by both terrorists and police forces. As the Paz y Justicia coordinator, he traveled widely over the continent. In 1974 he had launched a campaign on behalf of the Indians in Ecuador. During a trip to Brazil [in 1975], he was briefly imprisoned, and he was arrested again in Ecuador in 1976. In the same year, the Paz y Justicia headquarters were occupied and ransacked by security forces.

Among the books banned in 1977 were *La Economía alemana bajo el nazismo* (originally in French 1946, Madrid), by **Charles Bettelheim** (1913–), and *Historia del 36* (Madrid 1974), by **Max Aub** (1903–72), **Luis Romero** (1916–) and **J. Leon Ignacio**. In January 1978 the distribution, sale, and circulation of a series of booklets, *Historia de las revoluciones* (Buenos Aires 1973) was banned for its "subversive" contents. In March 1979 the film *Las Largas vacaciones del '36* (1977; The Great Holiday of '36), by Spanish director **Jaime Caminos**, was banned by the Third Army Region chief commander. Also banned was *Novecento*, a 1976 film by **Bernardo Bertolucci**, because it was "offensive to the moral order and to the Christian ethic". In June the Ministry of Education and Culture banned the work *Universitas: Gran enciclopedia del saber* (Barcelona 1979) from the public schools particularly because its second volume, *La Historia*, was allegedly inspired by the Marxist approach, especially in describing industrialization. In May 1980 Aries Films withdrew *The House on Garibaldi Street*, a 1979 film by American director **Peter Collinson** (1936–) telling the story of Adolf Eichmann from his capture in Argentina to his execution in Israel (1960–62), because extreme right-wing groups threatened the cinemas that showed it. After a bomb explosion in a cinema in Montevideo, Uruguay, it was permanently withdrawn. In September the ministry banned the twelve-volume *Enciclopedia Salvat Diccionario* (Barcelona 1978), used in the first years of the secondary schools, because of its alleged Marxist approach of history and society. In October the ministry deleted at least two works, labeled "Marxist", from a reading list for secondary-school history teachers: *De Mitre a Roca: Consolidación de la oligarquía anglo-criolla* (third edition; Buenos Aires 1975), by **Milcíades Peña** (died 1965), and *Buenos Aires: Sus hombres y su política, 1860–1890* (Mexico 1890, Buenos Aires 1952), by **Carlos D'Amico** (1839–1917), former governor of the Province of Buenos Aires. In November 1980 the four-volume *La Historia Presente* (1974–75), by **Guillermo Chiflet, Guillermo González, Hugo Cardozo, Enrique Bayona, Francisco Sánchez Toledo**, and **Gerardo Oliveira**, was banned because it allegedly had a bias in favor of terrorism, popular liberation movements, and armed struggle against capitalism, North American imperialism, and the military regimes supported by it. Cited as examples in a federal police report on the work were descriptions of Fidel Castro, Che Guevara, the Cuban Revolution, Patrice Lumumba, Salvador Allende, Pablo Neruda, and Juan and Evita Perón [q.v. 1945] and the Peronist movement. In April 1981 a journalist made a list of books that were banned from the official Book Fair: it included *La Guerra de las republiquetas*, by Argentinian president and historian **Bartolomé Mitre** (1821–1906), and *Estudios sobre los orígenes del Peronismo I* (Buenos Aires 1971), by **Miguel Murmis** and **Juan Carlos Portantiero**. A historical study, *Montoneros en caudillos*, was prohibited because its title contained the forbidden word Montonero (adopted by left-wing Peronists in memory of the irregular armies of gauchos who fought against Spanish troops during the wars of independence). Songs from the musical *Evita* (Perón's wife) were banned, on the assumption that they were favorable to the Peronists.

1981   In 1981 **Vicente Zito Lema** (1939–), poet, journalist, lawyer, and professor of art history at the Faculty of Arts, Buenos Aires University, lived in exile.

1983   **Fermín Chavez** (1924–), historian and editor of the Peronist monthly magazine *Movimiento*, received telephoned threats. In April the police intervened to prevent a bomb attack on his house.

1983–   Although the military declared that information on those "disappeared" during 1976–83 had been destroyed in 1983, some files were later found.

1989   In April the Fundación Plural (Plural Foundation), closely connected with the ruling UCR, decided not to broadcast part two of *El Galpón de la Memoria* (The Storehouse of Memory), a documentary on the history of Argentinian politics from 1930, just hours before it was due to be screened. After the first part had been broadcast, the army high command had complained that the program contained an anti-army bias. A government minister who had met the foundation board denied responsibility for the decision.

1992–93 In February 1992 the Carlos Meném government decided to grant historians and other researchers access to formerly secret police and intelligence files on Nazis who sought refuge in Argentina after the war, but requests for information reportedly produced little new evidence. Allegedly, Nazi criminal Joseph Mengele's file had several pages missing, and another on Nazi leader Martin Bormann was accidentally destroyed while in storage. Historians feared that many documents had been destroyed. Nazi crimes researcher Simon Wiesenthal said that the government tried to hide the extent to which Argentina had collaborated with Nazi officials. Government files released in December 1993 apparently revealed that successive administrations had been active in blocking attempts to bring suspected war criminals and Nazi collaborators to justice.

1996 In July eleven young people were arrested in Buenos Aires and allegedly beaten in a police station. Some were held incommunicado for seventeen hours and interrogated about their attendance at a public meeting organized by Hijos por la Identidad y la Justicia contra el Olvido y el Silencio (Children for Identity and Justice Against Oblivion and Silence), a group formed by children of the "disappeared".

1998–99 In August the Supreme Court refused **Carmen Aguiar de Lapacó**'s petition for access to the military and civilian archives in an attempt to trace her daughter Alejandra, who had "disappeared" under the military government (1976–83). The court denied access on the grounds that the case had been legally closed, although prosecution was stated not to be the plaintiff's aim. In September, however, the Supreme Court upheld the right of a man to access the government files in order to determine the whereabouts of his brother (a guerrilla leader killed in a confrontation in 1976 and whose body was subsequently hidden by the military government). In the Lapacó case, the government acknowledged and guaranteed the right to the truth as a right unaffected by statutes of limitations in November 1999.

Also see El Salvador (1970–: Pérez Brignoli), Spain (1948: Nicolás Sánchez Albornoz), United Kingdom (1984–92: Ponting), Uruguay (1971–85: Galeano).

SOURCES

AIDA, *Argentine, une culture interdite: Pièces à conviction 1976–1981* (Paris 1981) 68–70, 80, 98, 100–101, 171, 181–83.
———, *Argentina: 100 Artists Disappeared* (Paris 1982) 28.
Alexander, R.J., *Juan Domingo Perón: A History* (Boulder 1979) 44–47.
——— ed., *Biographical Dictionary of Latin American and Caribbean Political Leaders* (New York 1988) 349–51.
Amnesty International, *Report* (London) 1978: 98; 1981: 113; 1982: 113; 1997: 75; 2000: 35.
Article 19, *Information, Freedom and Censorship: World Report 1991* (London 1991) 74.
Avellaneda, A., *Censura, autoritarismo y cultura: Argentina 1960–1983* (Buenos Aires 1986) 94–95, 116, 125, 128, 131, 181, 200–202, 204–5, 214.
Barager, J.R., "The Historiography of the Río de la Plata Area since 1830", *Hispanic American Historical Review*, 1959: 610–12, 617, 634.

Bethell, L. ed., *The Cambridge History of Latin America*, vol. 8 (Cambridge 1991) 138.

Blanksten, G.I., *Perón's Argentina* (Chicago 1953) viii–xii.

Boia, L. ed., *Great Historians of the Modern Age: An International Dictionary* (Westport 1991) 651, 678–79, 681–82.

Boyd, K. ed., *Encyclopedia of Historians and Historical Writing* (London/Chicago 1999) 510–12, 1012–13.

Braslavsky, C., "Schulbücher in ihrem Kontext: Argentinien 1975–89", in: M. Riekenberg ed., *Lateinamerika: Geschichtsunterricht, Geschichtslehrbücher, Geschichtsbewusstsein* (Frankfurt/Main 1990) 54.

Chiaramonte, J.C., & P. Buchbinder, "Die Institutionalisierung der Geschichte in Argentinien am Beispiel der Historischen Akademie", in: Riekenberg ed. 1994: 189.

Comissão de Familiares de Mortos e Desaparecidos Políticos, Instituto de Estudo da Violência do Estado & Grupo Tortura Nunca Mais-RJ e PE, *Dossiê dos mortos e desaparecidos políticos a partir de 1964* (Recife 1995) 408.

Current Biography 1981 (New York) 321–24 (Pérez Esquivel).

Duffy, J., M. Frey, & M. Sins eds., *International Directory of Scholars and Specialists in African Studies* (Waltham, Mass. 1978) 181.

Gorman, R.A. ed., *Biographical Dictionary of Neo-Marxism* (Westport 1985) 153–54.

———, *Biographical Dictionary of Marxism* (Westport 1986) 272–74.

Hispanic American Historical Review, 1989: 559–61 (Barba).

Human Rights Watch, *World Report 1999* (Washington 1998) 101.

Index on Censorship, 1/75: 83; 3/78: 19, 21–22; 4/81: 24–27, 29; 4/82: 41; 4/83: 40; 4/85: 46; 6–7/89: 77; 4/92: 34; 4/93: 34; 1–2/94: 231; 6/98: 88; 1/01: 169.

Instituto Panamericano de Geografía e Historia, *Guía de personas que cultivan la historia de América* (México 1967) 18–19, 30, 41–42, 190, 223.

Keesings historisch archief, 1998: 631.

Liss, S.B., *Marxist Thought in Latin America* (Berkeley/Los Angeles 1984) 59–63.

Malagón, J., "Los historiadores y la historia", in: *El exilio español de 1939*, vol. 5 (Madrid 1978) 300–301.

Nunca Más (Never Again): A Report by Argentina's National Commission on Disappeared People (London/Boston 1986) 382–83.

Pérez Brignoli, H., personal communication, August 1994.

Rafetseder, H., *Bücherverbrennungen: Die öffentliche Hinrichtung von Schriften in historischen Wandel* (Vienna 1988) 278.

Riekenberg, M., "Zum politischen Gebrauch der Geschichte in Argentinien und Guatemala (1810–1955): Ein Vergleich", in: Riekenberg ed. 1994: 127.

——— ed., *Politik und Geschichte in Argentinien und Guatemala (19./20. Jahrhundert)* (Frankfurt/Main 1994).

Rock, D., *Authoritarian Argentina* (Berkeley 1993) 212, 220–22.

Simpson, J., & J. Bennett, *The Disappeared: Voices from a Secret War* (London 1985) 214, 219, 228.

Tenenbaum, B.A. ed., *Encyclopedia of Latin American History and Culture* (New York 1996) vol. 3, 171; vol. 4, 539, 596, 601.

Thomas, J.R., *Biographical Dictionary of Latin American Historians and Historiography* (Westport 1984) 123–24, 298–99, 308–9, 343–44.

Tucker, M. ed., *Literary Exile in the Twentieth Century: An Analysis and Biographical Dictionary* (Westport 1991) 469–70.

Walter, R.J., *Student Politics in Argentina: The University Reform and Its Effects, 1918–64* (New York/London 1968) 158–59, 161.

Wright, I.S., & L.M. Nekom, *Historical Dictionary of Argentina* (Metuchen 1978) 388, 758–59, 802–3, 1000.

ARMENIA

pre-1991 *See* Union of Soviet Socialist Republics (USSR).

1995–98 In late July 1995, archeologist **Vahan Hovhannisian**, leader of the opposition Armenian Revolutionary Federation (or Dashnaktsutiun), was arrested with thirty others for allegedly planning an assassination campaign and staging an armed coup on 29 July. The fairness of his trial (March and April 1996–December 1997) was widely criticized. Shortly after President Levon Ter-Petrossian resigned in February 1998, Hovhannisian was released and his party unbanned. His work on Bronze Age and later prehistoric materials from Transcaucasia, identifying Proto-Armenians with Proto-Indo-Europeans, was called tendentious by various archeologists.

SOURCES

Amnesty International, *Report* (London) 1996: 79; 1997: 76; 1998: 87.

Chernykh, E.N., "Postscript: Russian Archaeology after the Collapse of the USSR—Infrastructural Crisis and the Resurgence of Old and New Nationalisms", in: Kohl & Fawcett eds., 1995: 144.

Human Rights Watch, *World Report* (Washington) 1996: 197; 1997: 198–99; 1998: 230–31.

Index on Censorship, 2/95: 169; 2/98: 80.

Kohl, P.L., & C. Fawcett eds., *Nationalism, Politics, and the Practice of Archaeology* (Cambridge 1995).

Kohl, P.L., & G.R. Tsetskhladze, "Nationalism, Politics, and the Practice of Archaeology in the Caucasus", in: Kohl & Fawcett eds. 1995: 158, 173.

AUSTRALIA

In Australia historians were harassed for a diversity of motives. In addition, there were several cases of tensions between scholars and Aboriginals.

1959–62 A dissertation by **Allan Healy** (1929–) about the history of the Australian colonial administration of Papua New Guinea was put under lock and key in the library of the Australian National University, probably under instructions from the Department of Territories (which controlled the colonial administration). At that time, Australian control over Papua New Guinea (which lasted until 1975) was considered by the government to be vital to national security, whereas the dissertation presented the case for more rapid political devolution of power to Papua New Guinea. According to Healy, efforts had also been made to deny him any academic job. In 1959 he had been obliged to sign a form that granted prepublication approval to the department as a condition of access to official documents on the territory. Shortly before the presentation of the dissertation, he had published several articles criticizing colonial policy in a general way (without referring to specific documents).

1977–82   In 1977 the court ruled that *Nomads of the Australian Desert* (Adelaide 1976), a book by anthropologist **Charles Mountford** (1890–1976) about Central Australian Aboriginal lifestyles, art, and myths, had to be withdrawn from sale in the Northern Territory because it reproduced images of tribal sites and items of cultural and religious significance forbidden to uninitiated members of the Pitjantjatjara people. The Pitjantjatjara Council proved that an obligation of confidence had been placed on Mountford when he took the photographs during a 1940 field trip. In 1982 the court ruled that the slides taken by Mountford belonged to the Pitjantjatjara Council.

[1980s]   Aboriginal communities in Western Australia were offended when a female archeologist visited ceremonial sites forbidden to women. They withdrew permission for the excavation. Elsewhere, in Tasmania, the so-called Crowther Collection of skeletal material, reportedly lumped together in an appalling way, was returned to the Aboriginal community. It underwent traditional cremation in 1985.

1992   On 3 June the High Court recognized that the concept of terra nullius (Australia as an uninhabited continent before European settlement began in 1788) was a fiction, thereby strengthening Aboriginal claims to ancestral lands. This "Mabo judgment" (after Aboriginal leader Eddie Mabo), called historic, reversed a historical view of Australia's past in which the role of Aboriginals was downplayed.

1993–97   In June 1993 American-born **David Rindos** (?1947–96), senior lecturer in archeology (1989–93) at the University of Western Australia (UWA), Perth, was denied tenure and dismissed. In December 1990 he had written a memo to the Head of UWA's Division of Agriculture and Science, detailing what was described in a December 1991 Archaeology Department Review Report as "serious allegations of misconduct" against the Foundation Professor of Archaeology. The memo was the start of a conflict leading to Rindos's dismissal. After Rindos waged a long legal battle to get access to the relevant UWA files, and to review and appeal his dismissal, the Western Australian Parliamentary Standing Committee on Government Agencies decided to investigate the case in March 1996. In May 1997 the investigation was continued by the Legislative Council's Standing Committee on Public Administration, which reported in December that Rindos "did not have adequate and fair opportunities to present his case and has not, in all circumstances, been afforded common law procedural fairness." Rindos had died in December 1996, possibly in connection with the case. In the process, the Department of Archaeology and the Center for Prehistory were closed in July 1992, allegedly partly under pressure from a mining company because the Center for Prehistory was finding too many sacred sites around proposed mining leases.

1994–95   In mid-1994 **Jim Allen** and **Tim Murray**, two archeologists of La Trobe University, Melbourne, Victoria, sought to renew permits for the possession for research purposes of 400,000 cultural artifacts (including food remains, stone and bone tools, animal feces, and bits of shell) removed from four cave sites in the Southern Forests region of Tasmania in 1987–91, but the application for renewal was rejected. In June 1995 the La Trobe Archaeology Department was closed. In July–August 1995 the Federal Court in Melbourne ruled that the artifacts be returned to Tasmania and stored until they were given back to the Tasmanian Aboriginal Palawa community.

On 6 October 1995, the Federal Court found "fatally flawed" a December 1994 report of the Merit Protection Review Agency (MPRA), containing allegations of workplace harassment against **Brendon Kelson**, Australian War Memorial (AWM) director (1990–94), and **Michael McKernan**, AWM military historian (1981–95) and deputy director, because it had framed too broad a definition of workplace harassment. It also found that Kelson and McKernan had been denied natural justice. The allegations had been made between August and December 1994 by unidentified former and current AWM staff at MPRA's invitation. Some suggested that the MPRA inquiry was part of a plan to prevent McKernan from succeeding Kelson as AWM director after the latter's retirement on 1 January 1995 and to have appointed a military successor instead. Prime Minister Paul Keating appointed General Gower as AWM director. McKernan left the public service.

1996   In October Federal Parliament decided to ban photographs of the 1991 Dili massacre in East Timor, Indonesia, from an exhibition about the island to be held at Parliament House because they were "offensive".

Also see Indonesia ([?]: Sutjipto Wirjosuparto; 1987: Abeyasekere), Malaysia (1975: Healy), Portugal (1940s: Childe), Singapore (1998: Weir).

SOURCES

Bahn, P.G., *The Cambridge Illustrated History of Archaeology* (Cambridge 1996) 360–61.

Blakeney, M., "Intellectual Property in the Dreamtime—Protecting the Cultural Creativity of Indigenous Peoples" (November 1999), *Oxford Electronic Journal of Intellectual Property Rights* (WWW-text 2000).

Cribb, R., personal communication, September 2000.

Davis, R., personal communication, October 2000.

De Maria, W., *Deadly Disclosures: Whistleblowing and the Ethical Meltdown of Australia* (Kent Town 1999) 39, 92, 105–18, 176–91, 262–64, 273–75.

Index on Censorship, 3/72: 185–95; 1/97: 103.

Janke, T., *Our Culture: Our Future; Report on Australian Indigenous Cultural and Intellectual Property Rights* (1998) (WWW-text 2000) 72–74, 84–85.

Keesing's Record of World Events, 1992–93 (CD-rom version) (Terra Nullius).

Martin, B., C.M.A. Baker, C. Manwell, & C. Pugh eds., *Intellectual Suppression: Australian Case Histories, Analysis and Responses* (North Ryde NSW/London 1986) 50–58, 79–86, 165.

Moyal, A., personal communication, November 2000.

Renfrew, C., & P. Bahn, *Archaeology: Theories, Methods and Practice* (London 1991) 465–66.

Ritchie, J. ed., *Australian Dictionary of Biography*, vol. 15 (Melbourne 2000) 432.

AUSTRIA

The central preoccupation in Austria was the legacy of Nazism and World War II. Scores of historians went into exile after 1934 and 1938; others were dismissed for their collaboration with the Nazis.

1934–   Among the historians and others concerned with the past who emigrated after the February 1934 Civil War (and living in exile after 1944) were the following: **Ernst Gombrich** (1909–), **Otto Pächt** (1902–88), **Karl Polanyi** (1886–1964), **Karl Popper** (1902–94), **Arnold Reisberg** (1904–80), **Leo Stern** (1901–82), and **Arnold Wiznitzer** (1899–1972).

1938–   Among the historians and others concerned with the past who emigrated from Austria after the 1938 Anschluss to Nazi Germany (and living in exile after 1944) were the following: **Alfred Apsler** (1907–82), **Heinrich Benedikt** (1886–1981), **Otto Benesch** (1896–1964), **Paul Diamant** (1887–1966), **Friedrich Engel-Janosi** (1893–1978), **Max Ermers** (1881–1950), **Walter Federn** (1910–67), **Robert Friedmann** (1891–1970), **Bernhard Geiger** (1881–1964), **Alexander Gerschenkron** (1904–78), **Rudolf Glanz** (1892–1978), **Gustave von Grunebaum** (1909–72), **Arnold Hauser** (1892–1978), **David Herzog** (1869–1946), **Robert Kann** (1906–81), **Eric Koll-**

mann (1903–81), **Samuel Krauss** (1866–1948), **Gerhart Ladner** (1905–), **Alfred Low** (1913–), **Max Neuburger** (1868–1955), **Leo Oppenheim** (1904–74), **Adolph Placzek** (1913–2000), **Franz Schehl** (1898–?), **Heinrich Schwarz** (1894–1974), **Felix Strauss** (1918–81), **Walter Ullmann** (1910–83), **Eric Voegelin** (1901–85), **Johannes Wilde** (1891–1970), and **Hersch Zimmels** (1900–74).

Among the young refugees who became historians in their new country were **Walter Grab** (1919–2000), **Raul Hilberg** (1926–), **Gerda Lerner** (1920–), **Sidney Pollard** (formerly **Siegfried Pollak**) (1925–98), **Peter Pulzer** (1929–), **Uriel Tal** (1929–), and **Eric Wolf** (1923–99).

1945–   Art historian **Arpad Weixgärtner** (1872–1961), director at the Museum of Art History and head of the secular and ecclesiastical treasury in Vienna (1900–43), was immediately dismissed in 1943 because he refused to turn over the treasury key to the Nazis. His apartment was burned. In 1945 he emigrated to Sweden at the invitation of King Gustav VI Adolf and became a professor of art history at various Swedish universities.

Among the historians dismissed for their collaboration with the Nazis were the following:

Otto Brunner (1898–1982), historian and archivist at the Haus-, Hof- und Staatsarchiv in Vienna (1923–31), professor of Austrian medieval history at Vienna University (1931–45) and director of the Institut für österreichische Geschichtsforschung (1942–45), was dismissed, degraded, and forced into retirement. His *Adeliges Landleben und europäischer Geist* (1949; Noble Rural Life and the European Spirit) reestablished his reputation, and he returned to academic life in 1954, when he became a professor of economic history at Hamburg University (1954–68).

Oswald Menghin, archeologist and Minister of Education and Culture under the Nazi regime, was dismissed. He spent the rest of his life in South America, where he continued to excavate and publish.

Heinrich Ritter von Srbik (1878–1951), professor of modern history at Vienna University (1922–45), minister of education (1929–30), member of the German Reichstag (1938–45), president of the Austrian Academy of Sciences (1938–45), adviser to the Nazi Reichsinstitut für Geschichte des neuen Deutschlands, and biographer of Klemens von Metternich (1773–1859), was briefly imprisoned and deprived of his professorship. Although his gesamtdeutsche historical interpretation was attacked by strict Nazi historians before 1945 (as it was by the kleindeutsche school), he was accused of pan-

German views and found guilty of collaboration with the Nazis after the war. He lived in retirement until his death. His successor at Vienna University was the Benedictine monk and historian **Hugo Hantsch** (1895–72), who had spent the war at Buchenwald concentration camp (1938–?45).

Among the other historians temporarily suspended were the following: **Rudolf Egger** (1882–1969), professor of Roman history and epigraphy at Vienna University (1929–45), dismissed on political grounds; **Adolf Helbok** (1883–1968), professor of economic and regional history at the universities of Berlin (1934–36), Leipzig (1936–38) and Innsbruck (1938–45); **Walther Kienast** (1896–1985), medievalist at Graz University, dismissed during 1945–60, then at the University of Frankfurt am Main (1960–); and **Helmut Rössler**, Innsbruck University.

1966   In May 1966 historian **Taras von Borodajkewycz** (1902–84), a teacher with an active Nazi past (1934 until his 1945 dismissal) and professor of social-economic history at the Hochschule für Welthandel (1955–66) in Vienna, was forcibly retired. His public anti-Semitic statements, inter alia, in his winter 1961–62 classes and at a televised press conference in March 1965 had led to a wave of protest and violence, in which one person died, and to a lawsuit, in which he was found guilty of anti-Semitism. This led to his suspension and later compulsory retirement (which was confirmed in 1971). He remained active in extremist circles.

1982   In June a bomb exploded at the front door of the house of Nazi crimes researcher **Simon Wiesenthal** (1908–) in Vienna. One German and several Austrian neo-Nazis were arrested for the bombing. The German was sentenced to five years' imprisonment.

2000   In May a Vienna court found Innsbruck University political science professor **Anton Pelinka** (1941–) guilty of "defaming the character" of Jörg Haider, former leader of the far-right Freedom Party, because he had declared in an interview on an Italian television station in May 1999 that Haider trivialized Nazism. Pelinka was fined. In April 2001, the Supreme Court acquitted him. Haider's former lawyer, Dieter Böhmdorfer, who had initiated the case, was serving as Austria's minister of justice at the time of the court's ruling. In another case (about comparisons Pelinka had made to Cable News Network in the spring of 1999 between Haider's linking of Austria's level of unemployment with the number of foreigners in the country and the Nazis' linking of high unemployment rates with the size of the Jewish population), the court dismissed the defamation charge in October. At least one other similar defamation trial (lost by Haider against *Kurier* newspaper) took place.

Also see Argentina (1992–93: Wiesenthal), Hungary (1944–45: archives), USSR (pre-1949–54: Reisberg).

SOURCES

American Association for the Advancement of Science, Human Rights Action Network Case, *AU0003.pel* (17 July 2000).

Arnold, B., & H. Hassmann, "Archaeology in Nazi Germany: The Legacy of the Faustian Bargain", in: P.L. Kohl & C. Fawcett eds., *Nationalism, Politics, and the Practice of Archaeology* (Cambridge 1995) 75.

Boia, L. ed., *Great Historians of the Modern Age: An International Dictionary* (Westport 1991) 47–48, 56–57.

Boyd, K. ed., *Encyclopedia of Historians and Historical Writing* (London/Chicago 1999) 147–48, 530–31, 710–11, 1142–44.

Bruch, R. vom, & R.A. Müller eds., *Historikerlexikon: Von der Antike bis zum 20. Jahrhundert* (Munich 1991) 38–39, 124–25, 131, 295–97.

Cannon, J. ed., *The Blackwell Dictionary of Historians* (Oxford 1988) 53–54, 390.

Dokumentationsarchiv des österreichischen Widerstandes ed., *Rechtsextremismus in Österreich nach 1945* (Vienna 1981) 145–46, 175, 188, 199, 209–10, 227–28, 239, 294–96, 403.

Hanisch, E., *Der lange Schatten des Staates: Österreichische Gesellschaftsgeschichte im 20. Jahrhundert* (Vienna 1994) 324, 480–81.

Index on Censorship, 4/00:86; 6/00: 9, 166; 1/01: 100.

Keller, F., *Wien, Mai 68—Eine heisse Viertelstunde* (Vienna 1988) 30–31.

Rafetseder, H., *Bücherverbrennungen: Die öffentliche Hinrichtung von Schriffen in historischen Wandel* (Vienna 1988) 275–76.

Schulze, W., *Deutsche Geschichtswissenschaft nach 1945* (Munich 1993) 126, 315, 322–33, 329.

Simon Wiesenthal (1908–): A Short Biography (WWW-text 1998).

Strauss, H.A., & W. Röder eds., *International Biographical Dictionary of Central European Émigrés 1933–1945*, vol. 2 (Munich 1983) 407–8, 508, 710–11, 917, 931, 1151, 1233, 1257.

Weber, W., *Biographisches Lexicon zur Geschichtswissenschaft in Deutschland, Österreich und der Schweitz: Die Lehrstuhlinhaber für Geschichte von den Anfängen des Faches bis 1970* (Frankfurt/Main 1987) 72, 120–21, 204–5, 561–62.

Woolf, D.R. ed., *A Global Encyclopedia of Historical Writing* (New York/London 1998) 113, 861–62.

AZERBAIJAN

pre-1991   *See* Union of Soviet Socialist Republics (USSR).

1994   In December 1994 historian **Movsum Aliyev** was arrested for insulting President Heidar Aliyev in a September 1993 article he wrote for the newspaper *Azadliq*, entitled "The Answer to the Falsifiers of History". He was held in an overcrowded prison in Baku for several months before his release in February 1995.

[1996–97]   In 1996 or 1997, the Ganja local government confiscated all 2,400 copies of a book about the nineteenth-century Russian occupation of Ganja.

SOURCES

Amnesty International, *Azerbaijan: Allegations of Ill-Treatment in Detention* (EUR 55/ 01/96; London 1996) 4, 6.
Index on Censorship, 2/91: 6; 1/95: 233.

B

BAHAMAS

British Bahamas

1940s–50s   After 1945 the assembly commissioned an official history, but the chosen historian, Hilary St. George Saunders (1898–1951), died after two years' research. Novelist **Henry Ernest Bates** (1905–74) completed the work, but the manuscript, comparing a group of influential white merchants, known as the Bay Street Boys, to the pirate Blackbeard (?1680–1718), was considered offensive and was never published.

SOURCES

Craton, M., "Historiography of the Bahamas, Turks and Caicos Islands, Cayman Islands and Belize", in: B.W. Higman ed., *General History of the Caribbean*, vol. 6 (London/Oxford 1999) 671.

BAHRAIN

1976–   Among the books banned were *Bahrain: Social and Political Change since the First World War* (London 1976), by **M.G. Rumaihi**; *Tribe and State in Bahrain: The Transformation of Social and Political Authority in an Arab State* (Chicago/London 1980), by **Fuad Khuri** (1935–), professor of social anthropology at the American University of Beirut; and *Bahrain 1920–1945: Britain, the Shaikh and the Administration* (London 1987), by **Mahdi Abdalla al-Tajir** (1940–).

SOURCES

Anonymous personal communication, November 1999, February 2000.

BANGLADESH

pre-1971   *See* Pakistan.

1998   In February distribution of the Calcutta-based *Desh* weekly was
            banned because its special issue had carried an article by **Badruddin
            Umar**, former history professor and specialist in the history of the
            February 1952 Language Movement of Bangladesh, in which he
            stated that the then-imprisoned Sheikh Mujibur Rahman, leader of
            the Awami League and later first prime minister of Bangladesh
            (1971–75), was not involved in the Language Movement that made
            Bengali a state language in Pakistan. *Desh* apologized, withdrew the
            issue, and brought out a new one in which the article was replaced.
            The article, however, was republished in other magazines and on
            the Internet.

Also see Pakistan (1971: Ahmed, Bhattacharya, Khair).

SOURCES

GOB & Desh Censor Historian Badruddin Omar (WWW-text 1998).

BELARUS

President Alyaksandr Lukashenka's policy of integration with Russia since his
July 1994 election led to pressure to present a sanitized historical account of
Russian-Belarussian relations. Among the censored topics were the Stalinist re-
pression and the Belarussian independence movement during the Soviet era.

pre-1991   *See* Union of Soviet Socialist Republics (USSR).

pre-1994   *History of Belarus* (1925), a textbook for college students written
            by historian **Mitrafan Dounar-Zapolski** (1867–1934) and confis-
            cated in 1925 because the Soviet nationalities policy had changed,
            was published in Minsk (the capital) only in 1994. Because of his
            historical and political views, Dounar-Zapolski had to leave Minsk
            for Moscow in 1926. Accused of "national democratism", he was
            prevented from ever returning to Belorussia (Belarus's former
            name).

1995–   Since 1995 two history textbooks by **Vladimir Orlov**, a writer, his-
            torian, and vice president of Belarussian PEN in Minsk, have been
            banned. The first, *Where We Are From*, a book of stories on

Belarussian history for schoolchildren, contained a chapter explaining the historical roots of the national symbols of Belarus (the Pahonya or Charging Knight and the white-red-white flag) dating back to the Grand Duchy of Lithuania-Rus (1238–1569) and reinstated in 1991 but subsequently banned and replaced with Soviet-era symbols in 1995. Upon refusal by the state publisher of Belarus to publish the book as had been agreed with the Ministry of Education, Orlov received funding from the Belarussian Soros Foundation, which enabled Batkovshchina (Fatherland) publishers to publish it in 1996. It received few reviews and the ministry did not grant permission for its use in the schools. In early 1997 the authorities seized the remaining copies of the book and held them in damp conditions for a year. Once freed from seizure, the book was not stocked by the state bookshops. Only a few private bookstores sold it. The second book, *Ten Centuries of Belarussian History*, written by Orlov and historian **Gennady Saganovich** and already prepared for publication, was not published by the state publisher Mastatskaya Literatura. The publisher had reportedly received a letter from the State Press Committee in which state funding for the book was refused because, inter alia, it was written in a "tendentious, russophobic manner". In 1997 Orlov was dismissed from Mastatskaya Literatura, in which he had been responsible for the books on Belarussian culture and history.

1995   In August the Lukashenka government issued a Council of Minister directive ordering the removal of all high school history textbooks produced in the post-Soviet period (written in Belarussian) and their replacement by Soviet editions (written in Russian). Lukashenka reportedly said that the history textbooks were "politically biased" and that they developed a nationalist version of the Belarussian past while he preferred the Russophile version. In anticipation of new textbooks, old pre-1991 Soviet texts had to be used. The government later denied having issued the directive. In practice, an outright ban was not imposed, owing to textbook shortage. The issuing of the directive prompted the resignation of two deputy ministers of education.

1996   In early 1996 the printing of the third volume of the official *Encyclopedia of Belarussian History* (1996) was brought to a halt, reportedly to be purged of all material which represented a "negative" attitude to the USSR and Tsarist rule. Belarussian historians were considering a boycott of all future encyclopedia volumes.

1996–   In August 1996 **Zenon Pazniak** (1944–), archeologist, head of the Belarussian branch of the Historical-Enlightenment Society Memorial, cofounder and leader of the opposition party Belarussian Popular Front (1989–), outspoken critic of "Russian imperialism", presidential candidate in 1994 (with almost 14 percent of the first-round votes), and in hiding after antigovernment demonstrations in April, went into exile in the United States and Poland. In 1988 Pazniak had discovered 510 mass graves in the Kurapaty forest near Minsk. An official investigation into his allegations that Soviet interior ministry (NKVD) troops had executed some 200,000 Belarussian and Baltic citizens there in 1937–41 was initiated in 1994. It refuted his findings and stated that the number of victims was far smaller and that they were in fact Jews of different nationalities executed by the Nazis during World War II.

1996   In September the minister of culture and the press suspended the license of Chata publishers for one year for publishing the book *The Pahonya in Your Heart and Mine*. By praising the Pahonya, the book posed "a threat to civic order". The order was reportedly issued on official notepaper which still had the Pahonya on it.

1997–98   In May 1997 the General Procurator issued an official warning to the independent newspaper *Nasha Niva* (Our Land) because in March it had published an article by a historian [name unknown] with recollections of people from the Slominsky district, Grodno region, who related how Soviet partisans had wiped out civilians from 1943 to 1944. This allegedly "infringed the morality, honor, and dignity of citizens". When the newspaper demanded an investigation into these mass crimes, the General Procurator replied in June 1998 that the warning would not be revoked and that the facts had been "verified by the Belarussian [security service] KGB".

1997   In May Lukashenka reportedly criticized the university institutes of history and economics for destabilizing Belarus.

              Belarus's official independence day was moved from 27 to 3 July by Lukashenka to coincide with the 1944 liberation of Minsk by the Red Army. Demonstrators celebrating the anniversary of the nation's 1991 independence on 27 July were detained.

              In [November] **Pavel Zhuk**, publisher of the Minsk opposition newspaper *Svaboda*, received warnings from the State Press Commission that the paper could face criminal prosecution for publishing a series of articles which compared the government to Stalin's.

1998   In [January] **Liubov Lunyova**, who worked as a lecturer in ancient and medieval history on a fixed-term contract at the Belarussian State University history department, Minsk (1992–98), was dismissed, probably for being an activist for the human-rights organization Minsk Spring 96. When she applied for a job at another school, the principal told her that he "would be fired within half an hour" if he gave her a job. Others whose research was obstructed included **Nina Stuzhinskaya**, a doctoral student at the State National Academy of Sciences History Institute in Minsk working on a thesis entitled "The Anti-Soviet Movement in Belarus, 1917–1929".

In February the Belarussian Helsinki Committee held the conference "Political Repression in Belarus in the Twentieth Century" in Minsk. Among the historians attending were Stuzhinskaya [q.v. 1998], **Igor Kuznetsov, V. Karbalevich**, and possibly **A. Zalessky**, chair of the Belarussian Republican Association "Historical Knowledge". They also wrote articles later published by the committee in the collection *Political Repression in Belarus in the Twentieth Century: Materials from the Conference*. In October the state newspaper *Slavyansky Nabat* (Slavic Alarm Bell) published an article encouraging criminal charges against the conference organizers and the book authors because they were "guilty of humiliating the honor and dignity of the president". Despite their repeated attempts, the accused academics were denied the opportunity to respond to the article in the state newspapers.

The first issue of the Belarussian Association of Students newspaper, published in March, contained an article on the first page about the uprising in Kalinovsky in April 1863, in which students seized power in the town. In April one of the students responsible for the publication was questioned by, among others, a KGB officer.

In March up to fifty men and women were arrested and beaten by the police following a peaceful demonstration in Minsk to mark the eightieth anniversary of Belorussia's independence.

SOURCES

Amnesty International, *Report 1999* (London 1999) 92.

Article 19, *Ifex Alert*, 5 August 1998: 3.

Chernykh, E.N., "Postscript: Russian Archaeology after the Collapse of the USSR—Infrastructural Crisis and the Resurgence of Old and New Nationalisms", in: P.L. Kohl & C. Fawcett eds., *Nationalism, Politics, and the Practice of Archaeology* (Cambridge 1995) 144.

Davies, R.W., *Soviet History in the Yeltsin Era* (Basingstoke 1997) 4–5.

Human Rights Watch, *Republic of Belarus: Turning Back the Clock* (WWW-text 1998) 4–5.

———, *Republic of Belarus: Violations of Academic Freedom* (New York 1999) 5, 9, 12–18, 26–27, 37–38.

———, *World Report* (Washington) 1997: 203; 1999: 453; 2000: 237, 459.

Index on Censorship, 9/89: 41; 3/93: 4; 3/95: 64–67; 5/95: 170; 1/96: 114–17, 121–26,
    130, 170–71; 3/96: 102; 4/97: 105; 5/97: 165; 1/98: 79–81.
Keesings historisch archief, 1990: 290–91; 1994: 453; 1996: 459, 738; 1998: 147; 1999:
    427; 2000: 158.
Nekrich, A.M., "Perestroika in History: The First Stage", *Survey: A Journal of Soviet
    and East European Studies*, 1989, no.4: 39–40.
Zaprudnik, J., *Historical Dictionary of Belarus* (Lanham/London 1998) 98, 120, 124,
    171.

BELGIUM

The most sensitive historical subject seemed to be King Leopold's Congo Free
State (1885–1908).

pre-1945   Among the historians who emigrated before 1945 (and living in
            exile after 1944) were **George Sarton** (1884–1956) and **Henri Gré-
            goire** (1881–1964).

            Among the historians who were censored or persecuted during
            World War II (including in 1945) was **Léon-Ernest Halkin** (1906–
            98).

pre-1949   Until the late 1940s, the Congo Free State archives were treated
            carelessly. Twice, in 1895 and 1906–7, when the possible transfer
            to Belgium of sovereignty over the Congo was discussed, King Le-
            opold II gave detailed instructions to destroy or transfer the archives
            to the royal palace. "Je leur donnerai mon Congo, mais ils n'ont pas
            le droit de savoir ce que j'y ai fait" ("I shall give them my Congo
            but they have no right to know what I have done there"), he said.
            The massive destructions of 1906–7 led to a parliamentary question
            and to protests by the Association of Belgian Archivists and Li-
            brarians in 1910 (after Leopold's death). Not until the measures
            taken by Pierre Wigny, minister of colonies (1947–50), did the re-
            maining archives receive much attention (the German occupier of
            these archives in World War I excepted).

1945–59   In January 1945 politician, lawyer, and historian **Hendrik Elias**
            (1902–73) was interned in southern Germany by the Germans after
            he had refused to continue his collaboration with the German lead-
            ership in Belgium. In May he was arrested there by the French for
            his wartime collaboration with the Germans as the mayor of Ghent
            (December 1940–) and leader of the pro-German Vlaamsch Natio-
            naal Verbond political party (October 1942–). Until October he was
            interned in several camps and then transferred to Brussels. In March
            he had been sentenced to death in absentia by a military court in
            Ghent. In March–April 1947, after a long period of investigations,

his case was reconsidered; in May (and later on appeal) his sentence was confirmed and in April 1951 it was commuted into life imprisonment. In the fall of 1959, Elias was transferred to the hospital and then released in December. In prison, he did the preparatory work for his future historical research; he became a historian of the Flemish Movement. In 1931 the francophone historian Émile Lousse (1905–) was allegedly appointed professor of modern history and the history of law at Leuven University instead of Elias because of the latter's Flemish-nationalist convictions.

1945–   In 1945 historian **Robert Van Roosbroeck** (1898–1988) was sentenced to death in absentia for his wartime collaboration with the Germans. In 1941 the Free University of Brussels had been closed after its board had canceled Van Roosbroeck's appointment by the Germans, after which Van Roosbroeck had been appointed a history professor at Ghent University (1941–[45]). In 1945 Van Roosbroeck went into hiding and in 1947 he went into exile in the Netherlands until his death. After World War I, he had been dismissed as a schoolteacher for his Flemish activism and collaboration with the Germans. He edited the six-volume *History of Flanders* (Antwerp/ Amsterdam 1936–49).

1959–   Twice, in March and July, the Académie Royale des Sciences Coloniales refused to publish the papers of its member, missionary **Edmond Boelaert** (1899–1966), a historian and ethnologist who wanted to publicize abuses committed in the Congo under European direction. In both cases, the decision was the result of lively discussion and taken by vote. The papers, entitled *L'Occupation du District de l'Equateur dans les Souvenirs Indigènes* and *Les Débuts de la S.A.B. [Société Agricole et Commerciale de la Busira et du Haut-Congo] à Coquilhatville*, were deposited in the academy archives. The latter paper was finally published in the *Annales Aequatoria* of 1988, the former one was replaced by the publication of the sources for this text in the same journal in 1995–96.

1967–   From 1967 **Jan Dhondt** (1915–72), a medievalist who occupied the new chair of contemporary history at Ghent University since 1966, published the *Bulletin critique d'histoire de Belgique* (an annotated annual bibliography of the history of Belgium under his editorship) on his own. From 1953 to 1966, it had been published by the *Revue du nord* in Lille, France, but Dhondt was inspired to publish independently after at least two complaints from the Royal Commission of History, which he had criticized, and the ensuing pressure from the *Revue du Nord* board to omit certain extracts from the 1966 edition. In the same year (1967), the *Revue du Nord* started a rival *Bulletin d'histoire de Belgique*.

1975–   From 1975 diplomat **Jules Marchal** (1924–) did research and published several books in Dutch and French (1986–94) on the crimes in the Congo Free State under the pseudonym of A.M. Delathuy. For eight years he did not gain access to the Ministry of Foreign Affairs archives, particularly those on the 1904–5 official commission of inquiry into King Leopold II's misgovernment of the Congo Free State.

1986   In March retired Lieutenant-General Émile Janssens, chief of staff of the Force Publique (the army in the Belgian Congo) until 1960 and president of the patriotic movement Pro Belgica 1830–1980, wrote a letter to Minister of National Education Daniël Coens about historian and anthropologist **Daniel Vangroenweghe** (1938–). Janssens accused Vangroenweghe of libeling King Leopold II in his book *Red Rubber: Leopold II and His Congo* (Brussels/Amsterdam 1985) and in conferences and interviews between August 1984 and February 1986 by criticizing the crimes committed in the Congo Free State. Janssens also questioned Vangroenweghe's position as a history teacher at the Royal Atheneum of Ostende. In April he wrote a letter to Omer Marchal, director of Didier Hatier Éditions in Brussels, a publisher who prepared the French translation of Vangroenweghe's book, *Du sang sur les lianes: Leopold II et son Congo* (Brussels 1986). Apparently as a result of the letter, a publisher's note was printed in the French edition to warn the reader of its controversial character. Vangroenweghe was asked to sign a statement that he would take áll responsibility in the eventuality of a lawsuit. Although the French edition sold out in a few months, it was not reprinted. Pro Belgica asked a military historian to refute Vangroenweghe's "lies"; his report was distributed on a limited scale. Former Force Publique officer Andreas Louwagie made a similar attempt. Members of Parliament who sympathized with Pro Belgica asked two questions about the affair in Parliament. Coens established a commission of school inspectors, who interrogated Vangroenweghe (for one hour) and his superior and colleagues at Ostende. Coens stated that the charges were unfounded, but Vangroenweghe never received official confirmation of them or of the commission's conclusion. In the course of the affair, he was threatened in anonymous letters, and his public lectures on the subject were interrupted by former colonials and attended by the secret police. Later he was a guest lecturer (1992–95) and researcher on AIDS in Africa (1996–) at the Ghent University Department of African Studies. In 1994 he became a member of the Biographical Commission of the Académie Royale des Sciences d'Outre-Mer/Koninklijke Academie voor Overzeese Wetenschappen (successor of the Académie Royale des Sciences Coloniales), despite the possible protest of one academician because of his 1985 book.

[1990]   **Luc Huyse** (1937–), a professor of sociology at Leuven University who published extensively on Western European politics and studied the judiciary's role in transitions to democracy, had his research about the purges of Nazi collaborators—published as *Undigested Past: Collaboration and Repression in Belgium, 1942–1952* (Leuven 1991) and co-written by Steven Dhondt and Paul Depuydt—obstructed in several ways. The magistrate appointed by the university as a referee for the project disapproved of its funding on the grounds that social-scientific research about judicial decisions could not be trusted. Access to certain sources proved impossible, although they were not embargoed under the archive law. Lobbying by members of the judiciary reportedly tried to hamper the distribution of the published findings. The attorney general of the Cour de Cassation, Jacques Velu, wrote a letter to the director of the francophone television channel in order to prevent use of the findings for the series *Jours de guerre.*

1994–95   **Gie Van den Berghe** (1945–), a moral philosopher who specialized in Nazi-camp and Holocaust eyewitness research at the Navorsings- en Studiecentrum voor de Geschiedenis van de Tweede Wereldoorlog (Research and Study Center for the History of World War II) in Brussels and campaigner against Holocaust deniers, was himself implicitly categorized as someone who minimized the Holocaust by Dutch journalist Philo Bregstein in an article about anti-Semitism published in *Histoire de l'antisémitisme 1945–93* (Paris 1994), edited by French historian Léon Poliakov (1910–97). Bregstein denounced the fact that Van den Berghe, in his book *The Exploitation of the Holocaust* (Antwerp/Baarn 1990), not only attacked and refuted Holocaust denial but also described and criticized the alleged political exploitation of the Holocaust by some Israeli leaders. In the course of 1994, Van den Berghe sent several protest letters to Bregstein and Poliakov, who did not publicly reply until September 1995 but did not retract the accusation. In November 1994 seventy-six colleagues of Van den Berghe, including his director at the research and study center, José Gotovitch, and Jewish historian Maxime Steinberg, signed a petition in his support. In February 1995 Van den Berghe was again accused, this time as an anti-Semite, by Louis Davids, chief editor of the *Belgisch-Israëlitisch Weekblad*, who retracted the accusation after new protests, among others, from Van den Berghe's director and colleagues at the research and study center. Possibly as a result of the two affairs, Van den Berghe was denied access to the library of the Auschwitz Foundation; his candidacy for compiling a bibliography at the American Holocaust Museum in Washington and his application for the post of archivist at a Jewish archive and museum in Malines, Belgium, were annulled; his subsequent books were poorly reviewed in the Dutch press. In 1996, however, he was awarded an important Flemish free-speech prize. He was also attacked by the Holocaust deniers themselves. Although prepared in the 1980s to refute the theses of Holocaust deniers in a debate with them, he gradually distanced himself from this strategy. In 1992 he was charged with libel by some Holocaust deniers because he had denounced the so-called *Leuchter Report*, which denies the use of the gas chambers for murder, but in 1996 the case was dismissed. Early in 1994 (around the time of the Bregstein accusation), he was attacked in a book by Vrij Historisch Onderzoek (Free Historical Research), a group of Holocaust deniers, reportedly distributed to all libraries and history teachers in Dutch-speaking Belgium.

1996   In early 1996 the Institut Jules Destrée reportedly convinced bookshops in French-speaking Wallonia to sell the book *Les Grands Mythes de l'histoire de Belgique, de Flandre et de Wallonie* (Brussels 1995), edited by historian Anne Morelli, only if accompanied by a rectification of one of its essays. In the essay, historian **Jean-Philippe Schreiber** mentioned and analyzed the anti-Semitism of socialist politician Jules Destrée (1863–1936).

1996–   In March 1996 the newspaper *De Morgen* revealed that in November 1995 the Belgian Military Espionage Service (ADIV) and the Judicial Police of Brussels had planned to destroy parts of the Judicial Police's archives concerning political terrorism in Belgium and Europe during the 1980s, particularly concerning the group Cellules Communistes Combattantes. Parts of the archives were reportedly not destroyed but secretly kept and summarized by ADIV. A June 1997 confidential report investigating the matter and leaked to *De Morgen* confirmed the revelations.

1997   In March 1997 liberal politician Jean Pede threatened to sue historian **Patrick Duportail** (1973–) for libel because in an interview for a local paper about his historical study on war resistance in the village of Bottelare the latter had declared that Jean Pede's father Hubert had joined the anti-German resistance only after the Liberation in September 1944 and at the same time earned a large sum of money by hiding collaborators. In his letter to Duportail, Jean Pede's lawyer included evidence supporting the view that Hubert

Pede had been in the resistance from May to October 1944. In a rectification in the local paper, Duportail endorsed this view. Duportail's 1995 study was awarded a provincial history prize. In the manuscript of his book version (to be published in 2001) Duportail maintained that Pede's wartime activities were controversial, reaffirming his earlier version but also mentioning Pede's, both based on three testimonies.

Also see Congo (Belgian Congo), Rwanda (Belgian Ruanda-Urundi).

SOURCES

Bulletin de l'Académie royale des sciences coloniales, 1959: 508–11, 844–45.

Catoire, P., "Mythes, identités et vulgarisation", *Clio, Revue de l'association des historiens de l'UCL*, 1996, nos.108–9: 56–57.

Dhondt, J. ed., *Bulletin critique d'histoire de Belgique, 1966–67* (Ghent 1967) i–ii.

Encyclopedie van de Vlaamse beweging (Tielt/Utrecht 1973) 479–82, 1356.

File Duportail: "Interview Patrick Duportail: Een klein dorp in een grote oorlog", *De Beiaard*, 21 February 1997; letter by P. Laghaert (J. Pede's lawyer) to Duportail (10 March 1997) with evidence supporting Pede's version; Duportail's rectification, *De Beiaard*; case file from P. Duportail with evidence supporting his statements; personal communication, P. Duportail (October 2000).

File Van den Berghe: The accusation by Holocaust deniers in *Dr. Gie van den Berghe, Wetenschapper of moraalfilosofische kwakzalver?* (Antwerp 1994, 160 pages). The accusation by Bregstein, "Le Paradoxe néerlandais", in L. Poliakov ed., *Histoire de l'antisémitisme 1945–1993* (Paris 1994) 111–14; also in Dutch in: *De Groene Amsterdammer*, 20 April 1994: 14–18, repeated 12 July 1995; reply by Van den Berghe and reaction by Bregstein and Poliakov in the 13 September 1995 edition: 22–23; repetition of the accusation in: P. Bregstein, *Het kromme kan toch niet recht zijn: Essays en interviews* (Baarn 1997) 67, 70, 77–78. The accusation by Davids in: *Belgisch-Israëlitisch Weekblad*, 17 February 1995: 5 (also editions of 3 February 1995: 5; 24 February 1995: 4 for similar opinions); protests in the 1995 editions of 24 February: 4 and 17 March: 4; retraction 7 April; reply by Van den Berghe, 28 April. Articles about the affairs in *De Morgen*, 8 July 1994; *Vrij Nederland*, 9 July 1994: 12; *Markant*, 14 July 1994: 26; *Knack*, 15 March 1995: 35–39 and 8 September 1995: 10; *La Libre Belgique*, 1 June 1995: 4; *Humo*, 16 August 1995: 4–5; *Ter Herkenning*, 1995: 270–74; personal communication, G. Van den Berghe (January–February 1997, November–December 2000).

File Vangroenweghe: *Humo*, 14 March 1985: 47–54 (interview); Janssens's public accusations and author's reply in *Brugsch Handelsblad*, 24 and 31 May 1985; publisher's note in French edition; copies of two 1996 letters by Janssens (17 March to the minister, 7 April to Marchal); copy of Vangroenweghe letter to two school inspectors, 10 June 1986; personal communication, D. Vangroenweghe (December 1996; January 1997).

Hochschild, A., *King Leopold's Ghost: A Story of Greed, Terror, and Heroism in Colonial Africa* (New York 1998) 296–99.

Humo, 14 January 1997: 17 (Huyse).

Huyse, L., personal communication, January–February 1997.

Louwagie, A., *Rubber zonder kleur (Wat Vangroenweghe verzweeg)* (s.l. 1986).

Morelli, A., "Histoire, vulgarisation et politique: Les Termes d'un débat" (unpublished paper; Louvain-la-Neuve; April 1996) 7–9.

——— ed., *De grote mythen uit de geschiedenis van België, Vlaanderen en Wallonië* (Berchem 1996) 9–10, 283.

De Morgen, 2 July 1997: 1, 4.

Nieuwe encyclopedie van de Vlaamse Beweging (Tielt 1998) 1058, 1060–63, 2655–56.

Reynebeau, M., "Het water is te diep: De media als brug over de kloof tussen geschiedenis en openbaarheid", *Revue belge d'histoire contemporaine*, 1994–95: 209.

Stengers, J., "Études historiques", in: Académie royale des sciences d'outre-mer, *Livre blanc/Witboek*, vol. 1 (Brussels 1962) 121–22.

———, "Belgian Historiography since 1945", in: P.C. Emmer & H.L. Wesseling eds., *Reappraisals in Overseas History* (Leiden 1979) 164–65, 180.

Storme, M., "E.P. Edmond Boelaert, m.s.c.", *Mededelingen der zittingen van de KAOW*, 1967: 170, 192.

Van-Grieken-Taverniers, M., "L'Histoire de l'état indépendant du Congo et les archives du ministère du Congo Belge et du Ruanda-Urundi", *Archives, bibliothèques et musées de Belgique*, 1959, no.1: 3–8 (quote Leopold II: 4).

———, "Archives", in: Académie royale des sciences d'outre-mer, *Livre blanc/Witboek*, vol. 1 (Brussels 1962) 57–58.

Vangroenweghe, D., *Rood rubber: Leopold II en zijn Kongo* (Brussels/Amsterdam 1985, 1986).

Verhaegen, B., "Les Violences coloniales au Congo belge", *Cahiers d'actualité sociale*, March 1987: 3, 6.

Vinck, H., personal communication, June 1999.

Volmuller, H.W.J. ed., *Nijhoffs geschiedenislexicon: Nederland en België* (The Hague/Antwerp 1981) 174.

Winters, C. ed., *International Dictionary of Anthropologists* (New York/London 1991) 69–70.

BELIZE

1984–89   During the rule of the United Democratic Party government led by Manuel Esquivel, nationalist texts published after independence (1981) were virtually banned. They probably included *A History of Belize: Nation in the Making* (Belize City 1983), a history textbook anonymously written by sociologist and historian **Nigel Bolland** and former Minister of State **Assad Shoman** (1943–) and sponsored by the Ministry of Education, and *Readings in Belizean History* (Belize City 1984), edited and published by the staff of St. John's College.

SOURCES

Craton, M., "Historiography of the Bahamas, Turks and Caicos Islands, Cayman Islands and Belize", in: B.W. Higman ed., *General History of the Caribbean*, vol. 6 (London/Oxford 1999) 683–84.

BOLIVIA

1946–   Historian **Roberto Prudencio** (1908–), a representative of Bolivian neo-indianismo, chairman of the faculty of philosophy at the University of San Andrés, La Paz, broke with the Movimiento Nacionalista Revolucionaria (Nationalist Revolutionary Movement), a political party in which he had been active as a journal editor, and its philosophy, and went into exile in Chile, where he was appointed professor of philosophy at the Catholic University in Santiago.

1971–   After the military coup of August led by colonel Hugo Banzer, the original prints of *El Coraje del Pueblo* (The Courage of the People) by **Jorge Sanjinés** (1936–), director of the Bolivian Cinematographic Institute (1964–69), were smuggled out of Bolivia and edited in Italy. The film, a documentary reconstruction of a massacre of Indian miners in the town of Siglo XX in 1967, was banned and Sanjinés went into exile until the fall of the Banzer government in 1979. The film identified government and military officials responsible for the massacre. Survivors of the massacre actively participated in the film by recreating their activities before and during the bloodbath.

1980   After the 17 July 1980 military coup led by General Luis García Meza, the book *Historia del Cine Boliviano* (History of Bolivian Cinema), by filmmaker and journalist **Alfonso Gumucio Dagrón**, already at the printer, was censored by the publisher himself. Gumucio's home was raided and he had to hide. He sought asylum in the Mexican embassy and escaped to Mexico.

pre-1981   A 1981 report stated that the archives suffered much from political instability and official indifference.

1999   In March distribution of the magazine *Informe R* was obstructed because it carried an article about human-rights violations under South American dictators of the 1970s, including Banzer, dictator in 1971–79 and president in 1997–2001.

SOURCES

Arnade, C.W., "The Historiography of Colonial and Modern Bolivia", *Hispanic American Historical Review*, 1962: 371–74.

Blakewell, J.R., & P.J. Blakewell, "Bolivia: Preámbulo", in: J.J. TePaske ed., *Research Guide to Andean History* (Durham 1981) 2.

Index on Censorship, 4/81: 23, 30–31; 6/86: 3.

Keesings historisch archief, 2000: 98.

Nicholas, T. ed., *International Dictionary of Films and Filmmakers*, vol. 2 (Chicago/London 1991) 733–34.

BOSNIA-HERZEGOVINA

pre-1991   *See* Yugoslavia.

1992   In May, after the outbreak of the civil war in Bosnia-Herzegovina,
            Serbian historian **Milorad Ekmečić** (1928–), reported survivor of
            the Ustasha pogrom during World War II, professor of nineteenth-
            and twentieth-century national and general history at Sarajevo Uni-
            versity, and coauthor of *History of Yugoslavia* (1972; English 1974),
            was arrested and tortured by Bosnian Muslim paramilitary forces for
            his prominent role in Radovan Karadžić's Serbian Democratic Party
            (SDS). He was reportedly able to escape and went to Belgrade where
            he took a post as a Serbian Academy of Sciences and Arts history
            professor.

1993–97   In 1993 historian **Fadila Memisević** (?1940–), cofounder in May
            1992 of a research center in Zenica to document war crimes and
            "ethnic cleansing" in Bosnia, did not return to Bosnia-Herzegovina
            after presenting a list of 1,350 perpetrators to the United Nations
            Commission on Human Rights in Geneva because she had allegedly
            received death threats. She continued her work in Göttingen, Ger-
            many—with a three-month interruption in 1994 when she returned
            to Bosnia—and provided the International Criminal Tribunal for the
            Former Yugoslavia, The Hague, with much valuable information.
            Early in 1997 she reportedly returned to Bosnia.

SOURCES

Banac, I., "Historiography of the Countries of Eastern Europe: Yugoslavia", *American
    Historical Review*, 1992: 1090–91, 1102–3.
Bangert, Y., "Drei Preise für Menschenrechtsarbeit: Tilman Zülch, Fadila Memisević und
    die GfbV wurden 1996 geehrt", *Pogrom*, December 1996/January 1997: 40–41.
Grémaux, R., & A. de Vries, "Het omstreden verleden van een verloren land: Historio-
    grafie en nationaal bewustzijn in Bosnië-Herzegovina", *Groniek*, 1995: 107–10.
Humo (Belgium), 8 June 1995: 164–67 (Memisević).
Marès, A. ed., *Histoire et pouvoir en Europe médiane* (Paris 1996).
Marjanović, V., "L'Histoire politisée: L'Historiographie serbe depuis 1989", in: Marès
    ed. 1996: 287.
———, "L'Historiographie contemporaine serbe des années 80: De la démystification
    idéologique à la mystification nationaliste", in: Marès ed. 1996: 162–63.
NRC-Handelsblad, 1993 (7 July: 5 [Memisević], 30 December: 5 [Ekmečić]).
Šuster, Z.E., *Historical Dictionary of the Federal Republic of Yugoslavia* (Lanham/Lon-
    don 1999) 107.
Woolf, D.R. ed., *A Global Encyclopedia of Historical Writing* (New York/London 1998)
    210.

BOTSWANA

See Zimbabwe (pre-1974: Mudenge).

BRAZIL

During the military dictatorship (1964–85), dozens of historians were dismissed, persecuted, or exiled, especially those suspected of left-wing sympathies. The São Paulo University history department was purged. Above all, censorship affected contemporary history; analytical studies of current conditions were especially unpopular with the government, and publishers consequently shifted to past history or issued little on Brazil.

1945   At the end of President Getúlio Vargas's authoritarian Estado Novo (1937–45), a fire, allegedly started deliberately, destroyed the archives of the political police headed by Felinto Müller.

1947–   In 1947 Marxist historian and politician **Caio Prado** (1907–90) was elected deputy of São Paulo state for the Partido Communista Brasileiro (PCB; Brazilian Communist Party). When in 1948 the PCB was declared unconstitutional, all mandates, including his, were annulled. He spent a term in prison. With a thesis especially written for the purpose, he competed for the São Paulo University chair of political economy in 1954. He was appointed, not as the chair holder but as a "free lecturer" in political economy. In April 1964 (after the coup), the fifty-second issue of the *Revista brasiliense*, which he founded and edited (1955–64), was destroyed by the security services before distribution and the publication was banned. From that time, he was interrogated several times and frequently stayed in short-term detention. In 1968 governmental decree DL-477 forced him out of his post at São Paulo University and deprived him of his political rights. In the same year, he participated in another contest, this time for the chair of Brazilian history, with a thesis entitled "History and Development: The Contribution of Historiography to the Theory and Practice of Brazilian Development" (1968, 1978). He was reportedly the best candidate but the contest was never completed because of political interference. After an inquest (October 1967) and a military court trial (1968), he was sentenced to four and a half years' imprisonment (reduced to eighteen months on appeal) for a "subversive" interview with two philosophy students in *Revisão* (Revision), a student-sponsored magazine dedicated to theoretical debates. Apparently, the tribunal was in doubt whether the "struggle" mentioned in the interview meant "armed struggle". However, his book *The Brazilian Revolution* (1966, 1978) was understood to have inspired a new generation of urban guerrillas. He was imprisoned for a year, and after being found not guilty by the Supreme Military Court, he was released in 1971. Prado had often been harassed after he joined the PCB in 1931. In 1935 he became the vice president of the Aliança Nacional Libertadora (National Liberation Alliance), a coalition of opposition parties. In July the Alliance was declared illegal and he was imprisoned (1935–37). A book of his, *USSR: A New World* (1934, 1935), the result of his 1933 visit to the USSR, was destroyed in the period 1935–64. In 1937 he went into exile to France, where he joined the French Communist Party, and he participated in the Spanish Civil War. He returned in 1939.

1964–   In February 1964, five out of ten volumes of a new history textbook for secondary schools, *História nova do Brasil* (A New History of Brazil), were published by the Ministry of Education and Culture. They were written by General **Nélson Werneck Sodré** (1911–), Marxist historian, professor of military history at the Escola do Estado Maior do Exército (Army General Staff School) (1948–50), and head of the history department at the Instituto Superior de Estudos Brasileiros (ISEB) (1954–64), who was considered by many as the official PCB historian, with the collaboration of **Mauricio Martins de Mello, Pedro de Alcântara Figueira, Pedro Celso Uchôa Cavalcanti Neto**, and **Ruben Cesar Fernandes**, young history teachers educated at the National Faculty of Philosophy, São Paulo University, and **Joel Ruffino dos Santos** (?1942–), a history student at that faculty. There were heavy protests in several newspapers and on television against the plan to make the textbook obligatory reading throughout Brazil. The Brazilian Historical and Geographical Institute issued a document in which the Marxist model was condemned. In March two volumes were out of print. A decision to reprint and to continue with subsequent volumes to be published by the Editora Brasiliense in São Paulo encountered a hostile atmosphere shortly after the military coup of 31 March. Already controversial before the coup, the textbook focused on the Brazilian people and emphasized the economic dimension in history. It was deemed subversive and the ministry withdrew its support. Articles by Sodré and others in July and September 1965 provoked further investigations, and the military police imprisoned and tortured the authors. Sodré was imprisoned for several months and for a time thereafter prohibited from public speaking and writing. Harassment continued after habeas corpus was used to secure his release from prison. The authors were deprived of all opportunities to lecture and, with the exception of Sodré, had to go into exile for many years. The textbooks were confiscated in the bookshops, burned and banned, and ISEB was closed. For Joel Ruffino dos Santos, it was already the second arrest. An editor-contributor to the journal *Opinão*, once an exile in Bolivia, he "disappeared" in December 1972 when boarding the bus from São Paulo to Rio de Janeiro.

In [March], **José Honório Rodrigues** (1913–87), historian of historiography and of the colonial period, former director at the National Library Division of Rare Books and Publications (1946–58), was removed as director of the National Archives (1958–64) just before or after the coup. He became a visiting professor at the University of Texas, Austin (1963–64, 1966), and Columbia University, New York (1970), but declined offers of tenure in the United States. He was a member of the Academia de Letras (1970–87). He wrote the multivolume *História da história do Brasil* (1979–88). His collection of essays *História combatente* (Rio de Janeiro 1982) included previously banned articles on the role of chance in the historical process and on the role of the military in the period of Pedro I (1822–31).

During the dictatorship years, economic historian **Eulália Lahmeyer Lobo**, specialist in immigration during the colonial period, went into exile in the United States.

A book by social historian **Manuel Maurício**, *The Social Formation of the Brazilians*, was censored.

Under 1964 Institutional Act No. 1, lawyer and historian **Jânio Quadros** (1917–92), former president of Brazil (January–August 1961), was deprived of his political rights (April 1964–August 1979) and in 1968 placed in internal exile for 120 days in the town of Corumbá, Mato Grosso, because of his public statements. *História do povo brasileiro* (History of the Brazilian People) a book he cowrote with Afonso Arinos de Melo Franco, could be published in São Paulo in 1967. Later Quadros made a comeback as mayor of São Paulo (1985–88).

Under 1964 Institutional Act No.1, historian **Edmar Morel** was deprived of his political rights.

After the March 1964 coup, **Celso Furtado** (1920–), a dependency economist well known for his retrospective studies, staff member of the United Nations Economic Commission for Latin America (1948–58), Santiago de Chile, and first Brazilian Minister of Planning (1962–64), was immediately dismissed. He lost his political rights. He took refuge in the Mexican embassy and went into exile in Chile, the United States (where he worked at Yale University), and France, where he became a professor at the Sorbonne (1965–79). He visited

Brazil briefly in 1968 and regularly from 1975. He was granted amnesty in August 1979 and returned to Brazil, where he eventually became ambassador to the European Economic Community (1985–86) and minister of culture (1986–88). His work *La economía iberoamericana desde la conquista ibérica hasta la revolución cubana*, was banned in Chile. In a catalog sent out by the Editorial Universitaria publishers in Santiago after the September 1973 coup, it was deleted.

After the March 1964 coup, the radical sociologist, dependency economist, and economic historian **André Gunder Frank** (1929–), associate professor of sociology at Brasília University (1963–64), went into exile in Chile, where he became professor of sociology and economics at the Faculty of Economics, University of Chile, Santiago (1968–73), and adviser to President Salvador Allende. After the September 1973 coup there, he fled to (the Federal Republic of) Germany, his country of origin, where he worked at the Berlin University Lateinamerika-Institut and the Max-Planck-Institut, Starnberg (1974–78). Later, he worked at the University of East Anglia, Norwich, United Kingdom (1978–82), and the Free University of Amsterdam (1982–). He had left Germany as a child in 1933, when his family went into exile in Switzerland and later in the United States. There Frank studied economics at the University of Chicago. In the 1970s he was consistently denied visas to participate in scholarly meetings and to serve as a lecturer in American universities because of his "affiliation with various communist causes". He was the author of, inter alia, *Capitalism and Underdevelopment in Latin America* (New York 1967).

1968   In December **Roberto Lobo Neto** (?1899–), philosophy professor at São José dos Campos University, was prosecuted for lectures he had given in education history. He was accused of promoting Marxist-Leninist indoctrination and of attacking the Brazilian regime.

1969   In February governmental decree DL-477 forced university lecturer **Maria Emília Viotti da Costa**, historian of the independence period, to retire from her work. It deprived her of her rights. In a military police inquest in São Paulo, she was accused of spreading subversive propaganda in her university classes. Her dismissal came in the midst of legal proceedings against students and staff at the São Paulo University History and Geography Department, who were accused of participating in groups known as "parity committees for educational reform", set up in 1968.

Historian **Sérgio Buarque de Holanda** (1902–82), active socialist, journalist, professor of the history of Brazilian civilization at the São

Paulo University (1957–69), and director of its Institute of Brazilian Studies (1958–68), resigned in protest against the government's mass dismissal of staff. Later he declared that, in the absence of a free press, he wanted the departmental minutes to bear witness to the arbitrary official acts. In 1936 he had published *Raízes do Brasil* (Roots of Brazil; twenty-two editions by 1995). As an assistant professor of economic history and comparative literature at the University of the Federal District, Rio de Janeiro (1936–39), he had lost his position when the institution was closed after conflicts with President Vargas. In 1945 he cofounded the Democratic Left (later the Brazilian Socialist Party).

1970–74   In 1970 **Afonso Henrique Martins Saldanha** (1918–74), professor of history, geography, and sciences at various schools in Rio de Janeiro, author of some entries on education in the *Encyclopaedia Britannica*, federal inspector of the Ministry of Education and Culture, and president of the teachers' union of Rio de Janeiro (1967–69, reelected 1969), was imprisoned and tortured. After forty-two days he was released, but in December 1974 he died of complications resulting from the torture.

1971   In May **Ivan Mota Dias** (1942–), militant of the Vanguarda Popular Revolucionária and history student at Fluminense Federal University, Niterói (Rio de Janeiro State), living in hiding in Rio de Janeiro after his preventive detention had been decreed in December 1968, "disappeared". His family received an anonymous telephone call with the news of his imprisonment. According to two witnesses, he was imprisoned, tortured, and executed but, despite several habeas corpus pleas, authorities denied having detained him.

1971–79·   In June historian **Ciro Flamarion Cardoso** (1942–), who upon completion of his doctorate in France was unable to return to Brazil, was offered a position at the University of El Salvador but denied a visa. The University of El Salvador, however, co-funding the Programa Centroamericano de Ciencias Sociales (Central American Program of Social Sciences), linked to the Consejo Superior Universitario Centroamericano in San José, Costa Rica employed him there instead (August 1971–mid-1976). From August 1976 to January 1979, Cardoso worked at the Centro de Investigaciones Históricas of the Instituto Nacional de Antropología e Historia, Mexico City. In February 1979, after the amnesty, he returned to Brazil, where he became a professor at Fluminense Federal University (1979–).

1972   **[José Augusto Guilhon de] Albuquerque** and **Gerson [Moura]**, two professors at the Catholic University of Rio de Janeiro history department, were reportedly in a psychiatric hospital suffering from physical injuries after their arrest. They were possibly suspected of "subversive activities".

Journalist and amateur historian **Hélio Silva** (1904–95) interrupted the chronological order in the publication plan of his multivolume series on twentieth-century Brazilian political history (1965–) in order to avoid description of sensitive years (probably the Vargas years 1937–45). In January 1977 he was one of the intellectuals who presented an anticensorship petition to the minister of justice.

In October **Antonio Benetazzo** (1941–72), leader of the Movimento de Libertação Popular, was detained and tortured. He died on 30 October. According to the official version, he died in a traffic accident. His imprisonment, however, was acknowledged in January 1973. Until 1969, he had been a history teacher, active in the PCB and the Ação Libertadora Nacional, who had tried to transmit a critical vision of history to the students who prepared their college entrance exam at São Paulo University. In 1969 he had gone underground.

1973–   One night in February **Luiz Basílio Rossi** professor of Brazilian history at Penápolis University, São Paulo, was abducted by the military and tortured apparently because of his friendship with politically active people. Later that night, the security forces barred the house to prevent his wife and daughters from telling what had happened. In April his wife saw him alive at the military police headquarters in São Paulo but was forced to sign a fake letter stating that he was not tortured. After an international campaign, he was released on bail in October. In February 1974 he left for Belgium. In March 1975 his trial took place while he was in exile. He was not sentenced, but an arrest order was issued.

1974   **Vandick Reidner Pereira Coqueiro** (1949–?74), militant of the Partido Comunista do Brasil, economy student, and history teacher, guerrillero in Araguaia from February 1971, "disappeared". According to the official version, he died in January 1974.

1979–85   In July 1985 the book *Brasil: Nunca mais (Brazil: Never Again)* was published in Petrópolis. It was the summary of an unpublished twelve-volume 6,946-page report called "Project A". This "Project A" was an analysis of more than one million pages of verbatim transcripts of military trials, constituting the complete proceedings of nearly all the political cases (707) tried in military courts between April 1964 (the coup) and March 1979 (shortly before the August 1979 amnesty law), and fragmentary records for dozens of others. They included defendants' testimonies, a list of 444 torturers (made public separately in November 1985), and more than 10,000 pamphlets, manifestos, booklets, and correspondence confiscated by the police. All these records, stored in the Brasília archives of the Supreme Military Court, were secretly photocopied and microfilmed by a team of twelve lawyers and about twenty others working with the Catholic Church and funded by the World Council of Churches. The lawyers had been granted piecemeal access to the records because they had to prepare the amnesty requests by political prisoners. Microfilm duplicates were stored outside Brazil. The copying (1979–82) and analysis of the materials (1979–85) were done in complete secrecy because the 1979 amnesty law deterred investigation. In addition, when caught, the lawyers could have been subject to reprisals, and the archives in danger of destruction. The team maintained its anonymity even after the book was published. It became the single best-selling book of nonfiction in Brazilian literary history.

1988   In November the relatives of forty people who "disappeared" under the military dictatorship (1964–85) submitted a petition to the Supreme Court to gain right of access to personal files, including those held by the security services, under the so-called 1988 habeas data constitutional provision. In late 1988 the court had not issued a judgment.

1994   In June poet and historian **Hermógenes da Silva Almeida Filho** and a lawyer were shot dead in Rio de Janeiro. Both were advisers to the opposition Workers Party and members of the local council human-rights commission which monitored the investigation into two massacres of street children. Both had also reported that they had been receiving threatening notes, apparently related to their activities on behalf of black people and homosexuals.

2000   In April the police decision to impede a march organized by two thousand indigenous leaders from throughout Brazil during celebrations of the arrival of the first Portuguese explorers to Brazil in 1500 and the violence employed by shock troops against indigenous activists led the president of the government's indigenous institute FUNAI to resign in protest.

Also see Argentina (1976–: Basso; 1977–: Pérez Esquivel), USSR (1938–: Eisenstein).

SOURCES

Alexander, R.J. ed., *Biographical Dictionary of Latin American and Caribbean Political Leaders* (New York 1988) 371–72.
Amnesty International, "Luiz Basilio Rossi" (WWW-text 1996).

————, *Report* (London) 1969–70: 30; 1970–71: 62; 1972–73: 47; 1973–74: 38; 1974–75: 66; 1989: 110; 1995: 80; 2001: 56.

————. *Annual Obituary 1992* (Chicago/London) 38–41 (Quadros).

Beloch, I., & A. Alves de Abreu, *Dicionário histórico-biográfico brasileiro 1930–1983* (Rio de Janeiro 1984) 1417, 2855.

Benewick, R., & P. Green eds., *The Routledge Dictionary of Twentieth-Century Political Thinkers* (London/New York 1992) 60–62.

Boia, L. ed., *Great Historians of the Modern Age: An International Dictionary* (Westport 1991) 86–88.

Boyd, K. ed., *Encyclopedia of Historians and Historical Writing* (London/Chicago 1999) 550–51, 955–57, 1002–4.

Bruch, R. vom, & R.A. Müller eds., *Historikerlexikon: Von der Antike bis zum 20. Jahrhundert* (Munich 1991) 40.

Cannon, J. ed., *The Blackwell Dictionary of Historians* (Oxford 1988) 55–56, 341, 355.

Cardoso, C.F., personal communication, September 2000.

Carneiro Benevides, C.A., L.M. Paschoal Guimarães, & N. Leonzo, "Nationalisme et marxisme dans l'enseignement de l'histoire du Brésil", unpublished paper presented at the 18th International Congress of Historical Sciences, Montréal 1995.

Comissão dos Familiares dos Mortos e Desaparecidos Políticos, Instituto de Estudo da Violência do Estado (IEVE) & Grupo Tortura Nunca Mais—RJ e PE, *Dossiê dos mortos e desaparecidos politicos a partir de 1964* (Recife 1995) 135–36, 235, 311–12, 396.

Current Biography (New York) 1961: 377–79, 1992: 642 (Quadros).

Dassin, J., "Time up for Torturers? A Human Rights Dilemma for Brazil", *Nacla: Report on the Americas*, April–May 1986: 4–5.

———— ed., *Torture in Brazil: A Report by the Archdiocese of São Paulo* (originally Portuguese 1985; New York 1986) ix–xviii, 4–7, 116–17, 133–34.

Flynn, P., *Brazil: A Political Analysis* (London 1978) 80–84.

Gorman, R.A. ed., *Biographical Dictionary of Neo-Marxism* (Westport 1985) 148–51.

————, *Biographical Dictionary of Marxism* (Westport 1986) 268–69, 312–13.

Hispanic American Historical Review, 1982: 13 (Holanda); 1983: 147–50 (Holanda); 1984: 222, 227 (Rodrigues); 1988: 573–76 (Rodrigues).

Human Rights Watch, *World Report* (Washington) 1999: 107; 2001: 105.

Iglesias, F., "Situation de l'histoire et des historiens du Brésil", in: R. Rémond ed., *Être historien aujourd'hui* (Paris 1988) 55–56.

———— ed., *Caio Prado Júnior* (São Paulo 1982) 13–21, 29, 32–34, 36.

Index on Censorship, 3–4/72: 113; 2/73: i; 1/74: 10; 3/74: 79; 4/79: 8–10; 5/80: 9; 5/81: 14; 4–5/94: 232.

Instituto Panamericano de Geografía e Historia, *Guía de personas que cultivan la historia de América* (México 1967) 109, 175.

Johnson, P.T., "Academic Press Censorship under Military and Civilian Regimes: The Argentine and Brazilian Cases, 1964–1975", *Luso-Brazilian Review*, Summer 1978: 6, 10, 22–23.

Keesings historisch archief, 1977: 202; 1988: 424; 2000: 680.

Leonzo, N., personal communication, 1995–96.

Levine, R.M., *Historical Dictionary of Brazil* (Metuchen 1979) 177, 198.

Liss, S.B., *Marxist Thought in Latin America* (Berkeley/Los Angeles 1984) 116–19, 123–26.

Love, J.L., *Crafting the Third World: Theorizing Underdevelopment in Rumania and Brazil* (Stanford 1996) 152–57, 178–80, 192.

Martinière, G., "Problèmes du dévelopment de l'historiographie brésilienne", *Storia della storiografia*, 1991, no.19: 137, 139.

Martins, E. de Rezende, personal communication, August 1995.

Pereira, I.X., *O direito à nossa história: A luta dos familiares dos mortos e desaparecidos políticos* (Brasília 1996).

Rodrigues, J.H., *História da história do Brasil*, vol. 1 (São Paulo 1979) ix–x.

Sater, W.F., "A Survey of Recent Chilean Historiography, 1965–1976", *Latin American Research Review*, 1979, no.2: 85.

Skidmore, T.E., "The Historiography of Brazil, 1889–1964", *Hispanic American Historical Review*, part 1 (1975): 727, 729; part 2 (1976): 89–90, 99.

———, *The Politics of Military Rule in Brazil, 1964–1985* (New York 1988) 132, 317, 353.

Tenenbaum, B.A. ed., *Encyclopedia of Latin American History and Culture* (New York 1996), vol. 2: 631; vol. 3: 200–201; vol. 4: 464–65; 503–4, 589–90; vol. 5: 139–40.

Weschler, L., *A Miracle, a Universe: Settling Accounts with Torturers* (New York 1990) 7–79.

Woolf, D.R. ed., *A Global Encyclopedia of Historical Writing* (New York/London 1998) 108, 420.

The Writer's Directory 1988–90 (Chicago/London 1988) 325.

BULGARIA

In 1991 the director of the Bulgarian Academy of Sciences (BAN) History Institute Mito Isusov enumerated the "zones of silence" in communist historiography in an essay on the future tasks of historical scholarship in Bulgaria: "Bulgarian-Russian and Bulgarian-Soviet relations, the positive tendencies and phenomena in the [interwar] policies of the bourgeoisie and its political parties [especially the Agrarian Union], the characterization of popular, independent and contradictory historical figures, and the dramatic and tragic periods in Bulgaria's relations with its neighbors" [until the mid-1960s, primarily the Macedonian Question: the post-1878 debate on the future of the Macedonian territory]. He pointed at the implementation of censorship, which "restricted the creative disobedience of historical thought" and induced moods of "autocensorship". Another sensitive topic was undoubtedly Bulgaria's Ottoman past (1393–1878), which was considered a dark period, inter alia during the campaigns of enforced assimilation of the ethnic Turkish minority (e.g., in 1984–89). The psychological damage incurred by historians subjected to scrutiny or not allowed to teach was considered the worst effect of the communist regime on Bulgarian historians. As late as 1981, certain Bulgarian historians who advised a German historian while he wrote an overview of Bulgarian historical writing on the 1876–1914 period preferred to remain anonymous. Access to the archives was extremely difficult.

1944–56   Among the "suspected" works in the early period (1944–56) were those of the former leading "bourgeois" historians **Dimitûr Mishev**, Byzantinist and archeologist **Petûr Mutafchiev** (1883–1943), Byzantinist **Petûr Nikov** (1884–1938), **Ivan Ormandzhiev, Ivan Pastuchov, Nikola Stanev**, and medievalist **Vasil Zlatarski** (1866–1935). On the First National Conference of Historians in 1948, Ormandzhiev defended his 1943 history of Bulgaria in vain.

1944   One of the first directives of the new government established in 1944 enjoined teachers "not to expound the positive actions of monarchs in history lessons but to stress the tyrannical quality of their rule and the struggle of the oppressed people".

1945   Archeologist and politician **Bogdan Filov** (1883–1945), director of the Bulgarian Institute of Archeology (1920–), specialist in Thracian archeology and BAN president (1937–44), was sentenced to death by the Fatherland Front government and executed in February 1945. In February 1940 he had become prime minister and in August 1943 president of the regency after the death of Tsar Boris III.

            Medievalist **Ivan Duychev** (1907–77) was forced to leave the chair of Bulgarian, Byzantine, and Balkan history (1943–45). In 1947 it was given to Aleksandûr Burmov, a confirmed Marxist.

1954–   Criticism by noncommunist Bulgarian historians of the two-volume BAN *History of Bulgaria* (1954–55), containing a pro-Soviet version of Bulgaria's history, could reportedly be leveled at great risk only.

pre-1960s   Until the late fifties, traditional topics such as cultural history and the history of nonrevolutionary ideas were neglected.

1967   *Fascism*, completed in 1967 by philosopher and political scientist **Zhelyu Zhelev** (1935–), did not appear until 1982, when it was sold for three weeks and then banned. Zhelev was dismissed as a senior researcher at the Institute of Culture, Sofia (1974–82). The book, an analysis of German, Italian, and Spanish fascisms, was intended and understood as criticism of the Bulgarian communist regime. A new edition appeared in 1989 after the fall of the communist regime. Zhelev became the first president of postcommunist Bulgaria (1990–96). When he was a philosophy student, his master's thesis had been rejected. In 1965 he was removed from Sofia State University after he had published an article in the *Deutsches Zeitschrift für Philosophie*. He was expelled from the Bulgarian Communist Party (BKP). From 1966 to 1972, he was unemployed and lived in internal exile in his wife's native village.

1973   A critical biography and source edition of Vasil Levski (1837–73; a national liberation fighter), written by historian **Nikolai Genchev** (1931–), which questioned the official thesis that the liberation struggle had a peasant character, was not reviewed in the professional journals. Genchev later became rector of Sofia University. After his death, historian Ivan Undzhiev revised the biography for the 1980 second edition but, while inserting new source material, omitted the critical argument. Another historian who defended theses similar to Genchev's, **Jono Mitev**, voluntarily engaged in self-criticism in 1977 when attacked by the leading official historian Dimitûr Kosev (1903–).

1976   Historian **Ilcho Dimitrov** had to abridge his relatively sympathetic portrayal of Tsar Boris III in the revised edition of a 1962 book about the 1934–39 period. In 1979 he became rector of Sofia University.

1989–   During the post-1989 transition period, some of the state security files, held under the control of the minister of the interior, were reportedly destroyed.

1990–   At least since 1990 organizations of ethnic Macedonians, such as Obedinena Makedonska Organizatsiya "Ilinden" (OMO Ilinden; United Macedonian Organization "Ilinden"), named after the August 1903 Ilinden Uprising, had been denied official registration because they were considered separatist organizations threatening the Bulgarian security. In April 1993, 1994, and 1995, police used force to prevent OMO Ilinden assemblies at Rozhen Monastery. The annual gathering commemorating the death of Yane Sandanski (1872–1907), a revolutionary and leader in the Macedonian Revolutionary Organization, was deemed anti-Bulgarian. In July 1995 OMO Ilinden members were forbidden to meet at Samuil Castle to commemorate the foundation of the Republic of Macedonia. A Bulgarian court upheld the ban, reportedly stating that "the territory of Bulgaria cannot be used as a place to celebrate events that have no relation to Bulgarian history".

1991–   In May 1991 the Bulgarian Socialist Party (the BKP's successor) refused to hand over documents from its archives relating to the 1944–48 period, when thousands of Bulgarians were killed for their opposition to the BKP. In August 1992 the head of the Central Archives Administration announced that the archives would be made accessible in early 1993.

1992–93   In July 1992 Parliament began consideration of a draft "Law for Additional Requirements for Scientific Organizations and the

Higher Certifying Commission" which proposed to prohibit, inter alia, anyone who had "taught history of the Communist Party of the Soviet Union [or] BKP history" from holding positions in the executive bodies of scientific organizations. This so-called Panev Law, adopted in December, required leading academics to provide a written statement about their previous employment and activities as BKP members. If they taught courses in certain communist-related areas of history and the social sciences, they would be dismissed. The law was annulled in 1993.

pre-1993   Studies of historians **Strasimir Dimitrov** and **Vera Mutafchieva** (1929–), in which the authenticity of a 1870 document by Metodi Draginov about the seventeenth-century enforced islamization of the South-Bulgarian Tchepino region was questioned, appeared in a work of conference proceedings with small circulation because their criticism contradicted the official view. Only in 1993 did they appear in a book with wide circulation.

1995   In August British archeologist **Douglas Bailey** was deported after having participated in an excavation project in northeast Bulgaria. Fourteen of his students were searched and interrogated at Sofia airport and accused of military espionage. When Bailey later returned to Bulgaria to reclaim confiscated equipment, his passport was seized and he was interrogated for three days before being deported on 24 August. Bulgarian project members had their offices and homes searched and documents confiscated.

Also see Vietnam (1997–: Pham Van Viem).

SOURCES

Amnesty International, *Report* (London) 1986: 272–75; 1987: 282–84; 1988: 195–96; 1989: 213–14; 1990: 51–53; 1991: 50–51; 1994: 82–83; 1995: 82; 1996: 102.
Bernath, M., & F. von Schroeder eds., *Biographisches Lexikon zur Geschichte Südosteuropas* (Munich) vol. 1 (1974) 515–16, vol. 3 (1979) 282–83.
Boia, L. ed., *Great Historians of the Modern Age: An International Dictionary* (Westport 1991) 98, 102–4, 107.
Bronkhorst, D., *Truth and Reconciliation: Obstacles and Opportunities for Human Rights* (Amsterdam 1995) 81–82.
Dellin, L.A.D., "Bulgarian History Revised", *Survey: A Journal of Soviet and East European Studies*, 1961: 105–12.
Detrez, R., "Geschiedschrijving en maatschappij op de Balkan", *De Vlaamse Gids*, 1993, no.6: 15–16.
———, *Historical Dictionary of Bulgaria* (Lanham/London 1997) 357–59.
Deyanova, L., "When Memory Plays Tricks", *UNESCO Courier*, May 1994: 35 (quote 1944).
Friedrich, W.-U., "Die bulgarische Geschichtswissenschaft im Spannungsverhältnis

zwischen ideologischem Anspruch und historischer Realität: Die Geschichts-schreibung der Befreiungsbewegung und der Anfänge des Nationalstaates", *Jahr-bücher für Geschichte Osteuropas*, 1981: 412, 414, 416, 421–22, 426–28, 435.

Helsinki Watch, letter to President Zhelyu Zhelev (28 August 1992).

Hoppe, H.-J., "Politik und Geschichtswissenschaft in Bulgarien 1968–78", *Jahrbücher für Geschichte Osteuropas*, 1980: 245–46, 253, 270–73, 279–81, 285.

Human Rights Watch, *World Report* (Washington) 1990: 352; 1992: 499, 501; 1993: 209–12; 1994: 208; 1995: 199; 1996: 208–9; 2001: 286.

Ilchev, I., "La Science historique bulgare au cours des années 70 et 80", in: A. Marès ed., *Histoire et pouvoir en Europe médiane* (Paris 1996) 175, 180.

Index on Censorship, 10/92: 43; 3/94: 166–67; 5/95: 171–72; 1/01: 188–93.

Jelavich, B., *History of the Balkans: Twentieth Century*, vol. 2 (Cambridge 1983) 233–34, 257–58, 292.

Petrova, D., "Bulgaria", in: A. Boraine, J. Levy, & R. Scheffer eds., *Dealing with the Past: Truth and Reconciliation in South Africa* (Cape Town 1997) 77, 79.

Todorov, T., "The Abuses of Memory", *Common Knowledge*, 1996, no.1: 18.

Todorova, M., "Historiography of the Countries of Eastern Europe: Bulgaria", *American Historical Review*, 1992: 1107, 1109–11 (quote from Isusov 1109), 1115.

Woolf, D.R. ed., *A Global Encyclopedia of Historical Writing* (New York/London 1998) 117.

BURKINA FASO

1983–92   Between October 1983 and 1992, **Joseph Ki-Zerbo** (1922–), history professor at Ouagadougou University (1957–), specialist in the history of Black Africa, founder (1970) and leader of the socialist opposition party Union Progressiste Voltaique, was forced into exile by the military regime, first in Ivory Coast, then in Senegal. In Senegal he was a researcher at the Institut Fondamental d'Afrique Noire, Cheikh Anta Diop University. He also reconstituted the center that he had founded in Upper Volta in 1980 as the Centre de Recherche pour le Développement Endogène. In June 1984 he was accused by the authorities of having been behind the conspiracy which had planned a coup for 27 May 1984. President Thomas Sankara called him "pro-imperialist" because of his contacts with the French Socialist Party. He was sentenced to a term of imprisonment in absentia. During his exile all his previous equipment and his library of 11,000 volumes had reportedly been destroyed or dispersed. In 1995 he was a member of Parliament for the opposition Parti pour la Démocratie et le Progrès and director of the Centre d'Études pour le Développement Africain. He was a member of UNESCO's Executive Council (1972–78) and occupied a position at the United Nations University. In 1997 he was awarded the Right Livelihood Award, an alternative Nobel Peace Prize.

SOURCES

Africa Contemporary Record, 1973: B 744–45.
Degenhardt, H.W. ed., *Revolutionary and Dissident Movements: An International Guide* (Harlow 1988) 30.
"Gewalt is die Software der Geschichte", *Südwind-Magazin*, September 1996: 28–30.
Index on Censorship, 2/86: 16, 18.
Joseph Ki-Zerbo (1997) (WWW-text 1997).
Keesings historisch archief, 1985: 110.

BURMA

See Myanmar.

BURUNDI

1972–   Successive governments have denied the genocide of Hutu in 1972. An estimated 80,000 to 100,000 Hutu (3.5 percent of the population) were killed by the government of Colonel Michel Micombero between 30 April and early July 1972 after an attempted coup on 29 April. An estimated 2,000 Tutsi were also killed. In 1985 an Anglican missionary reported that it had become "a tacit crime against the state . . . to mention 1972 in the open."

1980s   In the late 1980s, **Tharcisse Nsabimana**, a Burundian student (and later historian in Burundi) in historian Steven Feierman's graduate class in East African history at the University of Wisconsin–Madison in the United States resisted in writing an assignment on "the relationships between pastoralists and agriculturalists in Great Lakes history", on the grounds that "such a paper would be illegal in Burundi".

1988   In late August or early September, **Augustin Nsanze** (1953–), a history lecturer at Bujumbura University, was arrested with six others after signing an open letter to President Pierre Buyoya criticizing the government's policy toward members of the Hutu community and the killing, in August 1988, of thousands of Hutu by government troops. No formal charges were brought against them, but the authorities alleged that they had incited racial hatred. His whereabouts were not known. He was released later. He possibly went to Kenya and wrote two books on the contemporary political history of Burundi.

[1993–]   During the armed conflict many repositories and archives were destroyed.

SOURCES

Albada, J. van, " 'Memory of the World': Report on Destroyed and Damaged Archives", *Archivum*, 1996, no.42: 11.

Amnesty International, *Report 1989* (London 1989) 38.

Index on Censorship, 4/85: 30–31 (quote from missionary: 30); 10/88: 35.

Kuper, L., Foreword, in: I.W. Charny ed., *Genocide: A Critical Bibliographic Review*, vol. 2 (London 1991) xiv.

Lemarchand, R., *Burundi: Ethnic Conflict and Genocide* (Cambridge 1996) 32 (quoting Steven Feierman).

Vansina, J., personal communication, August 1999.

C

CAMBODIA

During the years of the Lon Nol government (1970–75), Marxist historiography was banned. At the time of the takeover of Cambodia by the communist Khmer Rouge (Red Khmer) who established Democratic Kampuchea (DK; 1975–79), the publishing and teaching of history came to a halt. A spokesman proclaimed that "2000 years of history had ended". Dissident historical views were suppressed. Many historic temples at Angkor and other religious shrines and monasteries were used as storehouses. Most of the books, bibliographical records, and newspaper collections in the National Library were burned, but the archives suffered less damage, although they clearly contained information contradicting the Khmer Rouge view of history.

1977   In April **Mau Khem Nuon**, a Khmer Rouge lecturer known as **Phom**, was arrested. He was a former student at the Khmero-Soviet Technical Institute, Phnom Penh, and, in the mid-1960s, a guerrillero. From April 1975 he was a Communist Party of Kampuchea (CPK) political instructor for Cambodian returnees from abroad on, inter alia, the history of the CPK from its foundation in 1951.

1978   On 23 December **Malcolm Caldwell** (1931–78), a Marxist economic historian at the School of Oriental and African Studies, University of London, and expert at the Russell International War Crimes Tribunal on the American intervention in Vietnam (1967), was killed by a death squad gunman. In the preceding weeks, he had been a member of the first group of independent Western observers allowed to visit DK. Although sympathetic to the DK, he had asked some critical questions during the visit. He had had a private interview with Khmer Rouge leader Pol Pot on 22 December, just hours before his death. The DK security service Santebal was probably responsible for the squad, all the members of which were executed after the murder, but it remained unclear whether it acted upon orders of Son Sen, the leader responsible for security, or Pol Pot himself. Caldwell's planned book on DK's rural policy remained unfinished, but the manuscript was published post-humously as *Malcolm Caldwell's Southeast Asia* (1979).

1979   On 7 January, when the Vietnamese were entering the capital Phnom Penh, part of the Tuol Sleng prison archives were destroyed by the Santebal. Nonetheless, over 100,000 pages documenting the Santebal activities were left behind.

1994–   In May the premises of the newspaper *Sokal* were surrounded by forces of the ministry of interior. The newspaper had suggested that King Norodom Sihanouk was responsible for more than one million deaths under the Khmer Rouge regime. Ten thousand copies of the paper were seized, and *Sokal* has reportedly been closed down since then.

Also see Vietnam (1945–: Malleret).

SOURCES

Chandler, D., "Cambodian Palace Chronicles (rajabangsavatar) 1927–1949: Kingship and Historiography at the End of the Colonial Era", in: A. Reid & D. Marr ed., *Perceptions of the Past in Southeast Asia* (Singapore 1979) 216.
———, "Seeing Red: Perceptions of Cambodian History in Democratic Kampuchea", in: D.P. Chandler & B. Kiernan eds., *Revolution and Its Aftermath in Kampuchea: Eight Essays* (New Haven 1983) 36, 49–50.
Chigas, G., "The Trial of the Khmer Rouge: The Role of the Tuol Sleng and Santebal Archives", *Harvard Asia Quarterly*, Winter 1999–2000 (WWW-text).
Hoeven, H. van der, *Lost Memory: Libraries and Archives Destroyed in the Twentieth Century,* part 1, *Libraries* (WWW-text 1996) 4.
Index on Censorship, 1/79: 7; 3/94: 167; 2/99: 167.
Kiernan, B., *The Pol Pot Regime: Race, Power and Genocide in Cambodia under the Khmer Rouge, 1975–79* (New Haven/London 1996) 39, 150–51, 155, 350, 442–50, 452.
Vickery, M., *Cambodia 1975–1982* (Boston 1985) 173, 234, 329, 339.
Woolf, D.R. ed., *A Global Encyclopedia of Historical Writing* (New York/London 1998) 135.

CAMEROON

[1984–]   The name of **Ahmadou Ahidjo,** president in 1960–82, was reportedly systematically eliminated from texts and speeches because of the part he supposedly played in the attempted coup of April 1984. A film made by a Cameroonian entitled *The Nigerian-Biafran War* was banned because Ahidjo appeared in some footage. When photographs were published, his image was obliterated or cut out.

1985   In March a decree announced that it was forbidden to import, possess, sell, distribute, or circulate a book of essays by **Ruben Um Nyobè**, *Le Problème national kamerounais* (Paris 1985; The National Problem in Cameroon), edited by historian Mbembe [q.v. 1980s]. The book was banned because it discussed the preindependence nationalist uprising led by Um Nyobè (executed in September 1958) and his revolutionary movement, Union des Peuples Camerounais, violently put down first by the French and then by the Cameroonian Army. Many archives on this episode, a taboo since 1958, were destroyed.

1980s   Historian **Achille Mbembe** (1957–) left Cameroon because of his political activities. He went to the United States and later to Senegal, where in [1996] he became secretary-general of the Conseil pour le Développement de la Recherche en Sciences Sociales en Afrique (Codesria; Council for the Development of Social Science Research in Africa).

[1990]   *Gaullist Africa: Cameroon under Ahmadu Ahidjo* (Enugu 1978), a book on the postindependence history of Cameroon dealing with the laws of repression and edited by historian **Richard Joseph** (1945–), was confiscated in a police raid on the Yaoundé University bookshop.

1994   The 6 April edition of the newspaper *Le Messager*, which carried a cover story of the tenth anniversary of the 1984 failed coup attempt, was banned by a province governor for "disturbing public order".

Also see Senegal (1961–: Diop).

SOURCES

Doortmont, M., personal communication, June 1995.
Index on Censorship, 5/85: 24–25; 2/88: 23; 2/91: 25; 3/94: 167.
Mbembe, J.-A., "Pouvoir des morts et langage des vivants: Les Errances de la mémoire nationaliste au Cameroun", *Politique Africaine*, 1986, no.22: 39–40, 58–60, 68–69.

CANADA

1970   Radical U.S. historian **Gabriel Kolko** (1932–), expert at the Russell International War Crimes Tribunal on the American intervention in Vietnam (1967), history professor at the University of Pennsylvania and at the State University of New York at Buffalo (1968–70), author of books on American foreign policy during the Cold War—including *The Politics of War: The World and United States Foreign Policy 1943–45*

(1968) and *The Roots of American Foreign Policy: An Analysis of Power and Purpose* (1969)—was temporarily denied an immigration visa by the Canadian government when he was offered a professorship (1970–92) at York University, Toronto, apparently for his criticism of the American involvement in Vietnam. He claimed that the Canadian government relied on United States intelligence for its information on prospective immigrants.

1981   In July **Vladimir Ustinov**, specialist in disarmament and the history of science, was refused entry to attend the thirty-first Pugwash Conference as a member of the Soviet delegation for "security reasons".

Also see Colombia (1992: Gordon), Hungary (1956–: Mészáros), Pakistan (1946–: Smith), Turkey (1946–: Berkes), United States (1954–: Ginger).

SOURCES

Boyd, K. ed., *Encyclopedia of Historians and Historical Writing* (London/Chicago 1999) 653–54.
Index on Censorship, 1/73: 57; 6/81: 105.

CENTRAL AFRICAN REPUBLIC

1966–79   Many written documents were reportedly destroyed under the presidency of Jean-Bedel Bokassa (1966–79). When French soldiers removed Bokassa during Operation Barracuda, they took his personal archives to an unknown destination.

SOURCES

Gallo, T.-J., *N'Garagba, la maison des morts: Un Prisonnier sous Bokassa* (Paris 1988) 11.
Titley, B., *Dark Age: The Political Odyssey of Emperor Bokassa* (Montreal 1997) 240.

CHAD

1974–77   In April 1974 French archeologist **Françoise Claustre** (1937–), who was investigating prehistoric tombs, was kidnapped by the Second Liberation Army of the Front de Libération Nationale du Tchad (FROLINAT; National Liberation Front of Chad; Toubou rebels led by Hissene Habré) in Bardai, in the Tibesti, northern Chad, and held as a hostage. Approached by the rebels as Chad's ally, France could not meet their demands. In August 1975 her husband Pierre Claustre was also captured when he attempted to negotiate her release. For a long time, the government did not appear to be in a position to influence the rebels. In January 1977, after Habré and Goukouni

Oueddei had temporarily ended their alliance in the FROLINAT in 1976, the Claustres were released and brought to Tripoli, Libya.

SOURCES

Amnesty International, *Report* (London) 1975–76: 58; 1977: 67.
Decalo, S., *Historical Dictionary of Chad* (Metuchen 1987) 87, 158.

CHILE

During the military regime of General Augusto Pinochet Ugarte (11 September 1973–1990), left-wing historians were persecuted and their views banned. Archival sources on the left and on labor were not as accessible as before. Attempts were made to obliterate the 1970–73 experience (the period of the Salvador Allende presidency) from memory. Even after 1990, it reportedly remained difficult to teach or write about contemporary history.

1951 **Julio César Jobet Búrquez** (1912–80), history professor at the University of Chile (1937–72), leading figure of the revisionist school of historiography, and Socialist Party spokesman, was denied an ambassadorship to Yugoslavia after he had published his *Ensayo crítico del desarrollo económico-social de Chile* (Santiago 1951; Critical Essay on the Social-Economic Development of Chile), which the Chilean Congress considered an assault on the national hagiography. After the 1973 coup, all Jobet's works were banned.

1973– After the coup, the archives of the University of Chile's Department of Cinema and its Cinemateca were seized, but some items were smuggled out of Chile. The archives of the Central Trade Union Confederation Film Department were destroyed. Several films with a historical content were completed in exile. **Gaston Ancelovici** and **Orlando Lübbert**, for example, finished a documentary history of the Chilean labor movement, *Puños Frente al Cañon* (Fists before the Cannon), in the Federal Republic of Germany (FRG). All exile films were archived in Spain with the support of the International Federation of Film Archives.

On 11 September **Mario Céspedes Gutierrez** (1921–), history professor at the University of Chile, author of several books, director of radio programs, and television commentator, was arrested. First he was detained at the National Stadium in Santiago, but in 1974 he was reportedly held at Chacabuco detention center near Antofagasta.

On 12 September, when he reported to navy authorities on property of the customs office, **Luis Sanguinetti Fuenzalida** (?1935–73), head of the customs office investigation department and history professor at the University of Chile active in the Socialist Party, was arrested. On 14 September he died on board the ship *Maipo* after he was reportedly tortured: in a fit of despair he dove into one of the ship's holds and died immediately.

1973–89   On 12 September **Luis Vitale Cometa** (1927–), Argentinian student of historian José Luis Romero, and Trotskyist historian at Concepción University (1968–73) and the State Technical University, Santiago (1973), was arrested and brought to the National Stadium. He was stripped of his Chilean citizenship. Until November 1974 he was detained in nine different torture houses and concentration camps. After his expulsion, Vitale went into exile and held professorships in Frankfurt (1975–77), Caracas (1977–84), and Río Cuarto, Córdoba, Argentina (1984–89) and lectured widely at many universities in Latin America and Europe. During all these years, his works were banned or reviewed unfavorably. In July 1989 he returned to Chile and became professor at the ARCIS y ARCOS University, Santiago (1989–94). From 1992 he was an editor of the left-wing *Punto Final*. He was a specialist in the history of labor, women, ecology, and indigenous peoples. He was a trade union leader of the Central Única de Trabajadores de Chile (1958–62). In 1963–64 he had to go into internal exile to Curepto for seven months because he had called for a general strike which demanded that the government continue its diplomatic relations with Cuba. In 1965 he was one of the founders of the Movimiento de Izquierda Revolucionario (MIR; Revolutionary Left Movement), which he left after a dispute in 1969. He published the four-volume *Interpretación Marxista de la Historia de Chile* (1967–73). The entire edition of the fourth volume, published shortly before the coup, was reportedly burned.

1973–84   **Hernán Ramírez Necochea** (1917–84), a revisionist historian who studied under Guillermo Feliú Cruz (1900–73) and specialized in nineteenth-century history—including the 1891 civil war—and the history of the Chilean Communist Party, was persecuted. He died in Paris.

1973–   **Marcelo Segall**, historian and author of a work on the role of the Chinese in Chile, was imprisoned after the coup but was able to go into exile in the Netherlands together with his wife, **Ruth Iturriaga Jiménez**, historian of the 1851 rebellion. In Amsterdam he worked at the Museum for Social History until 1985.

Marxist history professor **Jorge Barría Serón**, author of a history of the Chilean labor movement and coeditor of a 1971 work on Radical Party leader Manuel Recabarren (1827–1901), was reportedly persecuted after the coup and died in Santiago in the early 1980s. The inventory of the work was destroyed after 1973.

1973–90   **Alejandro Chelén Rojas** (died 1990), historian, socialist, and author of a work on the Socialist Party, editor at the Quimantú company that published the Recabarren volume by Barría [q.v. 1973–], was persecuted after the coup. He died in Santiago.

1973–   In late 1973 several other historians were arrested: **Patricio Donoso**, philosopher and historian, author of works on Chilean history, who was reportedly held at Chacabuco detention center in 1974; **Lucy Lortsch**, historian and author of *Chapters from the History of Chile*; and **Ricardo Nuñez**, professor of history and sociology and secretary-general of the State Technical University, who was held in the National Stadium in Santiago.

1974   Five research professors and all personnel at the economic and social history department of the Catholic University of Chile, Santiago, were dismissed. Not all professors were dismissed outright, some being transferred to other departments, but the newly appointed department heads refused to accept the reassigned professors, who thus had to leave. Similar incidents reportedly occurred at the economic history department, University of Chile, and the Center for Historical and Philosophical Studies, Catholic University, Valparaíso. Specialized historical libraries of the University of Chile were integrated in general libraries, with the loss and destruction of parts of their collections.

1974–   In September agents of the Dirección de Inteligencia Nacional (DINA; National Intelligence Directorate) arrested **Maria Cristina López Stewart** (?1953–), history and geography student and MIR activist, at her home in Santiago. In October released prisoners claimed that they saw her in solitary confinement in the José Domingo Cañas location, a secret police interrogation center in Santiago, and that she had been tortured. In November she was forced to telephone her parents with the message that she was free and in good health. Since then, she has "disappeared".

In November **Felix de la Jara Goyeneche** (?1948–), history student and MIR activist, was arrested. Witnesses saw him at the detention site The Discotheque (La Venda Sexy). He "disappeared" while in the hands of the DINA.

In December **Carlos Guerrero Gutiérrez** (?1953–), history student and MIR activist, was arrested. A number of witnesses testified that he was held at the detention site Villa Grimaldi and that he "disappeared" from there while in the hands of the DINA.

1976–   In [December] historian and university professor **Juan Fernando Ortiz Letelier** (1922–), member of the Communist Party Central Committee, was arrested in the presence of several witnesses. He was hooded and he "disappeared". A judge conducted an inquiry into his case and reported to the United Nations Commission on Human Rights in [1990].

1979   In December lawyer and historian **Gonzalo Vial Corea** resigned as the minister of education. He had presented a plan for university reform, but increasingly open criticism of the government by university professors met with Pinochet's reply that the campuses were undergoing an unacceptable "political upsurge". In 1990–91, Vial, then a designated senator, also was a member of the National Commission on Truth and Reconciliation. In January 1999 a group of Chilean historians published a manifesto in which they attempted to refute Pinochet's and Vial's historical views.

1981–82 On 10 December 1981, Human Rights Day, **Pablo Arturo Fuenzalida Zegers**, a historian who in 1974 had been removed from the university and leading member of the Chilean Human Rights Commission, was arrested by members of the security police for alleged membership of the banned political party Izquierda Cristiana (Christian Left), which was part of the Unidad Popular coalition (overthrown in 1973). Before his arrest, he had suffered constant harassment for months. In the five days after his arrest, he was held incommunicado and tortured with electric shocks, despite his neuropsychiatric illness. He declared that his captors threatened to torture his wife and that he was forced to pose with a gun for a camera and to write and sign self-criticisms. Sentenced to eighteen months' exile, he was released on bail and had his sentence suspended in December 1982.

1982–   In January 1982 **Jorge Osorio**, historian and secretary of the human-rights organization Paz y Justicia, was arrested by agents of the security service because of his alleged membership of the banned Izquierda Cristiana. He denied the charge, saying that he had ceased to be a member since 1973, but he was sentenced to eighteen months' imprisonment.

1982   In September the rector of Catholic University, Santiago, retired Rear Admiral Jorge Swett, expelled three students, including a history student (name unknown), following protests against the abduction of a philosophy student.

pre-1986 In or before 1986, historian **Peter Winn**, who did research for his book *Weavers of Revolution: The Yarur Workers and Chile's Road* *to Socialism* (New York 1986), was interrogated by the military for three days because he had interviewed workers and trade union leaders. He was summarily expelled from Chile.

1989   In August **Marcelo Barrios Andrade**, a history and geography student active in the Manuel Rodríguez Revolutionary Front (an organization engaged in political violence), was killed in a gun battle with members of the navy when they tried to arrest him at Cerro Yungay, Valparaíso.

[1990]–   The whereabouts of the documents of the primary repressive institutions of the military dictatorship DINA and Central Nacional de Informaciones (state security police) were unknown.

1998   In September, marches in Santiago to mark the twenty-fifth anniversary of the 1973 coup were met with large-scale repression by the carabineros (national police force). Hundreds of demonstrators were arrested.

1999–   In April the entire print run of *The Black Book of Chilean Justice* (Santiago), launched the day before and written by Miami-based journalist **Alejandra Matus Acuña**, was seized by the police on the instructions of the Santiago High Court and banned. It was considered insulting to the authorities. The product of six years' research, the book examined the conduct of the Chilean High Court between its inception in 1826 and 1998, with special emphasis on the 1973–90 period. Matus flew abroad to avoid arrest and was given political asylum in the United States; the two publishers were briefly arrested. Pirate copies of the book remained in circulation. In December 2000, a Chilean judge upheld Matus's conviction on contempt charges, but in July 2001, the Santiago Appeals Court annulled the arrest order against her.

2000   In May right-wing parliamentarians (unsuccessfully) tried to persuade the Ricardo Lagos government to withdraw a Ministry of Education primary school history textbook which covered the 1973 military coup. They complained about nineteen "tendentious" or "biased" assertions, including the use of the word "coup" instead of "pronouncement" to describe the 11 September 1973 events and the statement that the 1925 Constitution had recognized a "lay society" instead of freedom of religion.

In November, several Mapuche indigenous organizations filed a libel suit against historian **Sergio Villalobos** for a newspaper article that they called defamatory for the honor of the Mapuche people. The article, *Araucania: Errores ancestrales* (Araucania: Ancestral Errors), appearing in the 14 May 2000 edition of *El Mercurio*, dealt with events that took place in the sixteenth- and seventeenth-century colonization of the Araucanians (the ancestors of the Mapuche) by the Spanish conquistadores.

Also see Argentina (1976–: Basso; 1946–: Romero), Brazil (1964–: Frank, Furtado).

SOURCES

Amnesty International, *Boletin informativo*, March 1982: 7.

———, *Report* (London) 1982: 119–20; 1983: 122; 1999: 126.

———, *Verdwenen gevangenen in Chili* (Amsterdam 1977) 45, 48, 49, 132.

Axelsson, S., et al., *Chili: Le Dossier noir* (Paris 1974) 217, 297, 299–300, 309.

Drake, P.W., "Chilean Political History since 1925", in: J.J. TePaske ed., *Research Guide to Andean History* (Durham 1981) 109.

Dulk, M. den, "Controle op en restricties voor de geschiedenis in Chili" (manuscript; Groningen 1994) 29–32, 58–63, 72–73, 79–84 (letters from Luis Vitale).

González Quintana, A., "Les Archives des services de sécurité des anciens régimes répressifs: Rapport préparé pour l'UNESCO à la demande du Conseil international des archives", *Janus*, 1999, no.1: 17.

Gorman, R.A. ed., *Biographical Dictionary of Marxism* (Westport 1986) 153, 345–46.

Hispanic American Historical Review, 1982: 121–22 (Jobet).

Human Rights Watch, *Chile: Progress Stalled; Setbacks in Freedom of Expression Reform* (WWW-text; Washington March 2001).

———, *World Report* (Washington) 2000: 112, 114; 2001: 527.

Ifex Communiqué 8–46 (30 November 1999) *10–1* (9 January 2001), 10–28 (17 July 2001), (Matus).

Index on Censorship, 1/74: 15; 3/74: 79–80; 2/75: 79; 2/80: 4–5, 8; 3/80: 57; 6/82: 18–19; 2/90: 35; 6/90: 36–37; 4/99: 130–31; 5/99: 23–24, 126–27; 1/100: 92; 2/01: 99.

Instituto Panamericano de Geografía e Historia, *Guía de personas que cultivan la historia de América* (México 1967) 180.

International PEN Writers in Prison Committee, *Centre to Centre*, 2001, no.1: 2.

Knight, A., "Latin America", in: M. Bentley ed., *Companion to Historiography* (London/New York 1997) 745.

Liss, S.B., *Marxist Thought in Latin America* (Berkeley/Los Angeles 1984) 79–81, 84–89.

Manifiesto de historiadores: Un grupo de historiadores chilenos refutan las versiones de la historia chilena presentadas por Pinochet y sus partidarios (WWW-text; Santiago 1999).

Nunn, F.M., "Chile since 1973: Historical and Political Perspectives", *Latin American Research Review*, 1979, no.3: 287, 289.

Report of the Chilean National Commission on Truth and Reconciliation (Notre Dame/London 1993) 95–96, 309, 537, 544, 547, 573, 677.

Sater, W.F., "A Survey of Recent Chilean Historiography, 1965–1976", *Latin American Research Review*, 1979, no.2: 56, 58, 63, 71–72, 80–82, 84–85.

Solidarität mit den politischen Gefangenen in Chile: Rettet das Leben von Luis Vitale! (Frankfurt 1974) 3.

Thomas, J.R., *Biographical Dictionary of Latin American Historians and Historiography* (Westport 1984) 223–24.
Vitale, L., *Interpretación marxista de la historia de Chile*, vol. 4 (Santiago 1993) cover.

CHINA

Armed conflicts (1911–50) and civil disorder (1966–70) were partly responsible for the destruction of about 1,369,500 shelf meters of records and the damaging of another 150,000 meters. During the Japanese invasion and occupation (1937–45), the retreat of Chinese universities with the Nationalist armies into the southwest, and the communist-nationalist Civil War (1946–49), historical scholarship and historical publications continued, although it diminished greatly. After the victory of the communists, organized historical study was again possible on a national scale. From the 1950s, Tibet was regarded as an integral historical part of China and any challenging view was dangerous. With the start of the Cultural Revolution in late 1965, the so-called Four Olds (*sijiu*)—old ideas, old culture, old customs, and old habits—came under attack. Institutionalized historical and archeological research and training came to a halt. Archeology suffered heavy losses; excavations were disrupted and sites attacked. Many historic monuments were destroyed. Journals such as *Kaogu* (Archeology) and *Lishi yanjiu* (Historical Research) ceased to be published; the latter did not resume publication until June 1974, when it came under the influence of writing bands of the "Gang of Four". The history department of Beijing University (*Beida*) suffered great damage and the loss of several historians. The study of modern European history came to a standstill. The publication of collections of historical documents appears to have been the only undertaking without risk for personal safety. Only after 1976 did the situation for history and archeology normalize. In the 1970s the practice of earmarking certain historical books and periodicals for internal circulation only (*neibu*) limited their readership within China and made it illegal to export them; the action was partly inspired by political and security reasons. The 1989 Tiananmen Square massacre was officially called a "counterrevolutionary rebellion" and any deviating view was suppressed.

Among the historians who went into exile before or after the 1949 communist takeover were the following:

1948–50   **Fu Sinian** (Fu Ssu-nien) (1896–1950) was a leader of the 1919 May Fourth Movement and chief editor of its monthly *New Tide* and a historian who specialized in the Shang (or Yin; 1766–1027 BCE) and Zhou (1027–256 BCE) dynasties. Fu was also an administrator of historical scholarship who organized and directed the Academia Sinica Institute of History and Philology and its library (1928–50). During the Sino-Japanese war, he became de facto secretary-general of the Academia Sinica (1936–) and supervised its various evacuations. In 1938–48 he was a member of the People's Political Council and he participated in political consultations between the Nationalist government and the communists. Appointed an academician in 1948, he organized the evacuation of the Academia Sinica Institute of History and Philology and its library to Taiwan in 1948–49. In January 1949 he became chancellor of National Taiwan University (1949–50).

1948–65 **Jiang Tingfu** (Chiang T'ing-fu; Western name: T.F. Tsiang) (1895–1965), professor of diplomatic history at Nankai University, Tianjin (Tientsin) (1923–29), and Qinghua University, Beijing (1929–35); ambassador to the USSR (1936–38); director at the political department of the Executive Yuan of the Nationalist government (1935–36, 1938–); and permanent representative to the United Nations (1947–62), New York, stayed in the United States after the communist takeover. He defended his right to represent China, arguing that Jiang Jieshi (Chiang Kai-shek)'s government was the only legitimate one. In 1961 he was appointed ambassador of Taiwan to the United States (1961–65).

1948– **Lao Gan** (Lao Kan), a historian of the Han period (206 BCE–220 CE) who in 1943 had produced a four-volume mimeographed work on the thousands of wooden strips of the Han period discovered in 1930, went into exile.

Leading archeologist **Li Ji** (Li Chi) (1896–1979) was the head of the Academia Sinica archeology department (1928–) and excavation director at Anyang, the center of the Shang dynasty. The 1937 war virtually put an end to any significant fieldwork by his department, but he continued work in the southwest. In 1948 he was elected to the Academia Sinica. Li Ji assisted in removing the art treasures and archeological specimens from the mainland to Taiwan. In 1955 he became director of the Academia Sinica Institute of History and Philology there. In the same year, he was one of the accused in a campaign launched by the Chinese Communist Party (CCP) against the capitalist mentality in archeology and the handling of cultural relics.

Historians **Quan Hansheng** (Ch'üan Han-sheng) and **Yang Liansheng** (Yang Lien-sheng) went into exile.

Historian and archeologist **Zheng Dekun** (Cheng Te-k'un) went to the United States, where he became a lecturer in Far Eastern Art and Archeology at Harvard University, Cambridge, Mass.

Xiao Yishan (Hsiao I-shan) (1902–78), specialist in Qing (1648–1911) history and active supporter of the Nationalists in the civil war, went to Taiwan, where he taught at Taiwan University. Later he chaired the editorial committee of the official five-volume *General History of the Qing* (1962–63). While studying at Cambridge

University before the war, he had collected materials on the Taiping Heavenly Kingdom (1851–64), unavailable in China because of the Qing suppression of information on the rebellion.

Xiao Gongquan (Hsiao Kung-ch'üan) (also: K.C. Hsiao) (1897–1981), historian and professor of political science at Yanjing (1930–32) and Qinghua (1932–37) universities and at Beijing law academy, went to Taiwan and the United States, where he taught at the University of Washington, Seattle (1949–68).

1949–

Dong Zuobin (Tung Tso-pin) (1895–1963) was an archeologist and collaborator of the Academia Sinica Institute of History and Philology (1928–) who specialized in the study of oracle bone and turtle shell inscriptions. He was the first to suggest the systematic excavation of the Anyang site. Publication of his 1937 manuscript on the inscriptions was delayed by the Sino-Japanese war until 1947. He moved with the institute to its various refugee sites during the war. In 1949 he helped to evacuate the Academia Sinica to Taiwan, where he served as history professor at Taiwan University (1949–63) and director of the Academia's Institute of History and Philology (1950–55).

Feng Ziyou (Feng Tzu-yu) (1881–1958), born in Japan, was an early associate of Sun Zhongshan (Sun Yat-sen), the founder of the Republic of China. In 1902 a ceremonial meeting to commemorate the death of the last Ming emperor, planned by Feng and others engaged in anti-Manchu (or anti-Qing) activity, was prevented by the Tokyo police; it was later held in Yokohama. Feng served as Sun's fundraiser in Canada and the United States. After the successful October 1911 revolt, he was the confidential secretary (1911–12) of Sun, then provisional president of China. Later he was appointed director of the Office for Investigation of Revolutionary Merits because of his broad knowledge of the various pre-1911 anti-Manchu revolutionary operations (1912–13). After the outbreak of the so-called second revolution in 1913, he had to flee from Beijing. He continued his association with Sun but gradually ceased his political activities. He wrote a three-volume work about the pre-1911 revolutionary movement (1928–44) and a five-volume "unauthorized" history of the 1911 revolution (1939–47). In 1949 he went to Taiwan and became national policy adviser to Jiang Jieshi (1949–58).

Jian Youwen (Chien Yu-wen) (also: Ren Youwen [Jen Yu-wen]) (1896–), Protestant minister, member of the Legislative Yuan (1933–46), history professor at Zhongshan (Chung-shan or Sun Yat-sen) University, Guangzhou (Canton) (1946–49), and founder and director-general of the Institute of History and Culture of Guangdong

(Kwangtung) province, moved to Hong Kong, where he became a research fellow at the Institute of Oriental Studies at the University of Hong Kong (1953–59) and specialized in the Taiping Rebellion.

Qian Mu (Ch'ien Mu) (1895–1990) was a historian of ideas; history professor at Beida (1931–) and the refugee Southwest Associated University at Changsha and Kunming (K'un-ming) (which combined Qinghua, Beijing, and Nankai universities in 1939–46) during the Sino-Japanese war; and director of the Research Institute on Chinese Culture of West China Union University (1941–46). He wrote *Outline History of the Nation* (1940), probably the most widely used history textbook in China for the next few years. In the spring of 1949, he went to Hong Kong, where he founded and presided at the New Asia Academy (1951–65). He was an Academia Sinica member. A paper of his, "The Unpublished Manuscripts of Chang Hsüeh-ch'eng" [historian Zhang Xuecheng, 1738–1801], published during the war in Sichuan, was reportedly reprinted in Beijing without his name. Qian's assessment of pre-Qin (prior to 221 BCE) schools of philosophy was praised as the culmination of the Qing dynasty school of textual criticism.

Tao Xisheng (T'ao Hsi-sheng) (1899–) was a Marxist-inspired social-economic historian specialized in Chinese feudalism who in 1930 debated with Guo Moruo [q.v. 1966–] and others on the nature of Chinese society. A member of the Reorganizationist faction led by Wang Jingwei, he joined the latter in his efforts after 1938 to reach a peaceful settlement of the Sino-Japanese war, but he became disillusioned and in January 1940 defected to Hong Kong with copies of Wang's secret agreement with the Japanese. His family was taken into custody for a time. In 1942 he became Jiang Jieshi's personal secretary. He went to Taiwan with him. From 1943 to 1955, he was chief editor of the *Central Daily News*.

Local historian **Zhang Qiyun** (Chang Ch'i-yün) (1901–) taught history and geography for many years at National Central University, Nanjing (Nanking) (1927–36), National Zhejiang (Chekiang) University, Hangzhou (Hangchow) (1936–), and the refugee universities during the Sino-Japanese war and emigrated in June 1949. In Taiwan he became secretary-general of Jiang Jieshi's office (1949–50) and minister of education (1954–58). He reestablished three universities and founded the National Historical Museum. He also edited Sun Zhongshan's principal writings.

Zou Lu (Tsou Lu) (1884–1954), Conservative Guomindang leader, compiler of two Guomindang histories, chancellor of Zhongshan University (1932–40), went to Taiwan.

Luo Jialun (Lo Chia-lun) (1896–1969) was a leader of the 1919 May Fourth Movement (the term is his), editor of its monthly *New Tide*, and one of the three student representatives who entered the American legation at Beijing on 4 May 1919 to present a memorandum of grievances concerning the Paris Peace Conference decision on transferring the special rights in Shandong (Shantung) to Japan. Later he was president of Qinghua University, Beijing (1928–31), where he resigned after protests of alumni against his reorganization policies. He became president of the National Central University, Nanjing (1932–41), and served the Nationalist government as supervisory commissioner of Sinkiang (1943–45), vice chairman of the Guomindang's party history compilation committee, and ambassador to India (1947–50). Early in 1950 he left India and went to Taiwan, where he became chairman of the Guomindang's archives and history compilation committee. In 1953 he became editor of a multivolume collection of documents from Guomindang and Academia Historica archives. In 1958 he was appointed president of the Academia Historica, where the official history of the 1911 Revolution and the Chinese Republic was compiled.

1949–   After 1949 the research of at least three historians who studied Western historiography was reportedly confined under political pressure: **Qi Sihe** (Ch'i Szu-he) did not write much after 1949; **Wang Yangchong** (Wang Yang-ch'ung) was frequently questioned about his motivation in the 1950s and 1960s and had been shut off from academic work for decades as a rightist; the work of **Guo Shengming** (Kuo Sheng-ming) was subject to heavy political pressure. The American or European education of these historians was regarded an "inexcusable stain" on their backgrounds, which became a main cause for their sufferings in those years.

1950–51   In 1950 the film *The Inside Story of the Qing Court* (1948), written by **Yao Ke** and directed by **Chu Shiling**, was banned because the suppression of the Boxer Rebellion against foreigners (1898–1900) by the Empress Dowager of the Qing dynasty, Zixi, shown in the film, was deemed the counterrevolutionary suppression of a proletarian uprising. Later the opera and stage versions, directed by **Liu Ban**, were also banned. Another film banned in 1950–51 was *The Life of Wu Xun* (1950), directed by **Sun Yu**, about a late-nineteenth-century beggar who became rich and used his money to found schools. Praise of Wu Xun was considered to be negating the overthrow of the landlord class by the peasants and the inevitability of class struggle and revolutionary violence.

1950–52   In the "Land Reform" and "Anti-Corruption" campaigns of the early 1950s, private antiquarian collections suffered many losses.

1952–59 From March 1952 to April 1959, **Gu Jiegang** (Ku Chieh-kang) (1893–1980), a professor and historian famous for his critical discussions of Chinese antiquity, especially as editor and coauthor of the seven-volume *Discussions of Ancient History* (1926–41), had to endure several attacks. After his appointment as head of the history department at the Chinese Academy of Sciences (CAS) in September 1954 (1954–82), he made a public statement of self-criticism (December 1954) and attacked his former mentor Hu Shi [q.v. 1954–] (something he had already done in December 1951), admitting, however, that he had the same shortcomings as Hu. Reprints of his older works contained self-critical prefaces. During the Cultural Revolution (1966–76), he was branded a "reactionary academic authority", his research was suppressed, and he had to clean the desks and floors of the CAS history department. His library of 70,000 volumes was sealed. In spite of Red Guard inspections, he continued his research, relying mainly on his well-trained memory. He used a fountain pen and primary-school copybooks that he placed on his children's desks when Red Guards paid him a visit. His close colleagues **Tong Shuye** (T'ung Shu-yeh) (who was apparently forced at one time to write against Gu), **Li Jingche** (Li Ching-ch'e), and **Zhou Yutong** (Chou Yü-t'ung) (1898–1981) were persecuted to death or went mad during the Cultural Revolution. In 1971–77 Gu was gradually rehabilitated and given a leading position at the history department of the Chinese Academy of Social Sciences (CASS; established 1977). In 1980 another close colleague of Gu, Yang Xiangkui (Yang Hsiang-k'uei), who had attacked him in 1952, retracted his criticism. As a schoolboy Gu had lost a high school scholarship for criticizing a second-century Han commentator. A friend of Fu Sinian [q.v. 1948–50], he was one of the participants in the 1919 May Fourth Movement and the "New Tide" Society (1918–22) that promoted a critical spirit, scientific thinking, and reformed rhetoric. A research professor at Xiamen (Amoy) University (1926–[27]), Fujian province, he was obliged to depart after a conflict with the writer Lu Xun. In 1928, when he worked at Zhongshan University, a high school history textbook of his did not receive official authorization for use in the schools because Guomindang officials denounced his treatment of the Golden Age as a myth. During the war, he came under frequent political crossfire, with reduced salary or none at all.

1954– Several Chinese scholars outside the historical profession and some artists, living in China or abroad, were criticized for the viewpoints in their work. Among them were literary critic **Yu Pingbo** (Yü P'ing-po) (1900–90), philosopher **Hu Shi** (Hu Shih) (1891–1962), and philosopher **Feng Youlan** (Feng Yu-lan) (1895–1990).

In September–October Yu Pingbo came under violent attack because he had disobeyed a CCP 1953 order to interpret Chinese classics in Marxist-Leninist terms; in a 1954 article published without the approval of Hu Qiaomu [q.v. 1966–], he contended that the *Dream of the Red Chamber*, one of China's outstanding eighteenth-century novels, was not a critique of the feudal system but its author's autobiography. During the Cultural Revolution (1966–76), he was detained for two years and sent to a May Seventh Cadre School (rural camps to reeducate intellectuals through manual labor established after 7 May 1966) in Henan Province (1969–71).

From December 1954 to February 1955, fifteen forums were held to criticize the political, philosophical, and historical views of Hu Shi, a proponent of the so-called Chinese Enlightenment (1919 May Fourth Movement). A disciple of American philosopher John Dewey, he was a pioneer of Western historical method in China, China's ambassador to the United States (1938–42), a member of the Chinese delegation to the founding United Nations conference (1945), and chancellor of Beida (1946–48). He was considered Yu's mentor. One of the forums was devoted to his *Outline of the History of Chinese Philosophy* (1919; republished 1986). Hu went to the United States, where he lived in semiretirement. Later he became Academia Sinica president in Taiwan (1958–62). Among the anti-Hu campaigners were Gu Jiegang [q.v. 1952–59], Zhou Gucheng [q.v. 1964–], and Hou Wailu [q.v. 1966].

Feng Youlan, a neo-Confucian philosopher known for his two-volume *History of Chinese Philosophy* (1930–36; reprint 1961; English translation: 1937, 1953) and his philosophical system combining neo-Confucianism, Western realism and logic, and elements of Taoist thought, was a professor of philosophy at Qinghua University (1927–52)—including its refugee campus Southwest Associated University at Kunming (1939–46)—and at Beida (1952–), the director of its Department of Research in the History of Chinese Philosophy (1954–[66]), and chief of the division of Chinese philosophy at the CAS Research Institute of Philosophy (1954–66). He had voluntarily undergone a process of "thought reform" in 1950. In May 1956 he criticized the disregard for expert opinion. In January 1957 he published "The Problem of Inheriting the Philosophical Heritage of China", an article containing a doctrine of abstract inheritance which was criticized in 1957–59. On several occasions he was denounced as a revisionist. Early in 1958 he was accused, inter alia, of distorting former Soviet Politburo member and cultural ideologue Andrei Zhdanov's definition of the history of philosophy and of revising the theory that there had been no materialistic interpretation of history before Karl Marx. In June he published a confession. In May 1968, during the Cultural Revolution, he was denounced as a counterrevolutionary element and purged. He "reappeared" in February 1972 as professor at Beida. In September 1976 he "disappeared" again until December 1981, when he was named "a leading scholar".

1956 During the whole first term of 1956, the biology department and the Marxist-Leninist study group at Fudan University, Shanghai, organized biweekly meetings to criticize *The History of the Development from Ape to Man*, a book by biology professor **Liu Xian**.

Among the historians and others concerned with the past who were victimized during the Anti-Rightist Campaign (June 1957–58) and not already mentioned were the following:

1957– Archeologists **Chen Mengjia** (Ch'en Meng-chia) and **Zeng Zhaoyu** (Tseng Chao-yü) were incriminated as "rightists" and persecuted; they committed suicide.

  In the summer, **Lei Haizong** (Lei Hai-tsung) (1902–62), a historian known for his cyclic periodization of Chinese history and his studies of ancient Chinese culture, was labeled "bourgeois" (together with historian **Yang Renpian**) and forbidden to teach Chinese history because of his outspoken criticism of communism at a Tianjin conference of professors in April 1957 during the Hundred Flowers campaign (May 1956–June 1957). He had, inter alia, challenged the historical accuracy of Karl Marx and Friedrich Engels regarding the ancient "slave society". His teaching activities were limited to one course in foreign historiography. He was a history professor at Qinghua University, Beijing (1932–52), including at the refugee campus of Southwest Associated University at Kunming, where he served as chairman of the combined history department. An opponent of Marxism, he was transferred by the government to Nankai University, Tianjin, in 1952.

1957–59 In September 1957 Ming historian **Jiang Xingyu** (Chiang Hsing-yü), member of the Shanghai Cultural Office, was nearly branded a "rightist" because he had written a biography of Ming official Hai Rui (Hai Jui; 1515–87). In April 1959 he wrote a short story about Hai Rui (Wu Han [q.v. 1965–69]) in Shanghai's *Liberation Daily*, for which he had to endure many struggle meetings, some years in a May Seventh Cadre School, and some years as a factory hand.

1957 In October–December historian **Xiang Da** (Hsiang Ta) was accused of the fact that he had allegedly characterized post-1949 historiography as being "at the brink of death" because of its exclusive attention to the questions of periodization, the formation of the Han nation, the feudal land system, peasant wars, and capitalist experiments.

1958–69   In July–August 1958, historian **Chen Yinke** (or Chen Yinque) (Ch'en Yin-k'o or Ch'en Yin-ch'üeh, also Tschen Yinkoh) (1890–1969) was criticized by students of Zhongshan University as a leading representative of the bourgeois historians who denied the class struggle, exalted the role of the individual in history, and worshiped Western authors. He was a specialist in Chinese Buddhism, Sui (581–618 CE) and Tang (618–907 CE) institutions, Ming and Qing culture, and the relations between the medieval Chinese empire and neighboring areas in 220–960 CE. He served as professor of Chinese and history at Qinghua University, Beijing (1925–49), research fellow (1928–) and director at the Academia Sinica Institute of History and Philology, and member of the Academia's board of supervisors (1935–49). He was also a Palace Museum director and a Qing Archives editorial board member. After the outbreak of the Sino-Japanese war (July 1937), he taught at the University of Hong Kong (1937–). Appointed in 1938 to the chair of Chinese at Oxford University, he was prevented from teaching there by the war and then by blindness. He taught Chinese history at the refugee campus of Yanjing (Yenching) University, Chengdu (1942–). In December 1948 he was evacuated from besieged Beijing. After 1948 he taught and did research at Linnan (1949–52) and Zhongsan universities. In 1953 he declined the directorship of the CAS Institute of Medieval History because he did not accept Marxism-Leninism as the only theoretical framework for the study of history. In May 1955 he became a member of the CAS Department of Philosophy and Social Sciences. Criticism subsided in 1959. In January 1967 he was attacked by Guangdong Red Guards as an "authority of reactionary bourgeoisie" and he "disappeared", probably passing his last years in extreme adversity.

1958–60   **Shang Yue** (Shang Yüeh) (1902–82), history professor and department head at People's University, Beijing (1950–), was criticized and attacked with increasing severity by Liu Danian [q.v. 1966], Li Shu [q.v. 1966–] and Jian Bozan [q.v. 1966–68], among others, because of his viewpoint, expressed in *Outline of Chinese History* (1954) and *Preliminary Investigations into the Origin and Development of Capitalist Economic Relations in China* (1956), that incipient capitalist elements did already exist in the late Ming period (seventeenth century), in other words much earlier than the mid-nineteenth century, a thesis casting doubt on the crucial role assigned to foreign capitalism in transforming China into a "semicolonial" status since the first Opium War (1839–43), on the timing of the CCP's rise to power, on its role in modern Chinese history, and hence on its legitimacy. He elaborated themes already described in the 1940s by Hou Wailu [q.v. 1966], who in an intellectual history of early modern China had ascribed the appearance of "bourgeois" thought in China to the late Ming and early Qing periods (sixteenth to seventeenth centuries). Until Mao Zedong's death in 1976, Shang remained in eclipse. In 1979 he was reported in bad health.

1960s   In the early 1960s, a directive of Lu Dingyi (Lu Ting-yi) (1901–), head of the CCP Propaganda Department (1949–66), explicitly forbade writing CCP history. The only existing history, *Thirty Years of the Chinese Communist Party* (Beijing 1951) by Hu Qiaomu [q.v. 1966–], was banned during the Cultural Revolution.

1963   **Lo Ergang** (Lo Erh-kang), historian of the Taiping Rebellion, was attacked for his portrayal of the last Taiping General Li Xiucheng (Li Hsiu-ch'eng) as a hero. As early as 1952, he had to write a self-criticism on his "bourgeois" point of view.

         In October **Liu Jie** (Liu Chieh) (1901–77), Confucian philosopher in the history department of Zhongshan University, was attacked in numerous articles and meetings in Beijing and Guangzhou because in several 1962–63 articles he had rejected the class analysis of ancient Chinese history. He saw the search for harmony between human activities and the laws of nature as a key to understanding ancient thought and as transcending class and historical period.

1964–   In the Rectification Campaign (summer 1964–summer 1965), historian and aesthetician **Zhou Gucheng** (Chou Ku-ch'eng) (ca. 1900–) and philosopher **Feng Ding** (Feng Ting) came under attack. Already criticized in September 1963 and May 1964, Zhou, author of works on Chinese history (1939, reprinted 1956–57, 1980) and world history (*Shijie tong shi*; 1949, reprinted 1950, 1958), professor at Fudan University (1950–) and head of its history department and member of the presidium of the Chinese Peasant and Workers Democratic Party, was attacked between August 1964 and March 1965 for the alleged Eurocentrism of his works and for talking of a "unified consciousness" and a "spirit of the age". He maintained that such a "spirit of the age" could never be completely expressed by one individual or even one entire class. He downplayed the significance of class feelings and believed that contradictions could be eliminated and conflict resolved through art. He was purged in 1966. In the spring of 1957, Zhou had participated in scholarly discussions on the origin and function of beauty, but he was not made a prominent victim of the Anti-Rightist Campaign, although his history of China was strongly criticized for its bourgeois point of view, which failed to credit peasant rebellions as the motive force of history. In 1979 he was reported in bad health. Around 1990 he headed the government's Council on Education, Culture, Science, and Health. In September 1964 Feng, while a professor of Marxist philosophy at Beida, came under attack because he had declared that social history was the history of the pursuit of happiness by all men, inter alia in his work *The Historical Mission of the Working Class* (1953).

1966–   Several films, plays, and books with a historical dimension were denounced as "poisonous weeds" during the Cultural Revolution. *Red Sun*, a film based on a screenplay by **Qu Baivin**, was said to have seriously "tampered" with history. Four pieces which satirized the present through historical incidents were denounced: *King of Qi Looks for a General* (1962), a film directed by **Tao Jin**; *Hai Rui Dismissed from Office* (Wu Han [q.v. 1965–69]); *Xie Yaohuan* (1956), a stage play written by dramatist **Tian Han** (T'ien Han) (1898–1966); and *Li Huiniang* (1961), a ghost play written by **Meng Chao**. Also denounced were *Hai Rui's Memorial to the Emperor* ([1959]), a stage play by **Zhou Xinfang, Tao Xiong**, and **Xu Siyan**; *On Our Ancient Scholars' Spirit and Method of Study* (1961), a book by **Wu Tianshi** and **Ma Yingbo**; and *History of Chinese Motion Pictures* (1963), edited by **Cheng Xihua**. *The History of the Chinese Cinema* (1963), the publication of which had been canceled in 1957, was banned in 1966 for its "sweeping praise of thirties' cinema". Sales of photographs depicting the 1949 Proclamation of the People's Republic of China and showing Liu Shaoqi (Mao's chosen successor) and Lin Biao (Mao's second chosen successor) were stopped after Liu's purge, and then fully destroyed on Central Committee orders after Lin's 1971 "disappearance", notwithstanding the fact that thousands of copies had already been distributed.

Among the historians and others concerned with the past who were victimized during the Great Proletarian Cultural Revolution (November 1965–1976), and not already mentioned, were the following:

1965–69   On 10 November 1965, Ming historian **Wu Han** (1909–69), chairman of the China Democratic League (1953–66), vice mayor of Beijing (1949–66), member of the CAS Department of Philosophy and Social Sciences (1955–66), and president of Beijing Television University (1964–66), was attacked by Yao Wenyuan, a literary critic and future member of the Gang of Four, in a press article said to have been revised by Mao before publication. This article is believed by most to be the start of the Great Proletarian Cultural Revolution. It denounced Wu's 1961 play *Hai Rui Dismissed from Office*. In it the upright Ming official Hai Rui defends the peasants against bureaucratic arbitrariness; as a result, he is dismissed. At the time of its appearance, the play had created no great stir. Mao originally urged that Hai Rui's antibureaucratic criticism be emulated. He later believed—possibly erroneously—that Wu's Hai Rui was in fact a historical symbol for Peng Dehuai, the minister of defense whom Mao had dismissed in July 1959 for his criticism of the Great Leap Forward policies (1958–60). Thus the play was read as an indirect criticism of Mao. Before Yao wrote his article, Mao had already asked Peng Zhen, Beijing's mayor, to criticize his vice mayor, but Peng had tried to protect Wu. Another point of criticism was the zawen, sixty-seven short satirical essays written by Wu in 1961–64 with essayist Deng Tuo [q.v. 1966] and journalist Liao Mosha (Liao Mo-sha) (1907–) under the pen name Wu Nanxing (Wu Nan-hsing) in *Front Line* under the title "Notes from a Three-Family Village". Concerning historical topics, these essays were a barely veiled criticism of Maoist policies. In a reaction to Yao's article, Wu made a self-criticism in China's largest newspaper, *Renmin Ribao* (People's Daily) on 30 December 1965, but in a forum in Shanghai the next day, he was attacked again. Among the critics was Zhou Gucheng [q.v. 1964–]. Only Peng Zhen, Deng Tuo [q.v. 1966], and some others defended him. A second self-criticism on 12 January 1966 quickly isolated him. The Hai Rui play was debated in the Chinese press throughout February. A whole volume of essays was published (for limited circulation to educational establishments) to criticize the 1965 edition of his biography of the first Ming emperor, Zhu Yuanzhang (Chu Yuan-chang) (ruled 1368–98), which was classified as negative teaching material. The attacks lasted until May 1966. In the spring of 1966, Wu was placed under house arrest. After a few months, he was arrested and held in the Beijing Municipal Party School, where he reportedly underwent an intense thought reform process and from where he was dragged almost daily to endure mass struggle meetings held throughout the Beijing area. In preparation of these meetings, his background was scrutinized (including his claim that his grandfather was a tenant farmer and his father an ordinary "public servant", his relation with his mentor Hu Shi [q.v. 1954–], and the 1946 murder of his Democratic League colleague Wen Yiduo). In 1968 he was sent to prison. Wu died there on 11 October 1969, as a result of prolonged ill-treatment and refusal of medical attention (some report suicide), a few months after the death of his wife. His daughter became mentally ill and reportedly committed suicide in 1975 or 1976. The first reappraisal of Wu came in 1976. In 1978 he was officially rehabilitated. In February 1979 the Hai Rui play was restaged, and his zawen and historical work were republished and praised. An official publication was dedicated to his life and work. His early work of the 1930s had reportedly demonstrated an acute faculty for detecting tendentious or falsified documents. In the 1940s, when the Guomindang suppressed open discussion of contemporary problems, Wu made ready use of historical allegories in his zawen as a form of indirect criticism. When in 1947 the Democratic League was outlawed, Wu began to cooperate clandestinely with the CCP, and in late 1948, when blacklisted by the Guomindang, he joined them. In 1949–50 he wrote several self-criticisms. In the Anti-Rightist Campaign, he attacked Luo Longji, his colleague in the Democratic League. A concern for Chinese history made Wu an ardent promotor of mass popularization, and he increasingly directed his writings toward the general public. In 1962–63 he had been criticized for his views on the inheritability of values (he had argued that, after critical examination, the best features of feudal and capitalistic morality could be inherited by proletarian morality).

1966–   According to one source, the entire senior staff of the history department at Zhongshan University was hanged.

Xia Nai (Hsia Nai) (1910–85), China's leading archeologist and student of Li Ji [q.v. 1948–], egyptologist, deputy director (1950–62), director (1962–83), and honorary director (1983–85) of the CAS/CASS Institute of Archeology, "disappeared". In 1970 or 1971, however, he was rehabilitated because his expertise was needed for new excavations. He made his first reappearance at a reception by Prime Minister Zhou Enlai for American President Richard Nixon in February 1972. In 1982 he became CASS vice president. He had been an activist in the Anti-Rightist Campaign.

Historian **Shen Yuan** (Shen Yüan) was denounced for opposing the Cultural Revolution. The same happened to historians **Sun Zuomin** (Sun Tso-min); **Qi Xia** (Ch'i Hsia) (1923–), assistant professor at the history department of Hebei (Ho-pei) University, Baoding City, and specialist in the Song dynasty (960–1279); and **Cai Meibiao** (Ts'ai Mei-piao) (1928–), research fellow at the CAS Institute of Modern History (1953–) and specialist in the Song, Yuan (1279–1368), and Qing dynasties. The four were specialists on the subject of peasant movements and had denied that the peasants had any subjective revolutionary consciousness. They had already been accused of "abandoning the class stand of the workers" before the

Cultural Revolution. In 1962 Sun and Qi had reportedly modified substantially their earlier more negative conclusions under the pressure of radical criticism. In 1963 Qi had been accused again, this time of going too far to the other extreme and exaggerating the revolutionary consciousness of the peasants. In June 1966 he was criticized by all the teachers and students at Hebei University.

1966–71   In 1966–71 historian **Zhou Yiliang** (Chou I-liang), a specialist in the Wei-Jin (220–589 CE) and Sui-Tang (581–907 CE) periods, trained at Harvard University, and editor of a three-volume, six-book world history (*Shijie tong shi*; 1962, revised second edition 1972), was persecuted for his class background (his father was a capitalist with extensive mining and manufacturing interests prior to 1949). "Re-educated", he became a leading figure in a radical writing group closely associated with the Gang of Four in 1973. During the criticism of the Gang of Four, he claimed that he had been deceived by their twisted "ultra left" line. In 1979 his appointment at Beida was pending because he was not yet exonerated officially, but after his self-criticism was officially accepted, he regained his position at Beida, serving as the history department chairman there until the summer of 1983.

1966–   **Wu Tingqiu** (Wu T'ing Ch'iu) (1910–), history professor at Nankai University (1950–66), "disappeared" during the Cultural Revolution. In July 1980 he was elected president of the Society for the Study of Japanese History. In April 1988 his whereabouts were again unknown.

Pei Wenzhong (P'ei Wen-chung) (1904–82), a geologist and archeologist who discovered the skull of the Peking Man (Sinanthropus pekinensis) near Zhoukoudian, Henan Province (1929), "disappeared" during the Cultural Revolution (1966–73). In March 1973 he "reappeared". In April 1979 he was deputy director-general of the Chinese Society of Archeology. During the communist takeover in 1949, Pei had been subjected to a three-month period of political indoctrination.

Also, historians mostly known for their loyal attitude toward the regime went through difficult times. In April 1966 **Guo Moruo** (Kuo Mo-jo) (1892–1978), archeologist and historian of antiquity, pioneer of the Marxist study of Chinese history, CAS president (1949–78), CCP Central Committee member (1969–78), and Mao's personal friend, made a self-criticism at a meeting of the Standing Committee of the National People's Congress. He was reportedly removed from his posts for some time. When in 1971–74 he refused to join the campaign of Jiang Qing, Mao's wife, against Zhou Enlai, the resulting strain reportedly broke his health. In 1973 Jiang tried to line up a group at Beida for open criticism of Guo. In February 1974 Guo was taken to the hospital after another refusal. He was described as a "moral victim" of the Cultural Revolution. Guo lived in exile twice, once in Japan as an "enemy of the Nationalist government" (1927–37) and once in Hong Kong to escape increasing persecution of left-wing intellectuals (1947–48).

Hu Qiaomu (Hu Ch'iao-mu) (?1905/11–1992), Mao's political secretary (1941–62), CCP Central Committee member (1956–), the leading CCP ideologue reponsible for two CCP key resolutions on history (in 1945 and 1981), and author of several historical works, including the official *Thirty Years of the Chinese Communist Party* (Beijing 1951), was attacked and relieved of all his posts in August 1966. In January 1967 he was publicly denounced as a supporter of Liu Shaoqi and as a "three-anti element". After this incident he "disappeared". In September 1974 he "reappeared" as a member of the CCP Secretariat and Central Committee. From 1976 he issued hundreds of censorial remarks to the press about how to portray and judge historical figures such as Sun Zhongshan and Liu Shaoqi, who was posthumously rehabilitated in 1980. In 1977 Hu became the first CASS president (1978–82).

1966   **Gen Danru** (Ken Tan-ju) (?–1966), historian and professor at Fudan University, and a pioneer in the study of Western historiography in China, underwent physical and mental abuses by the "revolutionaries" and died.

Deng Tuo (Teng T'o) (real name: Deng Yunte) (1911–66), a colleague of Wu Han [q.v. 1965–69], was a veteran cadre from the 1930s, *Renmin Ribao*'s former editor (1949–59) and chief editor (1952–57), a poet and historian, and in 1965 secretary for culture and education in the Beijing Party Committee. In the 1930s he was wanted by the Nationalist authorities and spent several terms in prison for his revolutionary activities. In 1944 he edited Mao's first *Selected Works*. In June 1955 he became a member of the History Institute of the CAS Department of Philosophy and Social Sciences. During the Anti-Rightist Campaign, he participated in the prosecution of liberals who had criticized the CCP. From March 1961 to September 1962, he wrote a series of zawen in the *Beijing Wanbao* (Beijing Evening News), *"Evening Chats at Yanshan"*, under the pseudonym Ma Nancun (Ma Nan-ts'un), in which he lampooned Mao through the use of ancient characters and historical incidents. In December 1961 a report drafted under his direction confirmed Peng Dehuai's criticism of the Great Leap policies. In May 1966 Deng was publicly denounced. He was called the chief of the Three-Family Village Black Gang (Wu Han [q.v. 1965–69]). He was accused of attacking the CCP, socialism, Marxism-Leninism, and Mao Zedong thought in a speech he had made at an enlarged meeting of the editorial committee for *Booklet Series on Chinese History, Booklet Series on the History of Foreign Countries*, and *Booklet Series on Geography* in October 1962. On 18 May 1966, Deng was killed or committed suicide under duress. In August 1979 he was officially rehabilitated and his works were republished.

Historian **Zou Shiyan** (1933–), working at the Department of Higher Education, Hubei Provincial People's Government (1964–66), "disappeared". He "reappeared" after the Cultural Revolution and became vice president of the Red Cross Society of China (1984–93).

1966–68   From March to December 1966, historian **Jian Bozan** (Chien Potsan) (1898–1968), head of the history department (1952–?66) and vice president (1962–?66) of Beida, was subjected to a criticism campaign, including more than forty attacks in a dozen newspapers and journals. He was denounced as an antisocialist, anti-party bourgeois "academic authority" who sought to lay the ideological foundation for the restoration of capitalism. In late 1967 Nie Yuanzi, leader of the Red Guard rebel faction at Beida and foremost member of the "Big Five" Red Guard leaders of Beijing, and her assistant, Sun Pengyi, reportedly compiled a "black list" with the names of thirty teachers from the history department whom they regarded as reactionary academic authorities. Jian was one of five whom they eventually hounded to death. On 16 December 1968, he committed suicide together with his wife, according to one source, after he had heard that his name was publicly and officially cleared the same day. In September 1978 he was officially rehabilitated. In February 1979 a memorial service in his honor was held at the Babaoshan Cemetery for Revolutionaries in Beijing. In 1980 a collection of his essays was republished, and in November 1982 a commemorative conference was held at Beida. An ethnic Uighur, a member of the CAS Philosophy and Social Science Division, one of the founders of Marxist historiography in China and already imprisoned in 1927 (for his left-wing tendencies) and criticized in the early 1950s, Jian's dissent became clearly visible around 1957, when he criticized the leading CCP cadres for not going far enough with the liberalizing Hundred Flowers campaign. In 1958–61 he rejected the Great Leap Forward policies. Central in his criticism of the extreme left-wing ideological trend were his "historicism" (respect for the context and the complexity of historical facts and primacy of the empirical methodology) and his "concession theory" (which explained that, when confronted with a peasant rebellion, the ruling class made concessions to the peasants with the aim of restoring the established order). In a June

1962 speech to the Nanjing Historical Society, he attacked the slogan "Lead History with Theory". This became the basis for the charge that he had rejected the class-struggle view of history. At the dawn of the Cultural Revolution, during a speech on 21 December 1965, Mao himself attacked Jian's concession theory. In 1977–78 the Red Guard atrocities were denounced on posters at Beida. The history department came under the strongest attack. The posters suggested that those responsible for Jian's death were still in charge of the department. During a reorganization, three departmental leaders were dismissed.

1966   In June **Zhou You** (Chou Yu), the publisher of the works of Wu Han [q.v. 1965–69], Deng Tuo [q.v. 1966], Liao Mosha, as well as other historical works, was denounced.

1966–   In June and October, **Li Shu** (1912–88), historian of the twentieth century and chief editor of the leading official journal *Lishi Yanjiu* (Historical Research), was attacked in *Renmin Ribao* as a "bourgeois" authority in the field of historical studies, for suppressing truly revolutionary historians through his control of the journal and for publishing the work of "reactionary" historians. In the late 1950s, he had already been denounced as an "inner-party democrat". In 1979 he was still *Lishi Yanjiu*'s chief editor and director of the CASS Modern History Institute, Beijing. In the 1980s he encouraged the reevaluation of major historical questions. In 1986 the second print run of a book he had edited, *Theoretical Storm*, was not distributed, and in 1990 the publisher was ordered to destroy the remaining 20,000 copies.

1966   In June **Wan Shengnan** (Wan Sheng-nan), lecturer at the history department of Hefei (Ho-fei) Teachers College in Anhui (Anhwei), was denounced as a "loyal disciple" of Wu Han [q.v. 1965–69]; under the "pretext" of giving history lectures, Wan "sold counter-revolutionary black merchandise".

In June **Li Pingxin** (Li P'ing-hsin), history professor at East China Normal College in Shanghai, was denounced because he openly opposed using a present-day proletarian yardstick to measure historical figures and because he had a "bourgeois concept" of history.

In August **Lin Yang**, director of the Propaganda Department of the Party Committee of Inner Mongolia University in Hohhot (Huhehot) and director of the history and political science department at the same university, was suspended from his CCP and other posts "for creating a host of counterrevolutionary incidents".

In October **Liu Danian** (Liu Ta-nien) (1915–), *Lishi yanjiu*'s assistant editor (1955–), historian, deputy director of the CAS Modern History Institute (?1960–67), and author of a study of American "imperialist aggression" against China, endured severe criticism. He was branded as a member of a group of anti-party elements, as an anti-socialist historian, and as a sworn supporter of Li Shu [q.v. 1966–], Deng Tuo [q.v. pre-1966], Wu Han [q.v. 1965–69], Jian Bozan [q.v. 1966–68], and Hou Wailu [q.v. 1966]. In January 1967 he "disappeared" until July 1972. He was a presidium member (1980–) and executive chairman (1983–) of the History Society and director (1981–84) and honorary director (1984–) of the CASS Modern History Institute.

In November another editorial board member of *Lishi yanjiu*, **Hou Wailu** (Hou Wai-lu) (1903–?1987/92), deputy director of the CAS Institute of Medieval History, specialist in the history of Chinese thought and scholarship, was denounced for urging people to "censure the emperor", defending the "rightist opportunists", and advocating to "take vengeance" against the CCP. In 1980 he became CASS History Institute director.

1967– In August 1967 and February 1968 respectively, the radical historians **Lin Jie** (Lin Chieh) and **Qi Benyu** (Ch'i Pen-yü), members of a group that had attacked Lo Ergang [q.v. 1963] in 1963, and Wu Han [q.v. 1965–69] and Jian Bozan [q.v. 1966–68] in 1966, were themselves purged. Qi was criticized for exaggerating the revolutionary qualities of the Boxer Rebellion.

pre-1973 In 1973 historian **Shao Xunzheng** (Shao Hsun-cheng) (1909–73), head of the Qinghua University history department, died as a result of persecution. With Jian Bozan [q.v. 1966–68] and Hu Hua, he was the coauthor of *A Concise History of China*, a book published in six languages that came under fire during the Cultural Revolution.

1978–90 In 1978 **Li Honglin** (1927–), a deputy head of the theoretical bureau of the CCP Propaganda Department and a historian who had criticized CCP historiography, had written a memorial essay for Jian Bozan [q.v. 1966–68]. In 1985 he revealed that some of the views expressed in this essay had been criticized. In 1983 he had been purged from his position for his liberal ideas and was appointed director of the Fujian CASS, Jinshan, Fujian. Relieved from that post in 1987, he remained a CASS research fellow. In March 1989 he joined forty-two intellectuals in signing an open letter to the CCP leadership calling for the release of political prisoners and for greater freedom in China. In July he was arrested in Fuzhou and imprisoned for that reason. He was released in May 1990, along with Dai Qing [q.v. 1989–90] and others.

1980s

During the 1980s Hu Qiaomu [q.v. 1966–] instructed archivists to buy and hide away the memoirs of former Trotskyist leader **Zheng Chaolin** (?1900–). Zheng, a political theorist and linguist, joined the CCP in the early 1920s but was expelled from it as a Trotskyist in 1929. He was arrested by the Nationalist government in 1931 and imprisoned for seven years. After his release, he continued his political work and historical studies. He was arrested in Shanghai in December 1952, reportedly for refusing to compromise with the CCP. He was released in June 1979.

1986–

Yan Jiaqi (1942–), professor of philosophy, director of the CASS Political Sciences Institute, adviser to Prime Minister (from 1987 CCP Secretary-General) Zhao Ziyang and to Bao Tong [q.v. 1995–] (1986–87), and advocate of political reform, wrote *Turbulent Decade: A History of the Cultural Revolution* (originally in Chinese 1986; Honolulu 1996) with his wife, **Gao Gao**. Issued for public sale in 1986, it was suddenly reclassified for restricted circulation. It was subsequently banned during 1987 and Yan was denounced for "bourgeois liberalization". Thousands of unauthorized copies were reportedly printed in [1988]. In April and May 1989, Yan was one of the intellectuals supporting the student movement. In May he was elected president of the Beijing Independent Intellectuals Association. Accused of agitation, he escaped from China in June. In July he belonged to a group of dissident Chinese exiles who issued an open letter to the world leaders gathered in Paris for the French Revolution bicentennial, asking them to aid "combatants for democracy who are victims of repression". They unveiled a replica of the statue of the Goddess of Liberty. In August Yan was dismissed from the CCP and from public employment. In the same month, he was elected chairman of the Paris-based dissident Federation for a Democratic China but he resigned in late 1990. He resided in Paris and Princeton. Early in his career, after having participated in rural campaigns in 1966, Yan had assisted in editing the works of Marx, Engels, Lenin, Stalin, and Mao (1966–), had read many banned books in the fields of world and pre-1949 Chinese history (1967–71), had studied the history of political thought (1972–), and had written a philosophical novel in which he compared political systems since the eighteenth century (1979).

In April two Beida history students, **Zhang Xiaohui** and **Li Caian**, were arrested for "counterrevolutionary activities", allegedly for distributing pamphlets, which criticized the CCP and called for the creation of the new political party China Youth Party. Unofficial sources confirmed that they had written an article criticizing Marxism and CCP leadership but denied that they had attempted to form a political party. Both had reportedly participated in student demonstrations in late 1985. They had been kept under surveillance since then.

In October a directive from the State Publication Bureau in Beijing stated that all manuscripts dealing with the Anti-Rightist Campaign and the Cultural Revolution had to be submitted to the bureau for prepublication approval. The directive was taken to be the equivalent of a ban. Subsequently, a massive *Cultural Revolution Dictionary* project was reportedly canceled. Around the same time, some films that attempted a reevaluation of topics such as the 1937 Nanjing Massacre or the 1979 Sino-Vietnam conflict were banned.

1987–   In January 1987 a scholarly conference on the thirtieth anniversary of the Anti-Rightist Campaign, organized by journalist **Liu Binyan** (Liu Pin-yen) (1925–), physicist Fang Lizhi (Fang Li-chih), and Xu Liangying [q.v. 1994–], was canceled after heavy pressure from the authorities. The organizers were expelled from the CCP for "bourgeois liberalization" and their unpublished speeches were circulated for criticism. Liu had been branded as a "rightist" in July 1957 for his criticism of Chinese bureaucracy; he had his books banned and was sent to labor on a state farm. Rehabilitated in 1966, he was almost immediately denounced again during the Cultural Revolution, imprisoned for two years, and then "reeducated". Formally rehabilitated in 1978–79, he became a reporter for *Renmin Ribao* and was elected vice chairman of the All-China Writers' Association. In 1988 he went into exile in France and the United States and remained active in opposition circles. As a member of the Princeton University China Institute, he published *China Focus* (1992–99).

1987   In the summer **Sun Changjiang**, editor of the *Science and Technology Daily* newspaper, formerly a ghostwriter for CCP Secretary-General Hu Yaobang and a professor at Beijing Teachers' College with a degree in Chinese history, nearly lost his CCP membership for allegedly advocating "bourgeois liberalization". In a speech at an academic forum on feudalism and socialism in contemporary China, he had criticized the ignorance of Chinese history in left-wing policies and practices.

1989–   In May **Su Xiaokang** (1949–), ex-Red Guard factional leader turned journalist and lecturer at Beijing Broadcasting Institute, went into hiding. In July he was possibly detained for interrogation. He eventually was able to escape to Hong Kong and went into exile in France and the United States in September. He was the author of works on the history of the Great Leap Forward and coauthor of the screenplays for *River Elegy*, a controversial but very popular 1988 television documentary series in which the Chinese Confucian tradition was criticized as the source of the continuing failure to modernize. The series was broadcast twice, the second time in a slightly censored version. In the summer of 1989, his works were proscribed, the television series was virulently denounced, video sales of it proscribed, and the script, which was published as a book, pulped. A sequel to *River Elegy, May Fourth*, nearly completed in early 1989, was canceled. His work and the work of Dai Qing [q.v. 1989–90] were attacked in a speech by Hu Qiaomu [q.v. 1966–] in March 1990. In 1993 he was a member of the Princeton University China Institute. In 1999 he edited an on-line magazine called *Democratic China*.

1989   On 5 June, when student demonstrators were being removed from Tiananmen Square, China Central Television broadcast an old story from the archives in which the Israeli prime minister admitted that it was impossible to crush the Palestinian uprising by force. Thus a foreign news item was used to provide an indirect comment on the events.

The government reportedly banned the studying of history.

In June **Yang Tao** (?1970–), a Beida history student and one of the twenty-one student leaders of the Autonomous Federation of Beijing University Students listed by the government, was wanted for counterrevolutionary rebellion and arrested that month in Lanzhou, northwest China.

In June historian **Jin Guantao** (1947–), a CASS Science Policy and Management Research Institute fellow, was denounced by CCP authorities. He was in Hong Kong at that time and did not return to China. He had been adviser to *River Elegy*, by Su Xiaokang [q.v. 1989–], and editor with Bao Zunxin [q.v. 1989–92] of the *Toward the Future* series, in which his book *Behind the Phenomena of History* (1983) had appeared.

1989–97 In June 1989 **Yu Zhenbin** (?1962–), Qinghai Provincial Archives Bureau staff member, was detained in Xining, the capital of Qinghai Province. In January 1991 he was sentenced to twelve years' imprisonment. He was convicted of setting up the Democratic Opposition Parties' Alliance, an organization that the authorities claimed to be "counterrevolutionary". He was also accused of having made "reactionary speeches" and of having distributed leaflets in which current policies and leaders were criticized and political reforms called for. In June 1997 he was released after his twelve-year sentence was reduced to eight years.

1989–92   In June or July 1989, historian and philosopher **Bao Zunxin** (1937–), associate research fellow at the CASS Institute of Chinese History, former editor of the monthly *Reading*, a controversial intellectual journal, was detained and charged with counterrevolutionary propaganda and agitation. In August he was expelled from the CCP and dismissed. In January 1991 he was sentenced to five years' imprisonment. In February 1989 he had signed several open letters calling on the authorities to release Democracy Wall activist Wei Jingsheng. In May he had been one of the intellectuals publicly supporting the student movement. He was in poor health and made several suicide attempts in prison after discovering that the authorities had used his statements as a basis for arresting several other pro-democracy activists. In 1992 he was held in solitary confinement and he developed signs of mental illness. In December he was reportedly released on parole.

1989   In the summer **Li Zehou** (1930–), professor at the CASS Institute of Philosophy and historian of modern Chinese thought, was put under intensive investigation and urged to repudiate his writings for their "corrupting" influence. In internal documents, he was named a main target of official denunciation.

1989–   On 6 July 1989, **Wang Dan** (?1969–), a Beida history student who was number one on the list of the most wanted student leaders issued by the government on 13 June, was arrested when he made preparations to leave China. In 1988–89 Wang had taken the lead in organizing seventeen unofficial open-air "Democracy Salons" at Beida, at which participants were urged to discuss controversial political issues. In April 1989 the government attempted to close down the salons and officials later cited them as evidence that Wang had incited the student unrest. During the student uprising in the spring of 1989, he had been one of the top student leaders and chairman of the Autonomous Federation of Beijing University Students. He was charged with "counterrevolutionary propaganda and incitement" and held in solitary confinement for four months. Then he was sent to Beijing Prison No. 2, a "reform through labor camp", and reportedly held in a cell with five common criminals. In January 1991 he was tried and sentenced to four years' imprisonment and one year's deprivation of political rights. According to official sources, "he had shown repentance such as confessing his own crimes and exposing others". In February 1993 he was released on parole for good be-

havior. He stated that he had no regrets. He peacefully resumed his
activities to promote human rights, contributed articles on democracy
and human rights to domestic and overseas Chinese media as well
as to international media, and raised funds to help people suffering
repression. In February 1994 his civil and political rights were officially restored but he was harrassed and arrested for short terms by
the police ever since his release. He was denied permission to re-
register at Beida, and in January 1994 he began taking a correspondence course from the University of California. In March he was
sent on "vacation" outside Beijing to prevent "disruption" during the
visit of American secretary of state Warren Christopher. After he
received death threats from the police in December, he filed a lawsuit
against the Public Security Bureau to protest police harassment. In
May 1995 he was detained again as a leading signatory of pro-
democracy petitions. After being held incommunicado for seventeen
months, Wang was indicted on 11 October 1996 for "conspiring to
subvert the government" because of his study, articles, and fund-
raising. His parents were given only one day to choose a lawyer. On
30 October, after a four-hour closed trial, he was sentenced to eleven
years' imprisonment and two years' deprivation of political rights.
The verdict and sentence had apparently been decided in advance.
The domestic media were forbidden to report on the trial. On appeal
on 15 November, Wang was not allowed to testify and his sentence
was confirmed after a ten-minute hearing. In 1997 there were reports
that he was in poor health. In April 1998 he was released on medical
parole and expelled as part of a deal between China and the United
States. In 1999 he was a history student at Harvard University.

1989–90   On 14 July 1989, **Dai Qing** (real name: Fu Xiaqing) (1941–), former
missile technician and former intelligence agent, writer, and reporter
for the newspaper *Guangming Ribao* (1982–89), was detained after
the police searched her apartment and confiscated her manuscripts
and articles. Her detention was not officially confirmed and for some
time her whereabouts were unknown. In April–May 1989, she had
tried to mediate between the students and the authorities. On 4 June,
the morning of the Beijing massacre, she had publicly resigned from
the CCP and signed a protest letter to the government. In an official
report on the "counterrevolutionary rebellion", she was labeled an
advocate of bourgeois liberalization and an instigator of civil unrest.
In September she was attacked in the *Guangming Ribao* by her former colleagues. In January 1990 her detention was replaced by police surveillance. She was released in May. In the 1980s she had
established a reputation for her historical investigative journalism
concerning dissident intellectuals in CCP history, such as Chu An-

ping (a journalist and editor in the 1940s and 1950s). After her arrest, her books were banned and removed from the bookshops. She was forbidden to publish or give interviews, and her name could not be cited. The materials that some journalists had gathered to prepare a major seminar on her historical writings in Shanghai in 1989 were put under lock and key. Her daughter, **Wang Xiaojia**, was unable to continue her studies after graduating in history from Beida in 1990 because she had declined to denounce her mother.

1989   In September *Hainan Shiji*, a popular magazine specializing in contemporary (post-1949) history and CCP abuse of power, was forced to close down.

1989–   **Turgun Almas**, an Uighur historian and researcher at the Xinjiang Academy of Social Sciences in Urumqi, aged in his sixties, was severely criticized after publishing his book *The Uighurs* (1989). He was accused of supporting "separatism" because the book "elevated the historical importance of the Uighurs", "denied the harmony of the coexistence of the Chinese and Uighur people", and gave a "nationalistic" view of Uighur history. Almas was placed under house arrest and his family was harassed.

1990   In April part 1 of an Article 19 Report, *Starving in Silence: A Report on Famine and Censorship* (London 1990), entitled *The Feast of Lies: Censorship in China's Famine of 1959–1961*, was written by a scholar of Chinese history, politics, and contemporary culture who, because of his frequent visits to China, wished to remain anonymous. The author argued that the facts, statistics, origins, and consequences of the 1959–61 famine, in which at least fourteen million Chinese died, were systematically censored. For example, in the 1989 Chinese translation of *The Origins of the Cultural Revolution, Vol. 2: The Great Leap Forward 1958–1960* (Oxford 1983), by British historian **Roderick MacFarquhar**, professor of history and political science at Harvard University, the nationwide death statistics were omitted.

In [August] **Zhang Zhenglong**, a People's Liberation Army (PLA) propagandist, writer, and army officer, was briefly detained, presumably for "counterrevolutionary propaganda". In late 1989 he had published a book *White Snow, Red Blood*, an account of the pre-1949 civil war in northeast China. It was banned because it contained provocative descriptions of the actions of then-military commander Lin Biao, of the Nationalist army, and of the PLA siege of Changchun in which an estimated 150,000 civilians died. During the same purge of army publications, other accounts of pre-1949 CCP and army history were reportedly banned.

1991–93   Between 1991 and 1993, filmmaker **Tian Zhuangzhuang** (1952–) was harassed while making *The Blue Kite*, a 1993 historical film in which he paid homage to his parents' generation and which depicted the excesses of the Cultural Revolution and other politically sensitive periods. The film was banned in China and at a Hong Kong Film Festival, but the raw footage was smuggled to Japan and then released worldwide. In 1993 the ban on *Farewell My Concubine*, another Chinese film, was rescinded only after an international campaign. The film, about the violence and brutality unleashed during the Cultural Revolution, was significantly cut before showings resumed. In the same year, Oliver Stone was not given permission to make a movie in China about Mao.

1991–   The book *Wild Swans: Three Daughters of China* (New York 1991), a best-selling memoir written against the background of twentieth-century Chinese history by **Jung Chang** (Chinese: **Chang Jung**) (1952–), was banned.

In mid-1991 **Ulan Chovo** (?1954–), history lecturer at Inner Mongolia University, was arrested, charged with passing "confidential documents" to foreign journalists, and sentenced to five years' imprisonment. This happened in the context of a secret repression campaign, launched in May 1991, against ethnic Mongolian intellectuals in Inner Mongolia. Since 1990 they had gathered in small study groups and reprinted and circulated, inter alia, academic papers on Mongolian history.

1992–   In June **Wang Shengli** and **Liao Jia-an**, two postgraduate philosophy students at People's University, Beijing, were arrested and charged with "counterrevolutionary propaganda" for hanging up a banner at the university campus to commemorate the 1989 massacres, for publishing *Da Jia* (Everyone), the unofficial monthly of the student organization "Study Club" which they had founded, and for distributing *Tides of History*, a banned book of essays in support of the reformist faction in the CCP. The book was legally published in April 1992 by People's University Press but witdrawn from circulation after criticism by hard-line officials. In August 1993 Liao was sentenced to three years' imprisonment.

In June **Wang Wanxing** was arrested on Tiananmen Square, Beijing, for unfurling a banner commemorating the 4 June 1989 massacre. In July he was confined to a psychiatric hospital and forcibly given drugs. After a brief period of release in 1999, he was confined to the hospital again in November 1999.

In September 1992 Beida archeology student **An Ning** was detained. In September 1993 he was indicted on a charge of "counterrevolution" for possessing political leaflets, but the real reason for his arrest was believed to be his contact with dissident Shen Tong in August 1991. In November 1993 the trial was still going on. An had previously been arrested and imprisoned for his role in the 1989 pro-democracy movement.

1993   In March **Wan Jianguo** received a four-year prison term for reprinting some 60,000 copies of *Golden Lotus*, a 400-year-old Chinese erotic classic. The book, banned from public sale, was available to the CCP leadership under a system of restricted circulation.

1993–94   In September 1993 **Yao Kaiwen** and **Gao Xiaoliang**, two workers arrested in May, were secretly tried on charges of "forming a counterrevolutionary clique". Their activities allegedly included commemorating the fourth anniversary of the Tiananmen massacre. In October **Yu Zhuo**, a graduate student in Wuhan Polytechnic's department of economic management, Hubei province, was sentenced to two year's imprisonment for putting up more than thirty posters commemorating the massacre after having been held incommunicado since September 1992. In 1994 minor symbolic protests to commemorate the June 1989 events were dealt with harshly. When paper money, a traditional means of commemorating the dead, was burned at People's University in Beijing, all evening students were detained until the culprits could be interrogated and taken away.

1993   In December independent publisher **Liu Taiheng** was arrested in connection with *Citizens Sue the China-Invading Japanese Army*, a book on a movement to get compensation for abuses committed during the Japanese occupation of China. The book was banned.

1993–   In December 1993 researcher on CCP history **Bu Weihua** was reportedly detained with two others and in January 1994 charged with "leaking state secrets". Their alleged offense was to have printed a letter of self-criticism written by Deng Xiaoping in 1973 in a book, *The Stormy Twilight*. Deng's letter was reportedly banned at the time it was written and never distributed. It is unknown whether Bu was tried and where he was held.

1994–   In March 1994 **Xu Liangying** (Hsu Liangying) (?1920–), a retired physicist formerly working at the CASS Institute of the History of Science, translator of Albert Einstein's collected works, and one of the intellectuals publicly calling for free speech and the release of political prisoners, was placed under surveillance and virtual house arrest during the visit of foreign dignitaries to China. In October

1992 all copies of the fifth issue of the scientific journal *Future and Development*, containing several articles criticizing the lack of political reform in China, including Xu's *Without Democracy There Will Be No Reform*, had been confiscated. In May 1995 he was harassed by government officials after drafting and initiating a petition appealing to the government to free all political prisoners and signed by forty-five intellectuals, including Bao Zunxin [q.v. 1989–92] and Wang Dan [q.v. 1989–].

1995   When *The Gate of Heavenly Peace*, a BBC documentary on the events leading to the 1989 Tiananmen massacre, directed by Carma Hinton and Richard Gordon, was selected for the Human Rights Watch International Film Festival, New York, the Chinese government called it "insulting" and asked (in vain) that it be canceled, threatening to withdraw director Zhang Yimou's *Shanghai Triad*, which would open the festival. Also in 1995 another sensitive BBC documentary, *Mao Zedong: The Last Emperor*, was shelved by Hong Kong's number two commercial station TVB.

1995–   In May **Liu Nianchun** (?1950–), former editor of the Democracy Wall Movement's *Today* magazine, was arrested with others for taking part in events commemorating the 1989 Tiananmen massacre and for demanding an official condemnation of it. He was sentenced to three years' reeducation through labor plus seven months for "refusing to reform". In December 1996 his sentence was upheld on appeal. A second appeal in January 1997 led to an additional 216 days' detention for "refusing to reform". He was reportedly held in isolation and ill-treated. In December 1998 he was expelled to the United States.

Among those detained during the Fourth United Nations World Conference on Women, held in Beijing in September 1995, were **Ding Zilin** (?1937–) and her husband **Jiang Peikun**, whose son Jiang Jielian (?1972–89) was killed during the June 1989 massacre. In August they had been arrested in Wuxi City, Jiangsu province, apparently to prevent them from having contact with the conference delegates, and accused of "economic irregularities". They were released in October without explanation. From 1991 Ding, a supervisor of graduate students at People's University, had campaigned for an independent investigation into the killings. She compiled a list of those killed and wounded (220 names in March 1999), wrote *The Factual Account of a Search for the June Fourth Victims* (1994), and tried to persuade the government to reverse its opinion that the 1989 demonstrations were counterrevolutionary. She was frequently harassed by the police, she lost her supervisor status, her salary was reduced, and her CCP membership revoked. Her husband was dismissed after he had granted an interview to an American radio station. In June 2000 she issued a letter signed by 108 bereaved families. In a similar case, philosophy student and student leader **Li Hai** (?1954–) was harassed when trying to commemorate and investigate the June 1989 events. In 1996 he was sentenced to nine years' imprisonment on charges of "prying into state secrets" for attempting to gather information on those imprisoned after 4 June 1989. On the eighth anniversary of the massacre in 1997, dissident **Shen Liangqing**, former state prosecutor and political prisoner, sent a petition to the National People's Congress demanding, inter alia, a reassessment of the 1989 events. Two months later, he was ordered to evacuate his private residence and surrender it to the local authorities. In April 1999 the police warned reformist political thinker **Bao Tong**, former chief of staff of Prime Minister and CCP Secretary-General Zhao Ziyang, that his 25 March letter to the leadership, calling for an official reassessment of the 1989 Tiananmen massacre, "endangered state security". Bao had been imprisoned (1989–96) and under house arrest (1996–97) for opposing the 1989 crackdown. In the run-up to the tenth anniversary, police in several cities prevented those wishing to publicly commemorate it from laying wreaths or visiting cemeteries. An estimated fifty activists were detained. They included 1989 student leader **Jiang Qisheng** (?1948–), who had written and distributed an open letter in April 1999, advocating a reassessment of the massacre, and who in December 2000 was sentenced to four years' imprisonment. In June 1999 an estimated 60,000 people joined the annual vigil. Wang Dan [q.v. 1989–] did not receive a visa for Hong Kong to attend a commemorating conference there in May. In June 2000, **Huang Qi**, founder of a website with information on the massacre, was arrested on charges of subversion. In August 2001, he was secretly tried, but no verdict was released.

In December historian **Chen Xiaoya** (?1955–) was dismissed from the CASS as a result of the publication, in Taiwan, of her manuscript *The History of the 1989 Democracy Movement*, which was the result of research since 1993. She remained unemployed. The expulsion of Chen and some of her colleagues came after a secret conference in Xibobo attended by CASS commissars and held to discuss the growth of "rightism". Scholars attempting to revive traditional Chinese culture, such as **Cheng Ming**, publisher of the neo-Confucianist journal *The Original Way*, were also subjected to official criticism.

1996   Under the new regulations governing control of society and media in Hong Kong, revealed by China in October 1996, anti-China activities such as the annual 1989 Tiananmen massacre demonstrations were prohibited, and institutions were forbidden to organize events advocating "two Chinas". Restrictions imposed on the media included a ban on references to "Taiwan's independence" or "self-determination for Hong Kong".

1998   Plans by the Shanghai Kunju Opera Company to perform *Peony Pavilion*, a twenty-two-hour classical opera directed by **Chen Shizheng**, in New York, Paris, Caen, Sydney, and Hong Kong, failed after Shanghai censors called the opera "feudal, superstitious, and pornographic", impounded the sets and refused to let the cast leave China. From the time it was written by Tang Xianzu (1550–1616; called the "Shakespeare of China") in 1598, the opera, based on a love story, had never been performed in its entirety.

1998–   **Tohti [Muzart]**, an Uighur scholar at the Minorities Institute, Beijing, who had been a visiting scholar in Japan, was arrested when returning to China to visit his relatives. He was reportedly tried and sentenced to seven years' imprisonment for publishing a Chinese-language book on Uighur history while in Japan.

1999   In March the China News Publishing Agency banned further sales of a biography of Fidel Castro, *The Last Revolutionary of the Twentieth Century*, written by a CASS historian, after a complaint from the Cuban embassy that it "hurt" Cuba's image.

1999–   In August 1999 **Song Yongyi** (1949–), a Chinese-born librarian and historian working at Dickinson College, Carlisle, Pennsylvania, United States (1989–), who specialized in contemporary Chinese history, was detained when he was in Beijing to collect published documents on the Cultural Revolution. He was confined and in December officially charged with "the purchase and illegal provision of intelligence to foreign people, and arrested". In January 2000 he was released. One source suggested that he was arrested because his research seemed to indicate that former Prime Minister Zhou Enlai—admired by Prime Minister Li Peng—played a more ruthless role in the Cultural Revolution than was generally accepted. During the Cultural Revolution, Song had had to interrupt his education to become a dockworker. In 1971–76 he had been imprisoned for organizing a book club with others interested in discussing political ideas. After the Cultural Revolution, he was cleared of all criminal charges.

1999   In December the essay *Fifty Years of Panic, Trials and Tribulations: Lonely Nighttime Thoughts on National Day*, by **Li Shenzhi**, retired CASS vice president and president of the China Society for American Studies, was posted anonymously on a Chinese website and read by thousands. It argued that the CCP had been the primary cause of instability in China and called for political reform. Li lost his position.

2000   The central government's Liaison Office warned Hong Kong Catholics to keep celebrations "low key" over the canonization of 120 victims of the Boxer Rebellion.

A blacklist of eleven banned journalists and academics, given to senior editors in Guangdong in December, included the names of historians **Liu Junning** and **Qian Liqun**. Earlier, in April, Liu's writings, frequently on issues of political and economic reform, had been banned from appearing in official publications and branded as "objectionable bourgeois-liberal" by the state propaganda department.

In July *Devils on the Doorstep*, a tragicomic film by **Jiang Wen** (winner of the 2000 Grand Prix Jury Prize at Cannes) about villagers collaborating with Japanese soldiers during the Sino-Japanese war, was banned by the Film Censorship Committee of the State Administration of Radio, Film and Television, allegedly because it "severely distorted history" and depicted the Chinese as "ignorant" and "not hating the Japanese troops as they should".

In December an Uighur history professor and an Uighur history teacher from Kashgar, Xinjiang, preferred to be cited under a pseudonym in a major article for a Dutch newspaper.

Tibet

1954–   Since at least 1954–55, history education at all levels in Tibet has been completely Chinese-centered and references to Tibetan culture and history have been dismissive. In addition, over six thousand monasteries (reportedly 97 percent of the total), including temples and historic buildings, and many religious and historic manuscripts were destroyed during the 1950s and 1960s. Many Tibetan treasures were sent off to China. From the early 1980s, many temples and monasteries have been rebuilt. In September 1983 thirty-two people were reportedly arrested while rebuilding the Ganden monastery (established in 1409 by Tsong Khapa, the founder of the Gelugpa tradition of Tibetan Buddhism to which the Dalai Lama belonged) which had been destroyed during the Cultural Revolution.

1972–   **Tsering Shakya** (?1959–) was among the young refugees who became historians in their new country (in his case the United Kingdom).

1981–87   Late in 1981 or early in 1982, **Geshe Lobsang Wangchuk** (?1914–87), a Tibetan lama and Buddhist scholar was arrested for writing leaflets on the history of independent Tibet. He disputed the Chinese claim that Tibet had always been part of Chinese territory. In February 1984 he was charged with "nurturing ideas to separate Tibet from the motherland" and sentenced to eighteen years' imprisonment. In November 1987 he died in prison in unknown circumstances. He was reportedly ill-treated in detention on several occasions, first in Drapchi prison, Lhasa, later in a labor camp at Kongpo Nyitri. His death was denied by the authorities, but exile sources said that his body was given to relatives for burial. He had undergone several prison terms since 1959.

pre-1986   In 1986 the traditional Tibetan Buddhist Monlam Chenmo or Great Prayer Ceremony (during which the monks of Lhasa's monasteries traditionally took over civil jurisdiction in Lhasa) took place the first time since 1966, and possibly since 1959.

1988   On 5 March, the last day of the Monlam Chenmo, at least sixty Tibetan monks were imprisoned after a demonstration for independence and held without charge for several months. Some of them were interrogated about Tibetan history. In September **Tsering Dondrup**, one of the monks who had been released in the meantime, argued about Tibetan history with a Work Team sent to Rato monastery. He maintained that Tibet had been independent for millennia and was backed by forty or fifty other monks. The same night he was arrested. In October his trial was announced. At the time, clandestine handwritten synopses of Tibetan history circulated. A number of Tibetan-language copies of *Tibet: A Political History* (1967, 1984), by **Tsepon Wangchuk Deden Shakabpa** (1907–), were smuggled into Tibet and circulated underground among Tibetan intellectuals in government offices, the university, and the monasteries. The book was, however, translated by the Chinese authorities into Chinese so that Chinese academics could publish critiques, which were widely distributed in China and also in translation abroad (e.g., *The Historical Status of China's Tibet*). Shakabpa had served as Tibet's secretary of finance (1930–50). In exile he had been the Dalai Lama's official representative in New Delhi (1959–66).

1991   The Chinese cultural attaché in Ottawa warned the National Film Board that the release of the documentary *A Song for Tibet* could have consequences. The film's version of Tibetan history ran counter to the official Chinese version.

           In March the Monlam Chenmo ceremony was forbidden in order to prevent protests during the commemoration of the 1959 revolt.

1994   **Lukhar Sham** was sentenced to eight years' imprisonment for pur-
            chasing classified documents and planning to send history and econ-
            omy books abroad.

1996–   In October 1996 the monk **Ngawang Tharchin** was administratively
            sentenced to three years' "reeducation through labor" because he
            had interrupted a lecture by a well-known Tibetan historian (name
            unknown) during a reeducation campaign at Drepung monastery,
            near Lhasa, and contradicted the claim that Tibet had been an in-
            tegral part of China since the thirteenth century. In 1997 the cam-
            paign continued and the monks were supposed to accept, inter alia,
            that Tibet had been part of China for centuries.

1997   In July a guidebook on seventeenth-century Tibetan history was of-
            ficially banned at the start of a new literature campaign.

Also see: Indonesia (1965–: Munandar), Japan (*passim*: Nanjing Massacre; 1975:
Nozue; 1982: textbook controversy; 1988: Bertolucci; 1993–94: Kasahara; 2000:
conference), Taiwan (1966–76: Lee Ao), United Kingdom (1995–97: Hong
Kong), United States (1953–63: *FRUS;* 1950–: Lattimore, Schram; 1950: Levenson; 1951: Fairbank).

SOURCES

Albada, J. van, " 'Memory of the World': Report on Destroyed and Damaged Archives",
    Archivum, 1996, no.42: 19, 66.
Algemeen Dagblad, 20 February 1992: 6 (Tsering Shakya).
American Association for the Advancement of Science, *Directory of Persecuted Scien-
    tists, Engineers, and Health Professionals* (Washington) 1992: 6–7, 13, 15; 1994:
    36–40; 1997–98: 4, 35, 47.
———, Human Rights Action Network, *Case CH9539* (23 May & 5 June 1995); *Case
    CH9621.Dan* (28 October 1996, 22 April 1998).
Amnesty International, *No One Is Safe: Political Repression and Abuse of Power in the
    1990s* (London s.d.) Chapter 2: 1.
———, *People's Republic of China: Gross Violations of Human Rights in the Xinjiang
    Uighur Autonomous Region* (WWW-text of ASA 17/18/99; London 1999).
———, *People's Republic of China: Preliminary Findings on Killings of Unarmed Ci-
    vilians, Arbitrary Arrests and Summary Executions since 3 June 1989* (ASA 17/
    60/89; London 1989) 30, 35.
———, *People's Republic of China: State Secrets, a Pretext for Repression* (WWW-
    text of ASA 17/42/96; London 1996).
———, *Report* (London) 1978: 157; 1985: 205–8; 1987: 225–27; 1988: 155; 1989: 169;
    1991: 65; 1992: 88; 1993: 94; 1994: 99–100; 1996: 118; 1997: 119–20; 1998:
    131; 1999: 129; 2000: 73, 75; 2001: 71.
———, *Urgent Action 248/89* (18 July 1989).
Annual Obituary 1985 (Chicago/London) 328–29 (Xia Nai).
Ansley, C., *The Heresy of Wu Han: His Play "Hai Jui's Dismissal" and Its Role in
    China's Cultural Revolution* (Toronto 1971).

Article 19, *Information, Freedom and Censorship: World Report* (London) 1988: 68; 1991: 156, 158.

———, "The Feast of Lies: Censorship in China's Famine of 1959–1961", in: Article 19, *Starving in Silence; A Report on Famine and Censorship* (London 1990) 15–87.

———, *The Year of the Lie: Censorship and Disinformation in the People's Republic of China 1989* (London 1989) 67.

Asia Research Center ed., *The Great Cultural Revolution* (Tokyo 1968) 91–115, 126–27, 132–33, 138–39, 155, 158, 161–62, 177–78, 181–82, 187–88, 196, 199–203, 420, 425.

Auer, L., "Archival Losses and Their Impact on the Work of Archivists and Historians", *Archivum*, 1996, no.42: 4.

Barmé, G., "History for the Masses", in: Unger ed. 1993: 272–73, 276, 278, 279.

———, "Memory As the Enemy of Tyranny", *Far Eastern Economic Review*, 19 May 1988: 49.

———, "My Friend the Memory Hole: A Comment on Living with Deng Xiaoping's 'Anti-Bourglib' Campaign", *Renditions*, 1987, Autumn: 6.

———, "Using the Past to Save the Present: Dai Qing's Historiographical Dissent", *East Asian History*, 1991, no. 1: 141–81.

——— & L. Jaivin eds., *New Ghosts, Old Dreams: Chinese Rebel Voices* (New York 1992) 28–29, 31–32, 62, 73, 138–64, 173–77, 180–82, 184, 291–92, 358–59, 362.

Barraclough, G., *Main Trends in History* (New York 1979) 210.

Bartke, W., *Die großen Chinesen der Gegenwart* (Frankfurt 1985) 87–91, 251–53, 258–59.

———, *Who's Who in the People's Republic of China* (Munich 1991) 127, 203–4, 355–56, 652.

———, *Who Was Who in the People's Republic of China* (Munich 1997) 55, 77, 101–2, 126–27, 186, 275–76, 360, 504, 511, 590, 699.

Beasley, W.G., & E.G. Pulleyblank eds., *Historians of China and Japan* (London 1961).

Biographical Profile of Yongyi Song (WWW-text 2000).

Boia, L. ed., *Great Historians of the Modern Age: An International Dictionary* (Westport 1991) 123–24, 127–32, 134, 141–42.

Boorman, H.L., "Mao Tse-tung As Historian", in: Feuerwerker ed. 1968: 327.

——— & R.C. Howard eds., *Biographical Dictionary of Republican China* (New York) vol. 1 (1967): 24–26, 259–61, 354–58, 366–71; vol. 2 (1968): 30–37, 43–46, 245–47, 276, 283–85, 289–92, 428–31; vol. 3 (1970): 67–69, 241–43, 317–18, 345–47, 425–430; vol. 5 (1971): 389–90.

Boyd, K. ed., *Encyclopedia of Historians and Historical Writing* (London/Chicago 1999) 198–200, 204, 206, 214, 493–94.

Brown, S., D. Collinson & R. Wilkinson eds., *Biographical Dictionary of Twentieth-Century Philosophers* (London/New York 1996) 230–32, 291–92, 351–52, 354–56, 460–61, 465–66, 640–41.

Bruch, R. vom, & R. A. Müller eds., *Historikerlexikon: Von der Antike bis zum 20. Jahrhundert* (Munich 1991) 121–22.

Burguière, A. ed., *Dictionnaire des sciences historiques* (Paris 1986) 122–24.

Cheek, T., "Deng Tuo: Culture, Leninism and Alternative Marxism in the Chinese Communist Party", *China Quarterly*, 1981: 470–91.

Chesneaux, J., "Les Travaux d'histoire moderne et contemporaine en Chine Populaire", *Revue historique*, 1956: 275–76, 280–81.

China Information, Winter 1989–1990: 24–27 (Su Xiaokang).

Chong, W.L., "Su Xiaokang on His Film *River Elegy*", *China Information*, Winter 1989–90: 44–55.

Copper, J.F., *Historical Dictionary of Taiwan* (Metuchen 1993) 26.

Demiéville, P., "Chang Hsüeh-ch'eng and His Historiography", in: Beasley & Pulleyblank eds. 1961: 176.

Ding Zilin, *Documenting Death: Reflections after Ten Years* (WWW-text 1999).

Dirlik, A., & L. Schneider, "The People's Republic of China", in: G. Iggers & H.T. Parker eds., *International Handbook of Historical Studies: Contemporary Research and Theory* (London/Westport 1979) 354–56, 358–61.

Edmunds C., "The Politics of Historiography: Jian Bozan's Historicism", in: M. Goldman, T. Cheek, & C.L. Hamrin eds., *China's Intellectuals and the State: In Search of a New Relationship* (Cambridge 1987) 65–106, 318–24.

Embree, A.T., et al. eds., *Encyclopedia of Asian History* (New York 1988) vol. 2: 426–27; vol. 4: 240.

Fang Lizhi, "The Chinese Amnesia", *New York Review of Books*, 27 September 1990: 30–31.

Fathers, M., & A. Higgins, *Tiananmen: The Rape of Peking* (London 1989) 21–22.

Feuerwerker, A. ed., *History in Communist China* (Cambridge 1968) viii–ix, 8–9, 18–21, 34, 42, 53, 70–71, 100, 209–10, 335–38.

Fisher, T., " 'The Play's the Thing': Wu Han and Hai Rui Revisited", in: Unger ed. 1993: 9–45.

Fokkema, D.W., "Chinese Criticism of Humanism: Campaigns against the Intellectuals 1964–1965", *China Quarterly*, 1966, April–June: 71–76.

Fowler, D.D., "Uses of the Past: Archeology in the Service of the State", *American Antiquity*, 1987: 237–38.

Goldman, M., *China's Intellectuals: Advise and Dissent* (Cambridge 1981) 51, 55, 71–72, 142.

———, "The Role of History in Party Struggle, 1962–4", *China Quarterly*, 1972: 502–3, 506–7, 509–12.

Gray J., "Historical Writing in Twentieth-Century China: Notes on Its Background and Development", in: Beasley & Pulleyblank eds. 202–4, 212.

Guillermaz, J., *The Chinese Communist Party in Power, 1949–76* (Boulder 1976) 52–53, 356, 362.

Hoeven, H. van der, *Lost Memory: Libraries and Archives Destroyed in the Twentieth Century,* part 1, *Libraries* (WWW-text 1996) 4, 7–8, 15–16.

Houn, F.W., *To Change a Nation: Propaganda and Indoctrination in Communist China* (New York 1964) 58–60, 85, 130–35.

Human Rights in China, *Prisoner Profile: Li Hai* (WWW-text 1997).

Human Rights Watch, *Ifex Alert*, 11 December 1996: 2; 15 January 1997: 3–4.

———, Letters, Academic Freedom Project to Song Jian (State Commission on Science and Technology) (16 February 1993) and President Jiang Zemin (7 November 1996).

———, *World Report* (Washington) 1993: 162; 1994: 152–53; 1995: 143–46; 1996: xxviii, 127, 133, 142, 148–49, 365, 376; 1998: 172–73, 177; 454–55; 1999: 177–78; 2000: 180, 182; 2001: 183–4; 187; 189.

Index on Censorship, 1/80: 13–15, 17, 46; 4/81: 16–18; 5/81: 4–5, 40; 6/81: 85–89; 6/
    85: 44; 4/86: 37; 2/89: 16–19; 4/89: 37; 8/89: 10, 12–14, 19; 1/90: 42; 5/90: 4–5;
    7/90: 35; 9/90: 26; 10/90: 35; 1/91: 17, 22, 34–35; 2/91: 36; 3/91: 37; 7/91: 12–
    14; 10/91: 53; 2/92: 35; 8/92: 3; 15–27, 28–30; 9/92: 42; 2/93: 35; 3/93: 35; 4/
    93: 35; 5–6/93: 43; 1–2/94: 235; 3/94: 169; 4/95: 173; 5/95: 174; 6/95: 80–81,
    172; 1/96: 173; 2/96: 84; 4/96: 97; 5/96: 104–5; 6/96: 171; 1/97: 56–57, 69, 76,
    95–97, 108, 114, 124; 5/97: 185; 1/98: 83, 101; 4/98: 11; 6/98: 141–45; 2/99:
    103, 166–67; 3/99: 100; 4/99: 131–32; 5/99: 90; 6/99: 41, 236; 1/00: 91–92; 2/
    00: 97; 3/00: 90–91; 4/00: 91–92; 5/00: 92–94; 02/01: 99.
International Herald Tribune, 2000 (19 January: Song Yongyi, 12 April: Li Shenzhi).
International PEN Writers in Prison Committee, *Half-Yearly Caselist* (London) 1997:
    26–27, 29; 1998: 25.
————, *Ifex Alert*, 8 June 1999, 23 January 2001 (Jiang Qisheng), 9 May 2001 (Tohti
    Muzart).
Jeffery, K., & C. Lennon, "Historians, Politics and Ideology: Report", in: *17th Interna-
    tional Congress of Historical Sciences*, vol. 2, *Chronological Section/Methodol-
    ogy* (Madrid 1992) 1066.
Jian Bozan, Shao Xunzheng, & Hu Hua, *A Concise History of China* (Beijing 1986) 244.
Journal of Asian Studies, 1982: 441–42 (Gu Jiegang).
Kasur Lodi, G. Gyari, "Tibet: The Right to Self-Determination", in: Unrepresented
    Nations and Peoples Organization, *The Question of Self-Determination: The
    Cases of East Timor, Tibet and Western Sahara* (Geneva 1996) 31.
Keesings historisch archief, 1991: 492; 1997: 277; 1999: 369, 428–29.
Kuiken, K., "Hong Kong and Macau" (manuscript for D. Jones ed., *Censorship: A World
    Encyclopedia* [London/Chicago 2001]) 5–6.
Landsberger, S.R., "The 1989 Student Demonstrations in Beijing: A Chronology of
    Events", *China Information*, Summer 1989: 37–56.
Letters American Association of University Professors, 6 January & 1 February 2000
    (Song Yongyi).
Leys, S., *Les Habits neufs du président Mao: Chronique de la "Révolution culturelle"*
    (Paris 1971) 50–51, 267–72, 286–87, 297–98.
————, *Ombres chinoises* (Paris 1974) 139–40.
Libération, 15 June 1989: 37 (Yang Tao).
Li Yu-ning, "Wu Han's View of History", in: *Collected Documents of the First Sino-
    American Conference on Mainland China* (Taiwan 1971) 413–26.
MacFarquhar, R., & J.K. Fairbank eds., *The Cambridge History of China*, vol. 14 (Cam-
    bridge 1987) 237–38, 453–54, 458–59, 472, 475.
————, *The Cambridge History of China*, vol. 15 (Cambridge 1991) 601.
Martin, D.A.L., *The Making of a Sino-Marxist World View: Perceptions and Interpre-
    tations of World History in the People's Republic of China* (Armonk, N.Y./Lon-
    don 1990) 22, 25, 27–28, 30–32, 35, 37, 55, 90, 94, 105, 112–13, 117–18.
Mazur, M.G., "Studying Wu Han: The Political Academic", *Republican China*, 1990:
    17–39.
Mok, K.H., *Intellectuals and the State in Post-Mao China* (London/New York 1998) 30,
    47–53, 64–65, 73–76, 109–12, 185–87.
Munro, R., "Settling Accounts with the Cultural Revolution at Beijing University 1977–
    78", *China Quarterly*, 1980: 309, 322–23, 329–30.

NRC Handelsblad, 14 December 1995: 4; 22 February 1997: 4 (Chen Xiaoya), 2 December 2000: 36–37 (Uighur historians).

O'Neill, H.B., *Companion to Chinese History* (New York/Oxford 1987) 2, 122.

Pak-wah Leung E., *Historical Dictionary of Revolutionary China 1839–1976* (New York 1992) 155–58.

Peschel, S. ed., *Die gelbe Kultur, der Film Heshang: Traditionskritik in China* (Bad Honnef 1991) 88–91, 102–3.

Price, R.F., *Education in Modern China* (London 1979) 164, 267.

Pusey, J.R., *Wu Han: Attacking the Present through the Past* (Cambridge 1969).

Richter, U., "Gu Jiegang: His Last Thirty Years", *China Quarterly*, 1982: 286–95.

————, "Zweifel am Altertum: Gu Jiegang und die Diskussion über Chinas alte Geschichte als Konsequenz der 'Neuen Kulturbewegung' ca. 1915–1923" (Stuttgart 1992) 176–78.

Schneider, L.A., "From Textual Criticism to Social Criticism: The Historiography of Ku Chieh-kang", *Journal of Asian Studies*, 1968–69: 772.

Schram, S. ed., *Mao Tse-tung Unrehearsed, Talks and Letters: 1956–71* (Harmondsworth 1974) 234, 237, 239, 256, 330–31, 336–37.

Schwarcz, V., *The Chinese Enlightenment: Intellectuals and the Legacy of the May Fourth Movement of 1919* (Berkeley 1986) 20, 28–29, 64, 99, 173, 180–81, 220, 230–32, 252, 255, 272–73, 279, 281.

————, "Strangers No More: Personal Memory in the Interstices of Public Commemoration", in: R.S. Watson ed., *Memory, History, and Opposition under State Socialism* (Santa Fe 1994) 53, 60.

Schwartz, R.D., *Circle of Protest: Political Ritual in the Tibetan Uprising* (London 1994) 104, 118–9, 130.

Shakabpa, T.W.D., *Tibet: A Political History* (New York 1984) cover.

Smith, W.W. Jr., *Tibetan Nation: A History of Tibetan Nationalism and Sino-Tibetan Relations* (Boulder 1996) 594, 607–8, 617.

Sullivan, L.R., *Historical Dictionary of the People's Republic of China 1949–1997* (Lanham 1997) 92, 98, 101–3, 121, 125, 234, 238.

Thurston, A.F., *Enemies of the People* (New York 1987) 133–34, 140, 145–46, 312.

————, "Memory and Mourning: China Ten Years after Tiananmen", *SAIS Review*, Summer–Fall 1999: 65–66, 71, 74–75.

———— & J.H. Parker eds., *Humanistic and Social Science Research in China: Recent History and Future Prospects* (New York 1980) 3, 11, 15, 17, 21–25, 29, 31, 34–35, 39–41, 43–46, 49–50, 55, 60.

Tong, E., "Thirty Years of Chinese Archaeology", in: P.L. Kohl & C. Fawcett eds., *Nationalism, Politics, and the Practice of Archaeology* (Cambridge 1995) 178, 182–83, 189–90, 193–97.

Trager, F.N., & W. Henderson eds., *Communist China, 1949–1969: A Twenty-Year Appraisal* (New York 1970) 240.

Trigger, B.G., "Alternative Archaeologies: Nationalist, Colonialist, Imperialist", *Man*, 1984: 359.

————, *A History of Archaeological Thought* (Cambridge 1989) 175–76.

Tucker, M. ed., *Literary Exile in the Twentieth Century: An Analysis and Biographical Dictionary* (Westport 1991) 649.

Uhally, S. Jr., "The Wu Han Discussion: Act One in a New Rectification Campaign", *China Mainland Review*, 1966, March: 24, 34–35.

Unger, J. ed., *Using the Past to Serve the Present: Historiography in Contemporary China* (Armonk 1993).

Unrepresented Nations and Peoples Organization, *"China's Tibet": The World's Largest Remaining Colony; Report of a Fact-Finding Mission and Analyses of Colonialism and Chinese Rule in Tibet* ([The Hague 1997]) 11–12, 62, 66.

Vermeer, E.B., "Geschiedschrijving en overheid in China", in: R.B. van de Weijer, P.G.B. Thissen, & R. Schönberger eds., *Tussen traditie en wetenschap: Geschiedbeoefening in niet-westerse culturen* (Nijmegen 1987) 72.

Wagner, R.G., "In Guise of a Congratulation: Political Symbolism in Zhou Xinfang's Play *Hai Rui Submits His Memorial*", in: Unger ed. 1993: 49, 54, 62–63.

Wakeman, F. Jr., "Historiography in China after 'Smashing the *Gang of Four*' ", *China Quarterly*, 1978: 891–92.

Wang, G., "Loving the Ancient in China", in: I. McBryde ed., *Who Owns the Past?* (Melbourne 1986) 190–91.

Wang, J., & N. Gyaincain, *The Historical Status of China's Tibet* (WWW-text; [Beijing] 1998).

Wang, Q., "Western Historiography in the P.R. China (1949 to Present)", *Storia della storiografia*, 1991, no. 19: 28–30, 33–35, 38–39, 46.

Weigelin-Schwiedrzik, S., "Parteigeschichtsschreibung und ihr Selbstverständnis— Zwischen Propaganda und Wissenschaft", *Periplus*, 1991: 90–91.

———, "Party Historiography", in: Unger ed. 1993: 154–55.

Winters, C. ed., *International Dictionary of Anthropologists* (New York/London 1991) 407–8, 532–33, 773–74.

Woolf, D.R. ed., *A Global Encyclopedia of Historical Writing* (New York/London 1998) 133–34, 156, 166, 169–70, 312, 384–85, 426, 428, 751–52, 830–31, 972–73, 976–77.

World University Service, *Academic Freedom* (London) 1990: 174; 1995: 122–24, 129, 133, 137.

Wu Han, *Le Tyran de Nankin: Empereur des Ming* (originally Chinese 1943; Paris 1991).

Wu Yuan-li, et al., *Human Rights in the People's Republic of China* (Boulder/London 1988) 167.

Zhelokhovtsev, A., "Guo Moruo: 'Hero' or Victim of the 'Cultural Revolution'?", *Far Eastern Affairs*, 1982: 129–30, 133–34.

COLOMBIA

1942–59   In 1942–44, 1945, and 1948–57, historian and diplomat **Germán Arciniegas** (1900–99) accepted a series of professorships at the University of Chicago, the University of California at Berkeley, and Columbia University in the United States because the political climate in which he served as Colombia's minister of education (1941–42, 1945–46), was too dangerous. Around 1954, while in exile, he was detained as a suspected communist at a New York airport on his return from a three-month European vacation and released only after a media campaign. Because of his writings against Latin American dictators, he was reportedly put on the hit list of Dominican

President Rafael Trujillo. Other dictators banned his books. In 1959 he resumed his diplomatic career as an ambassador to Italy, Israel, Venezuela, and the Vatican. He became president of the Academia Colombiana de Historia (Colombian Academy of History).

1985–   In 1985 a history textbook controversy took place. In several October and November issues of *El Tiempo*, Colombia's largest newspaper, Arciniegas [q.v. 1942–59] accused history textbook author **Rodolfo Ramón de Roux** (who with Fernando Torres Londoño had published the two-volume 1984 textbook *Nuestra Historia*) of omitting or ridiculing the most important figures of the independence period and of overemphasizing contemporary history. He labeled the New History approach in this and other textbooks Marxist and unpatriotic, as Roberto María Tisnés, another academy member, had already done in 1979. Despite the moral condemnation from the academy, the textbooks continued to be used in the schools. In 1988 a third volume in the textbook series was published, *Historia de Colombia*, written by **Silvia Duzzan** and **Salomón Kalmanovitz**, the latter probably a professor emeritus at the National University. Apparently, a judgment of the academy condemning the New History methodology used in the textbook was cited approvingly in the daily *El Siglo*. In the Medellín newspaper *El Colombiano* of 7 March 1989, an academy member added that it depicted Spaniards and Creoles unfavorably, thus inciting hatred against them. The academy reportedly urged the minister of education to censor the textbook. A petition from teachers and professors at the National University endorsed the textbook and criticized the academy's dogmatic attitude.

1992   In [May] Canadian archeologist **Steve Gordon** was apparently killed by the 34th Front of the Fuerzas Armadas Revolucionarias de Colombia (FARC) guerrilla movement in the De Los Katíos National Park in northern Colombia after being kidnapped in February.

1998   In April lawyer and professor of law **José Eduardo Mendoza** was killed by two unidentified persons, probably because he had attempted to reopen the inquiry into the 9 April 1948 assassination of liberal presidential candidate Jorge Eliécer Gaitán, a crucial event in Colombian contemporary history.

1999   In September the remains of historian **Darío Betancourt Echeverry** were found in a rural area outside Bogotá. He had been abducted by gunmen in April. A specialist on political violence, Betancourt had headed the social sciences department at the National Pedagogical University, Bogotá. Military intelligence files had reportedly linked his name to armed opposition groups. In 1998, however, the Twentieth Brigade of the Colombian army, responsible for military intelligence, had been disbanded after their involvement in human-rights violations against people on whom they had filed false information. The government repeatedly stated that it was committed to revising military intelligence archives in order to prevent further human-rights violations, but no such revisions had taken place.

SOURCES

Ambrus, S., "German Arciniegas: Guardian of our Distinct History", *Americas*, May/June 1997: 40–45.
American Association for the Advancement of Science, Human Rights Action Network, *Case CO9908*. Bet (23 June & 8 October 1999).
Amnesty International, *Urgent Action 103/99* (11 May, 15 September 1999).
Colmenares, G., "Der Schulbuchstreit in Kolumbien", in: M. Riekenberg ed. 1990: 97–100.
Index on Censorship, 3/98: 88; 4/98: 109–10.
Human Rights Watch, *State of War: Political Violence and Counterinsurgency in Colombia* (WWW-text; Washington December 1993).
———, *World Report 2000* (Washington 1999) xxvii, 458.
König, H.-J., "Die 'fahrenden Ritter des Patriotismus': zur Haltung der kolumbianischen Akademie der Geschichte gegenüber Problemen des sozialen Wandels", in: Riekenberg ed. 1990: 108, 110, 115.
Riekenberg, M. ed., *Lateinamerika: Geschichtsunterricht, Geschichtslehrbücher, Geschichtsbewusstsein* (Frankfurt/Main 1990).
Tenenbaum, B.A. ed., *Encyclopedia of Latin American History and Culture*, vol. 1 (New York 1996) 137–38.
World University Service, *Academic Freedom 1990* (London 1990) 18, 37.

COMOROS

1988   In March history teachers **Said Dhiofir** and **Said Nassur** were arrested together with two former government ministers on the island of Mohéli (Mwali), apparently because they distributed a leaflet signed by an organization called Comité pour la Défense des Intérêts de Mohéli, which criticized the government for discriminating against and marginalizing the Mohéli minority. All were released without charge after about two months.

SOURCES

Amnesty International, *Report 1989* (London 1989) 45.
Index on Censorship, 6/88: 35.

CONGO

After 1970, it was apparently very difficult for Zairese (Congolese) historians to write on postindependence history, especially contemporary political history.

President Joseph Mobutu Sese Seko's official policy of authenticity and return to the roots notwithstanding, freedom of speech restrictions reportedly made it impossible to develop any historical reflections that started from the present. The situation appeared to have worsened after the April 1990 political reforms.

Belgian Congo

1951   A bulaam (local community historian) of the Bushong, the ruling Kuba people, was possibly poisoned by the Bushong king for relating traditions to the European district commissioner that were reportedly harmful to the royal interest.

1953   In October another bulaam, **Shep Mathias**, was possibly poisoned on orders of the king with acid from a car battery, reportedly because he had told historian Vansina [q.v. 1971] "too many secrets".

Congo

1967   In April *Lumumba Patrice: Les cinquante derniers, jours de sa vie* (Brussels/Paris 1966), a book by **G. Heinz** and **H[enri] Donnay** about the house arrest, escape, imprisonment, transfer to Katanga, and assassination on 17 January 1961 of Congo's first prime minister, Patrice Lumumba (1925–61), was confiscated by the security services one day after its distribution and successful sale, including sale at the Parliament. The book, originally meant to be an element in an official campaign to rehabilitate Lumumba, suggested that some government members were implicated in the assassination and came at a moment when Mobutu (ruled 1965–98) wanted to abolish all political parties, including the one founded by Lumumba (and of which Mobutu had been a member before).

Zaire

1971   In June three history students (names unknown) "disappeared" when Lovanium University, Kinshasa, was closed. In protest, historian **Jan Vansina** (1929–), professor at the universities of Madison, Wisconsin, United States (1960–94) and Lovanium, resigned in the fall by taking a "leave of undetermined length". He was told that he could not return to Zaire anymore. Lovanium was nationalized and later merged with the universities of Kisangani and Lubumbashi into the National University of Zaire. In November the history department was transferred to Lubumbashi. Twenty years later it became known that two of the "disappeared" students had been sent to Ekafera concentration camp in the rain forests but had survived. The third student had not been heard from or seen since the abduction.

1981–   Philosopher, historian, and writer **Valentin-Yves Mudimbe** (1941–), professor at the National University of Zaire (1974–81), fled to the

United States to avoid punishment after refusing to enter the Central Committee of the Mouvement Populaire de la Révolution (Popular Revolutionary Movement; the only political party legally allowed), to which he had been named by presidential decree. He was appointed a professor of comparative literature and anthropology at Duke University, Durham, North Carolina, and later a professor of French and Italian at Stanford University.

In December 1981 **Ernest Wamba-dia-Wamba** (1942–), Zairese history and philosophy lecturer at Dar-es-Salaam University, Tanzania (1980–), was arrested when he entered Zaire for a visit to his parents and for research on opposition movements from 1963 to 1969. His travel documents were confiscated and he was searched. The Military Intelligence and Security Service G2 found some student papers, an incomplete manuscript, and his notes from a Washington conference. He was held incommunicado for more than a month and beaten at the OAU-2 prison. He was accused of possessing subversive documents and of having links with opposition movements. In 1971 he had resigned his post as a cabinet director in the ministry of social welfare, labor and housing, to protest the repression of the students at the closure of Lovanium, and gone into exile in the United States and Tanzania. In 1971–80 he studied and lectured at Boston College and Brandeis University, among other venues. He had been involved with a group of Zairese exile academics who had published commentaries on the developments in Zaire. At the time of his arrest, he was returning from a tour in the United States where he had participated in a conference organized by Zairese scholars in Washington, D.C. After an international protest campaign, including an intervention from Tanzanian President Julius Nyerere, he was released from prison without trial in January 1982. He had to report to the state security offices every other day until he was definitively released in October. He was forbidden to return to Zaire until 1992, when he was invited by the Sovereign National Conference to participate in its scientific group. He was the author, with historian Jacques Depelchin, of the *African Declaration against Genocide* (1997). In 1997 he was the president of the Conseil pour le Développement de la Recherche en Sciences Sociales en Afrique (Codesria; Council for the Development of Social Science Research in Africa) at Dakar, Senegal. From 1998 he has been a leader of the Rassemblement Congolais pour la Démocratie (RCD; Congolese Rally for Democracy), engaged in a rebellion against the government of Presidents Laurent-Désiré Kabila and Joseph Kabila.

1984   In [May] some official archives were reportedly burned in Lubumbashi.

Congo

2000　On 26 July BBC television producer **Caroline Parr** was detained in Kinshasa by the security services, along with her assistant and **Jonas Munkamba**, whom she was interviewing about the 1961 assassination of Lumumba.

Also see Belgium (1940s: Congo Free State archives; 1959–: Boelaert; 1975–: Marchal; 1986: Vangroenweghe).

SOURCES

Amnesty International, *Report* (London) 1982: 95; 1983: 96.

Boele van Hensbroek, P., personal communication, July 1999.

Boyd, K. ed., *Encyclopedia of Historians and Historical Writing* (London/Chicago 1999) 1252–53.

Brown, S., D. Collinson, & R. Wilkinson eds., *Biographical Dictionary of Twentieth-Century Philosophers* (London/New York 1996) 551–52.

Duffy, J., M. Frey, & M. Sins eds., *International Directory of Scholars and Specialists in African Studies* (Waltham, Mass. 1978) 300.

Index on Censorship, 1/82: 48; 2/82: 48; 4/82: 48; 5/82: 49–50; 1/83: 48; 5/00: 96.

Jewsiewicki, B., & D. Newbury eds., *African Historiographies: What History for Which Africa?* (Londen/Beverly Hills 1986).

Mbata Mangu Bétukumesu, A., "Zaire: Academic Freedom under Siege", in: Codesria, *The State of Academic Freedom in Africa 1995* (Dakar 1996) 155.

Mwa Bawele, M., "Authenticité, histoire et développement", *Authenticité et développement* (Kinshasa/Dakar 1982) 186–87.

———, "L'Évolution de l'historiographie en Afrique centrale: Le Cas du Zaïre", *Storia della storiografia*, 1991, no. 19: 100, 105–6.

——— & Sabakinu Kivilu, "Historical Research in Zaire: Present Status and Future Perspectives", in: Jewsiewicki & Newbury eds. 1986: 227, 229.

Slater, H., "Dar es Salaam and the Postnationalist Historiography of Africa", in: Jewsiewicki & Newbury eds. 1986: 257–58.

Vansina, J., *Living with Africa* (Madison 1994) 17–18, 154, 164–66, 219, 259–60, 285.

———, personal communication, August 1999.

Vinck, H., personal communication, July 1999.

"Wamba Dia Wamba, historien zairois: Les Intellectuels ont contribué au maintien du régime de Mobutu", *Le Jour*, 27 March 1997 (WWW-text).

Willame, J.-C., *Patrice Lumumba: La Crise congolaise revisitée* (Paris 1990) 477–79.

Woolf, D.R. ed., *A Global Encyclopedia of Historical Writing* (New York/London 1998) 915–16.

COSTA RICA

See Brazil (1971–79: Cardoso), Dominican Republic (1935–: Bosch), El Salvador (1970–: Pérez Brignoli, 1987–92: Argueta), Nicaragua (1975–77: Benavides).

CROATIA

pre-1991   *See* Yugoslavia.

1991   The museum in Vukovar, housing materials from the Copper Age, was destroyed in the Serbian siege.

1992   In January the Croatian television banned the screening of all films dealing with both World Wars and portraying Germany as the aggressor. Among European Community members, Germany took the lead in supporting Croatia's declaration of independence.

            In an open letter reported by Tanjug news agency in February, Serbian university professors and lecturers based in Croatia alleged that they were discriminated against and that the library of the Slavonian Orthodox eparchy at Pakrac, which contained many old manuscripts and documents as well as some 5,500 books, had been destroyed "in an effort to obliterate all traces of Serbs in these territories".

1995   In February members of Parliament launched a Croatian Statehood Campaign, in which they accused the media of being anti-Croatian and of falsifying Croatian history.

1996–98   In May 1996 **Viktor Ivančić**, chief editor of the satirical Split weekly *Feral Tribune*, and commentator **Marinko Čulić** were charged with "rudely and falsely slandering" President (and historian) Franjo Tudjman because in April they had published an article and photomontage, "Bones in the Mixer", criticizing Tudjman's plans to rebury the remains of Croatian fascists alongside their victims at the Jasenovac concentration camp. In the camp between 100,000 and 150,000 Serbs, Gypsies, Jews, and Croat partisans were killed during World War II. After a long trial, started in June 1996, with acquittal (September), appeal (October), annulment of appeal (May 1997), and many adjournments, the accused were acquitted in December 1998.

1996   In December **Ivo Banac** (1947–), history professor and master of Pierson College at Yale University, professor at the Central European University in Budapest, corresponding member of the Croatian Academy of Sciences and Arts, and board member of the human-rights organization Croatian Helsinki Committee, was labeled an "internal enemy" by Tudjman. Among the probable reasons was Banac's plea for the repatriation of Croatian Serbs at a June 1996 conference. In the fall of 1993, he had written an open letter to Tudjman in the journal *Erasmus*, together with five other Croatian intellectuals, including historian **Krsto [=Christopher] Cviić**, an editor for the BBC World Service (1964–69), journalist for *The Econ-*

omist (1969–90), and editor of the periodicals *The World Today* (1984–) and *Tjednik*. In the letter Tudjman was criticized for his policies and asked to resign.

SOURCES

Amnesty International, *Report* (London) 1997: 131; 1998: 146; 1999: 143.

Bahn, P.G., *The Cambridge Illustrated History of Archaeology* (Cambridge 1996) 365.

Banac, I., "Historiography of the Countries of Eastern Europe: Yugoslavia", *American Historical Review*, 1992: xiii.

Baudet, F., personal communication, October 1996, June 1997.

Human Rights Watch, *World Report* (New York) 1997: 212–13; 1999: 258.

Index on Censorship, 4/92: 40–41; 5/92: 35; 2/95: 173; 4/96: 22–24, 97; 6/96: 172; 4/97: 110; 1/98: 86; 2/98: 87; 2/99: 104.

International PEN Writers in Prison Committee, *Half-Yearly Caselist* (London) 1997: 45; 1998: 42.

Keesings historisch archief, 1998: 543.

Kolanović, J., "Archives en temps de guerre: L'Expérience de la Croatie", *Archivum*, 1996, no.42: 177.

Maletić, F. ed., *Who Is Who in Croatia* (Zagreb 1993) 31–33.

Stallaerts, R., & J. Laurens *Historical Dictionary of the Republic of Croatia* (Metuchen, N.J. 1995) 32, 72.

CUBA

After the victory of Fidel Castro's guerrilla forces on 1 January 1959, several leading historians went into exile. Study of the 1930s and early 1940s, when the pre-1959 Partido Socialista Popular (Communist Party) cooperated with the emergent military leader Fulgencio Batista, was sensitive. Following the severing of relations with the United States, contacts among Cuban and American historians and access to Cuban archival sources were seriously hampered.

[1952–]   In [1952] historian of Latin America **Manuel Moreno Fraginals** (1920–) was exiled by the Batista government and went to Venezuela, where he became a businessman. In 1959 he again took up his career as a historian in the United States, specializing in the history of Cuban slavery and sugar. He was denied the opportunity to teach at Havana University for political reasons. In 1997–98 he was a professor at Florida International University, in 2000 at Yale University.

1953–55   When imprisoned on Isla de Piñas, future Prime Minister Fidel Castro Ruz (1927–) was said to have organized a school for the study of history and philosophy, named the Abel Santamaría Academy, in order to give the other prisoners his understanding of political, social, and economic realities in Cuba.

Among the historians who went into exile after Castro came to power were the following:

1959–   **Herminio Portell Vilá** (1901–), a professor of history of the Americas at Havana University and adversary of the Castro government, went into exile in the United States where he taught and worked as a newspaper and radio commentator on international events in Washington, D.C. He had published historical works about the relations between Cuba, Spain, and the United States.

           Carlos Márquez Sterling y Guiral (1898–1991), politician and historian, author of many biographies, president of the 1940 Constitutional Assembly, minister of education (1942–43), and presidential candidate in November 1958, went into exile in the United States, where he worked at Columbia University, New York (1962–64), and at C.W. Post College (1964–79).

1959–68   **Emeterio Santovenia y Echaide** (1889–1968), historian, journalist, author, and director of the Cuban Archives, was arrested. As a statesman and former secretary to the president, he had been a loyal supporter of Batista throughout the 1950s. He opposed those governments that he believed were depriving the Cuban people of their rights. He died in Miami.

1960–   **Leví Marrero y Artiles** (1911–), geographer and professor of economic history at Havana University, went into exile. He taught in Venezuela (1960–65) and Puerto Rico (1965–72). He wrote the fifteen-volume *Cuba: Economía y Sociedad* (1974–[92]).

           Fermín Peraza y Sarausa (1907–69), historian, librarian, bibliographer, and director of the Municipal Library of Havana (1930–60), voluntarily went into exile. He continued his bio-bibliographical research in Colombia (1960–62) and the United States (1962–69). His *Anuario Bibliográfico Cubano* was published without interruption between 1938 and 1968.

           Historian of Latin American women **Asunción Lavrin** emigrated to the United States while a history student. She eventually became a history professor at Arizona State University, Tempe (1988–).

1961   According to an exiled teacher who had worked in a private school, books on religious history had been burned by government representatives a few months before the June 1961 nationalization of the private schools. One exiled school librarian told that she and her colleagues had been expected to eliminate the old history books completely; they had been given Marxist-inspired guidelines for the teaching of Cuban history.

1980–88   In 1980 **Ariel Hidalgo Guillén** (?1945–), historian, academic and writer, author of the textbook *Origins of the Worker Movement and Socialist Thought in Cuba* (1976), professor of philosophy and economics at the Manolito Aguiar Workers' College, was arrested when helping a friend who was being harassed by a mob because he wanted to leave Cuba. After three days Hidalgo was released but harassment began. In August 1981 he was rearrested and after a thirty-minute trial sentenced to eight years' imprisonment for "enemy propaganda". He was convicted because of his unpublished manuscript, "Cuba, the Marxist State and the New Class: A Dialectical-Materialist Study", which strongly criticized the new ruling class in Cuba and other communist countries from an orthodox Marxist viewpoint. In the trial transcript, he was called a "leftist revisionist", and his sentence specified that his books should be burned (it is unknown whether they were actually burned). Hidalgo spent the first fourteen months in solitary confinement in a special section of Combinado del Este Prison (Havana) known as the Rectangle of Death. In October and November 1986, he went on hunger strike as a protest against the arrest of several members of the unofficial human-rights group Comité Cubano Pro Derechos Humanos (CCPDH). Hidalgo had become CCPDH vice president in prison. He was said to have been fed intravenously. After his hunger strike, he was moved to a punishment cell in the Rectangle of Death, where he was held for five days without drinking water. He was solitarily confined for two or three more weeks. On 10 December 1987, Human-Rights Day, he staged a new hunger strike because food rations for common prisoners were less adequate than for political prisoners. He was again taken to the Rectangle of Death. In August 1988 he was released and went into exile in Miami, where he became active in a human rights information center.

1988   In 1988 **Enrique López**, a Roman Catholic intellectual and part-time history professor at Havana University, publisher of *Noticias Religiosas de Cuba* (1987–), suffered harassment. He was openly watched by his neighbors and had his telephone cut off when important foreign visitors were in Havana, as happened during the 1988 visit of the United Nations Commission on Human Rights. In 1989 *Noticias Religiosas de Cuba* had to suspend publication, unable to obtain newsprint and spare parts for its duplicator.

In February a CCPDH art exhibit, reportedly the first independent art exhibit in Cuba since 1959 and featuring the Afro-Cuban works of an artist who explored the legacy of nineteenth-century Cuban slavery, was disrupted by an aggressive crowd of "neighbors" presumably sponsored by the state security police.

1990–   In 1990 journalist and writer **Roberto Luque Escalona**, founder of
         the unofficial Cuban Democratic Party and human-rights activist,
         sent the manuscript of his book, *Fidel: El Juicio de la Historia*
         (Mérida 1990; *The Tiger and the Children: Fidel Castro and the
         Judgment of History*, New Brunswick 1992), a history of Cuba from
         1492 with emphasis on the twentieth century, to his daughter in
         Mexico, page by page, bound in the covers of the magazine *Economy
         and Development*, where he worked as a proofreader. After its pub-
         lication in Mexico, he was intimidated and finally imprisoned on the
         charge of "disrespect". In June 1992 he received permission to leave
         Cuba for Miami with his wife and son, but his son, a musician, was
         prevented from leaving at the last minute. He protested the decision
         by going on a hunger strike in September. A miniature edition of
         the book, small enough to fit into the palm of a hand, reportedly
         continued to circulate clandestinely in Cuba. In 1970 Luque had
         already been dismissed from his job at the Cuban press agency
         Prensa Latina after he had written an anti-Castro novel.

1991   According to a 1991 report, two senior historians (names unknown)
         decided not to publish accounts of the 1960s after being advised that
         their views did not coincide with Castro's.

1996   In August the government refused to renew the visa of **Robin Diane
         Meyers**, the United States Interests Section human rights officer,
         complaining, inter alia, that she had distributed "antigovernment lit-
         erature", including writings about José Marti (1853–95; the inde-
         pendence leader who could reportedly not be criticized either in
         Cuba or among Miami exiles).

1997   In April the authorities briefly detained **Fidel Tamayo**, father of one
         of several schoolchildren who had refused to sign the *Declaración
         de los Mambises del Siglo XX* (Declaration of the Mambises of the
         Twentieth Century) in March. The declaration, named after the mam-
         bises who fought for Cuban independence during the Ten Years'
         War (1868–78) and the Independence War (1895–98), was meant to
         support the Ley de reafirmación de la dignidad y soberanía cubanas
         (Law Reaffirming Cuban Dignity and Sovereignty), which created
         broad restrictions on free expression and was a response to the
         Helms-Burton law (which tightened the United States embargo of
         Cuba).

1997–   In July **Orestes Rodríguez Horruitiner**, leader of two opposition
         groups in Santiago, was arrested when during a house search books by
         prominent independence leaders—Marti, Máximo Gómez (1836–
         1905), and Antonio Maceo (1845–96)—were seized. They later

served as evidence in his trial. In November he was sentenced to four years' imprisonment for enemy propaganda. In April 2000 he was conditionally released.

Also see China (1999: book), Dominican Republic (1935–: Bosch), United States (1997: documents).

SOURCES

Americas Watch, *Human Rights in Cuba: The Need to Sustain the Pressure* (Washington 1989) 10–11, 28–30, 83, 88, 102–3.

Amnesty International, *Cuba: Recent Developments Affecting the Situation of Political Prisoners and the Use of the Death Penalty* (AMR 25/04/88; London 1986) appendix: 2.

———, *Political Imprisonment in Cuba* (AMR 25/06/86; London 1986) 7–8.

———, *Report* (London) 1986: 144; 1987: 153; 1988: 107; 1989: 117–18: 2001: 86.

———, *Urgent Action 334/86* (14 November 1986).

Article 19, *Information, Freedom and Censorship: World Report 1991* (London 1991) 97–99.

Boyd, K. ed., *Encyclopedia of Historians and Historical Writing* (London/Chicago 1999) 696, 836–37.

Chomsky, A., "Recent Historiography of Cuba", *Latin American Research Review*, 1994, no.3: 221.

Fagen, R.R., *The Transformation of Political Culture in Cuba* (Stanford 1969) 106, 252.

Gorman, R.A. ed., *Biographical Dictionary of Marxism* (Westport 1986) 66–67.

Human Rights Watch, *World Report* (New York) 1997: 95; 1999: 118.

Iglesias García, F., "Historiography of Cuba", in: B.W. Higman ed., *General History of the Caribbean*, vol. 6 (London/Oxford 1999) 377–78, 387.

Index on Censorship, 3/89: 18–19; 10/92: 44; 4/93: 32, 35; 1/98: 110.

Instituto Panamericano de Geografía e Historia, *Guia de personas que cultivan la historia de América* (México 1967) 165, 201–2.

International PEN Writers in Prison Committee, *"Dangerous Writers": Freedom of Expression in Cuba* (London 1997) 16.

Liss, S.B., *Marxist Thought in Latin America* (Berkeley/Los Angeles 1984) 265–66.

Oppenheimer, A., *The Secret Story behind the Coming Downfall of Communist Cuba* (New York 1992) 315–17.

Pacheco, R., & J. Hingson, *"Arroz con Mango": An Interview with Professor Manuel Moreno Fraginals* (WWW-text; 1997).

Pérez, L.A. Jr. "History, Historiography, and Cuban Studies: A Retrospective" (originally 1992), in: Pérez, *Essays on Cuban History: Historiography and Research* (Gainesville 1995) 177.

Provenzo, E.F. Jr., & C. Garcia, "Exiled Teachers and the Cuban Revolution", *Cuban Studies/Estudios Cubanos*, Winter 1983: 5, 7.

Suchlicki, J., *Historical Dictionary of Cuba* (Metuchen 1988) 174–76, 230, 256–57.

Thomas, J.R., *Biographical Dictionary of Latin American Historians and Historiography* (Westport 1984) 276–77, 315.

CYPRUS

1974–   After the 1974 Turkish occupation of the northern part of Cyprus, many
         Christian and Hellenic monuments were destroyed and archeological
         sites desecrated. The first-century city of Lamboussa, for example, was
         turned into a military zone and its Akhiropietos monastery was in use
         as a military warehouse. In 1976 a report on the destructions prepared
         for UNESCO by the Canadian Jacques Dalibard was kept confidential,
         apparently in the hope of avoiding a rupture with Turkey. The teaching
         of history was inspired by Turkish nationalism: balanced views of the
         Cyprus question and sympathy with the Kurdish political party PKK
         were reportedly grounds to denounce university history lecturers.

Also see Greece (1984: Nittis), Turkey (1946–: Berkes).

SOURCES

Freitag, U., personal communication, October 1999.
Hitchens, C., *Hostage to History: Cyprus from the Ottomans to Kissinger* (London/New
    York 1997) 112–18.

CZECHOSLOVAKIA

During the German occupation and World War II (1938–45), historical study
was brought to a standstill in Czechoslovakia. All Czech books in libraries in
the Sudetenland dealing with geography, biography, and history were confiscated. Many were burned, collections were totally destroyed or sent to Germany.
After the occupation of the rest of Czechoslovakia, some 2,000,000 volumes
were lost, including many manuscripts, incunabula, and codices. In February
1948 the communist takeover of government provoked a profound break in
Czechoslovak historiography. State agencies controlled and supervised all historical writing and teaching via a system of indoctrination, rewards, and pen-
alties. Historiography lost its independence and was forcibly isolated from
outside developments. Most of the precommunist historical institutions were
abolished. The *Český časopis historický* (Czech Journal of History), which had
resumed publication in 1946, ceased in 1949, and new institutions and journals
were established. Most of the noncommunist university lecturers, especially in
Prague, were dismissed and replaced by Marxist historians. In Slovakia many
historians were purged. The historical section of the Matica slovenská was dissolved. The Slovak Historical Society ceased to exist between the early 1950s
and 1957. The sensitive and controversial topics, often called "black holes",
were many, and included the age of Charles IV, Jan Hus, Comenius, the role
of religion in history, and the entire contemporary period since 1918: the 1918
establishment of the First Republic and its founders Tomáš Masaryk (1850–
1937), Edvard Beneš (1884–1948) and Milan Štefánik (1880–1919), the 1938

Munich Agreement, anti-Nazi resistance during World War II, the Slovak National Uprising of 29 August 1944, the Prague Uprising of 5 May 1945, the forced transfer of Germans from Czechoslovakia in 1945–47, the history of the Communist Party (CP-ČSSR) and Czech–Soviet relations, the history of labor and socialist movements and of the Communist International; later, the February 1948 seizure of power itself, and the political purges and trials of the 1950s. This situation lasted until 1956 at least.

Only in 1963 did a gradual political thaw begin to affect historiography. A controlled process of liberalization was initiated by the establishment historians. The emancipatory tendencies in official historiography culminated in the 1968 Prague Spring, when several works by proscribed historians of the older generation (re)appeared in print, but came gradually to a halt after the Warsaw Pact invasion of 21 August 1968. Historians of the History Institute of the Czechoslovak Academy of Sciences (ČSAV) issued statements protesting the invasion on at least two occasions: on the day of the invasion, the first statement was partially broadcast on the Czechoslovak radio after 11 P.M.; the second came on or after 28 August but was not broadcast. On 25 September they reaffirmed the principles of freedom of historical research. In the fall of 1968, some of them published a Black Book about the first invasion week. The limited edition of 2,900 copies was distributed throughout Czechoslovakia within hours of coming off the presses in order to avoid confiscation.

In the spring of 1970, the historiographical infrastructure was once more reshuffled. Not so harsh as twenty years before, the purges provoked by the so-called "normalization" were profound, and history was one of the hardest-hit fields, inter alia, because of its role in investigating the Stalinist purges of the late 1940s and 1950s and in rehabilitating the show trial victims. The ČSAV Institute for the History of the European Socialist Countries was reorganized as the Czechoslovak Institute of Sovietology, with historian Václav Král (1926–?83) as its new director. On 30 April 1970, the ČSAV History Institute was replaced by a new Institute of Czechoslovak and World History, and half its leading staff members, including its director Macek [q.v. 1969–], were dismissed. The staff of other institutes was similarly reduced. The Department of the History of the Working Class Movement at Charles University Philosophical Faculty in Prague, the Institute for International Politics and Economics of the Ministry of Foreign Affairs, and the Military Academy of Politics were dissolved. The Committee for the History of the Resistance and its periodical were abolished. The philosophical faculty lost one-third of its full professors. At the 13th International Congress of Historical Sciences meeting in Moscow in 1970, Stuttgart University historian Eberhard Jäckel (1929–) protested the dismissal of fifteen staff members at the ČSAV History Institute but he was criticized by the official Czechoslovak delegate Kořalka [q.v. 1969–]. Journals such as *Dějiny a současnost* (Past and Present) and *Revue dějin socialismu* (Journal of the History of Socialism) ceased to exist. A multivolume *World History*, a three-volume *History of the Resistance*, and a critical edition of sources in post-

1945 Czechoslovak history were discontinued. Estimates of historians dismissed varied from at least 145 to over 500. Of the historians affected, 90 percent were reportedly CP-ČSSR members. The highest percentage of dismissed historians was among those who dealt with twentieth-century history, especially political history and the history of the labor movement. The political interventions were generally less destructive outside the capital. Many of the persecuted historians had to survive by accepting physical labor or by going abroad. They were often barred from access to archival sources or to foreign publications and from legal publication and teaching for many years, their books were removed from the public libraries and often destroyed, and their earlier works could not be cited. In 1973 a procedure was reportedly started to deprive the dismissed historians of their academic titles. Self-censorship was extensive. The collection of data about persecuted historians itself was subject to police reprisal and punishment. Apart from official historians and historians operating in a "gray zone", a current of historiography independent of official ideological dogmas came into existence, with publications circulating on a limited scale in samizdat (self-publishing) or abroad. Many of the first samizdat manuscripts were composed while their authors were still in office. This current gained strength especially after the establishment of the human rights movement Charta 77 in 1977, in which many of the dismissed historians took part: the original charter was signed by forty historians, one-sixth of all signatories. These historians were able to present some of their best work at the International Congresses of Historical Sciences in 1975, 1980, and 1985. After the November 1989 Velvet Revolution, the obstacles for historical research were removed, institutions abolished or (re)established, some of the samizdat publications appeared in print, many historians returned from exile, and contacts with the international community of historians were restored. The historical profession reportedly complained of the public's loss of confidence in statements based on historical studies.

pre-1945   Among the historians and others concerned with the past who emigrated before 1945 (and living in exile after 1944) were the following: **Otakar Odložilík** (1899–) and **Hans Kohn** (1891–1971) before 1939; **John Buchsbaum** (1910–), **Konštantín Čulen** (1904–64), **Francis Dvorník** (1893–1975), **Victor Ehrenberg** (1891–1976), **Fred Hahn** (1906–), **Jozef Kirschbaum** (1913–), and **Oskar Rabinowicz** (1902–69) after 1939.

Among the historians and others concerned with the past who were censored or persecuted during World War II (including in 1945) were **Kamil Krofta** (1876–1945), **Zdeněk Nejedlý** (1878–1962), **Otto Peterka** (1876–1945), and **Arthur Stein** (1871–1950).

Among the young refugees who became historians in their new country were **Geoffrey Elton** [=**Gottfried Ehrenberg**] (1921–94), **Ernest Gellner** (1925–95), and **Theodore Rabb** (1937–).

1944–   From 1944 to the 1945 Prague Uprising, literary historian **Václav Černý** (1905–87) was imprisoned by the Nazis because of his resistance activities. In 1951 he was dismissed as a professor of comparative and general history of literature at Charles University (1945–51) during a university purge because of his anticommunist writings. In 1953 he was arrested and charged but apparently not imprisoned. He worked as a librarian and anonymous ČSAV collaborator. In 1968, during the reforms, he taught again at Charles University but he was dismissed and forced to retire in 1970. All his works were banned. He was a Charta 77 signatory and author of several samizdat studies, several of which (including two studies on Masaryk) were published in the samizdat series *Edice petlice (Padlock Editions)*.

1945–46   The so-called Prague Archive on Russia (about one million files collected since 1923–24 by White émigrés from the USSR living in Czechoslovakia during the interwar period) was confiscated by SMERSH ("Death to Spies", a Soviet security division) and in 1946 sent to Moscow.

1945–82   In 1945 the appointment as full professor of Catholic historian **Zdeněk Kalista** (1900–82), a specialist in Czech Baroque working at the Charles University Philosophical Faculty, was prevented allegedly because of pressure from the communists. The appointment had already been blocked in 1938–39 by the Nazis after he had drafted a protest appeal "To the Entire World of Learning" (against the 1938 Munich Agreement), signed by Czechoslovak intellectuals and published on 9 October 1938. After the communist takeover in 1948, he was one of the first dismissed. He became the target of an official criticism campaign. In August 1951 he was arrested and in July 1952 sentenced to fifteen years' imprisonment on charges of high treason and subversion. He was released before the expiration of his term in March 1960 and in June 1966 fully rehabilitated by court order. In June 1968 he was invited to teach history again at his old faculty, with the rank of professor extraordinary. However, "normalization" prevented him from taking up the post. From 1948 to 1966, he could publish nothing under his own name. From 1966 to 1971, he was able to publish again. He was the author of at least eighty-three books, more than a dozen of which, some of them multivolume, remained unpublished.

1945   Literary historian **Gerhard Gesemann** (1888–1948), professor of Slavonic studies (1922–45) at the German University in Prague, lost his personal library, which specialized in the Balkans, and many manuscripts.

1945–56   In April 1945 historian **František Hrušovský** (1903–56) was dismissed from his professorship of medieval Slovak history at Comenius University, Bratislava, to which he had been appointed two months before, because of his active defense of Slovak independence as a member of Parliament and chief inspector in the Slovak schools (1938–45) in 1939–45, when Slovakia was governed by the pro-Nazi regime of Jozef Tiso (1887–1947). Hrušovský went into exile in Austria, Italy, and the United States, where in Cleveland he cofounded the Slovak Institute.

1948–   During the communist period, the work of historian **Josef Pekǎr** (1870–1937) was banned and he was condemned as the leading ideologist of the counterrevolution, possibly because his name was allegedly misused in Nazi propaganda. From 1968, however, his work enjoyed recovery among the Czech public.

           Charles University history student **Zdeněk Dittrich** (1923–) went into exile in the Netherlands and became a professor of Eastern European history at Utrecht University.

1948–77   Jewish historian and diplomat **Josef Korbel** (1909–77), Jan Masaryk's personal secretary, head of the wartime broadcasting department of the Czech government-in-exile in London, ambassador to postwar Yugoslavia, and chairman of the United Nations Commission on India and Pakistan, which settled the Kashmir crisis, went into exile in the United States, where he taught international relations at Denver University and published many works on political and diplomatic history. His daughter Madeleine Albright became U.S. secretary of state (1997–2001).

1948–   In February 1948 playwright of historical plays and literary historian **Václav Renc** (1911–73) was dismissed as director of the Mahen Theater by the revolutionary "Action Committee". In May 1951 he was arrested by the secret police on the charge of espionage "on behalf of the United States in connection with the America-organized Green International". After a trial in 1952, he was sentenced to twenty-five years' imprisonment. In May 1962 he was amnestied after a severe illness. In 1965–69 he was able to publish his writings, but after 1969 he was censored again.

           The work of poet and art historian **Antonín Bartušek** (1921–74) was censored. In 1965–69 the improving political climate made publication of his work possible, after which censorship prevailed again.

           The works of historians **J. Slavika** and **Vsevlad Gajdos** (1908–78), were banned. Despite persecution Gajdos, a Slovak Franciscan, continued to work as a librarian and historian.

1949–50   In November 1949 communist essayist and historian **Záviš Kalandra** (1902–50) was arrested, accused of espionage, and denounced as a Trotskyist who actively directed those opposed to the party line toward "treason against the people, the nation and the State". He was hanged on 27 June 1950. In 1936 he had been expelled from the CP-ČSSR, inter alia, because he had cowritten a book, *Unmasking of Moscow's Mysterious Marxism* (1936), in which the purges then taking place in the USSR were denounced. Arrested in 1939 by the Gestapo, he spent six years in the Ravensbrück and Sachsenhausen prison camps.

1950s   In the 1950s art historian and writer **Miloslava Holubová** (1913–) was arrested and imprisoned. For almost twenty years she worked as an educator at the High School of Art and Industry. She was a Charta 77 signatory. Her work was banned and she was barred from writing and publishing. She was frequently interrogated by the police.

During the 1950s and 1960s, **Josef Zvěřina** (1913–), historian, art theoretician, theologian, and publicist who spent World War II in Nazi concentration camps, served thirteen years in prison. From 1970 he could not execute his profession nor his ecclesiastical duties. His work was banned. He was a Charta 77 signatory.

1950–   In 1950 **Daniel Rapant** (1897–1988), called the founder of modern Slovak historiography and rector of Comenius University, Bratislava (1945–50), was forced to leave the university because he was not prepared to compromise with the communist authorities. In 1952–58 he worked at the university library in Bratislava. He was put onto the compulsory retirement list in 1958. In 1967–69 he was gradually rehabilitated and he became a full member of the Slovak Academy of Sciences (SAV), but during the subsequent period of "normalization", he was censored again.

In 1950, following the dissolution of monastic orders, **Gabriel Povala** (1918–), a Roman Catholic priest who studied history at Comenius University, was sentenced to five years in a labor camp. In the 1960s he worked as an archeologist in local museums. From 1970 he looked after forcibly retired nuns in Zilina. In August 1981 the police raided his flat and confiscated his private papers and religious literature. In November he was sentenced to eight months' imprisonment for "obstructing the state supervision of the churches", a sentence upheld on appeal in February 1982.

1951–67   In 1951 Catholic art historian and archeologist **Růžena Vacková** (1901–82), a concentration camp survivor, was arrested on false charges of "espionage for the Vatican and the United States" and sentenced to twenty-two years' imprisonment. She was released in 1967. She became a Charta 77 signatory.

pre-1964   *The History of the Hussite Revolution*, an unfinished work of communist historian **Kurt Konrad (Kurt Beer)** (1908–41), who had died in a German prison because of his anti-Nazi resistance, was reissued.

1964–   In [July] 1964 Slovak historian **Milan Hübl** (1927–89) was dismissed as a lecturer in modern history and pro-rector (1962–64) of the CP-ČSSR Central Committee (CC) High School [or: Academy] of Politics for the "historically wrong conclusions" he had allegedly drawn in his writings on recent Slovak history, including on the political trials of the 1950s and their ramifications. His 1963 article "Social Responsibility, Scientific Methods and Ethics" supported the public demand by Slovak historians for a reevaluation of the Slovak Uprising and the rehabilitation of the so-called Slovak bourgeois-nationalists. In 1965–68 he was a researcher at the ČSAV Institute for the History of the European Socialist States, during which he produced an unpublished manuscript on the history of the Second International. In April 1968 Hübl was reinstated as rector of the high school. Between August 1968 and June 1969, he was a full member of the CP-ČSSR CC. From 1963 to April 1969, he worked for the rehabilitation and election as CP-ČSSR Secretary of Gustav́ Husák (who later presided over the "normalization" program). As he was allied with the Socialist Movement for Reform, however, Hübl was expelled from the CP-ČSSR (September 1969). In July 1970 he was dismissed from the high school; in October his wife was dismissed. Until 1972 he was unemployed or worked as an unskilled worker in Prague. In January or February 1972, he was arrested (together with Bartošek [q.v. 1969–]) for his editorship of a clandestine political monthly chronicle of current events and charged with leaking secret information to the Italian Communist Party. In the summer he was sentenced to six-and-a-half years' imprisonment. In November 1976 he went on a six-day hunger strike to protest prison conditions and the deliberate official restriction on his children's educational opportunities. When in December he was released from prison on three years' probation, he was almost blind. He allied himself openly with the dissident movement and published in the samizdat and émigré press. In 1977 he was a Charta 77 founder-member.

1965   CP-ČSSR leaders dismissed the entire editorial board of the popular historical monthly *Dějiny a současnost* because it had published a critical review of a recent book edited by CP-ČSSR historian Vaćlav Král. The monthly attacked him for presenting as complete some documents from which entire passages had been omitted.

1968– In August Charles University history student **Hans Renner** (1946–) went into exile in the Netherlands, completed his studies at Utrecht University, and became a professor of Eastern European history at Groningen University.

1969– Among the historians and others concerned with the past dismissed or otherwise persecuted during the period of "normalization" after the August 1968 invasion of the Warsaw Pact troops, were the following:

Jaroslav Barto (1930–), instructor at the Bratislava Institute of Technology, historian of Czech-Slovak constitutional relations, was dismissed in 1970. He became an unskilled worker (1970–).

Vladislav Bartoněk (1921–), CP-ČSSR CC Academy of Politics instructor, was dismissed and expelled from the CP-CSSR in 1970. He became a museum curator (1971–).

Karel Bartošek (1930–), ČSAV History Institute researcher (1960–69), specialist in the history of the anti-fascist resistance and the so-called Czech Question in the twentieth century, coauthor of a textbook of twentieth-century history for senior grammar school students, left the CP-ČSSR in 1969 and was dismissed in 1970. He became a stoker, school fireman, and factory worker (1970–82). In February 1972 he was arrested [q.v. 1964–: Hübl] and sentenced to one year of (suspended) imprisonment. He was a Charta 77 signatory. In December 1981 he was held in police custody for ninety-six hours and charged with expressing opposition to martial law in Poland. In July 1982 he was tried for "incitement to rebellion". In December he emigrated to France, where he became a collaborator at the Institut d'Histoire du Temps Présent, Paris (1983–96), and director of the journal *La Nouvelle Alternative*.

Ferdinand Beer (1926–), CP-ČSSR CC Academy of Politics instructor, historian of the resistance movement in World War II (about which he wrote a 1970 samizdat study), was expelled from the CP-ČSSR in 1970. He became a clerk in a construction cooperative (1970–).

Josef Belda (1920–), research associate at the CP-ČSSR CC Institute for the History of Socialism (1955–69) and specialist in post-1948 ČSSR history, was dismissed in 1969 and expelled from the CP-ČSSR in 1970. He became a stoker or fireman in a factory

(1971–). He was possibly tried and imprisoned for some time in [1972]. His books were reportedly banned in 1973.

Antonín Benčík (1925–), an Institute for Military History research associate and military historian specialized in the resistance movement during World War II who worked with Navrátil [q.v. 1969–] was dismissed, and expelled from the CP-ČSSR in 1970. He became a sculptor, factory worker (1970–73), and clerk in a construction firm (1974–).

Jan Beránek (1924–), Institute for Military History research associate, chief editor of the journal *History and the Army* (1955–69) and specialist in World War I, was expelled from the CP-ČSSR in 1970. He became a worker in road construction (1970–). He was a Charta 77 signatory.

Jiří Brabec (1929–), historian of literature, vice president of the Association of Czechoslovak Writers (1969–70), was unemployed in 1971–72. He became an attendant in Prague (1972–74). He was a Charta 77 signatory. Later he became a night watchman and stoker (1978–).

Vlastimil Brabec (1931–), historian of the political trials of the 1950s and CP-ČSSR History Institute staff member, was dismissed in 1969.

Radko Břach (1931–), professor of Czechoslovak history at the Military Political Academy and historian of Czechoslovak foreign policy in the 1920s (about which he wrote samizdat studies in 1970) was expelled from the CP-ČSSR in 1970. He became a construction worker (1970–).

Věra Břachová (1930–), editor of the journal *History and the Army* (1958–68) and specialist in interwar CP-ČSSR activity in the army, was expelled from the CP-ČSSR in 1970. She became an employee in various firms (1970–).

Zdeněk Bradáč (1928–), research associate at the CP-ČSSR CC Institute for the History of Socialism and specialist in interwar CP-ČSSR history, was expelled from the CP-ČSSR in 1970. He became a stoker or fireman in a factory (1970–).

Toman Brod (1929–), former Nazi concentration camp internee (1942–45), Institute of East European History research associate, specialist in Czechoslovak–Soviet relations, and historian of Czechoslovak military units in the West during World War II (about which he wrote samizdat studies in 1970 and 1979), was expelled from the CP-ČSSR in 1970. He became a worker and taxi driver (1970–). He was a Charta 77 signatory.

Bžoch (first name unknown), literary historian of Bratislava, was possibly imprisoned for (at least) several months.

Miroslav Caha (1924–), CP-ČSSR CC Academy of Politics instructor, specialist in the post-1945 nationality problem, was expelled from the CP-ČSSR in 1970. He became a depot worker (1969–).

Bohumil Černý (1922–), ČSAV History Institute researcher (1953–70), associate editor of *Československý časopis historický*, and specialist in the history of the German interwar emigration to Czechoslovakia and in the history of anti-Semitism, was expelled from the CP-ČSSR in 1970. He became a depot manager (1970–) and was the author of a samizdat study. In January 1985 the state security police entered his office at the State Saving Bank archives in search of leaflets allegedly issued in connection with the Palach Prize awarded to Hejdánek [q.v. 1977]. No leaflets were found, but ten copies of two volumes of the samizdat publication *Historické Sborniky* (Historical Almanac) were confiscated. Černý and Otáhal [q.v. 1969–], who was visiting his friend at the archives, were taken and interrogated for several hours. In 1991–93 Černý was a collaborator at the Institute for Contemporary History of the Academy of Sciences of the Czech Republic (AVČR).

František Červinka (1923–), writer and literary historian, lecturer in modern Bohemian history at Charles University, specialist in the history of nineteenth-century nationalism, and author of a biography of historian Zdeněk Nejedlý (1878–1962—a minister of education, deputy prime minister, and ČSAV president coresponsible for the postwar purges at the universities and for the silencing of several senior historians), was expelled from the CP-ČSSR in 1970 and dismissed in 1971. He became a disability pensioner (1971–). He was the author of samizdat studies about World War II (1979, 1980).

Milan Churáň (1931–), editor of the journal *History and the Present* (1959–70), specialist in recent Czechoslovak history, without CP-ČSSR affiliation, became an technical employee (1970–).

Bohumil Doležal (1940–), literary critic and historian, became a laborer and programmer (1970–). He was a Charta 77 signatory.

Jiří Doležal (1925–), ČSAV History Institute researcher (1957–70) and specialist in the 1944 Slovak Uprising and the cultural resistance during World War II, was dismissed and expelled from the CP-ČSSR in 1970. He was a depot worker and warehouse manager

(1970–79), a Charta 77 signatory, and author of several samizdat studies (1973–79). He became a historian in Tabor (1980–).

Karel Durman (1932–), lecturer in modern history at Charles University (1962–70) and specialist in the history of the Near East during 1918–59, was dismissed and expelled from the CP-ČSSR in 1970. Unemployed at first, he became a night watchman (1970–72) and a clerk in a technical library (1973–80). He was the author of unpublished manuscripts about Bulgarian, Russian, and USSR history (one anonymously prior to 1973, another in 1978, and a third written in 1979 under the pseudonym of Karel Kinsky). In February 1980 he emigrated to Sweden.

Eva Dvořáková (1932–), CP-ČSSR CC Academy of Politics instructor and specialist in CP-ČSSR history, was dismissed and expelled from the CP-ČSSR in 1970. She became a State Library employee (1970–).

Michal Dzvoník (1928–), lecturer at Comenius University Philosophical Faculty and historian of the Slovak Soviet Republic (1919), was dismissed and expelled from the CP-ČSSR in 1970. He became a librarian at the Bratislava Museum (1970–).

Juraj Fabián (1933–), instructor at Comenius University and historian of Hungarian irredentism against Czechoslovakia, was dismissed in 1969 and expelled from the CP-ČSSR in 1970. He remained without permanent work (1970–).

Samuel [= Samo] Faltán (1920–), SAV History Institute researcher (1962–70), specialist in the Slovak State (1939–45) and the antifascist struggle, and Secretariat member of the Communist Party of Slovakia CC (1968–70), was dismissed and expelled from the CP-ČSSR in 1970. He remained without permanent work (1970–).

Vojtěch Fejlek (1926–), head of the Archives for Military History (1961–72) and specialist in the history of the Czechoslovak army, was dismissed and expelled from the CP-ČSSR in 1972. He became an employee in a factory (1972–).

Ferda (first name unknown), secretary of a commission for the history of the resistance, was dismissed. He became a textile depot worker.

Jan Fiala (1929–), Institute for Military History research associate and specialist in the history of the Czechoslovak army, was expelled from the CP-ČSSR in 1970. He became a worker.

Edo Friš, SAV History Institute researcher and specialist in the international aspects of the Slovak Uprising, was expelled from the CP-ČSSR in 1970. He received a three-months' work contract, which amounted to a dismissal.

Koloman Gajan (1918–), former concentration camp internee, professor of modern history at Charles University Philosophical Faculty (1952–69), specialist in Franco– and German–Czechoslovak relations, and diplomatic historian, was dismissed in 1969 and expelled from the CP-ČSSR in 1970. He became a foreign-language teacher (1969–).

Alena Gajanová (1922–), ČSAV History Institute researcher and specialist in Czechoslovakia's interwar foreign policy, was dismissed in 1969 and expelled from the CP-ČSSR in 1970. First unemployed and then a housekeeper (1970–77), she became a translator (1977–).

Bohuslav Graca (1925–), director of the Institute for the History of the Slovak Communist Party, (1955–69), specialist in the history of the Slovak State, Communist Party of Slovakia CC member (1968–70), and chairman of the CP-ČSSR Ideological Commission (1969–70), was dismissed and expelled from the CP-ČSSR in 1970. He remained without permanent work (1970–).

František Graus (1921–89), professor of Czechoslovak medieval history at Charles University Philosophical Faculty, chief editor of *Československý časopis historický*, corresponding ČSAV member, was expelled from the CP-ČSSR in 1969 and dismissed. He went to Basel, Switzerland, and in 1970 to Gießen, Federal Republic of Germany (FRG). At both places, he was a professor of medieval history. As early as 1956, he had launched an appeal for more autonomy in historiography. On 24 August 1968, he had issued a statement of protest against the Warsaw Pact invasion, published in a special issue of *Československý časopis historický*. During World War II, he had been imprisoned in Theresienstadt, Auschwitz, and Buchenwald concentration camps (1940–45).

Ján Grivna (1924–), instructor at Prešov University Philosophical Faculty and specialist in sixteenth- and seventeenth-century Russian history, was dismissed in 1969 and expelled from the CP-ČSSR in 1970. He remained without permanent work. He eventually became a translator.

Jiří Hájek (1913–93) was a prisoner in a Nazi concentration camp (1940–45), CP-ČSSR member (1949–70), diplomat (1950–53), professor of history and diplomacy at Charles University (1953–55), deputy foreign minister (1958–62), and minister of education and culture (1965–68). As the minister of foreign affairs (April 1968–September 1968), he lodged a protest in the United Nations General Assembly on 24 August 1968 against the military intervention by the Warsaw Pact, an action for which he had to resign. He reportedly went back to the ČSAV History Institute. In September 1970 he was expelled from the CP-ČSSR and dismissed from all his posts. In 1976 he was deprived of his ČSAV membership. He was the author of samizdat works about human rights in historical perspective, the year 1968, and with Masaryk the coauthor of an anthology on freedom and power. All his writings were banned. He became a Charta 77 signatory and spokesman and was placed under police surveillance for ten years. In May 1981 he was arrested in Prague and awaited trial while at liberty [q.v. 1969–90: Mlynárik]. In 1987 the police prevented him from attending an underground conference in Prague marking Charta 77's tenth anniversary. He was the Czechoslovak Helsinki Committee chairman (1988–92). In December 1988 he was given permission to travel abroad for the first time in twenty years. After a critical speech in Bologna, however, he was denied permission to travel on three occasions, and after a similar speech during a visit to Scandinavia, his passport was withdrawn in July 1989. He was a critic of "lustrace" [q.v. 1977: Benda].

Miloš Hájek (1921–), arrested for his illegal political activity (1941–45), internee in a concentration camp (1945) and almost executed there, professor of general history and director (1968–69) at the CP-ČSSR CC Institute for the History of Socialism (1950–64), ČSAV History Institute staff member (1964–68), and specialist in the history of the labor movement and the Third International, was dismissed in 1968 and expelled from the CP-ČSSR in 1970. He became a disability pensioner (1968–). As a Charta 77 signatory and spokesman, he was repeatedly harassed by the police. He was the author of a number of samizdat publications, including, with Mejdrová [q.v. 1969–], *The Emergence of the Third International* (1976). His historical works about the Italian Communist Party were published in Italy. In July 1989, being a leader of the opposition group Obroda, Hájek was detained twice after he had written to CP-ČSSR members urging them to read the pro-reform petition "A Few Sentences" before condemning it.

Viliam Hanzel (1920–), CP-ČSSR CC Academy of Politics lecturer, specialist in post-1945 peasant history, and specialist in the history of farm labor, was dismissed in 1969 and expelled from the CP-ČSSR in 1970. He became a disability pensioner (1969–).

Slovak historian **L'udovít Haraksim** was expelled from the History Institute and forbidden to publish.

1969–90   **Milan Hauner** (1940–), a specialist in Central European history and international relations, went into exile (1968–90) in the United Kingdom and the United States, where he worked at the University of Wisconsin, Madison. He wrote on Czechoslovak historiography and the contemporary history of Afghanistan and India. In 1993 he worked at Charles University, Prague, and Georgetown University, Washington, D.C.

1969–   **Růžena Havránková**, Institute of East European History staff member and specialist in international relations, became unemployed.

František Helešic (1932–), research associate at the CP-ČSSR CC Institute for the History of Socialism and specialist in CP-ČSSR history, was dismissed in 1969 and expelled from the CP-ČSSR in 1970. He became a car mechanic (1969–). He was a Charta 77 signatory. In 1995 he was an AVČR Institute for Contemporary History staff member.

Tibor Hochsteiger (1927–), commander at the Institute for Military History in Prague (1963–70) and specialist in the history of the Czechoslovak army, was dismissed and expelled from the CP-ČSSR in 1970. He became a bricklayer.

Josef Hodic (1925–), professor of post-1945 Czechoslovak history at the Military Academy of Politics (1960–69), was dismissed in 1969 and expelled from the CP-ČSSR in 1970. He became a clerk (1969–). With Hoffman [q.v. 1969–] he was the coauthor of a 1969 unpublished manuscript about the year 1968. He was a Charta 77 signatory. He emigrated to Vienna in November 1977.

Rudolf Hoffman (1925–), Military Academy of Politics pro-rector (1962–70), specialist in the history of the European people's democracies, was expelled from the CP-ČSSR in 1970 and remained without permanent work (1970–).

Vladimír Hostička (1929–), research associate at the Institute of East European History and specialist in Czechoslovak–Russian relations, was expelled from the CP-ČSSR in 1970. He became a sales clerk in a music store (1970–).

Zdeněk Hradilák (1931–), research associate at the CP-ČSSR CC Institute for the History of Socialism (1958–70), specialist in CP-ČSSR history, and chief editor of the *Journal for the History of Socialism*, was dismissed and expelled from the CP-ČSSR in 1970.

He became an unskilled worker. He was the author of an unpublished manuscript on the communist movement in Czechoslovakia in 1932–35.

Marie Hromádková (1930–), historian and former CP-ČSSR borough committee secretary for industry in Prague and later member of the CP-ČSSR CC information department, was expelled from the CP-ČSSR in 1969, worked as an accountant in a construction firm, and became Charta 77 signatory and spokeswoman (1980–81). She was arrested for short periods several times. In November 1985 her residence was ransacked by the security police.

Anna Hučkova-Štvrtecká, research associate at the Institute for the History of the Slovak Communist Party, specialist in the history of the Slovak State and the anti-Fascist struggle, was expelled from the CP-ČSSR in 1970.

Václav Hyndrák (1923–), former concentration camp internee (1943–45), Institute of Military History research associate (1952–70), and specialist in the history of the Czechoslovak army, was dismissed and expelled from the CP-ČSSR in 1970. He became a stockroom manager. He was a Charta 77 signatory.

František Janáček (1932–), CP-ČSSR CC Academy of Politics lecturer and specialist in the history of the Czechoslovak National Front, was dismissed in 1969 and expelled from the CP-ČSSR in 1970. He became a depot manager (1969–). With Novotný [q.v. 1969–], he was the main editor of a collective work, *Czechoslovak Anti-Fascist Resistance 1938–1945*, vol. 1, *Occupation and Resistance 1938–1941* (1970), which was submitted to the publishers in January 1970 but never published. In 1995 he was an AVČR Institute for Contemporary History staff member.

Slovak historian Jablonický [q.v. 1973–].

Oldřich Janeček (1923–), research associate at the CP-ČSSR CC Institute for the History of Socialism and specialist in the history of Czechoslovak military units in the USSR, became a worker. He was the author of a samizdat study on the resistance during World War II.

Věra Jarošová (1930–), lecturer at the Institute for Social Policy of Charles University, specialist in the history of the Slovak labor movement, was expelled from the CP-ČSSR in 1970. She became a driver and was a Charta 77 signatory.

Květa Jechová (1930–), art historian, instructor at the Academy of Fine Arts, specialist in the history of the CP-ČSSR and its relations with the artistic avant-garde, was dismissed in 1969 and expelled from the CP-ČSSR in 1970. She became a clerk (1969–).

Ivan Jirous (1944–), art historian, journalist and poet, editor of the magazine *Art Work* (banned in [1969]), and since 1970 denied any possibility of working in his profession, became a night watchman and bricklayer. He was a Charta 77 signatory and one of the theorists of independent Czechoslovak culture in the 1970s. As the artistic director of the rock group Plastic People of the Universe, he organized various music festivals. He edited several samizdat collections and journals. In September 1973 he was sentenced to ten years' imprisonment for "defaming the nation" because he ate a copy of the CP-ČSSR daily *Rude Pravo* in the presence of a state security official. He was released [ten months] later. In the spring of 1976, he was one of several detained for investigation and charged with "public disturbance". In September he was sentenced to eighteen months' imprisonment. In October 1977, one month after his release, he was rearrested, and in April 1978 he was sentenced to eight months' imprisonment (later increased to eighteen months) for "breach of the public peace". In November 1981 he was arrested with three others for publishing and distributing the unofficial cultural journal *Vokno* (Window) and for possessing drugs. In July 1982 he was sentenced to three-and-a-half years' imprisonment and two years' police surveillance for "breach of the peace". His appeal was rejected in September. In October 1988 he was arrested because he codrafted and signed a petition in which a prisoner's death was denounced and the authorities were held responsible for the deaths of 8,000 people after the 1948 communist takeover, and sentenced—for the fifth time—in March 1989 to sixteen months' imprisonment. He was released in November.

Lenka Kalinová, research associate at the CP-ČSSR CC Institute for the History of Socialism and specialist in post-1948 Czechoslovakia, was expelled from the CP-ČSSR in 1970. She became a disability pensioner.

Ivan Kamenec was the author of a study on the Jewish question in Slovakia in 1938–45, which was accepted as a dissertation in 1971 but not allowed to appear in print.

Karel Kaplan (1928–), ČSAV History Institute researcher and lecturer (1964–70) and specialist in post-1945 history, secretary to the 1968 Piller Commission for the Rehabilitation of the Victims of Political Trials, attached to the CP-ČSSR CC (1968–69), and specialist in post-1945 CP-ČSSR history, was expelled from the CP-ČSSR in 1969. His monograph on the trials of leading communist functionaries in the 1950s was suppressed. In 1970 he was dismissed. He became a stoker. In February 1972 he was detained for three months on the charge of threatening to divulge state secrets, but after his release in April the charge was not dropped. He was the author of samizdat studies. In 1976 he emigrated to Munich, FRG, and reportedly smuggled part of his archive on the trials out of Czechoslovakia. In [1990] he published *Report on the Murder of the General Secretary*, about the 1951–52 trial of CP-ČSSR Secretary-General Rudolph Slánský (1901–52). In 1995 he was an AVČR Institute for Contemporary History staff member.

Jan Kapusta, art and music historian, director of a regional museum in Litomysl, East Bohemia, was dismissed in 1970 and became an unskilled worker at a local trout farm (until 1989).

Zdeněk Kárnik (1931–), lecturer in contemporary history at Charles University Philosophical Faculty and specialist in the history of the CP-ČSSR and the labor movement, was dismissed and expelled from the CP-ČSSR in 1970. He became a clerk (1970–).

Vladimír Kašík (1925–), professor of contemporary history at Charles University Philosophical Faculty (1957–70) and specialist in the history of the First International, was dismissed and expelled from the CP-ČSSR in 1970. He was unemployed in 1970–73. He was a Charta 77 signatory.

František Kautman (1927–), historian of literature, became an invalid pensioner (1974–). He was a Charta 77 signatory and author of several samizdat studies, including a large study on the Czech national identity.

František Kavka (1920–), professor of Czechoslovak medieval history at Charles University Philosophical Faculty (1955–70), specialist in the Hussite movement and in the history of Charles University, and biographer of King Charles IV (1316–78), was dismissed and expelled from the CP-ČSSR in 1970. He became a depot manager with the Jewish Museum in Prague (1970–85), after which he retired. He was the author of several samizdat studies.

Jaroslav Kladiva (1919–), former concentration camp internee, professor of contemporary history at Charles University Philosophical Faculty, and specialist in the problems of the cultural revolution (1945–48), was dismissed and expelled from the CP-ČSSR in 1970. He became a disability pensioner and was the author of a 1976 samizdat study of the Czech lands from the White Mountain battle (1620) to the mid-eighteenth century.

Vlasta Kladivová (1921–), lecturer in Russian and USSR history at Charles University Philosophical Faculty, was dismissed and expelled from the CP-ČSSR in 1970. She retired.

Arnošt Klíma (1916–), professor of contemporary history and deputy rector (1959–65) at the Pedagogical Academy in Prague, corresponding ČSAV member (1962–), and specialist in the 1848 revolution, was dismissed and expelled from the CP-ČSSR in 1970. He became a collaborator at the Institute of Pedagogics, Brandýs.

Libuše Klimešova (1926–), research associate at the CP-ČSSR CC Institute for the History of Socialism and specialist in CP-ČSSR history, was dismissed in 1969 and expelled from the CP-ČSSR in 1970. She became a cashier in a cinema (1969–).

Bohumír Klípa (1930–), Institute of Military History research associate and specialist in World War II history, was dismissed in 1969 and expelled from the CP-ČSSR in 1970. He became a laborer (1969–) and was a Charta 77 signatory.

Miroslav Klír (1920–), CP-ČSSR CC Academy of Politics lecturer and specialist in CP-ČSSR history, was dismissed in 1969 and expelled from the CP-ČSSR in 1970. He became an archivist (1969–).

Vladimír Kneř (1922–), research associate at the CP-ČSSR CC Institute for the History of Socialism and specialist in the nineteenth-century labor movement, was dismissed in 1969 and expelled from the CP-ČSSR in 1970. He became a stoker (1969–72) and worked at a university library (1972–).

Matej Kociský, instructor at Comenius University and specialist in the history of the working class in 1867–1914, was expelled from the CP-ČSSR in 1970.

Luboš Kohout (1925–), political science lecturer at Charles University Philosophical Faculty and specialist in the political systems of socialism and the history of Czechoslovakia, was dismissed in 1969 and expelled from the CP-ČSSR in 1969 or 1970. He became a laborer (1969–) and was a Charta 77 signatory.

Ivan Kolesár (1928–), associate at the Institute for Social Policy of Charles University and specialist in the history of the international labor movement in the 1930s, was dismissed in 1969 and expelled from the CP-ČSSR in 1970. He became a clerk (1969–).

Jiří Kořalka (1931–), ČSAV History Institute staff member and specialist in the Czechoslovak history of 1815–1914, was unemployed for a time. He was visiting professor at Kent University (1969), chief historian at the Hussite Museum in Tabor (1975–91), and research consultant to the AVČR History Institute (1992). In 1968–70 he helped to purge the History Institute. One of the few historians allowed to travel abroad, he allegedly collaborated with the secret police by reporting on Czech and Slovak refugee historians.

Květa Kořalková (1929–), historian, research associate at the Institute for International Politics and Economics, and specialist in the relations between people's democracies, was dismissed in 1969 and expelled from the CP-ČSSR in 1970. She became a clerk (1969–).

Václav Kotyk (1927–), research associate at the Institute for International Politics and Economics and specialist in the history of the socialist countries, was dismissed and expelled from the CP-ČSSR in 1970. He became a depot manager.

Karel Krátký (1930–), research associate at the Institute of East European History and specialist in the history of ČSSR military units in the USSR during World War II, was dismissed and expelled from the CP-ČSSR in 1970. He was unemployed at first and became a depot manager later.

František Kratochvíl (1927–), professor of contemporary political theories (1955–69) at the CP-ČSSR CC Academy of Politics, was dismissed in 1969 and expelled from the CP-ČSSR in 1970. He became a collaborator at a university library (1969–).

Jan Křen (1930–) lecturer in Czechoslovak history during World War II at the CP-ČSSR CC Academy of Politics (1953–69) and specialist in wartime emigration, was dismissed in 1969 and expelled from the CP-ČSSR in 1970. He became a laborer and night watchman (1970–) and was a Charta 77 signatory and author of several samizdat studies, including (with Kural [q.v. 1969–]) *Czechs and Slovaks in the Past* (1976). Between 1974 and 1986, Křen and Kural wrote a study of Czech–German relations from the late eighteenth century to 1918 (1986 samizdat edition, 1989 book published in Toronto, 1990 book officially published in Prague). In 1990 Křen became a professor at Charles University Philosophical Faculty, published a book on the blank spots of Czech history, written before November 1989, and became director at the Institute of International Studies at the social sciences faculty, Charles University, chairman of the History Club (Association of Bohemian, Moravian, and Silesian Historians), member of the Czech National Committee of Historians, and cochairman of the joint German-Czech history textbook revision commission. In the early 1960s, he had been member of a rehabilitation commission. In 1963 he had launched an appeal for more autonomy in historiography.

Jaroslav Křížek (1924–), Institute for Military History research associate and specialist in World War I history, was dismissed and expelled from the CP-ČSSR in 1970. He became a technical controller with a transport firm.

Marie Rút Křížková (1936–), literary historian and critic who had graduated in 1968, without CP-ČSSR affiliation, protested the Warsaw Pact invasion. Barred from publishing, she became a samizdat author. Consequently, she was dismissed and unemployed for over six months. She found employment as an assistant forestry worker for some years and, after contracting spinal trouble, as a forest warden. She was then dismissed and harassed by the state security police because she was a Charta 77 signatory. Later she was a night sorter with the post office and Charta 77 spokesperson. Her work was banned.

František Kružík (1931–), Institute for Military History research associate and specialist in the history of Czechoslovak participation in the Spanish Civil War, was dismissed and expelled from the CP-ČSSR in 1970. He became a bricklayer.

Karel Kučera (1932–), archivist at the Institute for the History of Charles University, was dismissed in 1969 and expelled from the CP-ČSSR in 1970. He became a librarian in the documents department of Charles University Law School (1969–).

Václav Kural (1930–), Institute of Military History research associate and specialist in the history of the resistance movement during World War II, was dismissed and expelled from the CP-ČSSR in 1970. He became a laborer (1970–) and was the author of several samizdat studies, some in collaboration with Křen [q.v. 1969–].

Vladimír Kuš (1927–), CP-ČSSR CC Academy of Politics instructor and specialist in the history of the Communist Party of the USSR, was dismissed in 1969 and expelled from the CP-ČSSR in 1970. He became a clerk at the Geodetical Archive.

Alexej Kusák emigrated. In 1975 he was an editor in Munich.

Petr Lesjuk (1930–), CP-ČSSR CC Academy of Politics instructor and specialist in CP-ČSSR history in 1945–48, was dismissed in 1969 and expelled from the CP-ČSSR in 1970. He became a clerk (1969–) and a company lawyer.

Milan Lichnovský (1930–), Institute for Military History research associate and specialist in the post-1945 history of the Czechoslovak army, was dismissed in 1969 and expelled from the CP-ČSSR in 1970. He became a stoker (1970–).

L'ubomír Lipták (1930–), SAV History Institute researcher (1956–70) and specialist in twentieth-century Slovak history, was dismissed from the History Institute and expelled from the CP-ČSSR in 1970. He was forbidden to publish. He remained unemployed at first and became a woodfeller later. He was the author of a 1970 samizdat study about Slovakia in 1938–41.

Bedřich Loewenstein (1929–), ČSAV History Institute researcher (1957–70) and specialist in nineteenth- and twentieth-century German history and in intellectual history, without CP-ČSSR affiliation, was dismissed in June 1970, probably because he had criticized the Warsaw Pact occupation of Czechoslovakia in a circular to participants in an August 1969 symposium about Fascism. Two of his books could not be published. He became a translator and interpreter at the German trade mission in Prague (1970–78) and was the author of several samizdat studies on the history of ideas, one of which was published in the FRG. In January 1979 he went into exile in the FRG, where he became a history professor at the Friedrich-Meinecke-Institut of the Free University Berlin (1979–94). The child of a Jewish-German-Czech family, he was forced to leave the secondary school during the war and to work in a factory. As a student of philosophy and history, he was banned from the university in May–June 1951 because as a Christian he had criticized the class struggle and North Korean policy in the Korean War. He was readmitted at the university as a history student in late 1953.

1969–87 **František Lukeš** (1933–87), head and research associate at the Institute for East European History and specialist in Czechoslovak history during 1938–39, was dismissed in 1969 and expelled from the CP-ČSSR in 1970. He became an archivist with ČSSR Television (1969–) and was the author of an unpublished manuscript. He was reportedly psychiatrically treated. Rehabilitated in 1984, Lukeš was physically weakened by a terminal disease.

1969– **Míla Lvová** (1930–), research associate at the CP-ČSSR CC Institute for the History of Socialism and specialist in the 1938 Munich Agreement and CP-ČSSR history, was dismissed and expelled from the CP-ČSSR in 1970. She became an aide at the Pedagogical Institute.

Josef Macek (1922–), ČSAV History Institute director (1952–69), corresponding (1952–60) and full (1960–69) ČSAV member, deputy to the National Assembly (1964–69), candidate (1962–66) and full (1966–69) CP-ČSSR CC member, member of its Ideological Commission (1963–69), and specialist in the history of the Hussite movement in Bohemia, the Italian Renaissance, and the Reformation, was dismissed in 1969 and expelled from the CP-ČSSR in 1970. He remained unemployed at first and was on the staff of the Old Czech Dictionary later. His book on the Jagiellonian period in Bohemia (fifteenth century) remained with the publisher for ten years. Many of his writings where published in Italy and France. On the day of the Warsaw Pact invasion, 21 August 1968, he had been one of the academicians who signed a telegram of protest to the USSR Embassy in Prague.

Jindřich Madry (1927–), Military Academy of Politics lecturer (1955–69) and specialist in CP-ČSSR military policy and the post-1956 struggle for reform, was dismissed in 1969 and expelled from the CP-ČSSR in 1970. He became an unskilled worker (1970–).

Emanuel Mandler (1932–), director of a publishing house, specialist in recent Czechoslovak history, writer and author of political and historical essays, and editor of the journal *History and Geography in School* (1957–60), without CP-ČSSR affiliation, worked in the toy business (1969–73). He became a programmer (1974–).

Jaroslav Marek (1927–), ČSAV History Institute researcher (1954–70) and specialist in late medieval urban history and in the history of historiography, was dismissed in 1970. He remained without permanent work (1970–73) and became a clerk at Brno University library (1973–).

Jan Měchýř (1930–), lecturer in contemporary history at Charles University Philosophical Faculty and specialist in the history of the labor movement, was dismissed and expelled from the CP-ČSSR in 1970. He remained without permanent work (1970–). In 1995 he was a staff member at the social history seminar, Institute for Economic and Social History, Charles University.

Květa Mejdřická (1920–), former Nazi concentration camp internee (1940–45), lecturer in modern history at Charles University Philosophical Faculty, and a specialist in Bohemian history and the French Revolution, was arrested in 1968, dismissed, and expelled from the CP-ČSSR in 1970. She retired.

Hana Mejdrová (1920–), lecturer in Marxism at the Academy of Chemical Technology and specialist in the interwar workers' youth movement, was arrested in 1968, dismissed, and expelled from the CP-ČSSR in 1970. She retired and was a Charta 77 signatory and author of a 1979 samizdat study about Czechoslovakia in 1926.

Vojtěch Mencl (1922–), Military Academy of Politics rector and specialist in the history of the first Czechoslovak Republic, was the author, with Menclová [q.v. 1969–], of a study about the political history of Czechoslovakia in the 1920s, which was submitted to a publisher in 1967 and suppressed in 1970. He was arrested and dismissed in 1968 and expelled from the CP-ČSSR in 1970. A disability pensioner since then, he was the author of an unpublished history of the Ottoman empire (1977), presumably the author of an anonymous manuscript "The Systems Theory and Problems of a General Outline of World History" (1978), and head of the governmental Commission to Analyze 1967–70, set up in February 1990.

Jarmila Menclová (1925–), research associate at the CP-ČSSR CC Institute for the History of Socialism and specialist in CP-ČSSR history, was arrested and dismissed in 1968 and expelled from the CP-ČSSR in 1970. She became a clerk at the Bureau of Statistics (1970–).

Slovak historian **Július Mésároš**, specialist in nineteenth-century history, was dismissed from the History Institute and forbidden to publish. Later he was allowed to participate in volume 2 (1526–1848) of the six-volume *Dějiny slovenska* (1986–92). (The preparation of volume 7 of this work was stopped after November 1989.)

Jaroslav Mezník (1928–), medievalist and diplomatic historian, ČSAV History Institute researcher at Brno, without CP-ČSSR affiliation, and specialist in medieval urban history, was arrested and dismissed in 1968. Again arrested in January 1972, he was sentenced in July to three-and-a-half years' imprisonment in connection with the formation of an illegal group between late 1970 and January 1972 whose aim was "to overthrow the Socialist state system" and which engaged "in hostile activities". Released in December 1974, he became a miner and worker in an elevator factory. He was a Charta 77 signatory and author of several samizdat studies and manuscripts, including a book (*Prague before the Hussite Revolution*) printed but destroyed after his 1972 arrest. In 1978 he retired. In 1995 he was a staff member at the Center for the History of Masaryk University, Brno.

1969–90   **Ján Mlynárik** (1933–), Slovak historian, lecturer in Marxism-Leninism at the Academy of Fine Arts, Prague, and specialist in the Slovak labor movement during 1900–38, was the target of a CP-

ČSSR condemnation in the 1960s because of his historical views. In 1968 he was arrested and dismissed, in 1970 expelled from the CP-ČSSR. He became a locksmith and assistant worker in a theater (1970–). He was a Charta 77 signatory. In 1982 he was deprived of his citizenship. He was the author of many samizdat studies and unpublished manuscripts, including censored works such as *Slovakia on the Eve of Independence* (1968), *Slovakia in the Czechoslovak State* (1969), and a biography of Štefánik (1969). In May 1981 he was arrested together with other Chartists and accused of participating in the production of antistate writings, of sending them abroad for publication, of smuggling them back into Czechoslovakia, and of distributing them there [q.v. 1977–81: Danubius]. They were charged with "subversion in collusion with foreign powers on a large scale". In May 1982, following appeals by other Chartists on his behalf, he was released from pretrial detention while he was in the prison hospital, but the charges were not dropped. In August he was refused emigration but in December he received permission and left for the FRG. His work was banned. In 1990 he returned to Czechoslovakia and was elected a member of Parliament.

1969– **Jan Moravec** (1927–), CP-ČSSR CC Academy of Politics lecturer and specialist in relations between people's democracies, was arrested in 1968, dismissed in 1969, and expelled from the CP-ČSSR in 1970. He remained unemployed (1969–72) and became a clerk (1972–).

Vladislav Moulis (1931–), research associate at the Institute of East European History and specialist in USSR history, was arrested in 1968, dismissed, and expelled from the CP-ČSSR in 1970. He remained unemployed at first and became a librarian later (1970–).

Jiří Muška (1929–), instructor at Charles University Philosophical Faculty and specialist in the history of the Czech Legion in World War I, was dismissed and expelled from the CP-ČSSR in 1970. He became an unskilled worker (1970–73) and a clerk at the Institute of Archeology (1973–).

Milan Myška (1932–), lecturer at the pedagogical faculty in Ostrava and specialist in historical demography, was expelled from the CP-ČSSR in 1970. He remained without regular employment.

Jaromír Navrátil (1926–), head of the Institute of Military History research department (1945–69) and specialist in army history, was dismissed in 1969 and expelled from the CP-ČSSR in 1970. He remained without permanent work for a time and became an unskilled worker (1970–). He was a Charta 77 signatory.

Jana Neumannová (1932–), research associate at the CP-ČSSR CC Institute for the History of Socialism (1956–69) and specialist in CP-ČSSR cultural policy, was dismissed in 1969 and expelled from the CP-ČSSR in 1970. She remained without permanent work (1970–) and was a Charta 77 signatory.

Ladislav Niklíček (1936–), instructor at Charles University Philosophical Faculty and specialist in CP-ČSSR history in the 1930s, was arrested in 1968, dismissed, and expelled from the CP-ČSSR in 1970. He became a clerk at the faculty of medicine (1970–).

Jan Novák (1930–), research associate at the CP-ČSSR CC Institute for the History of Socialism and specialist in CP-ČSSR and labor history in the 1930s, was dismissed in 1969 and expelled from the CP-ČSSR in 1970. He became a streetcar conductor (1970–).

Josef Novotný (1923–) research associate at the CP-ČSSR CC Institute for the History of Socialism and specialist in the history of the clandestine CP-ČSSR during 1938–45, was arrested in 1968, dismissed in 1969, and expelled from the CP-ČSSR in 1970. He became an unskilled worker (1970–) and was the author of a 1972 unpublished manuscript.

Dana Nývltová (1927–), Institute of Military History associate and specialist in the history of the Czechoslovak army during World War II, was arrested in 1968, dismissed, and expelled from the CP-ČSSR in 1970. She became a bookkeeper (1970–).

Věra Olivová (1927–), lecturer in Czechoslovak history at Charles University Philosophical Faculty and specialist in the political history of the first Czech republic, was expelled from the CP-ČSSR in 1970. A disability pensioner first, she became a clerk at a department of history and ethnology.

Jaroslav Opat (1922–), research associate at the Institute of East European History and specialist in the history of Southeast Europe, was dismissed in 1969 and expelled from the CP-ČSSR in 1970. Unemployed first, he became a stoker and bricklayer and lived with a disability pension later. He was a Charta 77 signatory and author of samizdat studies. In 1995 he was the director of the AVČR Masaryk Institute, reestablished in 1990.

Alexander Ort, research associate at the Institute for International Politics and Economics and specialist in the foreign policy of the first Czech republic, was dismissed in 1969 and expelled from the CP-ČSSR in 1970. He remained without permanent work (1969–).

Milan Otáhal (1928–), ČSAV History Institute researcher (1955–70), head of the Department of Modern Czechoslovak and World History, and specialist in post-1945 Czechoslovak history, was arrested in 1968, dismissed [q.v. 1969–: Prečan], and expelled from the CP-ČSSR in 1970. He became a disability pensioner. He was a Charta 77 signatory. Not allowed to publish in any Czechoslovak periodical, he was the author of several samizdat studies, including manuscript notes on *Dějiny a současnost* (an unofficial 1978 inquiry on Czechoslovakia's sixtieth anniversary among eighteen respondents, mostly historians). Between 1974 and 1989, he wrote, with psychiatrist **Petr Prihoda** and jurist, political scientist, and Charta 77 signatory **Petr Pithart** (?1941–), a survey of the Czech past from the Baroque period until the eve of World War II under the pen name Podiven, which was partially published in the exile quarterly *Svědectví* (Testimony; Paris), and published in full in Prague in 1991. From 1990 Otáhal has been an AVČR Institute for Contemporary History staff member [q.v. 1969–: Černý]. After his dismissal as a law professor, Pithart devoted himself to the reassessment of Czech history. A leading member of the opposition group Civic Forum, he became prime minister of the Czech Republic (1990–92) and a member of Parliament.

Libuše Otáhalová (1925–), ČSAV History Institute researcher and specialist in contemporary Czechoslovak history, was arrested in 1968 and dismissed. She was unemployed and lived on a disability pension (1970–).

František Palacký (1929–), instructor at the Pedagogical Academy in Ústi nad Labem and specialist in northern Bohemia's local history, without CP-ČSSR affiliation, was dismissed and became a teacher at a vocational school.

Ákoś Paulinyi (?1929–), instructor at Comenius University Philosophical Faculty, emigrated to Marburg, FRG.

Bohumil Pekárek (1923–), research associate at the CP-ČSSR CC Institute for the History of Socialism and specialist in the CP-ČSSR during 1938–45, was arrested in 1968, dismissed, and expelled from the CP-ČSSR in 1970. He became an unskilled worker (1970–).

Ivan Pfaff (?1925/28–), museum curator and specialist in nineteenth- and twentieth-century Czech cultural history, without CP-ČSSR affiliation, remained in administrative detention in [September] 1967 because he had written or publicized a manifesto of the Czechoslovak writer critical of prereform conditions. Released in 1968, he emigrated [in the fall] to Heidelberg, FRG, where he worked at the Rastatt Museum.

Karel Pichlíck (1928–), Institute of Military History research associate (1953–69) and specialist in World War I history, was arrested in 1968, dismissed in 1969, and expelled from the CP-ČSSR in 1970. He became a laborer (1970–). He was a Charta 77 signatory and author of an unpublished 1977 manuscript about theater history.

Věra Picková (1924–), Institute of Military History research associate (1951–69) and specialist in sixteenth- and seventeenth-century military history, was dismissed in 1969 and expelled from the CP-ČSSR in 1970. She became a clerk in a commercial office (1969–).

Jiřina Pokorná (1919–), research associate at the CP-ČSSR CC Institute for the History of Socialism and specialist in CP-ČSSR history in the 1930s, was expelled from the CP-ČSSR in 1970. She became a translator.

Pavel Polák, associate at the SAV Institute for the History of the European Socialist Countries and specialist in Russian-Czechoslovak relations in 1917–39, was dismissed and expelled from the CP-ČSSR in 1970.

Historian **Josef Polišenský** (1915–2001), a specialist in the history of international relations and European war, was dismissed at Charles University (1970–1989).

Zdeněk Pousta (1940–), archivist (1965–70) and specialist in CP-ČSSR history, was dismissed and expelled from the CP-ČSSR in 1970. He became a taxi driver (1969/70–).

Vilém Prečan (1933–) was a ČSAV History Institute researcher (1957–70), a specialist in the history of the resistance movements during World War II, particularly in Slovakia, and a CP-ČSSR member (1951–70). On 24 August 1968, he issued a statement against the occupation, which was published in a Czechoslovak historical journal. In 1969 two of his book manuscripts on Slovak history during World War II were suppressed for political reasons. In a September letter to CP-ČSSR Secretary Husák he wrote that he was stripped of his passport and prevented from doing research abroad and that a security official had made inquiries about his two weeks of research in the Central Archives of Bratislava in August. In April 1970 he was dismissed on the grounds of "political unreliability" but not tried or imprisoned. Later proceedings against him, Otáhal [q.v. 1969–], Seidlerová [q.v. 1969–], and Viktoria Čecková were started on the charge of compiling and publishing *Seven Days in Prague: August 21–27*, documenting the Warsaw Pact invasion and later called *The Black Book*. They were interrogated by the security police (Prečan eight times) and in April 1971 indicted on charges of instigation (in 1974 changed into "subversion"). The book was condemned by the Soviet authorities as a "gross falsification of the facts, having nothing in common with historical scholarship" and withdrawn. Among the first to protest this were British historians A.J.P. Taylor, Hugh Trevor-Roper, and Francis Carsten, American historian Paul Ward, and many other colleagues from Western Europe and the United States. In the spring of 1970, the multiauthor manuscript *An Outline of Czechoslovak History*, vol. 4, *1945–1948*, with Prečan as the editorial secretary, was suppressed for political reasons. A multivolume source edition about Slovakia in 1944 could not appear in print because he was the editor. The second part of his study *Nazi Politics and the Tiso Regime on the Eve of the Uprising* was not printed for similar reasons. From 1970 to 1976, he was a stoker in a hospital and a porter. During this period he received anonymous telephone calls and had his telephone tapped. He burned his "dangerous papers". In 1974–76 Prečan's 1973 text *Social Sciences in the Straitjacket of 'Consolidation'* was published under different names (Vratislav Prošek, Jiří Zemla) in short installments in two samizdat journals. In January 1975 he lost his job as a porter in a Prague wine café. In April his house was raided by the police, who seized a collection of exile journals and part of his library, archives, diary, and letters, most of which were returned to him in [June] 1976. In July 1975 he sent an Open Letter to the participants of the 14th International Congress of Historical Sciences, meeting in San Francisco in August–September, with details on his personal situation, which was read out by the German historian Heinrich August Winkler, University of Freiburg. The day after the Congress, Prečan was interrogated by the police. On 29 September he was called "an unprincipled enemy of socialism" during a further interrogation. In April 1976 the police made a raid on his house. In July he emigrated to Munich, Hannover, and Scheinfeld, FRG. In August 1977 he was stripped of his Czechoslovak nationality because of an article he had written for *The Times* (London). In 1980 he presented *Acta Creationis* to the 15th International Congress of Historical Sciences, meeting in Bucharest. The Czechoslovak government banned his work. In 1988, heading the Documentation Center for the Promotion of Independent Czechoslovak Literature in Scheinfeld-Schwarzenberg, Prečan started *Acta*, a quarterly magazine about unofficial Czechoslovak culture. In 1990 he founded the AVČR Institute for Contemporary History and was its director (1990–98) and chairman of the Czech National Committee of Historians.

Eva Prušinová (1930–), Institute of Military History associate (1956–69) and specialist in the history of the Czechoslovak army, was dismissed in 1969 and expelled from the CP-ČSSR in 1970. She became a postal clerk (1970–).

Michal Reiman (1930–), lecturer in CP-ČSSR history and the Russian Revolution at the CP-ČSSR CC Academy of Politics, was dismissed in 1969 and expelled from the CP-ČSSR in 1970. He became a translator (1969–) and was the author of samizdat studies. He emigrated to Tübingen, FRG, in 1976.

Pavel Reiman (1902–), director of the CP-ČSSR CC Institute for the History of Socialism (until 1968) and specialist in the history of the CP-ČSSR and the labor movement, was expelled from the CP-ČSSR in 1970. As a pensioner, he was the author of several samizdat studies.

Miroslava Rošková (1933–), instructor at the Bratislava Institute of Technology and specialist in the communist youth and students' organizations in the 1930s, was dismissed in 1969 and expelled from the CP-ČSSR in 1970. She remained without permanent work.

Jaroslav Šedivý (1929–), research associate at the Institute for International Politics and Economics and specialist in Czechoslovak foreign policy history, was dismissed in 1969, expelled from the CP-ČSSR in 1970, and imprisoned for some months. He became a window cleaner (1969–).

Irena Seidlerová (1926–), former Theresienstadt concentration camp internee (1943–45), ČSAV History Institute researcher, and specialist in the history of science, physics, and technology, was dismissed and expelled from the CP-ČSSR in 1970 [q.v. 1969–: Prečan]). She became a factory foreman.

Pavel Seifter (1938–), instructor at Charles University Philosophical Faculty and specialist in international labor history, was dismissed in 1969 and expelled from the CP-ČSSR in 1970. He became a window cleaner and was a Charta 77 signatory.

Zdeněk Šikl (1933–), chief editor of the journal *History and the Present* (1963–69) and specialist in the history of the first Czechoslovak republic, was dismissed in 1969 and expelled from the CP-ČSSR in 1970. He became an employee in a public health administration.

Jiří Sládek (1913–), research associate at the CP-ČSSR CC Institute for the History of Socialism and specialist in CP-ČSSR history, was dismissed and expelled from the CP-ČSSR in 1970. He retired.

František Šmahel (1934–), medievalist and ČSAV History Institute staff member, was dismissed. He became director at the AVČR Historical Institute (1990–98) and director of its department of early history (1998–). He also headed the seminar on medieval Bohemian history at Charles University Institute for Czech History.

Josef Smolka (1929–), ČSAV History Institute researcher (1955–69) and specialist in the history of natural sciences, was dismissed in 1969 and expelled from the CP-ČSSR in 1970. He became a clerk (1969–).

Antonín Šnejdárek (1914–), director of the Institute for International Politics and Economics at the Ministry of Foreign Affairs and specialist in World War II history and international politics, was dismissed. He emigrated to Paris, where he became a university professor.

Jiří Šolc (1930–), Institute of Military History research associate (1956–70) and specialist in the history of the Czechoslovak army during World War II, was dismissed and expelled from the CP-ČSSR in 1972. He became a construction worker (1971–).

Zdeněk Šolle (1924–), ČSAV History Institute researcher (1950–70) and specialist in nineteenth-century labor history, was dismissed and expelled from the CP-ČSSR in 1970. He became a ČSAV archival clerk (1971–). In 1995 he was a member of the Department for the History of Academic Institutions at the AVČR Archive.

Štefan Štvrtecký (1928–), associate at the SAV History Institute for the European Socialist Countries (1952–70) and specialist in the history of Slovak communists in the USSR, was dismissed and expelled from the CP-ČSSR in 1970. He remained without permanent work.

Milan Švankmajer (1928–), research associate at the Institute for East European History (1953–69) and specialist in eighteenth- and nineteenth-century Russian history, was dismissed in 1969 and expelled from the CP-ČSSR in 1970. He became a librarian (1970–).

František Svátek (1936–), professor of international relations at the CP-ČSSR CC Academy of Politics (1964–70), board member of *Dějiny a současnost*, and specialist in international labor history and in Czech historiography, was dismissed and expelled from the CP-ČSSR in 1970. He became a salesman in an antiquarian bookstore and samizdat writer. He became an AVČR Institute for Contemporary History staff member (1990–96) and professor at Charles University Philosophical Faculty.

Sáva Svatoň (1923–), former Auschwitz extermination camp internee (1944–45), Institute of Military History research associate (1952–69), and specialist in World War I history, was arrested in 1968, dismissed in 1969, and expelled from the CP-ČSSR in 1970. He became a laborer (1970–).

Mikuláš Teich (1918–), ČSAV History Institute researcher, emigrated to Cambridge, United Kingdom.

Alice Teichová (1920–), economic historian and lecturer at the Pedagogical Academy in Prague, emigrated to Cambridge, United Kingdom.

Jan Tesař (1933–), ČSAV History Institute researcher (1955–68) and specialist in World War II history, resigned from the CP-ČSSR in 1968. He became a night porter and was arrested in September 1969 but was released without trial after thirteen months' detention. Unemployed, he was the author of several samizdat studies and unpublished manuscripts such as *Motherland, Nation and History in Czech Thought during the First Years of German Occupation 1939–1942* (1968). He was one of the eight authors of the 1969 *Ten-Point Manifesto*, written at the occasion of the first anniversary of the August 1968 invasion. In November 1971 he was rearrested for printing and disseminating "antistate leaflets", distributed during the national elections, encouraging people to abstain from voting and criticizing the 1968 Warsaw Pact occupation. In July 1972 he was tried and sentenced to six years' imprisonment, during which he was allegedly ill-treated. Upon his release after nearly five years in October 1976, he was unemployed and asked permission to work abroad. He was a Charta 77 signatory. In April or May 1980, he was expelled to the FRG and deprived of his citizenship. He lived in Hannover.

František Tichý, historian and professor at a Litomysl high school, Social-Democrat before 1948, organizer of a solidarity meeting after the death of Palach [q.v. 1969], was barred in 1970 from teaching history for many years (but was permitted to teach German and Latin). He retired.

Miloš Tichý (1931–), instructor at Comenius University and specialist in Slovak regional history, was dismissed in 1969 and expelled from the CP-ČSSR in 1970. He remained without permanent work.

Miroslav Truc (1929–), instructor at Charles University History Institute and specialist in the sixteenth- and seventeenth-century history of Charles University, was dismissed in 1969 and expelled from the CP-ČSSR in 1970. He became a depot worker (1969–).

František Uličný (1932–), instructor at Prešov University Philosophical Faculty and specialist in the history of settlement in eastern Slovakia, was dismissed in 1969 and expelled from the CP-ČSSR in 1970. He remained without permanent work.

Zdeněk Ungermann (1918–?), lecturer at the Pedagogical Academy in Pilsen and specialist in local history, was expelled from the CP-ČSSR in 1970.

Otto Urban (1938–), specialist in Czech history from 1848 to 1918, remained at the Charles University history department but was not allowed to advance to the position of lecturer or professor or, at first, to lecture. His work was unfavorably received in official ČSAV circles but appreciated by other historians and awarded a prize in Vienna in 1990. In 1995 he was a member of the Czech National Committee of Historians.

Ján Ušiak (1928–), instructor at Comenius University and specialist in the history of the Protestant churches in Slovakia, was dismissed in 1969 and expelled from the CP-ČSSR in 1970. He remained without permanent work (1969–).

Antonín Václavů (1922–), former concentration camp internee (1940–45), research associate at the CP-ČSSR CC Institute for the History of Socialism, and specialist in twentieth-century agricultural history, was dismissed and expelled from the CP-ČSSR in 1970. He became a disability pensioner.

Vladka Václavů (1928–), instructor in Marxism at the Charles University law faculty, specialist in CP-ČSSR history in the 1930s, was dismissed in 1969 and expelled from the CP-ČSSR in 1970. She became a librarian (1969–).

Jaroslav Valenta (1930–), research associate at the Institute of East European History (1956–69) and specialist in Czechoslovak–Polish relations, was dismissed in 1969 and expelled from the CP-ČSSR in 1970. He became a disability pensioner (1970–). In 1995 he was a staff member at the department of nineteenth- and twentieth-century history of the AVČR History Institute and editorial board member of the Edvard Beneš Society.

Historian and essayist **Zdeněk Vašíček** was imprisoned in Prague in 1972–74 for writing and editing samizdat publications, inter alia, about the philosophy of history and the methodology of historiography. He was a Charta 77 signatory. He left Czechoslovakia in 1981 and became a lecturer at Bochum University, FRG.

Václav Veber (1931–), lecturer in political science at Charles University Philosophical Faculty and specialist in research on Lenin and on socialist ideologies, was arrested in 1969, dismissed, and expelled from the CP-ČSSR in 1970. A clerk from 1970 to 1974, he was unemployed thereafter.

Martin Vietor, professor at Comenius University law faculty and specialist in the Slovak Soviet republic and southern Slovakia under Hungarian occupation, was expelled from the CP-ČSSR in 1970.

Miroslav Vlašánek (1928–), CP-ČSSR CC Academy of Politics instructor and specialist in CP-ČSSR history in the 1930s, was arrested in 1968, dismissed in 1969, and expelled from the CP-ČSSR in 1970. He became a bricklayer (1970–).

Eva Vlčková (1924–), research associate at the CP-ČSSR CC Institute for the History of Socialism and specialist in the history of the German Social Democratic exiles in Prague, was dismissed and expelled from the CP-ČSSR in 1970. She became a disability pensioner.

Stanislav Zámečník (1920–), former Nazi concentration camp internee (1942–45), Institute of Military History research associate (1953–69), and specialist in the history of the 1945 Prague Uprising, was arrested in 1968, dismissed in 1969, and expelled from the CP-ČSSR in 1970. He became a laborer (1969–) and was the author of a 1969 samizdat study.

1969–80   Among the samizdat authors engaged in historical publications during 1969–80 and not yet mentioned were **Stanislav Biman, Joseph Carneades** (pseudonym), **F. Čermák** (pseudonym), **Albert Černý, Ivan Dérer** (died 1973), **Zdeněk Jelínek, Robert Kalivoda** (1923–89), **Božena Komárková** (1903–97), **Jan Malina, Tomáš Pasák, František Šamalík, František Silnický, Stanislav Šisler, Josef Sládeček** (pseudonym), **Oldřich Sládek, Zdeněk Sládek**.

1969   On 16 January **Jan Palach** (1948–69), history student at Charles University, set fire to himself on Wenceslas Square, Prague, to protest the Warsaw Pact occupation of Czechoslovakia. He died on 19 January. In 1989 the anniversary of his suicide was marked by demonstrations, despite a ban imposed by the authorities. On 16 January 1989, **Jana Petrova** and **Otakar Veverka**, members of unofficial peace groups, and playwright Havel [q.v. 1977] attempted to lay flowers on Wenceslas Square in memory of the twentieth anniversary of Palach's death. They were arrested and charged with public order offenses. Havel was sentenced to nine months' imprisonment for "hooliganism", and Petrova to eight months. Both were paroled after serving half their sentences. Veverka, sentenced to twelve months' imprisonment, was pardoned in late November.

1972   In May Ministry of Culture instructions to the librarians listed "publications defending the Czechoslovak Republic existing before the Munich Agreement (1938)", works by and on Masaryk and Beneš, and works by other "bourgeois politicians" in the category of "ideologically harmful publications". They were housed separately in locked rooms.

In November a seminar of communist historians took place in Prague. They published a list of twenty-one proscribed historians termed as "aggressive".

1973   In April a confidential official list of books which were to be withdrawn from circulation in the libraries included the complete work of Ferdinand Beer [q.v. 1969–], Belda [q.v. 1969–], Václav Černý [q.v. 1944–], historian **Jiří Frel**, Graus [q.v. 1969–], Hájek [q.v. 1969–], Hübl [q.v. 1964–], Kalandra [q.v. 1949–50], Kaplan [q.v. 1969–], Mencl [q.v. 1969–], Otáhal [q.v. 1969–], Pekař [q.v. 1948], Michal Reiman [q.v. 1969–], Pavel Reiman [q.v. 1969–], Renc [q.v. 1948–], **Aleksandr Solzhenitsyn** (1918–), and Teich [q.v. 1969–]. It also included one or some works of Červinka [q.v. 1969–], Doležal [q.v. 1969–], Durman [q.v. 1969–], Gajanová [q.v. 1969–], Kalista [q.v. 1945–82], Kavka [q.v. 1969–], Kořalka [q.v. 1969–], Křen [q.v. 1969–], Lukeš [q.v. 1969–87], Lvová [q.v. 1969–], Novotný [q.v. 1969–], Olivová [q.v. 1969–], Pfaff [q.v. 1969–], Pichlíck [q.v. 1969–], Šolc [q.v. 1969–], Šolle [q.v. 1969–], and Teichová [q.v. 1969–]. It further included the novel *The End of the Sixth Army* (1970), about the destruction of the sixth German army at Stalingrad, by novelist **Alexander Kluge** (1932–); a history of the Bible (1969) by **Stefan Andres** (1906–70); an anthology of the history of Czechoslovak philosophy (1963) edited by Kalivoda [q.v. 1969–80]; a history of political and legal ideologies (1965, 1967) by **Jiří Boguszak**; a work about Masaryk and the 1918 Washington Declaration (1968) by **S.B. Kozák**; a world history of sex (1969) by **Morus**; and a handbook of Czech and Slovak literary history (1966) by **Gregorec Páleníček** and **V.L. Petrak**. A similar list was issued in [early 1982].

1973–   In September 1973 the book *From Illegality into the Rising: Chapters from the History of Democratic Resistance* (1969), honored with a Socialist Academy prize in 1970, was removed from public libraries and bookshops. Its author was Slovak historian **Jozef Jablonický** (1933–), staff member (1960–74) and head of the Modern History Department at the SAV History Institute. A party-sanctioned condemnation shown to him said that he underestimated the communist resistance and overrated the noncommunist resistance during the 1944 Slovak National Uprising (seeing in the uprising an assertion of Slovak nationhood). The book also criticized the 1964 memoirs of CP-ČSSR Secretary Husák, who had participated in the uprising. In August 1974 Jablonický was dismissed from the SAV History Institute and removed to the Slovak Institute of Conservation of Monuments and Protection of Nature. His new study on the communist resistance could not be published. The state security investigated his case. His house was searched eleven times. During four house searches in November 1976, many of his books, periodicals, personal correspondence, research archives, and at least three manuscripts, including his study *The Slovak Communist Party in Anti-Fascist Resistance*, were confiscated and not returned. He was interrogated by the police, demoted, and expelled from the Slovak Communist Party. In February 1978 his permit for archival research was withdrawn. In August he completed a new text of *Bratislava and the Origins of the Slovak National Rising*, the original manuscript of which was seized by the police in November 1976. In 1979 he wrote two polemical articles against the gaps in official historiography (published in 1994). His study *The Failure of Malár's Army in the Carpathians* circulated in the Edice Petlice samizdat series. The first two versions of this study were seized by the police in November 1976 and June 1978; the third version was written while Jablonický simultaneously hid away remnants of his own archival collection and every completed page of his manuscript. In the same year, he became an alleged "perpetrator of antisocial activities" by obstinately insisting on his right to historical research. His writings were labeled "harmful to the interests of the state" and "contradicting official historical findings". In November 1979 he was arrested while visiting Prague, interrogated, briefly detained, and put back on the train for Slovakia. The police alleged that an illegal meeting connected with Charta 77 was to take place in his presence the following day. In May 1981 he was detained for four days. In August 1984 he had to appear at the customs administration because a customs official had allegedly found "objectionable printed material" (copies of émigré historical journals) in a parcel from Paris. He was charged with "incitement" and his flat, garage, and place of work were searched. His most recent papers on history as well as some reference documents were confiscated, possibly because they were considered particularly dangerous in the year of the fortieth anniversary of the Slovak Uprising. He was then interrogated. In the mid- and late-1980s, he published in the samizdat *Historické studie* (Historical Studies). He was a banned writer until November 1989. In 1990 he was able to resume his work at the Academy of Sciences Political Science Institute.

1974–75   Between April 1974 and August 1975, Loewenstein [q.v. 1969–], Bohumil Černý [q.v. 1969–], Macek [q.v. 1969–], Graus [q.v. 1969–], German historian Eberhard Jäckel, and American historian David Schoenbaum prepared a booklet, *Acta Persecutionis: A Document from Czechoslovakia*, that gave an overview of the persecution of the historical profession in Czechoslovakia and a list of 145 persecuted historians. Six thousand copies were distributed at the 14th International Congress of Historical Sciences, meeting in San Francisco in August 1975, together with a thousand copies of the open letter by Prečan [q.v. 1969–]. The list with names appeared in several newspapers and in the *Congressional Record* of the United States.

1975   The authorities ordered the suspension of the annual celebration of 28 October 1918, the Day of National Independence.

1977   Among the Charta 77 signatories not already mentioned were historians **Egon Čierny, Oldřich Jaroš, Jaroslav Jirů, Václay Komeda, Jaroslav Krejčí** (1916–). **Bohumil Pokorný, František Povolny, Miroslav Šumavský, Jiří Vančura, Václav Vrabec**; art historians **Anna Fárová, Ludvík Hlaváček, Vera Jirousová** (1944–), and literary historian **Karel Konstroun**.

Several persecuted philosophers were intensely involved in the historical debate. They included **Jan Patočka** (1907–77), a philosopher of history twice forced to give up lecturing (in 1948 and 1972), author of the 1975 samizdat study *Heretical Essays in the Philosophy of History*, and Charta 77 spokesman who died following interrogation in March 1977; **Ladislav Hejdánek** (1927–), a philosopher who since 1971 had been working as a night watchman and furnace stoker, a Charta 77 spokesman; **Milan Šimečka** (1930–90), former lecturer at Comenius University and the Slovak College of Musical Arts, Bratislava, philosopher, and essayist who was dismissed in 1970, assigned to various menial jobs, imprisoned for more than a year on charges of "subversion", Charta 77 signatory; playwright and philosopher **Václav Havel** (1936–), a Charta 77 spokesman, imprisoned several times, later president of Czechoslovakia (1989–92) and the Czech Republic (1993–); **Václav Benda** (1946–99), Catholic philosopher and Charta 77 spokesman, in

January 1991 the prime parliamentary sponsor of the original "lus-trace" resolution on the screening and disqualifying of members of Parliament and high government officials who had collaborated with the former communist regime; and **Miroslav Kusý**, professor of Marxist philosophy at Comenius University, one of the leading thinkers of reform socialism, dismissed in 1968 and assigned a minor job in the university library, dismissed because he signed Charta 77, unskilled worker since then, arrested between August and October 1989.

1977–84   In the course of 1977, a series of illegal seminar courses for young persons excluded from higher education was started in Prague, Brno, Bratislava, and other towns under Charta 77 auspices. They were informally known as the "Jan Patočka University". Participating historians included Mezník [q.v. 1969–], Vašíček [q.v. 1969–], and Tesař [q.v. 1969–]. In a course on the history of Czech literature, the lecturers chose works of nineteenth-century writers omitted from official school curricula because of the risk that students might draw parallels with contemporary events (e.g., works dealing with the Czech national struggle against the Austro-Hungarian authorities). Among the lectures most frequently disturbed by police raids were those on twentieth-century history. The seminars continued until 1984 at least.

1977–81   A large historical debate took place among samizdat historians about the forced transfer (*odsun*) of some three million Sudeten Germans from Czechoslovakia in 1945–47. The debate started with an article condemning the *odsun*, written in December 1977 (published in *Svě-dectví* in 1978) by **Danubius** (a pseudonym). It created a controversy among "independent" and exile historians such as Hübl [q.v. 1964–], Kohout [q.v. 1969–], a group of authors called **Bohemus** (including Otáhal [q.v. 1969–], Prihoda [q.v. 1969–], Pithart [q.v. 1969–]), and others. In early 1979 and again in 1981, police interrogated many persons, including Mlynárik [q.v. 1969–90], who after persistent denials admitted that he was Danubius.

1978–89   From January 1978 to 1989, twenty-six typed or mimeographed volumes of the samizdat journal *Historické studie* appeared. After 1985 special volumes of the *Library of Historical Studies* appeared. In addition émigré journals in Paris, Rome, and elsewhere published samizdat work.

1978   In August **Emil Fuchs** (?1921–), and **Václav Kimák** (?1950–), two employees of the national health institute of the uranium industry at Pribram-Zdabor, were charged with incitement. Kimák reportedly systematically collected printed material about the 1968–69 period and other contemporary materials linked to this period "under the pretext of studying history". Fuchs reportedly gave him *The Gulag Archipelago*, by Solzhenitsyn [q.v. 1973] and the magazines *Listy* and *Svědectví.*

1979   A two-volume work by historian **František Kutnar**, *Survey of the History of Czech and Slovak Historiography* (Prague 1973–77), and especially volume two, *From the Beginning of Positivist Historiography to the Threshold of Marxist History-Writing*, was severely criticized by J. Haubelt in *Československý časopis historický*. Subsequently, the book was withdrawn from the market and from use in the universities. The Historický Klub (Historians' Club) in Prague, a group of historians under Kutnar's presidency who produced politically independent studies, was temporarily interrupted in the mid-1980s.

1981–   From 1981 the School of Education History Department at Palacky University, Olomouc, remained closed. In 1982 the School of Education History Department at Charles University was closed down. It was partially reestablished in February 1992.

1984–85   A large historical debate took place among samizdat historians in 1984–85. It started in May 1984 with the publication of Charta 77 Document 11/1984 *The Right to History*, which included a negative assessment of official historiography, a defense of the Catholic view on history, and a reappraisal of several episodes and persons in Czechoslovak history. It also criticized the severely restricted access to archives, especially for post-1918 material. Reactions came from historians such as Miloš Hájek [q.v. 1969–], Hübl [q.v. 1964–], Kohout [q.v. 1969–], Křen [q.v. 1969–], Mejdrová [q.v. 1969–], Mezník [q.v. 1969–], Mlynárik [q.v. 1969–90], Opat [q.v. 1969–], Otáhal [q.v. 1969–], Tesař [q.v. 1969–], and others such as Catholic editor **Ladislav Jehlička, Radomir Malý**, Pithart [q.v. 1969–], psychologist **Jaroslav Šabata** (1927–), and engineer and human-rights activist **Petr Uhl** (1941–). Many texts appeared in Hübl's 1985 samizdat publication *Voices on Czech History*. On 21 August 1984, a Charta 77 document invoked the right to historical truth to denounce the short-term arrests of Charta 77 spokespersons on 16–18 August, which were carried out to prevent Charta 77 from commemorating the anniversary of the 1968 military intervention.

1987   In November 1987 the Catholic civil-rights campaigner **Ivan Polanský** was arrested after a house search disclosed that various of his notebooks contained samizdat writings on, inter alia, modern Slovak history. In June 1988 he was sentenced to four years' imprisonment.

1988   On 9 or 10 November, several people, including Jiří Hájek [q.v. 1969–] and Miloš Hájek [q.v. 1969–], were detained in connection with an unofficial international historical symposium, "Czechoslovakia 1988", due to open in Prague on 11 November.

[1989]   In [1989] the first of a series of conferences to be held in the Delta Club, Prague—a conference on the meaning of Czech history by Marek [q.v. 1969–]—was prevented by the authorities.

1989   In November, immediately after the Velvet Revolution, the Statni Bezpecnost (StB, or State Security Police) reportedly burned part of its archives. More than 15,000 of their confidential files were destroyed, predominantly current files of highly placed agents and officials.

            After the Velvet Revolution, Marxist historians **Miroslav Kropilák** and **Samuel Cambel** were forced into early retirement for their collaboration with the former regime.

1993–   *See* Slovakia.

Also see Germany (1956: Wolfgramm), Poland (1968–88: Geremek), USSR (1968: Baeva; 1968–: Pavlenkov; 1969–: Meshener; 1972–82: Pyotr Yakir; 1973–94: Solzhenitsyn).

SOURCES

Acta Persecutionis: A Document from Czechoslovakia (San Francisco 1975).
Afanasev, Y., "Rusland zoekt naar zijn ware geschiedenis", *Parool*, 27 April 1996: 7.
American Historical Review, 1993: 650–52 (Kořalka).
Amnesty International, *Report* (London) 1972–73: 63; 1975–76: 159; 1977: 241–43; 1978: 208–9; 1982: 261–62; 1983: 249–50; 1990: 80–81.
Andreas, K. [=B. Loewenstein], "Historici in Tsjechoslowakije", *Internationale spectator*, 1974: 272–75.
Annual Obituary (Chicago/London) 1989: 624–26 (Hübl), 1993: 733–35 (Jiří Hájek).
Bartošek, K., "Czechoslovakia: The State of Historiography", in: W. Laqueur & G.L. Mosse eds., *The New History: Trends in Historical Research and Writing since World War II* (New York 1967) 138.
———, "Les Historiens dans l'Histoire", *La Nouvelle Alternative*, 1986, no.1: 47–49.
Bernath, M., & F. von Schroeder eds., *Biographisches Lexicon zur Geschichte Südeuropas*, vol. 2 (Munich 1976) 41–42, 191–92.
Boia, L. ed., *Great Historians of the Modern Age: An International Dictionary* (Westport 1991) 154–57.
Boris, P., *Die sich Lossagten: Stichworte zu Leben und Werk von 461 Exkommunisten und Dissidenten* (Cologne 1983) 41–42, 52–53, 104, 131, 216, 224.
Boyd, K. ed., *Encyclopedia of Historians and Historical Writing* (London/Chicago 1999) 356–57.

Bronkhorst, D., *Truth and Reconciliation: Obstacles and Opportunities for Human Rights* (Amsterdam 1995) 81.

Bruch, R. vom, & R.A. Müller eds., *Historikerlexikon: Von der Antike bis zum 20. Jahrhundert* (Munich 1991) 249–50.

Bugajski, J., *Czechoslovakia: Charter 77's Decade of Dissent* (New York 1987) 20–22, 111–12.

ČSSR: Fünf Jahre "Normalisierung": 21.8.1968/21.8.1973 Dokumentation (Hamburg [1973]).

Czech National Committee of Historians, *A Guide to Historical Institutes, History Departments, Archives and Museums in the Czech Republic* (Prague 1995) 7–8, 10, 17, 19–20, 22, 26, 37, 42, 44, 47.

Dittrich, Z.R., B. Naarden, & H. Renner eds., *Knoeien met het verleden* (Utrecht/Antwerp 1984) 190, 192.

Ducreux, M.-E., "Les Tchèques et leur histoire", in: Marès ed. 1996: 205–6.

Erdmann, K.D., *Die Ökumene der Historiker: Geschichte der internationalen Historikerkongresse und des Comité international des sciences historiques* (Göttingen 1987) 357, 364–65, 368.

Gorman, R.A. ed., *Biographical Dictionary of Neo-Marxism* (Westport 1985) 223–24.

Hamsik, D., *Writers against Rulers* (London 1971) 103.

Hauner, M., "Recasting Czech History" [also "One Hundred Years of Czech History"], *Survey: A Journal of Soviet and East European Studies*, 1979, no.3: 214, 218–26.

Held, J., *Dictionary of East European History since 1945* (Westport 1994) 152–53.

Heneka, A., F. Janouch, V. Prečan, & J. Vladislav eds., *A Besieged Culture: Czechoslovakia Ten Years after Helsinki* (Stockholm/Vienna 1985) 25–29, 78–80, 92–94, 112–14, 199, 205–6, 218–19, 235, 238–39, 242, 249–51, 256, 275–77, 282–83, 287–89, 291–93, 295.

Historical Abstracts (CD-rom version) (Beer, Gajdos, Korbel, Prague Archive, Slavika).

Hoeven, H. van der, *Lost Memory: Libraries and Archives Destroyed in the Twentieth Century*, part 1, *Libraries* (WWW-text 1996) 8–9.

Index on Censorship, 1/72: 82; 2/72: 38, 41–43, 48, 50–51; 3–4/72: 115; 1/73: 104; 4/73: 91, 93–97; 3/74: 80, 93–94; 4/74: ii; 2/75: 87; 4/75: 53–57; 3/76: 27, 38–39, 63–71; 2/77: 64; 3/77: 26–29; 4/77: 68–69; 3/78: 35; 3/79: 55–56; 5/79: 62–63, 65; 4/81: 44–45; 5/81: 24–25; 6/81: 16; 3/82: 43; 4/82: 17, 44; 5/82: 34; 1/84: 6–10; 3/84: 45; 6/85: 20; 1/86: 57, 61; 4/86: 24–27; 3/87: 37; 3/88: 6, 14–21; 5/88: 52–54; 7/88: 34; 1/89: 28, 35; 2/89: 36; 4/89: 6; 10/89: 37; 2/90: 36; 10/90: 32; 6/92: 19; 5/99: 27.

Jablonický, J., *Glosy o historiografii SNP: Zneužívanie a falsovanie dejín SNP* (Bratislava 1994) 83–110.

———, personal communication, June 1996.

Jäckel, E., "Acta Liberationis", in: Prečan, Janišová, & Roeser eds. 1999: 271–98.

Keesings historisch archief, 1988: 184.

Keesing's Record of World Events, 1984: 32988A; 1989: 36400A, 37092B; 1990: 37736A.

Kirschbaum, S.J., *Historical Dictionary of Slovakia* (Lanham 1999) 126, 171–72.

Kořalka, J., "Historiography of the Countries of Eastern Europe: Czechoslovakia", *American Historical Review*, 1992: xiii, 1026–40.

Kotkin, S., "Terror, Rehabilitation, and Historical Memory: An Interview with Dmitrii Iurasov", *Russian Review*, 1992: 247.

Kusý, M., "On the Purity of the Historian's Craft", *Kosmas*, 1984–85, III/no.2 & IV/no.1: v, 29–38.

Lewytzkyj, B., & J. Stroynowski, *Who's Who in the Socialist Countries* (New York/Munich 1978) 370, 372, 432.

"Die Liste der verbotene Bücher und Autoren", in: ČSSR ([1973]) 298–307.

Littell, R., ed., *The Czech Black Book* (London 1969) ix, 3–4, 29, 62–63, 82, 106, 155–56, 284–86.

Loewenstein, B., "Kauza B.L./Die Akte B.L.", in: Prečan, Janišová, & Roeser eds. 1999: 299–351.

Marès, A. ed., *Histoire et pouvoir en Europe médiane* (Paris 1996).

Mazour, A.G., *Modern Russian Historiography* (Princeton 1958) 235.

Obrman, J., "Havel Challenges Czech Historical Taboos", *RFE/RL Research Reports*, 11 June 1993: 44–51.

Opat, J., "Zdeněk Kalista: Reflections on a Czech Historian's Eightieth Birthday", in: Prečan ed. 1980: 238–39, 243, 249–50.

Petruf, P., "L'Historiographie slovaque des années 80" and "L'Historiographie slovaque dans les années 1990–1992", in: Marès ed. 1996: 82, 84, 87–88, 92–94, 213.

Pithart, P., "Let Us Be Gentle to Our History", *Kosmas*, 1984–85, III/no.2 & IV/no.1: iii–vi, 17–22.

Prečan, V., "Comment and Controversy", *American Historical Association Newsletter*, September 1976: 15.

———, *Human Rights in Czechoslovakia: A Documentation, September 1981–December 1982* (Paris 1983) 13–15, 18–19, 21, 32, 42, 48, 93, 105, 107.

———, *Die sieben Jahre von Prag 1969–1976: Briefe und Dokumente aus der Zeit der "Normalisierung"* (Frankfurt 1978) 8–9, 12, 14–15, 28, 34–40, 43–44, 55–60, 67–70, 189, 198, 200–201, 213–22, 239–40, 248.

———, "A Slovak Historian Resists Coercion: The Case of Jozef Jablonický", in: Prečan ed. 1980: 22–24, 230–37, 235–36.

———, ed., *Acta Creationis: Independent Historiography in Czechoslovakia 1969–1980* (Hannover 1980) 4–65, 73, 252; supplement: xxxvi–lx.

Prečan, V., M. Janišová, & M. Roeser eds., *Grenzüberschreitungen oder der Vermittler Bedrich Loewenstein* (Festschrift; Prague/Brno 1999) 12–13, 361–67.

"Das Recht auf Geschichte: Kontroversen in der ČSSR um die Charta 77", *Osteuropa*, 1986: A370–84.

Renner, H., *A History of Czechoslovakia since 1945* (London/New York 1989) 23.

———, personal communication, October 1990, December 1996.

———, "Van brandstapel tot papiermolen: Over boekvernietigingen in Tsjechoslowakije", *Groniek*, 1983, no.83: 46.

Riese, H.-P. ed., *Bürgerinitiative für die Menschenrechte: Die Tschechoslowakische Opposition zwischen dem "Prager Frühling" und der "Charta '77"* (Cologne/Frankfurt 1977) 36–43, 54–59, 100–111, 194–98, 201, 223–31, 286–93, 318–20.

Röder, W., & H.A. Strauss eds., *Biographisches Handbuch der deutschsprachigen Emigration nach 1933*, vol. 1 (Munich 1980) 580.

Rosenberg, T., *The Haunted Land: Facing Europe's Ghosts after Communism* (New York 1995) 5, 70, 72, 106, 112–13, 409.

Rupnik, J., "Historian's Notebook: The Politics of History-Writing in Czechoslovakia", *History Workshop*, Spring 1981: 166–68.

Schmidt-Hartmann, E., "Lost Illusions", *UNESCO Courier*, May 1994: 32–34.

Schöttler, P. ed., *Geschichtsschreibung als Legitimationswissenschaft 1918–1945* (Frankfurt/Main 1999) 21.

Seibt, F., H. Lemberg, & H. Slapnicka eds., *Biographisches Lexikon zur Geschichte der Böhmischen Länder* vol. 3–2 (Munich 1986) 124.

Shafer, B.C., "The 14th International Congress of Historical Sciences", *American Historical Association Newsletter*, December 1975: 8.

Šimečka, M., "Black Holes: Concerning the Metamorphoses of Historical Memory", *Kosmas*, 1984–85, III/no.2 & IV/no.1: 23–28 (quote 24), iv.

Skilling, H.G., *Samizdat and an Independent Society in Central and Eastern Europe* (Oxford 1989) 99–122, 257–61.

———— & V. Prečan, "Real Socialism in Czechoslovakia and the Search for Historical Truth", *Kosmas*, 1984–85, III/no.2 & IV/no.1: v, 1–5.

Stewart, D.W., & C.V. Stewart, "Lustration in Poland and the Former Czechoslovakia: A Study in Decommunization", *International Journal of Public Administration*, 1995: 889.

Strauss, H.A., & W. Röder eds., *International Biographical Dictionary of Central European Émigrés 1933–1945*, vol. 2 (New York 1983) 261–62, 365–66, 933–34.

Stroynowski, J. ed., *Who's Who in the Socialist Countries of Europe* (Munich 1989) 67, 76, 80–81, 86, 134, 144, 165, 173–75, 184, 250, 268, 270, 274, 291, 294, 298, 332, 369, 376, 399, 406, 421, 437, 439, 451, 453–54, 457, 461, 482, 495, 500, 532, 534, 537, 559, 564–66, 569, 577, 581, 592, 605, 620–21, 625, 627, 633, 638, 649, 654, 680, 686, 691, 707, 710–11, 717, 728, 733, 755, 758–59, 766, 792, 800, 805, 816, 830, 842, 847, 851–52, 858, 873, 876, 905, 918, 920, 945–46, 952, 983, 999, 1052, 1057, 1067, 1091, 1095–96, 1141, 1146–47, 1195, 1199, 1221, 1236, 1241, 1244, 1247, 1256, 1266, 1338.

Svátek, F., "L'Historiographie tchèque des années 80", in: Mareš ed. 1996: 63–64, 71, 77, 79.

Tucker, A., "Shipwrecked: Patočka's Philosophy of Czech History", *History and Theory*, 1996: 196, 199.

Unfried, B., "Tchécoslovaquie: L'Historiographie indépendante depuis 1968", in: A. Brossat, S. Combe, J.-Y. Potel, & J.-C. Szurek eds., *A l'Est, la mémoire retrouvée* (Paris 1990) 468–88.

"Verfolgter Historiker", in: ČSSR ([1973]) 285–89.

Weber, W., *Biographisches Lexicon zur Geschichtswissenschaft in Deutschland, Österreich und der Schweitz: Die Lehrstuhlinhaber für Geschichte von den Anfängen des Faches bis 1970* (Frankfurt/Main 1987) 185.

Woolf, D.R. ed., *A Global Encyclopedia of Historical Writing* (New York/London 1998) 219, 500, 698–99, 762–63.

World University Service, *Academic Freedom 1990* (London 1990) 174–75.

"Zum Schicksal der Historiker in der Tschechoslowakei", *Geschichte in Wissenschaft und Unterricht*, 1973: 581–85.

D

DENMARK

1989   Several researchers called Danish archival access policy extremely restrictive. The policy reportedly forced historians and journalists to study contemporary Danish history in the archives of Washington and London and seriously hampered historical research.

SOURCES

Vandkunsten: Konflikt, politik og historie udgives af, 1989, no.1 (Special issue "Tanke-kontrol og historieskrivning: Arkivpolitik fra NATO til glasnost") 185–87.

DOMINICAN REPUBLIC

1930–61   The historiography of the Dominican Republic suffered greatly from the dictatorship of Rafael Trujillo and its official ideology of Hispanidad ("Hispanicity"). Research that would unveil the country's African past was largely forbidden. The Academia Dominicana de la Historia (Dominican Academy of History) was empowered to apply legal sanctions if its verdict in controversial matters was contested. The regime's historian, **Manuel Arturo Peña Battle** (1902–54), a minister of interior affairs (1943) and external affairs (1943–45), fell out of favor with Trujillo toward the end of his life: Peña Battle had rejected the positivist ideas of the liberal historian Eugenio María de Hostos (1839–1903) as incompatible with the country's Hispanic and Catholic character, but a survey among intellectuals commissioned by the government valued Hostos's work as beneficial in its time. Among those who worked outside the official system were historian and priest **Manuel Arjona Cañete** (known as Fray Cipriano de Utrera) (1886–1958), an expert on Dominican colonial history, and historian and biographer **Rufino Martínez**, who spent many years secretly writing a biography of Trujillo (published in 1965). Among the intellectuals living in exile were **José Ramón Cordero Michel** (1931–), a Marxist historian; **Juan Isidro Jimenes Grullón** (1904–83), a socialist historian and leader of the anti-Trujillo movement; **Félix Mejía; Luis Mejía; Pedro Mir** (1913–), a poet and historian of the early colonial period; and **Germán Ornes Coiscou** (1919–98).

1935–   Writer and historian **Juan Bosch** (1909–) went into exile in Cuba (1935–52, 1959–61) and Costa Rica (1952–59) and emerged as the major leader of the anti-Trujillo movement. In 1947 he led an unsuccessful military attack on the Trujillo regime. After his return in 1961, he became president of the Dominican Republic (February–September 1963), but, accused of being procommunist because of his land reform policy, he was ousted in a military coup. He went back into exile in Puerto Rico. A movement to restore Bosch to the presidency launched a revolt which was put down by an intervention from the United States in April 1965. After his return later in 1965, he was defeated by Joaquín Balaguer in the 1966 presidential elections. He again went into voluntary exile but returned in the late 1960s. He wrote, inter alia, *De Cristobal Colón a Fidel Castro: El Caribe Frontera Imperial* (Madrid 1970; From Christopher Columbus to Fidel Castro: The Caribbean As Imperial Frontier). In February 1973, Bosch briefly went into hiding when he was accused of complicity in an unsuccessful guerrilla invasion of the country from Cuba. He was a presidential candidate in elections up to 1990.

1956–   On 12 March 1956, the Spanish exile lawyer and historian **Jesús de Galíndez Suárez** (1915–56), author of several works of history, "disappeared" in New York and was almost certainly assassinated in retaliation against the imminent publication of his Columbia University doctoral dissertation, which exposed Trujillo as a dictator and was defended in late February. His body was never found. After the Spanish Civil War (1936–39), Galíndez had gone into exile in France and the Dominican Republic. As a legal adviser for the Dominican Department of Labor and National Economy, he had displeased Trujillo by arbitrating several strikes too favorably for the sugar workers. As a result, he was singled out for constant harassment. In 1946 he went into exile in the United States and became an activist among anti-Trujillo exiles. His doctoral dissertation *La Era de Trujillo: Un Estudio casuístico de una dictadura hispanoamericana* was published in 1956 in Santiago de Chile: seven printings were issued within six weeks. An almost identical edition was published in Buenos Aires. Galíndez was awarded the doctoral degree in absentia on 5 June 1956. An investigation during 1957 and 1958 ordered by Trujillo indicated that Galíndez was the representative of the Basque government-in-exile in the United States and that he was receiving money from the Central Intelligence Agency (CIA) to maintain contact with the anti-Franco underground in Spain. The case culminated in political and economic sanctions against the Dominican Republic in 1960.

1961–   Many valuable documents covering the Trujillo era were destroyed, stolen, or sold. After Trujillo's assassination in 1961, records were burned either to "cleanse the country of all traces of the hated tyrant", or, in the case of the voluminous secret police files, to prevent any future blackmail or the leaking of information concerning the repression that had taken place. Pro-Trujillo professors who had been responsible for the exclusion of those historians defined as Marxists were removed from the Autonomous University of Santo Domingo.

1992   In September a human-rights activist was killed during a demonstration against the celebrations planned to mark the 500th anniversary of Columbus's arrival in the Americas.

Also see Colombia (1942–59: Arciniegas), United States (1965–: Zea; 1970: Draper).

SOURCES

Amnesty International, *Report 1993* (London 1993) 116.
Bethell, L. ed., *The Cambridge History of Latin America*, vol. 7 (Cambridge 1990) 710.
Cassá, R., "Historiography of the Dominican Republic", in: B.W. Higman ed., *General History of the Caribbean*, vol. 6 (London/Oxford 1999) 400–13 (also 316, 328).
Galíndez, J. de, *The Era of Trujillo, Dominican Dictator*, ed. R.H. Fitzgibbon (Tucson 1973) ix–xv.
Instituto Panamericano de Geografía e Historia, *Guía de personas que cultivan la historia de América* (México 1967) 164.
Lentz, H.M. III, *Heads of States and Governments* (Jefferson, North Carolina, 1994) 231.
Malagón, J., "Los Historiadores y la historia", in: *El exilio español de 1939*, vol. 5 (Madrid 1978) 315, 329, 336–37.
Malek, R.M., "Rafael Leonidas Trujillo: A Revisionist Critique of His Rise to Power", *Revista/Review Interamericana*, 1977: 440 (quote), 443–44.
Scarano, F.A., "Slavery and Emancipation in Caribbean History", in: B. W. Higman ed., *General History of the Caribbean*, vol. 6 (London/Oxford 1999) 265.
Tenenbaum, B.A. ed., *Encyclopedia of Latin American History and Culture*, vol. 3 (New York 1996) 6–7.
Vázquez Montalbán, M., *Galíndez* (novel; Barcelona 1990).
Wise, D., *The Politics of Lying: Government Deception, Secrecy and Power* (New York 1973) 168–70, 546.

E

EAST TIMOR

See Indonesia.

ECUADOR

1992 In October five young artists, **Andrea Stark, Susana Tapia, Amparo Ponce, Joan Bagué**, and **Jean Marc Duray**, taking part in a peaceful public protest against the celebrations to mark Columbus's arrival in the Americas, were detained by members of the army in Quito. During their detention without charge, they were tortured and threatened with death. They were released three days later.

Also see Argentina (1950–: Blanksten; 1977–: Pérez Esquivel).

SOURCES

Amnesty International, *Report 1993* (London 1993) 117.
Monge, E., personal communication, September 1999.

EGYPT

Until at least the early 1960s, archives from the period before the military took over in 1952 were sometimes neglected for nationalistic reasons. Some archive custodians reportedly regarded pre-1952 history as a long period of foreign domination, the sources of which were allowed to perish. The archives were allegedly purged of controversial or embarrassing records. The state's archive section housing Turkish documents was closed down completely upon the death of its last surviving archivist. Documents pertaining to the history of revolutions and national movements were kept under lock and key in the presidential palace archives "because", as historian Anis [q.v. 1961] declared in 1962, "they are seething with snakes and scorpions and the authorities do not want to have accidents". Historical works dealing with the monarchy in the nineteenth and twentieth centuries in other than negative terms were not written. The most sensitive topic of post-1945 Egyptian historiography, however, was the relationship between Islam and history.

1952–   After the July 1952 Revolution, the blind writer and literary historian **Taha Husayn** (1889–1973), called the "dean of Arabic literature", was dismissed as rector (1942–52) of Farouk I University in Alexandria (which he founded in 1942). He continued as a part-time professor. His books were banned (some still were in 1992). In 1919 he completed the first doctoral thesis at the Egyptian University (renamed Fuad I University in 1928, later: Cairo University), on the social philosophy of historian Ibn Khaldun (1332–1406). He became a lecturer in ancient history (1919–25) and professor of Arabic literature (1925–) there. In 1926–27 his book *On Pre-Islamic Poetry* (1926), maintaining that great portions of pre-Islamic poetry were forged after the rise of Islam and doubting the historical reliability of some Koran chapters (including the one on Abraham's and Ismail's building of the sacred Kaba in Mecca), became the subject of a great controversy. A special al-Azhar University committee labeled the book blasphemous and banned it. Questions were asked in Parliament, legal charges of heresy were brought against him (but rejected in court), his resignation from the university was demanded, and his life was threatened. He was forced to withdraw the book. He publicly reaffirmed his belief in Islam and in 1927 published a revised version, *On Pre-Islamic Literature*, with the offending reference to Abraham and Ismail removed but the remainder of his argument expanded. In 1929–32 he served as the first Egyptian dean at the Faculty of Arts but in March 1932 he resigned because of the meddling of the government of Prime Minister Ismail Sidqi Pasha (1930–33) in university affairs and because he refused to endorse the honorary doctorate for a political personality proposed by King Fuad I. After a period of harassment (1932–36), he was reinstated with King Farouk I's accession (1936). From 1940 he intermittently worked at the Ministry of Education as the promotor of free education for all children. Husayn was minister of education (January 1950–January 1952) in the Wafd-led government.

             Historian **Abd al-Rahman Zaki** found himself isolated because of his close connections with court circles. He switched to art history.

1954–   Historian **Muhammad Sabri** (1894–1984), an expert on the 1919
             Egyptian Revolution, remained silent after 1954, a period described
             as an "enforced hibernation". He reportedly transferred his research
             efforts to less sensitive areas such as literary criticism and the me-
             dieval Arab influence in the Congo. Before World War II, his study
             of the 1919 Revolution had been confiscated by the government
             on three separate occasions and he had been requested by King
             Fuad I to delete some unflattering references to the Khedive Ismail
             (1863–79) from another of his works.

             Shafiq Ghurbal (1894–1961), considered the founder of modern
             Egyptian historiography and the first professor of modern history
             at the Egyptian University (1929–[58]), reportedly disappeared
             from the mainstream of historical activity in 1954, although the
             advent of President Gamal Abdel Nasser's regime coincided with
             his retirement and although he occupied important posts (such as
             director of the Arab League's Center for Arabic Studies and pres-
             ident of the Egyptian Historical Society, 1947–60). In 1941 he had
             used his position as deputy assistant director of the Ministry of
             Education to call for complete freedom of academic inquiry in the
             universities, independent from all control by his own ministry.

             A few months after the 1954 Revolution, **Ibrahim Abduh**, asso-
             ciate professor at Fuad I University's Institute of Journalism and
             author of many books on the history of the Arabic press, was dis-
             missed and, after a satirical piece of his was banned, he went into
             exile. He then worked as a journalist in Saudi Arabia and Kuwait
             and returned to Egypt to set up a private publishing house. He was
             reportedly amnestied by President Anwar al-Sadat.

             In [September] historian **Ahmad Shalabi** (?1914–), an assistant
             professor at the Cairo teacher-training college Dar al-Ulum (House
             of Sciences) sympathizing with the fundamentalist Muslim Broth-
             ers and criticizing military rule, was dismissed. He was also pre-
             vented from teaching in Iraq. He finally went to teach at the Islamic
             University of Indonesia, Yogjakarta (1955–63). In the 1960s he set
             up a department of history and Islamic civilization at the Islamic
             University of Omdurman in Sudan.

1954–66   **Sayyid Qutb** (1906–66), a former senior civil servant in the Min-
             istry of Education (1933–51) and the leading intellectual of the
             Muslim Brothers, author of several books with an Islam-centered
             view of history, was arrested and charged with conspiracy against
             the president after a Muslim Brother had attempted to assassinate
             Nasser. He was severely tortured but finally released in 1964 after
             a personal intervention of the Iraqi president. Upon his release

Qutb published *Milestones* (1964), his most controversial book written in prison. This resulted in his rearrest in 1965. He was sentenced to death on the same charge on 22 August 1966, hanged on 29 August, and buried in a secret plot in an unmarked grave. His writings were banned in Egypt, Syria, and Israel. In 1948–50 he had traveled in the United States after he had written a series of articles critical of Egyptian politics (1945–48). Upon his return Qutb became a member of the Muslim Brotherhood.

1960–65   In the early 1960s, **Rifat al-Said**, historian of the Egyptian communist movement, journalist for *Al Ahram* and *Al Talia*, was imprisoned because of his membership in the Egyptian Communist Party (ECP). When the ECP was dissolved and the communists joined the Arab Socialist Union (the only legal political party) in 1965, he was released. Later he became the secretary of the Central Committee of the Tajammu Party, the ECP heir. In 1978 he had reportedly been considered for investigation, following a draft law designed to curb Sadat's critics.

1961   **Muhammad Anis**, professor at Cairo University, probably Egypt's leading historian in the 1960s, discontinued all lectures for a period of one month in protest against a ruling of the Center for African Studies that no master's or doctoral theses would be accepted on a historical subject more recent than fifty years ago. Ghurbal [q.v. 1954–] apparently supported his opinion. In 1974 Anis decided to leave Egypt because of his close association with the Nasser era.

1966   **Abd al-Rahman al-Rafii** (1889–1966), politician, cabinet member in 1949, historian of Egypt's national movement, nominee for the Nobel Prize of Literature in 1964, wished to reprint his study *The Urabi Revolt and the British Occupation* (Cairo 1937; fourth edition 1983). In the book he expressed the opinion that the leader of the 1879–82 revolt, Colonel Ahmad Urabi, should have left politics to politicians (a conclusion probably unwelcome to President—and Colonel—Nasser). Unlike the first, 1937, edition, the reprint apparently had to be privately financed (like several of his other works). As early as the 1930s, several of his publications had been discouraged by the government and he had sometimes been denied access to important documents.

1970–81   During Sadat's presidency, **Hasan Hanafi** (1935–), a professor of the history of philosophy at Cairo University (1962–), could reportedly not directly criticize Islamic dogmatism.

During Sadat's presidency, clerical pressures reportedly led to the withdrawal of many mummified pharaohs from their display cases in the Cairo Museum. The official explanation was that offending religious sensibilities had to be avoided.

[1976–78]   Between [1976] and [1978], **Bezalel Porten**, a professor at Hebrew University, Jerusalem, was repeatedly denied permission by the Cairo Museum trustees to study the Aramaic papyri of Elephantine Island (near Aswan) stored in the museum's manuscript collections. He was finally allowed to enter Egypt in 1978, following the signing of the Camp David agreements. He visited the island and had relatively free access to the papyri, but his freedom to work in the museum was progressively restricted after Sadat's death (1981). Later a new application to study the papyri was rejected again. As early as the 1950s, the Nasser government had not welcomed the idea of a search for ancient Jewish remains at Elephantine Island because Egypt was officially at war with Israel at that time.

1979   In February the People's Assembly approved a motion confiscating all the works of Ibn al-Arabi (1165–1240), an Arab of Andalus (Spain) writing on Islamic mysticism. The government printing house was instructed to stop work on a new edition of his *Meccan Revelations* and to confiscate the volumes already distributed.

In April Egypt was not invited to the Federation of Arab Historians Congress in Benghazi, Libya, because it had signed the Camp David agreements with Israel.

1981–   U.S. historian **Peter Gran** (1941–) was repeatedly denied a visa to Egypt because, according to the Ministry of Interior, as a free-lance journalist in the Middle East in 1981 he had written reports which defamed Egypt. Gran had published *The Islamic Roots of Capitalism: Egypt, 1760–1840* (Austin 1979), but he denied that he had ever worked as a journalist. In 1996 he was an associate professor of history at Temple University, Philadelphia.

1981   In September **Latifa al-Ziyat**, assistant history professor at the Girls' Faculty, Ayn Shams University, Cairo, and chairwoman of the Committee for Preserving the National Culture, was removed from the university and detained together with hundreds of others in a purge of intellectuals. In November she was probably still in prison.

1985–   Act 102 of 1985 confined the role of the al-Azhar Islamic Research Academy to censoring books related to the Koran and Sunna only, but this role had reportedly expanded to include books discussing historical and intellectual issues in Islam from viewpoints differing from those of the academy.

1985   In April a judge ruled that a 150-year-old unexpurgated version of *A Thousand-and-One Nights*, a thousand-year-old Arabic classic, was pornographic and ordered it to be confiscated.

1990s   In the early 1990s, archeological sites in the Nile Valley, and tourists visiting them, became targets for terrorism.

1992   On 8 June **Farag Foda** [also: Fuda, Fudah, Fouda, Fawda] (1945–92), doctor of agricultural economics and human-rights activist, was shot and killed by two members of al-Gamaa al-Islamiya (the Islamic Group). In May an ad hoc committee of clerics from al-Azhar had decided that "everything he did was against Islam". The killers reportedly cited this fatwa (religious decree) as their justification for killing him. Foda had published books and articles on the history and politics of Islam, especially *The Wafd and the Future* (1983), concerning, inter alia, the 1919 Revolution, and *The Neglected Truth* (1985), in which the Islamic vision of history was attacked. Al-Azhar's council published *Who Killed Farag Foda?* In December 1992 Foda's collected works were banned. One of his killers was executed in February 1994.

1993–   In March 1993 **Nasr Abu-Zeid** (1943–), professor of Arabic literature at Cairo University, was denied promotion to full professor after a member of the review committee, Abd el-Sabour Shahin, called his writings an insult to Islam. Despite protests of the department professors, this minority report was endorsed by the university. In a mosque in April Abd el-Sabour Shahin publicly accused Abu-Zeid of apostasy. In May seven Islamist lawyers accused Abu-Zeid of apostasy under the Hisbah rule (Islamic personal status law allowing Muslims to file suits against those alleged to have violated religious law) because he had called for a historical interpretation and recontextualization of the Koran in his writings, particularly in *Criticism of Islamic Discourse* (1992, 1996), a semantic study of Islamic texts (in which he also repeated a 1988 attack against Islamic investment companies on behalf of one of which Abd el-Sabour Shahin had acted as a religious adviser before its collapse). In January 1994 the Giza Family Court ruled the case inadmissible but in June 1995 the Cairo Court of Appeals overturned the decision, declaring Abu-Zeid an apostate, and therefore ordering the divorce from his wife. In August 1996 the Court of Cassation confirmed the judgment. After the 1995 verdict, the militant Islamist group al-Jihad issued a death threat against Abu-Zeid and in September 1995 he and his wife went into exile in Spain and then the Netherlands, where he taught at Leiden University.

In September 1996 the Giza Court of Urgent Cases suspended implementation of the divorce order (this was confirmed in December). In later years he remained under threat of death.

1996   In April thirteen Muslim Brothers, including **Gamal Abd al-Hadi**, a lecturer in Islamic history at al-Azhar University, were arrested, tried by a military court in June, and charged with membership in an illegal organization which "aimed to overthrow the regime". Eight of them were sentenced to three years' imprisonment but al-Hadi was acquitted.

1998   In January the artistic production police raided Sinai publishers and confiscated fifteen copies of two books by **Khalil Abdel Karim**, *The Yathrib Society* (Yathrib being the pre-Islamic name for Medina) and *The Rabaa Songs on the Companions of Prophet Mohammed*, apparently because the Islamic Research Academy labeled them as blasphemous.

1999   Among the books banned at the American University of Cairo at the request of government censors was *The Prophet and Pharaoh: Muslim Extremism in Egypt* (originally in French 1984; London 1985), a history of the Muslim Brotherhood by French historian **Giles Kepel**.

Also see France (1947: Rodinson; 1951: Raymond), Indonesia (1994: Spielberg), Kuwait (1992: Anis), Lebanon (1978–: Chahine), Malaysia (1996: Husayn).

SOURCES

Al-Sayyid Marsot, A.L., "Egyptian Historical Research and Writing on Egypt in the 20th Century", *Middle Eastern Studies Association Bulletin*, 1973, no.2: 5.
———, "Survey of Egyptian Works of History", *American Historical Review*, 1991: 1422, 1424–25, 1427.
Amnesty International, *Report* (London) 1993: 119, 120; 1994: 122; 1995: 121; 1996: 143; 1997: 143; 1998: 158; 1999: 157; 2000: 96; 2001: 94.
———, *News Release* (MDE/12/1996; London, 20 August 1996).
Article 19, *Information, Freedom and Censorship: World Report 1991* (London 1991) 357.
Bahn, P.G., *The Cambridge Illustrated History of Archaeology* (Cambridge 1996) 370.
Boia, L. ed., *Great Historians of the Modern Age: An International Dictionary* (Westport 1991) 14–15, 21–22.
Boom, M. van den, "De denker als profeet: Hasan Hanafi", in: R. Peters & R. Meijer eds., *Inspiratie en kritiek: Moslimse intellectuelen over de Islam* (Muiderberg 1992) 17.
Choueiri, Y.M., *Arab History and the Nation-State: A Study in Modern Arab Historiography 1820–1980* (London 1989) 65–67.
Collins, R.O., "Egypt and the Sudan", in: R.W. Winks ed., *The Historiography of the British Empire-Commonwealth: Trends, Interpretations, and Resources* (Durham 1966) 287.

Crabbs, J. Jr., "Politics, History and Culture in Nasser's Egypt", *International Journal of Middle Eastern Studies*, 1975: 389–90, 393, 399, 400–404, 414–16, 419–20.

Current Biography 1953 (New York) 290–92 (Husayn).

Dagher, C., "In the Footsteps of Taha Hussein", *UNESCO Courier*, March 1990: 48–49.

Donohue, J.J., "Rewriting Arab History", in: *Arab Society 1978–79: Reflections and Realities*. Cemam Reports no.6 (Beirut 1981) 162.

El-Ghobashy, M., "Shredding the Past: Why Do the Second-Oldest Archives in the World Have So Few Documents?", *Cairo Times*, 19–25 April 2001 (WWW-text).

Ende, W., *Arabische Nation und islamische Geschichte: Die Umayyaden im Urteil arabischer Autoren des 20. Jahrhunderts* (Beirut 1977) 197.

Faris, N.A., "Development in Arab Historiography As Reflected in the Struggle between 'Alî and Mu'âwiya", in: B. Lewis & P.M. Holt eds., *Historians of the Middle East* (London 1962) 439.

Gordon, D.C., *Self-determination and History in the Third World* (Princeton 1971) 63–64.

Haddad, Y.Y., "Sayyid Qutb: Ideologue of Islamic Revival", in: J.L. Esposito ed., *Voices of Resurgent Islam* (New York 1983) 68–69, 77–78.

Human Rights Watch, Letter, Committee for International Academic Freedom to President of Cairo University (1 July 1993).

———, *World Report* (Washington) 1994: 354; 1997: 267, 279, 353; 2000: 325, 347.

Index on Censorship, 6/78: 56; 3/79: 66; 5/81: 39; 1/82: 37; 4/85: 51; 5/85: 65; 1/87: 40; 2/92: 23–24; 6/92: 33; 7/92: 90; 9/92: 43; 3/93: 35; 7/93: 33, 36; 1–2/94: 125, 127–28, 237; 1/96: 33; 4/96: 30–39, 43, 157; 5/96: 88; 2/98: 89; 4/99: 16.

International PEN Writers in Prison Committee, *Half-Yearly Caselist* (London 1997) 6.

———, *Ifex Alert*, 20 June 1995, 6 August 1996.

Keesings historisch archief, 1992: 637–38, 1999: 617.

Kerkhof, P., personal communication, March 1997.

King, J.W., *Historical Dictionary of Egypt* (Metuchen 1984) 524–25.

Meijer, R., "Een Egyptische 'Historikerstreit' op het Nederlands Instituut te Cairo", in: P. Aarts ed., *Midden-Oosten en Islam publicaties, witte reeks nr. 14* (Nijmegen 1989) 8, 12–13, 167.

Middle East Watch, *Syria Unmasked: The Suppression of Human Rights by the Asad Regime* (New Haven 1991) 127.

Nayed, S., "Academic and Intellectual Freedom in Egypt", in: Codesria, *The State of Academic Freedom in Africa 1995* (Dakar 1996) 139–41.

Reid, D.M., *Cairo University and the Making of Modern Egypt* (Cambridge 1990) 133–34, 147–49, 172, 198–99, 223.

———"Cairo University and the Orientalists", *International Journal of Middle East Studies*, 1987: 66–68.

Rejwan, N., *Nasserist Ideology, Its Exponents and Critics* (New York 1974) 15 (quote Anis), 43–48.

Shimoni, Y., *Biographical Dictionary of the Middle East* (New York 1991) 107.

Silberman, N. A., *Between Past and Present: Archaeology, Ideology and Nationalism in the Modern Middle East* (New York 1989) 160, 177, 182–85.

Simon, R.S., P. Mattar, & R. W. Bulliet eds., *Encyclopedia of the Modern Middle East* (New York 1996) 824–25, 1506–7.

Waardenburg, J.-J., *Les Universités dans le monde arabe actuel*, vol. 1 (Paris/The Hague 1966) 92, 96, 226–27.

EL SALVADOR

1970– Argentinian historian **Héctor Pérez Brignoli** (1945–) was expelled
       from El Salvador. Later he worked in Honduras and at the University
       of Costa Rica.

1972– Historian **David Luna** lived in exile after 1972.

1981   In January Venezuelan filmmaker **Nelson Arrieti**, professor of film
       history at Mérida University, Venezuela, was abducted in a hotel in
       San Salvador where he was working as a film director. After a period
       in clandestine detention, he was expelled from El Salvador.

1983   In September **Italo López Vallecillos** (died 1983), history professor
       at the University of Central America, reportedly died after the Ejér-
       cito Secreto Anticomunista (ESA; Secret Anti-Communist Army)
       planted a bomb at his home.

1985   In June historian **Jorge Gálvez Paz** was detained by the army. He
       was reportedly giving humanitarian assistance to people in the de-
       partment of San Miguel when he was seized in an army counterin-
       surgency operation.

1987–92 The novel *Cuzcatlan* (Tegucigalpa 1986; Cuzcatlan was El Salva-
       dor's ancient Nahuatl name), in which resistance against the auto-
       cratic rule of El Salvador was linked with pre-Columbus roots, was
       banned until the 1992 peace accords. The author, **Manlio Argueta**
       (1935–), lived in exile, mostly in Costa Rica.

Also see Brazil (1971–79: Cardoso).

SOURCES

Acuña, V.H., personal communication, August 1994.
Index on Censorship, 3/81: 74; 2/84: 9; 5/85: 65; 5/97: 140, 145.
Pérez Brignoli, H., personal communication, September 2000.

ERITREA

See Ethiopia (1976: Bahru).

ESTONIA

See Union of Soviet Socialist Republics (USSR).

ETHIOPIA

Archeology appeared to be a particularly vulnerable field in Ethiopia.

1957   According to a former official of the Press and Information Department
       of the Imperial Government of Haile Selassie, the following were

among eleven subjects "best left untouched" in March 1957: "Cold War polemics" and "the United States, France, United Kingdom and Portugal in colonial contexts".

1972   In March **Patrick Gilkes**, a British history professor conducting private research in Ethiopia, and Moira Larson, an American sociology lecturer at Addis Ababa University, were detained on suspicion of involvement in local student activities and expelled ten days later.

1975   In early 1975, a few months after Major Mengistu Haile-Mariam's military had abolished the monarchy in September 1974, an old film, *Prince Valiant*, depicting the ascent to power of a crown prince after his throne had been usurped, was televised. The censoring officer, a captain, was reportedly heavily punished. Around the same time, it was instructed that the terms *feudalism* and *imperialism* were banned until further notice.

1976   Within two weeks of his return from the School of Oriental and African Studies, University of London, to Ethiopia to take up a lectureship in the Addis Ababa University history department, **Bahru Zewde** was arrested. Later, he became a professor in modern history at that university, the author of *A History of Modern Ethiopia 1855–1974* (Addis Ababa 1991; updated up to 1991 in 2001), and a specialist in the causes for the Ethiopia-Eritrea conflict.

1978   In August Ethiopian Security asked American archeologist and geologist **Jon Kalb** to leave Ethiopia because of (unsubstantiated) rumors that he was connected with the Central Intelligence Agency.

1982   In October the government of Ethiopia brought to a halt all foreign prehistorical expeditions. The archeological teams of **Desmond Clark** and **Tim White**, and of **Donald Johanson**, both teams from the University of California, Berkeley, were the first to be hit by the moratorium. Reasons suggested for the ban were that foreign teams had exploited Ethiopian resources while giving little attention to training local scholars or to developing local facilities. In addition the book *Lucy: The Beginnings of Humankind* (New York 1981), by Johanson and Maitland Edey, had angered Ethiopians because the authors had described how they had removed a leg bone from a recent Ethiopian grave for comparison with a fossil knee joint some three million years old. This act was considered to be a desecration of the grave.

1988–   The government suspended archeological field research near Kassala, presumably because of constant military action in the region.

1997–   In October two writers were arrested, allegedly for their activities as journalists for the Oromo newspaper *Urji* and their membership in the

Ethiopian Human Rights League. They were held in solitary confinement for five months and denied any visits from their families.
Thereafter they were charged with armed conspiracy and involvement
with the Oromo Liberation Front. **Gamachu Malka Fufa** (pen name:
Moti Biyya) (?1957–) was a journalist and social anthropologist interested in the Oromo identity, and through his books he provided Oromo
society with a historical background. He had published *Oromia, the
Hidden Atrocities* (1995), a political analysis of the colonization of the
Oromo people by successive Abyssinian groups, and *Abyssinocracy or
Democracy?* (1997), in which he compared the situation of the Oromo
minority under the Mengistu government (1974–91) and its successor.
Garuma Bekele (?1960–) was a journalist who had published, inter
alia, a historical novel, *One Day in Afaan Oromo*, on the problems
Oromo had in East Africa from the 1950s to 1989. In July 1999 Garuma was charged with violating the press law and with engaging in
"terrorist activities". In April 2000 Gamachu was unexpectedly released
on bail. In May 2001 Garuma was also released.

2000– On 22 December up to 200 Oromo students from Addis Ababa University were beaten by police when they were arrested after a fight
between Oromo and other students, which started after a Tigrayan student had presented a sociology class paper about the Oromo which
offended Oromo students. Among the arrested was fourth-year history
student **Badada Bayene**. Up to 150 students, including Badada, were
taken into police custody and were reportedly at risk of torture. Later
they were released.

SOURCES

Amnesty International, *Report* (London) 1999: 162; 2000: 102; 2001: 100.
———, *Urgent Action 07/01* (12 & 19 January 2001).
Human Rights Watch, *World Report* (Washington) 199: 42–43; 2001: 17, 47–48.
Index on Censorship, 2/72: 90–91; 4/78: 17, 19; 1/83: 44; 5/99: 130; 1/00: 14–15.
———, International PEN Writers in Prison Committee, *Centre to Centre*, October 1998:
    4; 2000 no.3: 6.
———, *Half-Yearly Caselist* (London) 1997: 6; 1998: 7.
———, *Ifex Alert*, 19 November 1998.
———, *Rapid Action Network*, 23 July 1999.
Lewin, R., "Ethiopia Halts Prehistory Research", *Science*, 14 January 1983: 147–49.
Prouty, C., & E. Rosenfeld, *Historical Dictionary of Ethiopia and Eritrea* (Metuchen
    1994) 28.
Review of African Political Economy 1976, no. 3: 3.
Tesfaye Deressa, personal communication, March 1999.

F

FINLAND

See Union of Soviet Socialist Republics (USSR) (1967–Kan; 1973–94: Solzhenitsyn; 1981: Kholodkovsky).

FRANCE

Among the most sensitive areas of French history were World War II and the colonial and mandate policies in North Africa (Algeria in particular) and the Middle East. A relatively high incidence of cases was settled in court.

pre-1945	Among the historians and others concerned with the past who were censored or persecuted during World War II were **Fernand Braudel** (1902–85), **Henri Brunschwig** (1904–), **Claude Cahen** (1909–91), **Jacques Godechot** (1907–89), **Maurice Halbwachs** (1877–1945), **Louis Henry** (1911–91), **Georges Lefebvre** (1874–59), and **Gaston Maspero** (1883–1945).
1945–49	Among the historians dismissed for their collaboration with the Nazis was **Michel Lhéritier**. He had been appointed a lecturer at the Sorbonne without the consent of the staff during World War II. After a period of unemployment, he became professor at the University of Aix-en-Provence in 1949. He was not reinstated in his position of secretary-general of the International Committee of Historical Sciences (1926–45).
1947	**Maxime Rodinson** (1915–), an orientalist specializing in Semitic languages and early Islamic history working at the (Free) French antiquities service for Lebanon and Syria (1940–47), reported that he was "practically expelled" from Lebanon and Syria by the French

government in 1947 because, as a member of the French Communist Party (PCF) (1937–58), he had been active with the Lebanese and Syrian communists. He had made speeches on the radio and taught courses on Marxism in Beirut. He became librarian at the Bibliothèque Nationale (1947–55) and chair of Old Ethiopic and Old South Arabian studies at the École Pratique des Hautes Études, Paris (1955–84). Circulation of his biography *Mahomet* (Paris 1961; *Mohammed*, 1971) was restricted in Islamic countries. In May 1998, for example, the Egyptian minister of higher education officially requested that the American University in Cairo remove it from its curriculum because it allegedly contained "fabrications harmful to the respected Prophet and to the Islamic religion." The book, available in Egypt since the 1970s, was withdrawn from the reading lists and removed from the library and campus bookstore.

1951   In 1951 **André Raymond** (1925–), historian of the Middle East, later a history professor at the University of Aix-en-Provence and Princeton University, and, inter alia, vice president of the Institut du Monde Arabe in Paris, was appointed as a teacher at Bordeaux rather than Paris, as he had requested for his research, reportedly because of a negative administrative report about his stay at the Collège Sadiqi in Tunis, where as a high school teacher he had defended communist political opinions and had been engaged in trade union activities. Later he spent only one of at least three planned years in Egypt because the 1956 Suez Crisis cut his stay short. While making a survey of Ottoman Cairo in the early 1960s, he occasionally suffered minor harassments from the Cairo police.

1952   The sale in North Africa of *L'Afrique du nord en marche: Nationalismes musulmans et souveraineté française* (1952; North Africa on the March: Muslim Nationalism and French Sovereignty) by **Charles-André Julien** (1891–1989), professor of the history of colonization at the Sorbonne, Paris (1947–61), was stopped by the colonial administration. The book aroused much controversy for its anticolonialist stance. His first book, *Histoire de l'Afrique du nord: Tunisie, Algérie, Maroc* (1931; *History of North Africa: From the Arab Conquest to 1830*, 1970), supporting demands of North African nationalists for colonial reform, had already earned him the hostility of many French in the Maghrib.

1956   Historian **Henri-Irénée Marrou** (1904–77), a specialist in early Christianity, Christian humanist, and collaborator on *Esprit*, was visited by the police because in an April 1956 article in the newspaper *Le Monde* he had characterized the torture, summary executions, and collective reprisals in Algeria as crimes.

1957–77   From 1957 to 1977, the antiwar film *Paths of Glory* (United States, 1957), directed by **Stanley Kubrick** (1928–99) and dealing with a French general who massacres his own troops in an ill-judged action during World War I, was banned.

1960   Around 1960 **Louis Massignon** (1883–1962), orientalist and historian of Islam, assistant to the high commissioner of France in Palestine and Syria (1917–19), and professor of the sociology of Islam at the Collège de France (1926–54), was picked up several times by the police on the streets of Paris while he demonstrated for the Palestinian refugees and against torture in Algeria. During his retirement, Massignon was a proponent of the Muslim-Christian dialogue and an activist against the war in Algeria.

Historian **Pierre Vidal-Naquet** (1930–), a lecturer in ancient history at Caen University (1956–60), was suspended. He had signed the *Manifesto of the 121*, a "Declaration on the Right of Insubordination in the War in Algeria" of 121 intellectuals on 6 September 1960 issued during their campaign against torture in Algeria. The suspension interrupted his career for a year. Later he worked at Lille University (1961–62), the Centre National de la Recherche Scientifique (CNRS; National Scientific Research Agency; 1962–64), and Lyon University (1964–66). He eventually became director of the Centre Louis-Gernet de Recherches Comparées sur les Sociétés Anciennes at the École des Hautes Études en Sciences Sociales in Paris (1966–). In 1963 he published a work about the colonial torturers. As a Jew he incessantly refuted the theses of Holocaust deniers.

1962–68   From 1962 to 1968, **Jacques Soustelle** (1912–90), anthropologist specialized in Mesoamerican (particularly Aztec) history, minister of information (1945) and of colonies (1945), governor-general of Algeria (1955–56), minister of information (1958–59), and minister for Sahara and atomic questions (1959–60), lived in exile because he was charged with subversive activities after having been involved in the terrorist Organisation de l'Armée Secrète (Secret Army Organization), which struggled against Algerian independence and envisaged assassinating President Charles de Gaulle. Amnestied in 1968, Soustelle became a member of the Académie Française in 1983.

1965   In November a Paris court cleared historian **Michèle Cotta** of the charge that she had wrongly attributed facts of betrayal to Jean Lousteau in her book *La Collaboration 1940–44* (Paris 1964). Lousteau had argued that, as he had been amnestied for his deeds, they should not be mentioned anymore. The court emphasized her honest method of work and allowed her to write about sentences which had been amnestied later. The facts could also be mentioned in other works, as has been done by Pascal Ory in his *Les Collaborateurs* (Paris 1980).

1968   President de Gaulle's wife, Yvonne Vendroux, attempted to have a film version of *La Religieuse*, a book by Denis Diderot (1713–84), banned because it presented the eighteenth-century Catholic Church in an unfavorable light.

1971–79   For a decade the state television ORTF refused to show *The Sorrow and the Pity*, a documentary (1971) by **Marcel Ophüls** on the extensive French collaboration with the Jewish deportation during the Vichy regime (1940–44). When shown in [1979], it was denounced by a senator, himself an ex-member of the resistance, as "destroying myths of which the French still have need".

1976   The French government allegedly tried to prevent the distribution in its ex-colonies of *Les Confettis de l'Empire*, a book by **Jean Guillebord** which described the last phase of colonialism. The government finally did not ban it. The attempt provoked extra publicity for the book.

1983   In May a Paris judge refused permission to confiscate *L'Affaire Papon* (Paris 1983), a book by **Michel Slitinsky** about Maurice Papon, secretary-general of the Bordeaux prefecture under the Vichy regime and later chief of police in Paris, National Assembly deputy, and cabinet minister.

1983–84   In February 1984 a Paris judge ruled in a case that began in October 1983 that two extracts from the book *Ni droite ni gauche: L'Idéologie fasciste en France* (Paris 1983; revised and expanded in 1987; *Neither Right nor Left: Fascist Ideology in France*, Berkeley/ Los Angeles 1986), the third volume in a trilogy by Israeli historian **Zeev Sternhell** (1935–), director of the Center for European Studies, Hebrew University, Jerusalem, were libelous against economist Bertrand de Jouvenel, whereas six other extracts were not. The extracts presented him as one of the theorists of French Fascism with pro-Nazi sympathies. Examining Sternhell's good faith, the judge recognized his right to judge de Jouvenel's words but not his actions and reproached him for not having interviewed the witnesses still alive, including de Jouvenel himself. Sternhell and his publisher, Le Seuil, had to pay one French franc in damages. They were also fined but were not obliged to print the judgment in the book.

1983–85   In January 1985 a Versailles judge ruled that history professor **Laurent Wetzel** (1950–) and his publisher, Philippe Meaulle, were not guilty of defamation. In October 1983 the Association Française

Buchenwald-Dora et Commandos and the Fédération Nationale des Déportés et Internés Résistants et Patriotes had sued them because Wetzel had written in Meaulle's paper *Courrier des Yvelines* that Marcel Paul (died 1982), a former communist minister of industrial production, on having been deported to Buchenwald concentration camp during the war, had become one of the prisoners' leaders and in that capacity decided about life or death of numerous prisoners, taking into account principally the Communist Party's interests. The judge said that Wetzel had acted in good faith and with intellectual honesty and respected the rules of the historical profession by verifying his information and not distorting it.

1984   In July Henri Frenay, founder of the resistance movement *Combat*, lost a defamation suit against the Institut National de l'Audiovisuel. He had sued the institute because they had made a documentary in which they had shown part of his testimony only and juxtaposed his views on the links between resistance leader Jean Moulin and the Communist Party with those of another resistance member, Daniel Cordier. The judge ruled that the institute's method had been correct.

pre-1985   In July the television documentary *Des terroristes à la retraite* (1985; Terrorists in Retirement), by **[Vincent?] Mosco**, banned from transmission earlier, was finally shown. The film accused the PCF of exploiting political refugees such as Jews and Armenians and of not acknowledging their role in the French resistance during World War II. Earlier the PCF had led a campaign against showing the film when they were part of President François Mitterrand's government.

1985   In [August] Defense Minister Charles Hernu vetoed a plan for a commemorative statue of the Jewish Captain Alfred Dreyfus (1859–1935) in the courtyard of the Military School in Paris, apparently after pressure from senior army officers. In the same courtyard Dreyfus had been wrongfully cashiered in 1894. Dreyfus was not acquitted; he was not rehabilitated until 1906. Discussion of the Dreyfus Affair remained sensitive, especially on radio and television stations. In 1994 a film based on *L'Affaire* (Paris 1984)—a book by historian, lawyer, and former Minister of Justice Jean-Denis Bredin—was made by Yves Boisset, after two earlier plans, one by Constantin Costa-Gavras (1933–) and one (in the 1960s) by André Cayatte, had failed.

1990   In February a Paris judge ruled that historian and medical researcher **George Wellers** (1905–91), a specialist in World War II history working at the Centre de Documentation Juive Contemporaine who had called Robert Faurisson, a professor of literature notorious for his denial of the Holocaust, a "falsifier of the history of the Jews during the Nazi period", was not guilty of defamation.

[1991]   *Euskuda Gaduan*, a book about the history of the Basque independence struggle published in the Spanish Basque Country, was banned on the grounds that it threatened public order.

1991–93   In February and March 1991, **Georges Boudarel** (1926–), historian at the University of Paris–VII (until 1992) and expert in Southeast Asian history, especially the history of Vietnamese communism, was accused of crimes against humanity by several hundred demonstrators in Paris. They asked Minister of Education Lionel Jospin to dismiss him, but the minister refused. The university defended Boudarel's position and provided some physical protection against violent attacks. A committee of some forty intellectuals, including Vidal-Naquet [q.v. 1960], supported him. In April he was charged with crimes against humanity but in December the court of appeals did not accept the charges. The Cour de Cassation confirmed this judgment in April 1993. A French communist and philosophy teacher in Saigon, Boudarel had defected to the Vietminh (League for the Independence of Vietnam) in December 1950. He arrived in North Vietnam in late 1952. From at least January 1953 until January 1954, he was a political instructor in Camp 113, there responsible for the reeducation of French prisoners, under the nom de guerre of Daï Dong. He allegedly subjected the prisoners to "moral and psychological torture". Sentenced to death in France for insubordination and desertion, he stayed in Vietnam as an exile until April 1964 and subsequently went to Prague. In January 1967 he returned to Paris following the June 1966 general amnesty for colonial crimes in France. Boudarel reportedly never denied or concealed the 1953–54 events.

1993–95   In June 1995 **Bernard Lewis** (1916–), historian at Princeton University and specialized in Middle Eastern history, was ordered to pay one French franc in damages to the Forum des Associations Arméniennes de France and to the Ligue contre le Racisme et l'Antisémitisme because the judge found him not prudent enough when he remarked in an interview to *Le Monde*, published on 16 November 1993, that the qualification of genocide attributed to the 1915 massacres of Armenians perpetrated by the Ottoman Turks was "the Armenian version of history". He also maintained that there was no proof of the existence of an official extermination plan or policy. **Gilles Veinstein**'s appointment as professor of Turkish and Ottoman history at the Collège de France in November 1998 was criticized because he had taken a position similar to Lewis's in an April 1995 article in *L'Histoire*.

1994   In September a Paris judge ruled that **Emmanuel Chadeau** (1956–), historian at Lille University, had fulfilled his obligations as a biographer and historian when in his book *Saint-Exupéry* (Paris 1994) he had suggested that the disappearance of pilot Antoine de Saint-Exupéry, author of *The Little Prince*, during a flight to Germany in 1944 was possibly a disguised suicide. Surviving relatives of Saint-Exupéry had sued Chadeau. The judge also ruled that Chadeau and his publisher Plon had illicitly divulged unpublished documents on Saint-Exupéry.

1996   Among the books that the far-right mayor of Orange Jacques Bompard had refused to purchase for the new municipal library in July because they "offended good morals", was a history of World War II.

1996–99   The 17 October 1996 issue of the Algerian daily *Liberté* was seized by the French police because it carried an article entitled *When the Seine Rolled with Corpses*, commemorating the thirty-fifth anniversary of a 17 October 1961 proindependence demonstration by Algerians in Paris and mentioning a toll of deaths and disappearances of perhaps as many as two hundred instead of the official three deaths and sixty-four injured. In January 1998 the French government announced that it would not make public a report about the incident because it could interfere with a trial for war crimes against Papon [q.v. 1983: Slitinsky] who headed the Paris police in 1961. In July 1998 Papon, convicted of war crimes the same year, sued **Jean-Luc Einaudi**, a historian working at the Ministry of Justice, for libel. Einaudi, the author of a book on the 1961 events, had written in *Le Monde* in May 1998 that they constituted a "massacre perpetrated by the police on Papon's orders". In addition he had denounced the disappearance or destruction of several relevant archives, including those of the Service de Coordination des Affaires Algériennes. The trial took place in February–March 1999. The judge ruled that Einaudi's statement was libelous, but Einaudi was not ordered to pay damages because his method had been "serious, pertinent, and complete". In addition the judge recognized the "extreme violence" of the 17 October 1961 repression. In their oral and written trial testimonies before the judge on 11 February 1999, archivists Brigitte Lainé and Philippe Grand had confirmed, notwithstanding the unexplained absence of part of the records, the existence of records substantiating Einaudi's accusation. They were, however, condemned for misconduct by both the French Archives

Directorate and the French Association of Archivists on the grounds that they had defied legally defined restrictions on access to information. The association cited provisions of the 1996 Code of Ethics of the International Council on Archives. In June 1999 the National Assembly acknowledged having fought a "war" against Algerian nationalists in 1954–62 and unanimously abandoned the official viewpoint that the event had only been "an operation for keeping order".

1997   The author of the introduction and conclusion of *Le Livre noir du communisme: Crimes, terreur, répression* (Paris 1997; *The Black Book of Communism: Crimes, Terror, Repression*, Cambridge, Mass. 1999), historian **Stéphane Courtois** (1947–), CNRS research director and director of the journal *Communisme*, was forced to drop the original title, *Le Livre des crimes communistes* (The Book of Communist Crimes), when two of the six contributing historians, Jean-Louis Margolin, historian of Southeast and East Asia at the University of Aix-en-Provence, and Nicolas Werth, researcher of Soviet history at the Institut d'Histoire du Temps Présent, Paris, threatened to withdraw. They also questioned Courtois's introductory and concluding remarks on the centrality of mass crimes in communist repression; the extent to which communist doctrines explain criminal practice; the reliability of crime statistics; and the comparisons between communist and Nazi terror. On 14 November the book was discussed in the National Assembly (because the PCF participated in the government).

1997–98   In April 1998 a Paris judge ruled that journalist and historian **Gérard Chauvy** (1952–) and his publisher Albin Michel were guilty of "public defamation" because in his book *Aubrac, Lyon 1943* (Paris 1997) Chauvy had reproduced as an appendix a document called "Klaus Barbie's Testament," in which Barbie, wartime Gestapo chief at Lyon, suggested that resistance army fighters Raymond and Lucie Aubrac had betrayed resistance leader Jean Moulin in June 1943, leading to Moulin's arrest and death after torture. Although Chauvy had written in his conclusion that no archival document proved the alleged betrayal and declared that he had acted in good faith, the judge said that Chauvy, by publishing the document and citing it at least forty-four times, had given it excessive weight and that he had not been prudent enough in applying the historical method.

Also see Algeria (French Algeria; 1965–: Harbi; pre-1996–: Stora), Chad (1974–77: Claustre), Egypt (1999: Kepel), Germany (1998: Rittersporn), India (1996: Foucault), Ivory Coast (1982–92: Gbagbo), Korea (1985: Soboul), Laos (French Laos), Senegal (1961–: Diop), South Africa (1960–90: Garaudy), Sri Lanka

(1994: Sabalingham), Tunisia (French Tunisia), Turkey (1971–: Garaudy; 1995–: Ternon), United States (1970–72: Ahmed), USSR (1938–: Eisenstein), Vietnam (French Vietnam; 1945–: Malleret).

SOURCES

"L'Affaire Aubrac: vérité et mensonges", *L'Histoire*, June 1997: 78–85.

Amnesty International, *Report 2001* (London 2001) 21–22, 103.

Annual Obituary 1990 (Chicago/London) 510–12 (Soustelle).

Article 19, *Information, Freedom and Censorship: World Report 1991* (London 1991) 263.

Assouline, P., "Enquête sur un historien condamné pour diffamation", *L'Histoire*, June 1984: 98–101.

Azéma, J.-P., & G. Kiejman, "L'Histoire au tribunal", *Le Débat*, November–December 1998: 45–51.

Bédarida, F., "La Reconstruction du CISH après la Seconde Guerre Mondiale: Entretien avec Charles Morazé", *Bulletin d'Information du Comité international des sciences historiques*, no.21 (Paris 1995) 44.

Boyd, K. ed., *Encyclopedia of Historians and Historical Writing* (London/Chicago 1999) 628–29, 719–20, 782–83, 1000–1001.

Bredin, J.-D., "Le Droit, le juge et l'historien", *Le Débat*, November 1984: 104–5, 108–10.

Burguière, A. ed., *Dictionnaire des sciences historiques* (Paris 1986) 239, 441–42.

Calvocoressi, P., *Freedom to Publish* (Stockholm 1980) 98–99.

Cannon, J. ed., *The Blackwell Dictionary of Historians* (Oxford 1988) 245.

Erdmann, K.D., *Die Ökumene der Historiker: Geschichte der internationalen Historikerkongresse und des Comité international des sciences historiques* (Göttingen 1987) 253–60.

European Court of Human Rights, *Case of Lehideux and Isorni versus France: Judgment* (WWW-text; Strasbourg, 23 September 1998).

Gallagher, N.E. ed., *Approaches to the History of the Middle East: Interviews with Leading Middle East Historians* (Reading, UK 1994) 67, 74–75, 78, 87, 115–16, 120.

Groene Amsterdammer, 3 April 1991 (Boudarel).

Halimi, S., "Tapis rouge médiatique," *Le Monde diplomatique, Manière de voir 40* (July–August 1998) 21.

Harris, V., "Knowing Right from Wrong: The Archivist and the Protection of People's Rights", *Janus: Archival Review*, 1999, no.1: 36.

Human Rights Watch, *World Report 1999* (Washington 1998) 349, 453.

Index on Censorship, 2/76: 13; 4/81: 5; 5/85: 65; 6/85: 32; 6/95: 29; 5/96: 89; 1/97: 113; 1/98: 88; 4/98: 111; 2/99: 38, 56; 5/99: 130.

Instituto Panamericano de Geografía e Historia, *Guía de personas que cultivan la historia de América* (México 1967) 208.

Jeanneney, J.-N., *Le Passé dans le prétoire: L'Historien, le juge et le journaliste* (Paris 1998) 35–43, 48, 73–74, 105–10, 114–18, 124–25, 132–33.

Judt, T., "The Longest Road to Hell", *New York Times*, 22 December 1997: 27.

Julliard, J., & M. Winock eds., *Dictionnaire des intellectuels français* (Paris 1996) 764–65, 995–96, 1077–78, 1158–59.

Keesings historisch archief, 1998: 82, 736.

Kiejman, G., "L'Histoire devant ses juges", *Le Débat*, November 1984: 117–18, 123–24.

Le Monde, 1991 (14 March: 1; 19 March: 11; 20 March: 12; 22 March: 13; 16 September: 9; 17 September: 12; 21 December: 34); 1993 (3 April: 13; 16 November: 2; 27 November: 2), 1994 (1 January: 2); 1995 (19 May: 14; 23 June: 11; 10 July: 7); 1996 (14–15 July: 20); 1997 (25 October: 20); 1998 (20 May: 14; 19 June: 8; 11 September: 11; 31 October: 28; 10 November: 6; 14 November: 1, 16; 18 November: 17; 21 November: 2; 27 November: 15; 1 December: 36; 5 December: 1; 20 December: 1, 16); 1999 (5 February: 1, 8; 6 February: 9; 8 February: 9; 13 February: 13; 15 February: 8; 24 February: 14; 27 February: 11; 29 March: 1) (Bompard, Boudarel, Courtois, Einaudi, Lewis).

New York Times, 21 November 1997: 9 (Courtois).

Osiel, M., *Mass Atrocity, Collective Memory, and the Law* (New Brunswick/London 1997) 179.

Perrault, G., "Les Falsifications d'un 'Livre Noir' ", *Le Monde diplomatique, Manière de voir 40* (July–August 1998) 18–20.

Rebérioux, M., "Le Génocide, le juge et l'historien", *L'Histoire*, November 1990: 92.

Said, E., *Orientalism* (London/Henley 1978) 270.

"Sur la liberté de l'historien en correctionnelle à Versailles, le 17 Janvier 1985", *Vingtième siècle*, October–December 1985: 117–21.

Stengers, J., "L'Historien face à ses responsabilités", *Cahiers de l'école des sciences philosophiques et religieuses*, 1994, no.15: 27–28.

Thomas, Y., "La Vérité, le temps, le juge et l'historien", *Le Débat*, November–December 1998, no.102: 23–25.

Trouw, 27 March 1991: 5 (Boudarel).

Turley, W.S. ed., *Vietnamese Communism in Comparative Perspective* (Boulder 1980) xi.

Volkskrant, 26 March 1991: 4 (Boudarel).

Vidal-Naquet, P., *Torture: Cancer of Democracy* (Harmondsworth 1963) inside cover, 68–69, 147–48.

Winters, C. ed., *International Dictionary of Anthropologists* (New York/London 1991) 651.

Wohl, R., "French Fascism, Both Right and Left: Reflections on the Sternhell Controversy", *Journal of Modern History*, 1991: 91–98.

G

GAMBIA

See Uganda (1971–79: Heddle).

GEORGIA

pre-1991   *See* Union of Soviet Socialist Republics (USSR).

1992   In October, during the civil war between Georgians and Abkhazians
            (1992–94), the National Archives in Sukhumi, kept in the Abkhaz
            Institute of Language and Literature, were burned. An estimated 90
            percent was destroyed. Georgian-controlled militia reportedly im-
            peded volunteers from putting the fire out.

1993   In [June] **Behan Yavakhia**, history lecturer at Tbilisi State Univer-
            sity, was dismissed together with four other lecturers, possibly as a
            result of their political views and their public support of ex-President
            Zviad Gamsakhurdia.

1997   In [December] President Eduard Shevardnadze categorically op-
            posed the opening of the former archives of the security service
            KGB, arguing that it would give rise to "a new wave of resistance,
            mistrust and hatred" and would "reopen old wounds".

SOURCES

Auer, L., "Archival Losses and Their Impact on the Work of Archivists and Historians",
    Archivum, 1996, no.42: 3.
Human Rights Watch, Letter, Committee for International Academic Freedom to Rector
    of Tbilisi State University (2 August 1993).

————, *World Report 1993* (Washington 1992) 232.
Index on Censorship, 2/98: 90.
Larin, M., & W. Banasjukevich, "Ausnahmesituationen und Erhaltung von Archiven: Die Lage in Russland", *Archivum*, 1996, no.42: 202, 205.

GERMANY

The 1933 Nazi measures provoked what was perhaps the greatest wave of exile of historians in the twentieth century. Most of the refugee historians did not return. In World War II many historians were persecuted. The war also left the archives ravaged. In 1945–49 German historiography was restructured. The denazification by the occupying powers led to the dismissal or suspension of historians who had collaborated with the Nazi regime. The history textbooks were rewritten. In 1947–49 non-Marxist historians were removed from their posts in the Sowjetische Besatzungszone in Deutschland (SBZ; Soviet Zone of Occupation, from 1949 the German Democratic Republic, GDR) or went into the Western occupation zones.

pre-1933   Among the historians and others concerned with the past who emigrated before 1933 (and still living in exile after 1944) were the following: **Emil Gumbel** (1891–1966), **Peter Olden** (1905–) **Max Raphael** (1889–1952), **Henry Sigerist** (1891–1957), **Ernst Simon** ([1899–]), and **Alfred Vagts** (1892–1986).

1933–   Among the historians and others concerned with the past who emigrated after the 7 April 1933 Gesetz zur Wiederherstellung des Berufsbeamtentums (Law for the Restoration of the Professional Civil Service) and still living in exile after 1944 were the following:

1933   Abusch [q.v. 1950–52], **Erwin Achterknecht** (1906–88), **Paul Alexander** (1910–77), **Hannah Arendt** (1906–75), **Max Beer** (1864–1949), **Richard Bernheimer** (1907–58), **Margaret Bieber** (1879–1978), **Gertrude Bing** (1892–1964), **Franz Borkenau** (1900–57), **Ernest Bramsted** (1901–78), **Helmut Callis** (1906–82), **Ernst Cassirer** (1874–1945), **Frederick Cramer** (1906–54), **David Daube** (1909–), **Ludwig Edelstein** (1902–65), **Norbert Elias** (1897–1990), **Julius Epstein** (1901–75), **Lion Feuchtwanger** (1884–1958), **Horst Gerson** (1907–79), **George Hallgarten** (1901–75), **Ernst Hamburger** (1890–1980), **Gerhard Harig** (1902–66), **Fritz Heichelheim** (1901–68), **Georg Herlitz** (1885–1968), Heym [q.v. 1965–89], **Frederick Heymann** (1900–83), **Helmut Hirsch** (1907–), **Hajo Holborn** (1902–69), **Ernst Honigmann** (1892–1954), **Paul Honigsheim** (1885–1963), **Hubert Jedin** (1900–80), **Erich von Kahler** (1885–1970), Kamnitzer [q.v. 1955–], Alfred Kantorowicz [q.v. 1957–], **Richard Krautheimer**

(1897–1994), **Stephan Kuttner** (1907–), **Carl Landauer** (1891–1983), **Karl Lehmann** (1894–1960), **George Lichtheim** (1912–73), **Otto Maenchen-Helfen** (1894–1969), **Golo Mann** (1909–94), **Hans Mottek** (1910–), **Franz Neumann** (1900–54), **Fritz Neumann** (1897–1976), **Sigmund Neumann** (1904–62), **Karl Obermann** (1905–87), **Henry Pachter** (1907–80), **Walter Pagel** (1898–), **Nikolaus Pevsner** (1902–), **Hans-Georg Pflaum** (1902–79), **Martin Plessner** (1900–73), **Edgar Rosen** (1911–), **Hans Rosenberg** (1904–88), **Eugen Rosenstock-Huessy** (1888–1973), **Erwin Rosenthal** (1904–), **Nicholas Rubinstein** (1911–), **Alfred Salmony** (1890–1958), **Boris Sapir** (1902–89), **Fritz Saxl** (1890–1948), **Ernst Sceyer** (1900–), **Albert Schreiner** (1892–1979), **Karl-Israel Schwarz** (1885–1962), **Charlotte Sempell** (1909–), **Raphael Straus** (1887–1947), **Veit Valentin** (1885–1947), **Martin Weinbaum** (1902–), **Herta Wescher** (died 1971), **Hellmut Wilhelm** (1905–), **Karl With** (1891–), and **Sergius Yakobson** (1901–79).

1934   **Elias Bickerman** (1897–1981), **Henry Bruehl** (1879–1946), **Fritz Epstein** (1898–1979), **Richard Ettinghausen** (1906–79), **Paul Frankl** (1878–1962), **Albrecht Goetze** (1897–1971), **George Hanfmann** (1911–), **Uriel Heyd** (1913–68), **Ernst Kitzinger** (1912–), **Richard Koebner** (1885–1958), **Wilhelm Koehler** (1884–1959), **Paul Kristeller** (1905–), **Otto Kurz** (1908–75), **Gustav Mayer** (1871–1948), **Alfred Meusel** (1896–1960), **Franz Michael** (1907–), **Carl Misch** (1896–1965), **Sibyl Moholy-Nagy** (1903–71), **Dora Mosse** (1916–65), **Otto Neugebauer** (1899–1990), **Erwin Panofsky** (1892–1968), **Joseph Schacht** (1902–69), **Erika Spivakovsky** (1909–), **Leo Strauss** (1899–1973), **Wolfgang Volbach** (1892–), **Martin Weinberger** (1893–1965), **Bernard Weinryb** (1905–82), **Helene Wieruszowski** (1893–1978), and **Karl Wittfogel** (1896–1988).

1935   **Ludwig Bachhofer** (1894–), Bartel [q.v. 1945–53], **Clemens Bosch** (1899–1955), Engelberg [q.v. 1985–], **Walter Friedländer** (1873–1966), **Frederick Gaupp** (1897–1979), **Dietrich Gerhard** (1896–1985), **Felix Hirsch** (1902–82), **Ernst Hoffman** (1912–), **Paul Jacobsthal** (1880–1957), **Horst Janson** (1913–82), **Jacob Katz** (1904–), **Guido Kisch** (1889–1985), **Benno Landsberger** (1890–1968), **Edith Lenel** (1909–), **Richard Löwenthal** (1908–), **Gerhard Masur** (1901–75), **Ulrich Middeldorf** (1901–), **Heinz Mode** (1913–), **Walter Mohr** (1910–), **Alfred Neumeyer** (1901–73), **Ernst Rabel** (1874–1955), **Israel Rabin** (1882–1951), **Jakob Rosenberg** (1893–1980), **Walter Ruben** (1899–1982), **Willy Schwabacher** (1897–1972), **Georg Steindorff** (1861–1951), **Wer-**

ner Weisbach (1873–1953), **Kurt Weitzmann** (1904–), and **Hans Julius Wolff** (1902–83).

1936   **Francis Carsten** (1911–), **Herman Dicker** (1914–), **Andreas Dorpalen** (1911–82), **Hans Güterbock** (1908–2000), **Emmy Heller** (1886–1956), **Ernst Herzfeld** (1879–1948), **Werner Jaeger** (1888–1961), **Bruno Kisch** (1890–1966), Kuczynski [q.v. 1957–59], **Ernst Levy** (1881–1968), **Theodor Mommsen** (1905–58), **Fritz Redlich** (1892–1978), **Werner Richter** (1888–1969), **Wolfgang Stechow** (1896–1974), and **Joseph Walk** (1914–).

1937   **Arnold Bergstraesser** (1896–1964), **Justus Bier** (1899–), **Alexander Dorner** (1893–1957), **Wolfram Eberhard** (1909–89), **Erich Eyck** (1878–1964), **Helmut Gernsheim** (1913–), **Hans Huth** (1892–1977), **Hans-Paul von Lilienfeld-Toal** (1897–), **Christian Mackauer** (1897–1970), **Johannes Quasten** (1900–87), **Friedrich Ranke** (1882–1950), **Richard Salomon** (1884–1966), **Ernst Stein** (1891–1945), and **Paul Zucker** (1888–1971).

1938   **Kurt Badt** (1890–1973), **Hans Baron** (1900–88), **Bernard von Bothmer** (1912–), **Dietrich von Bothmer** (1918–), **Otto Brendel** (1901–73), **Henry Dittmar** (1913–), **Leopold Ettlinger** (1913–), **Aron Freimann** (1871–1948), **Yochanan Ginat** (1908–79), **Ernest Jacob** (1899–1974), **Ernst Kantorowicz** (1895–1963), **Hellmut Pappe** (1907–), **Raimund Pretzel** (1907–99; pseudonym: Sebastian Haffner), **Franz Rosenthal** (1914–), **Hans-Joachim Schoeps** (1909–80), **Frederick Sell** (1892–1956), **George Swarzenski** (1876–1957), **George Urdang** (1882–1960), and **Mark Wischnitzer** (1882–1955).

1939   **Hans Bach** (1902–77), **Eberhard Bruck** (1877–1960), **Fritz Caspari** (1914–), **Ludwig Feuchtwanger** (1885–1947), **Ernst Fraenkel** (1891–1971), **Max Friedländer** (1867–1958), **Paul Friedländer** (1882–1968), **Felix Jacoby** (1876–1959), **Adolf Katzenellenbogen** (1901–64), **Georg Karo** (1872–1963), **Adolf Kober** (1879–1958), **Heinrich Kurtzig** (1865–1946), **Franz Landsberger** (1883–1964), **Richard Laqueur** (1881–1959), **Adolf Leschnitzer** (1899–1980), **Wilhelm Levison** (1876–1947), **Hans Liebeschütz** (1893–1978), **Toni Oelsner** (1907–), **Erwin Palm** (1910–), **Ernst Posner** (1892–1980), **Fritz Pringsheim** (1882–1967), **Hermann Ranke** (1878–1953), **Hanns Reissner** (1902–77), **Judah Rosenthal** (1904–), **Hans Rothfels** (1891–1976), **Guido Schoenberger** (1891–1974), **Fritz Schulz** (1879–1957), **Otto von Simson** (1912–), **Bruno Strauss** (1889–1969), **Karl Süssheim** (1878–1947), and **Luitpold Wallach** (1910–86).

1940   Ernst Breisacher (1889–1971), and Kurt Rosenow (?1907–).

1941   Eugen Täubler (1879–1953) and Selma Stern-Täubler (1890–
            1981).

1943   Herbert Strauss (1918–).

[?]   Year of emigration unknown: Berthold Altmann (1902–), Henry
            Blumenthal (1911–87), Rosy Bodenheimer (1900–), and Char-
            lotte Littauer-Blaschke (1897–).

            Among the young refugees who became historians in their new
            countries were Gabriel Baer (1919–), Otto Benfey (1925–), Gerd
            Buchdahl (1914–), Julius Carlebach (1922–), Klaus Epstein
            (1927–), son of Fritz Epstein [q.v. 1934], Ulrich Eyck (1921–),
            son of Erich Eyck [q.v. 1937], Edgar Feuchtwanger (1924–), son
            of Ludwig Feuchtwanger [q.v. 1939], André Gunder Frank
            (1929–), Saul Friedlander (1932–), Hans Gatzke (1915–), Peter
            Gay (1923–; born Frölich), Hanna Gray (1930–; born Holborn),
            John Grenville (1928; formerly Hans Gubrauer), Alfred Grosser
            (1925–), Peter Hennock (1926–), Eric Hobsbawm (1917–), Fred-
            erick Hoeniger (1921–), Henry Huttenbach (1930–), Robert
            Huttenback (1928–), Georg Iggers (1926–), Hans Jaffé (1915–),
            Henry Kissinger (1923–), Helmut Koenigsberger (1918–), Wal-
            ter Laqueur (1921–), Leonhard [q.v. 1949–], Karl Leyser (1920–
            92), Wolfgang Liebeschütz (1927–), son of Hans Liebeschütz
            [q.v. 1939], Frederick Mayer (1921–), Wolf Mendl (1927–),
            Georg Mosse (1918–99), Werner Mosse (1918–), Peter Paret
            (1924–), Arnold Paucker (1921–), Fritz Ringer (1934–),
            Günther Rothenberg (1923–), Joseph Rothschild (1931–), Wolf-
            gang Ruge (1917–), Jürgen Schulz (1927–), Peter Selz (1919–),
            Walter Simon (1922–71), Fritz Stern (1926–), Theodore von
            Laue (1916–), Gabriel Warburg (1927–), and Gerhard Wein-
            berg (1928–).

pre-1945   Among the historians and others concerned with the past who were
            censored or persecuted during World War II (including in 1945)
            were Karl Bittel (1892–1969), Ludwig Dehio (1888–1963), An-
            ton Eitel (1882–1966), Carl Erdmann (1898–1945), Eberhard
            Kessel (1907–86), Ulrich Noack (1899–1974), Erich Paterna
            (1897–1982), Gerhard Ritter (1888–1967), Heinrich Scheel
            (1915–), Alexander Graf Schenk von Stauffenberg (1905–64),
            Heinrich Sproemberg (1889–1966), Max Steinmetz (1912–),
            Hermann Strasburger (1909–85), Joachim Streisand (1920–80),
            and Heinz Tillmann (1917–).

1939–46   During World War II, an estimated one-third of all German books were destroyed, including many historical maps, manuscripts, incunabula, and old printed works. Allied air raids had a disastrous effect on the State Archives in Hannover (September/October 1943), the State Archives in Würzburg (March 1945), and the Military Archives in Potsdam (April 1945). Large holdings of the latter were deliberately set on fire by American troops. The holdings of a number of municipal archives were virtually annihilated. Many civilian and military archives were confiscated by the Allied occupation forces and taken away from Germany. After the war the German Historical Association called upon the Allies not to return the files taken in 1945 until they had all been fully investigated and microfilmed. When the Wehrmacht (German Army) fled before the advancing Red Army in Central Europe in 1944–45, they destroyed a large number of documents stored in castles and abbeys there after they had been stolen by the Geheime Staatspolizei (Gestapo; Secret State Police) from Western European countries under German occupation. The remaining documents were discovered by the Red Army in 1945–46 and transferred to Moscow.

1945–   The Allied Powers banned all history textbooks which had been in use in the Third Reich. For a time no history lessons were given in the reopened schools, or textbooks dating from pre-Nazi periods were utilized instead. All the new books were subjected to Allied censorship. Forty-five Nazi films with a historical character were put under seal. In May 1946 the Coordinating Council of the American Military Government in Germany ordered Nazi memorials to be destroyed, but this order, issued as the anniversary of the 10 May 1933 book burning by the Nazis was being observed, caused sharp comment. Books of Adolf Hitler, Joseph Goebbels, Benito Mussolini, and Karl Marx were placed on restricted lists in libraries or in some instances pulped.

After the war several university history professors working in the later FRG were dismissed as part of a denazification strategy. Most could resume their work in the 1950s, but those who could not were replaced by refugee historians. The postwar situation at the history faculties was chaotic. In Göttingen, for example, only octogenarian historian **Karl Brandi** (1868–1946) could teach because all the others were ill, had been dismissed, or remained prisoners of war. Denazification in the SBZ implied the changing of street names, the removal of statues, and the destruction of buildings such as the Berliner Schloss.

Among the historians dismissed for their collaboration with the Nazis were the following:

1945– In May **Walter Frank** (1905–45), leading Nazi historian, committed suicide. He had been president (1935–41) of the Reichsinstitut für Geschichte des neuen Deutschlands (Reich Institute for the History of the New Germany) and of its special Forschungsabteilung Judenfrage (Research Department for the Jewish Question) until he was ousted in late 1941 after a conflict with a rival institute under NSDAP (National Socialist German Workers' Party; Nazi Party) auspices—the Institut des NSDAP zur Erforschung der Judenfrage.

Frank's teacher and collaborator, **Karl Alexander von Müller** (1882–1964), specialist in modern history at Munich University, NSDAP member, pro-Nazi president of the Bavarian Academy of Sciences who in February 1935 took over the editorship of the *Historische Zeitschrift* after Meinecke [q.v. 1948] resigned it, was dismissed from all his posts. Publication of the *Historische Zeitschrift* had been halted in 1943 (two issues already printed were destroyed) and resumed in May 1949 only, under a new editor, Dehio [q.v. pre-1945].

Theodor Mayer (1883–1972), rector at Marburg University (1939–42) and president of the Reichsinstitut für ältere deutsche Geschichtskunde (the Monumenta Germaniae Historica [MGH], renamed by the Nazis) (1942–45), was dismissed in 1945. He remained active as a medievalist.

Helmut Berve (1896–1979), historian of Greek antiquity, particularly Sparta, Kriegsbeauftragter der deutschen Altertumswissenschaft, professor (1927–43) and rector (1940–43) at Leipzig University, professor at Munich University (1943–45), was suspended (December 1945–48). In 1949–50 he was reinstated and went to work at the universities of Regensburg and Erlangen (1954–62). From 1960 to 1967, he was chairman of the Kommission für Alte Geschichte und Epigraphik. He tried to help some of his persecuted colleagues at Leipzig University.

Percy Schramm (1894–1970), medievalist and specialist in the iconography of rulership, professor of medieval and modern history at Göttingen University (1929–63), was the official recordkeeper for the Oberkommando der Wehrmacht (Army High Command) (1943–45) and rescued many records by disobeying explict orders to destroy them. He was suspended from teaching for a trimester while British intelligence launched an investigation into his wartime career and Nazi affiliations and then dropped it because they wanted to equalize denazification policy with the other Allied Powers. Another source indicated that he was a prisoner of war working at Versailles for the United States Army Historical Division, reconstructing Germany's last western campaign. In the fall of 1946, Schramm had fully resumed his work. He was a member of the MGH board of directors. The multivolume war diary of the Army High Command was published in 1961–69.

Joseph Vogt (1895–1986), in 1940–44 historian of Roman antiquity at the University of Tübingen (where he had already been professor in 1926–29), was reportedly transferred to the University of Freiburg im Bresgau (1944–46). He resumed his work at Tübingen in 1946 (1946–62).

In part as a result of the scarcity of trained professional archeologists after 1945, many prehistoric archeologists who had been active during the Third Reich, especially scholars of the SS-Ahnenerbe (a research and cultural propaganda organization) such as **Herbert Jankuhn** (1905–90), were reinstated in their old or related departments after denazification had temporarily removed them from their posts. Leading Nazi archeologist **Hans Reinerth** (1900–), who had purged the discipline of "undesirable elements", was not reinstated.

Among the historians temporarily suspended for their collaboration with the Nazis were the following:

1945–   **Willy Andreas** (1884–1967), history professor (1923–45) and rector (1932–33) at Heidelberg University, temporarily dismissed (1946–48); **Erich Botzenhart** (1901–56), specialist in modern history at Göttingen University (1939–45), Reichsinstitut collaborator, dismissed in 1945, then archivist; **Ulrich Crämer** (1907–), specialist in modern history at the universities of Jena and Munich, NSDAP member, dismissed in 1945; **Heinrich Dannenbauer** (1897–1961), medievalist at Tübingen University, dismissed (1945–49) and reinstated; **Wilhelm Engel** at Würzburg University (1938–45); **Eugen Franz** at Würzburg University; **Günther Franz** (1902–92), specialist in medieval and modern history at Strassburg University, NSDAP member, member of the SS (Schutzstaffel, Defense Corps; special NSDAP security force), dismissed (?1944–?57); **Werner Frauendienst** at Friedrich-Wilhelms-University, Berlin (1942–45); **Erwin Hölzle** (1901–76), specialist in modern history at Berlin University, dismissed in 1945; **Willy Hoppe** (1888–1960), medievalist, NSDAP member, Reichsinstitut collaborator, dismissed in 1945; **Ulrich Kahrstedt**; **Gerhard Kallen** (1884–), medievalist at Cologne University; **Gerhard Krüger** (1902–72); **Johann von Leers** (1902–65), dismissed at Jena University in 1945 and exiled in Italy (1945–50), Argentina (1950–55), and Egypt (1955–65); **Erich Maschke** (1900–82), medievalist at the universities of Jena (1936–42) and Leipzig (1942–45), dismissed and imprisoned in the USSR (1945–53), lecturer and professor of social-economic history at Heidelberg University (1954–68), later director of the Scientific Commission for the History of German Prisoners of War; **Heinz Maybaum** (1896–

1955), medievalist at Rostock University, dismissed in 1945; **Wilhelm Mommsen** (1892–1966), specialist in modern history at Marburg University (1929–), already dismissed in 1936 as coeditor of *Vergangenheit und Gegenwart*, dismissed by the American Occupying Power in 1945; **Franz Petri** (1903–93) at Cologne University; **Walter Platzhoff** (1881–1969), specialist in medieval and modern history, rector at the University of Frankfurt am Main, dismissed in 1945; **Gustav Rein** (1885–1979), specialist in modern history, rector at Hamburg University (1933–38), NSDAP member, dismissed in 1945; **Otto Scheel** (1876–1954) at Kiel University; **Paul Schmitthenner** (1884–1963), specialist in medieval and modern history at Heidelberg University, dismissed in 1945; **Wilhelm Schüssler** (1888–1965), dismissed at Berlin University in 1945; **Otto Graf zu Stolberg-Wernigerode** (1893–1984), specialist in modern history at Rostock University, dismissed (1945–55), then professor at the Hochschule für Politische Wissenschaften, Munich; **Fritz Taeger**; **Fritz Valjavec** (1909–60), specialist in modern history at Berlin University, dismissed (1945–50), professor of Southeast European culture and economy at Munich University (1958–60); **Hans Volkmann** (1900–1975) at Greifswald University; **Wilhelm Weber** (1882–1948) at Berlin University; **Lothar Wickert** (1900–89), historian of antiquity at Cologne University; **Egmont Zechlin** at Berlin University; **Ludwig Zimmermann** (1895–1959) at Erlangen University.

1945–50   From 1945 to 1950, German and Japanese representatives were excluded from the Conseil Permanent of the Union Internationale des Sciences Préhistoriques et Protohistoriques because these countries were still regarded as enemy belligerents.

1945–48   In April 1945 **Fritz Kern** (1884–1950), a medievalist and world historian who tried to negotiate the capitulation of Germany on behalf of the military resistance in 1944–45, fled to Switzerland. In 1948 he returned to Germany (the later Federal Republic of Germany, FRG), where he eventually became a cofounder of the Institut für Europäische Geschichte, Mainz. He had already been detained briefly in 1937. He initiated the project for the ten-volume world history *Historia mundi* (1952–61).

1945–53   The past of historian **Walter Bartel** (1904–92) was screened three times, in 1945, 1950, and 1953. A member of the Kommunistische Partei Deutschlands (KPD), trained in Moscow (1929–32), and involved in the illegal resistance (1932–33), he had been imprisoned in the correction house Brandenburg-Görden (1933–35). Then he had gone into exile in Czechoslovakia, where he had been excluded from the KPD because of a confession to the Gestapo. Interned in the Buchenwald concentration camp (March 1939–April 1945), Bartel became one of the leaders of the resistance and, ultimately, self-liberation. From 1945 he lived in the SBZ/GDR and he was the personal secretary of first GDR President Wilhelm Pieck for SED (Sozialistische Einheitspartei: Socialist Unity Party) questions (1946–53). He became, inter alia, professor of modern history at Karl Marx University in Leipzig (1953–57), director of the Deutsche Institut für Zeitgeschichte, Berlin (1957–62), and professor of modern history at Humboldt University, East Berlin (1962–70). His research into the resistance in the Dora-Mittelbau concentration camp, near Nordhausen, formed the basis of his report on the 1968 trial against the camp's leader.

1948   Philosopher **Karl Jaspers** (1883–1969) left Germany and accepted a professorship of philosophy at Basel University, Switzerland. The most important reason for his emigration was his disappointment with the unwillingness of the Germans to confront the past. Reception of his essay *Die Schuldfrage* (1946) about the war guilt had been slow and often negative. Another of his works was *Vom Ursprung und Ziel der Geschichte* (1949).

Among the non-Marxist historians who were removed from their posts in the SBZ, or went to the Western occupation zones, were the following:

1947   **Friedrich Baethgen** (1890–1972), medievalist at Humboldt University (1939–47), became MGH president in Munich (1947–58).

1948   **Friedrich Meinecke** (1862–1954), considered the doyen of German historians, professor at Friedrich-Wilhelms-University, Berlin (1896–1901, 1914–32), fled and became the first rector of the newly established Freie Universität (Free University), Berlin (1948–51). In 1935, under Nazi rule, he had resigned his editorship of the *Historische Zeitschrift* (1896–1935).

1949   Constitutional historian **Fritz Hartung** (1883–1967) resigned his chair of modern history at Friedrich-Wilhelms-University, Berlin (1923–49) after a row over academic freedom. He remained a member of the Deutsche Akademie der Wissenschaften (DAW) (1939–53). In the 1930s he had been an adviser to the Reichsinstitut für Geschichte des neuen Deutschlands (Frank [q.v. 1945–]). From 1945 to 1949, he repeatedly tried to reconcile GDR and FRG historiographies. He remained the editor of the *Jahresberichte für deutsche Geschichte* (1925–58).

Federal Republic of Germany

1956   In March **Eberhard Wolfgramm** (1908–) fled to the GDR because
        he feared the resurgence of fascism. He was a former Ostforscher (an
        academic studying eastern Europe), member of the Sudeten German
        Party, author of a brochure *Germans and Czechs in History* and lead-
        ing Nazi in the Sudetenland but increasingly distanced himself from
        his past after the war. He became a lecturer in Slavonic languages at
        Stuttgart University and member of the German-Soviet Friendship
        Society. This membership proved incompatible with the official pol-
        icy concerning "enemies of democracy," but Wolfgramm refused to
        sign a declaration renouncing his political contacts and, consequently,
        lost his right to teach in Baden-Württemberg. At Karl Marx Univer-
        sity in Leipzig, he cowrote a book denouncing Ostforschung.

1964   In February, after the intervention of historian Gerhard Ritter, the
        Minister of Foreign Affairs Gerhard Schröder rescinded the Goethe
        Institute travel funds awarded **Fritz Fischer** (1908–99), professor of
        contemporary history at Hamburg University (1942–78), for a lecture
        tour of the United States. This happened in the wake of the so-called
        "Fischer-Kontroverse", during which Fischer's book *Griff nach der
        Weltmacht: Die Kriegszielpolitik des kaiserlichen Deutschland 1914–
        1918* (Düsseldorf 1961; *Germany's Aims in the First World War*,
        1967), depicting Germany as actively preparing for an international
        conflict, was hotly debated. Through the efforts of a dozen American
        scholars, led by Klaus Epstein (1927–), the tour came about.

1965   A journalist (name unknown) who had attacked the "Kolonialle-
        gende" (the emphasis on Germany's achievements in her pre-1918
        colonies without mentioning the violence) on television received
        death threats. Another person (name unknown) abroad, who had
        pointed out parallels between the genocide of the Herero in South
        West Africa in 1904 and that of the Jews and the Poles had to cope
        with censorship threats by the foreign office.

1970s   In the early 1970s, a book on the history of the Siemens company
        appeared with long passages deleted after Siemens had taken the case
        to court. The deletions included information on Siemens's use of
        labor from concentration camps during the Third Reich.

1975   A history of German anarchists in Chicago, *1886, Haymarket: Die
        deutschen Anarchisten von Chicago; Reden und Lebensläufe* (Berlin
        1975), edited by **Horst Karasek** (1939–), was seized by the Bavarian
        authorities because it explained how to make explosives. The pub-
        lisher appealed against this decision and won his case.

1970s   In the late 1970s, a historical atlas was banned from use in schools in Baden-Württemberg on the grounds that, since the name FRG was not spelled out in full, the atlas was unsuitable for educational purposes.

[1990]–   **Anja Rosmus** (1960–), who investigated Passau's war past, was sued for defamation by the brother of Emil Janik, a man whose collaboration with the Nazis she had described. She produced documents to support her case and the charges were dropped. The threats she underwent during her research were the object of a 1990 film, *Das schreckliche Mädchen (Nasty Girl)*. In 1993 a Passau court threatened her with prison or fines if she persisted in alleging that the late Franz-Maria Clarenz, a local obstetrician, had performed forced abortions on slave laborers. She was due to publish the allegations in a new book, *Wintergreen: Suppressed Murders*, in September 1993. When her children were threatened, she emigrated to the United States, where she was offered a position in a Holocaust museum.

German Democratic Republic

From October 1949 to October 1989, GDR historiography was dominated by Marxist-Leninist thought as formulated by the SED. Among the sensitive, falsified, or taboo subjects (called blank spots or Weiße Flecken) were the following: Martin Luther, Frederick II the Great, Otto von Bismarck; labor history; the 1848–49 and November 1918 revolutions; the history of German communism (KPD and SED), including the Stalinist purges of the 1930s and 1940s; the 23 August 1939 Molotov-Ribbentrop nonaggression pact; the 1940 Katyń forest massacre; the Holocaust; the historical development of the GDR, including the SBZ administration, the purges in the SBZ/GDR in the 1940s and 1950s, the 17 June 1953 Workers' Revolt, and the 1961 building of the Berlin Wall. Ancient and medieval topics were generally less affected than modern and contemporary topics, but the older fields also received fewer personnel. In the 1950s one group of historians fled the GDR, while others who stayed were reprimanded. Control reportedly slackened after a Rat für Geschichtswissenschaft was established in June 1969. In the 1970s a group of history students were purged. Only a small number of historians had (restricted) access to the GDR archives, the inventories of which contained many blackened parts. After the Wende (fall of the wall between East and West Berlin, 9 November 1989) and especially after the Wiedervereinigung (reunification; 4 October 1990), GDR historiography was restructured.

1949–61   About half the 110 historians who obtained a doctorate in history in the SBZ/GDR between 1945 and 1955 left the country before the Berlin Wall was built in August 1961.

Among the historians who fled the GDR before 1961 were the following:

1949   Historian of antiquity **Franz Altheim** (1898–1976), who worked at
            the University of Halle-Wittenberg (1936–49), fled and became pro-
            fessor at the Free University, Berlin (1949–64).

            Johannes Kühn, modern historian at Leipzig University, went into
            exile.

            In March **Wolfgang Leonhard** (until 1945: Wladimir or Wolodja
            Leonhard) (1921–), history lecturer at the SED Hochschule Karl
            Marx (1947–49), went into exile in Yugoslavia (1949–50) because
            he did not agree with the June 1948 eviction of Yugoslavia from the
            Cominform. In 1950 he went to the FRG, where he became a jour-
            nalist. In [1963] he went to the United States, where he eventually
            became a guest professor (1966–72) and history professor (1972–
            89) at Yale University specializing in the history of international and
            Soviet communism. In September 1933 he had gone into exile from
            Germany to Sweden, then to the USSR. As a member of the
            German-speaking minority there, he was sent into exile in Kazakh-
            stan in September 1941, where he studied history at Karaganda
            (1941–42). In 1945 he had returned to Germany.

1951–   **Helmut Plechl**, historian at Humboldt University, went into exile.

1955–   **Albrecht Timm** (1915–81), medievalist at the universities of Ros-
            tock (1947–49), Halle-Wittenberg (1949–52), and Berlin (1952–55),
            went into exile. He became a professor of economic history at the
            universities of Hamburg (1956–66) and Bochum (1966–).

1956–   **Willy Flach** (1903–58), historian at Humboldt University (1953–
            56), became a professor at Bonn University (1957–58).

1957–   After refusing to sign a Writers' Union resolution against the 1956
            Hungarian Revolution, **Alfred Kantorowicz** (1899–1979), journalist
            and literary historian, professor of modern German literary history
            at Humboldt University, escaped to West Berlin in August 1957. He
            lived in Munich and Hamburg. In Munich the authorities refused to
            acknowledge him as a Nazi persecutee because of his past commun-
            ist association. A KPD member since 1931, he had gone under-
            ground and escaped to France after a warrant for his arrest was
            issued in 1933. His German citizenship was revoked in November
            1934. He deployed antifascist cultural activities, especially concern-
            ing the books burned by the Nazis on 10 May 1933, and fought in
            the Spanish Civil War. In 1939 he was temporarily interned in a
            French concentration camp. In March 1941 he emigrated to the
            United States, where he analyzed German radio programs for Co-

lumbia Broadcasting System. In December 1946 he had returned to the SBZ.

1958– **Hans Haussherr** (1898–1960), student of Hartung [q.v. 1949] and Meinecke [q.v. 1948], economic and modern historian at Halle University (1946–58), went into exile.

Irmgard Höss (1919–), specialist in medieval and modern history at Jena University (1952–58), went to Erlangen University, FRG.

Helmut Thierfelder, historian of antiquity at Leipzig University, went into exile.

[?] *Year of emigration unknown*: **Manfred Hellmann** and **Hermann Mau**.

Instances of censorship or harassment among those who stayed include the following:

1949 Historian **W. Eckermann** had to withdraw a monograph about "new historical writing" because his Marxist colleagues had sharply criticized it.

1950–52 **Alexander Abusch** (1902–82), Jewish journalist, historian, and author of *Der Irrweg einer Nation: Ein Beitrag zum Verständnis deutscher Geschichte* (Mexico 1945), was temporarily dismissed from all his functions after a screening (1950–52) of his exile years in Mexico (which is where he wrote the book). He was blamed, inter alia, for his pro-Zionist viewpoint as chief editor of the journal *Freies Deutschland* there. Consequently he was enlisted as an informer of the Ministerium für Staatssicherheit (MfS or Stasi; the State Security) for the field "Emigration-Trotzkismus" (1951–56). He became a member of the SED Central Committee (1957–), member of the Volkskammer (Parliament) (1958–), and minister of culture (1958–61). An active KPD member since its foundation (1918), Abusch was twice charged with treason in 1922. He went into hiding in Thüringen. He worked illegally in the Ruhr area until his exile into the Saar area (which was under the authority of a League of Nations High Commissioner). Thereafter he went to Czechoslovakia in 1935 and to France in 1937, where he was imprisoned (1939–40). He escaped and participated in the anti-Nazi resistance in southern France. He emigrated to Mexico (1941–46). Upon his return in 1946 in the SBZ, he became active in the KPD again.

1951 In 1951 **Walter Markov** (1909–93), history professor specializing in world history at Leipzig University (1949–74), director of the Institut für Kultur- und Universalgeschichte (later Institut für Allgemeine Geschichte) (1949–68) and of the Institut für Geschichte der Europäischen Volksdemokratien (1951–58), was temporarily expelled from the SED on the charge of "Titoism" and lost his status as a victim of National Socialism. He became vice president of the GDR Nationalkomitee der Historiker (1960–74). In 1961 he became a member of the Deutsche Akademie der Wissenschaften (DAW). In 1992 he was the honorary chairman of an alternative commission of inquiry into German contemporary history. In April 1945, then a historian and assistant at Bonn University, Markov had released himself from Siegburg correction house, where he had been interned in 1936 after being sentenced (1935) for his illegal KPD activities.

1951–   In 1951 **Ernst Niekisch** (1889–1967), history professor and director of the Institut zur Erforschung des Imperialismus (Institute for Research on Imperialism) at Humboldt University (1948–51), refused SED verification of his past. He resigned from the SED after the 1953 Workers' Revolt. He lost his status as a victim of National Socialism. Niekisch had been a member of the Arbeiter- und Soldatenräte (workers' and soldiers' councils established in November 1918). After the Räterepublik in Bayern was defeated in 1919, he had been imprisoned for two years. He had been active in the anti-Nazi resistance. In 1935 his journal *Der Widerstand* (1928–35; The Resistance) had been banned. Imprisoned on the charge of conspiracy and treason in 1937, he had been sentenced to life imprisonment in 1939 and put in the correction house of Brandenburg-Görden.

1953   The works of Karl Marx and Friedrich Engels were expurgated or rewritten "with historically important additions".

1954–   In 1954 **Hermann Weber** (1928–), KPD/SED member (1945–54), was arrested as a leading member of the Freie Deutsche Jugend, which had been declared illegal. The same year he resigned from the SED and fled to the West. He began a study of history and political science (1964–70), which led to a professorship of political science and contemporary history at Mannheim University (1970–). An expert of German communism and GDR history, he served two truth commissions (named Aufarbeitung von Geschichte und Folgen der SED-Diktatur in Deutschland and Überwindung der Folgen der SED-Diktatur im Prozeß der deutschen Einheit).

1955   **Heinz Kamnitzer** (1917–), professor of modern history at Humboldt University (1950–54), coeditor of the *Zeitschrift für Geschichtswissenschaft* (1953–55) and first director of the Institut für Geschichte des deutschen Volkes (1952–54), resigned after a long period of inactivity. He became a freelance writer of popular history and was active in the PEN-Zentrum Ost-West. In 1978–89 he was an MfS Inoffizieller Mitarbeiter (Unofficial Collaborator). Imprisoned in the fall of 1933 for his anti-Fascist activities and then released, Kamnitzer had fled to the United Kingdom (1933–35, 1936–40, 1942–46), Palestine (1935–36), and Canada, where he was interned (1940–41). In 1946 he returned to the SBZ/GDR and studied history (1946–50).

1956   A single copy of the third volume of the autobiography of Jewish historian **Simon Dubnov** (1860–1941), was rediscovered and served as the basis for a new complete edition in 1957, entitled *Book of Life: Memoirs, Thoughts* (New York). The volume, completed in 1940, had been published in Russian in Riga, Latvia, as *Book of Life* (1940), shortly before the German occupation; the Nazis had putatively destroyed the entire printing. Dubnov had lived as an exile from the USSR (1922) and Nazi Germany (1933). In the weeks before his death in December 1941, his library was seized. He was obliged to hide his manuscripts. Cut off from his daily work, he began chronicling life in the ghetto of Riga. His notebooks were smuggled out of the ghetto to Latvian friends in the city. During one of the roundups, a Gestapo officer (a former student of his, according to some) murdered him. According to his daughter, Dubnov repeatedly exclaimed in the minutes before his death: "People, do not forget. Speak of this, people; record it all."

1956–64   In November 1956 **Wolfgang Harich** (1923–), philosopher who specialized in the history of philosophy, was imprisoned because he had written a program for the radical democratization of the GDR and the socialist reunification of Germany. In March 1957 he was sentenced to ten years in a correction house on charges of forming a subversive group. In December 1964 he was amnestied and released. In 1990 he was rehabilitated.

1956–58   Several members of the *Zeitschrift für Geschichtswissenschaft* editorial board were replaced by others more loyal to the SED. The "revisionist" essays by Streisand [q.v. 1945] and board member Kuczynski [q.v. 1957–59] were sharply criticized.

1957   Historian **Fritz Klein** (1924–) was dismissed as *Zeitschrift für Geschichtswissenschaft* chief editor (1956–57), which he had cofounded in 1953. He was accused of "objectivism and revisionism" and reprimanded by the SED because of his connections with the "subversive Harich [q.v. 1956–64] group". He went to work at the DAW Institute of History (1957–91), where he was in charge of general history. He was a specialist in World War I history.

1957–59   Accused of revisionism, apparently for his reflections on the role of the masses in history and his proposals for a Marxist sociology, economist and economic historian **Jürgen Kuczynski** (1904–97) was formally reprimanded by the SED in 1959. He had been a leading KPD member (1930–) active in the illegal anti-Nazi resistance (1933–), inter alia, in the Revolutionäre Gewerkschafts-Opposition. He had gone to the United Kingdom, where he orchestrated many resistance activities. In 1940–41 he had been interned. In 1944–45 he was a U.S. Army statistician attached to the U.S. Strategic Bombing Survey. In 1945 he had returned to Berlin, worked for the Sowjetische Militäradministration in Deutschland (SBZ), and become professor of economic history at Humboldt University (1946–56), GDR Volkskammer member (1949–58), DAW member (1955–) and founder-director of the economic history department of the History Institute (1956–69). He was the National Committee of Economic Historians chairman (1965–79), an adviser to SED Secretary-General Erich Honecker for foreign economic policy, and a prolific writer about social and economic history.

1957–90   In 1957 **Günther Mühlpfordt** (1921–), professor of Eastern European history and director of the Institute for Eastern European History, Martin Luther University, Halle-Wittenberg (1954–58), was accused of "objectivism and revisionism". In April 1958 he was suspended, expelled from the SED, and given a Berufsverbot (blacklisted for civil service) which lasted until 1983. In 1962 he was dismissed. He became a private scholar. In 1983–90 he did research for the DAW Zentralinstitut für Geschichte. In 1990 he was rehabilitated. During World War II, he had been a Canadian prisoner of war.

1964   **Thomas Ammer** (1937–), a student of medicine who had been sentenced to fifteen years in a correction house for treason in 1958 because he had participated in a resistance group at Jena University, was released early and went into exile in the FRG via a Freikauf procedure (by which the prisoner is "purchased"). There he studied law, political science, and history.

pre-1965 Until 1965 some historians reportedly omitted sensitive facts and names of persons fallen into disgrace and falsified documents and images. **Stefan Doernberg**'s *Kurze Geschichte der DDR* (Berlin 1964) was cited as an example: in the 1964 edition, Soviet leader Nikita Khrushchev was cited on twenty pages and shown in two pictures; in the 1965 edition, after Khrushchev's downfall, he was cited on five pages and not shown anymore. In the works of SED leader Walter Ulbricht, passages not in accordance with the SED position were omitted, such as in volume 2 of *Zur Geschichte der deutschen Arbeiterbewegung* (1953) his 1946 remarks on the "special German path to socialism" and in volume four (1958) some negative remarks on Tito and laudatory ones on Stalin.

1965–89   In 1965 poet and novelist **Stefan Heym** (pseudonym of Hellmuth Fliegel) (1913–) fell into disgrace after the West German weekly *Die Zeit* printed his article on Stalin's declining importance and impact on communism. In 1973 the official SED newspaper announced that three previously banned historical novels—*Lassalle* (1969), about labor leader Ferdinand Lassalle (1825–64), *The Queen against Defoe* (1970; *Die Schmähschrift*), a novel with the year 1703 as the time of action, and *The King David Report* (published simultaneously as *Der König David Bericht*, 1972), in which a biblical setting in 800 BCE was used for an analysis of the problems of history writing in a totalitarian state—would be published in the GDR on the occasion of Heym's rehabilitation. In September 1974 his GDR publisher suddenly reneged on plans to publish his historical novel *Fünf Tage im Juni* (Munich/Vienna 1974; *Five Days in June*), the first comprehensive interpretation of the 1953 Workers' Revolt written by a GDR citizen. Heym was told that his interpretation (the revolt followed a breakdown of communication between the SED and the workers) "does not fit in with our views". The ban fomented the sales in the FRG and the smuggling of the book into the GDR. All his novels were published abroad. In 1979 he was fined for royalties received from abroad and expelled from the Writers' Union. Most of his work was banned until late 1989. In 1933 Heym had made public his opposition to Nazi policies and gone into exile to Prague (1933–35) and the United States, where he was employed in various jobs in Chicago (1935–). He served in the U.S. Army psychological warfare division (1943–45) and edited *Frontpost*, an American publication for German soldiers. He was the American delegation head at the 1950 World Peace Conference in Warsaw. In 1952 he was transferred back to the United States to face an investigation into his alleged pro-communist attitude. In 1953 he returned to Germany (GDR).

1968–   After the DAW reform of 1968–69 (with the DAW renamed as Akademie der Wissenschaften, AdW), in which a Zentralinstitut für Alte Geschichte und Archäologie was established, historian **Reinhard Koerner** (1926–1987) obligatorily switched from Greek epigraphy, his specialty since 1954, to politicized research about the early Greek polis. He refused to utilize ideological language and was called a "Faktologischer Querulant" (a person querulous about facts). He lived in professional isolation and under permanent fear that his large but unwelcome project on early Greek epigraphic law texts, begun in November 1973 and continued until a few months before his death, would be canceled. The project manuscript was published posthumously in 1993.

1969–90   Non-Marxist historian **Karlheinz Blaschke** (1927–), a specialist in Saxon history, had to resign as an archivist at the Sächsisches Landeshauptarchiv Dresden (1951–68) because of his criticism of official history. He became a history lecturer (1969–90) and professor (1990–92) at the Theologische Seminar (Kirchliche Hochschule), Leipzig. He was also an honorary professor at Marburg University (1990–), and professor of Saxon history and head of the history department at Dresden Technical University (1992–).

1971   On 19 April historian **Gert Sudholt** was denied access to the Archiv des Reichskolonialamtes in Potsdam for his research on the German colonial policy in South West Africa up to 1904. In 1998 his 1975 book was called "one of the most elaborate denials" of the genocide of the Herero.

1972–90   In 1972 history student **Rainer Eckert** (1950–) and thirteen others were removed from Humboldt University because they were "left radicals", advocated a "democratic socialism", and distributed banned books. Eckert was forbidden to leave the GDR. He worked in the construction sector and studied history at the Open University (1972–75). From 1975 he was an AdW collaborator. In 1982 his first doctoral topic ("The Nazi Persecution of Jews As Reflected in Exile Publications") was canceled for political reasons. His new dissertation, completed in 1984, was on the Nazi occupation of Greece. He was a member of the Unabhängige Historiker-Verband (Independent Union of Historians; founded in 1990). He was a lecturer at the Humboldt University History Institute (1992–).

           History student **Stefan Wolle** (1950–) was removed from Humboldt University on political grounds. While earning his living as an unskilled worker, he continued his study (1973–76) and became a collaborator at the AdW Zentralinstitut für Geschichte (1976–90). In 1984 he completed his doctoral research on Russian historical writing in German. Rehabilitated in 1990, he went to work at the Gauck-Behörde (Gauck Authority; MfS archives) (1990–91). In 1990 Wolle and Mitter [q.v. 1991] published *Ich liebe Euch doch alle! Befehle und Lageberichte des MfS, Januar–November 1989*, the first book on the MfS. Wolle became an assistant at Humboldt University (October 1991–).

1972   History student **Mechthild Günther** was sentenced and imprisoned. She went to West Berlin via a Freikauf procedure. In 1998 she worked at the Berlin-Hohenschönhausen Memorial Foundation (dedicated to the history of SBZ/GDR political prisons).

1973–   **Guntolf Herzberg** (1940–), a philosopher who also studied history and worked at the DAW/AdW Zentralinstitut für Philosophie (1966–73), was expelled from the SED because of his "non-Marxist ideas, club activities, and conduct detrimental to the Party", dismissed, given Berufsverbot, and barred from publishing. Having founded an unofficial discussion group (Freitagsrunde) in 1972, he was watched by the MfS. While a freelance translator, writer, lecturer, and active dissident (1973–84), Herzberg reportedly wrote about 100 texts and lectures (some published in 1990). In 1976 he defended his doctoral dissertation ("Wilhelm Dilthey and the Problem of Historicism"). Unemployed and harassed by the MfS when applying for an exit visa in 1984–85, he moved to West Berlin in March 1985 and became a professor at the Institut für Philosophie, Free University, Berlin (1987–). He was a member of the Unabhängige Historiker-Verband. In 1993–94 he was a collaborator at the Gauck-Behörde. In 1994 he was also a collaborator at the Institut für Philosophie, Humboldt University.

1977–   In 1977 **Bernd Florath** (1954–), history student at Humboldt University, was banned from the university because he refused to support the abrogation of singer Wolf Biermann's citizenship in November 1976. He continued his study in 1978. He became a collaborator of the AdW Zentralinstitut für Geschichte (1981–91) and completed his doctoral research on the theories of Wittfogel [q.v. 1934–] on oriental despotism (1987). He was a member of the Unabhängige Historiker-Verband. In 1994 he worked at Humboldt University.

1977–92   In 1977–78 historian **Ibrahim [= Manfred] Böhme** (1944–), who had left the SED in protest against the persecution of intellectuals, was in administrative detention for antistate propaganda for fifteen months. He was also forbidden to teach history. After his detention he worked at a theater in Neustrelitz, but he was dismissed there in 1981 because of his public sympathy with the Polish Solidarity trade union. He then had several manual and other jobs, including librarian and teacher of German to Vietnamese guestworkers. In 1989 he was a supporter of the Initiative für Frieden und Menschenrechte. In October 1989 he became a founding member and first secretary of the Sozialdemokratische Partei (SDP; Social Democratic Party) and in January 1990 its chairman. In March he was accused of having been an Unofficial Collaborator of the MfS. In April he resigned as SDP chairman and in October his SDP membership was suspended, although the accusation of collaboration was substantiated only later. In 1992 he was expelled from the SDP. In 1965 he had been imprisoned briefly because of a lecture on dissident Robert Havemann. In 1966–67 he had interrupted his Open University study of history and German, reportedly on political grounds. He became an SED member in 1967, was briefly imprisoned in 1968, and later frequently censored. It was in this period that he became an Unofficial Collaborator of the MfS.

1979   The American television series *Holocaust* (1979) was reportedly never shown in the GDR, but many people in the border areas tuned into FRG television stations.

1979–89   From 1979 to 1982, the MfS kept a file on British historian **Timothy Garton Ash** (1955–). From 1982 until 1989, he was banned from the GDR, although he briefly visited it twice as a member of official British delegations. From December 1981 until the spring of 1983, he was also refused entry into Poland. He wrote a book about his experience, *The File* (1997).

1983–   In December 1983 **Ulrike Poppe** (1953–), a historian working at the Museum für Deutsche Geschichte, Berlin (1976–88), and other members of the group Frauen für den Frieden (Women for Peace) were arrested in East Berlin and had their homes searched and books and papers seized. The four had met Barbara Einhorn, a New Zealand citizen who wrote for a publication of the Campaign for Nuclear Disarmament. All were charged with "treasonable passing on of information". After Poppe had gone on a hunger strike in January 1984, she was released. She remained active in peace and human-rights groups. In September 1989 she was a cofounder and spokeswoman of Demokratie Jetzt (Democracy Now). She worked at the Evangelische Akademie Berlin-Brandenburg (1992–).

1985–   After 1985, volume 1 of the Bismarck biography (1985) of historian **Ernst Engelberg** (1909–), in which the first chancellor of Germany, Otto von Bismarck (1815–98), was favorably reinterpreted, reportedly had to be sold under the counter inside the GDR, whereas it could be bought freely abroad. A communist engaged in antifascist activities, Engelberg had briefly been arrested by the Gestapo in 1934 (which prevented the publication of his doctoral thesis on Bismarck's social policy) and sentenced to eighteen months in a correction house on the charge of "preparations for treason". He went to Switzerland (1935–39) and Turkey (1940–47), where he was a teacher of German at Istanbul University. In 1948 he had returned to Germany (SBZ/GDR), where in 1949 he had become a history professor at Karl Marx University, Leipzig, director of the Institut für Geschichte des deutschen Volkes (1951–60), Leipzig, first president of the Deutsche Historikergesellschaft (1958–65), president of the Nationalkomitee der Historiker der GDR (1960–80), and director of the DAW Institute of History (1960–69).

1988   In November the German language edition of the Soviet monthly press digest *Sputnik* was banned and struck off the list of admissible journals for allegedly carrying "reports that distort history" because its October issue had been critical of Stalin's role in World War II and of the 1939 Molotov-Ribbentrop Pact. Probably for the same reason, five Soviet films, *The Commissar* by **Aleksandr Askoldov** (made in the 1960s but released in the 1980s), *The Theme* by **Gleb Panfilov** (a film about Jewish émigrés, banned in the USSR), *And Tomorrow There Was War* by **Juri Kara**, *The Cold Summer of 1953* by **Alexander Proshkin**, and *Games for Schoolchildren* by **Leida Laius** and **Arvo Iho**, all shown at a film festival in East Berlin and all dealing with aspects of USSR and GDR history, were withdrawn from general release.

1989–90   In October 1989, immediately after Honecker's downfall, and in November, parts of the MfS archives, especially the names of collaborators, files on high-ranking SED and state officials, files on MfS support of terrorist groups, and files on foreign intelligence were shredded or burned, although some may have been saved by secret microfilming. Many files were also lost when in December 1989–January 1990 members of the civil movement occupied the MfS archives. In March 1990 the hard disk of central MfS records was erased after the Volkskammer had voted to destroy it. Destruction of foreign intelligence records identifying individual agents and informers continued until the early summer.

Between the Wende and the Wiedervereinigung (reunification), changes in GDR historiography were relatively small. AdW and SED historical institutions continued to exist, but with less personnel or with another name. The Institut für Marxismus-Leninismus was succeeded by the new Institut für Geschichte der Arbeiterbewegung; the journal *Geschichtsunterricht und Staatsbürgerkunde* was renamed *Geschichtsunterricht und Gesellschaftskunde*. The Rat für Geschichtswissenschaft was abolished on 5 December 1989, and its first and only chairman, historian **Ernst Diehl** (1928–), went into early retirement in 1990 and became a porter in a Berlin factory. In December 1989 the old history textbooks were withdrawn from the schools. On 17 June 1990, the 1953 Workers' Revolt was officially commemorated for the first time.

1990–   After the Wiedervereinigung, changes were more significant. On 31 December 1991, the AdW and its Institutes für Deutsche Geschichte, für Allgemeine Geschichte, für Wirtschaftsgeschichte, and für Alte Geschichte und Archäologie and the Museum für Deutsche Geschichte were abolished. Most Traditionskabinette (miniature museums in schools and factories summarizing great moments in GDR history) were removed. After an evaluation, at least half the AdW Institute of History staff was reappointed, generally in temporary positions. Everywhere in the ex-GDR, the history departments were remolded according to the West German model. Whereas at Leipzig University nearly 50 percent of the East German historians kept their positions, fewer did so at the universities of Halle and Jena, and only 20 percent kept their chairs at Humboldt University. Among the several hundred teachers subject to dismissal from Saxon schools in 1991 and early 1992 because of their political association with the GDR regime were many history teachers. In 1992 historian and archivist Klaus Oldenhage, director of the Bundesarchiv (Federal Archive) in Potsdam, estimated that probably no more than 5 percent of the archivists from the former GDR Staatsarchiv were dismissed (with the exception of MfS officials who also worked there).

Among those dismissed were **Dieter Schulte**, curator of the history museum in Potsdam for seven years, **Kurt Pätzold** (1930–), specialist in Fascism and the Holocaust, history professor, head of the Humbold University history department (1973–92)—who had reportedly been active in the purges of scholars (1956–58) and history students (1968, 1971–72, 1976–77)—and **Ralf Preuß**. On 1 October 1990, **Joachim Hermann** (1932–), historian and archeologist specializing in the history of the Slavs, resigned under heavy pressure from his collaborators as the director of the AdW Zentralinstitut für Alte Geschichte und Archäologie (1969–90).

Germany (unified)

1991   In March **Armin Mitter** (1953–), historian and former AdW collaborator (1979–90) and Wolle [q.v. 1972–90], cofounders and board members of the Unabhängige Historiker-Verband (1990), were dismissed as staff members of the Gauck-Behörde because they had criticized its work. In three newspaper articles in January 1991, they had denounced the last GDR prime minister, Lothar de Maizière, as an Unofficial Collaborator of the MfS, and criticized his rehabilitation by Minister of Interior Affairs Wolfgang Schäuble. As a result, de Maizière resigned as deputy chairman of the Christian Democratic Union political party later that year. They also wrote that access to the archives was being hampered by the government since Germany's reunification. Mitter became an assistant at Humboldt University (October 1991–). He served as expert for the Enquete-Kommission Aufarbeitung von Geschichte und Folgen der SED-Diktatur in Deutschland (1995). Another Gauck-Behörde staff member, historian **Jochen Laufer**, resigned for similar reasons in February 1991. In 1994 he worked at the Forschungsschwerpunkt Zeithistorische Studien in Potsdam.

1995   In January customs officials in Wuppertal reportedly seized the entire print run of a book by left-wing author and historian **Karl-Heinz Jahnke** (probably *Hitlers letztes Aufgebot: Deutsche Jugend im sechsten Kriegsjahr, 1944/45* [Essen 1993]). The book, printed in Hungary, was banned in Germany for "reasons of national security".

In February the book *An Eye for an Eye* (New York 1995) by **John Sack** (1945–) was withdrawn by the publisher before any copies had been sold. It argued that Stalin deliberately chose Jews to oversee concentration camps in postwar Poland. The book was labeled "anti-Semitic fodder" by a literary critic.

1996   In June Pope **John Paul II** (1920–) was censored by his own bishops on a visit to Germany. From his homily delivered at the stadium built by Adolf Hitler for the 1936 Olympics, they excised a passage praising the Catholic hierarchy's "glorious" record of resisting Nazism.

1998   In April a researcher of the French Centre National de la Recherche Scientifique (CNRS; National Scientific Research Agency), Hungarian-born historian **Gabor Rittersporn** (1948–), working at the Marc-Bloch Franco-German Center for Social Sciences in Berlin, sued the newspaper *Berliner Zeitung* because it had attributed revisionist arguments (particularly that the existence of the Nazi gas chambers had not been proved) to him. Rittersporn had denied the allegations and condemned Holocaust denial. He told the court that some members of his family, itself part-Jewish, had perished in the Holocaust. He won the case. The allegations against Rittersporn had followed revelations that in the 1970s and 1980s he had been a member of extreme left-wing groups that favored free expression for Holocaust deniers.

Also see Argentina (1992–93: Nazi files), Brazil (1964–: Frank), Czechoslovakia (1977–81: Bohemus; 1977–81: Danubius; 1945: Gesemann; 1949–50: Kalandra), Indonesia (1994: Spielberg), Korea (1985: Wolf), Mexico (1967–68: Palerm), Namibia (1996: Groth), Poland (1944–49: Roos), Turkey (1948–52: Eberhard, Güterbock, Landsberger; 1995–: Kaiser), United States (1950: Edelstein, Kantorowicz; 1968–: Epstein), USSR (1941–55: Ruge; 1949–54: Reisberg; 1952: Kennan; 1974: Repatria).

SOURCES

Ackerman, B., *The Future of Liberal Revolution* (New Haven/London 1992) 80–89, 136–39.

Alter, P. ed., *Out of the Third Reich: Refugee Historians in Post-War Britain* (London/New York 1998) xvii–xviii, 73–97, 119–32.

Amnesty International, *Report* (London) 1980: 270; 1984: 284.

Arnold, B., & H. Hassmann, "Archaeology in Nazi Germany: The Legacy of the Faustian Bargain", in: P.L. Kohl & C. Fawcett eds., *Nationalism, Politics, and the Practice of Archaeology* (Cambridge 1995) 73–74, 80.

Auer, L., "Archival Losses and Their Impact on the Work of Archivists and Historians", *Archivum*, 1996, no.42: 4.

———, "Archival Losses since the Second World War", *Janus: Archival Review*, 1994, no.1: 71.

Bak, J., "Percy Ernst Schramm (1894–1970)", in: H. Damico & J.B. Zavadil eds., *Medieval Scholarship: Biographical Studies on the Formation of a Discipline*, vol. 1, *History* (New York/London 1995) 247, 249.

Banisar, D., *Freedom of Information around the World* (WWW-text; Privacy International Report; London 2000).

Barth, B.-R., et al. eds., *Wer war Wer in die DDR: Ein biographisches Handbuch* (Frankfurt/Main 1996) 13–14, 37, 76, 83–84, 135–36, 166–67, 275, 298, 302–3, 353–54, 376–77, 421–22, 480, 509–10, 518–19, 539–40, 558, 576–77, 812–13.

Baumgartner, G., & D. Hebig eds. *Biographisches Handbuch der SBZ/DDR 1945–1990* (Munich 1996) 1–2, 24–25, 70, 121–22, 161, 279–80, 310–11, 373–74, 397, 446, 512, 599.

Bley, H., "Unerledigte Deutsche Kolonialgeschichte", *Entwicklungspolitische Korrespondenz: Zeitschrift zur Theorie und Praxis der Entwicklungspolitik*, 1977, nos.5–6: 5.

Boia, L. ed., *Great Historians of the Modern Age: An International Dictionary* (Westport 1991) 297–98, 536–37.

Boraine, A., J. Levy, & R. Scheffer eds., *Dealing with the Past: Truth and Reconciliation in South Africa* (Cape Town 1997) 72.

Boris, P., *Die sich lossagten: Stichworte zu Leben und Werk von 461 Exkommunisten und Dissidenten* (Cologne 1983) 25–26, 114–16, 159–60, 289–91.

Boyd, K. ed., *Encyclopedia of Historians and Historical Writing* (London/Chicago 1999) 324–25, 386–87, 440–41, 518–19, 667–68, 721–22, 796–97, 841–42, 1020, 1066–67, 1285–86.

Brinks, J.H., personal communication, February 1997.

———, *De rechterflank van Duitsland* (Amsterdam 1994) 85.

———, "De wonderbaarlijke wederopstanding van Pruisen: Het nieuwe Duitse nationalisme in de DDR en de 'Wiedervereinigung' ", *De Gids*, 1988: 532–33.

Bruch, R. vom, & R.A. Müller eds., *Historikerlexikon: Von der Antike bis zum 20. Jahrhundert* (Munich 1991) 4, 6–7, 17–18, 28–29, 95–96, 126–27, 166–67, 200–205, 219–20, 282–83, 322.

Bruhns, H., "Allemagne: Entre historiens de l'Est et historiens de l'Ouest, le mur est encore là: Dans les têtes . . .", *Le Monde*, 18 March 1993: ix.

Burguière, A. ed., *Dictionnaire des sciences historiques* (Paris 1986) 17.

Burleigh, M., *Germany Turns Eastwards: A Study of Ostforschung in the Third Reich* (Cambridge 1988) 309–10.

Buruma, I., *The Wages of Guilt: Memories of War in Germany and Japan* (New York 1994) 88, 178, 215, 232, 234, 239–42, 262–75.

Butler, D., "French Research Agency to Seek Ruling on Holocaust Sceptics", *Nature*, 23 April 1998: 745.

Calvocoressi, P., *Freedom to Publish* (Stockholm 1980) 47.

Cannon, J. ed., *The Blackwell Dictionary of Historians* (Oxford 1988) 179, 274–76.

Cantor, N.F., *Inventing the Middle Ages: The Lives, Works and Ideas of the Great Medievalists of the Twentieth Century* (New York 1991) 91–92, 423–24.

Černý, J. ed., *Wer war Wer—DDR: Ein biographisches Lexikon* (Berlin 1992) 9, 24, 50, 82, 102, 167–68, 186, 217–18, 232–33, 259–60, 334.

Christ, K., *Neue Profile der alten Geschichte* (Darmstadt 1990) 80–81, 176–79.

Dance, E.H., *History the Betrayer: A Study in Bias* (London 1964) 31, 62–63.

Darnton, R., *Berlin Journal 1989–1990* (New York/London 1991) 93–94, 122, 129–37, 212–13.

De Schryver, R., *Historiografie: Vijfentwintig eeuwen geschiedschrijving van West-Europa* (Leuven/Assen 1990) 326.

Dorpalen, A., "Die Geschichtswissenschaft der DDR", in: Faulenbach ed. 1974: 121–37.

Dubnov-Erlich, S., *The Life and Work of S.M. Dubnov: Diaspora Nationalism and Jewish History* (originally 1950; Bloomington/Indianapolis 1991) 245–47 (quote 247).

Eckert, R., I.-S. Kowalczuk, & I. Stark eds., *Hure oder Muse? Klio in der DDR: Dokumente und Materialien des Unabhängigen Historiker-Verbandes* (Berlin 1994) 18, 112–13, 115, 123–25, 153–54, 256–57, 266–69, 277–78, 304, 359, 396–97, 434.

Eckert, R., W. Küttler, & G. Seeber eds., *Krise-Umbruch-Neubeginn: Eine kritische und selbstkritische Dokumentation der DDR-Geschichtswissenschaft 1989/90* (Stuttgart 1992) 202, 204–7, 222, 435–38, 480–84, 488, 492.

Ehrenburg, I., & V. Grossman, *The Black Book: The Ruthless Murder of Jews by German-Fascist Invaders throughout the Temporarily-Occupied Regions of the Soviet Union and in the Death Camps of Poland during the War of 1941–1945* (New York 1981) 310–11, 333.

Eich, H., *Die mißhandelte Geschichte: Historische Schuld- und Freisprüche* (Munich 1983) 72.

Erdmann, K.D., *Die Ökumene der Historiker: Geschichte der internationalen Historikerkongresse und des Comité international des sciences historiques* (Göttingen 1987) 235, 339.

Faulenbach, B. ed., *Geschichtswissenschaft in Deutschland: Traditionelle Positionen und gegenwärtige Aufgaben* (Munich 1974).

Faulenbach, B., M. Meckel, & H. Weber eds., *Die Partei hatte immer Recht—Aufarbeitung von Geschichte und Folgen der SED-Diktatur* (Essen 1994).

Fischer, A., & G. Heydemann, "Weg und Wandel der Geschichtswissenschaft und des Geschichtsverständnisses in der SBZ/DDR seit 1945" (originally 1989), in: Eckert, Küttler & Seeber eds. 1992: 128–30, 133, 141–42, 146.

Fryskén, A., "Archives for Millennia", *Archivum*, 1996, no.42: 330–31.

Garton Ash, T., *The File: A Personal History* (New York 1997) 20, 86–87, 156, 163, 166, 208–12.

Gauck, J., "Zum Umgang mit den Stasi-Akten—eine Zwischenbilanz", in: Faulenbach, Meckel, & Weber eds. 1994: 30–31.

Guardian Weekly, 27 February 1994 (archives).

Gutman, I. ed., *Encyclopedia of the Holocaust*, vol. 2 (New York/London 1990) 526–27.

Haight, A.L., *Banned Books* (New York 1955) 122–23.

Hallof, K. ed., *Inschriftliche Gesetzestexte der frühen griechischen Polis: Aus dem Nachlaß von Reinhard Koerner* (Cologne 1993) xv–xviii, 593–603.

Herwig, H.H., "Clio Deceived: Patriotic Self-Censorship in Germany after the Great War", in: K. Wilson ed., *Forging the Collective Memory: Government and International Historians through Two World Wars* (Oxford/Providence 1996) 18, 107, 114–16, 126.

Heydemann, G., *Geschichtswissenschaft im geteilten Deutschland: Entwicklungsgeschichte, Organisationsstruktur, Funktionen, Theorie- und Methodenprobleme in der Bundesrepublik Deutschland und in der DDR* (Frankfurt/Main 1980) 141, 144, 152, 155, 171–72, 179, 198.

Hobsbawm, E., "The Historians' Group of the Communist Party", in: M. Cornforth ed., *Rebels and Their Causes: Essays in Honour of A.L. Morton* (London 1978) 22–23, 34.

Hoeven, H. van der, *Lost Memory: Libraries and Archives Destroyed in the Twentieth Century*, part 1, *Libraries* (WWW-text 1996) 9–11, 15.

Hoffman, C., "The Contribution of German-speaking Jewish Immigrants to British Historiography", in: W.E. Mosse ed., *Second Chance: Two Centuries of German-Speaking Jews in the United Kingdom* (Tübingen 1991) 164–65.

Index on Censorship, 4/76: 31–32; 4/78: 21; 3/79: 19–20; 4/81: 15; 2/84: 45; 3/84: 46; 6/85: 20–21; 6/88: 36; 1/89: 35–36; 2/89: 4–5; 8/90: 36; 10/90: 36; 10/93: 44; 1/95: 239; 2/95: 175; 4/96: 6.

Jonassohn, K., & K.S. Björnson, *Genocide and Gross Human Rights Violations in Comparative Perspective* (New Brunswick/London 1998) 78–79.

Kaplan, J., "The Historiography of National Socialism", in: M. Bentley ed., *Companion to Historiography* (London/New York 1997) 555–59.

Keesings historisch archief, 1990: 428–30; 1991: 8.

Keesing's Record of World Events, 1989: 36624A; 1990: 37259A.

Kocka, J., "Nachwort", in: Eckert, Küttler, & Seeber eds. 1992: 468–69, 477–78.

Kowalczuk, I.-S., "Die Etablierung der DDR-Geschichtswissenschaft 1945 bis 1958", in: R. Eckert, I. S. Kowalczuk, & U. Poppe eds., *Wer schreibt die DDR-Geschichte? Ein Historikerstreit um Stellen, Strukturen, Finanzen und Deutungskompetenz* (Berlin-Brandenburg 1995) 12, 18.

Lehmann, H., & J. Sheehan eds., *An Interrupted Past: German-Speaking Refugee Historians in the United States* (Cambridge 1991) 227.

Maibaum, W., "Geschichte und Geschichtsbewußtsein in der DDR", in: R. Thomas ed., *Wissenschaft und Gesellschaft in der DDR* (Munich 1971) 96, 203, 205.

Materialien der Enquete-Kommission "Aufarbeitung von Geschichte und Folgen der SED-Diktatur in Deutschland", vol. 7-1 (ed. Deutsche Bundestag; Frankfurt/Main 1995) 254–56.

Müller, W., "Hermann Weber 60 Jahre", *Internationale wissenschaftliche Korrespondenz zur Geschichte der deutschen Arbeiterbewegung*, 1988: 357–60.

NRC-Handelsblad, 4 February 1992: 9 (MfS archives); 16 July 1993: 5 (MfS archives); 13 January 1996: 5 (Eckert).

Otterspeer, W., "Huizinga before the Abyss: The von Leers Incident at the University of

Leiden, April 1933 (introduction and afterword, L. Gosman)", *Journal of Medieval and Early Modern Studies*, Fall 1997: 432.

Pohl, K.H., ed., *Historiker in der DDR* (Göttingen 1997) 147.

Preuß, R., "Berliner Historiker fordert Wissenschaftler der Humboldt-Universität auf sein Leben zu erforschen", *Hochschule Ost*, 1994, no.3: 110–13.

Röder, W., & H.A. Strauss eds., *Biographisches Handbuch der deutschsprachigen Emigration nach 1933*, vol. 1 (Munich 1980) 2–3, 163, 346–47, 365–66, 400–401, 433.

Rosenberg, T., *The Haunted Land: Facing Europe's Ghosts after Communism* (New York 1995) 291–93, 295.

Roth, C. ed., *Encyclopaedia Judaica*, vol. 6 (Jerusalem 1971) 252–58.

Schöpflin, G. ed., *Censorship and Political Communication in Eastern Europe: A Collection of Documents* (London 1983) 157–58, 163.

Schöttler, P. ed., *Geschichtsschreibung als Legitimationswissenschaft 1918–1945* (Frankfurt/Main 1999) 7–30.

Schreiner, K., "Führertum, Rasse, Reich: Wissenschaft von der Geschichte nach der nationalsozialistischen Machtergreifung", in: P. Lundgreen ed., *Wissenschaft im Dritten Reich* (Frankfurt/Main 1985) 200–201, 216–17.

Schüddekopf, O.-E., "History of Textbook Revision 1945–1965", in: Schüddekopf, et al., *History Teaching and History Textbook Revision* (Strasbourg 1967) 23.

Schulze, W., *Deutsche Geschichtswissenschaft nach 1945* (Munich 1993) 87, 121–30, 207–9, 221–22, 313–31.

———, "Das traurigste Los aber traf die Geschichtswissenschaft: Die DDR-Geschichtswissenschaft nach der 'deutschen Revolution' ", in: Eckert, Küttler, & Seeber eds. 1992: 217–22.

Schwabe, K., & R. Reichardt eds., *Gerhard Ritter: Ein politischer Historiker in seinen Briefen* (Boppard/Rhein 1984) 585–88.

Shaw, T., "The Academic Profession and Contemporary Politics: The World Archeological Congress, Politics and Learning", *Minerva*, 1989: 63, 84.

Stern, F., *The Varieties of History: From Voltaire to the Present* (New York 1961) 330, 342–46.

Stieg, M.F., *The Origin and Development of Scholarly Historical Periodicals* (Alabama 1986) 160–65.

Strauss, H.A., & W. Röder eds., *International Biographical Dictionary of Central European Émigrés 1933–1945*, vol. 2 (Munich 1983) 46–47, 78–79, 165, 180, 201, 228–29, 264–65, 268, 293–94, 339–40, 360–61, 414, 416, 421–22, 506, 525, 547–50, 562, 593, 639, 694, 728, 790, 835–36, 888, 890, 997; 1054–55, 1074, 1086, 1123–24, 1196–97, 1208, 1221.

Sudholt, G., *Die deutsche Eingeborenenpolitik in Südwestafrika: Von den Anfängen bis 1904* (Hildesheim 1975) 9–10, 215.

Taal, G., "Fritz Fischer (geb. 1908)", in: A.H. Huussen, E.H. Kossmann, & H. Renner eds., *Historici van de twintigste eeuw* (Utrecht/Antwerpen 1981) 257.

Timm, A., *Das Fach Geschichte in Forschung und Lehre in der sowjetischen Besatzungszone Deutschlands seit 1945* (Bonn/Berlin 1966) 24, 46, 170–73.

Tucker, M. ed., *Literary Exile in the Twentieth Century: An Analysis and Biographical Dictionary* (Westport 1991) 313–16.

Verbeeck, G., " 'Aus der Geschichte lernen, heisst siegen lernen'; Terugblik op de DDR-historiografie: Een Literatuuroverzicht", *Revue belge d'histoire contemporaine*, 1992: 212.

―――, "Contemporaine geschiedschrijving in Duitsland na de Hereniging", *Contactblad van de Vereniging voor de geschiedenis van de twintigste eeuw*, December 1995: 62.

Watt, D.C., "The Political Misuse of History", *Trends in Historical Revisionism: History As a Political Device* (London 1985) 11.

Weber, H., "Die Aufarbeitung der DDR-Geschichte und die Rolle der Archive", in: Faulenbach, Meckel, & Weber eds. 1994: 44–45.

―――, *Die DDR 1945–1986* (Munich 1988) 105–15.

―――, " 'Weisse Flecken' in der DDR-Geschichtsschreibung" (originally 1990), in: Eckert, Küttler, & Seeber eds. 1992: 369–91.

Weber, W., *Biographisches Lexicon zur Geschichtswissenschaft in Deutschland, Österreich und der Schweiz: Die Lehrstuhlinhaber für Geschichte von den Anfängen des Faches bis 1970* (Frankfurt/Main 1987) 5–6, 8–9, 22–23, 42, 99–100, 129, 205–6, 215, 296, 365–67, 394, 603–4, 623.

―――, *Priester der Klio: Historisch-sozialwissenschaftliche Studien zur Herkunft und Karriere deutscher Historiker und zur Geschichte der Geschichtswissenschaft 1800–1970* (Frankfurt/Main 1984) 316–17, 429–30.

Weinreich, M., *Hitler's Professors: The Part of Scholarship in Germany's Crimes against the Jewish People* (New York 1946) 45–62.

Wengst, U., "Geschichtswissenschaft und 'Vergangenheitsbewältigung' in Deutschland nach 1945 und nach 1989/90", *Geschichte in Wissenschaft und Unterricht*, 1995: 192, 202.

Wer ist Wer? Das Deutsche Who's Who (Lübeck 1998) 351.

Werner, K.F., "Die deutsche Historiographie unter Hitler", in: Faulenbach ed. 1974: 89, 93.

Wieczynski, J.L. ed., *The Modern Encyclopedia of Russian and Soviet History*, vol. 10 (Gulf Breeze 1979) 22–24.

Wielenga, F., *Schaduwen van de Duitse geschiedenis: De omgang met het Nazi en DDR-verleden in de Bondsrepubliek Duitsland* (Amsterdam 1993) 32–34, 89, 120, 130.

Wistrich, R.S., *Who's Who in Nazi Germany* (London/New York 1995) 64, 152–53.

Woolf, D.R. ed., *A Global Encyclopedia of Historical Writing* (New York/London 1998) 203, 318–19, 363, 608–9, 695, 815–16.

GHANA

Gold Coast

1945–52   Anthropologist **Eva Meyerowitz** studied the Akan traditions of origin during this period. She was often denied detailed information connected with the origin of the various royal houses because the royal houses did not want to inform their own people that they were of foreign origin and had, in most cases, superimposed themselves on an aboriginal people. Due to this secrecy, these historical circumstances had almost been forgotten. An old Nzima man refused to see her because he feared that the Evalue overlords of Axim might take revenge if he passed on information about chief Ano Asaman. In 1480 this chief presumably brought the Nzima from the northern Ivory Coast south to the Gold Coast, where they founded the Axim State on the western coast. When that state was destroyed in 1515 after a conflict with the Portuguese and the Evalue, the Portuguese allowed the Evalue to install themselves at Axim. Meyerowitz's work with oral sources was much criticized.

Ghana

1977–93   In October 1977 a lecture of **Albert Adu Boahen** (1932–), a history professor at the University of Ghana, Legon (1971–85) and a prolific writer on West African history, was broken up by what was described as the hired thugs of Colonel Ignatius Acheampong, the president. In his lecture on the Union Government (UNIGOV; a presidential plan for a political system without political parties), Boahen had linked political instability in Africa to the intervention of the military in politics. On 5 April 1978, Acheampong banned all movements that had campaigned against UNIGOV. As a leader of the Association of Recognized Professional Bodies and the People's Movement for Freedom and Justice, Boahen was arrested. He was released on 6 July, one day after Acheampong's overthrow. In 1985 Boahen retired from the university reportedly as a silent protest against the way in which the vice chancellor was appointed. On 15–17 February 1988, he delivered the J.B. Danquah Memorial Lectures for a large audience, under the title *The Ghanaian Sphinx: Reflections on the Contemporary History of Ghana 1972–1987*. Advertisements for the lectures in the local media were apparently stopped after the initial announcements had been made. In the lectures Boahen criticized military interventions in Ghana's recent history and denounced the culture of silence. After the last lecture, Lieutenant General Arnold Quainoo, the general officer commanding the armed forces, gave a short reply in which he dismissed the notion that military interventions were entirely responsible for Ghana's problems. Unconfirmed reports suggested that Boahen had been picked up briefly for questioning afterward. Press coverage of the lectures was negative. As the chairman of the Movement for Freedom and Justice (1990–) and the leader of the most important opposition party, New Patriotic Party (1992–), Boahen was arrested, interrogated, and harassed several times. In the November 1992 presidential elections, he finished second with 30 percent of the votes. In December he was charged with obstructing the court for refusing to testify in a case of bomb attacks because he did not consider the court to be independent of government influence. In January 1993 his passport was seized.

SOURCES

Amnesty International, *Report* (London) 1993: 137; 1994: 139.
Boahen, A.A., *The Ghanaian Sphinx: Reflections on the Contemporary History of Ghana 1972–1987* (Accra 1989).
Boyd, K. ed., *Encyclopedia of Historians and Historical Writing* (London/Chicago 1999) 97–98.
Index on Censorship, 2/86: 15; 3/93: 36.
Keesings historisch archief, 1978: 523, 556; 1991: 837; 1993: 109.
McFarland, D.M., *Historical Dictionary of Ghana* (Metuchen 1985) 51.
Meyerowitz, E.L.R., *Akan Traditions of Origin* (London 1952) 15, 21, 84–85, 131.
West Africa, 1988 (21 March: 501–2; 28-March: 540–41) and various 1992 and 1993 issues.
Woolf, D.R. ed., *A Global Encyclopedia of Historical Writing* (New York/London 1998) 94.
Wright, H.M., "British West Africa", in: R.W. Winks ed., *The Historiography of the British Empire-Commonwealth: Trends, Interpretations, and Resources* (Durham 1966) 268.

GREECE

Chronic political instability and professional insecurity made historians cautious about probing into controversial issues (such as the Axis occupation of Greece during World War II and the ensuing civil war between October 1946 and October 1949) or raising questions potentially offensive to the established authority. During the 1950s and during the 1967–74 junta of the colonels, the prevailing climate of conservatism, anticommunism, and anti-intellectualism reportedly forced nonconservative historians to remain silent or seek refuge abroad. Despite a certain relaxation in the early 1960s, historical work produced in Greece until 1974 was confined to fields that were not "ideologically sensitive", for instance, the Greek war of independence (1821–28) and the question of Hellenic continuity. The collapse of the military dictatorship in 1974 encouraged the return of émigré historians and favorably influenced the development of Greek historiography.

1940s   During the 1940s journalist and Marxist historian **Yiannis Kordatos** (1891–1961) was among the communists who were persecuted and imprisoned. He was a cofounder of the Socialist Workers' Party of Greece (1918; from 1920 the Communist Party of Greece, KKE). As one of its leaders (1918–24), Kordatos spent most of his time in prison. He withdrew from the KKE in 1924 because he disagreed with the KKE's decision in favor of the demand for autonomy of Macedonia and Thrace. During the German occupation of Greece (1941–44), he was involved in the leftist resistance organization National Liberation Front (EAM).

1946/48– In 1946 or 1948, during the civil war, historian **Nicolas Svoronos** fled to France for political reasons. His *Histoire de la Grèce moderne* (Paris 1953) was the first Marxist-oriented short history of Greece. He inspired a new generation of Greek economic historians in Paris (including Constantine Tsoucalas, Spiros Asdrachas, and Vasilis Panayiotopoulos).

1947–62 In the fall of 1947, during the civil war, communist journalist, economist, and historian **Serafím Máximos** (1898–1962) went into voluntary exile in Paris (1947–48), Prague (1948–50), and Vienna (1950–62). A KKE Politburo member, Máximos (like Kordatos [q.v. 1940s]) disagreed with the KKE's 1924 decision in favor of the demand for autonomy of Macedonia and Thrace, although he accepted it in the end. He became an intraparty dissident and was finally ousted from the KKE in 1935–36. Between 1922 and 1941 he was often persecuted by the police of various dictatorships, including short-term arrests, a prison term (1925–27) for treason (because of the KKE position on Macedonia and Thrace), and exile in Paris (1936–39), where he studied political science and Greek economic history (including with Ernest Labrousse, 1895–1988) at the Sorbonne. During World War II he was active in the underground press.

1967 On 21 April the government of Prime Minister and historian **Panayotis Kanellopoulos** (1902–86), inaugurated on 3 April 1967, was ousted by a military coup led by Colonel Georgios Papadopoulos. Although arrested and first kept in detention, then under close surveillance, Kanellopoulos actively opposed the colonel's regime. After democracy's return (1974), he declined the premiership in favor of Constantinos Karamanlis and became a member of parliament. In 1932 he had become the first professor of sociology at the University of Athens (1932–35). During the dictatorship of General Ioannis Metaxas (1936–41), he had opposed the abolition of parliamentary politics and had gone underground. In February 1937 he had been arrested and sent into internal exile on three isles (1937–40). There he wrote his two-volume *History of the European Mind* (1940 and 1947; 1966–). During the Italian war (1940–41), he was a soldier in Albania. During the German occupation, he formed his own resistance group and in March 1942 fled to Egypt to join the Greek government-in-exile. After the liberation he was briefly prime minister (November 1945) and served as a minister in various governments.

At the time of the coup, **Rodis Roufos**, historian, novelist, and former diplomat, resigned his post in the foreign service.

1967–69   In August 1967 the student of Indian archeology and poet **Yiannis Leloudas** (?1939–) was arrested. After the coup he had granted an interview to three foreign television stations. His apartment served as a hiding place for then-left-wing composer Theodorakis [q.v. 1978–81] and communist leader Constantine Filinis. During his pretrial detention, he was tortured and held in a solitary confinement cell for fifteen days. In November he and thirty-one other members of the communist resistance organization Patriotic Front were charged with attempting to overthrow "the existing regime and prevailing social order". He was sentenced to life imprisonment but amnestied in December. Although under police surveillance, he escaped together with his wife to France in the spring of 1969. He became a Patriotic Front representative abroad.

1967   In October archeology student **Andreas Lendakis** (?1935–) was arrested as a Patriotic Front member. While in prison he was tortured.

1972   Among the books reportedly banned were the following: *The Unfinished Revolution* by Polish-born Trotskyist historian **Isaac Deutscher** (1907–67) and *History of the Russian Revolution* by Soviet leader and historian **Leon Trotsky** (1879–1940).

1975–   In 1975 some 3,000 files amassed by the military police during the dictatorship (1967–74) were destroyed. In 1982 the two communist parties claimed that much historical documentation about their post-1940 history had been destroyed by the army and police during 1967–74.

1978–81   In October 1978 a film by **Maria Karavela** containing interviews with participants in the wartime resistance was banned as likely to "inflame political passions". In February 1979 police interrupted the showing of a film by **Dimitris Makris**, *The Wrought-Iron Gate*, in an Athens cinema and confiscated the film on the grounds that it "inflamed political passions". This occurred shortly after the owners of five Athens cinemas were prosecuted (but acquitted) for having shown the entire film, including two censored scenes, one of which portrayed the death of a civil war partisan on the run from the police. In March a film by **Nicos Koundouros**, *1922*, depicting the Turkish massacre of Greek and Armenian Christians in Izmir (Smyrna) in August–September 1922, was banned. In a statement the Ministry of Foreign Affairs said that the film content did not correspond to the present realities of Greco-Turkish relations and would unnecessarily offend or provoke Turkey. In April *Neighborhoods of the World*, a record by the composer **Mikis Theodorakis** (1925–) with words by the poet **Yannis Ritsos** (1909–90) was banned by the national radio and television network ERT apparently because of its treatment of the December 1944 conflict in Athens and the subsequent civil war. In [1981] the prime minister's office stopped author **Olympia Papadouka** from adding an explanatory introduction to the (allowed) recording of a collection of "Prison Songs" because it "referred to an unhappy period in our country's history" (probably 1967–74) and could lead to political unrest. In March 1981 the prime minister's office banned *The Trial of the Junta*, a documentary film directed by **Theodosis Theodosopoulos**, consisting mainly of material shot during the various trials of the junta leaders during 1974–75.

1984   In February the Ministry of Education ordered the immediate dismissal of **Dion Nittis**, a Greek-American or Greek-Cypriot teacher in an Anglo-American school in Athens following complaints that he was engaged in pro-Turkish propaganda. He had asked his class to write an essay on the 1974 Turkish invasion of northern Cyprus from the Turkish viewpoint and to compare it with the Greek view. He had included a few official Turkish government publications in the recommended reading. This led the ministry to invoke a 1931 law which prohibited foreign schools in Greece from holding any kind of educational materials deemed to be unfavorable to the Greek nation.

1989   On 29 August, the fortieth anniversary of the civil war's official end was celebrated by burning all the police files from the postwar period. It was denounced as an act of historical vandalism, notably by historian Philippos Iliou.

1992   A number of Greeks reportedly were prosecuted for criticizing the government's nonrecognition of FYROM (Former Yugoslav Republic of Macedonia) as long as it claimed the name "Macedonia".

In December **Michalis Papadaki** (?1975–) was arrested for distributing leaflets saying Alexander the Great was a war criminal and sentenced to one year's imprisonment for "disturbing public peace".

1995   In May and June, two trials of the nationalist weekly *Stohos* for having incited violence against the antinationalist and controversial historian **George Nakratzas** were postponed until November. In that month the weekly was acquitted. Nakratzas worked on the ethnic relationship between contemporary Greeks, Bulgarians, and Turks.

1998   A leader of the ethnic Macedonian Rainbow party was awaiting trial on charges of incitement for having brought calendars from Macedonia bearing the names of Greek towns in Macedonian and praising the KKE's interwar pro-Macedonian policy. Many ethnic Macedonians who fled Greece as a result of the 1946–49 civil war were not allowed to enter Greece in 1998 (and possibly much earlier), even for brief visits, or to attend events related to the fiftieth anniversary of their exodus in July.

Also see United Kingdom (1995–96: Karakasidou).

SOURCES

Becket, J., *Barbarism in Greece: A Young American Lawyer's Inquiry into the Use of Torture in Contemporary Greece, with Case Histories and Documents* (New York 1970) 59–65, 94–96.

Bernath, M., & F. von Schroeder eds., *Biographisches Lexicon zur Geschichte Südeuropas*, vol. 2 (Munich 1976) 334–36, 479–80.

Boia, L., ed., *Great Historians of the Modern Age: An International Dictionary* (Westport 1991) 329–31.

Bronkhorst, D., *Truth and Reconciliation: Obstacles and Opportunities for Human Rights* (Amsterdam 1995) 49.

Clogg, R., "The Greeks and Their Past", in: D. Deletant & H. Hanak eds., *Historians As Nation-Builders: Central and South-East Europe* (London 1988) 29.

European Court of Human Rights, *Case of Sidiropoulos and Others versus Greece: Judgment.* (WWW-text; Strasbourg, 10 July 1998).

Fleischer, H., "The Last Round of the Civil War: Developments and Stagnation in Historiography Concerning Axis-Occupied Greece, 1941–44", in: Macrakis & Diamandouros eds. 1982: 153, 155–56.

González Quintana, A., "Les Archives des services de sécurité des anciens régimes répressifs: Rapport préparé pour l'UNESCO à la demande du Conseil international des archives", *Janus*, 1999, no.1: 18, 29.

Greek Helsinki Monitor & Minority Rights Group—Greece, *1995 Activity Report* (WWW-text 1995) (Nakratzas).

Hokwerda, H., personal communication, February & September 2000.

Human Rights Watch, *World Report 1999* (Washington 1998) 266.

Index on Censorship, 1/72: 148; 2/72: 135–36; 2/79: 66; 3/79: 67; 4/79: 65; 5/79: 66; 4/81: 45; 6/81: 107; 3/84: 46; 2/86: 11; 3/93: 36; 2/95: 175; 3/95: 174; 5/95: 178; 6/95: 179.

Keesings historisch archief, 1986: 847.

Kitroeff, A., "Continuity and Change in Contemporary Greek Historiography", *European History Quarterly*, 1989: 270–72, 291.

Kitromilides, P.M., "Historiographical Interpretations of Modern Greek Reality: An Exploratory Essay", in: Macrakis & Diamandouros eds. 1982: 8–9.

Le Monde, 9 April 1993: 4 (Papadaki).

Macrakis, A.L., & P.N. Diamandouros eds., *New Trends in Modern Greek Historiography* (Hanover 1982).

McGrew, W., "Introduction", in: Macrakis & Diamandouros eds. 1982: xii-xiii.

Pridham, G., & S. Verney, "The Coalitions of 1989–90 in Greece: Inter-Party Relations and Democratic Consolidation", *West European Politics*, October 1991: 59, 69.

Veremis, T.M., & M. Dragoumis, *Historical Dictionary of Greece* (Metuchen 1995) 104–5.

Woolf, D.R. ed., *A Global Encyclopedia of Historical Writing* (New York/London 1998) 380, 510–11.

GRENADA

1983–85   Caribbean historians and journalists protested the removal of eight tons of documents relating to the government of Prime Minister Maurice Bishop (1979–83) following the 1983 U.S. invasion of Grenada and their subsequent partial publication in the United States. The American authorities gradually returned most of the documents between 1983 and 1985.

SOURCES

Index on Censorship, 5/85: 65.

GUATEMALA

The central topic, at least during the later years, was the demand to know the truth about the human-rights violations during the 1960–96 civil war, a conflict that, although widely varying in intensity over the years, dominated the collective memories.

[?]   Several Guatemalan historians were living in exile for many years: **Julio Castellanos Cambranes** in Spain (reportedly a self-imposed exile); **Severo Martínez Peláez** (died 1998) in Mexico, where he became a professor at the Universidad Autónoma de Puebla; and **Arturo Taracena Arriola**, in France in 1967–70, in Mexico in 1971–77, and in Costa Rica from 1982.

1977   In June **Abilio Berganza Bocalletti**, history student at the University of San Carlos (USAC), Guatemala City, was shot dead. The police claimed that he was a member of the Rebel Armed Forces. His fellow students denounced the act as a political assassination. Soon after the killing, the USAC School of History was raided and the records of the school's council of directors, of which Berganza was a student member, were confiscated.

1980s   In the early 1980s, American historian of colonial Guatemala **Christopher Lutz** was threatened and forced out of Guatemala. In 1996 he was the editor of *Mesoamérica* and director of the Centro de Investigaciones Regionales de Mesoamérica, Antigua.

1980 In June USAC history student **Edgar Celada Quezada** was arrested by the police during a traffic surveillance in Guatemala City. He "disappeared".

1980/83 In 1980 or 1983, **Luis Colindres**, a history student working on the economics faculty, "disappeared".

1981 On 3 October **Ligia Martínez Urrutia**, USAC history student and teacher at the Instituto Belga, was assassinated. In 1971 she had participated in the Catholic Church's Operación Uspantán in a poor rural area of Quiché.

1982 In September **Rolando Medina Cuellar**, USAC history professor and literary critic, was abducted from the School of History parking lot.

1984 In May USAC history professor and archeologist **Carlos Ericastilla García** was captured and left for dead on the USAC campus. He died later as a result of the beating and torture to which he had been subjected.

1992 In February **Manuel Estuardo Peña**, USAC history professor and director of the Guatemalan Teachers' Association, was shot dead by two unidentified men outside his Guatemala City flat. His assistant Pedro Us Soc, USAC lecturer and leader of teachers' and indigenous organizations, and the latter's wife, Floridalma Ixtahualan, secretary at the Hermandad Presbiterios Mayas, subsequently received death threaths. The circumstances of the murder suggested security force involvement. Peña had been working with a local community project involving people displaced by the armed conflict. He was known for his left-wing views and had received anonymous death threats before. The judicial investigation into his death had produced no suspects by December.

1995– In April 1995 the Catholic bishops launched the project Recuperación de la Memoria Histórica (REMHI; Recuperation of Historical Memory). The project came about in response to popular frustration with the official Comisión de Esclarecimiento Histórico (CEH; Commission to Clarify Past Human Rights Violations and Acts of Violence That Have Caused the Guatemalan Population to Suffer), originally a June 1994 idea for a commission scheduled to spend only six months investigating thirty-six years of violence. On 26 April 1998, two days after the publication of the voluminous interdiocesan report *Guatemala: Nunca más; Informe del proyecto interdiocesano REMHI* (Guatemala: Never More), auxiliary archbishop and REMHI founder-director **Juan Gerardi Conedera** (?1923–98) was murdered. The four-volume report, based on three years' research by nearly 600 investigators, was a study of more than 55,000 testimonies about human-rights violations committed during the 1960–96 civil war and identified the army as responsible for approximately 80 percent of these violations. It was widely believed that military personnel engineered Gerardi's death, although the army denied involvement in the murder. The government's poor handling of the investigation was criticized. The case remained unresolved. Several witnesses, two judges, and the prosecutor were intimidated. Other REMHI supporters and collaborators, including researcher **Pietro Notta**, forensic anthropologist **Carlos Reyes López**, and Archbishop **Próspero Penados del Barrio** received death threats. As the bishop of Quiché in the 1980s, Gerardi had withdrawn from the region after he had escaped an attempted ambush. He was then forbidden reentry into Guatemala for several years. The REMHI findings were submitted to the CEH, which in August 1997 had started its work. The authorities withheld vital information requested by the CEH and restricted access to certain military installations. Although it also withheld information, the United States released thousands of pages of declassified documents in 1997–99 that aided the CEH in understanding the Guatemalan abuses and the American role in them. CEH submitted its 3,400-page report *Guatemala: Memories of Silence* in February 1999. Based on evidence from 9,000 witnesses and survivors on the cases of 42,000 victims, it concluded that the Guatemalan state had been responsible for acts of genocide against indigenous Mayan communities as well as massive human-rights violations, that 83 percent of fully identified victims were Mayans, and that state forces and related paramilitary groups were responsible for 93 percent of the violations documented by the CEH. It also referred to the direct and indirect role of the U.S. Central Intelligence Agency in supporting illegal operations since the 1960s. In a reaction, former President (1986–91) Vinicio Cerezo said that the American government knew about the extrajudicial executions carried out by army death squads and that they prevented him from revealing the facts while he was in office. During a March 1999 visit to Guatemala, President Bill Clinton expressed regret for the role of his country in Guatemala's conflict. In 2000 the Guatemalan President Alfonso Portillo called the Gerardi murder and its bungled investigation a "national embarrassment", publicly committing himself to bringing those responsible to justice. In June 2001, three army officers and a priest were sentenced to between twenty and thirty years' imprisonment in the Gerardi case.

1996   In early September former military commissioners threatened to commit mass murder on 15 September, the day that a group of widows planned to commemorate the massacres of their husbands by army and civil patrols in the Rabinal area in the early 1980s.

In [October] several students from the School of Anthropology and History Association were threatened and intimidated by unknown persons.

1997–   Forensic workers and observers at various clandestine cemetery sites around Guatemala, including Reyes López [q.v. 1995–] and **Marlon García**, were threatened and intimidated.

1997–98 In February 1997 the Inter-American Commission on Human Rights admonished the government to actively investigate the 1982 Plan de Sánchez massacre of 268 people. In response, forensic reports and ballistic evidence disappeared from the public prosecutor's office. The entire file of another massacre of thirty-five men at Chichupac, Rabinal, also disappeared in 1998.

1999   In May several American groups released a copy of a military log-book that documented the activities of a Guatemalan military unit responsible for kidnapping, torturing, and executing suspected leftists between 1983 and 1985. The log was smuggled out of military files by a military official. Its authenticity was challenged. The military was reportedly engaged in the destruction of all such incriminating documents early in 1999.

Also see United States (1997: documents).

SOURCES

American Association for the Advancement of Science, *Directory of Persecuted Scientists, Engineers, and Health Professionals* (Washington 1992) 26.
———, Human Rights Network, *Case GU9615.LOP* (10 July, 11 October 1996).
Amnesty International, *Is Guatemala Falling Back to Its Tragic Past?* (London 1998).
———, *Report* (London) 1993: 141; 1997: 165; 1998: 179; 181; 1999: 178–80; 2000: 14, 114–15; 2001: 113–14.
———, *Urgent Actions 173/96* (8 July 1996), *139/98* (1 May, 15 May, 1 December 1998, 7 January 1999), *142/98* (1 May 1998).
———, *Worldwide Appeal* (NWS 22/02/99; February 1999).
BBC News Online (WWW-text; London) 8 June 2001.
Benjamin, T., personal communication, November 1996.
Guatemala: Memoria del silencio—vol. 5: Conclusiones y recomendaciones—Informe de la Comisión para el esclarecimiento histórico (Guatemala 1999) 21, 25, 52, 56–57, 102–3.
Guatemala: Nunca Más (REMHI report summary; June 1998).
Human Rights Watch, Letter, Committee for International Academic Freedom to President Serrano, (30 September 1992).
———, *World Report* (Washington) 1993: 114; 1997: 102; 1998: 118, 120; 1999: xxviii, 91, 95, 123–28; 2000: 97, 130–33; 2001: 126–27.

Index on Censorship, 1/83: 44; 5/92: 36; 4/95: 176; 1/97: 113; 4/98: 113; 1/99: 29; 2/
    99: 108; 4/99: 134–35; 6/99: 240; 3/00: 95.
Keesings historisch archief, 1998: 345; 1999: 605–8.
Kobrak, P., *Organizing and Repression in the University of San Carlos, Guatemala,
    1944 to 1996* (Washington 1999) 124, 131, 138, 141, 145, 154, 156.
Organisation Mondiale Contre la Torture, *Case GTM 251196* (Geneva 1996).
Organization of American States, Inter-American Commission on Human Rights, *Fourth
    Report on the Situation of Human Rights in Guatemala* (Washington 1993) 92.
Taracena, A., personal communication, August 1994.
Tuyuc R., "We Can't Forgive Until We Have Justice", *UNESCO Courier*, December
    1999: 21.
Ulltveit-Moe, T., personal communication, March 2000.
Webre, S., personal communication, August 1995.

GUINEA

1992   Among the lecturers of Conakry University forcibly transferred in April
        by the Head of the Department of Higher Education and Scientific Re-
        search was the historian **Hamadi Seck**. The decision was a result of the
        violent clashes between students and police in January–February.

SOURCES

Sow, C., & I. Fox, "Guinea: Violations of the Rights of Students and Teachers", in:
    Codesria, *The State of Academic Freedom in Africa 1995* (Dakar 1996) 147–48.

GUINEA-BISSAU

1998   During the armed rebellion in the summer, the Instituto Nacional de
        Estudos e Pesquisa (INEP; National Institute of Studies and Research)
        was heavily damaged. The National Archives and Audiovisual Archives
        at INEP were scattered, shredded, and exposed to rain and dirt. Hundreds
        of audiocassettes which recorded the history of the national liberation
        struggle and of the various regions had disappeared. This loss of sources
        would seriously hamper the writing of a first general history of Guinea-
        Bissau. After the 25 August ceasefire, INEP continued to be a military
        camp. INEP staff was forbidden to rehabilitate or save INEP from fur-
        ther destruction.

SOURCES

Amnesty International, *Report 1999* (London 1999) 182–83.
Cahen, M., "The NISR Endangered by War" (WWW-text 1998).
Index on Censorship, 2/99: 81–82.

GUYANA

1974–96   After his expulsion from Jamaica, historian **Walter Rodney** (1942–
80) returned to University College of Dar es Salaam, Tanzania,
where he had already taught (July 1966–January 1968), and worked
there until 1974. His most famous book, *How Europe Underdevel-
oped Africa*, was published in 1972. In 1974 he returned to Guyana
because he was offered a history professorship by the senate of the
University of Guyana, Georgetown. However, the appointment was
withdrawn by the board of governors as a result of political intervention by the government of President Forbes Burnham. At the
same time, he and his wife were blocked from all employment reportedly because of Rodney's reputation as an activist. In 1975 he
became a founder and leader of the left-wing opposition party Working People's Alliance (WPA), with a revolutionary and multiracial
program. In July 1979 several WPA leaders, including Rodney, were
arrested by the security forces and charged with arson and possession
of arms. The day before, an antigovernment demonstration had taken
place and during the night an explosion and fire had destroyed several government buildings and the ruling party's headquarters. The
trial was adjourned three times for lack of evidence and Rodney was
released on bail. In April 1980 the authorities tried to prevent his
presence at the Zimbabwe independence celebrations. On 13 June
1980, Rodney was killed by a bomb concealed in a walkie-talkie in
his brother's car in Georgetown. His brother Donald survived but
was implicated in his death by the government. It was generally
believed that the government itself was involved in the assault. In
January 1981 the government terminated the state press agency's
contract with a Barbados-based firm because its coverage of Rodney's death was deemed unsatisfactory. In the same year, Rodney's
book, *A History of the Guyanese Working People 1881–1905*, published posthumously (Baltimore 1981), was banned. Four academics
faced disciplinary charges because they had referred to Rodney's
death in their reports for the 1979–80 academic year. In October
1987 the government ordered an inquest into his death. In February
1988 the final verdict of the inquest was "death by accident or mis-
adventure". In June 1996 a former soldier in the Guyana Defense
Force living in French Guiana was charged with the murder of Rodney.

Also see Jamaica (1968: Rodney).

SOURCES

Alpers, E.A., & P.-M. Fontaine eds., *Walter Rodney: Revolutionary and Scholar* (Los
Angeles 1982) 186–87.

Amnesty International, *Report* (London) 1980: 145; 1981: 156; 1982: 145; 1983: 144–45; 1984: 164; 1988: 117; 1989: 128; 1997: 169.

Button, J., *The Radicalism Handbook* (London 1995) 283–84.

Boyd, K. ed., *Encyclopedia of Historians and Historical Writing* (London/Chicago 1999) 1001–2.

Gorman, R.A. ed., *Biographical Dictionary of Marxism* (Westport 1986) 292–93.

Index on Censorship, 6/79: 66; 5/80: 32; 3/81: 75; 4/81: 46; 6/81: 26–30; 6/85: 52–54; 5/88: 127.

———, *Guyana: Suspicious Death of Leading Opposition Intellectual* (briefing paper, June 1980).

Journal of Peasant Studies, 1983, no. 4: 250–52 (Rodney).

Race and Class, Autumn 1976: 109–28 (Rodney).

Slater, H., "Dar es Salaam and the Postnationalist Historiography of Africa", in: B. Jewsiewicki & D. Newbury eds., *African Historiographies: What History for Which Africa?* (London 1986) 249–60.

Sutton, P., "The Historian As Politician: Eric Williams and Walter Rodney", in: A. Henessy ed., *Intellectuals in the Twentieth-Century Caribbean*, vol. 1 (London 1992) 98–114.

Wallerstein, I., "Walter Rodney: The Historian As Spokesman for Historical Forces", *American Ethnologist*, 1986: 330–37.

H

HAITI

1947–   A law required that all history teachers in primary and secondary schools be Haitian citizens. The law still existed in the 1990s.

1957–71 Under the government of President François Duvalier (1957–71), some left-wing history teachers were reportedly killed; others were purged or exiled. Those who stayed in Haiti rarely published. Historian **Hénock Trouillot** had privileged access to several archives.

1960–   In 1960 **Leslie Manigat** (1930–), a historian, political scientist, and foreign ministry official, was accused of rebellion against Duvalier. He was deemed responsible for a wave of student unrest and sentenced to two months' imprisonment. In 1963 he broke with Duvalier and spent the next twenty-three years in exile, first in the Argentinian embassy, then in Washington, New York, Paris (where he completed his doctoral thesis on history), Trinidad and Tobago, and finally Caracas. There he was a professor of political science, founded the political party Rassemblement des Démocrates Nationaux Progressistes d'Haïti and established an anti-Duvalierist "government-in-exile" between 1978 and 1985. After Duvalier's 1986 overthrow, he came back to Haiti. In November 1987 his house was fired on. On 17 January 1988, he became the first civilian president in more than thirty years, with 50 percent of the votes in controversial elections. Other important candidates had withdrawn after earlier elections had been called off due to violence. On 20 June Manigat was removed by General Henri Namphy after a conflict with the army leadership. He then went into exile again in the Dominican Republic and the United States. In his numerous writings about Haitian, Caribbean, and Latin American history, he adopted a noiriste position, emphasizing Haiti's African heritage.

1982–   In August 1982 historian and sociologist **Laënnec Hurbon** was detained overnight at San Juan airport, Puerto Rico, but allowed entry by the U.S. Immigration Service the next day, possibly because the French Centre National d'Investigation which had mandated him to carry out a study of religion there had criticized the treatment of Haitian refugees, many of them without documentation and temporarily detained in Puerto Rico. In 1994 Hurbon, then a professor at the University of Quisqueya, reportedly worked with a civilian mission of the United Nations and the Organization of American States on the planning of civic education programs. Possibly for this reason, his house was searched several times. He stayed abroad for reasons of safety. In 1999 he was a director of research at the Centre National de la Recherche Scientifique (CNRS; National Scientific Research Agency) in Paris, specialized in the sociology of religion in the Caribbean.

1987–   In April professor **Roger Gaillard**, dean at the State University of Haiti and historian of the United States occupation period (1915–34), was dismissed while developing a university reform project in cooperation with the academic community. In August 1993 he was reportedly president of a university council again.

Also see United States (1994: documents).

SOURCES

Amnesty International, *Report 1989* (London 1989) 129.
Bellegarde-Smith, P., *Haiti: The Breached Citadel* (London 1990) 158–60, 174.
Index on Censorship, 6/82: 47.
International Who's Who 1988–89 (London 1988) 980.
Keesings historisch archief, 1988: 81–83, 609–13.
Keesing's Record of World Events, 1988: 35695A.
Trouillot, M.-R., "Historiography of Haiti", in: B.W. Higman ed., *General History of the Caribbean*, vol. 6 (London/Oxford 1999) 468 (also 160, 693), 471–73.
World University Service, *Academic Freedom 3* (London 1995) 209, 211–12.

HONDURAS

1981–88 In September 1981 student leader **Angel Velásquez Rodríguez** was abducted by security force undercover agents in Tegucigalpa. He subsequently "disappeared". The Inter-American Court of Human Rights investigated the case and in 1988 concluded that Honduras was responsible for the involuntary "disappearance" and had a legal duty to carry out a serious investigation of similar violations committed within its jurisdiction. For the first time, a state was held accountable not only for a "disappearance" but also for not investigating it. This principle of obligatory investigation of past abuses even after a change of regime was considered the first recognition of the right to know the truth about past abuses.

1995   In June the national human-rights commissioner Leo Valladares said that he would ask the United States embassy to declassify documents relating to the "disappearance"of 184 Honduran civil leaders during the 1980s. The Honduran Armed Forces burned all their files on the "disappearances". In September 1997 the United States declassified the documents.

1997   On 12 October, Día de las Razas (Day of the Races), demonstrators destroyed a statue of Christopher Columbus in Tegucigalpa. On 29 October police prevented four hundred Indians from erecting a statue of their historical leader, Lempira, in its place.

Also see United States (1998: documents).

SOURCES

Amnesty International, *"Disappearances" and Political Killings: Human Rights Crisis of the 1990s: A Manual for Action* (Amsterdam 1994) 108, 138, 164–66.
————, *Report 1994* (London 1994) 153.
Index on Censorship, 4/95: 177.
Keesings historisch archief, 1998: 111.

HONG KONG

1945–   *See entry on China* (1949–: Jian Youwen, Qian Mu, Tao Xisheng; 1958–69: Chen Yinke; 1989: Jin Guantao; 1989–: Wang Dan, Su Xiaokang; 1991–93: Tian Zhuangzhuang; 1995: BBC documentary; 1996: anti-China activities; 1998: Chen Shizheng).

pre-1997   *See entry on the United Kingdom* (1995–97: textbooks; 1996: protestors).

HUNGARY

In the early communist period (1948–53), and to some extent also later, numerous professional historians were "eliminated in an administrative way" from historical journals and research posts at the universities, the Hungarian Academy of Sciences, and elsewhere. In 1950–51 the Academy of Sciences, its History Institute, and the National Archives were reorganized. The Hungarian Heraldic and Genealogical Association (founded in 1883) was banned from 1949 until

1983 because the auxiliary sciences of history were considered to be "feudalistic disciplines". Some historians had to make statements of self-criticism. The idealist schools of history such as the Geistesgeschichte School and the Ethnohistory School came to an end. According to one source, research on the Middle Ages and early modern history was consciously reduced in 1949–57 but another source indicated that the further back the period that was being studied lay in the past, the more possibility there was of pronouncing an independent judgment on it. Until 1956–57 it was reportedly forbidden to mention the name of Béla Kun, leader of the 1919 Hungarian Soviet Republic and victim of the Stalinist terror in the 1930s. He was omitted from the history of the Hungarian workers' movement. Similar was the fate of nineteenth-century reformer Count István Széchenyi, leader of the 1848 uprising, Lajos Kossuth, and Count Mihály Károlyi, prime minister (October 1918–January 1919) and first president of the Hungarian Republic (January–March 1919). Even after the 1956 Revolution, many historians resorted to self-censorship, several were imprisoned or silenced otherwise, others emigrated or went into exile to continue historical work in their host countries. Among the "white spots" of communist historiography were the following: historical coats of arms; the World War II victims; the history of the 1956 Revolution (officially labeled a "counterrevolution"); Warsaw Pact membership and the stationing of Soviet troops in Hungary; Soviet–Hungarian relations, and Soviet foreign policy and Comecon (Council for Mutual Economic Assistance). As late as the 1970s, typewriters and copying machines in factories and offices were locked away before 23 October in order to forestall the production of leaflets on the anniversary of the 1956 Revolution. In the 1980s parables in a historic setting, used as veiled criticism, were tolerated. Archival access remained very difficult. Despite several institutional changes, no purges of communist historians were reported after 1989.

pre-1945   Among the historians who emigrated before 1945 (and living in exile after 1944) were **Oszkár Jászi** (1875–1957) and **György Pálóczi-Horváth** (1908–).

1944–45   Many archives containing Hungarian source materials in Vienna and Transylvania were destroyed during the war campaign without ever having been examined.

From 19 March 1944 to 4 April 1945 (the German occupation of Hungary), historian **Gyula Szekfű** (1883–1955), leader of the Geistesgeschichte (intellectual history) School, sought asylum with ecclesiastic friends and spent a year in hiding. He had burned many of his personal papers. Upon his return, he found his library totally ruined. During World War II, he had been the editor of the anti-Nazi daily *Magyar nemzet*. Ambassador to Moscow in 1945–48, he resigned this post in 1948 due to ill health and returned to his chair at Budapest University but lived in seclusion. In 1953 he became a member of Parliament (1953–55) and in 1954 member of the Presidium of the People's Republic of Hungary. His earliest works, *Rákóczi in Exile* (1913) and *Der Staat Ungarn* (1917; The Hungarian State), written while working at the Haus-, Hof- und Staatsarchiv in Vienna (1913–16), had been attacked for their pro-Habsburg point of view. The 1913 work had been publicly burned by nationalists.

1945 Historian **Elemér Mályusz** (1898–1989), founder of the Hungarian Ethnohistory School and professor of medieval history at Budapest University (1932–45), was obliged to retire at the age of forty-six owing to his conservative political views. Although forced to function at the periphery of the profession, he became a member of the Hungarian Academy of Sciences History Institute (1954–68).

After his return from a German concentration camp, where he had been interned after the German occupation of Hungary, historian and liberal statesman **Gusztáv Gratz** (1875–1946), a former member of Parliament and twice a minister for brief terms (1917, 1921), looked in vain for a publisher for his manuscript on the interwar history of Hungary. In 1921 he had been detained briefly for his support for the return to Hungary of King Charles IV.

1945– The return of Northern Transylvania to Romania led to the forced retirement of **Vencel Bíró** (1885–1962), until then professor of East European history at the University of Kolozsvar (Cluj). In 1948 Catholic priest **György Balanyi** (1886–1963) was dismissed from the same university, where he had been professor of European history (1943–48).

1945–48 Sometime between 1945 and 1948, constitutional and cultural historian **Ferenc Somogyi** (1906–) left Hungary because the Marxist approach to history became dominant.

1946 Social historian and philosopher of history **István Dékány** (1886–1965) was dismissed from his chair of social philosophy (1942–46) at Budapest University.

1947– **András Alföldi** (1895–1981), historian of Roman antiquity at the University of Budapest (1930–47), fled to Switzerland, leaving much of his notes and documents behind. He became a professor at the Universities of Bern (1948–52) and Basel (1952–55) and then went to the School of Historical Studies at the Institute of Advanced Studies, Princeton, N.J., United States (1955–65).

1948– **François (= Ferenc) Fejtő** (1909–), an expert on the history of Eastern Europe, went to France.

József Deér (1905–74), a professor of Hungarian history at the Universities of Szeged (1932–40) and Budapest (1940–44, 1945–48) who believed in the biologically inheritable charisma of Hungarian kings, left Hungary. He went to Switzerland, where he became a history professor at Bern University (1950–71).

In December **Ladislas Szabó**, a writer who had been in hiding from the Nazis (1944–45) and who was a professor of art history at the Academy of Arts in Budapest (1945–48), went into exile in Italy (1949–51) and the United Kingdom, where he became a BBC collaborator.

In December historian and archivist **Gyula Miskolczy** (1892–1962) was dismissed as history professor at Budapest University and as director at the Hungarian Institute in Vienna (1935–48). He became an honorary professor at Vienna University.

After 1948 historians **Domokos [= Dominic] Kosáry** (1913–), **Kálmán Benda** (1913–), and **László Makkai** (1911–89), who attempted to continue the tradition of conservative-liberal historiography after 1945, were periodically excluded from the profession. In 1949 Kosáry, history professor at Eötvös College (1938–49) and Budapest University (1946–49), specialist in eighteenth- and nineteenth-century social and cultural history and historical bibliography, was dismissed as director of the Academy of Sciences History Institute and sent to work as a librarian at the Agricultural University in Gödöllő (1954–57). He participated in the 1956 Revolution. In 1958 he was arrested and in June sentenced to four or five years' imprisonment because he had compiled a documentation of the 1956 events and deposited it at the university library. He was released in 1960 and entirely rehabilitated later. The president and secretary-general of the International Committee of Historical Sciences, Italian historian Federico Chabod (1901–60), and French historian Michel François (1906–), had intervened on his behalf. Kosáry held the post of archivist at the Archives of Pest County (1960–68) and worked at the Hungarian Academy of Sciences History Institute again (1968–89). In 1990 he distanced himself from Marxism and was elected president of the Hungarian Academy of Sciences (1990–96).

Benda was the editor of the official historical journal *Századok* (Century). Upon his dismissal as its editor, publication of its 1948 volume was prevented, but he saved the galleys and the 1948 volume was finally printed in 1989. Benda also had difficulties with a four-volume chronology. He was an archivist (1951–56), deputy director of the History Institute after 1957, and vice president of the Hungarian Association of History.

1949–56   In 1949 historian **Zoltán Horváth** was imprisoned. He was reha-
           bilitated just before the 1956 Revolution. He became a history pro-
           fessor in Budapest.

1949   Literary historian **George Cushing** (1923–96), then a student at Eöt-
           vös College in Budapest, was expelled from Hungary as a suspected
           British agent. The notes for his thesis about nineteenth-century Hun-
           garian literature were confiscated. He became a teacher of Hungarian
           at the School of Slavonic and East European Studies, London.

1950–61   **Erik Fügedi** (1916–93), medievalist, archivist in charge of the res-
           cue and conservation of private collections, libraries, and archives
           (1945–49), head of the Archival Research Center (1950), was
           persecuted for political reasons and became a clerk in a cannery for
           ten years. A research fellow at the Historical Association (1961–),
           he joined and headed the historical demography research group
           (1965–80) and became professor at Eötvös Loránd University
           (1980–), specializing in the sociological and psychological approach
           of the history of elites.

1953   **Bálint Hóman** (1885–1953), professor of Hungarian medieval his-
           tory, president of the Hungarian Historical Society (1933–45) and
           minister of culture in various governments that supported the
           German political orientation (1932–38, 1939–42), died in prison.
           When the Red Army approached Hungary (December 1944–April
           1945), he had fled to Austria, but from there he was extradited by
           the United States Army to Hungary, where he was sentenced to life
           imprisonment. With Szekfű [q.v. 1944–45] he wrote an eight-
           volume *Hungarian History* (1928–33). Another historian, **Ödön
           Málnási** (1898–1970), was sentenced to forced labor for his pro-
           Nazi sympathies (date unknown).

1956   In late October **Erzsébet Andics** (1902–86), the communist presi-
           dent of the Historical Society from 1949 who had denounced the
           old historiography as being a servant of the ruling classes, went
           temporarily into exile in the USSR.

1956–   On 4 November 1956, when Soviet troops encircled the parliament
           building, Hungarian minister of state, judge, and historian **István
           Bibó** (1911–79) was the only one to remain at his post at the Par-
           liament, writing a protest against the forcible removal of the legal
           government and an appeal for passive resistance. He further elabo-
           rated his viewpoint in *Political Testament*, written in hiding six
           weeks later, smuggled out, and published in the West a few months
           after his May 1957 arrest. In a note appended to the text, he had
           explicitly requested publication regardless of the personal conse-

quences. He was imprisoned without trial until August 1958. He was then charged with "counterrevolutionary conspiracy" and sentenced to life imprisonment in a secret court. In 1963 he was given amnesty. He became a librarian at the Central Statistical Office in Budapest (1963–71). During World War II, after having forged documents for the persecuted, Bibó had briefly been arrested (1944). Thereafter he had gone underground. Until 1948 he had been a leading member of the National Peasant Party (in 1956 renamed the Petőfi Party) and undersecretary in the Ministry of Interior (1945–49). After the communist takeover in 1948, he had returned to his chair at Szeged University (1946–50), and then had become a clerk working at the National Széchenyi Library in Budapest (1950–56). On 2 November 1956, he had joined the government.

In November, at the time of the Soviet invasion, Marxist philosopher and historian **István Mészáros** went into exile in Italy (1956–59), the United Kingdom (1959–73), and Canada (1973–) because he was against the oppression and advocated civil liberties. In February 1972 he was offered a five-year contract by the Division of Social Science at York University, Toronto, but in July he was refused landed immigrant status by the Canadian government because it would be "contrary to Canadian public interest". He was considered a "security risk" possibly because of rumors that he was a Russian secret service agent. In September an appeal lodged by the university was rejected and Mészáros, who visited Canada, was threatened with deportation. After the Canadian elections, his reapplication was accepted by the new minister of Manpower and Immigration and he left for Canada with his family in January 1973. In 1999 he was a professor emeritus of philosophy at the School of European Studies of the University of Sussex, United Kingdom.

1956–89   In November historian **Béla Király** (1912–), military commander of the 1956 Revolution, went into exile in Austria and the United States, where he became a professor of military history at Brooklyn College and New York University. From 1977 he had edited the *Studies on Society in Change* series on problems of Eastern European and Hungarian history. In 1989 he returned to Hungary and was elected member of the first postcommunist parliament (1990–94). In 1950 Király had been appointed general and served as the director of the Miklós Zrínyi Military Academy, but in 1951 he had been imprisoned because of "anti-Soviet propaganda" and sentenced to death, then to life imprisonment (1951–56). Once released in October 1956, he played a leading role in the 1956 Revolution, but after the invasion he went into hiding and escaped.

1956   On 6–8 November Soviet artillery bombardment of the National Archives building and the subsequent fire destroyed the Ministry of Justice archives (covering 1867–1944). In 1944 part of the archives had already been destroyed during the siege of Budapest.

1956–   After 1956 **Péter Gosztonyi** (1931–), a former army officer who participated in the Revolution, went into exile in Switzerland, where he studied military history (1957–61) at Zürich University, became director of the East European Library in Bern (1963), and published about Hungarian history.

1957–   Journalist and historian **Miklós Molnár** (1918–), editor of *Irodalmi ujság* (Literary Gazette) until his dismissal (1955), and active member of the opposition led by 1956 revolutionary leader Imre Nagy, emigrated and became a university professor in Geneva. He was the author of several books on the 1956 Revolution.

In January **László Révész** (1916–), professor of the history of law and president of the October 1956 Revolutionary Committee at Budapest University, went into exile in Switzerland, where he became a professor of Eastern European Studies at Bern University and lecturer at the Universities of Zürich and Fribourg.

1959   **Tibor Méray** (1924–)—Imre Nagy's biographer—Molnár [q.v. 1957–], and others prepared the documentation *The Truth about the Nagy Affair*, published by the Petőfi Circle in Exile in Brussels in 1959. In June 1988 Méray, then director of the *Gazette littéraire hongroise* in Paris, took the initiative to erect a symbolic monument for Nagy at the Pére-Lachaise cemetery. In June 1989 his book *Life and Death of Imre Nagy* (?1979) was published in Hungary.

Sándor Fekete (1927–), literary historian and journalist of *Szabad Nép*, the central organ of the Hungarian Socialist Workers' Party (HSWP; the communist party) (1952–56), was sentenced to nine years' imprisonment because of his anti-Kádárist activities and because of his pamphlet written under the pseudonym Hungaricus. The pamphlet, dealing with the history of the Hungarian communist movement from its beginnings to 1956, began to circulate illegally in December 1956 (first part) and February 1957 (second part). It was soon smuggled out of Hungary and circulated abroad. It was called the first Hungarian critical analysis of the 1956 Revolution. Fekete was amnestied in 1963. Together with him, the last resistance group from the former inner-party opposition, including historian **György Litván** (1929–), was tried. Litván was sentenced to six years' imprisonment. After his release he became a librarian, a fellow at the Hungarian Academy of Sciences History Institute, director of the Institute for the History of the 1956 Hungarian Revolution (1990–), and professor of sociology at ECTE University (1993–). He wrote many books on Jászi [q.v. pre-1945].

1968   Philosopher **Zsádor Tordai** (1924–), who had been a research assistant (1951–57) at the History Institute of Cluj University, Romania, was expelled from the HSWP for criticizing the Warsaw Pact troops' invasion of Czechoslovakia.

1972   A two-volume collection of documents, *Turning Points*, edited by historian and director of the Central Archives of the Trade Unions **Elek Karsai** (1922–), was withdrawn from the bookshops allegedly because it contained five documents with vague references to the violent actions of Soviet soldiers during their 1956 campaign in Hungary.

     Sociology student **Gábor Demszky** was suspended from Budapest University for organizing a left-wing demonstration on the anniversary of the 1919 Hungarian Soviet Republic. In late 1981 he launched the first independent publishing house, AB: Independent Publishers.

1973–   Historian **Ferenc Fehér** (1933–), assistant to philosopher György Lukács (1967–70) and scholar at the Hungarian Academy of Sciences History Institute (1970–73), resigned for political reasons. In 1977 he left for Australia.

1978   A biography of Béla Kun by **György Borsányi**, historian at the Institute of Party History, was withdrawn from the bookshops because it contained several references to the cooperation between the Comintern (the third Communist International, 1918–43) and the Soviet secret police, and to Kun's role in the 1920 communist terror in the Crimea.

1978–79   In 1978 or 1979, historian **Mihály Hamburger** was dismissed by the Trade Union Theoretical Research Institute allegedly because he and another historian, **Gyula Benda**, had jointly replied to a questionnaire on Marxism. All the replies to the questionnaire were in the book *Marx in the Fourth Decade*, edited by **András Kovács** (1925–), a lecturer in oral history at Budapest University. Kovacs had been oppressed for many years, during which he earned money as a life-story interviewer. After the book came out, he was dismissed from Kossuth publishers. Benda was also dismissed and subsequently worked as a researcher in an ethnographic museum. In the early 1980s, he was a member of a samizdat (self-publishing) group studying social history. Hamburger became an auto fuel pump attendant.

1978   In September Hungary's unofficial university, sometimes referred to
            as repulo ovoda (Flying Kindergarten), was established. The Lectures
            which regularly attracted large audiences, mostly students, dealt with
            topics such as twentieth-century Hungarian history. The first lecture,
            given by historian Miklós Szabó (?1940–), discussed the thoughts
            of Bibó [q.v. 1956–].

1979–   When Bibó [q.v. 1956–] died, an opposition group began preparing
            a samizdat collection of articles in his honor (Bibó emlékkönyv,
            1981). Certain contributors were summoned to the HSWP head-
            quarters and subjected to a severe "discussion", others were allowed
            to retain their jobs but not to teach at the university, and still others
            were dismissed and unable to find state employment for years. A
            fourth group, finally, was subjected to official monitoring and intim-
            idation.

1980   An essay by historian and former government minister **Miklós Mes-
            ter**, Where Did We Go Wrong? The National Equality of the Peoples
            of the Danube Valley, circulated as an unofficial publication. His
            memoirs were smuggled out of Hungary.

1981–82   The underground press published about the following topics: the
            1956 Revolution (including documents collected by Krassó [q.v.
            1984–] and appearing in Napló [Diary], a hand-copied "journal"),
            the historical and current situation of Hungarian minorities in neigh-
            boring countries, and the history of imprisonment and labor camps
            in Hungary during the Stalinist years (in a series called The Hun-
            garian Gulag). British historian and peace campaigner E.P. Thomp-
            son's book Beyond the Cold War was translated in September 1982.
            In 1983 Beszélő (The Speaker), the most widely read underground
            newspaper, devoted a special issue to the memory of the victims of
            1956.

1981   In April **Bill Lomax**, a sociology lecturer at Nottingham University,
            United Kingdom, was searched by customs officers and had his
            books and notes confiscated as he was about to leave Hungary after
            three weeks' research on the 1956 Hungarian Revolution. Following
            protests to the Foreign Ministry, all the material was returned to him
            in May. In December 1982 he was expelled, although he was in
            possession of a valid visa. His 1976 book about the Hungarian Rev-
            olution (Hungary 1956) was smuggled into Hungary and soon trans-
            lated by Krassó [q.v. 1984–] but it was not published in Hungarian
            until 1989.

1984–   In June 1984 economist **György Krassó** (1932–91) was questioned
            by the police about his interview on the imprisonment, trial, and
            1958 execution of Imre Nagy and other leaders of the 1956 Revo-

lution to the samizdat periodical *Hirmondó* (The Messenger) in December 1983 and published there as *The Memory of the Dead*. He was released nine hours later. In October he was again detained. His flat was searched and many samizdat materials were confiscated; he was fined for possessing and distributing them. He was the organizer of the samizdat October Free Press. From November 1984 to October 1985, he was put under strict police surveillance. In December 1984 nearly 300 people signed a letter of protest to the authorities about his treatment. In late 1985 he emigrated to the United Kingdom, where he worked at the BBC and led a Hungarian news agency. In 1989 he returned to Hungary and founded the Hungarian October Party. In July he was brought to court following demonstrations in Budapest's Ferenc Münnich Street, during which the nameplates of the street were covered over with plates bearing the street's older name, Nador Street. He was given verbal warnings. In the early fifties, Krassó had been expelled from the HSWP and from Karl Marx University of Economics. For his participation in the 1956 Revolution, he had been sentenced in 1957 to ten years' imprisonment but he had been released under the 1963 amnesty. Ever since, but especially after February 1979, he had attempted to correct the official view of "1956" in oral or written form, "to give back to the people their own, forgotten history". Since 1963 he had been repeatedly harassed by the police and denied permission to travel to the West.

1986   Historian **Péter Hanák** (1921–97), specialist in the early-twentieth-century Habsburg empire and its successor states, department chairman at the Hungarian Academy of Sciences History Institute, history professor at Eötvös University, Budapest, and since 1991 in charge of the History Institute of the Central European University, was elected to the Academy of Sciences after long having been bypassed for membership because he had refused in 1956 to join the reconstituted HSWP.

On 3 March historian **György Gadó**'s flat was searched as was his mother's. Manuscripts and materials printed without a licence were taken away. On 7 March he was fined 10,000 forints and on 11 March his flat was searched again. His notebook and some private letters were confiscated.

On 15 March police broke up an unofficial peaceful procession of four to five hundred people commemorating the anniversary of the 1848 Hungarian Revolution.

1986–   On 20 October **László Rusai** (?1956–), a former teacher from Hatvan active in opposition circles, was arrested after he had hung a poster from his window commemorating the thirtieth anniversary of the 1956 Revolution. He was forcibly confined in a mental hospital until his release in November. In November 1987 he was rearrested and charged with "violating the community" after slogans were chalked on a monument to the Soviet army's losses in World War II. Six days earlier, he had hung a flag commemorating the 1956 Revolution in his window. He denied the charges but remained detained without trial in the psychiatric wing of Budapest Prison in late 1987.

1988   On 16 June, the thirtieth anniversary of Nagy's execution, several members of the Committee for Historical Justice (TIB; founded in the spring of 1988 by, inter alia, Litván [q.v. 1959]) were arrested when police used force to break up a large demonstration in the center of Budapest. TIB demanded a reassessment of the 1956 Revolution and the rehabilitation of its leaders.

1989   In the spring publications on the 1956 Revolution, prepared for circulation as samizdat literature, were in practice distributed freely. On 16 June the ceremonial reburial of Nagy took place. He was entirely rehabilitated on 6 July. Other reburials were those of historian and sociologist Jászi [q.v. pre-1945] and of Admiral Miklós Horthy, regent in 1920–44.

During the 1989 events, many communist monuments with a historical-documentary value were destroyed.

1994   In December Radio Budapest reported that the government had abolished the Historical Investigation Committee (established 1989). Part of the committee's role was to account for the omissions in history books left by censors under the communist regime. The investigations had proved uncomfortable for some of the politicians elected to power in the spring of 1994.

Also see Germany (1957–: Alfred Kantorowicz), Italy (1946: Chabod), Romania (1972–: Tamas; 1980–96: history and geography teachers; 1986: Köpeczi; 1992: statue), South Africa (1960–90: Lukács), Turkey (1948: Halasi-Kun), Ukraine (1996: monument), United Kingdom (1981: E.P. Thompson).

SOURCES

Amnesty International, *Report* (London) 1985: 271; 1986: 288; 1987: 298–99; 1988: 205.
Auer, L., "Archival Losses and Their Impact on the Work of Archivists and Historians", *Archivum*, 1996, no.42: 4.
————, "Archival Losses since the Second World War", *Janus*, 1994, no.1: 71.
Benda, G., "Des Coquelicots dans un champ de blé", in: Marès ed. 1996: 230–31, 235.

————, "L'Historiographie hongroise des années 80", in: Marès ed. 1996: 118, 120, 123–24.

Bernath, M., & F. von Schroeder eds., *Biographisches Lexicon zur Geschichte Südeuropas* (Munich) vol. 2 (1976): 84–85, 176–77; vol. 3 (1979): 223; vol. 4 (1981): 256–58.

Boia, L. ed., *Great Historians of the Modern Age: An International Dictionary* (Westport 1991) 341–42, 346–47.

Boris, P., *Die sich lossagten: Stichworte zu Leben und Werk von 461 Exkommunisten und Dissidenten* (Cologne 1983) 99, 232–34.

Borsody, S., "Modern Hungarian Historiography", *Journal of Modern History*, 1952: 402–3, 405.

Boyd, K. ed., *Encyclopedia of Historians and Historical Writing* (London/Chicago 1999) 425–26, 1166–67.

Bozóki, A., "Censorship in the 1980s", *Hungarian Quarterly*, 1995, no.139: 102, 107–8.

Brossat, A., S. Combe, J.-Y. Potel, & J.-C. Szurek eds., *A l'Est, la mémoire retrouvée* (Paris 1990).

Bruch, R. vom, & R.A. Müller eds., *Historikerlexikon: Von der Antike bis zum 20. Jahrhundert* (Munich 1991) 3, 145, 306.

Burguière, A. ed., *Dictionnaire des sciences historiques* (Paris 1986) 336–37, 339.

Cannon, J. ed., *The Blackwell Dictionary of Historians* (Oxford 1988) 399–400.

Christ, K., *Neue Profile der alten Geschichte* (Darmstadt 1990) 40–41.

Czigány, L., "The Passionate Outsider: Professor George Cushing", *Hungarian Quarterly*, 1996, no.142: 101.

Deák, I., "Historiography of the Countries of Eastern Europe: Hungary", *American Historical Review*, 1992: 1049–51, 1053–55, 1057–58.

Deletant, D., & H. Hanak eds., *Historians As Nation-Builders: Central and South-East Europe* (London 1988) xv.

Epstein, I.R., *Gyula Szekfü: A Study in the Political Basis of Hungarian Historiography* (New York/London 1987) 2–3, 254–59, 266–68, 273–77, 320, 326, 331.

Erdmann, K.D., *Die Ökumene der Historiker: Geschichte der internationalen Historikerkongresse und des Comité international des sciences historiques* (Göttingen 1987) 335–36.

Fekete, M. ed., *Prominent Hungarians Home and Abroad* (London 1985) 54, 189.

Glatz, F., & A. Pók eds., "The Soviet System and Historiography, 1917–1989: The Influence of Marxism-Leninism on the Historical Sciences" (unpublished papers; Budapest 1995).

Greenberg, S., "Les Funerailles nationales d'Imre Nagy", in: Brossat et al. eds. 1990: 126, 130–31, 134, 136, 139, 146–47.

Held, J., *Dictionary of East European History since 1945* (Westport 1994) 246–47, 267, 273–74.

Horváth, Z., "Hungary: Recovering from the Past", in: W. Laqueur & G.L. Mosse eds., *The New History: Trends in Historical Research and Writing since World War II* (New York 1967) 222–23, 226, 228–30, 232–33.

Index on Censorship, 3–4/72: 114; 1/73: ii, 53–59; 6/78: 21; 2/80: 16; 4/81: 46; 2/83: 3–5, 12; 5/84: 49 (quote Krassó), 50; 1/85: 62; 2/85: 54; 1/86: 53; 5/86: 13–14; 7/88: 35; 4/89: 37; 6–7/89: 63; 10/89: 38; 1/95: 240.

Kammer, H., personal communication, May 1997.

Kosáry, D., "The Idea of a Comparative History of East Central Europe: The Story of a Venture", in: Deletant & Hanak eds. 1988: 126–27, 130–31.

Lakos, J., "Die Zerstörung des Archivsmaterials des Ungarischen Königlichen Justizministeriums während der Revolution von 1956", *Archivum*, 1996, no.42: 255–65.

Litván, G. ed., *The Hungarian Revolution of 1956: Reform, Revolt and Repression 1953–56* (originally Hungarian 1991; London/New York 1996) xii, 104–5, 115–16, 119–20, 142–43, 157, 159–63, 196, 198, 202–3, 205–6.

Lomax, B., *Hungary 1956* (London 1976) 171–74.

Marès, A. ed., *Histoire et pouvoir en Europe médiane* (Paris 1996).

Mucsi, F., "Die Bewertung der Sozialdemokratie und des Bürgerlichen Radikalismus in der Ungarischen Geschichtsschreibung (1948–1989)", in: Glatz & Pók eds. 1995: 54–56.

The National Archives of Hungary: Its History and Holdings (Budapest 1999) 8–9.

Papp, N.G., "The Paradox of Recent Hungarian Historiography: The Limits of Revision", *East European Quarterly*, 1986: 229, 235, 237–39.

Passerini, L. ed., *International Yearbook of Oral History and Life Stories*, vol. 1, *Memory and Totalitarianism* (Oxford 1992) ix.

Rainer, J.M., "István Bibó: A Great Political Diagnostician", *Hungarian Quarterly*, 1993, no.132: 32, 37.

Schöpflin, G., "Opposition in Hungary: 1956 and Beyond", in: J.L. Curry ed., *Dissent in Eastern Europe* (New York 1983) 77.

Schuitema, A. ed., *Schrijvers in ballingschap* (originally English; Amsterdam [1954]) 316.

Sipos, P., "Hungarian Historical Scholarship and Marxism-Leninism", in: Glatz & Pók eds. 1995: 96, 99, 101, 103.

Soulé, V., "La Guerre des blasons", in: Brossat et al. eds. 1990: 150–61.

Stokes, G., *The Walls Came Tumbling Down: The Collapse of Communism in Eastern Europe* (New York/Oxford 1993) 88–89, 95–96.

Stroynowski, J. ed., *Who's Who in the Socialist Countries of Europe* (Munich 1989) 82, 297, 533, 598, 1212.

Szücs, G., "Sickle Amnesia", *New Hungarian Quarterly*, 1991, Autumn: 73.

Várdy, S.B., *Historical Dictionary of Hungary* (Lanham 1997) 161–62, 331, 341, 356–60, 384–85, 423, 433–34, 475–76, 657–59.

———, *Modern Hungarian Historiography* (Boulder 1976) 98, 115, 119–20, 150, 173, 195, 199.

Weber, W., *Biographisches Lexicon zur Geschichtswissenschaft in Deutschland, Österreich und der Schweiz: Die Lehrstuhlinhaber für Geschichte von den Anfängen des Faches bis 1970* (Frankfurt/Main 1987) 3–4, 101–2.

Woolf, D.R. ed., *A Global Encyclopedia of Historical Writing* (New York/London 1998) 432–33, 590, 873.

I

INDIA

Three areas of historical research and teaching were of long-standing preoccupation in India: the relations between Hindus and Muslims, the relations between communalism and secularism, and the 1947 partition and the ensuing relations with Pakistan.

British India

1930–45   In the 1930s and 1940s, **Jawaharlal Nehru** (1889–1964), future prime minister of India (1947–64), wrote two history books in prison: *Glimpses of World History, Being Further Letters to His Daughter, Written in Prison, and Containing a Rambling Account of History for Young People* (two volumes, 1934–35), written between October 1930 and August 1933 in various prisons while he was serving sentences for his anticolonial activities; and *The Discovery of India* (1946), written between August 1942 and June 1945 when he remained under rigorous confinement after riots following the rejection of the spring 1942 proposals of Sir Stafford Cripps (proposals done to resolve an impasse between the British government and the Indian nationalist leaders). In the first work Nehru cited Benjamin Disraeli on Hugo Grotius: "Other men condemned to exile and capitivity, if they survive, despair; the man of letters may reckon those days as the sweetest of his life". Between 1921 and 1945, Nehru spent nine terms (totaling nine years) in British prisons. *Glimpses* made him the first non-Western world historian.

1946–47   Historian and politician Sir **Shafaat Ahmad Khan** (1893–1947) was stabbed in Simla by a Muslim extremist. He ultimately died from the effects of the attack. Khan was head of the history department of Allahabad University, Uttar Pradesh (1921–40), India's high commissioner to South Africa (1941–45) and minister of education in the interim government of India (1946). As a historian he played a significant role in spreading the European model of historiography within India. As a politician he was an active advocate of Muslim separatism before 1940 but later he joined the Indian National Congress and opposed the demand for an independent Pakistan. This change of ideas made him persona non grata with the orthodox Muslims.

1946   **Rajendra Prasad** (1884–1963), Congress Party leader, president of the Constituent Assembly (1946–49) and future president of India (1950–62), wrote his book *India Divided* (Bombay 1946) in prison (1942–45), where he had been detained because he had opposed the British war effort. Arguing from an Indian nationalist viewpoint but emphasizing the unity between the historical traditions and political ideals of Hindus and Muslims, it had gone through three editions before India was partitioned in 1947.

pre-1947   Before the independence of British India (1947), Marxist-inspired "economic nationalist" interpretations of Indian history (pleas for autarchy based on historical arguments, criticism of "landlordism" and nineteenth-century deindustrialization) were banned at schools and universities.

India

1952–57   In December 1952 the Ministry of Education appointed an editorial board to compile an official history of the Indian freedom movement, to be published on the centenary celebrations of the 1857 revolt of Indian soldiers (sepoys). In May 1953 **Romesh Chandra Majumdar** (1888–1980), professor of ancient history at Calcutta University (1913–21), professor (1921–42), and vice chancellor (1937–42) at Dacca University, and general editor of the Bharatiya Vidya Bhavan's *History and Culture of the Indian People* (Bombay 1951–77), was appointed project director. In 1954 he presented the draft of the first volume to the other editorial board members and after a delay he learned from the minister of education that some of them had criticized it as exaggerating the role of Bengal in the freedom movement. Equally controversial was the starting point of the freedom movement, situated by Majumdar in 1870, while others preferred the 1857 revolt, or even the thirteenth century—implying that Muslims were foreigners in India, an assumption undermining the Congress Party's ideal of India as a secular democracy. A third point of conflict was the nature (a national war of independence or not) of the 1857 revolt. Majumdar resigned in 1955. On 31 December 1955, the editorial board was dissolved. The government entrusted the work to Surendra Nath Sen, director of the National Archives of India in New Delhi, who published *Eighteen Fifty Seven* in 1957. The same year Majumdar published his findings as *The Sepoy Mutiny and the Revolt of 1857.* Later he wrote a three-volume *History of the Freedom Movement in India* (Calcutta 1961–62).

1970s– In the 1970s or 1980s, a historian (name unknown) at Punjabi University, Patiala, drew the anger of orthodox Sikhs for his views on one of their gurus.

1973 **P.V. Ranade**, a historian at Marathwada University, Aurangabad, Maharashtra, was suspended for having written a critical article on Shivaji (1627–80), who opposed Mughal domination and became founder of the Maratha State. After protests from his colleagues, including the Indian History Congress (IHC), Ranade was reinstated.

1975– **Romila Thapar** (1931–), a history professor at the Center for Historical Studies at Jawaharlal Nehru University, New Delhi (1970–93), was harassed under the Emergency (1975–77) after she had refused to sign a 1975 communication on Indian democracy initiated by Prime Minister Indira Gandhi. Her income tax assessments for a decade were reopened. In 1976 Thapar, Gopal [q.v. 1977–78], Mukhia [q.v. 1977–78] and other historians were signatories to an appeal against Gandhi's extension of her rule.

1975 In June newspaper editors were no longer allowed to print extracts from speeches by Jawaharlal Nehru [q.v. 1930–45], Mahatma Gandhi (1869–1948), or Rabindranath Tagore (1861–1941) which related to freedom or touched on the kinds of measures introduced by Indira Gandhi's government during the Emergency.

1977 The Supreme Court ruled that products of serious historical research could not be punished or proscribed under the Penal Code, even if some of the facts unearthed as a result of such research were unpalatable to followers of a particular religion.

1977–78 From May 1977 until March 1978, a history textbook controversy took place. On 27 May 1977, the principal secretary to Morarji Desai, then prime minister of the newly elected Janata government (1977–79), sent a note to the minister of education saying that the prime minister's attention had been drawn to the contents of four books on Indian history (written at the insistence of educational authorities, for use in the higher school classes and the primary stage of college instruction and already prescribed in certain institutions).

The secretary endorsed a detailed anonymous memorandum, dated 18 May, to the prime minister which stated that the contents of these textbooks were prejudicial to the study of Indian history. The minister of education was asked to consider withdrawing recognition from them. The textbooks were *Medieval India* (1967) by Thapar [q.v. 1975–], *Modern India* (1970) by **Bipan Chandra** (1928–), *Freedom Struggle* (1972) by **Amales Tripathi, Barun De** (1932–) and Chandra, and *Communalism and the Writing of Indian History* (1970) by **Harbans Mukhia** (1939–), Thapar, and Chandra. During the controversy a fifth textbook, *Ancient India* (1977) by **Ram Sharan Sharma** (1920–), was added after it was denounced at a mass meeting. Mukhia was a history professor at the Center for Historical Studies at Jawaharlal Nehru University. Marxist historian Chandra was the head of that Center and professor of modern Indian history, Sharma was the head of the history department first at Patna University, Bihar, later at Delhi University, and for some years the director of the Indian Council of Historical Research (ICHR; the national organization of Indian historians). Tripathi was head of the history department and De was director of the Institute for Social Sciences, both at Calcutta University, West Bengal State. The textbooks had not been criticized before that time. The Education Ministry referred the matter to the National Council for Educational Research and Training (NCERT), financed by the ministry and publisher of three of the books. NCERT examined them and dismissed the criticism as untenable. A virtual ban on the use and reprint of the books did nevertheless apparently occur.

The most disputed feature of the textbooks was the interpretation of "medieval" Indian history, the period in which Muslim rule prevailed in much of India (1200–1757), deemed by some as antinational, anti-Hindu, and pro-Muslim. Much discussion centered around the question whether Muslim rule should be called "indigenous" or "foreign". Other important points were the authors' attention to social-economic history and their propensity to explain conflict among elites primarily in political rather than religious terms. What one side called demystification of the past was called denigration of the past by the other. The controversy took place in the press (inter alia, between Thapar, who defended the secularist view, and Majumdar [q.v. 1952–57], who argued from the communalist point of view), journals of opinion and Parliament. A leaflet against the authors was distributed, but teachers and students at two New Delhi universities signed petitions in their favor. At the same time a more general campaign was allegedly waged against so-called communist historians and social scientists. Historian **Sarvepalli Gopal** (1923–), professor of contemporary history at Jawaharlal Nehru

University (1972–83) and biographer of Nehru [q.v. 1930–45], for example, was attacked in Parliament from the government benches as a supporter of communist causes.

Sharma's book, published at the height of the controversy and about to go into a second edition, was withdrawn from the syllabus in the 1,100 schools affiliated to the Central Board of Secondary Education in July 1978. The books by Thapar and Chandra were not formally withdrawn, but their distribution was de facto sharply reduced. Fourteen other history textbooks were on a list of works to be withdrawn. In October 1977 Sharma had already been denied a passport and thus prevented from leaving India as the head of an ICHR delegation to attend a conference on the Aryans in the USSR. By then he had already been relieved from his ICHR directorship. The ICHR publication program was reportedly affected by the government measures. After the IHC strongly supported the textbook writers, the Janata government encouraged the creation of a rival organization, the Indian History and Culture Society. In May 1981 cultural historian Niharranjan Ray became ICHR chairman. He suspended the research grants of ten historians appointed under Janata auspices.

1978   Late in the year, a member (name unknown) of the history department at Dibrugarh University, Assam, published a research paper in the department journal, quoting critical comments on nineteenth- and twentieth-century Assamese society. As the article was written by a Bengali, it was supposed to contain anti-Assamese sentiments. Although the university had impounded all copies of the journal within a week of its issue, the comments aroused the anger of the public and some academics. The author and the editor, who was also the department head, were suspended by the university authorities despite protests from academics outside the university, including the IHC.

1970s   In the late 1970s, the Bihar government demanded action against a teacher in an undergraduate college (name unknown), who during a lecture advocated the theory that the Aryan-speaking people came from outside India, a theory generally held among scholars.

[1981]   **Irfan Habib** (1931–), history professor of medieval India at Aligarh Muslim University (AMU), Uttar Pradesh, gave an interview to the newspaper *Indian Express* in which he declared that he had been the victim of attempted physical violence after he had exposed irregularities in the admission and examination of AMU students. This was regarded as an act of misconduct and an attempt to malign the AMU and he was issued a charge-sheet by the vice chancellor, allegedly after pressure from local Muslim political groups. An AMU Action Committee demanded Habib's resignation. In a letter to the vice chancellor, the president of the Students' Islamic Union of India wrote that he wanted every AMU teacher to be loyal to the Islamic faith and not to do anything detrimental to the interests of Islamic culture, community, and the university: "Not only the present statement of Irfan Habib, but his attitude in the past as well, was always inimical to Islam and the community. . . . Therefore, in this case, taking advantages of loopholes in the law, we have to throw him out of the University. . . . If you fail now, there would arise not one but hundreds of Irfan Habibs from amongst our staff". In 1982 Habib published *An Atlas of the Mughal Empire*. He was IHC president and ICHR chairman.

1984   In January the British documentary film *The War of the Springing Tiger*, dealing with the history of the Indian National Army during World War II, was banned by the Indian television. The Minister of External Affairs, later Prime Minister, Narasimha Rao, said that the film could be shown only when "objectionable features and offending passages" had been changed.

1988   The Supreme Court, asked to adjudicate on a plea to ban the popular television series *Tamas* (Darkness) by filmmaker **Govind Nihalani**, on the grounds that it might inflame communal passions, refused to sanction the ban. It considered the educative value, the sober tone, and the fidelity to historical facts of the series. *Tamas* was based on Bhisham Sahni's novel about the violence during the 1947 partition of British India (1988).

1989   In April *The Oxford Illustrated Encyclopaedia*, vol. 4, *World History from 1800 to the Present Day* (1988) was banned because it contained critical statements concerning former Prime Minister Indira Gandhi.

In April historian **M. Kalburgi** received death threats from militants of the Hindu Lingayat community (founded in the twelfth century) because they alleged that his book *One Way* blasphemed a twelfth-century saint, Basaveshwara.

1992   In May 1992 **Mushirul Hasan**, professor of modern Indian history and pro–vice chancellor at the Jamia Millia Islamia, Jamia Nagar, New Delhi, was forced to stay off campus after receiving death threats from students. In April he had said in a magazine interview that the ban on Salman Rushdie's *Satanic Verses* should be lifted even though the book offended Muslims because banning it would only endow it with notoriety and cause India to gain a reputation for being "intolerant and undemocratic". The university was closed for three months after riots sparked by his remarks. In November a committee appointed by the minister for human resources and development found that his remarks had amounted to "an act of indiscretion" but that, in view of his subsequent apology, no further action was necessary. On 4 December (two days before the destruction of the Ayodhya mosque), his first day back at work, he was attacked by three students with iron bars and knives but he did not resign. On 31 October 1996, he returned to the university, amid heavy police deployment and protests from a section among the students.

On 6 December, a mosque at the sacred city of Ayodhya, Uttar Pradesh, built in the sixteenth century allegedly by destroying a temple that stood at the birthplace of the Hindu deity Rama, was demolished by Hindu nationalists. It was the climax of the so-called Babri Masjid-Ram Janmabhumi controversy that had started in January 1986 (preceded by conflicts in the nineteenth century and 1947–50). The ensuing violence all over India, in which two thousand people died, was said to be the worst since independence. Out of revenge a Hindu temple in Lahore was destroyed on 8 December 1992 by radical Muslims. In October 1994, when considering the case, the Supreme Court refused to intervene in the historical problem whether the 1528 mosque had been built on the razed temple. Writers defending the Hindu view in the controversy alleged that some nineteenth-century and twentieth-century sources in their favor had been suppressed or censored.

1994   In March Ramesh Singla, youth-wing president of the Congress Party in Punjab, and an Amritsar organization both reportedly offered substantial rewards for the murder of the Pakistani **Sadique Hussain**, author of the book *History of Warriors*.

1996   The following books were reportedly banned: *Nine Hours to Rama* (1962), a reconstruction of the plot to kill Mahatma Gandhi that reportedly sympathetically portrays the killer, written by **Stanley Wolpert** (1927–), lecturer (1958–68) and history professor (1968–) at the University of California; *The History of Sexuality* (New York 1978; originally French 1976) by French philosopher **Michel Foucault** (1926–84); *Reclaiming the Past? The Search for Political and Cultural Unity in Contemporary Jammu and Kashmir* (London 1995) by **Vernon Hewitt** (1961–), a book critical of Pakistan and India. The Hewitt and Foucault books were held up at customs; Foucault's book had previously been freely available.

1997   On 15 August, Independence Day, the film *Train to Pakistan*, by **Pamela Rook**, was denied broadcasting permission shortly before its scheduled showing. The story, based on a novel by Khushwant Singh (1915–), concerned communal tension in a Punjabi village during India's 1947 partition. The Central Board of Film Certification asked the director to remove the word *Muslim* (recurring throughout the screenplay) and all indirect references to Mahatma Gandhi.

1998   In July the minister of cultural affairs of Maharashtra banned a play because it portrayed Mahatma Gandhi unfavorably.

1999–   In December 1999 (or earlier), the ICHR allegedly decided to order Oxford University Press to suspend publication of two volumes in its *Towards Freedom* series (a documentation project on the 1938–47 period) by social historians **Sumit Sarkar**, Delhi University, and **K.N. Panikkar**, Jawaharlal Nehru University, and return them to the ICHR for review. The volumes, about the years 1940 and 1946, were submitted in 1995 and 1996 and were already in press. The authors and general series editor Gopal [q.v. 1977–78] were informed of the suspension by the ICHR on 11 February 2000. On [15] February dozens of historians and academics from the four New Delhi universities protested in front of the ICHR office. A statement signed by over thirty academics, including three former ICHR chairpersons (Sharma [q.v. 1977–78], Habib [q.v. 1981], and Ravinder Kumar [1959–]), denounced the withdrawal of the volumes as "the grossest form of censorship". Panikkar declared that the volumes were withheld because the militant Hindu organization Rashtriya Swayamsevak Sangh, close to the Bharatiya Janata Party (ruling since 1998), wanted a prominent place in the freedom movement by emphasizing that Sangh leaders like (Prime Minister) Atal Vajpayee and organizations like Hindu Mahasabha played an important role in it. On 3 March the Rajya Sabha (Council of States) discussed the affair. In August 2000 the New Delhi High Court appointed an arbitrator to decide whether Oxford University Press was within its rights to go ahead with the publication of the two volumes. **Basudev Chatterji**, a specialist in the intellectual history of the late nineteenth and early twentieth centuries in India, editor of the three-volume second part, *1938* (1999), and full-time coordinating editor of the entire series (1989–2000), was dismissed by the ICHR.

Also see Iran (1989–: Rushdie), Pakistan (1946–: Smith; 1984–88: Wolpert), United States (1952–: Thorner).

SOURCES

Abraham, A.S., "Dispute over Textbook 'Censorship' ", *Times Educational Supplement*, 9 September 1977: 10.

————, "India: Book Ban Angers Liberals", *Times Higher Education Supplement*, 7 July 1978: 6.

Amnesty International, *Report* (London) 1993: 154; 1994: 159; 1999: 194; 2000: 126.

Ballhatchet, K., "The Rewriting of South Asian History by South Asian Historians after 1947", *Asian Affairs*, 1984, no. 1: 28, 30–31.

Banerjee, T., "Ramesh Chandra Majumdar: The Historian of Indian Nationalism", *Journal of Indian History*, 1981: 347–60.

Bayly, C.A., "Modern Indian Historiography", in: M. Bentley ed., *Companion to Historiography* (London/New York 1997) 682.

Boia, L. ed., *Great Historians of the Modern Age: An International Dictionary* (Westport 1991) 354–55, 357–58, 366.

Boyd, K. ed., *Encyclopedia of Historians and Historical Writing* (London/Chicago 1999) 478–79, 1177–78.

Brass, P.R., *The New Cambridge History of India*, vol. 4–1, *The Politics of India since Independence* (Cambridge 1994) 239–47.

Chopra, P.N., & P. Chopra, *Encyclopedia of India* (New Delhi 1988) 233.

Crane, R.I., "India", in: Winks ed. 1966: 369.

"Debate on History", *Mainstream*, 1977 (10 December: 31–34; 24 December: 29–32).

Elst, K., *Ram Janmabhoomi vs. Babri Masjid: A Case Study in Hindu–Muslim Conflict* (New Delhi 1990) 7–9.

Eswaran, K.S.V., "Advocacy of National, Racial and Religious Hatred: The Indian Experience", in: S. Coliver ed., *Striking a Balance: Hate Speech, Freedom of Expression and Non-discrimination*. (London 1992) 173, 176.

Gopal, S., "The Fear of History", *Seminar*, January 1978: 71–73.

Gopinath, R., "Report of Protests Regarding Ordered Suspension of Publications of Professors Sumit Sarkar and K.N. Panikkar by the Indian Council of Historical Research" (WWW-text 2000).

Gottlob, M., "Writing the History of Modern Indian Historiography: A Review Article", *Storia della storiografia*, 1995, no.27: 145.

Handa, M.L., "Indian Historiography: Writing and Rewriting Indian history", *Journal of Asian and African Studies*, 1982: 218, 233.

Hasan, M., *Legacy of a Divided Nation: India's Muslims from Independence to Ayodhya* (New Delhi 1997) viii–x, 324–25.

Heehs, P., "Myth, History, and Theory", *History and Theory*, 1994: 12–14.

Hilton, R.H., "Censorship in India", *Past & Present*, November 1977: 142.

The Hindu, 2000 (WWW-texts; daily from 15 to 29 February; 2, 4, 8, 16, 17 March; 11 April 2000).

Human Rights Watch, *World Report* (Washington) 1997: 159–60; 1999: 184, 186; 2001: 198, 467.

Index on Censorship, 3/75: 50; 2/84: 45–46; 6–7/89: 78; 8/89: 38; 7/92: 45; 3/93: 36; 3/94: 175; 2/96: 90; 166, 168; 3/97: 8; 5/97: 171; 6/97: 67, 86–87; 5/99: 74; 3/00: 95.

Keesings historisch archief, 1990: 38–39, 472; 1991: 127–28, 492–93; 1992: 271–72, 275, 576, 577–78; 1993: 132, 135, 137–38, 586–87; 1995: 216; 1998: 686, 692.

Majumdar, R.C., "Indian Historiography: Some Recent Trends", in: Sen ed. 1973: xxi–xxii.

————, *The Sepoy Mutiny and the Revolt of 1857* (second edition; Calcutta 1963) i–xvii.

Mansingh, S., *Historical Dictionary of India* (Lanham 1996) 111–12.

Mathur, L.P., *Historiography and Historians of Modern India* (New Delhi 1987) 27, 203, 221, 225–26.

"Mythifying History: A Symposium on the Making of Myths Claiming to Be Historical" *Seminar*, December 1989 (special issue).

Nandy, A., "History's Forgotten Doubles", *History and Theory*, 1995: 60–65.

Narain, H., *The Ayodhya Temple-Mosque Dispute: Focus on Muslim Sources* (New Delhi 1993) 74–77.

Nehru, J., *Glimpses of World History, Being Further Letters to His Daughter, Written in Prison, and Containing a Rambling Account of History for Young People* (originally 1934–35; New Delhi 1989) vii–viii, 949 (quote).

"Past and Prejudice", *Frontline*, 4–17 March 2000 (WWW-text).

Philips, C.H. ed., *Historians of India, Pakistan and Ceylon* (London 1961).

Prasad, B., "Sir Shafaat Ahmad Khan", in: Sen ed. 1973: 147.

Prasad, R., "Further Reports on the Indian Council of Historical Research Issue" (WWW-text 2000).

Ray, S., "India: After Independence", in: W. Laqueur & G.L. Mosse eds., *The New History: Trends in Historical Research and Writing since World War II* (New York 1967) 123–24.

Rosser, Y., personal communication, November 2000.

Rudolph, L.I., & S. Hoeber Rudolph, "Cultural Policy, the Textbook Controversy and Indian Identity", in: A.J. Wilson & D. Dalton eds., *The States of South Asia: Problems of National Integration* (London 1982) 135, 139–50.

Scholars at Risk, *December 2000 Profiles* (WWW-text; Chicago 2000).

Sen, S.N., "Writings on the Mutiny", in: Philips ed. 1961: 373–84.

Sen, S.P. ed., *Historians and Historiography in Modern India* (Calcutta 1973) xiii–xv.

Sharma, R.C., et al., *Historiography and Historians in India since Independence* (Agra 1991) 100–101, 215, 229–30, 235.

Siddiqi, M.H., "History-Writing in India", *History Workshop*, Autumn 1980: 186–90.

Singhal, D.P., "Pakistan", in: Winks ed. 1966: 403–4.

Smith, W.C., "Modern Muslim Historical Writing in English", in: Philips ed. 1961: 324, 331.

Thapar, R., "Academic Freedom and [the] AMU Crisis", *Radical Humanist*, April 1981: 13–14.

———, "L'Histoire en Inde", in: R. Rémond ed., *Être historien aujourd'hui* (Paris 1988) 278–79.

———, "Sources of Encroachment on Academic Freedom", *Radical Humanist*, February 1979: 12–13.

Wesseling, H.L., "Overseas History", in: P. Burke ed., *New Perspectives on Historical Writing* (London 1991) 73.

Winks, R.W. ed., *The Historiography of the British Empire-Commonwealth: Trends, Interpretations, and Resources* (Durham 1966).

Woolf, D.R. ed., *A Global Encyclopedia of Historical Writing* (New York/London 1998) 459.

INDONESIA

Under the Japanese occupation (March 1942–August 1945), the teaching of the history of Western countries was forbidden in the schools. Historical research and the publication of books and journals on Indonesian history and culture were almost completely stopped. During President Sukarno's "Guided Democracy" era (1959–65), historical discussion and research were restricted. Historians were expected to support and justify the revolution as defined in the president's political manifesto. During the reign of President Suharto (1967–98), the attorney general regularly banned foreign and domestic books that challenged the official account of history. Among the sensitive topics were Indonesia's independence struggle (1945–49), communism, and the attempted coup of 30 September 1965 and its aftermath of large-scale killings during which Suharto rose to power. Historians inspired by Islam reportedly found it difficult to express their opinion in their work due to the policy that anything which discredited a people, religion, or race could not be published because it would damage national unity. Access to relevant archival sources, especially those in the hands of military authorities, was very difficult.

1943–45 Sumatran teacher, journalist, and writer **Sanusi Pané** (1905–68), head of the Office of Cultural Affairs under the Japanese occupation (1942–45), published his four-volume *History of Indonesia*, which became very popular and served as a school textbook. Its Indonesian nationalist tone was muted, reportedly owing at least partly to the wishes of the Japanese authorities who sponsored it. This probably also explains why the first 1945 edition of the fourth volume did not give an overview of the development of the nationalist movement such as the one appearing in the 1950 edition.

1945 **Willem Mansvelt** (1891–1945), writer of the two-volume *History of the Dutch Trading Company* (1924–26) and head of the Central Office of Statistics at Batavia (from 1942: Jakarta), put together a number of economic-historical-statistical publications in 1937–39, intended as preliminary studies for a work on the cultivation system (a system established in 1831–33 forcing peasants to grow specific export crops to be auctioned in Europe by the Dutch Trading Company). Before he could carry out the work, he was murdered by Indonesian extremists at Batavia, presumably because of his nationality.

1946–48 A follower of Tan Malaka [q.v. 1965–], **Muhammad Yamin** (1903–62), a lawyer, politican, writer, and nationalist historian, was involved in a 1946 coup attempt [q.v. 1983: Puradisastra]. In June 1946 he was arrested and later sentenced to four years' imprisonment but pardoned on Independence Day (17 August) of 1948. The arrest was related to his opposition to the willingness of the Republican forces to negotiate and compromise with the Dutch regarding the scope of Indonesian independence. From 1951 to 1962, he held many posts, including minister of education and minister of information. He wrote profusely on history and was called the foremost architect of the Indonesian view of history. In 1973 he was declared a national hero. Under Japanese rule he had been imprisoned.

1956–   Dutch teachers, including history teachers, were gradually expelled from Indonesia.

1965–66   The attempted coup of 30 September 1965 and its aftermath led to the loss of many important books and documents, especially in the Ministry of Foreign Affairs archives and the Ministry of Information library.

1965–   After the attempted coup, many Indonesian leaders who had shown a keen interest in history in their oral and written work fell into disgrace. Among them were **Sukarno** (1901–70), the former president (1945–67), who had already explained his ideas on history in his defense in December 1930, when he was tried for "subversive" action against the Dutch government, and **Dipa Nusantara Aidit** (1923–65), ideologue and Secretary-General (1951–65) of the Indonesian Communist Party (PKI), author of *A Short History of the Communist Party of Indonesia* (New Delhi 1955), who was assassinated. Sixteen years before, in 1949, another communist politician interested in history, **Tan Malaka** (1897–1949), nationalist, PKI leader, and dissident, a leader of the Murba Party, had been executed by the Indonesian Army.

At the time of the attempted coup, political scientist **A. Munandar** (?1924–) was a student in the German Democratic Republic (GDR) who sympathized with the PKI. He went into exile in the GDR and China, where he studied history but was unable to teach due to the Cultural Revolution. In 1985 he went to the Netherlands.

[1965?]   Historian **Sutjipto Wirjosuparto** (1915–71), dean of the Faculty of Arts (1961–64), University of Indonesia, Jakarta, whose historical works were often seen as an apology for Sukarno's Guided Democracy and Pancasila ideology, probably went into exile after 1965. From 1967 he had taught at the Australian National University, where he died in 1971 while giving a lecture.

1967–   Beginning in the spring of 1967, **Benedict Anderson** (1936–), political scientist and historian working at Cornell University, Ithaca, N.Y. (1967–)—first as a doctoral student in the Cornell Modern Indonesia Project (CMIP), then as a professor—was repeatedly denied a visa. He was twice expelled from Indonesia, in April 1972 (when he wanted to do research on the 1959–65 period) and August 1981 (when he was to have chaired a conference on polylingualism). After the first expulsion, he was blacklisted. The reasons were his coauthorship of *A Preliminary Analysis of the October 1, 1965, Coup* *in Indonesia*, an internal Cornell paper of January 1966 (eventually published in its original form in 1971) which became known in the press in March 1966, and his testimonies on human-rights abuses in Indonesia and East Timor before two subcommittees of the United States Congress in March 1976, February 1978, and January 1980, and before the United Nations General Assembly's Fourth Committee (Decolonization) in October 1980. Anderson is the author of *Imagined Communities: Reflections on the Origin and Spread of Nationalism* (1983, 1991). A 1972 essay of his, arguing that Suharto shared many Javanese conceptions with Sukarno, was censored when it was published in Bahasa Indonesia.

In December 1981 and April 1984, **Audrey Kahin**, another historian at Cornell University, did not receive a visa to do research into the history of West Sumatra. As early as 1975, when she was still a doctoral student, her application for a research visa had been delayed for several months. The reason was that her husband, **George McT. Kahin**, a political scientist with historical training and the CMIP director, had consistently backed the authors of the 1966 paper. The Kahins were taken off the blacklist in 1991.

1970s   **Adil Rakindo**, a researcher of the history and role of the Chinese in Indonesia, lived in exile in Western Europe.

1971   A book by **Slametmuljana** (1922–), professor of Bahasa Indonesia at the University of Indonesia and specialist in the history of the Srivijaya (675–1006 CE) and Majapahit (1293–1527) empires, was banned. In the book, *The Demise of the Hindu-Javanese Empires and the Birth of Muslim States in the Indonesian Archipelago* (Jakarta 1968), it was argued that Islam had been introduced to Indonesia from China and not from Arabia or India (implying perhaps that it was less "pure"). This 1968 study and a later one from 1976, both reportedly based on dubious sources, created a stir among Indonesian Muslims.

1972   In April a book by Australian journalist **Peter Polomka** (1934–), *Indonesia since Sukarno* (Harmondsworth 1971) was withdrawn from circulation and banned.

1973   *Romusha*, a film depicting the sufferings of Indonesians forced into hard-labor gangs during the Japanese occupation, which had already obtained the Indonesian Film Censorship Board's approval for distribution, was banned by the Indonesian Department of Information after strong pressure from the Japanese government.

1974–   In January 1974 **Soedjatmoko** (1922–89), journalist, socialist politician, historian, and former ambassador to the United States (1968–

71), was accused of being one of the "brains" behind a student-led riot against the visiting Japanese prime minister (the "Malari Affair"). After three weeks of intensive interrogation, he was released. Although Soedjatmoko was a special adviser to the Indonesian Planning Agency at the time of the affair, he was banned from traveling abroad for thirty months. He had his passport confiscated. Later he became rector of the United Nations University in Tokyo (1980–87). In 1943 he had already been imprisoned for organizing a student strike against the Japanese authorities. Upon his release he had been expelled from medical school and barred from enrolling elsewhere. He spent the next two years in virtual exile at his parents' home under surveillance of the Japanese military police. In 1947–52 he was a member of the Permanent Indonesian Delegation to the United Nations. In 1955 he served as adviser to the Indonesian delegation at the Conference of Bandung. In December 1957 he made a controversial statement at the national history seminar at Gadjah Mada University, Yogyakarta, which brought him into conflict with the nationalist historians. In the same year he refused to join Sukarno's new Cabinet and, as a result, he was reportedly blacklisted in official circles. During the same period, the Socialist Party was banned and the daily newspaper *Pedoman* and the weekly magazine *Siasat*, both of which he directed, were closed down. He remained effectively unemployed for almost four years. However, he was apparently a member of the Constituent Assembly in 1956–59. Although a major work such as *An Introduction to Indonesian Historiography* (1965) was completed under his direction in 1962, he increasingly moved away from historical writing.

At the time of the Malari Affair, **Deliar Noer** (1926–), political scientist, former member of Suharto's personal political advisory staff (1966), and president of the Jakarta Teacher's College (1974), was believed by the government to have harbored "independent ideas". As a result he was barred from "teaching at any university". He wrote about the Muslim movement in Indonesia from 1900 to 1942 and was independence leader Mohammad Hatta's biographer. He was also acting rector of the Universitas Nasional Jakarta.

1974   In August the Sixth Congress of the International Association of Historians of Asia, meeting at Yogyakarta, took place behind closed doors, at least officially at the beginning. According to one source, a paper entered as "The Biro Chusus of the PKI: Its Origin, Organization and Functioning" may have been responsible for this confidentiality. Neither the paper nor its author were present at the meeting in the end.

1975–   In March archeologist **I Made Sutayasa** (?1940–) was arrested at
            Jakarta airport when he returned from an archeology conference in
            Sydney, reportedly because ten years earlier he had been a member
            of the Balinese student movement Konsentrasi Gerakan Mahasiswa
            Indonesia, associated with the PKI. After his arrest he was dismissed
            from his post at the National Research Center of Archeology in mid-
            1975. In October he was transferred to a prison in Denpasar, Bali,
            without charge or trial.

1977–   In April the Indonesian Film Censorship Board banned *Saija dan
            Adinda* (or: *Max Havelaar*), a Dutch-Indonesian film directed by
            Fons Rademakers (1920–). The 1976 film, an adaptation of a novel
            by Multatuli (pen name of nineteenth-century Dutch writer Eduard
            Douwes Dekker), told the story of the corrupt and exploitative prac-
            tices of the local gentry under Dutch colonial rule in Indonesia. The
            board declared that the ban was imposed because the film created
            the impression that colonialism was good and that the people were
            exploited by the local gentry rather than the Dutch.

1981–   In May 1981 two historical novels of a quartet by journalist and
            writer **Pramoedya Ananta Toer** (1925–) were banned. The books,
            This Earth of Mankind (1980) and *A Child of All Nations* (1981),
            were stories about the early Indonesian nationalist movement in
            1896–1916, told by Pramoedya to his fellow prisoners on Buru Is-
            land in 1973 and written down in 1975 during his confinement
            without trial there. They were published after his release in late 1979
            and were highly successful during the months that they were allowed
            to circulate. The first printings of the novels (tens of thousands of
            copies) were sold out immediately, but further printings were
            banned, confiscated, or burned in Jakarta. Book reviews and letters
            to the editor were not allowed, and university libraries were forbid-
            den to buy or hold copies of the books. Students who circulated
            them clandestinely incurred long prison sentences. The attorney gen-
            eral claimed that the books represented a threat to security and order
            and that Pramoedya "had been able by means of historical data to
            smuggle in Marxist-Leninist teachings". The ban was reportedly also
            inspired by fear that analogies would be drawn between the historical
            abuses of power described in the quartet and those occurring at the
            time. Pramoedya and his publishers were arrested. Whereas Pra-
            moedya Ananta Toer was released after interrogation, his publisher
            spent several months in police custody. The remaining volumes of
            the quartet, *Footsteps* (1985) and *House of Glass* (1988), were im-
            mediately banned upon publication. The attorney general reportedly
            linked each of the four books with a precise category of leftist ide-
            ology: the first with bringing out the value of class struggle, the

second with advocating internationalism, the third with representing the *Communist Manifesto*, and the fourth with being a proponent of communist society. Pramoedya's history is one of house burning (October 1965); city arrest (1979–); harassment; manuscript confiscation or destruction (1947, 1965, 1979), including *A Preliminary Study of the History of the Indonesian Language*; archive and library destruction, including documentation for an encyclopedia (1965); and burning or banning of his work. He was detained and tortured under three different administrations: in 1947–49 under Dutch colonial rule as a nationalist revolutionary; in 1960–61 under Sukarno for publishing the popular history *The Chinese Question in Indonesia* (relaunched in 1998); in 1965–79 under Suharto for his leadership of the left intelligentsia from the late 1950s until 1965. Among his other books was *The Initiator* (1985), a political biography of Tirto Adhi Suriyo (1880–1918), the turn-of-the-century proto-nationalist journalist and protagonist of the above quartet, and a book on Kartini (1879–1904), a Javanese forerunner of the women's movement. He wrote many novels in prison.

1982–83   Journalist **Subagijo Ilham Notodidjojo** (1924–) reportedly omitted important but painful details from his historical biographies of such figures as S.K. Trimurti (1982) or Sudjono (1983).

1982   In January a book by **Siauw Giok Tjhan** (1914–81) carrying testimony on the 1948 and 1965 coups was banned because "it could arouse social unrest".

1982–   In October **Sunardi**, a lawyer who had made public requests in 1981 and 1982 to investigate allegations about Sukarno's role in the 1965 coup, was found guilty of slandering the president and sentenced to forty months' imprisonment.

1982–   *The Year of Living Dangerously*, a 1982 film by Australian director
2000   **Peter Weir** (1944–) about the 1965–66 killings, was banned. In 2000 it was screened to a sell-out crowd at the Jakarta International Film Festival. The Censorship Board released the film on the condition that its single showing would be to a private audience only.

1983   An article by **S.I. Puradisastra** (1923–) (pseudonym), suggesting that the popular General Sudirman, Republican Army chief commander during the Revolution (1945–49), had been sympathetic to the conspirators in the Tiga Juli affair (who wanted to push Prime Minister Sutan Sjahrir aside in 1946 because of his inclination to compromise with the Dutch [q.v. 1946–48: Yamin]), was banned.

1986–88   **Sugiarso Surojo** (1921–), a former intelligence agent with access to some secret documents, could not find a publisher for his controversial 1986 manuscript in which he accused Sukarno of planning the 1965 coup. He founded his own publishing company and published his book in 1988. The book provoked a storm of protest and its author was harassed and threatened with death. In 1988 **Bambang Siswoyo** (1950–) wrote a pamphlet to refute the assertion in the book but it was banned by the intelligence service.

1987   *Jakarta: A History* (Oxford 1987), by Australian academic **Susan Abeyasekere**, was banned because of its criticism of successive Indonesian governments.

1989   It reportedly took twenty-three years to translate an official account of the 1965–66 killings from English into Bahasa Indonesian. **Nugroho Notosusanto** and **Ismael Saleh**'s *Coup Attempt of the "September 30 Movement" in Indonesia* (1966) appeared as *Tragedi nasional: Percobaan Kup G30S/PKI di Indonesia* (G30S is a code for the September 30th Movement) in Jakarta as late as 1989.

Schools in Central Java were instructed to stop using three English-language encyclopedias, including *Human Heritage: A World Story* and *Encyclopaedia of Historic Places,* vol. 1 because "they contained items offensive to the Indonesian state."

1989–   In May the attorney general banned *Tan Malaka: The Struggle for the Republic*, a biography by Dutch scholar **Harry Poeze** (1947–), on the grounds that it might disrupt public order. He declared that the book, which had sold 2,700 copies by the time it was banned, could result in the spread of Marxist-Leninist teachings. It was still banned in 1995. Other books banned around the same time were *Chinese, Javanese and Madurese in the Context of the Founding of Surabaya*, a historical account of ethnic relationships in Surabaya; the Indonesian translation of *The United States and the Overthrow of Sukarno* by American scholar **Peter Scott** (1929–); *Respect for Those Who Have the Right: Bung Karno Was Not Involved in G30S/PKI* by **Manai Sophiaan** (1915–), a leader of the Indonesian Nationalist Party in the 1960s.

1990   The attorney general banned *Permesta, the End of Hope* (1988) by **K.M.L[umban] Tobing**, an account of the Permesta rebellion in Sulawesi during the late 1950s, because it "contained analyses that conflict with the work *Aspects of the History of Struggle of the National Army*, a work published by the armed forces.

One contributor to Robert Cribb ed., *The Indonesian Killings of 1965–66: Studies from Java and Bali* (Clayton 1990) preferred to remain anonymous.

In July a best-selling eyewitness testimony depicting Sukarno in a sympathetic light, *The Devious Dalang: Sukarno and the So-Called Untung Putsch* (1974)—transcripts of fourteen interrogations in 1970 about the 1965 events by former adjutant **Bambang Widja-narko** (1927–)—was classified as "unsuitable" for use in schools. It was banned because it "could generate feelings both for and against Bung Karno [Sukarno] and could tend to generate public disturbance/anxiety".

1991   In September the attorney general banned the circulation of four publications, including *Under the Red Lantern*, a study on the emergence of the Indonesian nationalist movement Sarekat Islam (Islamic Association; founded in 1909) by **Soe Hok Gie** (1942–1969), on the grounds of "religious incitement".

1993   In September the third volume of the four-volume series *Thirty Years of Indonesian Independence* (fifth edition; Jakarta 1981), covering the period 1965–73 and for which the authors had privileged access to the archives, was withdrawn because it contained two different and allegedly false versions of the 11 March 1966 *Surat Perintah Sebelas Maret (SuperSemar)*, a lost letter by which Sukarno transferred power to Suharto.

1994   In February *Schindler's List*, a film by **Steven Spielberg** (1947–) about the Holocaust, was banned because it contained nudity and violence scenes. The Indonesian Ulama Council and other Muslim leaders rejected the film as "Zionist propaganda". The film was also banned in Dubai, Egypt, Jordan, and Lebanon. It was first banned and then withdrawn from Malaysia. Thai and Philippine censors hesitantly approved the film.

In April writer and Protestant teacher of religion **Wimanjaya Liotohe** (1933–) was interrogated by the police in connection with *Prime Sin: Wimanjaya and the Indonesian People Accuse Suharto's Imperium* (1994), a collection of documents for submission during an intended lawsuit to accuse Suharto of being behind the 1965 move to overthrow Sukarno. The collection was banned in January, and Wimanjaya Liotohe, briefly arrested, faced up to seven years and four months' imprisonment for insulting the president, but he was eventually released. In September 1997 he nominated himself as vice president for the 1998 elections, but he was arrested on charges of insulting the president.

The book *The 30 September Movement: The Rebellion of the Indonesian Communist Party*, containing an anonymous official version of the 1965–66 killings and published in late 1994, had a small printing run, reportedly out of fear of arousing too much interest in communism.

1995   *Sintesa*, a publication of students at the political and social science department of Gadjah Mada University, was banned after featuring an article on the death toll following the 1965 coup attempt.

1996   In April *Shadows of the PKI* (1995), a collection of essays and transcripts of seminar presentations on the 1965 events published by the Institut Studi Arus Informasi (Institute for Studies on the Free Flow of Information), Jakarta, was banned because it "inverts or obscures facts on the history of G30S/PKI and includes tendentious explanations . . . that could lead [readers] to an erroneous viewpoint, leading the public astray and ultimately disturbing public order". The book included interviews with eyewitnesses and a contribution by historian **Ong Hok Ham** (1933–), until 1992 history professor at the University of Indonesia.

East Timor

1991   On 12 November **Kamal Bamadhaj** (?1971–91), a Malaysian student of Asian history and politics at the University of New South Wales, Australia, who had arrived in East Timor in October as an observer, was one of dozens of people killed when government troops opened fire on a peaceful procession at the Santa Cruz cemetery in the capital Dili. The procession commemorated a young man killed by government forces two weeks earlier. Bamadhaj was shot while he escaped from the cemetery. He was buried in a mass grave.

1997   On 11 November **Lynn Fredriksson**, an American freelancer covering a ceremony commemorating the 1991 massacre of civilians by the military, was expelled from East Timor.

Also see Australia (1996), Netherlands (pre-1945: Wertheim), Singapore (1998: Weir).

SOURCES

Ali, M., "Historiograhical Problems", in: Soedjatmoko et al., *An Introduction to Indonesian Historiography* (Ithaca 1965) 21–22.
Amnesty International, *Indonesia* (London 1977) 111–12.
———, *Power and Impunity: Human Rights under the New Order* (London 1994) 20, 22, 95.
———, *Report* (London) 1968–69: 27; 1977: 59–61, 68–69; 1980: 199; 1982: 200–201; 1983: 200; 1989: 178; 1998: 197.
Anderson, B., *Language and Power: Exploring Political Cultures in Indonesia* (Ithaca/ London 1990) 6–12.

————, "Radicalism after Communism in Thailand and Indonesia", *New Left Review*, November–December 1993: 9–10.

————, "Scholarship on Indonesia and Raison d'État: Personal Experience", *Indonesia*, October 1996: 2, 4–8, 10, 15, 17.

Anonymous, "Additional Data on Counter-Revolutionary Cruelty in Indonesia, Especially in East Java", in: Cribb ed. 1990: 169–76.

Article 19, *Information, Freedom and Censorship: World Report* (London) 1988: 143; 1991: 176–77.

————, *Surveillance and Suppression: The Legacy of the 1965 Coup in Indonesia* (Censorship News no.43; London 1995).

"Bibliographical Appendix: South-East Asian Historical Writing", in: Reid & Marr eds. 1979: 417.

Blussé, L., F.-P. van der Putten, & H. Vogel eds., *Pilgrims to the Past: Private Conversations with Historians of European Expansion* (Leiden 1996) 89–90.

Boia, L. ed., *Great Historians of the Modern Age: An International Dictionary* (Westport 1991) 610–11, 621–23.

Boyd, K. ed., *Encyclopedia of Historians and Historical Writing* (London/Chicago 1999) 30–31, 1344–45.

Bzzlletin, September 1981: 34–44 (Pramoedya).

Caldwell, M. ed., *Ten Years' Military Terror in Indonesia* (Nottingham 1975) 296.

Calvocoressi, P., *Freedom to Publish* (Stockholm 1980) 45.

Coolhaas, W.P., "Dutch Contributions to the Historiography of Colonial Activity in the Eighteenth and Nineteenth Centuries", in: Hall ed. 1961: 231–32.

Cribb, R., *Historical Dictionary of Indonesia* (Metuchen 1992) 498–99.

———— ed., *The Indonesian Killings of 1965–1966: Studies from Java and Bali* (Clayton, Victoria, Australia 1990).

————, personal communication, September 2000.

De Casparis, J.G., "Historical Writing on Indonesia (Early Period)", in: Hall ed. 1961: 147–48.

Dengel, H.H., "Indonesier schreiben ihre Geschichte: Tendenzen der Historiographie in Bahasa Indonesia", *Periplus*, 1991: 87.

————, *Neuere Darstellung der Geschichte Indonesiens in Bahasa Indonesia: Entwicklung und Tendenzen der indonesischen Historiographie* (Stuttgart 1994) 8–9, 16–17, 48, 52–54, 74, 77, 90–92, 97, 182, 228–29, 267–69.

"Flogging the Official Version", *Tapol Bulletin*, April 1995: 20–21.

Foulcher, K., "Making History: Recent Indonesian Literature and the Events of 1965", in: Cribb ed. 1990: 103.

Gorman, R.A. ed., *Biographical Dictionary of Marxism* (Westport 1986) 20–21, 322–23.

Hall, D.G.E. ed., *Historians of South-East Asia* (London 1961).

Human Rights Watch, *Academic Freedom in Indonesia: Dismantling Soeharto-Era Barriers* (New York 1998) 3, 6, 15, 21, 29, 45, 47–52 (quote Shadows PKI: 51–52), 69, 84.

————, *World Report* (Washington) 1997: 165; 1998: 433.

Index on Censorship, 3–4/72: 117; 4/73: 90; 2/78: 52; 5/78: 49–53; 1/81: 61–62; 5/81: 41; 6/81: 35–37; 2/82: 45; 1/83: 44; 3/85: 5; 4/86: 38; 7/87: 5; 9/88: 4, 37; 3/89: 37; 2/90: 37; 3/90: 37; 6/90: 38; 1/91: 36, 44; 9/92: 45; 3/94: 176; 3/95: 177; 6/95:

105, 176; 182; 3/96: 110; 4/96: 103; 6/96: 162–63; 2/97: 66–69; 1/98: 90; 3/98: 98; 1/01: 109.

Indonesia, 1990: 132–37 (Soedjatmoko).

International PEN Writers in Prison Committee, *Half-Yearly Caselist* (London 1997) 32.

Jones, R., "International Association of Historians of Asia: Sixth Congress, Held at Yogyakarta 26–30 August 1974", *Indonesia Circle*, November 1974: 17–18.

Klooster, H.A.J., *Bibliography of the Indonesian Revolution: Publications from 1942 to 1994* (Leiden 1997) 50, 416.

———, *Indonesiërs schrijven hun geschiedenis: De ontwikkeling van de indonesische geschiedbeoefening in theorie en praktijk 1900–1980* (Dordrecht 1985) 48–50, 89–94, 129–33, 159–61, 223.

———, "Muhammad Yamin en de geschiedenis van Indonesië", *Spiegel Historiael*, 1981: 609–13, 639.

———, personal communication, June 1999.

———, "Some Remarks on Indonesian Nationalist Historiography", in: G. Schutte & H. Sutherland eds., *Papers of the Dutch–Indonesian Conference Held at Lage Vuursche, the Netherlands, 27–28/6/1980* (Leiden/Jakarta 1982) 54–55.

May, B., *The Indonesian Tragedy* (London 1978) 334.

Newland, K., & K.C. Soedjatmoko eds., *Transforming Humanity: The Visionary Writings of Soedjatmoko* (West Hartford 1994) 5–15.

NRC Handelsblad, 22 January 2000: 33 (Munandar).

Oetomo, B., "Some Remarks on Modern Indonesian Historiography", in: Hall ed. 1961: 75–76, 78–79.

Poeze, H., personal communication, May 1995.

Pramoedya Ananta Toer, "My Apologies, in the Name of Experience" (originally Indonesian 1992), *Indonesia*, April 1996: 4, 9–11.

Reid, A., "The Nationalist Quest for an Indonesian Past", in: Reid & Marr ed. 1979: 290.

——— & D. Marr eds., *Perceptions of the Past in Southeast Asia* (Singapore 1979).

Roeder, O.G., & M. Mahmud, *Who's Who in Indonesia: Biographies of Prominent Indonesian Personalities in All Fields* (Singapore 1980) 275.

Termorshuizen, G., "De almachtige vrijheid: Pramoedya Ananta Toer, mens en schrijver", in: R.J.C. Cornegoor et al., *Literatuur in verdrukking* (Muiderberg 1983) 35–50.

Wertheim, W.F., "Indonesië herinnert zich 1965", *Politiek en cultuur*, 1995: 106–7.

Woolf, D.R. ed., *A Global Encyclopedia of Historical Writing* (New York/London 1998) 465–66, 980.

Wordt vervolgd, December 1997: 28 (Bamadhaj).

IRAN

Vital issues in Iranian historiography were Islam and secularism. During the reign of Shah Muhammad Reza Pahlavi (1941–79), the positions of both proponents and adversaries of Shiism were at stake. When a new regime took power in 1979, its leader, Ayatollah Ruhollah Khomeini, soon (in his New Year speech of 21 March 1980) ordered Iranians to forget the pre-Islamic past. A systematic campaign was launched against the Persian classical heritage. The Shahnameh

(Book of Kings; Iran's national epic) was banned; in special programs, the state-owned media tried to portray its heroes as "corrupt" and "irresolute". New history books depicted Iran's kings such as Cyrus the Great as "cruel tyrants". Great events of history were reportedly rewritten entirely in accordance with the Koran. Some historical monuments were destroyed either through neglect or while deliberately describing them as "relics of the Age of Idolatry". The plundering of museums and official or private collections reportedly resulted in a loss estimated at about 90 percent. Under Sadegh Gotbzadeh, Khomeini's "spiritual son", documentary films about the 1979 Revolution were doctored: all evidence that intellectuals and academics had participated in the revolution disappeared. The archives of the Iranian Radio and Television were destroyed, with the exception of certain revolutionary marches. Under the supervision of the Ministry of Islamic Guidance, the Assessment Department of the Central Office of Press and Publications monitored all historical publications.

pre-1946   On 11 March 1946, at the last session of preliminary hearings on charges brought against him, **Ahmad Kasravi** (1890–1946), historian of Shiism and Iran, jurist and polemicist against religion and Sufism, was murdered in Teheran by the Fedaiyan-e Islam (Devotees of Islam), a radical political group founded in 1945 to pursue the goal of an Islamic state. In 1911 Kasravi had left the clerical establishment because of his liberal ideas and modernistic tendencies and joined the constitutionalists. He worked at the Ministry of Justice (1919–29) but was forced to resign when as a judge he returned a verdict against the royal court in favor of a group of peasants. He briefly taught history at Teheran University, which he left in 1934 because he refused to retract his criticism of much of classical Persian literature. Among his many books were a history of Khuzistan (1933), a six-volume history of Azerbaijan (1934–40), a three-volume history of the Iranian Constitutional Revolution of 1905–11 (1940–42), and a study of the pre-Seljuk dynasties of northwestern Iran. He criticized the imams' power of intercession and the emphasis of Shiism on past issues and events irrelevant to current life. Kasravi and his group of supporters instituted an annual "festival of book burning" to destroy harmful writings which they had owned before joining the group. They met with violent opposition: some of Kasravi's books were banned; his supporters, united in the Azadegan Society (founded 1941), were often persecuted and socially ostracized. At the instigation of the speaker of Parliament and the Ministries of Education and Justice, Kasravi was charged with "slandering Islam" and called "the most notorious enemy of Islam". In 1944 Khomeini wrote an unsigned tract, *Secrets Exposed*, in which he attacked contemporary secularists such as Kasravi and his disciple Ali Akbar Hakamizadeh, a former cleric who had written the book *Secrets of a Thousand Years*, in which he tested the historical authenticity of the central Shii myths. Khomeini issued a *fatwa* (religious decree) against Kasravi for ridiculing Islam and many connected the fatwa with his assassination. Kasravi had already been the target of an assassination attempt in [April] 1945. Mohammad Sadr, prime minister from June to October 1945, had brought formal charges against him for propagating "heretical ideas". After Kasravi's death his body remained unburied for a number of days because no religious authority wanted to perform the funeral rites. A high military tribunal acquitted his two murderers.

1957–77   As a part-time student at Mashhad University, Mashhad, Khorasan (1956–59), the future sociologist and historian **Ali Shariati** (1933–77) was arrested in 1957, together with his father, for activities on behalf of "The God-Worshipping Socialists", a group trying to revive the National Front of former Prime Minister Muhammad Musaddiq (founded in 1951). Shariati was imprisoned for eight months. As one of the best students, he had the right to a scholarship abroad but he was not allowed to leave for a year. He completed his doctoral studies of religious history and sociology in Paris (1959–64). Upon his return to Iran in 1964, he was arrested at the border and imprisoned for six months without trial for importing banned books and for his oppositional activities in France, including his membership of the religious-nationalistic group Nihzat-i Azadi (Freedom Movement). After his release he applied for a teaching position at the faculty of arts, Teheran University, but as a politically suspect person he was turned down. In 1966 he became a professor of Islamic history at the Mashhad University history department. In 1970 he was dismissed because of his radical sociological approach to Islamic history and his free and popular methods of teaching. He was blacklisted and thus prevented from teaching at any Iranian university. In 1972 he was forced to move to Teheran, where he began lecturing at the Husainiya-yi Irshad, a progressive center for religious education. In his lectures, which had an enormous nationwide impact, he criticized the shah by means of historical comparisons with the pharaoh or the Umayyad Caliph Yazid. It took the secret police SAVAK six months to realize what was going on. His books were forbidden but they circulated secretly. In the fall of 1973, the center was closed down temporarily, probably because of the guerrilla activities of the Mudjahidin-i Khalq who were inspired by Shariati's ideas. Shariati went into hiding, but after some time he gave himself up in order to secure the release of his father, who was being held hostage. He was arrested for propagating "Islamic Marxism" and imprisoned without charge or trial. International pressure and the fact that his solitary confinement stimulated public interest in his writings led to his release after eighteen months in March 1975. Subsequently he was kept under strict surveillance in Mazinan, his home town in Khorasan, and barred from teaching and publishing. In late May or early June 1977, he was permitted to leave Iran for the United Kingdom, where he died on 19 June, possibly from a heart attack. The mysterious circumstances of his death, however, have led many to believe that the SAVAK was involved. He was buried in Damascus next to the mausoleum of Imam Husayn's sister. Many of his lectures were recorded and distributed on tape, transcribed, and published widely. During the shah's reign, thousands of Iranians were reportedly imprisoned and tortured for possessing his books or tapes. He was called "the Ideologue of the Iranian Revolution", but his strong criticism of the traditional Shii clergy (ulama) led to the banning of his works by the Khomeini government. In the mid-1980s his widow, a politically suspect person too, reportedly could not find employment as a teacher. Dozens of his followers were arrested. Three of them were executed in late 1992. Another, a refugee in Sweden, was abducted in February 1994 but was able to escape his interrogators. In 1995–97, despite official denials, at least ten of his Mudjahidin followers were serving long prison terms after unfair trials. In November 1998 translator and author Majid Sharif, a key member of the Committee for Research into the books of Dr. Shariati, was found dead.

pre-1962   The absence of outright Marxist histories in Iran was ascribed by one observer in 1962 to the political conditions in the country.

1977   In the course of a large-scale demonstration at Aryamehr University, Teheran, that was protesting the disruption of a meeting of the Writers' Association of Iran in November, **Homa Nateq**, history professor at Teheran University and member of the association, was questioned at a police station, then taken out of Teheran and ill-treated by SAVAK thugs, who also tried to rape her. Several years later, in February 1981, Nateq and Fereidun Adamiyat, also a history professor at Teheran University, were among the signatories of two public statements against the human-rights abuses and repression of intellectuals under the new regime.

1977–79   From late 1977 to February 1979 (the final collapse of the monarchy), hundreds of titles known as *cap-e safid* (with blank covers) were published in Iran, including many previously banned books on the political history of Persia.

[?]   For years a history of modern poetry in Iran by writer **Shams Langaroudi** [Javaheri Gilani] (1951–) had been banned.

1980s   The first part of the sixth volume of *Social History of Iran* by **Mor-
             teza Ravandi** was published in a volume which also contained a
             text, approved by the Ministry of Islamic Guidance, which dismissed
             Ravandi's views as un-Islamic.

1989–   On 14 February 1989, Khomeini issued a fatwa against **Salman
             Rushdie** (1947–), a writer who studied history at Cambridge Uni-
             versity (1965–68) and showed special interest in the history of early
             Islam and independent India. Muslims everywhere were asked to
             kill him and his publishers and translators for writing and publishing
             an allegedly blasphemous novel, *The Satanic Verses* (London 1988).
             Rushdie's statement of regret was rejected. The book was banned
             and burned in many countries, and Rushdie was forced to go into
             hiding (1989–). During the international debate following the fatwa
             it was remarked that the Islamic historian al-Tabari (839–923) had
             written about the "satanic verses" more than thousand years ago and
             not faced death threats. In September 1998 the government an-
             nounced that it dissociated itself from the fatwa and from the reward
             offered for the killing, but several senior religious figures and mem-
             bers of Parliament continued to support it. Indian-born Rushdie had
             written several historical novels before 1988, including *Midnight's
             Children* (1981; banned in India) and *Shame* (1983; banned in Pak-
             istan). 1997 BBC plans to make a five-part television serial *Saleem's
             Story*, based on *Midnight's Children*, were unsuccessful because In-
             dian and Sri Lankan authorities did not allow shooting the film in
             their territory after Muslims had protested earlier permissions.

1991–92   In order to monitor male-female contacts closely, the Sazman-e
             Miras-e Farhangi (Cultural Heritage Organization) strictly applied
             Islamic principles and instructed female archeologists not to engage
             in archeological activities outside a designated area. The effects of
             this restriction became so extensive that the universities canceled the
             excavation course for female students so that they lost one semester
             in the field. As a result women were appointed to work in museums
             only.

1994   In March liberal writer and historian **Ali Akbar Saidi-Sirjani** (died
             1994) was arrested together with another writer and publicly accused
             of drug abuse, brewing alcohol, homosexual acts, links with espio-
             nage networks, and receiving money from "counterrevolutionary"
             circles in the West. However, the real reason for his arrest appeared
             to be his 1990 open letters to Ayatollah Ali Khamenei, Khomeini's
             successor as Iran's spiritual leader, in which he had ridiculed Kha-
             menei, contested his claim to the rank of ayatollah, and demanded
             why all his—Sirjani's—books were lying "rotting in publishers' ware-

houses" (most of his writings were effectively banned). After his arrest he reportedly publicly renounced his former writings, including the open letters. In April 1994 an intelligence officer declared that he had confessed several capital offenses. He was held incommunicado until 27 November, when he reportedly died of a heart attack in a Teheran hospital. His family and friends claimed that he died because of medical neglect. In October 1997 poetess **Simin Behbehani**'s speech about, among others, Sirjani was interrupted at the Grand Hall of Art in Teheran, when the sound system was disconnected and lights switched off before she could finish.

1995– Beginning in September 1995, militant students from the Ansar-e Hezbollah (Partisans of the Party of God) intimidated **Abdolkarim Soroush** (1945–), philosopher and historian of philosophy and science, research fellow at the Institute for Research in the Humanities, and lecturer at Teheran University. They interrupted his lectures or prevented him from delivering them, including a May 1996 lecture at Amirkabir Technical University, Teheran. The Intelligence Ministry repeatedly summoned and threatened him. He was attacked by the clergy and in the press. In a 9 May open letter to President Hashemi Rafsanjani, he denounced this situation and wrote that no one dared to offer teaching posts to him and that he was allocated only one course (the philosophy of social sciences) at Teheran University. In one of his articles, he advocated that rationality, not religious jurisprudence, should be the basis for the organization of society and the running of government. Reputedly a moderate in the Shiite world, called by some the "Luther of Islam", Soroush was accused by militants of undermining religion under the guise of scientific discourse. In 1997 the Ministry of Information seized his passport, preventing him from attending academic seminars to which he was invited in Germany, Malaysia, and the United Kingdom. He was banned from teaching and warned that he faced possible imprisonment if he continued to speak his mind. He has been repeatedly harassed since.

1996– In 1996 **Karamollah Tavahodi** (?1927–), Kurdish writer, historian, and retired director of the university library of Mashhad, was arrested and held incommunicado until his trial. In January 1997 he was sentenced to one or two years' imprisonment for "propagating non-Islamic ties" following official objections to the content of volume five of his *Historical Movement of Kurds in Khorasan*, a book based on research into Kurdish tribal migrations from Kurdistan to Persian regions over four centuries ago. His files, the product of thirty years' research, were reportedly confiscated.

1998   In June hojatoleslam **Sayed Mohsen Saidzadeh** (1958–), cleric and writer, was arrested and held for four months without charge or access to counsel, presumably for advocating equal opportunities for women and for writing an article for the newspaper *Jameah* in which he constructed legal arguments for a progressive view of Islam. A judge in the revolutionary courts of Kermanshah until 1986, he became a scholar of Islamic law and in 1995 an adviser and researcher for the Ministry of Justice. He was the author of a two-volume local history of his hometown Qaen and he addressed many historical subjects. In October 1998 the Ministry of Islamic Guidance refused to allow publication of his new book, *Freedom of Women during the Time of Mohammad*, charging that the book showed disrespect to the Prophet. In December 1998 he was released but his status as a clergyman was rescinded.

     In July **Mohammed Reza Zaeri**, publisher of *Khaneh*, was arrested for publishing an anonymous letter criticizing Khomeini for having been responsible for the deaths of hundreds of thousands of youths during the Iran–Iraq war (1980–88) and causing Iran's international isolation by issuing a fatwa against Rushdie [q.v. 1989–]. He was fined and given a six-month suspended sentence.

2000   On 5 August Iranian authorities arrested hojatoleslam **Hassan Youssefi Eshkevari**, director of the Ali Shariati Research Center and author of several books on Iranian history, after his return from Berlin, where he had presented a paper on *Dictatorship and Its History*. He was held in solitary confinement for two months and tried in October before a Special Court for the Clergy on charges of apostasy and "being corrupt on earth", which carry the death penalty. By the end of 2000, his sentence had not been made known.

Also see India (1992: Hasan), United States (1953–59: Keddie; 1997: documents).

SOURCES

Abrahamian, E., "Kasravi: The Integrative Nationalist of Iran", *Middle Eastern Studies*, 1973: 274–79, 283, 287, 289–91.
———, *Khomeinism: Essays on the Islamic Republic* (London/New York 1993) 9, 124.
Akhavi, S., "Islam, Politics and Society in the Thought of Ayatullah Khomeini, Ayatullah Taliqani and Ali Shariati", *Middle Eastern Studies*, 1988: 404–30.
Amnesty International, *Iran: Human Rights Violations against Shi'a Religious Leaders and Their Followers* (MDE 13/18/97; London 1997).
———, *Iran: Official Secrecy Hides Continuing Repression* (MDE 13/02/95; London 1995) 14–15.
———, *Report* (London) 1990: 124; 1992: 145; 1993: 161, 163; 1994: 163, 165–66;

1995: 164–66; 1996: 179–80; 1997: 185–86; 1998: 201–2; 1999: 199–201; 2001: 130.

Appignanesi, L., & S. Maitland, *Het internationale Rushdiedossier* (originally in English; Amsterdam 1989) 13–17, 157–58.

Article 19, *Information, Freedom and Censorship: World Report* (London) 1988: 252, 254, 311; 1991: 171, 182, 212, 291, 360–61, 363.

Avery, P., G. Hambly, & C. Melville eds., *The Cambridge History of Iran*, vol. 7 (Cambridge 1991) 748, 752, 756–58, 868, 1023.

Bayat-Philipp, M., "Shi'ism in Contemporary Iranian Politics: The Case of Ali Shari'ati", in: E. Kedourie & S.G. Haim eds., *Towards a Modern Iran: Studies in Thought, Politics and Society* (London 1980) 155–68.

Benewick, R., & P. Green eds., *The Routledge Dictionary of Twentieth Century Political Thinkers* (London/New York 1992) 208–10.

Bosworth, C.E. ed., *Encyclopaedia of Islam*, (Leiden) vol. 4 (1978) 732–33, vol. 9 (1996) 328–29.

Boyd, K. ed., *Encyclopedia of Historians and Historical Writing* (London/Chicago 1999) 633–35.

Daneshvar, P., *Revolution in Iran* (Houndmills 1996) 83–85, 91, 207–8.

Farhang, M., "Resisting the Pharaohs: Ali Shariati on Oppression", *Race and Class*, Summer 1979: 31–40.

Haffenden, J., *Novelists in Interview* (London 1985) 231–53.

Hanson, B., "The 'Westoxication' of Iran: Depictions and Reactions of Behrangi, Al-e Ahmad, and Shari'ati", *International Journal of Middle Eastern Studies*, 1983: 1–23.

Human Rights Watch, *World Report* (Washington) 1997: 283; 1998: 330, 332, 436; 1999: 204, 355, 357, 436, 491; 2000: 354, 356–57, 504; 2001: 354, 381, 468, 528.

Index on Censorship, 2/78: 60; 5/78: 12–13; 3/81: 59–62; 3/83: 26–27; 6/83: 2; 10/88: 33, 42; 3/90: 1; 4/90: 9–25; 2/91: 34; 4–5/91: 10–11; 3/92: 18; 4/92: 3; 6/92: 28–29; 10/93: 40–41; 3/94: 176; 1/95: 7, 241; 2/95: 176–77; 6/95: 177; 4/96: 8, 104, 165–78; 6/96: 176; 5/97: 38; 1/98: 90, 100; 2/98: 93; 4/98: 160–62; 5/98: 88; 6/98: 97, 113; 1/99: 87; 2/99: 108; 4/00: 97; 1/01: 109; 2/01: 39; 3/01: 109.

International PEN Writers in Prison Committee, *Centre to Centre*, 2001, no.2: 3, 4.

———, *Half-Yearly Caselist* (London) 1997: 60, 65; 1998: 56.

Kazemzadeh, F., "Iranian Historiography", in: B. Lewis & P.M. Holt eds., *Historians of the Middle East* (London 1962) 431–34.

Keddie, N.R., *Roots of Revolution: An Interpretative History of Modern Iran* (New Haven/London 1981) 199–200, 202, 206, 215–25, 295.

Keesings historisch archief, 1989: 129–35, 169–74; 1999: 360.

Kielstra, N., "Alî Sharî'âtî: Voorloper van de Iraanse revolutie", in: R. Peters & R. Meijer eds., *Inspiratie en kritiek: Moslimse intellectuelen over de Islam* (Muiderberg 1992) 70–76.

Lewis, B., "Behind the Rushdie Affair", *American Scholar*, 1991: 185–96.

Manguel, A., *A History of Reading* (London 1996) 223.

Parameswaran, U., "Handcuffed to History: Salman Rushdie's Art", *Ariel*, October 1983: 34–45.

Pathak, R.S., "History and the Individual in the Novels of Rushdie"; M.M. Rao, "Time and Timelessness in Rushdie's Fiction"; S.B. Singh, "R. Wiebe, P. Scott, and

S. Rushdie: Historians Distanced from History", all in: *Commonwealth Review*, 1990: 118–56.

Sachedina, A., "Ali Shariati: Ideologue of the Iranian Revolution", in: J.L. Esposito ed., *Voices of Resurgent Islam* (New York/Oxford 1983) 192–96.

Simon, R.S., P. Mattar, & R.W. Bulliet eds., *Encyclopedia of the Modern Middle East* (New York 1996) 98.

Srivastava, A., " 'The Empire Writes Back': Language and History in 'Shame' and 'Midnight's Children' ", *Ariel*, October 1989: 62–78.

Steenhuis, A., *In de cakewalk: Schrijvers over de twintigste eeuw* (Amsterdam 1990) 247–56 (Rushdie).

Tucker, M. ed., *Literary Exile in the Twentieth Century: An Analysis and Biographical Dictionary* (Westport 1991) 589–96.

Wordt vervolgd, January 1998: 6–7 (Soroush).

World University Service, *Academic Freedom 3* (London 1995) 141, 155–56.

Yarshater, E. ed., *Encyclopaedia Iranica*, vol. 5 (Costa Mesa 1992) 139–40.

IRAQ

None of Iraq's governments, including the monarchy (1921–58), have permitted academic freedom. Professional academic work on modern history has been restricted severely. Most work has been written on the basis of information available abroad by scholars outside Iraq who could not or did not go there. Several historians were living in exile.

1963–70   When President Abd al-Salam Arif came to power (1963), **Taha Baqir** (1913–), curator at the Iraqi National Museum (1941–53), vice director (1953–58), and director (1958–) of antiquities, vice president of Baghdad University (1961–63), and an archeologist of Mesopotamia's pre-Islamic past who defended the theory of the cultural and ethnic continuity between ancient Mesopotamians and modern Iraqis, was relieved of all his posts and forced to retire. He spent the years 1965–70 in Libya and was then recalled by the Baath government (ruling since their July 1968 coup) and restored to his professorship at Baghdad University. In 1971 he became a member of the Academy of Sciences.

[1968]–   **Abdul-Aziz al-Duri** (?1919–), social-economic historian of Iraq and the Arab world, dean of the faculty of arts and science, University College of Baghdad (1949–58), professor of Islamic history [1961–65], and rector at Baghdad University (1963–68), went into exile after the Baath Party took power, reportedly because of his royalist sympathies. He went to Jordan, where he became a history professor at the history and archeology department of the University of Jordan, Amman, and member of the Royal Academy for Islamic Civilization

Research. Later he went to the Center for Contemporary Arab Studies at Georgetown University, Washington D.C.

Around the same time, archeologist and anthropologist **Abdul Jalil Jawad**, a specialist in northern Mesopotamian archeology, left Iraq and went to the Netherlands.

1968–   Among the historians marginalized after the Baath came to power were economic historian **Muhammad Salman Hasan**, historian of medieval Basra **Salih al-Ali**, and historical sociologist **Ali al-Wardi** (1913–). Al-Wardi was forced into retirement because he had emphasized the importance of Iranians in Iraqi history.

[?]   The works of Arab historian **Ibn Khaldun** (1332–1406) were banned for a while because of his critical comments on the Arabs, especially his alleged negative description of the Arabs before Islam.

1991   When in October a television channel of the Patriotic Union of Kurdistan started its broadcasts in Kurdish-controlled northern Iraq, once-banned histories and heroes were said to be among the topics treated in the programs.

1992–93   Eighteen tons of official state documents, especially from the secret police, captured by Kurdish parties in the March 1991 uprising (after the Gulf war) were shipped to the United States for safekeeping and analysis. They contained evidence of gross human-rights violations, including the use of chemical weapons, against the Kurds in the 1987–89 period, particularly during the 1988 Anfal campaign.

Also see Iran (1996–: Tavahodi), Syria (1966: Aflaq), United Kingdom (1953: Kedourie; 1984–92: Ponting).

SOURCES

Baram, A., *Culture, History and Ideology in the Formation of Ba'thist Iraq 1968–1989* (New York 1991) 51–52.

Esposito, J.L. ed., *The Oxford Encyclopedia of the Modern Islamic World*, vol. 1 (New York/Oxford 1995) 389–90.

Farouk-Sluglett, M., & P. Sluglett, "The Historiography of Modern Iraq", *American Historical Review*, 1991: 1408–9, 1421.

Gran, P., *Beyond Eurocentrism: A New View of Modern World History* (New York 1996) 79–80, 86.

Hamarneh, S.K., "A.A. Dûrî, an Outstanding Contemporary Arab Scholar", *Folia Orientalia*, 1974: 277–80.

Human Rights Watch, *Bureaucracy of Repression: The Iraqi Government in Its Own Words* (Washington 1994) ix–x.

Jawad, F., personal communication, February 1997.

Labande, E.-R., & B. Leplant, *Répertoire international des médiévistes* (Poitiers 1971) 222.

Lewis, B., *History Remembered, Recovered, Invented* (New York 1987) 79.

Who's Who in the Arab World (Beirut 1974–75) 1530 (al-Duri).

Wild, S., "Der Generalsekretär und die Geschichtsschreibung: Saddam Husayn und die irakische Geschichtswissenschaft", in: I.A. El-Sheikh, C.A. van de Koppel, & R. Peters eds., *The Challenge of the Middle East: Middle Eastern Studies at the University of Amsterdam* (Amsterdam 1982) 162, 164, 170.

Zimmerman, A., "Kurdish Broadcasting in Iraq", *Middle East Report*, July–August 1994: 21.

IRELAND

pre-1976   The first release of cabinet records of independent Ireland was delayed until 1976. The sensitive topic of the civil war (1922–23) following independence in 1921 contributed to the reluctance of successive governments to open official records.

2000   In March the Irish Censorship Board unbanned 420 books, including *Marriage Past, Present and Future: An Outline of the History and Development of Human Sexual Relationships* (London 1930), by **Ralph De Pomerai**, banned in 1931.

Also see United Kingdom (Northern Ireland: 1970s, 1988–94).

SOURCES

Fanning, R., "The Great Enchantment", in: C. Brady ed., *Interpreting Irish History: The Debate on Historical Revisionism 1938–1994* (Dublin 1994) 151.

Index on Censorship, 3/00: 15, 97.

ISRAEL & OCCUPIED TERRITORIES

The content of Palestinian history, especially where it conflicted with Israeli historical views and claims, was the main sensitive subject in Israel.

Palestine

1947–91   For decades access to the Dead Sea Scrolls—a collection of about six hundred Hebrew and Aramaic manuscripts from 200 BCE to 68 CE first discovered at Qumran, Jordan, in 1947—was severely restricted by a small international editorial committee appointed in 1953. Its de facto monopoly, considered unfair by many, was broken in September 1991 only, when a complete set of photographs of the scrolls was put at the disposal of scholars by the Huntington Library, San Marino, Calif., United States, and, consequently, the Israeli Antiquities Authority agreed to grant unrestricted access to the scrolls.

Israel & Occupied Territories

pre-1948   *See* previous page under Palestine heading.

1948–   The 1948 war led to the exile of **Abdel-Latif al-Tibawi** (1910–81),
            Palestinian historian and teacher on education and on the Middle
            East, and to his search for a new career in London. From 1931 to
            1948 he had held important posts, including that of a senior edu-
            cation officer. He went to work at the London University Institute
            of Education (1963–) and published about modern Middle Eastern
            history.

1960–   In 1960–61 in a cave in the Judean desert, general and archeologist
            Yigael Yadin (1917–84) recovered a set of thirty-five personal doc-
            uments concerning a Jewish woman, Babatha, who had fled the re-
            volt launched by the Jewish rebel Simon Bar Kokhba in 132–35 CE.
            The documents, indicating harmonious relations between Jews and
            Arabs in the territory south of the Dead Sea in postbiblical times,
            reportedly remained unpublished for nearly twenty-five years.

1964   Soon after his appointment as a visiting professor at Bar-Ilan Uni-
            versity, Ramat Gan, **Cecil Roth** (1899–1970), historian and former
            reader in Jewish Studies at Oxford University (1939–64), was ac-
            cused of unorthodoxy in a pamphlet which quoted a citation from
            his *Short History of the Jewish People* (1936) on doubts expressed
            by others about the historicity of Moses but omitting Roth's refu-
            tations of these doubts. Although supported by the university au-
            thorities and others, he suffered a heart attack and resigned from the
            university. He became, inter alia, chief editor of the *Encyclopaedia
            Judaica* (1966–70). Also a scholar with a special interest in Italy,
            he had been elected a member of Italian learned societies before
            1939 but he had resigned his membership as a protest against Mus-
            solini's anti-Jewish legislation (November 1938).

1967   The Palestine Archeological Museum and its library were confis-
            cated by the Israeli authorities.

1981   **Amin Madani**'s *Arab History and Geography* ([1971], [1976]), **Ab-
            duh Mubassir**'s *Sinai, the Place and History* (1978), and **Abdul-
            Kader Yassin**'s *Struggle of the Palestinian Arab People before
            1948* were banned in the West Bank, according to two lists issued
            in May and June. Similar lists existed for the Gaza Strip. Also pro-
            hibited were a *History of Jerusalem*, geography books containing
            maps of pre-1948 Palestine, and most accounts of Middle East his-
            tory by both Arab and European authors which took issue with Is-
            raeli policies toward the Palestinians. Palestinian history professors
            reportedly found it almost impossible to draw up course read-

ing lists without putting their students at risk. The condemned titles included works that "express, instill or foster Palestinian-Arab national feelings and national heritage". The works were deemed a risk to "public order and security". Concomitantly, little or no attention was paid to Palestinian history and culture in the Hebrew and Arab school curricula. However, the banned works on Palestinian history could allegedly be found in Israeli university libraries.

1981–   In September 1981 thousands of ultra-orthodox Jews held a demonstration in Jerusalem against the alleged desecration of graves at a major excavation in the city. Archeologists were seeking to uncover the biblical city of King David. One of the protesters, rabbi **Uri Blau**, was charged with illegal assembly and sentenced to three months' imprisonment with a six-month suspended sentence. Similarly, in August 1986, an important archeological project at Tel Haror in the Negev desert was vandalized, probably by members of Atra Kadisha, an ultra-orthodox group dedicated to preserving the sanctity of Jewish cemeteries.

1981   In December **Abdul-Wahhab Kayyali** (1939–81), Palestinian nationalist, historian, publisher, and author, was shot dead by unidentified gunmen (possibly members of a rival Palestinian faction) at his office in Beirut. As a child he had moved to Lebanon with his family in the late 1940s. He had been an Executive Committee member of the Palestine Liberation Organization (PLO) and a member of the Baath Party's Iraqi Regional Command (1970–77). He was the founder (1970) and director of the Arab Institute for Research and Publishing in Beirut and had been one of the leading publishers in the Middle East.

1982–   In September 1982, concomitantly with the Sabra and Shatila massacres, the Israeli army occupied and looted the Palestine Research Center in West Beirut and shipped its archives to Tel Aviv. They also destroyed rare pre-1948 historical documents and the private libraries and homes of Lebanese and Palestinian personalities. In February 1983 the center was bombed, killing more than twenty persons. The attack was believed to be the work of the Phalangist security forces of Lebanese president Amin Gemayel. In June the Lebanese authorities closed the center. On 19 December 1984, Resolution 38/180B of the 38th United Nations General Assembly condemned Israel for seizing and taking away archives and documents concerning Palestinian history and culture during its 1982 occupation of Beirut (adopted with 121 votes for, 1 against, and 20 abstentions). The archives were later returned.

1983–   In May 1983 Palestinian poet **Sami Kilani**, living in Yaabad, was taken to the military court in Nablus, West Bank, for publishing a collection of poetry, *A New Promise to Iz al-Din al-Oassam*. The reference in the title and in one poem to Syrian-born Izzedin al-Qassam (1882–1934), the first leader of the Palestinian revolution in 1934 killed in a clash with British troops in Yaabad, was called "inciting". In 1984 Kilani was under town arrest in his village.

1983   On 22 October an exhibition of the Palestinian Heritage was opened at Bethlehem University. The Israeli authorities confiscated the exhibit material because it allegedly incited to anti-Israeli hatred. The university authorities were surprised by the confiscation and by the fact that the Israelis had arrested the whole student council on 27 October after a violent student demonstration against the confiscation. When the students became concerned about the fate of their arrested colleagues, they threw stones on 1 November. This led to an intervention of the Israeli army. On 2 November (Balfour Day, named after the British Balfour Declaration of 2 November 1917, which officially approved a "Jewish national home" in Palestine) the Israeli authorities ordered the university to close for two months.

1985   Historian **Basir Sulayman** was dismissed from an-Najah University, Nablus. In his book *Another History* (1985) he argued that the period of the fifth Umayyad caliph, Abd-al Malik (685–705), was more important to Islamic history than the preceding periods and that the Koran had to be treated as a historical source. The book was banned in the West Bank and in Jordan.

1988   In March an international conference at Birzeit University, West Bank, on "Two Decades of Occupation" was obstructed by a refusal to allow its keynote speaker **Edward Said** (1935–), professor of English and comparative literature at Columbia University, New York (1963–), critic of orientalism and imperialism, and member of the Palestine National Council (1977–91), to enter Israel. In 1984 Said had allegedly been threatened with death by Fatah dissidents within the PLO for his viewpoint that a more realistic strategy was needed after the PLO's exit from Beirut in 1982. Born into a Palestinian Christian family in Jerusalem, Said left Palestine in 1948 at the onset of the war. He studied English and history at Princeton University and comparative literature at Harvard University.

In July the Israeli authorities closed the Arab Studies Society in East Jerusalem for one year and put its director **Faisal Husseini** under administrative detention for six months. The society (founded 1980) provided information about, inter alia, Palestinian history. Its archives section collected materials and leaflets issued in Palestine since 1918. The authorities apparently held the opinion that the archives were collected for purposes of inciting unrest.

1989   Among the books banned at Ketziot detention camp in October were *The Story of Mankind* (1921) by the Dutch-American historian of culture **Hendrik Willem van Loon** (1882–1944), and *August 1914* and *Cancer Ward* by **Aleksandr Solzhenitsyn** (1918–). Among those banned in the Occupied Territories was *Studies in the History of Palestine during the Middle Ages* by **P.P. Bartholdy**.

1991   Television and radio directors were ordered by the general director of the Israeli Broadcasting Authorities to replace the Arabic names of villages and sites in the Occupied Territories with their ancient biblical ones. The Occupied Territories themselves had to be called by their Hebrew names Judea and Samaria, and pre-1967 border demarcations were no longer allowed on maps.

1992   On 19 January American archeologist **Albert Glock** (died 1992), head of the archeology department of Birzeit University and co-founder of its Archeological Institute, was killed by an unidentified gunman in Birzeit. The investigations by both the Israeli authorities and the PLO into the murder, which remained unsolved, were deemed by some to be unsatisfactory. Glock had challenged the political use of archeology by Israel.

1993–94 Academics with West Bank and Gaza identity cards were banned from specialized libraries and archives, conferences, seminars, bookshops, and numerous cultural institutions in Jerusalem.

1995   Occupied Territories: *see* next page under Palestinian Authority heading.

1995   Prime Minister Yitzhak Rabin rejected calls for an investigation into allegations that Israeli soldiers killed Egyptian prisoners during the 1956 and 1967 wars. Egypt demanded a full inquiry.

1998   In March and April, **Ronit Weiss-Berkowitz** received death threats from Jewish extremists for her contribution to a twenty-two-part television series *Tekuma* (Rebirth) marking Israel's fiftieth anniversary and analyzing Israel's history from 1936 to 1995. Her views on the fate of the Arab population after Israel's foundation in 1948, the confiscation and administration of their territories, and the Palestinian refugee problem since 1948 challenged the traditional Israeli view of history.

2000   The Minister of Justice Yossi Beilin denied a request by **Benny Morris** (1948–), a historian working at Ben-Gurion University, Beersheba, to release 1948 excised cabinet statements and other classified documents which could throw light on the nature of the exodus (was it an expulsion or not?) of more than 600,000 Arabs during the 1948 war. Classified documents are to be released after forty years, but state archivist Evyatar Frizel said that opening the material would harm Israel's foreign relations (particularly the negotiations with the Palestinians). Morris wanted the documents for revisions of his book *The Birth of the Palestinian Refugee Problem 1947–1949* (Cambridge 1987).

Teddy Katz (?1943–), a historian who studied at Haifa University, was sued for libel by the Organization of Veterans of the Alexandroni Brigade (a Hagana militia) after his study on a forgotten massacre in the village of Tantura on 15 May 1948 (the day Israel came into being) had implicated the brigade in the killings of 200 villagers.

Palestinian Authority

pre-1948 *See* page 299 under Palestine heading.

1948–95 *See* pages 300–304 under Israel & Occupied Territories heading.

1995 In December **Maher al-Alami**, a senior editor at the Arabic-language daily *al-Quds* was summoned for questioning in Jericho and detained for six days, apparently because he put a story on page 8 and not on the front page. The story was about the Greek Orthodox patriarch granting President Yasser Arafat, PLO chairman and head of the Palestinian Authority, symbolic custody of Christian holy sites in Jerusalem by likening him to seventh-century Caliph Umar (634–44) who delivered Jerusalem to Islam. After a personal reprimand from Arafat, al-Alami was released.

1996– In April 1996 **Wael Ali Farraj** (?1975–), history student at the Islamic University in Gaza, was arrested by members of the General Security Services. He had his house searched. He was interrogated about his membership in Hamas (an Islamist political movement) and possession of weapons. During the first three days of his detention, he was hooded, severely beaten, and deprived of sleep and food. He was detained in solitary confinement without charge or trial. In August 1997 Farraj was moved to Gaza Central Prison, where his treatment improved. The attorney general's office informed his father that it could not intervene because his case was "political". Although the High Court of Justice ordered his immediate release in February 1999, he remained in detention.

1999– Among eleven academics and critics arrested in November 1999 for signing a petition which accused the Palestinian political leadership of corruption and political mismanagement was **Abd al-Sattar Qas-**

sim (?1949–), professor of history or political science at An-Najah National University, Nablus. He was arrested by the General Security Services and held in Jericho. In December his documents and papers were confiscated during a house search. In January 2000 he was released without charge. He was rearrested in February. Although the High Court of Justice ordered his immediate release in July, he remained in detention. Qassim had also been shot in 1995 after writing an article criticizing Arafat.

2000   Said [q.v. 1988] criticized Palestinian Authority history textbooks for obliterating the history of post-1948 Palestinian-Israeli relations with the aim of not disturbing the Oslo peace process.

Also see Egypt (1976–78: Porten), France (1960: Massignon; 1984: Sternhell), Syria (1975–: Ebla); Turkey (1978–85: Armenian genocide), United Kingdom (1994–: Zuroff), USSR (1948: Ehrenburg, Grossman).

SOURCES

American Association for the Advancement of Science, Human Rights Action Network, *Case Number PA9915*, 9 December 1999.
———, *Report on Science and Human Rights*, 1991, no. 13/1: 2.
Amnesty International, *News*, November 1998: 7.
———, *Palestinian Authority Defying the Rule of Law: Political Detainees* (MDE 21/03/99; April 1999) 14.
———, *Report* (London) 1982: 332; 1996: 187; 2000: 187; 2001: 187.
———, *Urgent Action 319/99* (15 & 20 December 1999, 10 January 2000), *50/00* (25 February & 24 July 2000).
Annual Obituary 1981 (Chicago/London) 657–58 (al-Tibawi), 734 (Kayyali).
Article 19, *Information, Freedom and Censorship: World Report* (London) 1988: 265, 269, 298; 1991: 376.
Baigent, M., & R. Leigh, *The Dead Sea Scrolls Deception* (London 1991) xi–xix, 82–83, 225–36.
Bowersock, G.W., "Palestine: Ancient History and Modern Politics", in: Said & Hitchens eds. 1988: 185–86, 190.
Boyd, K. ed., *Encyclopedia of Historians and Historical Writing* (London/Chicago 1999) 866, 1043–44.
Button, J., *The Radicalism Handbook* (London 1995) 293–94.
Christian Science Monitor (WWW-text, 3 January 2001).
Glock, A., "Archaeology As Cultural Survival: The Future of the Palestinian Past", *Journal of Palestine Studies*, 1994, no.3: 70–71, 79.
Gush Shalom, *New Historian Teddy Katz Needs Help* (WWW-text; Tel Aviv 2000).
Human Rights Watch, *World Report* (Washington) 2000: 366; 2001: 353, 358, 395–96.
Index on Censorship, 6/80: 63; 5/81: 39–40; 4/82: 25; 5/83: 45; 4/84: 33–35; 3/86: 36–37, 41; 9/88: 4–5; 3/90: 28; 1/91: 42; 6/95: 177; 2/96: 73, 98; 3/98: 76–77; 4/98: 115; 1/00: 100; 2/00: 108; 3/00: 102–3.
International PEN Writers in Prison Committee, *Half-Yearly Caselist* (London 1998) 58.
Keesing's Record of World Events, 1984 (CD-rom version) (Palestinian archives).

"Israel in Lebanon: Excerpts from the McBride Report", *Race and Class*, Spring 1983: 469–70.

Nawas, J.A., "De moderne Arabische geschiedbeoefening: Problemen en praktijk", in: R.B. van de Weijer, P.G.B. Thissen, & R. Schönberger eds., *Tussen traditie en wetenschap: Geschiedbeoefening in niet-westerse culturen* (Nijmegen 1987) 149.

Nazzal, N.Y., & L.A. Nazzal, *Historical Dictionary of Palestine* (Lanham 1997) 175.

New Encyclopaedia Britannica: Micropaedia, vol. 3 (London 1994) 937–38.

Palestinian Center for Human Rights, *Press Release*, 1 March 1999.

Renfrew, C., & P. Bahn, *Archaeology: Theories, Methods and Practice* (London 1991) 465, 481.

Roberts, A., B. Jörgensen, & F. Newman, *Academic Freedom under Israeli Military Occupation: Report of WUS/ICJ Mission of Inquiry into Higher Education in the West Bank and Gaza* (London 1984) 48, 55–56, 65.

Roth, C. ed., *Encyclopaedia Judaica*, vol. 14 (Jerusalem 1971) 326–27.

Said, E., "Dark at the End of the Tunnel", *Al-Ahram Weekly*, (WWW-text, 20–26 July 2000).

―――, *The Politics of Dispossession: The Struggle for Palestinian Self-determination 1969–1994* (London 1994) xxv–xxvi, xxxii, 71–72, 119.

Said, E., & C. Hitchens eds., *Blaming the Victims: Spurious Scholarship and the Palestinian Question* (London 1988) 17.

Silberman, N.A., "Lure of the Holy Land", *Archaeology*, November/December 1990: 31.

Trigger, B.G., *A History of Archaeological Thought* (Cambridge 1989) 184.

Tucker, M. ed., *Literary Exile in the Twentieth Century: An Analysis and Biographical Dictionary* (Westport 1991) 598–601.

Woolf, D.R. ed., *A Global Encyclopedia of Historical Writing* (New York/London 1998) 790.

World University Service, *Academic Freedom* (London) 1990: 89; 1995: 168; 1996: 213.

ITALY

Fascism and its consequences, including the exile of several historians, appeared to dominate the historiographical landscape long after 1945.

pre-1945   Among the historians and others concerned with the past who emigrated before 1945 (and living in exile after 1944) were **Giorgio Levi Della Vida** (1886–1967), **Roberto Lopez** (1910–86), **Arnaldo Momigliano** (1908–87), **Gaetano Salvemini** (1873–1957), and **Lionello Venturi** (1885–1961) and his son **Franco Venturi** (1914–94).

1945   In February **Piero Pieri** (1893–1979), a military historian at Turin University (1939–74), and his entire family were arrested and briefly imprisoned by the special "black police" of Benito Mussolini's Nazi-backed Italian Social Republic Salò (September 1943–April 1945).

1946   After five years of silence, the *Rivista storica italiana* resumed publication under the directorship of Giorgio Falco (1888–1966) and Federico Chabod (1901–60). Chabod, professor at Rome University

(1946–60), director of the Croce Institute in Naples, historian of the Renaissance and postunification Italy, had helped his then-teacher Salvemini [q.v. pre-1945] to escape in 1925 and played an important role as a leader of the Piedmontese partisan movement. He actively supported his colleagues who had fallen out of grace after the November 1938 race laws (for example, he reemployed the dismissed ancient historian **Mario Attilio Levi** [1902–], a student of Gaetano De Sanctis (1870–1957), and arranged the publication of some of his studies under a pseudonym). Chabod became president of the International Committee of Historical Sciences (1952–60).

1926–47   The *Quaderni del carcere (Selections from the Prison Notebooks*, 1971), thirty-four notebooks written in prison between 1929 and 1935 by political and cultural theorist, historian, philosopher, co-founder and leader of the Italian Communist Party **Antonio Gramsci** (1891–1937), were smuggled out of prison and later published in, inter alia, the twelve-volume *Opere di Antonio Gramsci* (Turin 1947–72; *Collected Works*). Imprisoned from November 1926 to April 1937, Gramsci died one week after his release.

1981   In July American author **Robert Katz** (1933–) was convicted of defaming Pope Pius XII (1876–1958) in his book *Death in Rome* (New York 1967) and sentenced to thirteen months' imprisonment. He was released on bail pending an appeal. The defamation charge was brought by a niece of the pope, who denied the truth of Katz's claim that the pope had been aware of wartime Nazi plans to take reprisals against Italian partisans for the killing of German SS soldiers and had done nothing to prevent them.

1996   A Molotov cocktail was thrown at the house of historian **Renzo De Felice** (1929–96), founder-editor of the journal *Storia contemporanea*, biographer of fascist leader Mussolini, and professor of the history of political parties and movements at the University of Rome.

1997   In May **Giuseppe Segato**, an amateur historian with allegedly secessionist views on Venetian history, was briefly detained after the campanile (belltower) of the San Marco square was occupied by separatists inspired by his historical theories. With their action the eight separatists wanted to commemorate the fall of the Venetian Republic in May 1797, which put an end to more than a thousand years of Venetian autonomy. In July 1997 they received sentences of up to six years and a fine for this and other actions.

2000   In November Francesco Storace, a member of the far-right Alleanza Nazionale, voted for the creation of a commission to evaluate history textbooks in the Lazio region. This sparked a controversy because professional historians feared that it was the first step of a process in which right-wing political parties would demand the end of the antifascist paradigm, a condemnation of the communist experience and a reevaluation of the Republic of Salò which fought against the partisans after the 1943 armistice.

Also see Israel (1964: Roth), Libya (1977: al-Zawi).

SOURCES

Boia, L. ed., *Great Historians of the Modern Age: An International Dictionary* (Westport 1991) 389–92, 406, 420–22.

Boyd, K. ed., *Encyclopedia of Historians and Historical Writing* (London/Chicago 1999) 192–94, 292–93, 481–82, 776, 918–19.

Bruch, R. vom, & R. A. Müller eds., *Historikerlexikon: Von der Antike bis zum 20. Jahrhundert* (Munich 1991) 50–51, 87.

Burguière, A. ed., *Dictionnaire des sciences historiques* (Paris 1986) 387–88.

Cannistraro, P.V. ed., *Historical Dictionary of Fascist Italy* (Westport 1982) 114, 253–54, 557.

Davis, J.A., "Modern Italy—Changing Historical Perspectives since 1945", in: M. Bentley ed., *Companion to Historiography* (London/New York 1997) 593.

Erdmann, K.D., *Die Ökumene der Historiker: Geschichte der internationalen Historikerkongresse und des Comité international des sciences historiques* (Göttingen 1987) 324.

Frankfurter Rundschau, 16 November 2000: 2.

Galtung, J., & S. Inayatullah eds., *Macrohistory and Macrohistorians: Perspectives on Individual, Social, and Civilizational Change* (Westport 1997) 128–32.

Gorman, R.A. ed., *Biographical Dictionary of Neo-Marxism* (Westport 1985) 178–83.

Index on Censorship, 5/81: 45; 1/01: 13–14.

Keesings historisch archief, 1997: 764.

NRC-Handelsblad, 28 May 1996: 10 (De Felice); 13 May 1997: 7 (Segato).

Salomone, A.W., "Federico Chabod: Portrait of a Master Historian", in: H.A. Schmitt ed., *Historians of Modern Europe* (Baton Rouge 1971) 262–64, 271–74.

———, "Italy", in: G. Iggers & H.T. Parker eds., *International Handbook of Historical Studies: Contemporary Research and Theory* (London/Westport 1979) 242–45.

Visser, R., personal communication, May 1997.

Woolf, D.R. ed., *A Global Encyclopedia of Historical Writing* (New York/London 1998) 151–52, 374–75, 477.

IVORY COAST

1982–92   In February 1982 **Laurent Gbagbo** (1945–), history lecturer, director at the Institut d'Histoire, d'Art et d'Archéologie Africaines, National University of Abidjan (1981–82), and student-union and teacher-union activist since 1969, circulated a suppressed speech on democracy and the advantages of a multiparty system that he had intended to deliver. He may have been arrested. The cancellation of the lecture entitled "Youth and Democracy on the Ivory Coast" sparked off student unrest in February and led to several retaliatory measures by the government against universities and secondary schools. Gbagbo went into self-imposed exile in France for more than six years. In September 1988 he returned to Ivory Coast. In December he was summoned to a meeting and reprimanded by President Félix Houphouët-Boigny for unspecified subversive activities. In November 1989 the socialist opposition party Front Populaire Ivoirien (Ivorian Popular Front) that he had cofounded in 1982 was legalized and challenged Houphouët-Boigny in the October 1990 elections, the first since independence in 1960. In February 1992 he and his wife were arrested with other opposition party leaders because they were held responsible for the riots that had followed antigovernment student demonstrations earlier that month. These had been organized because Houphouët-Boigny had refused to accept the findings of a commission of inquiry into a military raid on Yopougon University campus in May 1991. In March 1992 Gbagbo was sentenced to two years' imprisonment for "acts of violence and destruction of public property" despite his parliamentary immunity. In protest, all other opposition members of Parliament resigned. In July Gbagbo was released after the National Assembly had adopted an amnesty law. In October 2000 he became president of Ivory Coast after controversial elections. Gbagbo had also been imprisoned in 1969 and 1971.

Also see Nigeria (1970–84: Ojukwu).

SOURCES

Amnesty International, *Report 1993* (London 1993) 104–5.
Index on Censorship, 3/82: 45–46; 5/92: 35; 6/92: 35; 9/92: 43.
Keesing's Record of World Events (CD-rom version).
Mundt, R.J., *Historical Dictionary of the Ivory Coast* (Metuchen 1987) 72.

J

JAMAICA

1968   On 15 October **Walter Rodney** (1942–80), a Marxist history lecturer
from Guyana at the University of the West Indies, Kingston, since January, was refused reentry in Jamaica after having attended a Black Writers' Conference in Montréal and was sent back to Canada. As a history
lecturer, he had organized many popular off-campus lectures for non-
academic audiences, including Rastafarians and the urban poor, in which
African history and the concept of Black Power were discussed. This
was considered a security threat to the government. The vice chancellor,
however, refused to terminate his contract and therefore Rodney was
served with a banning order. His writings were banned. In the wake of
the ensuing student protests, serious riots (known as the Rodney Riots)
took place on 16 and 17 October. The university was kept under a state
of siege for over a week. In an emergency debate in the House of Representatives broadcast live throughout Jamaica on radio and television,
Prime Minister Hugh Shearer accused Rodney of communist views.

Also see Guyana (1974–96: Rodney).

SOURCES

Payne, A., "The Rodney Riots in Jamaica: The Background and Significance of the
Events of October 1968", *Journal of Commonwealth and Comparative Politics*,
1983, no.2: 158–74.

JAPAN

Since the adoption of the Fundamental Law of Education (1947), the Ministry
of Education has screened all history textbook manuscripts at primary and sec-

ondary school levels. This screening system tightened after the adoption of two laws in 1956 and 1963. Many believed that the textbook authorization system (*kentei seido*), in conjunction with other measures such as textbook selection, national examinations, and teacher job rating reports, led to a narrow and centralized view of the past. Sensitive topics in Japanese historiography included the emperor, the royal family, and their relationship to Shintoism; the national flag and anthem; the foundation of the nation; the 1889 Meiji Constitution; the Korean Independence Movement of 1 March 1919; armed forces atrocities during the Pacific War (1931–45), such as the invasion of China by the Japanese Imperial Army in the 1930s, the December 1937 Nanking (Nanjing) Massacre, and the bacteriological experiments of Unit 731 at Harbin; the conscription of Koreans and Chinese into forced labor in Japan during 1939–45; the 1941 Russo-Japanese nonaggression pact; the question of the "comfort women", and the 1945 battle of Okinawa.

pre-1945   Among the historians censored or persecuted during World War II (including 1945) were **Hani Goro** (1901–83) and British historian **Charles Boxer** (1904–2000).

1939–45   During World War II, the Marxist *Rekishigaku Kenkyukai* (Society for Historical Study) or *Rekken* was suppressed. Virtually no publication in the historical field appeared in 1943–45.

1945–   At the end of the Pacific War and shortly thereafter, the Japanese government and military authorities destroyed many official documents relating to their wartime crimes. This contributed to the denial by many Japanese of the 1937 Nanking Massacre (Nanking was the capital of the Chinese nationalists). For example, a mass meeting on "Did the Nanking Atrocities Really Happen?", held in Tokyo in June 1994, maintained that the massacre was fabricated by the International Military Tribunal for the Far East (1946–48).

1945–52   In September 1945 officials of the Education Ministry issued detailed orders to amend wartime textbooks. Following this order teachers and students all over Japan deleted objectionable passages in wartime textbooks with ink and scissors as they saw fit. From late October 1945, the Supreme Commander for the Allied Powers (SCAP) gradually asserted control over the textbooks, culminating in a total ban on the use of wartime textbooks on Japanese history on 31 December 1945. The first postwar history textbook was published by the Education Ministry in October 1946: it contained no glorification of militarism, ultranationalism, and Shintoism. SCAP censors also distrusted anything they associated with "feudalism": therefore they banned sword-fight films, samurai dramas, and 98 Kabuki theater plays; anthologies of medieval poetry were scrutinized for signs of ultranationalist sentiments; depiction of Mount Fuji, long the object of Shintoist nature worship, was not allowed. Only scientific texts about the A-bomb were allowed to be published: as late as 1949, the film project *No More Hiroshimas* was canceled because SCAP objected to scenes that depicted the sufferings caused by the A-bomb; in 1950 the title of a painting had to be changed from *Atomic Bomb* to *August 6, 1945*.

1945–   After the war the study of expansion history underwent a long crisis because of its connection with prewar nationalism and expansionism. Most prewar historians of expansion refrained from writing about it.

After Japan's surrender, all historical research at Taihoku Imperial University (later National Taiwan University) was interrupted and the Japanese staff was repatriated. Historian **Yanai Kenji** (1910–), a specialist in Japanese-Philippine relations and the history of Kyushu, was forced to leave his research notes behind.

Among the historians purged from public life by SCAP was historian and journalist **Tokutomi Soho** (1863–1957), for his support to the wartime government. A Class A war-criminal suspect, he was put under house arrest only because of his age. He renounced all his previous honors and positions. Around 1895 Tokutomi's position had moved from liberalism to imperialistic nationalism. His newspaper was twice (1905, 1913) put to the torch by mobs angered by his support for the government. In 1911 he was appointed to the House of Peers (1911–45). He wrote the one-hundred-volume *History of the Japanese Nation in Early-Modern Times* (1918–52). After the war Meiji Shoin publishers refused to publish the last twenty-four volumes because of SCAP's objections, but another publisher was found.

1945–50s   Historian **Itazawa Takeo** went into self-chosen seclusion because his writings as the chair of Japanese history and director of the Historiographical Institute at Tokyo University during the war had reportedly been colored by war propaganda. In the 1950s he was called back and began teaching at Hosei University, Tokyo. On a more general level, as late as 1955, almost no academic historian at Tokyo University reportedly covered post-1868 history.

1946   SCAP banned *The Japanese Tragedy*, a film by left-wing director **Kamei Fumio** which criticized the emperor's wartime role, after Prime Minister Yoshida Shigeru had complained that the film was subversive.

1963–   In 1963 the Education Ministry refused to approve the fifth revised edition of a high-school history textbook *A New History of Japan*, written by **Ienaga Saburo** (1913–), history professor at Tokyo Kyoiku (Education) University (1949–77) and specialist in Japanese cultural and legal history. Ienaga was asked to modify about three hundred items, although almost all these items had appeared in the same form in the first edition. This first version, approved in 1953 (after having been rejected in 1952), had been used constantly for a decade. In June 1965 Ienaga filed a suit, the first of a series known as the kyokasho saiban (textbook cases). In these cases he challenged the official textbook authorization system as an unconstitutional transgression of his freedom of expression, his academic freedom, and the children's right to education. In the June 1965 suit, he sought compensation for damages from the ministry for not approving his textbook and asked the screening system to be declared unconstitutional. He maintained that the suit was the first of its kind in the world.

It became the longest-running case in Japanese legal history, with court decisions in July 1974, March 1986, March 1993, and May 1994. In June 1967 he filed a second, administrative suit to have the rejection of his textbook repealed. Court decisions came in July 1970, December 1975, April 1982, and June 1989. After the July 1970 decision had ruled that screening, if interfering with textbook contents, constituted censorship and was unconstitutional and illegal, right-wing extremists threatened the judge, Sugimoto Ryokichi, and Ienaga and his lawyers. The decision was later overruled.

In January 1984 Ienaga filed a third lawsuit concerning the unacceptable and increasingly severe textbook screening procedures. He argued that officially approved textbooks showed a fundamental bias. In 1980 the ministry had demanded the revision of nearly four hundred items in the new edition of a Japanese history book that he had submitted for approval. Another factor that contributed to his decision to file this third suit was the 1982 history textbook controversy [q.v. 1982]. Court decisions in the case were taken in October 1989, October 1993, and August 1997. Ienaga partially won his case in 1997, when the Supreme Court ruled as illegal the deletion of references to Unit 731 activities and the 1937 Nanking Massacre. At the same time, it upheld the ministry's constitutional right of textbook screening, arguing that it did not constitute censorship because it did not prohibit the book from being published commercially. The court declared that the Education Ministry's power had been abused in expunging cases of well-documented atrocities from textbooks. From the beginning Ienaga received wide and organized support from many researchers and educators and from the Japan Teachers' Union (which regularly published a critique of textbooks in use). In [1992], for example, 500 Japanese historians signed an appeal for fairness in the textbook cases.

One of Ienaga's supporters was **Munakata Seiya**, whose history textbooks were also censored and who was asked by his publisher to resign. Another historian active in protests and lawsuits directed against the government was a student of Hani Goro [q.v. pre-1945], **Inoue Kiyoshi** (1913–).

While a student at the Tokyo University history department (1934–), Ienaga had written many articles for the journal of the Shigakkai (Historical Society), but ultranationalistic students had reportedly edited these articles and changed the arguments in one of them without his permission so as to present diametrically opposing views from those in the original version. Later they had rejected his protests. After graduation (1937), Ienaga worked at the Institute of Historiography of Tokyo University. An article of his had been accepted by *Rekishi Chiri*, a journal edited by some institute members. Because of its ideological position, however, he had been asked to withdraw it and he had reportedly regretfully complied. In 2001 Ienaga was nominated for the Nobel Peace Prize.

1975   **Nozue Kenji**, was accused of treason after publishing a book about the Hanaoka Incident (on 30 June 1945) in which many Chinese slave workers died during a rebellion. During the twenty years of research for the book, he and his family were frequently threatened. He later wrote three other books on the subject.

1981   **Kojima Yoshio**, professor of modern Chinese history at Nihon University, Tokyo, and five others submitted the draft of a world history textbook to the Education Ministry. Under pressure from the ministry, the authors reluctantly changed the word *shinryaku* (invasion) to *shinnyu* (infiltration) in connection with Japan's activities in Korea in the second half of the sixteenth century. A ministry examiner reportedly told the authors that descriptions which might give Japan a bad image were undesirable.

[1981]   A textbook manuscript by **Uno Shunichi**, professor of modern Japanese history at Chiba University, Chibashi, was criticized by an Education Ministry examiner for its "one-sided" description of the 1937 Nanking Massacre. Uno was instructed to place the description in a footnote. He also had to revise a section concerning the Japanese seizure of land in Korea in 1908.

1982   From 26 June, when the Japanese press reported on a new generation of history textbooks, to 24 November, an international controversy took place. Picking up the news from the Japanese press, many Asian countries, led by South Korea and China, disputed the ways in which these new textbooks portrayed Japanese military imperialism in Asia (1910–45). On 26 July China lodged an official protest, and in South Korea widespread anti-Japanese demonstrations broke out. One of the points raised in the debate was the extent to which foreign governments could interfere in the writing of a country's national history. On 26 August, the Japanese government announced that it would correct the textbook accounts and that the textbook authorization criteria would be revised. Korea and China accepted this promise. In September Japanese students clashed with riot police at demonstrations in which grievances were expressed over various issues, including the revision of history textbooks. In November a new policy for textbook examination and authorization was adopted with, however, several exemptions. During the controversy it was noted that the initial press reports which sparked off the controversy were partly mistaken: the press reported that in connection with the war in China the word *invasion* in the original manuscript of one high school world history textbook had obligatorily been changed into *advance*. Verification showed that the reports were wrong in this respect.

1986   In September Minister of Education **Fujio Masayuki** was dismissed after a controversial remark in an interview with *Bungei Shunju* magazine whitewashed Japan's 1910 annexation of Korea. He also said that the 1937 Nanking Massacre was "just part of war", that the number killed had been highly exaggerated, and that the 1946–48 International Tribunal was a "racial revenge" intended to "rob Japan of her power". The remarks were made in the context of a discussion of Japan's high school textbooks.

1987   A textbook manuscript, *New Edition: Japanese History*, written by the private group "National Congress to Protect Japan" and compiled under the direction of historian **Murao Jiro** was approved by the Education Ministry on the condition that some eight hundred "inappropriate" expressions be revised. The authors reluctantly made some changes after protests from China, North and South Korea, Hong Kong, and the Philippines about its contents, which, these countries thought, distorted history from a conservative viewpoint, for example by denying or justifying the excesses of Japanese militarism. The textbook was subsequently approved and used in the schools. Murao had served as a textbook examiner in the Education Ministry (1956–75) and appeared as a government witness in the suits of Ienaga [q.v. 1963–].

1988   In January scenes of Japanese troops committing atrocities against
             unarmed Chinese during the 1937 Nanking Massacre were deleted
             from the first showing in Tokyo of *The Last Emperor*, a 1987 film
             by **Bernardo Bertolucci** (1940–) about China's last emperor, Pu
             Yi. After complaints from Bertolucci and the British producer, the
             thirty-second cut was restored by the Japanese distributors, Sho-
             chiku Fuji.

             In October a Japanese publisher announced that he would delete a
             chapter on Japanese atrocities in Malaysia during World War II
             from a forthcoming English-language textbook for high school stu-
             dents. This apparently happened after pressure from a group of Lib-
             eral Democratic Party politicians demanding that the Education
             Ministry withdraw certification for the textbook because the chapter
             was "inappropriate from the point of view of proper education".

1988–90   In January 1990 mayor of Nagasaki, **Motoshima Hitoshi**
             (?1923–), was shot and seriously injured apparently by right-wing
             extremists. Motoshima had received death threats for publicly rais-
             ing the question of Emperor Hirohito's war guilt in December 1988.
             Other politicians as well as publishers and writers who debated the
             late emperor's behavior and actions were also threatened by far-
             right groups.

1989   In January a BBC television documentary about Emperor Hirohito
             discussing his complicity in war crimes was shown in the United
             Kingdom and later attacked by the Japanese Foreign Ministry as
             "historically of no value whatsoever". Japanese television networks
             were reportedly "too scared" to broadcast the program, and Japa-
             nese participants in it had received death threats from extreme right-
             wing groups.

             A Japanese publisher who wanted to publish a Japanese translation
             of the biography *Hirohito: Behind the Myth* (1989) by journalist
             and historian **Edward Behr** (1926–) was threatened and withdrew
             the plan. A Japanese version was eventually published in [1995].

1993–98   In 1993 **Takashima Nobuyoshi** (?1942–), former teacher of social
             studies in Tokyo and writer of many textbooks, later professor at
             Ryukyu University, sued the state because after revision the Edu-
             cation Ministry had proposed to change almost the entire text of
             his four-page manuscript about Emperor Hirohito, the Japanese
             army, Japanese colonialism, and the Gulf War (1991), to be in-
             cluded in a reader. He had already faced problems with textbook
             certification in 1989 and 1992. In April 1998 a district court ruled
             that two changes in his textbook demanded by the ministry were

illegal. One passage quoted philosopher Fukuzawa Yukichi (1835–1901), who described other Asian nations as "savage", the other stated that Japan should have consulted other Asian countries before sending minesweepers to the Persian Gulf in 1991. The court ordered the ministry to pay damages to Takashima.

1993–94   The authors of the textbook manuscript *The History of the World B* were pressured to change two passages on the 1937 Nanking Massacre chosen by historian **Kasahara Tokushi**. The authors amended the sections but were still attacked in some press articles in 1993 and 1994. In April 1994 another textbook, *Japanese History for High School B*, was approved, but the Education Ministry required eight revisions on the 1937 Nanking Massacre afterward, allegedly as a result of pressure from a member of Parliament.

1994   In April two armed men held newspaper executives hostage for six hours at the newspaper *Asahi Shimbun* in Tokyo in protest against the paper's coverage of the 1946–48 International Tribunal which, they said, blasphemed the spirits of the dead. The men surrendered after riot police surrounded the building.

           In May Justice Minister Nagano Shigeto was forced to resign for saying to the newspaper *Mainichi Shimbun* that the 1937 Nanking Massacre was a fabrication and that Japan was not an aggressor in World War II.

1995–96   In February 1996 New Zealand author **James Mackay** received death threats from an anonymous man in an apparent attempt to prevent publication of his forthcoming book on Japanese war crimes. In late 1995 Mackay had reportedly refused bribes to cancel the book.

1996   In March curators at the Atomic Bomb Museum, Nagasaki, removed controversial photographs and texts from an exhibition. Items depicting the 1937 Nanking Massacre and the Bataan Death March (Philippines) were replaced by pictures of victorious Japanese soldiers and the 1941 attack on Pearl Harbor. The items, introduced at a late stage to give a balanced overview of the war, were removed after a formal protest from conservative city council members. In June the museum replaced a picture of the 1937 Nanking Massacre by order of the mayor. The prime minister instructed the Foreign and Education Ministries to investigate whether photographs of Japanese military aggression in museums around Japan were real or fabricated.

1997   In a January article, the newspaper *Yomiuri Shimbun* accused the Kanagawa Human-Rights Center of "oppressing freedom of speech" because the center had protested local politicians' statements on Korean "comfort women" and the Japanese colonization of Korea.

In [May] an elementary school history textbook was reportedly banned in the Miyagi prefecture because of its presentation of the Sino-Japanese war and the 1937 Nanking Massacre.

In [December] no cinema in Tokyo was willing to screen the film *Don't Cry Nanjing*, a 1995 China–Hong Kong coproduction depicting the 1937 Nanking Massacre. The first showing went ahead in Nagoya on 8 December to an audience of thirty.

2000   The Chinese government repeatedly expressed indignation to Japan for allowing a conference entitled "The Biggest Lie of the Twentieth Century: Documenting the Rape of Nanking" to proceed in January in Osaka. Osaka officials refused to halt the conference "because it would infringe the constitutional right of free speech". The government, while confirming that the massacre occurred, said it was a matter for Osaka authorities to decide.

Also see China (1949–: Feng Ziyou; 1993: Liu Taiheng), Germany (1945–50), Indonesia (1973: Romusha; 1974–: Soedjatmoko), Korea (1987–: Chang Ui-gyun), United States (1995: exhibit), USSR (1982: Batrovin).

SOURCES

Albada, J. van, " 'Memory of the World': Report on Destroyed and Damaged Archives", *Archivum*, 1996; no.42: 20, 92.

Amnesty International, *Human Rights Are Women's Right* (London 1995) 53–56.

Article 19, *Information, Freedom and Censorship: World Report 1991* (London 1991) 178–82.

Bellah, R.N., "Ienaga Saburô and the Search for Meaning in Modern Japan", in: M.B. Jansen ed., *Changing Japanese Attitudes toward Modernization* (Princeton 1965) 369–423.

Blussé, L., "Japanese Historiography and European Sources", in P.C. Emmer & H.L. Wesseling eds., *Reappraisals in Overseas History* (Leiden 1979) 194, 196–97, 209–10, 217.

Blussé, L., F.-P. van der Putten, & H. Vogel eds., *Pilgrims to the Past: Private Conversations with Historians of European Expansion* (Leiden 1996) 216.

Boia, L. ed., *Great Historians of the Modern Age: An International Dictionary* (Westport 1991) 453–54.

Brownlee, J.S. ed., *History in the Service of the Japanese Nation* (Toronto 1983).

Buruma, I., *The Wages of Guilt: Memories of War in Germany and Japan* (New York 1994) 51, 100, 113–14, 119, 126, 176, 189–201, 249–50, 285–87, 318.

Caiger, J., "Ienaga Saburō and the First Postwar Japanese History Textbook", *Modern Asia Studies*, 1969, no.1. 1–8.

Cogan, J.J., & R.E. Weber, "The Japanese History Textbook Controversy . . . and What We Can Learn from It", *Social Education*, 1983: 253–57.

Dore, R.P., "Textbook Censorship in Japan: The Ienaga Case", *Pacific Affairs*, 1970: 548–56.

Elsevier, 11 December 1993: 54–61 (Takashima).

Guardian Weekly, 22 August 1982: 6 (Unit 731).

Hall, J.W., "Historiography in Japan", in: H.S. Hughes ed., *Teachers of History* (Ithaca 1954) 297.

Hérail, F., "Les Révisions de l'histoire nationale par les Japonais", in: G. Gadoffre ed., *Certitudes et incertitudes de l'histoire* (Paris 1987) 105–14.

Herzog, P.J., *Japan's Pseudo-Democracy* (Sandgate 1993) 196–217.

Horio, T., *Educational Thought and Ideology in Modern Japan: State Authority and Intellectual Freedom* (Tokyo 1988) 171–212.

Human Rights Watch, *World Report 1999* (Washington 1998) 197.

Huntsberry, R., " 'Suffering History': The Textbook Trial of Ienaga Saburō", *Journal of the American Academy of Religion*, 1976: 239–54.

Ienaga, S., "The Historical Significance of the Japanese Textbook Lawsuit", *Bulletin of Concerned Asian Scholars*, 1970, no.4: 3–12.

———, *Japan's Last War: World War II and the Japanese, 1931–1945* (originally Japanese 1968; Oxford 1979) 254–56.

———, "War in Japanese Education", *International Security*, Winter 1993/94: 123–28, 130–32.

Index on Censorship, 5/82: 9; 3/83: 34–36; 5/86: 6; 4/88: 37; 1/89: 36; 3/89: 37; 1/90: 38; 4/90: 36; 7/91: 17; 3/94: 177; 3/95: 68–71; 3/96: 111; 5/96: 94; 2/97: 9; 4/97: 116; 6/97: 114; 2/98: 94; 3/98: 48–52; 4/98: 115; 2/00: 104.

Iwao, S. ed., *Biographical Dictionary of Japanese History* (Tokyo 1978) 497–98.

Kasahara, T., "Control of Expression in Japan and the Historians' Struggle against It: The Case of the Nanking Massacre" (paper presented at the 18th International Congress of Historical Sciences; Montréal 1995) i, 4–8.

Keesings historisch archief, 1998: 259.

Kim, P.S., "Japan's Bureaucratic Decision-Making on the Textbook", *Public Administration*, 1983: 283, 288–94.

Kodansha Encyclopedia of Japan, vol. 3 (Tokyo 1983) 261.

Miura, S., "Don't Leave History to the Historians", *Japan Echo*, 1982, no.4: 29–35.

Nagahara, K., "Reflections on Recent Trends in Japanese Historiography", *Journal of Japanese Studies*, 1984, no.1: 180–82.

National League for Support of the School Textbook Screening Suit, *Truth in Textbooks, Freedom in Education and Peace for Children: The 28 Year Struggle of the Ienaga Textbook Lawsuits* (Tokyo 1993).

Osiel, M., *Mass Atrocity, Collective Memory, and the Law* (New Brunswick/London 1997) 190.

Pyle, B.K., "Japan Besieged: The Textbook Controversy", *Journal of Japanese Studies*, 1983: 300.

Shermer, M., & A. Grobman, *Denying History: Who Says the Holocaust Never Happened and Why Do They Say It?* (Berkeley 2000) 231–37.

Sinh Vinh, "The Achievement of a Nationalist Historian: Tokutomi Sohō (1863–1957)", in: Brownlee ed. 1983: 145, 148.

Tchoubarian, A.O., "Power, Liberty, and the Work of the Historian (The Implications of Political, Economic, and Cultural Controls on the Organization of Historical Research and Publication)", in: 18th International Congress of Historical Sciences, *Proceedings* (Montréal 1995) 144–48.

"Textbook Flap: Editor's Comment", *Japan Echo*, 1982, no.4: 15–16.

Tiedemann, A.E., "Japan Sheds Dictatorship", in: J.H. Herz ed., *From Dictatorship to Democracy: Coping with the Legacies of Authoritarianism and Totalitarianism* (Westport/London 1982) 194.

Uyenaka, S., "The Textbook Controversy of 1911: National Needs and Historical Truth", in: Brownlee ed. 1983: 113–14, 119–20.

Woolf, D.R. ed., *A Global Encyclopedia of Historical Writing* (New York/London 1998) 444–45, 468–69, 486–87, 893.

Yamanouchi, Y., "Japan", in: G. Iggers & H.T. Parker eds., *International Handbook of Historical Studies: Contemporary Research and Theory* (London/Westport 1979) 271.

Yamazaki, M., "History Textbooks That Provoke an Asian Outcry", *Japan Quarterly*, 1987: 51, 55.

Yayama, T., "The Newspapers Conduct a Mad Rhapsody over the Textbook Issue", *Journal of Japanese Studies*, 1983: 307–10.

JORDAN

1956   When the Department of Antiquities on the West Bank was transferred to Amman after Jordan's annexation of the West Bank in 1948, its British director [name unknown] was dismissed. He was considered a "holdover" from the mandate period (1918–46).

Also see Indonesia (1994: Spielberg), Iraq (1968–: al-Duri), Israel (1947–91: Dead Sea Scrolls; 1985: Sulayman).

SOURCES

Glock, A., "Archaeology As Cultural Survival: The Future of the Palestinian Past", *Journal of Palestine Studies*, 1994, no.3: 77.

K

KAZAKHSTAN

pre-1991   *See* Union of Soviet Socialist Republics (USSR).

[1996]   **Karasaev Khusein**, a writer about Kazakh epic storytellers, was imprisoned as a member of the "Social Turan Party", a party which was reported not to exist.

1998   In May the procuracy opened an investigation into allegations that the Kazakh mass media had committed 273 violations of the Press Law in 1997, including "incitement of national enmity . . . aimed at instigating disputes and controversy over the country's history and sovereignty".

2000–01   On 6 July 2000, retired historian and dissident **Karishal Asanov** wrote an article critical of President Nursultan Nazarbayev in the opposition weekly *SolDat*, printed in Russia. Although the issue containing the article was seized by Kazakh customs police and never distributed within Kazakhstan, a trial for defamation of the president was started against Asanov and *SolDat*'s chief editor in March 2001. On 3 April Asanov was acquitted for lack of evidence. The chief editor was sentenced to one years of imprisonment, but immediately pardoned under a presidential amnesty. The court ordered that the 6 July print run of *SolDat* be burned. In 1992–93 Asanov had already been charged with insulting the president. After a trial, retrial, and appeal, he was acquitted.

SOURCES

Amnesty International, *Report* (London) 1993: 178; 1994: 181.
Human Rights Watch, *World Report* (Washington) 1997: 365; 1999: 270; 2001: 300–301.
Index on Censorship, 5/00: 100–101; 3/01:111.
International Press Institute, *Ifex Alert*, 14 March and 18 April 2001.

KENYA

The interpretation of Kenya's colonial history and independence movement, particularly the Mau Mau rebellion (1952–56), was the predominant subject of debate among Kenyan historians, the conclusions of which had implications for the legitimacy of the leadership.

British Kenya

pre-1963–   Many official records on the Mau Mau rebellion were destroyed before and after independence.

Kenya

1977–   On 31 December 1977, the Marxist-inspired novelist and playwright **Ngugi wa Thiongo** (born James Ngugi) (1938–), educated in the history of English literature and language at Makerere University College, Kampala, Uganda, and head of the department of literature, Nairobi University, was arrested and detained "for reasons of public security" without charge or trial in Kamiti Maximum Security Prison at Kiambu. This followed the ban on a play in Gikuyu on which he collaborated, *I Will Marry When I Want*. It dealt with the issue of *kamatimu*, the Kenyans who collaborated with the colonial administration by serving in the Home Guard during the Mau Mau rebellion. It also treated the struggle over land between a peasant farmer and a rich landowner. In the words of a government official, it "promoted the class struggle". On 2 October 1977, the twenty-fifth anniversary of the declaration of the anti–Mau Mau emergency, the play's premiere had taken place. Shortly after the play was staged, a strike in the local shoe factory broke out. On 16 November its performance license was revoked on the grounds that it was "too provocative, would make some people bitter and was opening up old graves". The arrest was probably linked also with Ngugi's 1977 novel *Petals of Blood*. The 1977 staging of another play on which he collaborated, *Mzalendo Kimathi*, about the trial of Mau Mau leader Dedan Kimathi (1920–56), was also controversial. During Ngugi's arrest, part of his private library was confiscated. On 6 January 1978, his detention was announced. For two weeks there was no news about his whereabouts and neither his pregnant wife nor his lawyer was allowed to see him. He was allegedly ill-treated in prison during the first months. From the books sent to him in prison, some, such as *Kenya from Within: A Short Political History* (London 1927) by **William MacGregor Ross**, discussing British colonialism in Kenya in the 1920s, *Roots* (Garden City 1976) by **Alex Haley** (1921–92), and *The Second Word: More Essays on Kenyan History* by Ochieng [q.v. 1985–86], were returned to the senders. Ngugi was released on 12 December 1978 in an amnesty for political prisoners, two months after the inauguration of President Daniel arap Moi. One of the many who had pleaded for his release was historian Ali Mazrui, who had written a letter to President Jomo Kenyatta (January 1978) and a paper *The Detention of Ngugi wa Thiongo: Report on a Private Visit* (April 1978; published in 1990). Nairobi University, which had advertised Ngugi's position as vacant following his arrest, did not reinstate him despite a petition signed by 400 academics. In March 1979 Ngugi was briefly rearrested. His family was harassed, he remained unemployed, and his books were removed from the school reading lists. While in prison he wrote a novel in Gikuyu on toilet paper, in 1982 published as *Devil on the Cross: Free Thoughts on Toilet-Paper.* About his prison experience he wrote *Detained: A Writer's Prison Diary* (1981), banned in Kenya. In February 1982 the performances of *Mother, Sing for Me*, a 1981 musical play dealing with colonial repression and rebellion in the 1930s and showing historical slides, were canceled because they received no license. The theater was broken up by the police in March. In June 1982 Ngugi went to the United Kingdom to promote *Devil on the Cross* and, on learning of his impending arrest in Nairobi after an attempted coup during his absence, asked for asylum there. In August 1984 his views on the Mau Mau rebellion were attacked at a conference of the Historical Association of Kenya. As an exile he founded the London-based association Umoja (Unity) in 1987, which stood for a radical redistribution of land. Later he went to the United States and became a professor of comparative literature at New York University. His first novels, *Weep Not, Child* (1964), *The River Between* (1965), and *A Grain of Wheat* (1967), also dealt with Mau Mau (in 1955 his family house and village had been razed in an anti-Mau Mau campaign). In January 1969 he had resigned as a lecturer in English at University College, Nairobi (1967–69) in protest against Kenyatta's suppression of academic freedom but he had resumed teaching there in 1971.

1981–89   In May 1981 the passports of twelve lecturers, including **David Mukaru Nganga**, lecturer in history and development studies at Nairobi University, and **E.S. Atieno-Odhiambo** (1946–), lecturer at the Nairobi University history department, were seized as a result of campus riots. Mukaru Nganga, who was also a staff union's executive officer, had already been arrested earlier in 1981 for "abusing the chair of the Muranga County Council". In June 1982 a group of five lecturers, including Mukaru Nganga, was arrested after Moi had accused certain unnamed lecturers of "teaching subversive [Marxist] literature aimed at creating disorder in the country". Mukaru Nganga had published critical research about the Mau Mau rebellion and publicly stated that Kenyans had the right to form a political party. He was dismissed and detained without charge or trial under the Preservation of Public Security Act (PPSA). Released in April 1984, he was rearrested under the PPSA in April 1986 while preparing to leave Kenya for a teaching position at Dar-es-Salaam University, Tanzania. Held incommunicado, he was not officially detained until July. His continued detention was allegedly motivated by official displeasure over his suit against the government for torture and illegal detention. He was reportedly pressed to withdraw his case in return for release but he refused to do so. In June 1989 he was released. In December 1992 Mukaru Nganga was the presidential candidate for the radical opposition party Kenya National Democratic Alliance. Atieno-Odhiambo was arrested in May 1986 and released without charges in June. He went to the United States.

1982–89   On 3 June 1982, five police officers of the Criminal Investigation Department (CID) searched the house of **Maina wa Kinyatti** (1944–), Marxist senior lecturer (1975–82) and leading University Staff Union member at the history department, Kenyatta University College, Nairobi, without warrant in his absence. They confiscated many books and personal files, including unpublished manuscripts on the history of the Kenyan independence struggle and Mau Mau. The next day he was arrested when he reported to CID headquarters. He was charged with possessing a one-page student leaflet entitled *Moi's Divisive Tactics Exposed* (April 1980)—which did not advocate violent overthrow of the government. He claimed that the leaflet had been inserted later among the papers removed during the search. In early June he was interrogated under severe duress, inter alia, about his historical research. He was held in custody in Nairobi Remand Prison without bail for more than four months. During his trial in late September and early October, he was held in the prison's maximum security section reserved for "criminally insane" inmates. There he contracted a serious eye disease. During the trial the leaflet was not read out and his book *Thunder from the Mountains: Mau Mau Patriotic Songs* (Nairobi/London 1980; some songs of which were used in *Mzalendo Kimathi* by Ngugi [q.v. 1977–]) and an unpublished manuscript in a file entitled "Current History of Kenya 1979–80" were cited to support the case for conviction. *Thunder from the Mountains* was removed from the university syllabus. His persecution was probably primarily due to his radical (and controversial) research focus. In October Maina was sentenced to six years' imprisonment and held in Kamiti Prison. In 1983 two appeals were rejected and in 1986 he was denied release on remission. During his detention he was held in solitary confinement for periods of up to one month on several occasions. His opportunities to study, to write letters, to have visitors, and to receive medical attention were minimal and frequently revoked. He was reportedly beaten as the police attempted to extract a confession that he was involved in the underground opposition movement Mwakenya. During his detention his edition of Dedan Kimathi's letters and documents was published. In October 1988 he was released but found himself unemployed. In March 1989 he fled to Tanzania and from there to the United States in April. In the 1950s and 1960s, his father and brother had been detained as Mau Mau suspects for many years, several of them in Kamiti Prison. While a student at Michigan State University, United States, Maina had published polemical articles in a student journal, including one in which he had attacked as racist the university's African Studies Center and its staff, which had led to pressure for him to leave.

1982–   On 4 August three student leaders, including first-year history student **David Onyango Oloo**, were arrested following a coup attempt on 1 August. In November he was sentenced to five years' imprisonment for possessing (and possibly writing) a "seditious document", apparently a handwritten unfinished pamphlet or essay.

1983   An article on Mau Mau in *Race and Class: A Journal for Black and Third World Liberation* (London) appeared anonymously because, according to the editor, this "was in the nature of authoritarian regimes".

1984   In July the tenth congress of the International Primatological Society (IPS) took place in Nairobi without two South African participants (names unknown). A September 1983 letter had informed all IPS members that, in line with the Organization of African Unity policy, all South African passport holders were banned from Kenya. One of the two South Africans was an invited symposiast, the other an editor of the *International Primatological Journal*. Both were known for their opposition to racism and apartheid.

1985–86   In April 1985 **William Ochieng** (1943–), senior lecturer and director (1980–86) at the history department, Kenyatta University College, was interrogated by the police for forty-eight hours over an article in which he questioned the capitalist system. A meeting of Mau Mau veterans in February 1986 demanded that his writings, known for their neoconservative interpretation of the Mau Mau rebellion, be banned from the schools. The veterans also decided to commission the "correct" historiography of the rebellion. In an official reaction, Moi declared that he could not allow history to be written in a way that might divide the Kenyans and that any history of the rebellion should provide a correct account of independence.

1994–98   In 1994 paleoanthropologist **Richard Leakey** (1944–), son of pre-historians Louis and Mary Leakey, discoverer of the bones of Homo erectus in 1984, director of the National Museums of Kenya, re-signed his directorship of the Kenya Wildlife Services (KWS) (1988–) after pressure from his critics. He had reformed the organization, dismissed 1,700 employees, and initiated an interna-tional ivory ban. When he founded the Safina (Noah's Ark) oppo-sition party, Moi accused him of being a colonialist and a foreigner. In August 1995 when he and other Safina members intended visiting an opposition leader in Nakuru prison in the Rift Valley, they were attacked by about fifty men armed with whips and clubs. Witnesses identified the attackers as members of the local youth wing of the ruling Kenyan African National Union political party. In 1998 Lea-key became a member of Parliament and a member of the commis-sion to revise the constitution. He was also reappointed as KWS director.

Among the books banned between January 1994 and November 1998 was *Kenya: Return to Reason* (1993), by former cabinet min-ister and opposition leader **Kenneth Matiba**, a concise record of Kenya's political, economic, and human-rights history.

Also see Uganda (1973–: Mazrui).

SOURCES

Africa Watch, *Academic Freedom and Human Rights Abuses in Africa* (New York 1991) 20–23, 25.

Ahluwalia, P., "Founding Father Presidencies and the Rise of Authoritarianism: Kenya, a Case Study", *Africa Quarterly*, 1996, no. 4: 66.

Amnesty International, *Report* (London) 1978: 56–57; 1979: 23; 1983: 48–49; 1984: 57–58; 1985: 54–55; 1987: 57, 61, 63; 1988: 48; 1989: 59–60; 1990: 139; 1996: 196.

American Association for the Advancement of Science, *Directory of Persecuted Scien-tists, Engineers, and Health Professionals* (Washington 1997–98) 31.

Anonymous, "Mau Mau after Thirty Years", *Race and Class*, Winter 1983: ii, 259–66.

Article 19, *Information, Freedom and Censorship: World Report 1988* (London 1988) 36.

Atieno-Odhiambo, E.S., "The Production of History in Kenya: The Mau Mau Debate", *Canadian Journal of African Studies*, 1991: 302, 304.

Brinkman, I., "Het Gevecht om Mau Mau: Censuur en geschiedenis in Kenia", *Derde wereld*, 1993, no.1: 52.

Brockman, N.C., *An African Biographical Dictionary* (Santa Barbara 1994) 188.

Buijtenhuijs, R., " 'Free Thoughts on Toilet-Paper': Schrijverschap, staat en ideologie in Kenia", *Groniek*, 1985, no.91:9.

Duffy, J., M. Frey, & M. Sins eds., *International Directory of Scholars and Specialists in African Studies* (Waltham, Mass. 1978) 330.

Furley, O.W., "The Historiography of Mau Mau", in: B.A. Ogot ed., *Politics and Nationalism in Colonial Kenya* (Nairobi 1972) 130.

Index on Censorship, 2/78: 61; 3/78: 7–10; 6/78: 78–79; 2/79: 67; 6/79: 67–68; 3/80: 20–24; 3/81: 41–46; 6/81: 80–82; 3/82: 46; 4/82: 41–42, 49–50; 5/82: 35; 6/82: 45; 1/83: 22–26, 45; 2/83: 49; 4/83: 30, 34; 4/85: 53; 2/86: 19–22; 5/86: 3–4, 39; 6/86: 39; 1/87: 23–29; 6/87: 22–25; 1/88: 38, 42; 4/88: 38; 5/88: 91–94; 1/89: 37; 8/89: 38; 7/92: 53; 1–2/94: 242; 5/95: 180; 1/99: 90.

————, *Kenyan Academic Life at Risk* (briefing paper; August 1982).

Keesings historisch archief, 1993: 486; 1998: 316–17.

Kigotho, W., "Detained Lecturers Set Free", *Times Higher Education Supplement*, 26 February 1988: 10.

Maina wa Kinyatti, *Kenya's Freedom Struggle: The Dedan Kimathi Papers* (London 1987) xiii–xvi.

————, *Mother Kenya: Letters from Prison, 1982–1988* (London/New York 1997) ix–xiv, 15–20, 250–51.

———— ed., *Thunder from the Mountains: Mau Mau Patriotic Songs* (Nairobi 1980) 1–9.

Mutunga, W., & M. Kiai, "The State of Academic Freedom in Kenya 1992–94", in: Codesria, *The State of Academic Freedom in Africa 1995* (Dakar 1996) 81, 88, 97.

Network for the Defense of Independent Media in Africa, *Ifex Alert*, 13 December 1996, 16 June 1997, 16 November 1998.

Ngũgĩ wa Thiong'o *Detained: A Writer's Prison Diary* (London/Nairobi 1981) xvii–xxiii, 5–8, 33, 132–33, 159.

Ochwada, H., "Men of Literature and Kenya's Historiography: An Appraisal of the Writings of Ngugi wa Thiong'o", *Transafrican Journal of History*, 1995: 151–61.

Prunier, G., "Mythes et histoire: Les Interprétations du mouvement Mau Mau de 1952 à 1986", *Revue française d'histoire d'outre-mer*, 1987: 418–23, 428.

Savage, D.C., & C. Taylor, "Academic Freedom in Kenya", *Canadian Journal of African Studies*, 1991: 314–17.

Sicherman, C., *Ngugi wa Thiong'o: The Making of a Rebel: A Source Book in Kenyan Literature and Resistance* (London 1990) 4–5, 11–16, 33–40, 92, 150–51, 170–71.

Tobias, P.V., "Prehistory and Political Discrimination" (originally 1985), *Minerva*, 1988: 588.

Tucker, M. ed., *Literary Exile in the Twentieth Century: An Analysis and Biographical Dictionary* (Westport 1991) 514–16.

Widner, J.A., *The Rise of a Party-State in Kenya: From "Harambee!" to "Nyayo!"* (Berkeley 1992) 177.

KOREA

Unwelcome versions of some themes of Korean history—among them the Japanese occupation (1910–45), the independence struggle (1919–45), partition (1945–48), war (1950–53), and possible reunification of Korea—were liable to censorship.

North Korea

1950   Cultural historian and journalist **Chong In-bo** (1892–1950) was abducted by the North Korean Army during the Korean war (1950–53). Under Japanese occupation he had helped refute the Japanese view of Korean history and participated in the underground independence movement, for which he had been imprisoned.

1960s–   After the establishment of North Korea, **Paek Nam-un** (1895–?1974/ 79), social-economic historian and pioneer of Marxist history in Korea, became minister of education (1948–), member (1953–61) and president (1956–61) of the Academy of Sciences, chairman of the Supreme People's Assembly (1961–), and member of the Central Committee of the Korean Workers Party (1961–). In the early 1960s, he "disappeared". In 1938–41 Paek had been persecuted by the Japanese authorities and imprisoned for his anti-Japanese activities.

1970s–   From the 1970s chu-cheism (the spirit of national sovereignty) has replaced Marxism-Leninism as the official view of history. The history of the national liberation movement was reduced to President Kim II Sung's biography and family. He was depicted as personally responsible for the "Korean Revolution" in every detail. The roles of rival factions of Korean communists (1926–45) and of the USSR and China in the foundation and preservation of North Korea (1945–53) were omitted from the account. The Museum of the Korean Revolution contained no reference to either Soviet or Chinese connections or support.

South Korea

1949–50   In 1949 **Choe Nam-son** (1890–1957), historian, journalist, and student of Korean folklore, was prosecuted and found guilty of betraying Korea because he had been a coauthor of *History of Korea* ([1930]), designed to justify Japanese colonialism. After his release in 1950, he published many historical works. Choe drafted the Korean Declaration of Independence during the 1 March 1919 movement, which had led to his imprisonment by the Japanese colonizers for about two years, but later he tended to support Japanese rule of Korea.

1981–88   In June 1981 publisher and labor activist **Lee Tae-bok** (?1950) was arrested and accused of setting up student and labor leagues and of printing and distributing banned foreign books, mostly by Marxist authors. His publications included translations of works by British historians **Maurice Dobb** (1900–76) and **Christopher Hill** (1912–). Allegedly tortured, Lee was sentenced to life imprisonment in January 1982 on charges of trying to incite a revolution and establish a socialist government. In May an appeal court confirmed the sentence, but it was commuted to twenty years' imprisonment in August 1983. In 1988 he was released.

1985   In May the government banned hundreds of books previously admitted, including *Without Parallel: The American–Korean Relationship since 1945* (New York [1974]), a collection of articles on recent South Korean history edited by **Frank Baldwin** and translated as *Contemporary History before and after the Division of the Nation; Economic History of Korea* (1945) by Marxist scholar **Chon Soktam**; the first volume of *The Origins of the Korean War* (Princeton 1981), a revisionist work by **Bruce Cumings** (1943–), history professor at the University of Chicago, which circulated in pirated or xeroxed form in the English original among the student and intellectual population; *The History of Russian Thought* by **Isaac Deutscher** (1907–67); *Economic Growth and Backward Nations* by Dobb [q.v. 1981–88]; *Forty-Year History of Japanese Colonial Rule*, a work initially published in Japan by historian **Kang Cheon**; *A Critical History of Contemporary Korean Literature* by **Kim Yungsik**, a standard textbook for Korean college students; *The French Revolution 1789–99* (New York 1974) by French historian **Albert Soboul** (1914–82); *Peasant Wars of the Twentieth Century* (New York 1969) by **Eric Wolf** (1923–99); and books by **André Gunder Frank** (1929–) and **Antonio Gramsci** (1891–1937). The ban also included books about the May 1980 Kwangju incident, in which at least two hundred people were killed by the army after demonstrations against martial law.

1985–   In July 1985 **Mun Yong-shik** (?1959–) and **Ahn Byung-ryong** (?1959–), student leaders and history students at Seoul National University, were arrested amid violent antigovernment demonstrations at the university campuses after the publication of a booklet, *The Flag Advocating Left-wing Violent Struggle against the Government*. They were reportedly ill-treated during interrogation. In January

1986 they were among eleven dissident students sentenced to prison terms ranging from two to seven years for organizing a "pro-Communist group" and circulating "left-wing publications".

1987–   In February 1987 publisher **Nah Pyong-shik** was arrested under the National Security Law (NSL) and charged with publishing "impure" books which "contain ideology sympathetic to North Korea". He had published *The History of the Korean Masses*, a book containing a Marxist analysis of history and describing a number of antigovernment incidents. Seven of his employees were interrogated. In August he received a two-year suspended sentence.

In July 1987 **Chang Ui-gyun** (?1951–), a publisher specializing in books on ancient Korean history, was arrested shortly after his return from Japan and held incommunicado for twenty-five days. Later he claimed that he had been subjected to torture. From 1985 to 1987, he had studied ancient Korean history at Kyoto University. In Japan he had met a journalist of Chochong-nyon, an organization sympathizing with North Korea, and discussed with him North Korean proposals for the reunification of the Korean peninsula. He also visited the library and attended classes at the pro-North Korean University Chosen Daiggako. In May 1986 he organized a meeting on Korean reunification where a song which he had written on the subject was performed. He was accused of having passed on information about South Korea to a North Korean agent in Japan and of trying to infiltrate South Korean opposition groups as a North Korean spy, but he denied the accusation. In December 1987 he was charged with espionage and sentenced to eight years' imprisonment.

1987   In October students **Kim Sung-yong** and **Song Ki-yong** were arrested on charges of producing pro-North Korean publications. According to the authorities, an edition of one of these, *Plaza for Democracy*, carried an article referring to the United States Army presence in South Korea after World War II as an "occupation" and the entry of the USSR into North Korea as a "liberation" from Japanese colonial rule.

1987–88   In November 1987 poet **Lee San-ha** was arrested for the publication of *Halla Mountain*, a poem challenging the official version of the 3 April 1948 Cheju rebellion. (This alleged communist rebellion on Cheju Island, off South Korea, was violently suppressed and tens of thousands of islanders, allegedly communists or communist sympathizers, were massacred.) He was released in October 1988.

1987   In November Seoul Metropolitan Police seized thousands of copies of over 100 titles, including *A History of Western Philos-*

ophy (New York 1945) by philosopher **Bertrand Russell** (1872–1970).

1989–   In July 1989 dissident painter **Hong Song-dam** (?1955–) was arrested, inter alia, for sending photographic slides of a large mural depicting Korean popular uprisings and entitled *A History of the National Liberation Movement* to North Korea, where they were reproduced for exhibition at the World Festival of Youth and Students in Pyongyang in early July. He was tortured. During his trial in September his mural was described as "imbued with North Korean ideology". He was also charged with espionage for North Korea because he had sent books to a Korean in the Federal Republic of Germany. In January 1990 he was found guilty and sentenced to seven years' imprisonment, reduced on appeal to three years.

1990–   In 1990 writer **Lee Sung-hwan** was reportedly sentenced to one year in prison for his book *The Contemporary History of Korea's Independence Movement*.

1990   In January the police and Agency for National Security Planning (ANSP) agents raided the publishing company Labor Literature History Co. and seized nearly 46,000 copies of books, magazines, original writings, and address books of labor organizations.

In February **Oh Pong-ok** (?1961–) was arrested after writing a poem, *Red Mountain, Black Blood*, which the authorities said praised the role played by North Korean leader Kim Il Sung during the Japanese occupation. He was released in May with a two-year suspended sentence. The 1989 book in which the poem was published, treating the Korean resistance during the Japanese occupation, was edited by **Song Ki-won** (?1943–), who in May 1990 was sentenced to six months' imprisonment and twelve months' suspension of civil rights.

1992–   In January poet **Park Yong-hee** was detained and accused of espionage under the NSL for illegally visiting North Korea in October 1991 as part of his research on mining conditions in Korea during the Japanese occupation. Reportedly tortured in prison, he was sentenced to fifteen years' imprisonment.

1994–   In March publishers **Lee Song-woo** and **Kim Byong-hak** were arrested and accused of producing pro-North Korean publications. Several books and diskettes were confiscated, including *The History of the Party*. Kim was released the same day.

1995   In March 1995 **Kim Mu-yong** (?1961–), a history professor at Bangsong Tongshin University History Institute who had published several theses on the liberation movement during the Japanese occupation, was arrested under the NSL for "possessing, distributing, and producing" writings on the Korean guerrilla movement (1948–53). The police confiscated some of his books, pamphlets, cassette tapes, and computer diskettes. The charges related to a July 1993 lecture on the Korean guerrilla movement and to documents he had distributed to those attending the lecture, entitled *Post-Liberation History of the Guerrilla Struggle*. He was also charged with having arranged four tours of guerrilla areas in North Cholla and South Kyungsang Provinces (South Korea) and having written the guide pamphlet *Modern Korean History and the Guerrilla Movement* with details of the itinerary and of guerrilla activities. Awaiting trial in Seoul Prison, he risked up to seven years' imprisonment. A colleague of his was also arrested for distributing the pamphlets. He was further charged with writing the lyrics of some guerrilla songs found in his notebooks and written down during a meeting with a former prisoner convicted of guerrilla activities for North Korea.

1995–98   In April 1995 **Park Chang-hee** (?1932/33–), history professor at the Foreign Language University of Korea, author of books and theses on Korean history and the Japanese occupation, was arrested under the NSL at his home in Seoul and interrogated by the ANSP for twenty days after his arrest. Some of his research papers were confiscated. While interrogated, he was threatened and ill-treated. In June he was charged with having met a "pro-North Korean agent" in Japan, leaking state secrets and praising North Korea. In October he was sentenced to seven years' imprisonment, in February 1996 reduced by half. He was released under a presidential amnesty in March 1998.

1995   An August 1995 report stated that the concept of historical materialism was still strictly prohibited by law: in [1994] some professors had been prosecuted under the NSL and risked expulsion from the university, allegedly for their use of the concept.

1997–   In November 1997 **Suh Jun-sik** (?1949–), editor, columnist, and director of the human-rights group Sarangbang (1993–), was arrested and charged with, inter alia, violating the NSL for screening the South Korean documentary *Red Hunt* at the 1997 Sarangbang Film Festival. The film detailed government collusion in the 1948 Cheju massacre and contained survivors' testimonies and comments by historians. Although Suh was released on bail in February 1998 after protests, the charges against him were not dropped. At his September 1999 trial, he was found guilty of violating the NSL and placed on probation. In 1971–88 and 1991, he had already been imprisoned for seventeen-and-a-half years. Earlier in 1997 the film had already been shown at another film festival without any of those involved being detained. The filmmaker himself was briefly detained after Suh's arrest and subsequently released without charge.

Also see Japan (1981: Kojima, Uno; 1982: textbook controversy; 1986: Fujio; 1997: Kanagawa).

SOURCES

Amnesty International, *Newsletter*, August 1990: 2; January 1992: 4, 6.
————, *Report* (London) 1982: 210–11; 1983: 207, 210; 1984: 236; 1986: 236; 1988: 167; 1989: 183–84; 1990: 144; 1991: 138; 1992: 164; 1994: 188; 1996: 202; 1998: 226; 1999: 225; 2001: 150.
————, *South Korea: History Lecturer Arrested under National Security Law* (ASA 25/ 11/95; 10 May 1995).
————, *South Korea: On Trial for Defending His Rights: The Case of Human Rights Activist Suh Jun-sik* (WWW-text of ASA 25/18/98; London 1998).
Article 19, *Information, Freedom and Censorship: World Report* (London) 1988: 151, 153; 1991: 190–91.
Boia, L. ed., *Great Historians of the Modern Age: An International Dictionary* (Westport 1991) 461–62.
Great Soviet Encyclopedia (New York/London) vol. 21 (1978) 180; vol. 29 (1982) 180.
Handbook of Korea (Elizabeth 1994) 109.
Human Rights Watch, *World Report* (Washington) 1999: 467, 493; 2000: 474.
Index on Censorship, 2/82: 47; 2/84: 4–7; 3/86: 40; 4/86: 31–32, 40; 7/86: 45; 4/87: 39; 5/90: 39; 7/90: 39; 8/90: 39; 9/90: 40; 10/90: 13, 38; 1/91: 39; 2/91: 39; 3/95: 187; 4/95: 186; 2/98: 101.
International PEN Writers in Prison Committee, *Half-Yearly Caselist* (London) 1997: 39–40; 1998: 38.
————, *Ifex Alert*, 11 April & 21 June 1995.
Lim Jie-Hyun, "The Nationalist Message in Socialist Code: On the Court Historiography in People's Poland and North Korea" (unpublished paper, 19th International Congress of Historical Sciences; Oslo 2000) 2, 7–12.
Lim Sang-woo, "History As a Vocation: A Weberian Perspective on the Development of Historical Institutions in Modern Korea" (unpublished paper, 18th International Congress of Historical Sciences; Montréal 1995) 5–6.
Nahm, A.C., *Historical Dictionary of the Republic of Korea* (Metuchen 1993) 72.
Woolf, D.R. ed., *A Global Encyclopedia of Historical Writing* (New York/London 1998) 172–73, 513–14, 687.
Wordt vervolgd, 1994, nos. 7–8: 34.

KUWAIT

1992   Historian **Abdulazzim Anis** was on a list of forty-seven Egyptian writers and artists to be banned throughout the Gulf region. The list, compiled by the Kuwaiti Information Office in Cairo for the Gulf Cooperation Council, targeted those who had been critical of Kuwait's ruling al-

Sabah family, their role in the Gulf War, their personal behavior, and the treatment of Palestinians in Kuwait. It was leaked and published in September.

1998   In August, forty men of the Salab tribe ransacked the offices of the daily *Al-Qabas* in Kuwait City in response to the republication of a picture from the 1940s showing Salab women dancing without veils in front of men. The caption explained that the Salab acted this way because they were "a mix of Arabs and other peoples who came to Islam later".

1999   Political scientist **Ahmad al-Baghdadi** and historian **Sulaiman al-Badr** from Kuwait University were criticized by some clerics because in 1996 they had written in a student magazine that the Prophet Mohammed had failed to convert unbelievers during his time in Mecca. Al-Badr publicly apologized, but al-Baghdadi was found guilty of blaspheming Islam and given a suspended six-month sentence in May 1999. On appeal his sentence was reduced to one month. He was imprisoned on 5 October. The court had found him guilty of "spreading views that ridicule, scorn or belittle religion." He went on a hunger strike. After Emir Sheik Jaber al-Ahmad al-Sabah pardoned him, he was released on 18 October.

SOURCES

Amnesty International, *Report 2000* (London 2000) 151.
Frankfurter allgemeine Zeitung, [6] October 1999.
Human Rights Watch, Letter, Academic Freedom Committee to Emir of Kuwait (13 October 1999).
————, *World Report* (Washington) 2000: 325; 2001: 466–67.
Index on Censorship, 10/92: 46; 1/93: 28; 6/98: 100; 6/99: 245; 1/100: 99.

KYRGYSZTAN

See Union of Soviet Socialist Republics (USSR).

L

LAOS

French Laos/Laos

1946–   In 1946 **Sisana Sisane** (1922–) fled to Thailand at the time of the French reconquest of Laos because he had participated in the seizure of power by the nationalist Lao Issara in 1945. In 1948 he became a member of the Lao Committee of Resistance in the East. In July 1959 he was imprisoned with other Pathet Lao representatives, but they escaped in May 1960. He then became director of Radio Pathet Lao (1961–75) and minister of information, propaganda, culture, and tourism in the Lao People's Democratic Republic government (1975–83). In 1983 he was demoted for expressing anti-Soviet sentiments and internally exiled. Rehabilitated in 1985, he was appointed director of the Institute of Social Sciences, responsible for producing an official history of Laos and the Lao People's Revolutionary Party.

1946–49   In 1946 **Maha Sila Viravong** (1905–86) also went into exile in Thailand with the Lao Issara. He returned to Laos in 1949 and became the leading Lao historian. He wrote *History of Laos* (New York 1964).

SOURCES

Stuart-Fox, M., & M. Kooyman, *Historical Dictionary of Laos* (Metuchen 1992) 52, 84, 134.

LATVIA

pre-1945   Among the historians who emigrated before 1945 (and living in exile after 1944) was **Max Laserson** (1887–1951).

1945–91   *See* Union of Soviet Socialist Republics (USSR).

1998–   In March the prosecutor-general filed criminal charges against publicist **Juris Rudevskis** for a series of articles in the political weekly *Nacionala Neatkariba* (National Independence) in which he criticized Russia, citing numerous examples of massacres, court treachery, and murder from tsarist times to the communist era and discussing the role of the Russian Orthodox Church in supporting "state tyranny" through the ages. The charges—incitement of racial or ethnic hatred—carried a three-year sentence.

SOURCES

Index on Censorship, 3/98: 180.

LEBANON

1978–   The film *Alexandria . . . Why?* (1978), by the Egyptian filmmaker **Youssef Chahine**, was banned (as it was in many other Arab countries), inter alia, because of its satirical presentation of the Free Officers of the 1952 Revolution. When the ban was lifted, several scenes were cut, including a scene in which a group of Jewish war refugees arrived in New York and a scene portraying the burning of the King David Hotel in Jerusalem in 1946 by Jewish terrorists (because an Israeli flag was shown).

1978–83   Part of the historical treasures of the National Museum, Beirut, were damaged or destroyed by Syrian and Israeli troops. Director of Antiquities Amir Maurice Shihab (Emir Maurice Chehab) (1904–94) and his wife, Olga Chaiban, were able to hide most of it.

1999   In October *A Civilized People*, a film about the civil war (1975–90) by **Chahal Sabbag**, had fifty minutes cut out by the government censor because of "inflammatory remarks" against Christ, the Virgin Mary, and Islam. None of his previous films about the conflict had been screened in Lebanon.

Also see France (1947: Rodinson), Indonesia (1994: Spielberg), Israel (1981: Kayyali; 1982–: occupation of Beirut), Saudi Arabia (1979: al-Said), Syria (1952: Zurayq, 1985: Salibi).

SOURCES

Human Right Watch, *World Report 2001* (Washington 2000) 479.
Index on Censorship, 4/81: 39–40; 1/00: 173; 2/00: 106; 6/00: 108.
NRC-Handelsblad, 20 November 1998: 22 (National Museum).

LESOTHO

See Zimbabwe (pre-1974: Mudenge).

LIBERIA

1984   In late August President Samuel Doe dismissed the entire teaching staff of the University of Liberia, including history professor **J. Paul Chauduri**, because he held them responsible for the student demonstrations of 22 August, which were suppressed by the president's Executive Mansion Guard. The demonstrations were a protest against the arrest earlier that month of two academics for allegedly plotting a coup.

1989–97   During the civil war, many archives were destroyed.

SOURCES

Africa Watch, *Academic Freedom and Human Rights Abuses in Africa* (New York 1991) 31.
Albada, J. van, " 'Memory of the World': Report on Destroyed and Damaged Archives", *Archivum*, 1996, no. 42: 19.
Amnesty International, *Report 1985* (London 1985) 59–60.
Auer, L., "Archival Losses and Their Impact on the Work of Archivists and Historians", *Archivum*, 1996, no. 42: 4.

LIBYA

1973   During Colonel Muammar al-Qaddafi's April "Cultural Revolution", history textbooks were reportedly largely untouched where they dealt with ancient history (an important subject in Libya because of major Greek and Roman archeological remains) or with the first Islamic empires. For more recent periods, textbooks were extensively rewritten. The preeminent place given to the Sanusi family (to which former King Idris belonged) in accounts of the Ottoman and Italian periods was downgraded almost to the point of nonexistence.

1977   In October several articles in the official daily newspaper *al-Fajr al-Jadid*, reportedly inspired by Qaddafi, attacked the Grand Mufti, Shaykh **Tahir al-Zawi** (?1887–). The articles argued that he had failed to declare a jihad (holy war) against the Italians and opted for

Italian citizenship in the 1930s. In the aftermath of the debate, the mufti, one of the foremost chroniclers of modern Libyan history and an active opponent of imperialism in Libya, resigned. He was not replaced.

1984–85 In 1984 or 1985, Qaddafi ordered the removal of an ancient Greek statue from between the cities of Tripoli and Barqa because it was not Libyan.

Also see Chad (1974–77: Claustre), Egypt (1979: congress), Iraq (1963–70: Baqir), Syria (1970: doctoral student).

SOURCES

Anderson, L., "Qaddafi's Islam", in: J.L. Esposito ed. *Voices of Resurgent Islam* (New York/Oxford 1983) 140, 143, 149.
Davis, J., "The Social Relations of the Production of History", in: E. Tonkin, M. McDonald, & M. Chapman eds., *History and Ethnicity* (London 1989) 104–20.
Index on Censorship, 5/81: 10–12, 38–39; 5/87: 27.

LITHUANIA

See Union of Soviet Socialist Republics (USSR).

LUXEMBOURG

1960– Under the 1960 decree on state archives, the archives had to be open to the public, but citizens had to make a written request explaining why they wanted access. Ministers had broad discretion to deny such requests.

SOURCES

Banisar, D., *Freedom of Information around the World* (WWW-text; Privacy International Report; London 2000).

M

MACEDONIA

pre-1991   *See* Yugoslavia.

1999   In January Macedonian state radio commentator **Gorica Popova** was
             demoted from her editorial position to that of a "junior associate"
             after expressing her personal view on the stay of several foreign
             guests who were invited by the Macedonian government to honor
             the controversial leader of the Internal Macedonian Revolutionary
             Organization Todor Alexandrov (?–1924).

Also see Bulgaria (Macedonian Question; 1990: OMO-Ilinden), Greece (1992:
Papadaki, FYROM; 1998: Rainbow Party).

SOURCES

Greek Helsinki Monitor, *Ifex Alert*, 29 January 1999.
Human Rights Watch, *World Report 2000* (Washington 1999) 281–82.
Index on Censorship, 2/99: 113.

MALAWI

From 1968 to 1994, the Malawi Censorship Board banned hundreds of books,
including many important (and especially left-wing) works of history, one of
the disciplines most affected. The September 1964 cabinet crisis, in which President Hastings Banda eliminated a series of potential rivals from the government,
was the most important historical taboo. Politicians out of favor found their role
in Malawi's independence struggle obscured in history books. The names of
those who contributed to the rise of Malawian nationalism in the 1950s could

be mentioned only in secret. One source described the situation as follows: "During the show trial of Orton and Vera Chirwa in 1984, when Vera Chirwa began her testimony with the statement 'When I founded the Malawi Women's League', a tremor of excitement ran through the spectators. The simplest historical fact has become subversive."

1968   In a November speech, Banda strongly objected to a text on Malawi's history which referred to the role played by the predominantly Muslim Yao people of southeastern Malawi in the precolonial Arab slave trade, in order to avoid tribal conflict. At the same time, the Yao were unfavorably presented in official Malawian historiography.

1970s   In the 1970s the University of Malawi, Limbe, was purged of northern administrators and academic staff, including historian **Chifipa Gondwe**, as one of the measures to favor students from the Central Region (the region where Banda, John Tembo, and others in control of the Malawian government came from).

1972–   Historian **Landeg White** (1940–), lecturer at the University of Malawi (1969–72), was deported after *Vanguard*, a radical student magazine of which he was editorial adviser, had published a poem critical of old men. This was regarded as offensive to the government. White became a research fellow (1980–84) and director (1984–) at the Center for Southern African Studies of York University, United Kingdom. In 1999 he taught at the Universidade Aberta, Lisbon. He also worked in Trinidad and Sierra Leone.

1975–   Among the books banned as of 31 December were history books, particularly studies of the Russian Revolution, the overthrow of Ghana's first president, Kwame Nkrumah, and accounts of the problems of postindependence Africa. They included *The History of the Russian Revolution* (1929), written by **Leon Trotsksy** (1879–1940) while he was exiled in Turkey; *Impact of the Russian Revolution* by historian **Arnold Toynbee** (1889–1975); *Banda* (London 1974), a biography by journalist **Philip Short** (of which three thousand copies were destroyed in December 1972, a few weeks before its publication); and a history of Central Africa by **D.E. Needham**. Also banned was *Strike a Blow and Die* by Chief **Mwase Kasungu**, an account of the 1915 anti-British uprising of pastor John Chilembwe, the first founder of an independent church in Malawi, a document of prime importance for the study of Malawi's past. The book was edited by a non-African scholar whose work *The Rise of African Nationalism* was also banned because it was unacceptable to Banda. The book bans were cited as evidence for the reason that Malawian historians did little research on Malawi's modern history. One of the reasons for the ban on Short's book may have been Short's probing into Banda's exact age, a politically sensitive subject because it could affect the popular image of his heroic march to South Africa as a young person.

pre-1977   On 3 September 1977, **Albert Muwalo Nqumayo** (1927–77) was executed. A former secretary-general of the ruling Malawi Congress Party and a former minister of state in the president's office (1966–76), he was arrested in October 1976, found guilty of treason, and sentenced to death after an unfair trial with inadequate evidence by the Southern Regional Traditional Court in Blantyre in February 1977. Muwalo had allegedly been involved in a plot to assassinate Banda and overthrow the government. One of the charges was that he possessed the banned book *Animal Farm*, by **George Orwell** (1903–50), a historical study of the assassination of Zulu leader Shaka (?1787–1828), and political and historical works on the USSR. The judges found that, although these latter works were not banned, they undoubtedly would have been if they had been imported legally. Possession of them was deemed evidence of subversive intention. As an influential politician, Muwalo had been responsible for many detentions in 1975–76, particularly those of members of the University of Malawi's academic staff.

1982   In July a proposal of historians **Leroy Vail** and White [q.v. 1972–] to a meeting of Malawian historians and political scientists to hold a seminar on the 1964 cabinet crisis met with complete silence. Several people left the room.

1984–85   In 1984, at a conference on Malawi's development strategy held at Edinburgh University, a paper by **Andrew Ross**, containing reportedly privileged information on the 1964 cabinet crisis, was suppressed by the organizers. It was subsequently presented to a research seminar at York University in 1985.

Also see Zimbabwe (1962: federal project).

SOURCES

Africa Watch, *Academic Freedom and Human Rights Abuses in Africa* (New York 1991) 36, 38.
———, *Where Silence Rules: The Suppression of Dissent in Malawi* (New York 1990) 16, 33–36, 58, 71.
Amnesty International, *The Death Penalty* (London 1979) 48–49.
———, *Report* (London) 1977: 80–81; 1978: 58; 1979: 24.
———, *When the State Kills . . . The Death Penalty versus Human Rights* (London 1989) 170–71.

Article 19, *Information, Freedom and Censorship: World Report 1991* (London 1991) 28.

———, "Malawi's Past: The Right to Truth", *Censorship News*, November 1993: 11, 13.

Crosby, C.A., *Historical Dictionary of Malawi* (Metuchen 1993) 100.

Hodder-Williams, R. ed., *A Directory of Africanists in Britain* (Bristol 1990) 128.

Index on Censorship, 1/73: v; 2/73: xiii; 3/73: v; 6/79: 56–58; 2/88: 19–20; 5/97: 76.

Joffe, S.H., *Political Culture and Communication in Malawi: The Hortatory Regime of Kamuzu Banda* (Boston [1978]) 390–91.

Lwanda, J.L., *Kamuzu Banda of Malawi: A Study in Promise, Power and Paralysis; Malawi under Dr. Banda (1961 to 1993)* (Glasgow 1993) 5, 51.

Mazrui, A.A., "Subjectivism and the Study of Current History: Political, Psychological and Methodological Problems", in: UNESCO, *The Methodology of Contemporary African History* (Paris 1984) 30.

Searle, C., "Struggling against the 'Bandastan': An Interview with Attati Mpakati", *Race and Class*, 1980: 392.

Vail, L., and L. White, *Power and the Praise Poem: Southern African Voices in History* (London/Charlottesville 1991) 291–92, 317.

———, "Tribalism in the Political History of Malawi", in: L. Vail ed., *The Creation of Tribalism in Southern Africa* (London 1989) xiv, 182, 184 (quote).

World University Service, *Academic Freedom* (London) 1993: 63, 67, 71, 75–76; 1995: 34, 37–39, 41, 43–44.

MALAYSIA

Communal aspects of Malaysian society were the most contentious areas of historical research.

British Malaya

1948–55   From 1948 to 1955, journalist and historian **Ahmad Boestamam** (1920–) was imprisoned. He was reportedly one of the more extreme Malays who relied on history to propagate his cause. In 1976 he wrote an account of his imprisonment.

1953–   After his retirement as a Chinese affairs official, **Wilfred Blythe** embarked on a study of Chinese secret societies in Malaya in the nineteenth and twentieth centuries and had special access to secret government documents.

Malaysia

1975   In the first half of 1975, **Allan Healy** (1929–), an Australian historian and social scientist planning to do research on the history of education in Malaysia, could obtain a research visa for three months only, granted after two months of bureaucratic problems. His research project's title was written in his passport, and he had to promise to submit to the government a report of his findings before leaving Malaysia. His problems were probably linked with the sensitive communal aspects of his research and the tension between Malays and Chinese, especially since 1969.

1995   In October the prime minister ordered a review of the twenty-year-old ban on television programs featuring people in Chinese historical costumes after two such programs had to be withdrawn that month.

1996   In August, during a period in which the authorities were campaigning to curb the influence of Shiism, the UMNO (United Malays National Organization, the leading political party) Youth Movement at Terengganu called upon the religious authorities to ban a book on Islamic history which, it claimed, promoted Shiism. The first edition of this book, *Fitnah Terbesar Dalam Sejarah Islam*, by Egyptian literary historian **Taha Husayn** (1889–1973) was published by a state-owned press in 1992 but sold out.

Also see Australia (1959–62: Healy), Egypt (1952–: Husayn), Indonesia (1991: Bamadhay; 1994: Spielberg), Japan (1988: publisher).

SOURCES

Index on Censorship, 3/76: 73–75; 6/95: 179; 5/96: 96–97.
Kim, Khoo Khay, "Malaysian History in the Twentieth Century", in: A. Reid & D. Marr eds., *Perceptions of the Past in Southeast Asia* (Singapore 1979) 308, 413.
Turnbull, C.M., "Malaysia", in: R.W. Winks ed., *The Historiography of the British Empire-Commonwealth: Trends, Interpretations, and Resources* (Durham 1966) 473, 480.

MALDIVES

1995   On 21 April about a dozen police officers raided the home of **Ahamad Shafeeq** (?1928–), former civil servant, editor of the historical journal *Vanavaru*, author of a number of books on history, ornithology, and fiction. They arrested him and another writer. Shafeeq's diaries and other papers were seized probably because of comments made in them criticizing the cost of a newly constructed presidential palace. On 30 April he was given permission to receive medical treatment in India but on 10 May he was returned to the capital, Mal, in poor health. He was denied visits from his family. From July to December, he was held under house arrest without charge or trial.

SOURCES

Amnesty International, *Report 1996* (London 1996) 218–19.
International PEN Writers in Prison Committee, *Ifex Alert*, 9 June 1995.

MALI

1976   In 1976 the Mandenka jeli (oral traditionist or *griot*) from Krina **Waa Kamisoko** (Wa Kamissoko) (?1919–76) died and was given a state funeral. It was widely believed that he had been killed for revealing esoteric knowledge or for "attempting to become the equal of the great masters of the Komo" [initiation society]. Waa Kamisoko was an expert in Komo matters, though not a Komo initiate, as the jeliw (griots) were reportedly excluded from the Komo society. He was known for his critical stance toward past and contemporary Malian society. In 1977 oral traditionist and historian Amadou Hampâté Bâ (1900–91) remarked that by speaking extensively and publicly about certain subjects, Waa Kamisoko had displayed considerable courage and exposed himself to certain risks.

SOURCES

De Moraes Farias, P.F., "The Oral Traditionist As Critic and Intellectual Producer: An Example from Contemporary Mali", in: T. Falola ed., *African Historiography: Essays in Honour of Jacob Ade. Ajayi* (Harlow, Essex 1993) 14–15, 20, 23, 30, 34–35.

MAURITANIA

1983–   After an in camera trial by a military special court of justice, history teacher and former director of higher education **Mehmed Ould Ahmed** and sixteen others were sentenced to twelve years' imprisonment with hard labor in October 1983 on the charge of "complicity with a foreign power" and "membership in a banned organization" (a pro-Iraqi Baathist party in Mauritania). He had been arrested in August 1981 or March 1982. He was released in the general amnesty after the coup of December 1984. In 1988 he was reportedly tried again on the same charges by the same court.

1986–90 In September 1986 **Seydou Kane, Ibrahima Sall**, and **Abdoulaye Sarr**, history lecturers at Nouakchott University, were among thirty people arrested. They were charged with holding unauthorized meetings, displaying and distributing material harmful to the national interest, and creating racist propaganda. Inside and outside Mauritania, they had distributed a document *Le Manifeste du Négro-Mauritanien opprimé* (Manifesto of the Oppressed Black Mauritanian), alleging discrimination by the ruling Arab-Berber military government against the southern black population. They were held incommunicado in police custody and possibly ill-treated. On 25 September the group was tried and convicted on all charges. Sentences ran from six months' to five years' imprisonment with fines, to be followed by five and ten years' internal exile and loss of civil rights. In October the court of appeal confirmed all convictions and sentences. The historians were released in September 1990.

SOURCES

Amnesty International, *Report* (London) 1987: 72–73; 1988: 54–55; 1989: 68–69; 1991: 155.
Index on Censorship, 10/86: 47; 2/87: 38.

MEXICO

Historical episodes to be treated with particular prudence were found in all three periods of the Mexican past (indigenous era, Spanish colonial rule, epoch of the nation-state). Among recent events, the 1968 Tlatelolco massacre was the most traumatic. According to most estimates, 300 people, mainly students, died in the massacre on 2 October 1968.

1946   In 1946 historian **Luís González y González** (1925–), then a third-year law student (1943–46), was removed from the Universidad Autónoma de Guadalajara because of his Marxist sympathies. Subsequently he enrolled at the Centro de Estudios Históricos (Center of Historical Studies) of the Colegio de México (1946–49), of which he would become the director later (1963–65, 1970–73). In 1997 he was called the "dean of Mexicanists".

1950–51   From January 1950 to February 1951, a scientific commission that included archeologists **Manuel Gamio** (1883–1960) and **Alfonso Caso** (1896–1970) and historians **Manuel Toussaint** (1890–1955) and **Wigberto Jiménez Moreno** (1909–85) devoted thirty-seven sessions to verify the authenticity of the bones of Cuauhtémoc (the last Aztec emperor and a national symbol of resistance to European imperialism) which were "discovered" in the church of Ixcateopan, Guerrero, in September 1949. The commission found no proof of their authenticity and thus was unable to satisfy national pride. During its sessions and afterward, the commission was confronted with extreme hostility in the press. The bones were enshrined in a glass case in the local church. In 1975 a new commission came to the same conclusion as the 1951 group.

1960–90   For thirty years director **Julio Bracho's** film *La Sombra del caudillo* (1960), dealing with a general's power struggle in the 1920s, before the 1929 establishment of the Partido Nacional Revolucionario (1929; forerunner of the Partido Revolucionario Institucional, PRI:

Institutional Revolutionary Party), was banned. Based on events at the end of General Álvaro Obregón's presidency (1920–24), the film changed the protagonists' names. It was banned, apparently at the behest of the Mexican army, until October 1990.

1966–72 From April 1966 to March 1972, Mexican (Argentinian-born) writer, journalist, and historian **Adolfo Gilly** (1928–), then a left-wing journalist expelled from Cuba in October 1963 for his Trotskyist ideas, was imprisoned in Lecumberri prison on the baseless charge of conspiracy against the state. During the first five years of his prison term, he wrote *La revolución interrumpida: México, 1910–1920; Una guerra campesina por la tierra y el poder* (México 1971; *The Mexican Revolution*, London 1983). After scores of political prisoners were assaulted in prison on 1 January 1970 and the manuscript was in danger of loss, he began smuggling it out of prison. The book, appearing while Gilly was still in prison, became a best-seller (most recent revised edition: 1998; translations in English and French). In March 1972 Gilly was released and expelled to France, but later the Supreme Court annulled the charge. Returning to Mexico in November 1976, he became a professor at the faculty of economics and the Escuela Nacional de Antropología e Historia (1977–78) and at the Department of Political and Social Sciences of the National Autonomous University of Mexico (UNAM) (1979–). He received the Mexican nationality in 1982. Lecumberri prison now houses the National Archives.

1967–68 In 1967 or 1968, anthropologist and historian of civilizations **Angel Palerm Vich** (1917–80) was offered a leading position at the Museo Nacional de Antropología. He did not or could not accept it because of the attacks of some of his colleagues. In 1968 he resigned his post as professor of anthropology at the Escuela Nacional de Antropología e Historia (?1965–68) in protest against the Tlatelolco massacre. Earlier he had had some problems with the escuela, inter alia, because he reportedly protested the dismissal of a colleague for political reasons. He founded and directed the Department of Social Anthropology and the Instituto de Ciencias Sociales at the Universidad Iberoamericana (1967–80). In 1975–76 he was founder-director of the Centro de Investigaciones Superiores del Instituto Nacional de Antropología e Historia (INAH). He wrote, inter alia, on the history of anthropology and tried to adapt the thesis of the German-American historian Karl Wittfogel (1896–1988) on the hydraulic society to pre-Columbian history. In his early years, Spanish-born Palerm was an anarchist, later communist, student who fought in the 1936–39 civil war and in 1939 went into exile in Mexico, where he studied history and anthropology. He worked for the Organization of American States (OAS) (?1952–65) and the American University (1960–65) in Washington D.C. Reportedly expelled from the United States for political reasons, he was appointed OAS special representative for Latin America (1965–67).

1968–   After the 1968 Tlatelolco massacre, President Gustavo Díaz Ordaz dissolved the PIPSA, the state company which supplied newsprint. He reestablished it on 1 April 1970. Consequently, the newspapers—with the exception of the daily *Excélsior*—did not mention the massacre for years.

1970s   Students opposed the candidacy of historian and Catholic theologian **Carlos Herrejón Peredo** (1942–) for a position as professor of the philosophy of history at the University of Toluca, apparently for his clerical antecedents. The staff, however, approved it and after a public interview he was appointed.

pre-1971   *La noche de Tlatelolco: Testimonios de historia oral* (Mexico D.F. 1971; The Night of Tlatelolco: Oral History Testimonies), by **Elena Poniatowska** (1942–), could not be published until Díaz left office in 1970. The book about the 1968 massacre had thirty-two editions in seven years.

1972   **Pablo González Casanova** (1922–), neo-Marxist historian, professor of sociology and historical sciences at the UNAM (1952–66, 1972–77), and director of its Institute for Social Science Research (1966–70), resigned his UNAM rectorship (1970–72) after numerous strikes. He had reportedly been made rector because of his sympathy with radical students during the post-Tlatelolco months.

1975–78   Editorial Novaro refused to publish **Gonzalo Martre**'s novel *Los símbolos transparentes* (1975) because it primarily dealt with the 1968 Tlatelolco massacre. When it was ultimately published in 1978, it became a best-seller in six months.

1976   In June **Gastón García Cantú**, a leftist historian and political commentator for *Excélsior* who frequently wrote articles in which the speeches of presidential candidate José López Portillo were criticized, became one of the victims of a smear campaign. Directed against *Excélsior*, its editor, and several contributors in order to silence the newspaper, the campaign was possibly authorized by collaborators of President Luis Echeverría Álvarez. When editor Julio Scherer was dismissed, *Excélsior* collaborators resigned en masse. García Cantú was later appointed to the INAH by President López Portillo.

1981   Scholars with South African passports were excluded from the Tenth
            International Congress of the Union Internationale des Sciences Pré-
            historiques et Protohistoriques in Mexico City.

1982   A statue of conquistador Hernán Cortés, unveiled by López Portillo
            in Mexico City and dedicated to Mexico's mixed-blood heritage, was
            removed shortly after the president had left office.

1983   The UNAM planned the production of a play by **Vicente Leñero**
            (1933–), entitled *Martirio de Morelos* (Mexico 1981; The Martyr-
            dom of Morelos). The portrayal of priest and independence hero José
            María Morelos as someone who under torture betrayed the names,
            strategies, and troop strengths of other rebel commanders caused a
            great stir, especially because President Miguel de la Madrid had
            "adopted" Morelos as his spiritual mentor from the past. Some re-
            hearsals were reportedly interrupted, a controversial actor playing
            the part of Morelos was replaced, and precautions against violent
            protests were taken on opening night.

1985   When **Edmundo O'Gorman y O'Gorman** (1906–95), archivist at
            the Archivo General de la Nación (National Archives) (1938–52)
            and UNAM professor of historiography (1940–78), historian of ideas
            specialized in the discovery and conquest of America, submitted the
            text of the keynote address to be delivered at the fiftieth anniversary
            of the UNAM Instituto de Investigaciones Estéticas on 1 February,
            the Institute director asked him to delete or moderate some passages
            in which he criticized the writer Octavio Paz, who had said on tel-
            evision that the study of Mexican colonial art began with historian
            and art critic George Kubler rather than with the Institute's founder
            Toussaint [q.v. 1950–51]. O'Gorman, the Institute's oldest alumnus,
            refused and, after new invitations and programs were printed, the
            ceremony took place without him.

1987   In March, O'Gorman [q.v. 1985] resigned the presidency (1972–87)
            of the Academia Mexicana de la Historia (Mexican Academy of
            History) because his disagreement with historian Miguel León-
            Portilla (1926–), specialist of Aztec history and general coordinator
            of the Comisión Nacional Conmemorativa del V Centenario del En-
            cuentro de Dos Mundos (1986–87), did not lead to a change in the
            concept of the 1992 quincentenary marking Columbus's arrival in
            the Americas. In the debate O'Gorman challenged León-Portilla's
            view, which equated the discovery with an encounter between the
            Old and the New World.

1988   During the 1988 election campaign, thirty-seven episodes of the his-
            torical television series *Senda de gloria* (Path to Glory) written by

Fausto Zerón Medina and **Enrique Krauze** (1947–), historian and essayist for *Vuelta* (1976–), were canceled. The series gave a positive account of the late president Lázaro Cárdenas (ruled 1934–40), whose son Cuauhtémoc was an opposition candidate.

1989–90   Authorization to show the film *Rojo amanecer* (Red Dawn), a 1989 drama by **Jorge Fons** (1939–) based on the 1968 Tlatelolco massacre, was delayed until mid-1990, reportedly by order of the Presidential Guard.

[1990]   In [1990] historian and political scientist **Lorenzo Meyer** (1942–) was labeled "an enemy of the president [Carlos Salinas]". This was considered a dangerous identification.

1992   From August to October a history textbook controversy took place in the mass media about the contents of the new official mandatory history textbooks for nine- to twelve-year-olds. The new books, entitled *Mi libro de historia de México* (My Book of Mexican History), were intended to replace social science textbooks because the Ministry of Public Education had declared in May 1991 that the public had insufficient knowledge of national history. The protest was directed against what was called a biased interpretation of Mexican history, especially contemporary history, in support of the legitimation of the ruling PRI: traditional (nationalist) heroes were neglected; the 1910 Revolution was deflated; the Porfiriato (1876–1911), an epoch when President Porfirio Díaz attempted Mexico's modernization at great human cost, was depicted as a liberal and technocratic precedent and rehabilitated. As a result of the protests, the government withdrew the textbooks. In August 1993 revised editions that stopped Mexican history in 1964, thus avoiding description of the 1968 Tlatelolco massacre (which had been included in the 1992 books, much to the discontent of the army), aroused new criticism and they too were withdrawn. Ad hoc history-teaching materials were distributed instead.

1993–   On 2 October 1993, the twenty-fifth anniversary of the 1968 Tlatelolco massacre, intellectuals and human rights groups formed an unofficial truth commission and pressured the government to open official files on the massacre. The commission was denied access to them, however, and dissolved. On 2 October 1997, the Congress (under control of the opposition parties) decided to establish an official truth commission. The government promised to open official records in time for publication of the commission report on 2 October 1998, but many suspected that they were sanitized. The government released 3,000 boxes of papers stored at the National Archives, mainly from the Interior Ministry. Although many key documents appeared to be missing, some were useful as a basis for the report. But the commission was denied access to Defense Ministry records and many hours of footage of the massacre for national security reasons. The historians' consensus was reportedly that the government had orchestrated the violence to justify a broader crackdown on protesters, who were considered an embarrassment before the 1968 Olympics.

1994–   In May 1994 two unidentified men attempted to enter the Institute of Anthropological Advice for the Maya Region in San Cristóbal de las Casas, Chiapas, in order "to take away the computer". The institute compiled historical archives widely consulted by representatives of nongovernmental organizations and journalists covering the Chiapas uprising since January. The institute's coordinator, French historian and anthropologist **Andrés Aubry**, received several death threats accusing him of sympathy with the Ejército Zapatista de Liberación Nacional (EZLN) rebels. He and his wife, archivist and writer **Angélica Inda**, assisted the Comisión Nacional de Intermediación which was conducting peace talks between the government and the EZLN. In 1998 they and other scholars were intimidated and harassed. Attacks against them included attempted detention by unidentified security forces; theft of computers, notes, and manuscripts; and break-ins and vandalism of their home.

1996   In May **Javier Elorriaga Berdegué**, a historian and journalist who made video reports of the 1994 EZLN rebellion, was sentenced to thirteen years' imprisonment on the charge of terrorist activities because of his alleged EZLN membership. He was held in the Cerro Hueco prison in Tuxtla Gutiérrez. The trial was widely believed to be unfair. In June he was acquitted on appeal.

Also see Spain (1955–69: Zea), United States (1953–57: Cosío; 1965–: Zea; 1985–89: Randall).

SOURCES

American Association for the Advancement of Science, *Directory of Persecuted Scientists, Engineers, and Health Professionals* (Washington 1997–98) 36, 83–85.
———, Human Rights Action Network, *Case Me9815.Chi*, 16 November 1998.
Aguilar Camin, H., & L. Meyer, *In the Shadow of the Mexican Revolution: Contemporary Mexican History 1910–1989* (Austin 1994) 208–9.
Amnesty International, *Report 2001* (London 2001) 170.
Article 19, *Information, Freedom and Censorship: World Report* (London) 1988: 100; 1991: 112.
Bailey, D.C., "Revisionism and the Recent Historiography of the Mexican Revolution", *Hispanic American Historical Review*, 1978: 77.
Bethell, L. ed., *Cambridge History of Latin America*, vol. 7 (Cambridge 1990) 135.

Blanquel, E., "Sobre Toussaint ¿ Censura universitaria?, *La jornada*, 4 February 1985.

Boyd, K. ed., *Encyclopedia of Historians and Historical Writing* (London/Chicago 1999) 477–78, 709, 878–79.

Camp, R.A., *Who's Who in Mexico Today* (Boulder 1993) 86–87, 104, 133.

Cannon, J. ed., *The Blackwell Dictionary of Historians* (Oxford 1988) 306–7.

"Crea la Cámara Comisión Para Investigar el 68", *La jornada*, 3 October 1997 (WWW-text).

De Baets, A., "Mexico 1968: De spoken van Tlatelolco", *Spiegel Historiael*, May 1998: 186–88, 227.

Doyle, K., personal communication, February 2001.

———, "Tlatelolco Massacre: Declassified U.S. Documents on Mexico and the Events of 1968" (WWW-text 1998).

El exilio español en México 1939–1982 (Mexico 1982) 830.

Florescano, E., & R. Pérez Montfort eds., *Historiadores de México en el siglo XX* (Mexico 1995) 158–59, 256–57, 263, 267–68, 306, 351–52, 364–65, 395, 501–2.

Gilly, A., personal communication, August–September–December 2000.

———, *La revolución interrumpida: Edición corregida y aumentada* (originally 1971, Mexico 1998) 9–13.

Gorman, R.A. ed., *Biographical Dictionary of Neo-Marxism* (Westport 1985) 171–72.

Hayner, P.B., "Fifteen Truth Commissions, 1974 to 1994: A Comparative Study", *Human Rights Quarterly*, 1994: 606.

Human Rights Watch, *World Report 1997* (Washington 1996) 111.

Index on Censorship, 4/76: 34–38; 10/90: 4; 3/94: 179; 1/00: 165–66.

Keesings historisch archief, 1970: 171; 1996: 563–64, 771; 1999: 734–35.

Knight, A., "Latin America", in: M. Bentley ed., *Companion to Historiography* (London/New York 1997) 750.

Liss, S.B., *Marxist Thought in Latin America* (Berkeley/Los Angeles 1984) 229–33, 235–37.

Malagón, J., "Los Historiadores y la Historia", in: *El exilio español de 1939*, vol. 5 (Madrid 1978) 279.

Matute, Á., personal communication, September–October 2000.

Meyer, K.E., *The Plundered Past* (London 1974) 184.

Meyer, M.C., & W.L. Sherman, *The Course of Mexican History* (New York/Oxford 1995) 721.

New York Times, 1998 (21 February: A10; 14 September: A4; 4 October: 4–16), 1999 (29 June: A6) (Tlatelolco).

Ortega y Medina, J.A., "Antropología", in: *El exilio español en México 1939–1982* (Mexico 1982) 345–53.

Proceso, 26 October 1992: 12–15.

Radkau García, V., "Auf der Suche nach der Nation: Die Debatte um die staatlichen Geschichtslehrbücher in Mexiko", *Internationale Schulbuchforschung*, 1993, no. 1: 75–84.

Reid, M., "Mexico Rewrites Its History", *Guardian*, 21 August 1993: 12.

Riding, A., *Mexico: Inside the Volcano* (London 1987) 15–18, 311.

Shaw, T., "The Academic Profession and Contemporary Politics; The World Archaeological Congress: Politics and Learning", *Minerva*, 1989: 63, 68–69, 73, 118.

Tenenbaum, B.A. ed., *Encyclopedia of Latin American History and Culture* (New York 1996) vol. 3: 85, 354; vol. 4: 217.

Werner, M.S. ed., *Encyclopedia of Mexico: History, Society, and Culture* (Chicago/London 1997) 449, 650, 784.

Winters, C. ed., *International Dictionary of Anthropologists* (New York/London 1991) 101–2, 527–28.

Woolf, D.R. ed., *A Global Encyclopedia of Historical Writing* (New York/London 1998) 669.

Young, D.J., "Mexican Literary Reactions to Tlatelolco 1968", *Latin American Research Review*, 1985, no.2: 79.

MOLDOVA

1999   In February the offices of the daily *Flux* were attacked by a group of veterans from the war in Afghanistan (1979–89) because it had published a critical article regarding the tenth anniversary of the withdrawal of Soviet troops.

SOURCES

Index on Censorship, 3/99: 108.

MONGOLIA

In communist-controlled Mongolia (1921–90), the preceding period in which the Bogd Khaan ruled (1911–21) was either depicted negatively or blotted out from history. Buddhist historical biographies (*namtar*)—previously official texts—were confiscated but survived in limited clandestine circulation. A namtar of the eighth bogd (the Bogd Khaan) was said to exist in a restricted state archive. The bogd's *lungdeng* (edicts) continued to circulate secretly.

1930s–40s   Historian and writer **Byambyn Rinchen** (1905–77) was imprisoned for several years and heavily beaten and tortured because he refused to confess that he was "against the Revolution". Later he became a member of the Mongolian Academy of Sciences.

1962–   In February 1962 **Daramyn Tömör-Ochir**, a philosopher, history professor, and Politburo and Secretariat member of the Mongolian People's Revolutionary Party (MPRP), was charged with organizing the national celebrations of the 800th anniversary of the birth of Genghis Khan (?1162–1227) on 31 May. When the Soviet Communist Party newspaper *Pravda* published an attack on Genghis Khan and the "Mongol-Tatar empire" because it had placed Russia under its "yoke" for several centuries, the MPRP canceled the celebrations and issued a new and negative evaluation of the Mongol state's founder. In September Tömör-Ochir was deprived of his MPRP Politburo and Secretariat membership for allegedly intriguing against other MPRP leaders, being a careerist, trying "to create an unhealthy mood in public opinion and to inflame nationalist passions", supporting "nationalist tendencies directed at idealizing the role of Genghis Khan in Mongolian history", organizing a "pompous celebration" of the anniversary, and pursuing an "anti-Marxist nationalist line in the guise of struggle against the Choybalsan [MPRP leader 1939–52] personality cult". His dismissal was confirmed by the MPRP Central Committee in September. He retired and was eventually murdered with an ax under mysterious circumstances. He was rehabilitated in March 1990.

1982–84   In January 1982 historian **Bagaryn Shirendyb** (1912–), rector of Mongolian State University (1942–54), Academy of Sciences president (1961–82), member of the MPRP Politburo, and deputy chairman of the Great People's Hural (Parliament) (1966–?82), was removed from his posts for his alleged "lack of principle and party spirit". In the party newspaper *Unen* (Truth), he was accused of embezzlement and of ideological "mistakes" (such as ignoring valuable suggestions made by Soviet scholars). His dismissal was almost certainly linked with the dismissal of an academy vice president, whom he had supported in a conflict with Soviet scientists. After his dismissal, *Unen* printed two pages of denunciations from some of his former colleagues. One of the main charges was that he had apparently supported two fellow historians (names unknown) who in 1980 had published a book on Mongolian history, condemned for being "hostile to the Party's ideological line". The authors had apparently referred to Mongolia as once having been "part of China", a viewpoint not officially accepted and considered excessively "independent" and "nationalist". After the fall of Yumjaagiyn Tsedenbal from power in 1984, Shirendyb resumed his activities and was able to return to the Academy of Sciences as a counselor at its Institute of Oriental Studies.

SOURCES

Great Soviet Encyclopedia, vol. 29 (New York/London 1982) 601.
History of the Mongolian People's Republic (originally Mongolian 1969; Cambridge 1976) 630, 832–33, 835–36.
Humphrey, C., "Remembering an 'Enemy': The Bogd Khaan in Twentieth-Century Mongolia", in: R.S. Watson ed., *Memory, History, and Opposition under State Socialism* (Santa Fe 1994) 22, 27–28, 32, 37.
Index on Censorship, 4/82: 37.
Sanders, A.J.K., *Historical Dictionary of Mongolia* (Lanham 1996) 182–83, 195–96, 270.
Woolf, D.R. ed., *A Global Encyclopedia of Historical Writing* (New York/London 1998) 630–31.

MOROCCO

French Morocco

pre-1956   Due to political sensibilities, research in contemporary history at the
            Institut des Hautes Études at Rabat was ignored during the colonial
            period.

Morocco

1974–   In November 1974 **Brahim Mouatta** (1950–), a history and geog-
            raphy teacher in Khénifra active in the radical wing of the progres-
            sive political party Union Nationale des Forces Populaires, was
            arrested and held without trial until 1977. During the trial in Casa-
            blanca in January–February 1977, he was sentenced to twenty-two
            years' imprisonment. In 1982 he was held at Kénitra Central Prison.

1977–89   In February 1977 history and geography teacher **Said Asghen** was
            sentenced to twenty years' imprisonment for his alleged membership
            in a subversive organization. In May 1989 he was released after a
            royal pardon by King Hassan II.

pre-1981   Up to 1981 poems on the anticolonial resistance of the Berber tribes
            of the Rif in the 1920s and 1930s were completely banned in rural
            Morocco.

1984   **Abdallah Laroui** (1933–), history professor at Muhammad V Uni-
            versity, Rabat (1964–), and historian of Islamic and Moroccan civ-
            ilization, was deprived of his position for a few months before his
            reappointment in the same capacity at Casablanca University. He
            had been a counselor of foreign affairs for the Moroccan government
            (1960–63). His academic work often overlapped with various polit-
            ical activities (he was inspired by the leader of the Moroccan left,
            Mehdi Ben Barka), a cause of friction between him and the king.
            In 1985, however, he became the crown prince's official tutor.

1986   **Driss Bouissef** (?1947–), a political prisoner serving a twenty-year
            sentence since 1977, was refused permission to defend his doctoral
            thesis on Franco's Spain under the supervision of Toulouse Univer-
            sity, France.

2000   On 2 December Communications Minister Mohamed Achaari an-
            nounced a permanent ban on three weekly newspapers after they
            published a letter written by exiled opposition leader Mohamed
            Basri, in which he directly implicated Prime Minister Abderrahmane
            Youssoufi in an attempted coup against King Hassan II in 1972.

Also see France (1952: Julien).

SOURCES

American Association for the Advancement of Science, *Report on Science and Human Rights*, 1989, no.9/2: 7.
Amnesty International, *Report 2001* (London 2001) 172.
Autorenkollektiv 79 ed., *Länger als 1001 Nacht—Plus de 1001 nuits* (Tübingen 1982) 71–79.
Brown, S., D. Collinson, & R. Wilkinson eds., *Biographical Dictionary of Twentieth-Century Philosophers* (London/New York 1996) 438.
Boyd, K. ed., *Encyclopedia of Historians and Historical Writing* (London/Chicago 1999) 683–84.
Choueiri, Y.M., *Arab History and the Nation-State: A Study in Modern Arab Historiography 1820–1980* (London 1989) 165–67.
Index on Censorship, 2/81: 32–33; 8/86: 39; 1/01: 112.
Miège, J.L., "Historiography of the Maghrib", in: P.C. Emmer & H.L. Wesseling eds., *Reappraisals in Overseas History* (Leiden 1979) 72.

MOZAMBIQUE

1982   In August engineer and self-taught historian **Antonio Aquino de Bragança** (1918–86), director of the Eduardo Mondlane University Center for African Studies, Maputo, and one of the participants in the peace negotiations that led to the independence of the Portuguese colonies, was slightly injured in the explosion of a letter bomb which killed the South African exiled sociologist Ruth First, center's research director. In October 1986 Aquino de Bragança died in an airplane crash which also killed President Samora Machel, to whom he was an adviser.

Also see Zimbabwe (1996: Sinclair).

SOURCES

Azevedo, M., *Historical Dictionary of Mozambique* (Metuchen 1991) 38.
Index on Censorship, 6/82: 29–31, 46.

MYANMAR

Burma

1964   British linguist and art historian **Gordon Luce** (1889–1979), specialized in Burma's historical origins, particularly the Pagan period (eleventh–thirteenth centuries), and lecturer at Rangoon University (1922–), was required by the military government of President Ne Win (1962–81) to leave Burma. He went to the United Kingdom. During World War II, many of his research papers were lost.

Myanmar

1988–   After the 1988 military coup, cultural, historical, economic, or religious studies of ethnic minorities were suppressed.

U Kyaw Thiha, a history lecturer at Mandalay University, was detained under the martial law conditions enforced since September.

1990–91   In May 1990 **U Oo Tha Tun** (?1908–91), an Arakan (Rakhine) historian and election candidate for the Arakan League for Democracy, was detained and sentenced to three years' imprisonment with hard labor under the 1950 Emergency Provisions Law, which prohibited promoting disloyalty to the state. He died in prison.

1998–   In February 1998 **Ko Aung Tun** (1967–) was arrested and sentenced to seventeen years' imprisonment under various acts, including the 1962 Printers and Publishers Registration Act. The military government claimed that he was collaborating with "terrorist groups". Opposition sources stated, however, that the real reason for his arrest was his seven-volume history of the student movement in Myanmar. Ko Aung Tun had been active in the 1988 student-led prodemocracy movement. He had already been imprisoned in 1990–94. Businessman **U Myo Htun** assisted Ko Aung Tun in writing the book, which the authorities claimed was distributed "illegally". He was sentenced to ten years' imprisonment in March 1998. Both were held incommunicado in solitary confinement and tortured. Their health was precarious. A third author involved in writing and distributing the book was **U Ohn Myint** (?1917–), an unofficial adviser of the opposition party National League for Democracy. He was sentenced to seven years' imprisonment in April but released in January 1999 following the visit of United States Congressman Tony Hall.

1999–   In July history teacher **Ma Khin Khin Leh** (?1965–) was detained with eighteen others in Pegu, on suspicion that they were planning a pro-democracy march scheduled for 19 July (Martyrs' Day, commemorating the 1947 assassination of General Aung San, independence leader and father of opposition leader Daw Aung San Suu Kyi). The local Military Intelligence arrested her and her three-year-old daughter after officials from the State Peace and Development Council (military junta) attempted to detain her husband, Kyaw Wunna, a political activist and one of the march organizers, but could not locate him. The child was released after five days' detention. In December 1999 a Special Court sentenced Ma Khin Khin Leh to life imprisonment. In January 2000 she was transferred to an unknown location.

Also see Thailand (1984–: Sulak Sivaraksa).

SOURCES

American Association for the Advancement of Science, Human Rights Action Network, *BU0009.Daw* (5 December 2000).

Amnesty International, *Report* (London) 1991: 164; 1992: 194; 1999: 258.

———, *Urgent Action 163/98* (26 May 1998).

Article 19, *Information, Freedom and Censorship: World Report 1991* (London 1991) 202.

———, *State of Fear: Censorship in Burma (Myanmar)* (London 1991) 41–42, 68.

Human Rights Watch, *World Report* (Washington) 1999: 166; 2000: 170, 501.

International PEN Writers in Prison Committee, *Half-Yearly Caselist* (London 1998) 31–32.

Winters, C. ed., *International Dictionary of Anthropologists* (New York/London 1991) 428–29.

World University Service, *Academic Freedom* (London) 1993: 37–38; 1995: 99, 105.

N

NAMIBIA

[1990s] A Namibia Broadcasting Corporation radio program containing pre-independence archive material of detainees in the South West Africa People's Organization (SWAPO) exile camps was withdrawn at the last minute, apparently on the orders of the Minister of Information.

1996 On 6 March Namibian President Sam Nujoma attacked **Siegfried Groth**, German Lutheran Church pastor, and **Christo Lombard**, professor of theology at the University of Namibia, in a television broadcast to the nation. Groth was the author of *Namibia—The Wall of Silence: The Dark Days of the Liberation Struggle* (Wuppertal 1995; originally German 1995), a book with eyewitness accounts of the torture and "disappearance" of detainees in the SWAPO exile camps. The detainees had been accused of internal dissent or of spying for South Africa during Namibia's struggle for independence (1966–89). Lombard was the book's promoter. For many years both had actively supported SWAPO's antiapartheid struggle. On a 21 March rally in northern Namibia celebrating the sixth anniversary of Namibia's independence, some two thousand people called for the banning and public burning of the book. The book, officially launched by the civil rights movement Breaking the Wall of Silence Committee in the capital Windhoek on 30 March, had sold out about two weeks before.

Also see Germany (1965: Herero; 1971: Sudholt), United Kingdom (1986: World Archaeological Congress).

SOURCES

Article 19, *'Who Wants to Forget?' Truth and Access to Information about Past Human Rights Violations* (London 2000) 15.

Dauth T., "Review of Siegfried Groth's *Namibia: The Wall of Silence; The Dark Days of the Liberation Struggle*" (WWW-text 1996).

Media Institute of Southern Africa, *Ifex Alert*, 27 March 1996.

————, *So This Is Democracy? State of the Media in Southern Africa Report on 1996* (Windhoek 1997) 19–21.

THE NETHERLANDS

World War II and postwar military policy in Indonesia were the most sensitive areas of Dutch history. The security archives were the subject of a large debate.

pre-1945   Among the historians who emigrated before 1945 (and living in exile after 1944) were De Jong (q.v. 1971–73) and **Arthur Lehning** (1899–2000).

Among the historians and others concerned with the past who were censored, dismissed, or persecuted during World War II (including in 1945) were **Herman Colenbrander** (1871–1945), **Anton de Kom** (1898–1945, from Suriname), **Pieter Geyl** (1887–1966), **Johan Huizinga** (1872–1945), **David Koker** (1921–45), **Jaap Meijer** (1912–93), **Otto Oppermann** (1873–1946), **Nicolaas Posthumus** (1880–1960), **Jan Romein** (1893–1962), Rüter [q.v. 1955–59], and **W.F. Wertheim** (1907–98, in the Dutch East Indies).

1946–   In February 1946 **Jan de Vries** (1890–1964) was dismissed as a professor of ancient Germanic languages, religion, and history at Leiden University (1926–46). In May 1948 the court ruled that he was an "intellectual collaborator" with the Nazis. De Vries became a secondary-school teacher (1948–55).

1947–51   In November 1947 historian and Jewish leader **David Cohen** (1882–1967) was briefly arrested on charges of wartime collaboration with the Germans, but he was released in December. The case was dropped in 1951. The Jewish Honorary Council (Ereraad) temporarily excluded him from all Jewish functions. Dismissed from his professorship of ancient history at Amsterdam University (1926–53) in 1941, Cohen had acted as cochairman of the Joodsche Raad (Jewish Council), appointed by the German authorities (February 1941–September 1943). In 1943–45 he had been an inmate at Theresienstadt concentration camp.

1947   In 1947 the minister of education refused to confirm the appointment of historian and writer **Jacques Presser** (1899–1970) as professor

of contemporary history at the newly established faculty of political
and social sciences of the Municipal University of Amsterdam because of his left-wing views. He had written for several left-wing
magazines and protested McCarthyism in the United States and
Dutch policy in Indonesia. He was eventually appointed in 1949. As
a professor of modern and contemporary history at Amsterdam University (1959–69), he published an official two-volume history of
the persecution of the Dutch Jews during World War II (1965).
During that war, in November 1940, Presser, a Jew, had been dismissed at the Vossius gymnasium in Amsterdam. In 1941 he was
the main author of *The Eighty-Years War* (1568–1648), but the book
was published under the names of "J. Romein, B.W. Schaper, A.C.J.
de Vrankrijker, R.E.J. Weber, and J.W. Wijn". Presser "borrowed"
his colleague Schaper's name. From October 1941 to May 1943,
when he went into hiding after his wife's arrest, he taught at the
Jewish Lyceum, Amsterdam.

1955–59   In 1955 **Adolf Rüter** (1907–65), history professor at Leiden University, completed a manuscript commissioned by the Netherlands
State Institute for War Documentation (RIOD) about the 1944–45
railway strike. It criticized the lenience of the Dutch Railways management toward the Germans. For four years Dutch Railways, which
had funded the study, had tried first to change Rüter's interpretation
and some of his conclusions and later to persuade the government
not to publish it. The manuscript, however, was published unaltered
as *Running and Striking: The Dutch Railways during the War* (The
Hague 1960). In 1940, during World War II, Rüter had been dismissed from the International Institute of Social History, Amsterdam, by the Germans when they confiscated it.

1971–73   In 1971 H.W. van der Vaart Smit, a wartime member of the
Nationaal-Socialistische Beweging (National Socialist Movement),
sued historian and RIOD director **Loe de Jong** (1914–) for libel
because in part 1 of the official war history *The Kingdom of the
Netherlands in World War II* (thirteen parts in twenty-seven volumes; The Hague 1969–88) he had quoted another author who called
Van der Vaart Smit a "liar". In June 1972 the court rejected the
charge. The judgment was confirmed on appeal in April 1973 and
reconfirmed in cassation in December.

1972   In 1972 de Jong [q.v. 1971–73] had completed the manuscript of
part 4 of his *Kingdom of the Netherlands in World War II*. In it he
wrote about the Nederlandsche Unie (Dutch Union), a political party
founded in July 1940 (after the German occupation in May) by a
triumvirate. The Nederlandsche Unie aimed at cooperation between

Dutch and German authorities to create a national mass movement. Two triumvirate members, Jan de Quay and L. Einthoven, tried to prevent the manuscript's publication. De Quay, former prime minister (1959–63), approached another former prime minister, Louis Beel, who talked with a senior civil servant about the approval procedure for the work. In May Einthoven wrote to the minister of education and sciences that an official history written by someone who had not experienced the German occupation (de Jong escaped and spent the war as a journalist in London) but behaved as a prosecutor and judge at the same time, was unacceptable. In July Einthoven sent a request for de Jong's dismissal to the minister of scientific policy and education. In August De Quay spoke with Prime Minister B.W. Biesheuvel and the minister of education and sciences. The minister said that he had no scholarly responsibility for the content of the work (a view endorsed by the Council of Ministers), and did not intervene. The main point of difference between de Jong and the triumvirate was the degree to which the Nederlandsche Unie accommodated itself to the Third Reich. The triumvirate submitted several memoranda to de Jong later and met once with him. This led to many amendments in his texts for parts 4 and 5, although mostly on minor points.

1985–90   In 1985 part 11A of *The Kingdom of the Netherlands in World War II* was published. Dealing with the Dutch East Indies and the later Indonesia, it led to a protracted lawsuit (March 1985–April 1986; appeal June 1986–April 1990) which was finally decided against the petitioners (representatives of part of the community of those who formerly lived in the East Indies, organized as the Comité Geschiedkundig Eerherstel Nederlandsch-Indië, the Committee for the Historical Rehabilitation of the Dutch East Indies) in April 1990. They had accused de Jong [q.v. 1971–73] of portraying too negatively the role of the colonial administration, objected to passages about war crimes committed by Dutch troops against against Indonesian nationalists in 1945–49, and asked the state to commission "a less prejudiced historian" to rewrite the history of colonial relations. A January 1986 Freedom of Information request to make public the reading reports of the reviewers of de Jong's manuscript was refused in June 1989. The 1987 manuscript of part 12, also about Dutch–Indonesian relations in 1945–49, was leaked to the press by two military reviewers and evoked strong protests from veterans because it contained a 46-page section entitled "War Crimes". Some demanded nonpublication of part 12, others sued de Jong for libel or published denials. In the 1988 publication of part 12, the section was entitled "Excesses".

1994–95   In June 1994 author **Graa Boomsma** (1953–) was found not guilty
of insulting Dutch war veterans. The charges arose over comments
made by Boomsma in a March 1992 interview about his novel *The
Last Typhoon* (1992). In them he compared the Dutch army's conduct in Indonesia in the late 1940s to that of the Nazis during World
War II. An appeal launched against the Groningen Court decision
in July 1994 was dismissed in January 1995. Boomsma reportedly
received threatening telephone calls throughout January.

1995   In 1995 **Dirk Engelen** (1941–), historian and member of the Binnenlandse Veiligheidsdienst (BVD; Internal Security Service), published a BVD history commissioned by the minister of internal
affairs in 1990. He was given access to all the archives but could
not report on data that would endanger the BVD's functioning. A
commission of four historians supervising his doctoral research
asked and was given full access to the archives in order to enable
scholarly control. Other historians were denied full access to BVD
archives and had to start a procedure based upon the Wet Openbaarheid Bestuur (Freedom of Information Act) in order to gain
access to specified documents. Engelen's book was written against
a background of public debate about the intended destruction of
hundreds of thousands of files on persons and organizations in the
BVD archives. In May 1998 a parliamentary working group report
stated that the BVD illegally destroyed more than 500 file groups
between 1959 and 1990. Similar reports were heard on the External
Intelligence Service (IDB) and the Military Intelligence Service
(MID). On a more general level, historians repeatedly warned that
the historical interest (as distinguished from the administrative and
the civil interest) was not taken fully into account in the archival
selection process and that the 1962 and 1995 Archive Laws allowed
inadmissable levels of destruction of documents, especially those
concerning policy preparation and implementation.

Also see Belgium (1994–95: Van den Berghe), Indonesia (1945: Mansvelt;
1977–: Rademakers; 1981–: Pramoedya).

SOURCES

Amerongen, M. van, "De mislukte aanslag op het koninkrijk der Nederlanden in de
Tweede Wereldoorlog", *Vrij Nederland*, 22 October 1983: 3–4.
Boekholt, R., *De staat, dr. L. de Jong en Indië: Het proces van het Comité Geschiedkundig Eerherstel Nederlands-Indië tegen de Staat der Nederlanden over deel
11A van "Het Koninkrijk der Nederlanden in de Tweede Wereldoorlog" 29 maart
1986–10 april 1990* (Den Haag 1992) 209–14, 286–90, 369–75.

Charité, J. ed., *Biografisch woordenboek van Nederland* (The Hague/Amsterdam), vol. 1 (1979): 474–77, 508–11; vol. 2 (1985): 602–4; vol. 3 (1989): 101–4.

De Baets, A., "Gekruiste degens: Overheid, historici en archieven in Nederland", *Bibliotheek- en archiefgids*, 1996: 237–42, 277.

"Discussiedossier Archiefvernietiging", *Bijdragen en mededelingen betreffende de geschiedenis der Nederlanden*, 1993: 722–87.

Engelen, D., *Geschiedenis van de Binnenlandse Veiligheidsdienst* (The Hague 1995) 9, 377.

Hoogstraten, M. van, & S. Jansens, "Debat over de vernietiging van de BVD-archieven: Manipulatie van het verleden dreigt", *Historisch nieuwsblad*, 1993, no.5: 6–9.

Huussen, A.H. Jr., "Archiefbeheer: Selectie, vernietiging en behoud", *Groniek*, 1996: 328–33.

———, "Geschiedschrijving, archieven en vernietiging", *Nederlands archievenblad*, 1991: 304–7.

———, *Historical Dictionary of the Netherlands* (Lanham 1998) 58, 117.

Index on Censorship, 3/94: 179; 4–5/94: 245; 2/95: 181.

International PEN Writers in Prison Committee, *Ifex Alert*, 13 January 1995.

Jong L. de, *Het koninkrijk der Nederlanden in de Tweede Wereldoorlog* (The Hague/ Leiden) vol. 1 (1969): 491; vol. 12b (1988): 1011–12; vol. 13 (1988): 70–75, 83; vol. 14 (1991): 62–63, 291–97, 308, 320, 339, 762, 900–918, 931, 937–41.

Keesings historisch archief, 1998: 336.

Klep, P.M.M., *Archieven bewaren: Cultureel investeren in de toekomst; Discussienota over selectie en vernietiging van archiefbescheiden ten behoeve van de Rijkscommissie voor de archieven* (Nijmegen 1992) [summary in: *Bijdragen en mededelingen betreffende de geschiedenis der Nederlanden*, 1993: 190–97].

NRC-Handelsblad, 1994 (20 May: 7; 26 May: 11) (Boomsma).

"De ontwerp nieuwe archiefwet: Twee reacties", *Historisch nieuwsblad*, 1993, no.3: 30–33.

Pam, M., *De onderzoekers van de oorlog: Het Rijksinstituut voor Oorlogsdocumentatie en het werk van dr. L. de Jong* (The Hague 1989) 25–27, 81–86.

Presser, J., *The Night of the Girondists* (originally Dutch 1957; Groningen 1995) 67–74.

Romijn, P., "Fifty Years Later: Historical Studies of the Netherlands and the Second World War", in: N.C.F. van Sas & E. Witte eds., *Historical Research in the Low Countries* (The Hague 1992) 102–3.

Roth, C. ed., *Encyclopaedia Judaica*, vol. 5 (Jerusalem 1971) 668.

Rüter, A.J.C., *Rijden en staken: De Nederlandse spoorwegen in oorlogstijd* (The Hague 1960) vii–xii.

Voerman, G., " 'Dales versus Cleio': Dreigende kaalslag in BVD-archieven", *Socialisme en Democratie*, 1993: 454–57.

———, "Kleio mag niet vergeten worden bij vernietiging BVD-archieven", *Staatscourant*, 24 February 1994: 2.

———, "Kroniek van een aangekondigde vernietiging: Over de toekomst van de archieven van de BVD", *De nieuwste tijd*, 1996, no.6: 23–30.

Volkskrant, 1998 (29 January: 3; 2 February: 4; 14 May: 9) (BVD archives).

Volmuller, H.W.J. ed., *Nijhoffs geschiedenislexicon: Nederland en België* (The Hague/ Antwerp 1981) 126, 292, 468, 503.

NEW ZEALAND

pre-1954   A 1954 report stated that many archives were destroyed or neglected.

pre-1991   A 1991 report stated that many Maori (the indigenous population)
disliked having the past examined. The history they passed down
among themselves was reportedly secret and sacred information, not
for public discussion. They also often preferred to see human remains destroyed rather than dug up and preserved.

Also see Germany (1983–Poppe), Japan (1995–96: Mackay).

SOURCES

Beaglehole, J.C., "The New Zealand Scholar" (1954), in: P. Munz ed., *The Feel of Truth:
Essays in New Zealand and Pacific History* (Wellington 1969) 251.
Renfrew, C., & P. Bahn, *Archaeology: Theories, Methods and Practice* (London 1991)
466.

NICARAGUA

pre-1952   **Pedro Chamorro Zelaya** (1891–1952), historian, journalist, politician, and diplomat, was a strong advocate of the liberal principles
of free press and freedom of thought. His ideas led the Somoza
government to attack him and to silence his newspaper *La Prensa*
on several occasions. He eventually went into exile, but he returned
and resumed his work as a journalist.

1975–77   In October 1975 **Liana Benavides Grütter** (1952–), former history
student at the University of Costa Rica, was arrested by National
Guard troops in Chinandega. In November she was indicted for violent actions on behalf of the Frente Sandinista de Liberación Nacional (FSLN) on the basis of her own testimony. In early 1977 she
was sentenced to eighteen months' imprisonment for alleged crimes
against internal security—nearly equal to the period already spent
in pretrial detention—and released a few weeks later. She returned
to Costa Rica. According to various reports, she had been severely
tortured in Chinandega and held incommunicado for nearly two
months in the capital Managua. One of the tortures she had to undergo was "la capucha" (hooding), consisting of covering a person
with a black cloth for some weeks until all concept of time is lost.

1990–   After the Unión Nacional Opositora took over power from the FSLN
in February 1990, many of the close to 300 murals created from
1979 to 1990 and depicting the Sandinista view of Nicaraguan his-

tory were destroyed or painted over, especially in Managua under Mayor (and future President) Arnoldo Alemán Lacayo. A 1991 fourth-grade *History of Nicaragua* textbook reportedly passed over Sandinista heroes and achievements in silence.

1997   In October students at the former Instituto Autónomo Rigoberto Ló-pez Pérez, named after the Sandinista poet-fighter who assassinated former President Anastasio Somoza in 1956, went on strike after it was announced that the school was to be renamed after another poet. The episode fitted in an alleged government campaign to wipe out the last vestiges of Sandinismo by changing the national symbols. This included the replacement of Augusto Sandino's image on the banknotes with that of former President José Santos Celaya (in office 1894–1909).

SOURCES

Amnesty International, *Report 1977* (London 1977) 152.
————, *The Republic of Nicaragua: An AI Report, Including the Findings of a Mission to Nicaragua 10–15 May 1976* (London 1977) 64, 69–72.
Boia, L. ed., *Great Historians of the Modern Age: An International Dictionary* (Westport 1991) 653–54.
Index on Censorship, 1/98: 93.
Kunzle, D., *The Murals of Revolutionary Nicaragua 1979–92* (Berkeley/London 1995) ix, xi, xv, 12–26.
Thomas, J.R., *Biographical Dictionary of Latin American Historians and Historiography* (Westport 1984) 133–34.
Woolf, D.R. ed., *A Global Encyclopedia of Historical Writing* (New York/London 1998) 152.

NIGERIA

Ethnic tensions and military intervention in politics were the most precarious historical subjects in Nigeria.

1966   Late in 1966 historian **Kenneth Onwuka Dike** (1917–83), vice chancellor (1960–66) and director of the Institute of African Studies (1962–67) at Ibadan University, returned to his home province. He was an Igbo, and ethnic tensions had limited his freedom of move-ment in his administrative role at Ibadan University, located in Yo-ruba territory. An Eastern Nigeria History Project he had began together with historian Joseph Anene in 1966 at Ibadan was aborted by the civil war (May 1967–January 1970), as was his plan for a new university in eastern Nigeria. In 1971 he became the first pro-fessor of African history at Harvard University.

1970–84   From early 1970 (after the civil war) to 1982, **Chukwuemeka Ojukwu** (1933–), historian, army commander, and leader of the secessionist state of Biafra (1967–70), was exiled in Ivory Coast. In 1982 he was pardoned, and he returned to Nigeria. When Major General Muhammadu Buhari came to power on 31 December 1983, Ojukwu was imprisoned, probably on account of his former political activities. After his release in October 1984, he went into private business.

pre-1976   By 1976 economic historian **R.J. Gavin**, a representative of the so-called Ibadan school of historiography at Ahmadu Bello University, Zaria, was reportedly "forced out" of Zaria.

1978   In August or September, historian **Jacob Ajayi** (1929–), professor at Ibadan University (1958–72, 1978–89), was summarily removed from his post as vice chancellor at the University of Lagos (1972–78) after extensive rioting after a funeral in April, attributed to university students.

1989   Writer **Kole Omotoso** (1943–) declared that parts of *Just before Dawn* (Ibadan 1988), his novel about Nigerian history from 1918 to 1988, in which historical sources were copiously quoted, had been censored. According to Omotoso, the publishers were forced to excise large parts of the manuscript because they revealed details about the postindependence era, particularly about the role of senior army officers in politics. After publication of some excerpts two days before the novel's launch on 20 July 1988, General Olusegun Obasanjo, former and later head of state (1976–79, 1999–), objected to his being mentioned as one of those attending a 1983 meeting of senior military officers at which the decision was allegedly made for the army to intervene in Nigerian politics. The publisher complied with the demand and corrected the text by eliminating the list of names at the meeting on the penultimate page.

1989–90   In [June] 1989 **Yusufu Bala Usman**, a radical history teacher at Ahmadu Bello University and strong critic of President Ibrahim Babangida's government (in office 1985–93), was told in a letter that he was dismissed "in the public interest". In June 1990 a judge ruled that the dismissal was illegal. In May 1989 the minister of education had announced that all university teachers were forbidden by law to take part in partisan politics. Teachers were given until late May either to withdraw from politics or to face official action. Thereafter vice chancellors were asked to monitor the activities of their employees and compile a list of teachers who failed to comply with the new regulations for scrutiny by the National University Commission. Bala Usman was the first victim of these regulations. With his historical work as a point of departure, he had criticized the lack of democracy and the corruption of the political system (for example in his *For the Liberation of Nigeria*, 1979).

1990–   **Toyin Falola** (1953–), historian at Obafemi Awolowo University (1977–90), Ife, Oyo State, went into voluntary exile in Canada, where he worked at York University, Ontario (1990–91), and to the United States, where he was a professor of African history at the University of Texas, Austin (1991–). He was a specialist in the history of West Africa, Nigeria, and Yoruba-speaking people since the nineteenth century. The Buhari government (1983–85) disapproved of his book *The Rise and Fall of Nigeria's Second Republic 1979– 1984* (1985), with Julius Ihonvbere as coauthor. Falola was briefly detained under the Babangida government.

1990   In March *Quality* magazine editor **Bala Dan Musa** and former civilian governor (of Imo state) **Sam Mbakwe** were arrested by the State Security Service. No reason was given, but in a *Quality* interview **Mbakwe** had said that "the spirit of Biafra" lived.

Among those who felt the repercussions of the aborted coup of 22 April 1990, led by Major Gideon Orkar, were the following:

1990   **Lukman Abubakar**, lecturer at the history department of Usmanu Danfodiyo University, Sokoto, was dismissed, possibly in connection with the coup.

On 28 April 1990, **Obaro Ikime** (1936–), history professor and head of the Ibadan University history department, was arrested for soliciting prayers for the stability of Nigeria after the aborted coup. Some of his views on religion were reflected in the coup leaders' statement. He and others such as Osoba [q.v. 1990] were held for three months without charge and, when no evidence was found linking them to the coup, released on 1 August. After the Ministry of Education issued a letter requesting Ikime's retirement from the university on the grounds that "further or continued employment in the relevant service would not be in the public interest", he retired under compulsion on 1 September. The university's governing council was not consulted.

Another historian declared wanted in the wake of the aborted coup was **Segun Osoba**, although he was in the United Kingdom and the Caribbean at that time [q.v. 1990: Ikime]. Osoba worked at Obafemi Awolowo University for many years and was frequently harassed and put in detention by the Babangida government for criticizing the military. He was Nigeria's most sustained Marxist historian, and his university reportedly refused to elevate him to full professor because of his writings.

SOURCES

Africa Watch, *Academic Freedom and Human Rights Abuses in Africa* (New York 1991)
    45–46, 49, 51.
Alagoa, E.J., "Nigerian Academic Historians", in: Jewsiewicki & Newbury eds. 1986:
    191, 195, 203.
———, "Oral Tradition and Cultural History in Nigeria", *Storia della storiografia*, 1984,
    no.5: 70.
Amnesty International, *Report* (London) 1985: 79, 1991: 173.
Annual Obituary 1983 (Chicago/London) 496–97 (Dike).
Boia, L. ed., *Great Historians of the Modern Age: An International Dictionary* (Westport
    1991) 1–2.
Boyd, K. ed., *Encyclopedia of Historians and Historical Writing* (London/Chicago 1999)
    22–23.
Brockman, N.C., *An African Biographical Dictionary* (Santa Barbara 1994) 277–78.
Busia, N.K.A. Jr., "Towards a Legal Framework for the Protection of Academic Freedom:
    Perspectives on the African Human Rights System", in: Codesria 1996: 25.
Codesria, *Bulletin*, 1/91: 11.
———, *The State of Academic Freedom in Africa 1995* (Dakar 1996).
Duffy, J., M. Frey, & M. Sins eds., *International Directory of Scholars and Specialists
    in African Studies* (Waltham, Mass. 1978) 12–13, 125, 327–28.
Falola, T. ed., *African Historiography: Essays in Honour of Jacob Ade. Ajayi* (Harlow,
    Essex: 1993) viii, 1, 233.
———, personal communication, April 1996, September 1997, February 1999.
Index on Censorship, 1/79: 62; 5/81: 12–13; 2/86: 16–17; 2/89: 14–15; 6/90: 40; 1/91:
    31.
Jewsiewicki, B., & D. Newbury eds., *African Historiographies: What History for Which
    Africa?* (London/Beverly Hills 1986).
Lovejoy, P.E., "The Ibadan School and Its Critics", in: Jewsiewicki & Newbury eds.
    1986: 197–98, 203–4.
———, "The Ibadan School of Historiography and Its Critics", in: Falola ed. 1993: 199.
Middleton, J. ed., *Encyclopedia of Africa South of the Sahara*, vol. 1 (London 1997)
    466–67.
Mustapha, A.R., "The State of Academic Freedom in Nigeria", in: Codesria 1996: 111.
Nwala, U., "Academic Freedom in Africa: The Nigerian Experience", in: M. Mamdani
    & M. Diouf eds., *Academic Freedom in Africa* (Dakar 1994) 186–88.
Omotoso, K., "De verdraaide en vertekende geschiedenissen van Nigeria", in: *Het col-
    lectieve geheugen: Over literatuur en geschiedenis* (Amsterdam 1990) 81–91.
Oyewole, A., *Historical Dictionary of Nigeria* (Metuchen 1987) 106.
Woolf, D.R. ed., *A Global Encyclopedia of Historical Writing* (New York/London 1998)
    14–15, 237–38.
World University Service, *Academic Freedom 4* (London 1996) 63.

NORTH KOREA

See Korea.

NORTHERN IRELAND

See United Kingdom.

NORWAY

pre-1945   Among the historians and others concerned with the past who emigrated before 1945 (and living in exile after 1944) was **Halvdan Koht** (1873–1965).

pre-1991   A 1991 report stated that the Storting (Norwegian parliament) was very reluctant to let qualified historians examine its archives. The 1970 Public Access Act did not cover its records. It was further reported that the Norwegian National Archives had uncovered massive destruction of documents in the archives of many defense agencies; this was considered problematic because the shortage of accurate current information enhanced the value of historical records. Because of archival weeding and allegedly slow declassification, Norwegian historians had to rely to a large extent on United States archival sources in their work on Norwegian security topics. In recent years, however, access to the Storting archives and the security archives has become very liberal. At the same time, access to other sensitive contemporary archives (such as those on forced sterilization, lobotomy, insanity, espionage, secret surveillance) have been the object of controversy.

SOURCES

Article 19, *Information, Freedom and Censorship: World Report 1991* (London 1991) 288, 290–91.

Banisar, D., *Freedom of Information around the World* (WWW-text; Privacy International Report; London 2000).

Eriksen, K.E., personal communication, October 2000.

Sogner, S., personal communication, September 2000.

P

PAKISTAN

After General Zia ul Haq assumed power in July 1977, the Education Department started to revise syllabi at all educational levels in order to bring them into line with Islamic ideology and principles. The purged material reportedly included "atheistic" accounts of history. The rewriting of history books began in earnest in 1981, when ul Haq declared that teaching Mutalaa-i-Pakistan (Pakistan Studies) to all degree students was compulsory. The course was based on the Ideology of Pakistan, the creation of a completely Islamized state. Topics that were distorted included the historical origins of Pakistan and its archeological heritage (because of its largely non-Islamic nature); the sacrifices and anticolonialism of the Muslims in British India; the image of Ali Jinnah (1876–1948), Pakistan's leader in 1947; the role of the *ulama* (religious scholars) in the nationalistic Pakistan Movement before independence; secularism and regionalism; and the portrayal of Hindus. The 1947–77 period, including the 1948 war over Kashmir (fought when a civilian government was in power), the history of East Pakistan (including the 1971 civil war, the Indian invasion, and Pakistan's partition in December 1971), and Zulfikar Ali Bhutto's rule (1971–77), was almost entirely neglected in textbooks. After 1988, under Benazir Bhutto's government, some distortions were rectified; archival traditions and practices were poor.

British India

1946– The book *Modern Islam in India: A Social Analysis* (London), by **Wilfred Cantwell Smith** (1916–), Canadian lecturer in Islamic history at the Forman Christian College in Lahore (1940–46), later a professor of comparative religion and Islamic studies at McGill University, Montréal (1948–64), and Harvard University, Cambridge, Mass. (1964–73), was not allowed into India because of its alleged communist approach. In 1954 a pirated edition was published in Lahore as *Modern Islam in India and Pakistan* without the author's consent or knowledge, with interpolations and an additional chapter written by someone else. The 1946 books, describing the transformation of the traditional Muslim community into a modern society during the preceding seventy-five years, were a revision of the first edition (Lahore 1943), augmented with a pamphlet, *The Muslim League 1942–45*.

Pakistan

1958–69   Under Field Marshal Muhammad Ayub Khan's rule (1958–69), the archives of the All-India Muslim League and its heir, the Pakistan Muslim League, were seized by the police after the Pakistan Muslim League and all other parties were declared unlawful. Possibly half the archives were destroyed. The Bengal Muslim League's archives in Dacca were confiscated by the police and held for several years. The entire Punjab Muslim League's archives were destroyed in a fire, which started when the police raided the league's office. In addition, restrictions imposed on visits of Pakistani citizens to India meant that many archives on Pakistan's history remained inaccessible.

1961   The Pakistani censor cut the last part of the film *El Cid* (1961) because it showed El Cid's ghost leading the Christians to victory over the Moors.

1971   Among the Bengali intellectuals kidnapped by Al Badr death squads at Dacca University during the genocide (which led to the independence of East Pakistan, renamed Bangladesh) and murdered on 14 December were assistant history professor **Ghyasuddin Ahmed**, assistant history professor **Santosh Bhattacharya**, and associate history professor **Abul Khair**. Many historical documents and other collections were burned at the university.

A survey carried out after the independence war by Dacca Museum director Enamul Haque revealed that at least 2,000 Hindu temples had been destroyed or substantially damaged as a result of deliberate plunder and that some 6,000 pieces of sculpture had been removed or destroyed by looters in 1971. Thirty-five bronze sculptures were taken from the Archeological Museum at Mainamati, and the entire collection of the Dinajpur Museum was looted.

Among those who felt the repercussions of the July 1977 coup were the following:

1977–   Historian **Khursheed Kamal Aziz** (1927–), who had served as deputy official historian to the government of Pakistan, as chairman of the National Commission on Historical and Cultural Research (1973–77), and special policy adviser to Prime Minister Ali Bhutto, was suspended, harassed for ten months, and then forced to resign and leave Pakistan.

          Jinnah: Creator of Pakistan (London 1954), a book by **Hector Bolitho** (1898–1974) reprinted several times, was censored. Based on unpublished material and on personal interviews with Jinnah's friends and associates, it contained an account of Pakistan's 1947 origins and was considered a standard work. A book with radio interviews given by Jinnah's contemporaries shortly after his death could not be published. A documentary sponsored by the National Committee for Quaid-e-Azam Centenary Celebrations and entitled *A Portrait of the Quaid* [Ali Jinnah] (1976), which had been screened on television and in cinema houses throughout Pakistan, was withdrawn and later banned. The film's copies disappeared.

1977   In September the Martial Law Administration of the Punjab banned four books, including *A History of Pakistan* by **[Yuri] Gankovsky** and **Ludmila Gordon-Polonskaya**, and *Imperialism and Revolution in South Asia* (New York 1973) by **Kathleen Gough** (1925–90) and **Hari Sharma**.

          The unfinished film *The Blood of Hussain* by **Jamil Dehlavi** was banned. In the film a historic procession of mourning for Imam Hussain (a grandson of the Prophet Mohammed murdered by the forces of Umayyad Caliph Yazid in 680 CE) became the symbol of a modern peasant uprising against the military government. Before the film's seizure, Dehlavi managed to send the unedited material out of Pakistan. His passport was confiscated and for two years he was harassed, but he finally escaped on a forged passport to the United Kingdom, where he completed the film.

1984–88   *Jinnah of Pakistan: A Life* (New York 1984) by historian **Stanley Wolpert** (1927–), lecturer (1958–68) and history professor (1968–) at the University of California, was banned for four-and-a-half years because Wolpert refused to delete 28 lines considered objectionable (and related to Jinnah's eating habits) or to publish an abridged edition. He also turned down an invitation to visit Pakistan. Publisher **Najam Sethi** of Vanguard Books, Lahore, spent a month in prison (August–September 1984) on charges of attempting to pirate the book. He was released only after a storm of international protest and after he had proved that he had been negotiating with Oxford University Press in New York for reprint rights under royalty. By 1987–88, however, a pirated edition was openly available in bookshops in

Islamabad and sold well. Ul Haq himself presented copies of the confiscated first edition to dignitaries and visiting journalists. The book was finally published by Oxford University Press, Pakistan, following the repeal in September 1988 of the 1963 West Pakistan Press and Publications Ordinance.

1988   A Pakistani university professor abandoned his project of writing Jinnah's biography after he was denied access to Jinnah's and the cabinet's papers of 1947–48. Around the same time, many historical maps were reportedly classified and, therefore, beyond access. Historian Aziz [q.v. 1977–] spoke of excessive secrecy.

Facts Are Facts: The Untold Story of India's Partition ([Peshawar]), a book by **Khan Abdul Wali Khan** (1921–), son of Khan Abdul Ghaffar Khan and leader of the Pathans and the Awami National Party, was banned. Since the 1940s he and his father had been opposed to the Muslim League's demand for the creation of a separate homeland for the Muslims of British India because this would divide them. Like his father, Wali Khan was imprisoned several times (1947–53, 1958, 1968, 1972, 1975–78). Around December 1981 the Urdu weekly *Chattan* had been banned because it had published an interview with him.

Also see Bangladesh (1998: Umar), India (1946–47: Khan; 1992: Ayodhya; 1994: Hussain; 1996: Wolpert), Iran (1989–: Rushdie), United States (1970–72: Ahmed).

SOURCES

Amnesty International, *Report* (London) 1974–75: 97; 1975–76: 144–45; 1977: 206; 1978: 179.

Article 19 et al., *Global Trends on the Right to Information: A Survey of South Asia* (WWW-text; London 2001).

Aziz, K.K., *The Murder of History: A Critique of History Textbooks Used in Pakistan* (Lahore 1993) ix–xvii, 187–247.

———, *The Pakistani Historian: Pride and Prejudice in the Writing of History* (Lahore 1993) 7, 22–23, 25, 28, 31, 42–43, 74, 99–100, 103–5.

Bayly, C.A., "Modern Indian Historiography", in: M. Bentley ed., *Companion to Historiography* (London/New York 1997) 683.

Burki, S.J., *Historical Dictionary of Pakistan* (Metuchen 1991) 212–14.

Chaudhuri, K., *Genocide in Bangladesh* (Bombay 1972) 149–50.

Ferahian, S., *W. C. Smith Remembered* (WWW-text; 1996).

Hasan, M., *Legacy of a Divided Nation: India's Muslims from Independence to Ayodhya* (New Delhi 1997) 65–66.

Himmelmann, N., *Utopische Vergangenheit: Archäologie und moderne Kultur* (Berlin 1976) 107.

Hoodbhoy, P.A., & A.H. Nayyar, "Rewriting the History of Pakistan", in: M.A. Khan, *Islam, Politics and the State: The Pakistan Experience* (London 1985) 164–77.

Index on Censorship, 1/72: 33; 2/75: 88–89; 4/80: 57; 4/81: 21–22; 2/82: 46; 6/84: 47; 2/85: 28; 1/88: 38–39; 6/97: 65–66.

Jalal, A., "Conjuring Pakistan: History As Official Imagining", *International Journal of Middle East Studies*, 1995: 79–85, 89.

Mathews, T.D., *Censored* (London 1994) 98.

Meyer, K.E., *The Plundered Past* (London 1974) 7–8.

Niazi, Z., *The Web of Censorship* (Karachi 1994) 28–29, 108–12, 121–22.

Singhal, D.P., "Pakistan", in: R.W. Winks ed., *The Historiography of the British Empire-Commonwealth: Trends, Interpretations, and Resources* (Durham 1966) 400–401, 403–4, 407, 415.

Woolf, D.R. ed., *A Global Encyclopedia of Historical Writing* (New York/London 1998) 950.

World University Service, *Academic Freedom 4* (London 1996) 121–27, 134.

PALESTINE

See Israel & Occupied Territories (pre-1948).

PALESTINIAN AUTHORITY

See Israel & Occupied Territories (1995–).

PANAMA

1989   After the entry of United States forces in December which ousted President Manuel Noriega, almost all sixty murals painted by the Felicia Santizo Brigade were destroyed. The murals displayed nationalist, Marxist, antiimperialist, pro-Palestine, and pro-Sandinista themes.

SOURCES

Kunzle, D., *The Murals of Revolutionary Nicaragua 1979–92* (Berkeley/London 1995) ix, 22–23.

PAPUA NEW GUINEA

See Australia (1959–62: Healy).

PARAGUAY

During President Alfredo Stroessner's rule (1954–89), historical research withered, with only the official line being tolerated in schools and at the university.

pre-1945– Among the historians and others concerned with the past who emigrated before 1945 (and were living in exile after 1944) were **Justo Pastor Benítez** (1895–1962), **Pablo Ynsfran** (1894–1972), and **Efraím Cardozo** (1906–73).

1949–   **Juan Natalicio González** (?1896–1966), historian, publisher, and politician of the Partido Colorado (Colorado Party), of which he headed the authoritarian nationalist faction known as Guión Rojo, became president of Paraguay (August 1948–January 1949). Thereafter he was ousted and sent into political exile as an ambassador to Mexico. His personal historical library was acquired by the University of Kansas, Lawrence, United States.

Among those who felt the repercussions of Stroessner's rule were the following:

[1954–]   **Justo Pastor Prieto** (1897–), historian and politician active in the Liberal Party, former minister of education, justice, and foreign relations, resided in Argentina.

1954–89   The work of **Julio Correa**, considered the founder of modern Guaraní theater, was banned, including plays such as *Back to the Struggle, Yellowbellies*, and *During the War*, reportedly showing how the Paraguayan people were forced to fight in the Chaco War against Bolivia (1932–35) while the large landowners saved their children from the front line.

             Augusto Roa Bastos (1917–), a novelist and Chaco War veteran, lived in Argentina for several years and then taught at Toulouse University, France, until his 1985 retirement. His novel *Hijo de hombre* (1960; *Son of Man*, 1965) was a novelistic portrait of Paraguay in the last two centuries. In his 1974 novel *Yo el supremo* (*I the Supreme*, 1986), about Paraguay's first ruler José Gaspar Rodríguez de Francia (ruled 1814–40), he implicitly condemned Stroessner. In April 1982 he returned to Paraguay for a visit but he was expelled as a "Marxist subversive". After 1989 he returned from exile. As early as 1947, Roa Bastos had already been forced into exile in Brazil, Argentina, and France, as he had been a target of militarist forces.

1977   In September Spanish-born Catholic teacher **E. Pérez Barquín** was expelled from Paraguay. The minister of education accused him of "educating potential supporters and implementers of the Marxist ideas of communism". Among the evidence against him were books from his library by Austrian-born philosopher and historian **Ivan Illich** (1926–) and the book *World History of the Communist Parties*.

1988   In July four opposition politicians were arrested in the town of Itá after attending a religious service commemorating the 101st anniversary of the Liberal Party. They were detained incommunicado for three days without official explanation and then released without charge.

1989–   In February the municipality of Asunción prohibited the showing of a play, *Los tribunales de San Fernando*, by journalist **Alcibíades González Delvalle**, on the grounds that it was offensive to the memory of former president and dictator Francisco Solano López (ruled 1862–70). Despite a series of legal hearings, the ban remained a year later, although selling the text was permitted.

SOURCES

Amnesty International, *Report 1989* (London 1989) 143.
Article 19, *Information, Freedom and Censorship: World Report 1991* (London 1991) 128.
Barager, J.R., "The Historiography of the Río de la Plata Area since 1830", *Hispanic American Historical Review*, 1959: 623–24.
Bethell, L. ed., *The Cambridge History of Latin America*, vol. 8 (Cambridge 1991) 246–50.
Index on Censorship, 1/79: 27, 30; 4/83: 15–17; 6/85: 50–51.
Instituto Panamericano de Geografía e Historia, *Guía de personas que cultivan la historia de América* (México 1967) 97, 175.
Nickson, R.A., *Historical Dictionary of Paraguay* (Metuchen 1993) 260–61.
Tenenbaum, B.A. ed., *Encyclopedia of Latin American History and Culture* (New York 1996) vol.3: 83; vol. 4: 581–82.
Tucker, M. ed., *Literary Exile in the Twentieth Century: An Analysis and Biographical Dictionary* (Westport 1991) 580–82.

PERU

1949–57   While enjoying diplomatic asylum in the Colombian embassy in Lima (1949–54), **Victor Haya de la Torre** (1895–1979), founder of the Alianza Popular Revolucionaria Americana (1924), wrote a critique of the writings of world historian Arnold Toynbee (published in 1957). Haya de la Torre stressed the uniqueness of America's indigenous history. In 1954 he was given a guarantee of safe conduct to leave Peru. He returned in 1957.

[1972]–   Historian **Heraclio Bonilla** was reportedly criticized and possibly harassed by the military. This followed a debate about a book that he coedited, *La independencia en el Perú* (Lima 1972), a revisionist interpretation of the Peruvian independence movement which was criticized in the media as unpatriotically debunking the nation's traditional heroes and emphasizing too much the social-economic factors. A few years later, the debate about the "great men" historiographical tradition was continued in connection with the use of certain textbooks in high school classes.

1989   Several archeologists withdrew from the highlands because of the political violence in Peru.

pre-1997   Historian **Mark Thurner's** intention to carry out ethnographic and oral history research in the Huaraz region for his book *From Two Republics to One Divided: Contradictions of Postcolonial Nationmaking in Andean Peru* (Durham/London 1997) was thwarted by assassinations, bombings, power outages, and attacks in peasant communities during the conflict between the Peruvian state and the Maoist guerrilla movement Sendero Luminoso (Shining Path).

1997   In August investigative journalist **Cecilia Valenzuela** was summoned to the public prosecutor's office after a complaint lodged by the head of the National Archives, Adida Luz Mendoza. The complaint stated that in early August Valenzuela had removed a page of a typewritten index from the National Archives in order to use it in the television program *En persona* and in the magazine *Caretas*. She had returned the page intact the following day. In July an investigation of hers had raised doubt about President Alberto Fujimori's birthplace. Valenzuela has frequently been harassed for her work.

SOURCES

Alisky, B.M., *Historical Dictionary of Peru* (Metuchen 1979) 47.
Bahn, P.G., *The Cambridge Illustrated History of Archaeology* (Cambridge 1996) 370.
Davis, H.E., *History and Power: The Social Relevance of History* (Lanham 1983) 102–3, 107.
Drinot, P., "After the *Nueva Historia*: Recent Trends in Peruvian Historiography", *European Review of Latin American and Caribbean Studies*, April 2000: 67.
Instituto Prensa y Sociedad, *Ifex Alert*, 25 August 1997.
Keesing's Record of World Events, 1990: 37485A.
Klarén, P.F., "Sources for the Study of Twentieth-Century Peruvian Social and Political History", in: J.J. TePaske ed., *Research Guide to Andean History* (Durham 1981) 243.
Pérez Brignoli, H., personal communication, August 1994.
Sigmund, P.E. ed., *The Ideologies of the Developing Nations* (New York/London 1963) 282.

PHILIPPINES

1951–   Diplomat, columnist, political scientist, and revisionist historian **Renato Constantino** (1919–99) had to endure many years of harassment. An executive secretary of the Philippine Mission to the United Nations (1946–49) and a counsellor (1949–51) at the Department of Foreign

Affairs (1949–51), he was dismissed in 1951 after having been considered too radical by the Committee on Un-Filipino Activities (CUFA). In 1954 he was dismissed as a professor of political science and history (1951–54) at Far Eastern University, Manila, for being a "dangerous subversive". He was blacklisted at the universities and by 1959 he was barred from publishing until 1966. He became curator of the Lopez Memorial Museum (1960–72). Shortly after the declaration of martial law on 23 September 1972, he was placed under house arrest by the government of President Ferdinand Marcos. His satirical political columns in the *Manila Chronicle* and *Graphic*, gathered in the volume *Marcos Watch*, were banned from the bookstores. Publication of his book *The Philippines: A Past Revisited*, cowritten with his wife, **Letizia Roxas Constantino**, and scheduled for 1972, was delayed until 1975. From 1975 he occupied several short-term positions as a professorial lecturer, including in history. In 1978 Constantino was reportedly under constant surveillance. As a student in 1939, he had briefly been arrested and interrogated by the United States colonial authorities at Fort Santiago, Intramuros, Manila, because he had written an article exposing American atrocities perpetrated against the Filipino population during the "pacification campaign" in 1899–1902. He was released after he had said that his source was the book *The Conquest of the Philippines by the United States 1898–1925* (New York 1926) by Moorfield Storey and Marcial Lichauco. This incident reportedly made him determined to reexamine Philippine history.

1972   In December **Zeus Salazar**, history lecturer at the University of the Philippines, Quezon City, was arrested at his home in Manila. He was not officially charged, but the reason given for his arrest was that he had criticized certain factual errors in the historical material of Marcos's book *Today's Revolution: Democracy* ([Manila] 1971) in a review.

Also see Indonesia (1994: Spielberg).

SOURCES

Constantino, R., *The Aquino Watch* (Quezon City 1987) v.
———, "Identity and Consciousness: The Philippine Experience I", *Journal of Contemporary Asia*, 1976: 25.
———, *Neocolonial Identity and Counter-Consciousness* (New York 1978) 11–14.
Fast, J., & L. Francisco, "Philippine Historiography and the De-mystification of Imperialism: A Review Essay", *Journal of Contemporary Asia*, 1974: 344.
Index on Censorship, 3–4/72: 118; 2/73: vii; 3/78: 39.
Pineda-Ofreneo R., "Renato Constantino: Approximating a Self-Portrait", *Journal of Contemporary Asia*, 2000, no.3 (special issue 'Tribute to Renato Constantino') 324.

———, "Renato Constantino: Biographical Sketch, Ideological Profile", in: P. Limqueco ed., *Partisan Scholarship: Essays in Honour of Renato Constantino* (Manila 1989) ii, 3, 5–7.

Simbulan, R.G., "Renato Constantino: The Centennial Filipino Scholar, 1919–1999", *Journal of Contemporary Asia*, 2000: 405–9.

POLAND

During World War II and the German occupation of Poland (1939–45), historiography suffered considerable losses: half the historians active before 1939 died (in 1945 only 50 professors of history remained), the universities and institutions were closed, archives and libraries were pillaged and destroyed, and conducting research became impossible. The following archives were destroyed as a result of evacuation, fire, hostilities, and a deliberate policy on the part of the occupying powers: 100 percent of the Archives of Public Education, the Treasury Archives, and the Archives of the City of Warsaw; about 97 percent of the Archives of Earlier Records; about 80 percent of the Archives of Recent Records. Documents for the 1918–45 period suffered particularly severely. In 1947–48 the journal of the Society of Polish Historians, *Kwartalnik historyczny*, was criticized and appeared with much delay. At the first postwar meeting of Polish historians in 1948, Polish historiography became the object of rewriting according to communist views. In 1950, at the congress of Polish sciences, interwar historiography was condemned. In December 1951–January 1952, at the First Methodological Conference of Polish Historians at Otwock, a Marxist periodization of Polish history was imposed. The sovietization of Polish history extended to professional journals, university and school textbooks, series and institutions, especially the Polish Academy of Sciences (PAN). The gap between "official history" and "historical consciousness" was reportedly large.

The turning point of Marxist historiography was reached in 1953, and after 1956 a process of freeing history from ideological and political constraints began (initiated by philosophers, writers, and journalists). Episodes such as the Polish uprisings before and in 1863 and the landowning gentry that led them were partially rehabilitated. By 1969, when the Tenth Congress of Historians was held (postponed from 1968 to 1969 because of the political situation), the 1914–39 years were being hesitantly reexamined. This process of liberalization accelerated in 1978–81 but was completed only after 1989.

On the whole, popular history was more affected by the reigning dogmas of 1948–89 than academic history was, contemporary history more than the earlier periods. Censorship and self-censorship were widespread. Among the taboo or falsified topics, called *białe plamy* (blank spots or areas of darkness), were the following: the history of the aristocracy, the bourgeoisie, and the Catholic Church; the reign and person of Marshal Józef Piłsudski (1867–1935); the Soviet–German relations after the 1922 Rapallo Treaty; the history of the Polish United Workers' Party (PUWP; 1948–90) and its predecessors KPP (1918–38) and PPR (1941–48); the history of the USSR and of Russian– and Soviet–Polish relations (including the 1918 rebirth of Poland; the Polish–Soviet war of 1919–21; the secret protocols of the 23 August 1939 Molotov-Ribbentrop nonaggression pact, officially denied by the Soviet authorities until February 1990; the Soviet annexation of eastern Poland on 17 September 1939; the massive deportations from Polish territories seized by the USSR in 1939–41; the 1940 Katyń Forest massacre; the Polish military effort on the western front; the Polish government-in-exile in London; Polish–Soviet wartime cooperation; Moscow's attitude toward the Warsaw Uprising of August–October 1944; the Polish boundaries; the Polish wartime underground institutions; wartime Ukrainian–Polish relations and the 1947 Operation Vistula [or Weichsel, a mass deportation of Ukrainians and Lemko], and the repatriation of Poles from the USSR in 1944–47); the postwar polonization of the German territories; the history of the Polish People's Republic (PPR); the repression in the Stalin era; the October 1956 events; the anti-Semitic campaign of March 1968; the history of the Solidarity trade union; and, finally, the Soviet role in the 1981 events.

Censorship documents disclosed in the so-called *Black Book of Censorship* in the mid-1970s [q.v. 1977] contained instructions on how to deal with contemporary history in general and in detail, in scholarly and popular works and in death notices: there was a rule forbidding the mention of prewar decorations; certain facts and events at the disposal of scholars could not be mentioned in texts aimed at a wider readership; and reviews and positive mentions of any banned works were banned themselves. One of the instructions stated that "one and only one" line of assessment of the past was permissible. In 1981 the *Gazeta krakowska* ran a series on the "Blank Spaces in the History of Poland". By 1985 the Center for the Study of Public Opinion (CBOS) had established a list of blank spots. In 1988 Juzwénko [q.v. 1987–88] reported that in 1958–88 not a single uncensored book was officially published on the history of the labor movement, Poland's political systems, its place in Europe, or its relations with neighboring states. After the collapse of communism, the historical sciences were freed from their former ideological constraints as the blank spots were filled in. After 1989 some communist historians lost their key positions in the historical institutions. The PUWP History Center was abolished; the Institute of Military History was reorganized.

Among the historians and others concerned with the past who emigrated before 1945 (and were living in exile after 1944) were

pre-1939   **Adolf Berger** (1882–1962), **Stanisław Kot** (1885–1975), and **Moses Shulvass** (1909–).

1939–   **Isaac Deutscher** (1907–67), **Jedrzej Giertych, Oskar Halecki** (1891–1973), **Marian Kukiel** (1885–1973), **Leon Radzinowicz** (1906–), **Rafael Taubenschlag** (1881–1958), and **Isaiah Trunk** (1905–81).

pre-1945   Among the historians and others concerned with the past who were
            censored or persecuted during World War II (including in 1945)
            were **Bogdan Baranowski** (1915–), **Ludwig Fleck** (1896–1961),
            Gieysztor [q.v. 1968], **Marceli Handelsman** (1882–1945), **Zofia
            Kossak-Szezucka** (1890–1968), **Witold Kula** (1916–88),
            Stanisław Librowski (1914–), **Ernestyna Podhorizer-Sandel**
            (1903–84), and **Witold Zalewski** (1921–).

            Among the young refugees who became historians in their new
            country were **Lewis Namier** (born Ludwik Niemirowski) (1888–
            1960), **Richard Pipes** (1923–), and **Justus Rosenberg** (1921–).

1940–90   The most controversial of all blank spots was the massacre of some
            4,000 Polish army officers at Katyń forest near Smolensk, Russia,
            by the Soviet secret police NKVD in April 1940. In 1946 the Polish
            security apparatus had allegedly impeded the recovery by the Home
            Army (the partisan forces of the Polish underground state loyal to
            the government-in-exile in London) of the archives with evidence
            of the massacre gathered by the Germans in 1943. The topic was
            vigorously censored from the 1940s to the late 1970s. The 1977
            Black Book of Polish Censorship [q.v. 1977] included detailed cri-
            teria for evaluating material covering Katyń: "1. No attempts to
            charge the USSR with the responsibility for the death of the Polish
            officers in the Katyń forests should be permitted. 2. In scientific
            writing, memoirs and biographies, formulations such as the follow-
            ing may be permitted: 'shot by the Nazis in Katyń', 'died in Katyń
            or 'fell in Katyń'. If phrases such as 'fell in Katyń' are used with
            a date of death, the date may be given only as coming after July
            1941. 3. The term 'prisoners of war' should be stricken with ref-
            erences to Polish soldiers and officers interned by the Red Army in
            September 1939. The correct term is 'interned'. It is permissible to
            use the names of the camps: Kozielsk, Starobielsk and Ostaszków,
            in which Polish officers were interned and later shot by Nazis in the
            Katyń forests. 4. Necrologies, obituaries, religious services an-
            nounced for the intention of the victims of Katyń and information
            concerning other means of paying respect to their memory may be
            permitted only with the approval of the Central Office for the Con-
            trol of the Press, Publications, and Entertainment leadership. . . . If
            there are any violations of this prohibition, the prohibition must not
            be referred to, and its existence must not be revealed. [14 January
            1975]".
                Among the many historians who were hampered in investigating
            the topic in that period was **Jerzy Łojek** (pseudonym: Leopold Jer-
            zewski), whose father died in Katyń. In 1980, against the back-

ground of Solidarity's struggle for more openness, he published a work about Katyń. In April 1981 Katyń was called a Soviet massacre during a memorial service in Warsaw. It became one of the blank spots officially investigated by the Joint Commission of Party Scholars from the PPR and the USSR for Issues in the History of Relations between the Two Countries (established April 1987), co-chaired by Maciszewski [q.v. 1990], PAN rector, professor at the Warsaw University History Institute, historian of seventeenth-century Polish–Russian relations and member of Parliament, and **Georgy Smirnov**, academician and director of the Institute of Marxism-Leninism, Moscow. Early in 1988, however, censors prevented publication in the literary magazine *Miesiecznik literackie* of an article on Katyń containing evidence of Soviet responsibility. In January 1988 an interview with historian **Andrzej Ajnenkiel** (1931–) in the Warsaw *Tygodnik kulturalny* about the blank spots in Polish history was cut almost thirty times, mostly in connection with statements on Katyń. In February fifty-nine leading Polish intellectuals, including historians Holzer [q.v. 1979–], Kersten [q.v. 1980–82], Kieniewicz [q.v. 1968] and Samsonowicz [q.v. 1982], demanded in an open letter that Katyń be investigated. A speech by Soviet historian **Natan Eidelman** (?1929/30–89) at a symposium of Polish and Soviet filmmakers on the topic of "blank spots" (particularly Katyń) in Moscow in April was censored in four places when published in a Polish weekly. After (separate) research by historians Valentina Parsadanova, member of the Joint History Commission, and Natalia Lebedeva, supporter of the human-rights group Memorial and member of the USSR Academy of Sciences Institute of General History, in the hitherto secret Special State Archives, the Soviet authorities finally admitted their responsibility for Katyń on 13 April 1990. The Russian government of Boris Yeltsin apologized to Poland for the murders and transferred the essential documents to Poland in 1992, including a record of the Soviet Politburo meeting approving the massacres. In September 1993 the Polish minister of justice announced that there would be an independent investigation into the murders at Katyń and other Soviet prison camps in 1940.

1944–49 In 1944 German historian **Hans Roos** (1919–84), who fought on the eastern front, was imprisoned by the Polish Home Army and sent to a Soviet prisoner-of-war camp (1944–49). He then returned to Bochum University, Federal Republic of Germany (FRG), where he specialized in Polish history.

1946– In 1946–48 and again in 1949–54, historian and author **Władysław Bartoszewski** (1922–) was charged with espionage and imprisoned for his anticommunism but in 1955 he was rehabilitated. In 1960 he was dismissed as an editorial secretary of the weekly *Stolica* (the Capital). During the 1960s and 1970s, he was active in the opposition. As the secretary-general of the Polish PEN Club (1972–[81]), he was often refused permission to attend conferences abroad. From 1973 he was a lecturer in contemporary Polish history at Lublin Catholic University. In November 1979 his lecture for the TKN [q.v. 1978–] was interrupted by a Warsaw city council representative who announced that the meeting was dissolved. However, nobody left the flat and the lecture went ahead. Later that month he was fined about the equivalent of an average monthly salary on charges of organizing an illegal gathering. In 1980 he became an adviser of Solidarity. He was interned under martial law (13 December 1981) but released in April 1982 after many interventions from Poland and abroad. He lived in Austria and was a lecturer at various universities. In 1992 he became Poland's ambassador in Austria. Later he was Poland's minister of foreign affairs (1995, 2000–). During World War II, he had been a political prisoner at Auschwitz extermination camp (1940–41) and member of the Underground Army (1942–45). He organized the rescue of many Jews and fought as a lieutenant during the 1944 Warsaw Uprising. Since 1944 he had taken part in various commissions for the investigation of Nazi crimes in Poland, and nearly all his works were about the war and Polish–Jewish relations.

1949   The methodological work of historian **Władysław Konopczyński** (1880–1952), president of the Society of Polish Historians, specialist in prepartition (pre–1772) Polish history and first editor of the Polish Biographical Dictionary (1931–49), could not be published because of his criticism of historical materialism and despite the fact that his colleague, economic historian Jan Rutkowski (1886–1949), had agreed, upon Konopczyński's request, to add a chapter on historical materialism. He had to give up his position and functions.

[1952]– *The Political History of Post-Uprising Poland, 1864–1918* (1948; second edition Paris 1979), a book written by diplomatic historian **Henryk Wereszycki** (1898–1990), a former war prisoner (1939–45) and at that time an assistant professor at Wrocław University (1948–56), was withdrawn from circulation. It had been denounced by Communist historian Żanna Kormanowa. Wereszycki was virtually barred from the profession until after the October 1956 events. He then became history professor at Jagiellonian University, Cracow (1956–69). Barely tolerated by the establishment, he criticized the draft of the first volume of the official *History of Poland* (1957).

1957–   Sociologist and photographer **Jerzy Kosinski** (1933–91) emigrated to the United States for political reasons. In 1953 he had obtained an MA in history from Łódź University. He was the author of, inter alia, the novel *The Painted Bird*.

1958–60   At the Eighth Congress of Historians in 1958, leading historian and director of the PAN History Institute **Tadeusz Manteuffel-Szoege** (1902–70) gave a critical report on the negative effects of restricted archival access, political controls, and isolation from Western scholarship. It was not included in the 1960 five-volume congress publication.

1958–88   In March 1958 historian and journalist **Robert Moczulski** (1930–), specialist in the history of the September 1939 campaign, was charged with spying and arrested but found not guilty. In 1972 *The Polish War*, a work in which he questioned the Soviet role in Poland in 1939, was withdrawn from circulation. In May 1977 he was dismissed from *Stolica*, where he had directed the history section (1960–72). Later he worked for the underground journals *Opinia* and *Droga*. In June he was ousted from the leadership of the Movement for the Defense of Human and Civil Rights (ROPCiO) which he cofounded in March 1977, and in October 1978 he was expelled from ROPCiO. In 1979 he was cofounder and principal spokesman of the unofficial nationalistic group Confederation for an Independent Poland (KPN). In September 1980 he was arrested and charged with "slandering the dignity of the PPR and its organs" and "having participated in an organization with criminal objectives", following an interview with *Der Spiegel* in which he had described the KPN as an opposition party whose aims were "an independent sovereign Poland, free from Soviet rule and from the totalitarian dictatorship of the PUWP". In March 1981 he was officially indicted. He was released from preliminary detention in June but rearrested in July. He was sentenced to seven years' imprisonment in October 1982. Released under an amnesty for political prisoners in July 1984, he was rearrested in March 1985 during a meeting of the KPN Political Council, charged with "illegal association in order to foment public unrest", and sentenced to four years' imprisonment in April 1986. He was reportedly denied adequate medical treatment after suffering two heart attacks while in detention. He was released under an amnesty for political prisoners in September. He became a member of Parliament and in 1990 he was the KPN presidential candidate. In 1991, on the tenth anniversary of martial law, he introduced an impeachment resolution in the Sejm (House of Representatives) in order to prosecute the high officials of the former communist regime. Two of his works, *Rebirth of the Polish Republic* (1978) and *Revolution without Revolution* (1979; London 1984), appeared in samizdat (self-publishing).

1960–89   In 1960 literary critic and historian **Jan Józef Lipski** (1926–91),
active participant in the wartime resistance, member (1956–62) and
chairman (1957–58), of the anti-Stalinist discussion group "Crooked
Circle Club", was dismissed as editor and department head (1953–
60) at the State Editorial Institute. He became a PAN Institute of
Literary Studies researcher (1961–91). In March 1964 he was arrested because he had collected the signatures for the *Letter of the
34 Intellectuals* (signed by, inter alia, Gieysztor [q.v. 1968]) directed
at the prime minister and protesting censorship. He was soon released. From 1964 to 1976, he took part in many dissident actions,
and between 1968 and 1989 he was often detained. His works were
banned. In September 1976, he helped found the Committee for the
Defense of the Workers (KOR; later Committee for Social Self-
Defense, KSS-KOR, 1976–81) [q.v. 1961–88: Kuroń]. In March
1979 he was detained by the police when he and another KOR
member were to hold the first classes at a new farmer's university.
In 1981 he published a samizdat article on Polish megalomania and
xenophobia in historical perspective. A Solidarity member from
September 1980, he was arrested in December 1981 under martial
law for organizing a strike at the Ursus tractor factory but released
because of his poor health in May 1982. In September while in
London for medical treatment and in order to write *KOR: A History
of the Workers' Defense Committee in Poland 1976–81* (1983 samizdat; Berkeley 1984), proceedings were started against him in
absentia [q.v. 1961–88: Kuroń]. Upon his return on 16 September
1982, he was arrested. The government reportedly did not want him
to die in detention, and he was released and amnestied in June 1984.
In November 1987 he cofounded the reestablished Polish Socialist
Party (PPS), which had forcibly merged with the PUWP in 1948.
In February 1988 he and others temporarily resigned the PPS, claiming that it had been infiltrated by the security police. In June 1989
he was elected a Solidarity Civic Committee senator. He wrote a
major account of Solidarity's political development.

1961–88   In 1961 historian **Jacek Kuroń** (1934–) of Warsaw University was
expelled from the Polish Scouts Union, where he had been head of
the Program Department (1960–61). In 1962 he founded with Modzelewski [q.v. 1964–84] the "Political Debating Club" at Warsaw
University, but the club was closed in 1963. In November 1964 he
was expelled from the PUWP and in July 1965 sentenced to three
years' imprisonment [q.v. 1964–84: Modzelewski]. In [August]
1967 he was released. Active in students' circles in 1967–68, he
was again arrested during the student demonstrations on 10 March
1968. In January 1969 he was sentenced to three-and-a-half-years'

imprisonment on the charge of having inspired the riots. In September 1971 he was released [q.v. 1964–84: Modzelewski]. He became one of the most active dissidents. He was often harassed and arrested, inter alia, for his activities for KOR, of which he was a cofounder and spokesman (1976–81). He collected and published dates about persecutions in Poland in the underground periodical *Biuletyn informacyjny*. In 1977–78 he helped found TKN [q.v. 1978–] and lectured for it. His book *Principles and Ideas*, about the strategy and political objectives of the democratic opposition in Poland, was published by NOWa (Niezaleleżna Oficyna Wydawnicza, Independent Publishing House). In 1978 he was a cofounder and editorial board member of the underground political quarterly *Krytyka*. In November he was arrested in Warsaw on his way to give a TKN lecture on education and social life. Many of his 1979 TKN lectures were disrupted and he was often beaten. He was a Solidarity member and a personal adviser to Solidarity leader Lech Wałęsa. In July–August 1980 he was founder and chief of the Bank of Strikes Informations during the protests. On 21 August Kuroń and Michnik [q.v. 1965–86] were among fourteen KOR members arrested after they had collected and disseminated information on the strike situation for several weeks. Their release (occurring on 1 September) was the final condition of the agreement between the government and Solidarity on 31 August. He was interned under martial law (13 December). In September 1982, after widespread demonstrations against martial law on 31 August, four KOR members, including Kuroń and Michnik, were arrested in the internment camp on charges of "making preparations for the violent overthrow of the Polish sociopolitical system". In November 1982 Kuroń's wife Grażyna died after her release from detention in May because of ill health. In 1983, still under arrest, Kuron had turned down an offer to emigrate. The Kuroń/Michnik trial, scheduled to open on 13 July 1984, was postponed, but they were released under the 21 July amnesty for political prisoners. On 1 May 1985, Kuroń was arrested after leading a demonstration on May Day to counter the official Labor Day parades and sentenced to three months' imprisonment. He was released on appeal. In 1988–89 he was a Solidarity delegation member at the Roundtable Negotiations. In June 1989 he was elected a member of Parliament for Solidarity (later for the Union of Freedom caucus). He was minister of labor and social policy twice (1989–91, 1992–93). In the first round of the November 1995 presidential elections, he obtained 9 percent of the votes.

1962–   The émigré journal *Zeszyty historyczne* (Historical Notebooks) was founded in Paris. It published, inter alia, on the blank spots of contemporary history. The copies were illegally introduced in Poland, sometimes in miniature versions.

1964–   Historians **Ludwik Hass** and **Romuald Śmiech** were accused of founding a Trotskyist movement in Warsaw, tried in camera and sentenced to, respectively, three-and-a-half and three-years' imprisonment.

1964–84   In November 1964, medievalist and son of a historian and former Polish foreign minister **Karol Modzelewski** (1937–) and Kuroń [q.v. 1961–88] were arrested because they had written a dissertation critical of Poland's political reality. They were expelled from the PUWP on the charge of spreading antiparty propaganda. In January 1965 Modzelewski was dismissed as a history lecturer at Warsaw University (appointed 1959). In March he and Kuroń were arrested on the charge of advocating revolution because they had submitted a ninety-page *Open Letter to Party Members*, being a summary of the 1964 dissertation (published in Paris in 1966), to members of Warsaw University PUWP sections and the Union of Young Socialists. After a secret trial, Modzelewski and Kuroń were sentenced to, respectively, forty and thirty-six months' imprisonment in July. Their appeal was rejected in October. Their wives were dismissed from their jobs. In August 1967 Modzelewski was released on bail. In March 1968 he took part in the student protests, was rearrested on 10 March, and in January 1969 was sentenced to another forty months' imprisonment for activities violating the public order and for founding an illegal organization. He and Kuroń were not amnestied in July because they were held to be "recidivists". In September 1971 they were released. From 1972 Modzelewski was a researcher at the PAN Institute of Material Culture History in Wrocław. He was a Solidarity member and its national press spokesman (1980–April 1981). He reportedly coined the name "Solidarity". He was interned, together with his wife, under martial law (13 December 1981). In May 1982 he started a hunger strike at Białołęka prison near Warsaw, and in December he was arrested at an internees' camp. In [1983] he was charged with trying to overthrow the communist system and he risked five to eight years' imprisonment. He was released in July 1984. In 1989 he became a Solidarity Civic Committee Senator (1989–91). He remained a leading figure in Labor Solidarity.

1965–86   In March 1965 **Adam Michnik** (1946–) (pen names: Bartlomiej; Andrzej Zagozda), history student at Warsaw University, was arrested for two months for illegal activity: he had been involved in writing and disseminating the *Open Letter to the Party* [q.v.

1964–84: Modzelewski]. Previously, in 1961, he had given a speech on school reform to the "Crooked Circle Club", which had led to his expulsion from school for "illegal activity". In 1963 the newspapers reported that party leader Władysław Gomułka had attacked him by name in a PUWP meeting. Between 1965 and 1980, Michnik was detained over a hundred times. In 1966 he was suspended from Warsaw University for participating in a discussion in which the philosopher Kołakowski [q.v. 1966–] criticized the regime. On 6 March 1968, he was expelled from Warsaw University after he had helped organize a protest against the banning on 30 January of poet Adam Mickiewicz's play *Forefathers' Eve*, which portrayed nineteenth-century Russian despotism and the Polish freedom struggle, and after he had been in contact with a *Le Monde* newspaper correspondent. He was arrested after student protests against his expulsion on 9 May and sentenced in February 1969 to three years' imprisonment on the charge of organizing riots. Released after eighteen months, he worked as a welder and secretary. In 1972 he was subjected to preventive arrest during American President Richard Nixon's visit to Warsaw. Allowed to study again in 1973, he completed his history education at the night school of Poznań University in 1975. In September 1976 he helped found KOR. He then spent eight months in Western Europe. His book *The Church, the Left: A Dialogue*, in which he argued that the church had been the single staunchest defender of human and civil rights, was sent clandestinely to Paris and published in 1977. In 1977 he was an editorial board member of the underground literary quarterly *Zapis* and a NOWa representative. He was a cofounder and staff member of *Krytyka* [q.v. 1961–88: Kuroń]. In 1978 he helped found TKN [q.v. 1978–] and lectured for it. In February, in the course of a dawn raid on his house, police smashed down the door and used tear-gas grenades to disperse a group of 120 students who had gathered there to hear his lecture "Thirty Years of Communism in Poland". In the following weeks, three of his lectures were prevented. In December 1979 he was arrested, together with other dissidents, outside a Warsaw church where a mass was taking place in memory of fifty-six workers shot by police in the 1970 food riots. In 1980 he became a Solidarity member. He was interned under martial law (13 December 1981) and charged with advocating antistate violence. In September 1982 he was arrested in the internment camp and released in August 1984 [q.v. 1961–88: Kuroń]. He was rearrested in February 1985 at a meeting of senior Solidarity activists at Gdansk on the charge of plotting protest strikes and sentenced to three years' imprisonment in June. In February 1986 the sentence was reduced to thirty months' imprisonment. In August he was released under an amnesty for political prisoners. In 1988–89 he was a Solidarity delegation member at the Roundtable Negotiations. In May 1989 he became the chief editor of the first legally published noncommunist newspaper in decades, *Gazeta wyborcza* (Election Gazette). In June he was elected to the Sejm but did not seek reelection in 1991. In June 1990 Lech Wałęsa attempted to dismiss him from Solidarity. In October 1995, Wałęsa, then Poland's president, accused him of "highly unethical manipulation" in publishing the "unauthorized text" of an interview with him, which was "too frank". Most essays published in his *Letters from Prison and Other Essays* (1985) were first published underground in Poland and abroad.

1966–   In October 1966 philosopher **Leszek Kołakowski** (1927–), lector (1954–64), professor (1964–68) and chair of the history of modern philosophy (1959–68) at the faculty of philosophy of Warsaw University, and **Krzysztof Pomian** (1934–), a former student leader and a philosopher at Warsaw University, were expelled from the PUWP for their support of the freedom of expression of Modzelewski [q.v. 1964–84] and Kuroń [q.v. 1961–88]. They had also asked for the truth about the October 1956 events at Poznań and Warsaw during a discussion at the Warsaw University History Institute. In February 1968 Kołakowski was expelled from Warsaw University. In March he was dismissed for his protest against the January 1968 ban of Mickiewicz's play [q.v. 1965–86: Michnik] and for his (secretly recorded) speech "Polish Culture in the Past Twenty Years" to students at the History Institute. He went into exile in Canada (1968–69), the United States (1969–70), where he worked at the University of Chicago and Yale University, and the United Kingdom, where he became a senior research fellow at All Souls College, Oxford University (1970–95). He remained an active supporter of the dissident movement and was considered Poland's most important revisionist Marxist in the 1960s. He wrote the three-volume *Main Currents in Marxism* (New York 1976–78). Pomian was also dismissed and exiled. He worked at the Centre National de Recherche Scientifique (CNRS), Paris (1973–). He wrote, inter alia, on the history of ideas and the scientific and artistic culture of modern Europe.

[1967]   Reviews and positive mentions of *The Soviet Union, Its Years of Struggle and Success*, a book published for the fiftieth anniversary of the USSR but exposing the difficult moments in USSR history and the differences of opinion among Communist Party leaders, were banned.

1968   Publication in Polish of *History of Poland* (Warsaw: Polish Scientific Publishers, 1968), appearing in English under the general editorship of historian **Stefan Kieniewicz** (1907–), professor of Polish modern history (1961–77) at Warsaw University and a specialist in nineteenth-century history, was not allowed. Other contributors were medievalist **Aleksander Gieysztor** (1916–99), former prisoner of war, professor at Warsaw University, member (1965–85) and president (1980–85) of the International Committee of Historical Sciences, PAN member (1971–83) and president (1980–84, 1990–); **Janusz Tazbir** (1927–), vice director (1968–83) and director (1983–) of the PAN History Institute and specialist in the sixteenth and seventeenth centuries; **Emanuel Rostworowski** (1923–), PAN professor, specialist in the eighteenth century, and chief editor of the *Polish Biographical Dictionary* (1964–); and Wereszycki [q.v. 1952–]. In 1983 Kieniewicz published a text on Polish historiography in *Kwartalnik historyczny*, in which he openly referred to the achievements of the years 1980–81.

1968   The work of amateur historian **Pawel Jasienica** (1909–70), reportedly the most widely read historian in Poland in the 1960s, was criticized by official historians for its "heroistic personalism and optimism", but the criticism only added to the popularity of his volumes. Most likely because of this popularity, even Gomułka singled him out for attack. His essay *The Republic of Both Nations* was banned because of its presentation of Russia's role during the partitions (1772–95).

1968–93   In March 1968 historian **Antoni Macierewicz** (1948–), then a history student, was arrested after a students' strike at Warsaw University; he was released in July. Between 1968 and 1976, he was dismissed several times from the university, twice as a student and in October 1976 as a lecturer in Iberian Studies and specialist in Inca history at Warsaw University. As a KOR member, he was often arrested between 1976 and 1980. Working from May 1981 at the PAN History Institute, he was interned on 13 December. In August 1984 he was released from prison under an amnesty for political prisoners. In December 1991 he became minister of the interior and in June 1992 he sent to the Sejm a list with sixty-four names of politicians and officials—including the prime minister's most important political adversaries, among them then-President Wałęsa—suspected of being former security police agents during the period 1945–90. The list was drawn up on the basis of secret police files. In the controversy that followed—called *noc teczec* (night of the long files)—he was expelled from the political party ZChN. In July a Sejm committee investigating the list concluded that only six of the sixty-four had signed any agreement to collaborate. It accused

Macierewicz of actions which could have led to the destabilization of the state. The government of Jan Olszewski was dismissed. In September 1993 Macierewicz was charged with publishing state secrets.

1968–88   In August 1968 medievalist **Bronisław Geremek** (1932–), working at the PAN History Institute since the 1950s, resigned from the PUWP in 1968 in protest against the Warsaw Pact invasion of Czechoslovakia. Among the other historians who did so were Łepkowski [q.v. 1984] and Kersten [q.v. 1980–82]. Between 1976 and 1980, Geremek joined KOR. He was often arrested. In August 1980 he became a Solidarity member and key adviser to Wałęsa. He was interned at Białołęka camp under martial law (13 December 1981). Late that month he became the victim of a slander campaign. In early January 1982, he went on hunger strike for fifteen days, which reportedly put his life in danger. Thirty historians, including Kieniewicz [q.v. 1968], protested to chairman of the State Council Henryk Jabłoński (1909–), a former minister of education (1965–72) and also a historian. Later that month Geremek was transported to another camp. Although released in December, he was imprisoned again in May–July 1983 on the charge of having organized an illegal meeting and having spread misinformation about Poland. In April 1985 he was summarily dismissed from the PAN following "anti-Soviet remarks" made during a meeting with students in Gdansk in March and following a discussion on human rights with British Foreign Secretary Geoffrey Howe during the latter's official visit to Poland. In 1985 he was refused permission to attend the 16th International Congress of Historical Sciences in Stuttgart. His 1986 text for a centenary conference on French historian Marc Bloch (1886–1944) had to be read for him by Jacques Le Goff in Paris. In October 1987 thirty-six PAN professors, including Gieysztor [q.v. 1968] and Kieniewicz [q.v. 1968], signed an open letter calling for an end to political interference in their work; the letter cited the Geremek case. In March 1988 several opposition leaders, including Geremek (of Jewish origins) and Kuroń [q.v. 1961–88], were detained for questioning as a result of their having signed an open letter criticizing police repression during student demonstrations on 7 and 8 March at which the repression of the 1968 student protests and the ensuing anti-Semitic campaign were commemorated. Around that time Geremek suggested an "anticrisis pact" between the government and Solidarity. In June 1989 he was elected a member of Parliament and became a Solidarity spokesman (until November 1990). In 1991 he became the leader of the Democratic Union parliamentary group. He was the president of the constitutional reform and foreign affairs parliamentary commissions and minister of foreign affairs (1997–2000).

1968–   **Jan Tomasz Gross** (1947–), a student of physics and sociology at Warsaw University, was arrested for participating in the March 1968 student protests, expelled from the university, and imprisoned. Upon his release, he immigrated to the United States and earned a doctorate in sociology from Yale University. He became a political science lecturer at New York University and published widely on Polish contemporary history, especially World War II.

1968–69   In September 1968 history student **Barbara Toruńczyk** was arrested and in February 1969 sentenced to two years' imprisonment for her role in the March 1968 student protests. She was released under the July 1969 amnesty. In 1981 NOWa published her anthology of Polish political thought from 1895 to 1905.

1969   The first edition of a handbook for law students at Warsaw University, *The History of Polish Legal Institutions 1764–1939* (Warsaw 1969, 1970) by Ajnenkiel [q.v. 1940–90], **Bogusław Leśnodorski** (1914–85), and **Władysław Rostocki** mentioned the existence of the secret protocols of the Molotov-Ribbentrop pact probably for the first time in Poland: it was a two-sentence description (on page 242) without explanations. In 1986 Garlicki [q.v. pre-1970–] printed the text of the protocols.

pre-1970– Prior to 1970 a monograph on Piłsudski by **Andrzej Garlicki** (1935–) was banned. After having been rejected by several publishers, it was split into separate volumes, which appeared with two different publishers under different titles. Positive references to Piłsudski were eliminated from many texts until the late 1970s.

1972   In 1972 a work by professor **Maria Turlejska** (1918–) (pseudonym: L. Socha [q.v. 1984–86]), *Register for the First Decade 1944–1954*, which criticized the origins of People's Poland in 1944–54, was withdrawn from circulation for allegedly claiming that the USSR was responsible for the Cold War. Turlejska was a Marxist historian who wrote extensively on the occupation, Polish communism, and postwar Poland, mainly in *Krytyka*.

[1972]   A study of wartime Ukrainian–Polish relations never reached the bookshelves.

1976   Second-year history student **Marek Majla** was expelled from Warsaw University.

          In April the government censors met with the editors in Warsaw and gave them a list of topics which they were forbidden to publicize. On the list were "such facts in historical works as would attest to the creative role of the Catholic Church with regard to the nation and state".

1977   In the fall Tomasz Strzyżewski, a former censor of the Cracow Branch of the Central Office for Control of the Press, Publications and Performances, brought with him to the United Kingdom around 700 pages of confidential instructions and circulars, dating from February 1974 to February 1977, and published in Polish as the *Black Book of Polish Censorship*. The names of Kołakowski [q.v. 1966–] and Pomian [q.v. 1966], among others, could not be published and their scholarly contribution could not be emphasized in a positive sense. Reviews of *Repatriation of the Polish Population after World War II*, a book by Kersten [q.v. 1980–82], were controlled because "the publication contained many statements which contradict the current goals of propaganda work". A similar directive existed for *1859 days of Warsaw*, a book by Bartoszewski [q.v. 1946–]. Noncommunist (in the *Black Book*: "right-wing") accounts of the interwar period were forbidden. Other instructions read: "Obituaries and advertisements in the mass media announcing meetings at cemeteries, monuments or sites of battles etc., whether commemorating the anniversary of the Warsaw Uprising itself or any one episode of ex-soldiers of the Home Army or any right-wing organization which participated in the Warsaw Uprising, cannot be released for publication." Censorship was also strict in matters concerning the inadequate protection afforded to historical buildings and monuments. Furthermore, there were instructions dealing with history-related matters in countries such as Uganda or Iran.

1977–86   Historian and KOR member **Bogdan Borusewicz** (1949–) was often detained. In February 1978, while giving a lecture for the TKN [q.v. 1978–] in his flat, he was arrested and interrogated for forty-eight hours before being tried for "hooliganism" and sentenced to two weeks' imprisonment, prolonged on appeal to three weeks. The police also arrested eleven students attending the lecture, caused extensive damage to his flat, and confiscated books, tape recordings, and other materials connected with TKN. As a student, Borusewicz had already been arrested and sentenced to three years' imprisonment in 1968 but he was released under the July 1969 amnesty for political prisoners. A personal friend of Wałęsa's, Borusewicz helped organize Solidarity and played a crucial role in the formulation of the "Twenty-one Demands" during the August 1980 strike. After imposition of martial law (13 December 1981), he organized an occupational strike at the Lenin Shipyard at Gdansk. On 17 December he went into hiding. In January 1986 he was arrested and in February charged with "preparation to overthrow the state by force" and he reportedly was refused the lawyer of his choice. He was released under an amnesty for political prisoners in September. He became a member of Parliament, first for Solidarity, later for the Union of Freedom.

1978   The 1939 Molotov-Ribbentrop pact was not mentioned in *History of Poland 1864–1948*, a general synthesis written by professor **Józef Buszko** of Cracow University. It was republished in 1982 in a more objective version.

The poem *Short History* by **Jerzy Jarniewicz** (1958–) was banned on the grounds that it gave a "biased, defamatory account of the last forty years of Polish history".

1978–   In January 1978 a Towarzystwo Kursow Naukowych (TKN, Society for Academic Courses; popularly known as the Latajacy Uniwersytet [Flying University]) was set up within the dissident movement to teach, inter alia, the forbidden historical subjects, especially contemporary Polish history and the history of Polish–Russian relations. In addition, a special TKN working group of historians was formed to evaluate the official history curricula and to reveal all distortions and falsifications. The initiative formalized a series of educational self-help lectures that had started at private homes in October 1977. It was reminiscent of similar clandestine classes under Russian and German rule (1883–1919 and 1940–45). Among the signatories of the original declaration and the lecturers were Brandys [q.v. 1982], Cywiński [q.v. 1978–], Geremek [q.v. 1968–88], Gleichgewicht [q.v. 1978–79], Kersten [q.v. 1978–79], Lipski [q.v. 1960–89], and Wereszycki [q.v. 1952–] (all of whose contributions are treated elsewhere). Other contributors were Bartoszewski [q.v. 1946–], whose subject was "political geography of the Polish underground, 1939–1945"; **Jerzy Jedlicki**, a historian of the nobility in modern times, whose subjects were "social-political ideologies from the French Revolution to World War II" and "leading contemporary ideas", and who in 1995 became professor at the PAN History Institute; **Tadeusz Kowalik**, an economist whose subject was "economic history and the history of economy"; Kuroń [q.v. 1961–88], whose subject was "education and social life"; **Marian Małowist** (?1900–88), professor of social-economic history of the thirteenth–seventeenth centuries at the Warsaw University History Institute (1949–) and founder and chief editor of *Acta poloniae historica* (1958–); Michnik [q.v. 1965–86], whose subjects were "elements of the political history of People's Poland" and "contemporary history of Poland" (together with others); and **Andrzej Werner**, a writer and literature and film critic whose subject, "ideological aspects of the Polish cinema", was very historically oriented. The lectures on contemporary Polish history and on the history of social thought enjoyed the greatest success; they attracted audiences of a hundred and more. The texts of several lectures appeared in samizdat: they included those of Bartoszewski on the Polish Underground State, frequently reprinted, and those of Cywiński on the prewar problems of Catholic life in Poland. The TKN stressed the damage done by the political censorship of history and sociology textbooks and wanted to reinforce "the awareness of tradition and historical continuity which has been particularly weakened". In a March 1978 communiqué, the Polish episcopate affirmed that it would "support those initiatives which aim at presenting . . . the history of the nation in an authentic form". The regime's response was one of selective harassment.

In February 1978 TKN cofounder **Bohdan Cywiński** (1939–), Catholic historian and journalist, former chief editor of the underground Catholic monthly *Znak* (1973–77), and contributor to the underground monthly *Głos*, was arrested in Łódź during a TKN lecture. He remained a lecturer in modern church history in Eastern European countries during 1979–80 and later became a Solidarity official and personal adviser of Wałęsa. He was abroad on 13 December 1981, the day of the declaration of martial law, and went into exile in Switzerland to become a member of the Solidarity Foreign Bureau. Two of his books, inter alia, *The Polish Church between the Two Wars*, were published in samizdat, two others in Paris. In 1979 he published a pamphlet *Poisoned Humanistic Studies*, in which he specified a long list of falsehoods in the teaching of post-1918 history.

1978 In the fall the underground political quarterly *Krytyka* was founded. It was linked with the KOR and printed by NOWa. It sought, inter alia, to uncover and educate the public about the blank spots in Polish history. Among its editiorial board members were Kuroń [q.v. 1961–88]; Michnik [q.v. 1965–86]; Werner [q.v. 1978–]; **Marek Beylin**, a journalist, historian, KOR member, and, later, researcher at the PAN Institute of Political Studies; and **Jan Kofman**, specialist in interwar economic history of Poland and Eastern Europe, active in the opposition since the 1960s, later professor of history and political science at Warsaw University and the PAN Institute of Political Studies, chief editor and deputy director of Polish Scientific Publishers (PWN), the largest academic publishers, and in 1988–89 a Solidarity delegation member at the Roundtable Negotiations.

Among the authors published by *Krytyka* were Turlejska [q.v. 1972] and **Anna Bojarska**, a writer known for her historical novels.

In [December] a reference to Saint Stanisław, Poland's patron saint who was martyred by the king of Cracow in 1079, was deleted by the local censor from the pope's Christmas message to his former diocese of Cracow. The uncut text, published by a Roman Catholic newspaper, said that Saint Stanisław was a spokesman of the most essential human rights and rights of the nation.

1978–79   Other disrupted TKN lectures [q.v. 1978–] included the following: In March 1978 police raided the home of historian and professor **Bolesław Gleichgewicht** during a TKN lecture and detained twenty-seven students attending it. He was not at home at the time. In April a surgeon was fined for allowing professor **Edward Lipiński** (1888–1986)—an economist and specialist in the history of economic thought, PAN member (1952–), and KOR chairman—to hold a TKN lecture on the economic reforms of 1956 in his flat. In March 1979 thugs arrived at a TKN lecture on contemporary Polish history, given jointly by Michnik [q.v. 1965–86] and writer **Andrzej Szczypiorski** (1924–). The lecture had to be abandoned and some participants were beaten up. In May historian **Adam Kersten** (1930–?83), specialist in the history of France and Sweden, decided to abandon his TKN lecture "The View of History As Presented in School Textbooks" as a result of persistent heckling. In October three TKN lecturers, among them Kowalik [q.v. 1972] and Werner [q.v. 1978–], were detained by the police shortly before the lecture and forced to leave town. In November at least three scheduled TKN lectures (by Bartoszewski [q.v. 1946–], Jedlicki [q.v. 1978–], and Cywiński) were interrupted in Warsaw. Each time, the police raided the premises, photographed everyone present, demanded identity papers, and conducted a search.

1979–   In 1979 **Jerzy Holzer** (1930–), contemporary historian and specialist in Polish labor history, resigned from the PUWP. In 1980 he became an adviser to Solidarity. He was interned under martial law (13 December 1981) and was released in April 1982. His history of Solidarity, *Solidarność 1980–81: Genesis and History*, printed by the unofficial Krag [q.v. 1980–82], had a record run of 12,000 copies. It also appeared in Paris in 1984. In January 1988 he published an open letter advocating a "historic pact" to rescue the nation. In March 1996 he attended an international textbook meeting in Prague.

1979–86   At least 90 people in various cities were arrested before 11 November 1979, the sixty-first anniversary of the restoration of Polish independence. During the ten days preceding the commemoration on 13 December of striking workers killed during the 1970 riots in Gdansk, some 200 people were detained. A number of workers in Gdansk who took part in the demonstration were subsequently dismissed. On 16 December 1980 Solidarity erected a memorial at Gdansk for the 1970 victims (who were officially described as "counterrevolutionaries"). On 11 November 1986, student **Daniel Korona** was detained after leaflets calling for the commemoration of Poland's 1918 independence had been thrown out of a window in Warsaw. He was sentenced to a fine for distributing an illegal publication, a charge he denied. At least twenty-two people in Warsaw and Cracow alone were detained and fined for participating in peaceful demonstrations on 11 November.

1980   In 1980 the Polish Historical Association changed its bylaws, which until then had proclaimed Marxism to be the only method of historical scholarship.

1980–82   The political quarterly *Res publica*, whose chief editor was historian **Marcin Król** (1944–), a specialist in nineteenth-century conservative thought who in 2000 was the Warsaw University history department director, appeared in samizdat. Writer and literary historian **Wojciech Karpiński** (1943–), coeditor of *Res publica*, author with Król of *Political Silhouettes of the Nineteenth Century* (1974), was in the United States on the day of the declaration of martial law (13 December 1981) and became first a lecturer at Yale University and in 1982 a CNRS staff member in Paris. In 1982 he wrote *The Shadow of Metternich*.

1980   In May historian **Roman Wapiński** requested that his publisher withdraw his textbook on modern Polish history from circulation because high school students had protested its censored contents. The minutes of the Polish-Soviet historical commission to which textbooks such as Wapiński's were submitted for comment were published by the underground publishers Glos in 1980 and by *Zeszyty historyczne* in 1981.

1980–82   Between August 1980 and the introduction of a new censorship law in October 1981, there was a breakthrough in the defalsification of history. Two monographs on Polish modern history, *History of Postpartition Poland 1795–1921* by émigré historian Kukiel [q.v. pre-1945], minister of defense in the Polish wartime government-in-exile, and the multivolume *History of Poland 1866–1945* by **Władysław Pobóg–Malinowski** (1899–1962), were reprinted as underground publications, as were certain *Zeszyty historyczne* editions. The official press and publishers started publications on forbidden topics. Solidarity's national weekly, *Tygodnik Solidarność*, began publishing *A Political History of Poland 1944–56* by historian **Krystyna Kersten**, professor of modern history at the PAN History Institute. It was published in full without the author's permission by Krag (the Circle), Poland's largest underground publishers in 1982 (under martial law). *Tygodnik Solidarność* published extensive source materials on the events of 1956, 1968, 1970, and 1976, featured articles of general historical interest on forgotten historical figures, on the political terror of the late 1940s and early 1950s, and on historical controversies such as the circumstances of regaining independence in 1918. New editions of classics of Polish historiography by **Szymon Askenazy** (1865–1935), **Władysław Smoleński** (1851–1926), **Karol Szajnocha**, and others, which had never appeared in the PPR, were published. Among the books published by Krag in 1982 were *A Contemporary History of Poland 1918–1939* by **Andrzej Albert** (pseudonym of **Wojciech Roszkowski**, historian and senior lecturer at a Warsaw School of Economics); *Berlin Uprising 17 June 1953* by **Axel Bust-Bartels**; *Fire-Tested I: The Roots of Identity*, a contemporary history of the Catholic Church in Eastern Europe by Cywiński [q.v. 1978–]; *Letters from Białołeka* by Michnik [q.v. 1965–86]; *The Uprising of the Polish Nation 1830–31* by **Maurycy Mochnacki** (?1803–34); *Warsaw Uprising* by **Antoni Nowosielski**; *A Contemporary Political History of Poland*, vol. 3, *1939–1945* by Pobóg–Malinowski; *The Invasion of Czechoslovakia, August 1968; A Review Sent from Moscow: Polish History Handbooks*; and *Zeszyty historyczne*, nos. 1, 2, 52, 54, and 55.

1981–89   *Man of Iron*, a film by **Andrzej Wajda** (1926–) about the 1980 Gdansk shipyard strike and Solidarity's birth, was banned shortly after its 1981 premiere. In January 1982 the film was condemned as an incitement to social anarchy. In February 1989 it was screened again in Warsaw. Wajda was elected a Solidarity senator in 1989.

1981   In January academic historians denounced the limited access to archives, incomplete cataloging of documents, and the unavailability of émigré publications.

1981–83   After martial law was declared (13 December 1981), all academic sessions on the modern period were held under PUWP auspices or army research institutions. The Historical Association [q.v. 1980] was suspended but resumed activities in August 1982. The authorities did not crudely stifle scholarly discussion, but independent historical writings were driven underground, in the so-called "second circulation". The situation among school history teachers was worse:

many were reportedly arrested, dismissed, or harassed. But the Historical Association and the church were active on behalf of these lesser-known persons. Under martial law (1981–83), no discussion of current political affairs was possible. However, intense substitute historical polemics did take place. The repercussions of the Targowica Confederation in 1792–93—when, ominously, Polish traitors had called in the Russian army—were discussed, as were the policies of Poland's last king, Stanisław August (reigned 1764–95), the meaning of nineteenth-century uprisings, the introduction of martial law in 1861, and Piłsudski's policies.

1980s   *The Establishment of the Communist Rule in Poland 1943–1948* (Boulder 1991) by Kersten [q.v. 1980–82] was originally published in samizdat. Other synthetic studies on Polish history that circulated in abridged samizdat versions were those of **Stanisław Cat-Mackiewicz** and **Paweł Zaremba**.

Zdzisław Najder (1930–), an anticommunist literary historian who together with lawyer and future prime minister Jan Olszewski participated in the Polish Independence Compact (a group that published anonymous reports on historical and current issues), went into exile and worked as director of the Polish section of Radio Free Europe. The authorities sentenced him to death in absentia. Upon his return to Poland in [1990], he became chairman of the national Solidarity Civic Committee and adviser to Prime Minister Olszewski (1991–92). In 1992 journalist Jerzy Urban published extracts from the former communist political police archives revealing that in 1958 Najder had undertaken to cooperate with the secret police.

1982   Among the artists and writers reported arrested in January 1982 was **Marian Brandys** (1912–), former journalist and author of historical novels, many of which were published underground. The offices of the Polish PEN Club were closed down and its doors sealed. Among the leading PEN members arrested were historians Bartoszewski [q.v. 1946–], Lipski [q.v. 1960–89], Jedlicki [q.v. 1978–], and Geremek [q.v. 1968–88]. Of the TKN [q.v. 1978–] lecturers interned, many reportedly gave lectures to their fellow inmates. Bartoszewski, for example, delivered some seventy hours of lectures during his five-month internment. Also detained was church historian and medievalist **Jerzy Kłoczowski** (1924–) of Lublin Catholic University, PAN member (1968–), vice president of the Polish Historical Society (1980–), and Solidarity adviser. In 1944–45 he had been a war prisoner. In 1995 he was director of the Institute of East Central Europe at Lublin and president of the Polish National Commission at UNESCO.

[1982]   The so-called *Kubiak Report*, an analysis of Poland's postwar crises ordered by the Ninth PUWP Congress, was not allowed to be published in its original version (which contained many outspoken passages on the negative consequences of manipulating history), not even in internal PUWP bulletins, although it came out in the underground press and abroad.

1982   In January the authorities dismissed historian and medievalist **Henryk Samsonowicz** (1930–) from his post as elected rector of Warsaw University (1980–82) under protest of the university staff. He had already been expelled from the PUWP after he had protested the "verification" of university personnel (a screening process requiring "political conversations" and the signing of "loyalty declarations") and after he had invited TKN [q.v. 1978–] professors to present their lectures openly and legally on the campus. Later Samsonowicz became the minister of national education in the Tadeusz Mazowiecki government (1989–91).

1984–86   In 1984 the first volume of the Solidarity archives, *Szczecin: December–August—December* by **Malgorzata Sejnert** and **Tomasz Zalewski**, was published by NOWa. It also published *The Generations Black from Mourning: Those Sentenced to Death and Their Judges, 1944–1954* by **Lukasz Socha** [q.v. 1972: Turlejska] and *December 1970 in Gdynia* (1986) by **W. Kwasniewska**.

1984   A paper, "Polish Society between the Eighteenth and Twentieth Centuries: Rhythms of Development and Dynamics of Change", by historian and professor **Tadeusz Łepkowski** (1927–), head of the History of Latin America, Asia and Africa Research Center at the PAN History Institute (1969–) and chairman of the Solidarity Committee at the Institute (January–December 1981), was read at the Thirteenth General Conference of Polish Historians at Poznań in September 1984 but not included in the conference documents; only its title was mentioned with the note "was submitted to the editor". It circulated in the samizdat and émigré publishing circuit.

1985   A well-known Polish journalist specializing in historical subjects wrote an essay for *Index on Censorship* about Polish history; he wished to remain anonymous.

           Roman Korab-Żebryk's book *Operacja wilenska AK* (Warsaw 1985), about the postwar treatment of the Home Army, was censored.

[1985]   In [February] 650,000 copies of the history textbook *Modern History* by historian **Andrzej Szcześniak** were withheld by the censors and ordered to be shredded, apparently because it touched upon "sensitive" facts which had been passed over in previous textbooks.

1986–88   In 1986 *Birth of the System of Power*, a book by Kersten [q.v. 1980–82] about the June 1946 referendum, was published abroad. In late 1988 it was still banned but easily available in Warsaw, although expensive.

1986   In March historians **Teresa Sulej** and **Wlodzimierz Sulej** were given eight-month suspended sentences for possessing and distributing underground literature.

            In April **Agnieszka Sadlakowska**, archivist at Warsaw's Jewish Theater, was given an eight-month sentence suspended for five years for possessing illegal publications.

[1987–88]   In [1987] or [1988] an article by historian **Adolf Juzwénko**, which was accepted for publication in *Res publica*—then an independent but legally published monthly—was banned. The article, *The Right to Historical Truth*, describing the state of Polish postwar historiography, appeared in English in *Index on Censorship* (October 1988). The same or a similar article appeared in *Tygodnik Solidarność* in September 1989.

1987   In August historian **Wieslaw Wadyka** declared in an interview that a book about the 1956 events he had cowritten was not allowed to be published.

            In November the Poznań customs office confiscated seventeen publications sent to a Polish citizen from the FRG, including *The Gulag Archipelago* by **Aleksandr Solzhenitsyn** (1918–), and *Zeszyty historyczne* no.6 of 1984; published by the Paris Instytut Literacki, containing a biographical lexicon of the victims of terror in Poland (1944–64), and no.11 of 1963 containing articles concerning World War II.

1989   A text called *The Crime of the Partitions* (1919), by writer **Joseph Conrad** (1857–1924), was excluded from his *Complete Works* by the communist regime but unofficially published in a series on blank spots in history.

1990   In July the Mazowiecki government dissolved the PAN and dismissed its rector, **Jarema Maciszewski**, the co-chairman of the Joint Polish-Soviet History Commission.

1990–   In [September] 1990 the archive of the abolished Censorship Office was entrusted to the Archive of Recent Records. In November 1991 the Commission for the Investigation of Crimes against the Polish

Nation reported that secret documents on crimes committed during the Stalin era had been uncovered in the main military prosecutor's office. They were to be examined by a new National Remembrance Institute (established September 1998). In December 1992 the Defense Ministry announced that destruction of military archive documents dealing with martial law (1981–83) had been virtually total after 1989 and that ten persons accused of destroying the archives would soon be appearing in court. In December 1994 several dozens of writers and intellectuals issued an appeal to open the Security Administration Archives covering the Stalinist period (1944–56). In March 1995 the Interior Ministry announced that many files from the communist secret police archives would be made available to historians. Journalists seeking access to the archives would have to apply directly to the interior minister for permission.

1993 In June anti-Semitic Poles in Cracow attacked the film cast of Steven Spielberg's *Schindler's List*, a film about the Holocaust.

1997 In the spring American publishers Doubleday claimed that the Polish version of a biography of Pope John Paul II, *His Holiness: John Paul II and the Hidden History of Our Time* (New York 1996), by journalists **Carl Bernstein** (1944–) and **Marco Politi**, was doctored by its Polish partners, Amber Publishing, to avoid giving offense to Roman Catholics in Poland as well as to the (Polish) pope. Controversial references to Polish history, particularly passages referring to the Auschwitz extermination camp, were reportedly removed.

Also see Germany (1977–92: Böhme; 1979–89: Garton Ash), Greece (1972: Deutscher), Korea (1985: Deutscher), United Kingdom (1987: Samborski), United States (1955: Pipes), Union of Soviet Socialist Republics (USSR) (1969–: Karavansky; 1980: Kieniewicz; 1937–45: Liudkiewicz; 1973–94: Solzhenitsyn; 1989: Zakirov).

SOURCES

Ajnenkiel, A., "Blank Pages in Polish History", *Polish Review*, 1988: 333–41.
Amnesty International, *Report* (London) 1968–69: 25, 27; 1969–70: 19, 28–29; 1971–72: 43; 1977: 261; 1978: 223–24; 1980: 283–84; 1981: 311–12; 1982: 281, 283; 1983: 268–69, 294; 1984: 294; 1985: 277–78; 1986: 294; 1987: 306–8.
Annual Obituary 1991 (Chicago/London) 291–95 (Kosinski), 564–68 (Lipski).
Article 19, *Information, Freedom and Censorship: World Report* (London) 1988: 201, 311; 1991: 294.
Auer, L., "Archival Losses and Their Impact on the Work of Archivists and Historians", *Archivum*, 1996, no.42: 3.
———, "Archival Losses since the Second World War", *Janus*, 1994, no.1: 70.
Banisar, D., *Freedom of Information around the World* (WWW-text; Privacy International Report; London 2000).

Beauvois, D., "Être historien en Pologne: Les Mythes, l'amnésie et la 'vérité' ", *Revue d'histoire moderne et contemporaine*, 1991: 360–86.

Bentley, M. ed., *Companion to Historiography* (London/New York 1997) 474.

Bernard, M., & H. Szlajfer eds., *From the Polish Underground: Selections from Krytyka, 1978–1993* (University Park, Pa. (1995) 398, 401, 405, 407, 410, 415–16, 421–22, 428, 433–34, 439–42.

Biernat, A., "The Destruction and Reconstruction of Archives: The Case of Poland", *Archivum*, 1996, no.42: 147–55.

Biskup, J., personal communication, July 1997.

Boia, L. ed., *Great Historians of the Modern Age: An International Dictionary* (Westport 1991) 207, 475–76, 482–83, 495–96.

Boris, P., *Die sich lossagten: Stichworte zu Leben und Werk von 461 Exkommunisten und Dissidenten* (Cologne 1983) 35, 139–40, 153–54, 166, 188–89, 193–94, 203–4.

Boyd, K. ed., *Encyclopedia of Historians and Historical Writing* (London/Chicago 1999) 652–53, 851–52, 929–30, 935–36.

Bronkhorst, D., *Truth and Reconciliation: Obstacles and Opportunities for Human Rights* (Amsterdam 1995) 147.

Bruch, R. vom, & R.A. Müller eds., *Historikerlexikon: Von der Antike bis zum 20. Jahrhundert* (Munich 1991) 222–23.

Buczynska-Garewicz, H., "The Flying University in Poland, 1978–1980", *Harvard Educational Review*, 1985: 20–33.

Burguière, A. ed., *Dictionnaire des sciences historiques*, (Paris 1986) 528, 532.

Cannon, J. ed., *The Blackwell Dictionary of Historians* (Oxford 1988) 295–96.

Darnton, R., "Poland Rewrites History", *New York Review of Books*, 16 July 1981: 6–10.

Davies, N., *God's Playground: A History of Poland*, vol. 1 (Oxford 1981) 14–22.

Davies, R.W., *Soviet History in the Yeltsin Era* (Basingstoke 1997) 19.

Duby, G., & B. Geremek, *Passions communes: Entretiens avec Philippe Sainteny* (Paris 1992) 15–16, 51–58.

Duruflé-Lozinski, A., "Retour à Katyn", in: A. Brossat, S. Combe, J.-Y. Potel & J.-C. Szurek eds., *A l'Est, la mémoire retrouvée* (Paris 1990) 39, 41, 50.

Eich, H., *Die mißhandelte Geschichte: Historische Schuld- und Freisprüche* (Munich 1986) 179–81.

Ferro, M., *Comment on raconte l'histoire aux enfants à travers le monde entier* (Paris 1981) 212, 218–19, 221–22.

Geremek, B., "Marc Bloch, historien et résistant", *Annales ESC*, 1986: 1091–1105.

Gieysztor, A., "Les Sciences historiques dans la Pologne d'aujourd'hui", in: R. Rémond ed., *Être historien aujourd'hui* (Paris 1988) 147–48, 156.

Gorman, R.A. ed., *Biographical Dictionary of Neo-Marxism* (Westport 1985) 232–34, 248–49, 299–300.

Grabski, A.F., "Poland", in: G. Iggers & H.T. Parker eds., *International Handbook of Historical Studies: Contemporary Research and Theory* (London/Westport 1979) 301, 316–17.

Gross, J.T., "In Search of History", in: A. Brumberg ed., *Poland: Genesis of a Revolution* (New York 1983) 6–9.

Held, J., *Dictionary of East European History since 1945* (Westport 1994) 332, 341–43, 345–46.

Historical Abstracts (CD-rom version) (Roos).

Hoeven, H. van der, *Lost Memory: Libraries and Archives Destroyed in the Twentieth Century*, part 1, *Libraries* (WWW-text 1996) 9.

Human Rights Watch, *World Report 1993* (Washington 1992) 246.

Index on Censorship, 2/73: vii; 1/77: 63; 3/77: 69; 4/77: 71; 5/77: 69–70; 6/77: 66; 3/78: 66; 4/78: 28–29, 32 (second quote *Black Book*), 33, 65, 69; 5/78: 69; 6/78: 57–59; 1/79: 62; 2/79: 67–68; 3/79: 69; 4/79: 67; 5/79: 69; 6/79: 19–22; 2/80: 71–72; 3/80: 37, 65–66; 4/80: 73; 6/80: 70; 1/81: 37, 76; 3/81: 77; 1/82: 46; 2/82: 46–47; 4/82: 16–18, 29, 41, 46; 1/83: 46; 6/83: 23, 46; 1/84: 45; 3/84: 48; 5/84: 46; 6/84: 47; 1/85: 64; 2/85: 21–23, 36; 3/85: 52; 4/85: 4, 54; 5/85: 67; 6/85: 5, 10–13, 33; 3/86: 40; 4/86: 39; 7/86: 43; 8/86: 39–40; 1/87: 42; 3/87: 39; 5/87: 39; 7/87: 40; 9/87: 37; 2/88: 38; 3/88: 39; 4/88: 39; 5/88: 129; 7/88: 37; 9/88: 10–15; 1/89: 38; 2/89: 31, 39; 6–7/89: 4, 79; 9/89: 41; 1/90: 1; 8/90: 38; 1/91: 16; 2/92: 38; 4/93: 39; 10/93: 47; 6/94: 157–62; 1/95: 245; 3/95: 184; 6/95: 105; 1/96: 183; 2/96: 99–100, 152; 5/96: 145–47; 4/97: 11; 5/97: 117; 2/99: 166; 2/00: 124–25.

Keesings historisch archief, 1991: 221; 1992: 612–13, 758–59; 1993: 548, 843; 1999: 333–34.

Keesing's Record of World Events, 1983: 32445A; 1985: 33874A; 1988: 35649A; 1990: 37383B.

"Leading Polish Historian Is Dismissed", *Times Higher Education Supplement*, 10 May 1985: 9 (Geremek).

Lerski, G.J., *Historical Dictionary of Poland* (Westport 1996) 337.

Marès, A. ed., *Histoire et pouvoir en Europe médiane* (Paris 1996).

Michnik, A., *Letters from Prison and Other Essays* (Berkeley 1985) iv, x–xv, xix–xxi, 2.

Persky, S., & H. Flam eds., *The Solidarity Sourcebook* (Vancouver 1982) 35–56.

Raina, P., *Political Opposition in Poland 1954–1977* (London 1978) 32–33, 70–71, 74–77, 81–100, 112–19, 121–23, 125–27, 130, 133, 135, 146, 156, 170–73, 178–96, 247–49, 251, 265, 280–82, 299–302, 328, 335–36, 339, 346, 361, 364–66, 380–82, 427, 485–96, 500–501, 531–41, 545–48.

Redlich S., *What Happened One Day in Jedwabne* (WWW-text 2001).

Romek, Z., personal communication, December 1999.

Rosenberg, T., *The Haunted Land: Facing Europe's Ghosts after Communism* (New York 1995) 154, 163, 245–48, 250–51.

Ryszka, F., "Poland: Some Recent Revaluations", in: W. Laqueur & G.L. Mosse eds., *The New History: Trends in Historical Research and Writing since World War II* (New York 1967) 105–7, 112.

Samsonowicz, H., "Poland: Myths That Die Hard", *UNESCO Courier*, May 1994: 23–24, 31.

Sanford, G., & A. Gozdecka-Sanford, *Historical Dictionary of Poland* (Metuchen 1994) 76, 78, 86, 106, 111, 124, 128–29, 132, 214.

Schöpflin, G. ed., *Censorship and Political Communication in Eastern Europe: A Collection of Documents* (London 1983) 52, 54–56, 73, 77–78, 81 [first quote *Black Book*: 56.].

Schramm, T., "L'Historiographie polonaise 1976–1989" and "L'Historiographie polonaise de 1989 à 1994", in: Marès ed. 1996: 35, 37, 39–43, 195, 198–99.

Stern, F., "Historians and the Great War: Private Experience and Public Explication", *Yale Review*, 1994 no.1: 53.

Strauss, H.A., & W. Röder eds., *International Biographical Dictionary of Central European Émigrés 1933–1945*, vol. 2 (Munich 1983) 984.

Stroynowski, J. ed., *Who's Who in the Socialist Countries of Europe* (Munich 1989) 68, 128, 136, 208, 346, 353, 443, 533, 546, 551, 567, 579–80, 628, 650, 679–80, 690–91, 714, 727, 770, 794–95, 1000, 1023, 1164, 1191, 1238, 1278.

Szayna, T.S., "Addressing 'Blank Spots' in Polish–Soviet Relations", *Problems of Communism*, 1988: 37–57.

Time, 18 June 1990: 33 (Michnik).

Topolski, J., "Polish Historians vis-à-vis Marxism after World War II", in: F. Glatz & A. Pók eds., *The Soviet System and Historiography, 1917–1989: The Influence of Marxism-Leninism on the Historical Sciences* (unpublished papers; Budapest 1995) 79–88.

Tucker, M. ed., *Literary Exile in the Twentieth Century: An Analysis and Biographical Dictionary* (Westport 1991) 388–91.

Valkenier, E.K., " 'Glasnost' and Filling in the 'Blank Spots' in the History of Polish–Soviet Relations, 1987–1990", *Polish Review*, 1991: 247–68.

———, "The Rise and Decline of Official Marxist Historiography in Poland, 1945–1983", *Slavic Review*, 1985: 664, 666–82.

Wandycz, P.S., "Historiography of the Countries of Eastern Europe: Poland", *American Historical Review*, 1992: 1011, 1018–23.

Washburn, W.E., "The Academic Profession and Contemporary Politics", *Minerva*, 1988: 401.

Woolf, D.R. ed., *A Global Encyclopedia of Historical Writing* (New York/London 1998) 510, 589–90, 646, 721–23.

Zernack, K., D. Geyer, & H.A. Winkler, "Zur Politischen Rolle der Polnischen Historiker", *Geschichte in Wissenschaft und Unterricht*, 1982: 487–93.

PORTUGAL

During the Estado Novo (New State; 1932 until 25 April 1974), led until 1968 by Prime Minister António Salazar, the study of contemporary history virtually disappeared, at least until the 1960s. In 1954 the historian of Portuguese expansion Charles Boxer called government censorship "one of the seven deadly sins prone to afflict Portuguese historians." Access to archival materials was very limited.

pre-1945–	Among the historians who emigrated before 1945 (and living in exile after 1944) were the brothers **Jaime Cortesão** (1884–1960) and **Armando Cortesão** (1891–1977).
1940s–	The work of Marxist archeologist **Gordon Childe** (1892–1957), Australian-born professor of prehistory at Edinburgh University (1927–46) and director at the London University Institute of Archaeology (1946–56), reportedly did not have much impact on

Portuguese archeology despite his 1949 visit and the Portuguese translation of some of his books, presumably because almost all archeologists feared punishment from the regime when reading Marxist scholars. The Centro Piloto de Arqueologia (CPA; Pilot Center of Archeology) prevented four Portuguese archeologists (names unknown) from conducting fieldwork in Portugal because of their left-wing tendencies. After the 1974 Revolution, the CPA was disbanded under pressure from a group of fifty archeologists.

[1962]–74   After his participation in the January 1962 Beja military revolt, historian of mentalities **Joaquim Barradas de Carvalho** (1920–80), member of the clandestine Portuguese Communist Party (1940–), went into exile in France (?1962–64), Brazil (1964–70), where he worked at São Paulo University, and again in France (1970–76) together with his wife **Margarida**, also a historian. He returned to Portugal after the 1974 revolution and worked there as a history professor at Lisbon University.

1964–65   Some archives reportedly made foreign historians feel unwelcome, possibly because the sources consulted there were sometimes used to criticize Portugal's role in Africa.

1965–74   In 1965 historian **António de Oliveira Marques** (1933–) was forced to leave Portugal. He taught at Auburn University, Alabama, for one year and at the University of Florida, Gainesville, for three years. In 1968 he learned that the new prime minister, Caetano [q.v. 1974], a former professor of his, would tacitly allow him back in Portugal. Meanwhile he had been commissioned by Columbia University Press to write a two-volume *History of Portugal* (New York 1972). Although the book was not banned, Caetano sought to refute its theses in a long book review. After the 1974 revolution, Oliveira Marques was named National Library director in Lisbon.

1968–74   In March 1968 lawyer **Mário Soares** (1924–), who had a degree in history and philosophy from Lisbon University (1951), was deported to São Tomé but was able to return in 1969 during a brief liberalization period. As he attacked the dictatorship and its colonial policies in Africa, he was harassed by the political police. (During the 1960s he had already been arrested at least twelve times.) The 1969 elections in which he participated as an opposition candidate were rigged. He went into exile in France (1969–74), where he taught at the Sorbonne. In 1973 he helped to refound the Socialist Party. After 1974 he was prime minister on several occasions, and from 1985 to 1996 he was elected president twice.

1970	In June, when Salazar died, photographs from the 1930s showing him making the Nazi salute could not be published.
1970s	Historian **Fernando Rosas** (?1947–), a member of a Maoist group, was imprisoned twice for more than one year. In 1971 he was tortured three times and deprived of sleep for a week. After his release he went underground. He became an associate professor specializing in the history of the Estado Novo and the chairman of the Contemporary History Institute at the New University of Lisbon. A candidate for the Bloco de Esquerda (Left-Wing Bloc) political party in the January 2001 presidential elections, he received 3 percent of the votes.
pre-1974	**Vitorino Magalhães Godinho** (1918–), socialist and historian of the Portuguese discoveries and of economics, lived in exile in France, part of the time as a professor at Clermont-Ferrand University (1971–74). After the 1974 revolution, he was briefly minister of education and culture (July–November 1974), but he resigned after incidents at Lisbon University in October–November culminating in troops being brought in on 30 November to quell fighting between rival left-wing groups.
1974	After the 1974 revolution, **Marcello Caetano** (1906–80), prime minister (1968–74), historian of law, and political scientist, surrendered and went into exile in Brazil (1974–80), where he wrote his memoirs and histories of the Estado Novo period. In March 1962 he had resigned as rector of Lisbon University after a clash between students opposing the regime and the political police PIDE.
1975	**António da Silva Rego** (1905–86), priest and historian of Portuguese expansion in Asia and elsewhere, was reportedly forced to retire as director of the Centro de Estudos Históricos Ultramarinos and as professor at the Instituto Superior dos Estudos Ultramarinos, Lisbon, because he was closely associated with the former regime.
[1979]	The television series *The Years of the Century*, reportedly a left-wing historian's personal view of the Estado Novo, was canceled after complaints from the Catholic Church about the first episode. The film explicitly attacked the church's alleged support of the Estado Novo repression of black nationalists in the Portuguese colonies.
1996	In April a controversy took place about the accessibility of PIDE archives and the possible restitution of stolen letters, secret photographs, and telephone conversation recordings in these archives.

Also see: South Africa (1953–: Davidson).

SOURCES

Amnesty International, *Report 1967–68* (London 1968) 11.

Azevedo, M., *Historical Dictionary of Mozambique* (Metuchen 1991) 122.

Barradas de Carvalho, J., *A la recherche de la spécificité de la renaissance portugaise* (Paris 1983) v–vii.

Bender, G., & A. Isaacman, "The Changing Historiography of Angola and Mozambique", in: C. Fyfe ed., *African Studies since 1945: A Tribute to Basil Davidson* (London/ Edinburgh 1976) 222, 237.

Blussé, L., F.-P. van der Putten, & H. Vogel eds., *Pilgrims to the Past: Private Conversations with Historians of European Expansion* (Leiden 1996) 138, 142–43.

Boia, L. ed., *Great Historians of the Modern Age: An International Dictionary* (Westport 1991) 192–93.

Boxer, C.R., "Some Notes on Portuguese Historiography 1930–1950", *History*, 1954: 6, 10–11 (quote 10).

Index on Censorship, 2/72: 55; 4/79: 68.

Keesing's Record of World Events, 1974: 26685A; 1975: 27007B-08A.

Lillios, K.T., "Nationalism and Copper Age Research in Portugal during the Salazar Regime (1932–1974)", in: P.L. Kohl & C. Fawcett eds., *Nationalism, Politics, and the Practice of Archaelogy* (Cambridge 1995) 63, 67–69.

Mota, C.G., "Joaquim Barradas de Carvalho", *Estudos avançados*, 1994: 289–95.

NRC-Handelsblad, 1996 (25 April: 6; PIDE archives); 1999 (27 & 28 October: 1; Rosas).

Raby, D.L., *Fascism and Resistance in Portugal: Communists, Liberals and Military Dissidents in the Opposition to Salazar, 1941–1974* (Manchester/New York 1988) 237.

Wheeler, D.L., *Historical Dictionary of Portugal* (Metuchen 1993) 49–52, 165–66.

Winius, G.D., "Iberian Historiography on European Expansion since World War II", in: P.C. Emmer & H.L. Wesseling eds., *Reappraisals in Overseas History* (Leiden 1979) 102, 112, 115–16.

Winters, C. ed., *International Dictionary of Anthropologists* (New York/London 1991) 111–13.

Woolf, D.R. ed., *A Global Encyclopedia of Historical Writing* (New York/London 1998) 729–30.

Q

QATAR

See United Arab Emirates (Aqil).

R

ROMANIA

During the communist years (1948–89), most historians lived in isolation, except during a relatively liberal period from 1965 to the early 1970s. Some topics were described as "the great taboos of official communist historiography": the monarchy, the army, the parliamentary system, and the political parties (including the Romanian Communist Party, the history of Transylvania (a region with a large Hungarian-speaking minority), Bessarabia and northern Bukovina (annexed by the USSR in 1940), Russo-Romanian relations, and universal history. The history of religions could be added. Government decrees of 1947–48 outlawed the circulation of some seven hundred publications covering the former Romanian-ruled provinces of Bessarabia and Bukovina and the royal family. Several purges of historians took place, especially between 1947–48 and 1959. After the reform of education (1947) and of the Romanian Academy (June 1948), the most important historians were reportedly removed from their posts and often imprisoned. Their works and those of many Romanian historians of the past were banned from the library catalogs and the antiquarian bookshops, as they were called the legacy of the liquidated fascist regime. As a reaction, some historians reportedly took refuge in technical professionalism, others went into exile. Around 1965, some of the prewar historians, such as Constantin Giurescu [q.v. pre-1954] and Panaitescu [q.v. pre-1954], were rehabilitated and became active again. The state archives kept part of the prewar documents only. Those regarded as "sensitive" (such as documents relating to the royal family, the political parties, and the Ministry of Foreign Affairs) were placed in reserved archives, mainly those of the Romanian Communist Party (RCP) History Institute. Only some of these archives became accessible after 1990. In Transylvania the government "rationalized" archives and libraries. The 1948 law of nationalization, the 1971 National Archives Law, and the 1974 Law for the Protection of the National Cultural Patrimony placed all manuscript collections of historic value under the jurisdiction of the General Directorate of State Archives of the Ministry of Internal Affairs. The directorate operated under the control of a special section of that ministry, the Securitate (the security police in 1948–90). Most of these collections, especially private and ecclesiastical archives, suffered disorganization and losses and were inaccessible. In anticipation of such damages, valuable manuscripts were frequently hidden from the authorities. In the 1980s the Bucharest University History Institute did not buy any historical works from abroad: the only new historical works were gifts from the USSR. In the final days of President Nicolae Ceauşescu's government (who took power in 1965), on 25 December 1989, four historians wrote a declaration, which, signed by thirteen historians, was given to the press (access to the television was refused). It condemned the historical lies of Ceauşescu's regime and proposed the outline of a new program for Romanian historiography. Among the signatories were David Prodan (1902–92), medievalist and Romanian Academy member, and Henri Stahl [q.v. pre–1953] and Dionisie Pippidi [q.v. pre–1953], corresponding Academy members.

1945–   In 1945 **Mircea Eliade** (1907–86), historian, philosopher of comparative religion, lecturer in the history of religion and metaphysics at Bucharest University (1933–39), cultural attaché with the Royal Legation of Romania in London (1940) and Lisbon (1941–45), went into self-imposed exile because he was suspected of having supported the Romanian Fascist organization Iron Guard in his press articles of the late 1930s. During a brief return to Bucharest in August 1942, he had been watched by the Gestapo and Romanian secret service agents. He lectured at various Western European and Scandinavian universities (1945–56) before going to the United States, where he became professor and chairman of the history of religions department at the University of Chicago (1957–85). His works were banned in Romania until the 1970s. His multivolume *History of Religious Ideas* (French 1976–83, English 1978–85) was distributed to a list of people selected by RCP officials. Coming in the middle of an antireligious campaign, publication of the translated second volume, *From Gautama Buddha to the Triumph of Christianity* (French 1978, English 1982), was postponed. The third volume, *From Muhammad to the Age of Reforms* (French 1983, English 1985), did not appear on the bookshop shelves but was reportedly sold at high prices on the black market instead. In his early years, Eliade had founded *Revista universitară* (1926), which was suppressed after only three issues because of his critical review of *Essai d'histoire universelle* by Iorga [q.v. 1948–].

1947–53 In September 1947, historian and politician **Gheorghe Brătianu** (1898–1953), son of a princess and a prime minister, medievalist and byzantinist, professor of world history at Iasi University (1924–40), director of the Institute of World History in Bucharest (1940–47), specialist in the history of the civilizations in the Black Sea area, and active member of the National Liberal Party, was put under house arrest. In May 1950 he was arrested because of his alleged political (pro-monarchical, pro-German) viewpoints. In 1953 he committed suicide in prison. Publication of his works was forbidden for a long time. Some appeared posthumously, such as *La Mer noire: Des origines à la conquête ottomane* (Munich 1969; The Black Sea: From Its Origins to the Ottoman Conquest).

1948–54   Despite his record of service during the war, historian, RCP theoretician, and veteran leader **Lucreţiu Pătrăşcanu** (1900–54), an "early" communist nationalist, was excluded from the post-1944 Politburo. In February 1948, at the climax of the campaign against Yugoslav leader Tito, he was expelled from the RCP Central Committee (CC) and in April 1948 he was arrested on charges of national chauvinism and right-wing deviationism. According to rumor, he was lodged in the Lubianka prison in Moscow. He was ill-treated, convicted, and executed in April 1954. In 1965 an RCP inquiry commission showed that the secret police chief had personally assembled false charges against him. In 1968 he was rehabilitated. His most important historical study was *A Century of Social Unrest, 1821–1907*, written between 1933 and 1943, interrupted by spells of imprisonment and clandestinity.

1948–   In the spring of 1948, the works of historians such as **Nicolae Iorga** (1871–1940; a former prime minister [1931–32] killed by the Iron Guard) and **Vasile Pârvan** (1882–1927) were banned for more than a decade. The *Chronicle of the Antiquity of the Romano-Moldavians and Wallachians* (1719–22) by historian **Dimitrie Cantemir** (1673–1723) was also banned, probably for being too pro-Roman for the new pro-Slavic approach.

1948   **Randolph Braham** (1922–) was among the young refugees who became historians in their new country (in his case the United States).

1949–62   In January 1949 **Constantin Gane** (1885–1962), historian and biographer of royalty, former Iron Guard member, and ambassador in Athens (1940–41), was arrested and sentenced to twenty-five years' imprisonment, for his part as an extreme rightist. He died in prison.

1949–   After 1949 **Andrei Rădulescu** (1880–1959), professor of the history of Romanian law in Bucharest and president of the Romanian Academy (1946–48), was downgraded; he became an academy researcher.

pre-1953   Only after Stalin's death could historians of antiquity and the Middle Ages, such as **Maria Holban, Henri Stahl**, and **Dionisie Pippidi**, publish their works.

pre-1954   In 1954 two historians were released from prison, partly due to the efforts of Constantinescu [q.v. 1957–]: **Constantin Giurescu** (1901–77), political and institutional historian, professor of Romanian history at Bucharest University (1926–48, 1963–75), director of the Institute of National History (1931–48), and minister (1939–40), who had spent five years in prison, and **Petre Panaitescu** (1900–67), professor of Slavonic history at Bucharest University (1932–41) and researcher at the Nicolae Iorga Historical Institute in Bucharest (1954–65).

1957–   In June 1957 historian, sociologist, and politician **Miron Constantinescu** (1917–74) was forced to perform self-criticism at the CC plenum, under circumstances possibly connected with the fall of former Prime Minister Georgi Malenkov in the USSR. Imprisoned during the war for his communist activities, he became the youngest Politburo member in 1944 and the RCP's "official social scientist". In 1954–57 he was first deputy prime minister and minister of education. At the March–April 1956 Politburo sessions, he (and others) attacked the politics of RCP leader Gheorghe Gheorghiu-Dej, accusing him of the main crimes perpetrated during the Stalinist epoch. At the June 1958 CC plenum, Constantinescu was exposed as the symbol of an "anarcho-liberal" deviation in the RCP and in 1959 he was expelled from the CC. He became an associate history professor at the Institute of Postgraduate Pedagogical Studies in Bucharest and later a research associate at the Romanian Academy of Sciences History Institute, directed at that time by historian Andrei Oţetea (1894–1977). In November–December 1961, he was criticized for having devoted a prewar vacation to reading Karl Marx's *Das Kapital* in a convent. He was rehabilitated in 1965 by then RCP Secretary-General Nicolae Ceauşescu. As the president of the Academy for Social and Political Sciences (1970–) and CC secretary (1972–), he published profusely on social history and sociology. In March 1974 a book in which he tried to apply Marx's theses on oriental despotism to Romanian medieval social history was attacked within the RCP, and its distribution rights were withdrawn. Not long before his death, he was stigmatized by Elena Ceauşescu for allegedly intending to seize control of the RCP.

[?]   General **Ion Munteanu**, a member of Ceauşescu's team of profes-
                       sional ideologues and head of the Securitate's First Directorate (in
                       charge of supervising cultural and scientific activities), fell out of
                       favor after some of his colleagues had denounced him as the author
                       of an anonymous letter sent to Ceauşescu to protest the lack of
                       training of the historians representing Romania at international meet-
                       ings. After the December 1989 revolt, he was appointed director of
                       the State Archives. President Ceauşescu and his brother, Lieutenant
                       General Ilie Ceauşescu, were known for their special interest in his-
                       tory. Ilie Ceauşescu was a military historian. Both actively contrib-
                       uted to the official versions of the Romanian past.

1967   In 1967 historian **Ioan Lupaş**, (1880–1967), professor of Romanian
                       history at Cluj University (1919–46), head of the Institute of Ro-
                       manian National History (1920–45), and specialist in Transylvanian
                       and church history, reportedly died in prison.

1972–   As an editor of a literary weekly in Transylvania in 1972–78, his-
                       torian and philosopher **Gáspár Miklós Tamás** was frequently cen-
                       sored, in one case for writing an essay in which he drew a historical
                       parallel, while adding the words "mutatis mutandis". In the spring
                       of 1975, he was downgraded to the job of proofreader after he re-
                       fused to write about a new communist moral code drafted by Ceau-
                       şescu. He was interrogated by the Securitate two or three times a
                       week for a period of four months and subjected to "punitive" meet-
                       ings. From 1975 to 1977, he was banned from publishing. In 1978
                       he emigrated to Hungary. In 1982 he was dismissed there from his
                       teaching post at Budapest University because of his involvement in
                       the opposition movement (samizdat—or self-publishing—writing
                       and lectures at the unofficial "Flying University"). In 1983 he
                       worked as a librarian. In September 1984 he had been told to leave
                       Hungary, apparently for sending a letter to *The Times* (London),
                       published on 23 August, in which he wrote about the case of im-
                       prisoned Transylvanian intellectuals. The demand was reportedly
                       part of an official attempt to discourage calls by dissident intellec-
                       tuals for more vigorous action on behalf of the Transylvanian Hun-
                       garians. Tamás refused to emigrate. At the same time, he was
                       refused permission to travel abroad and had his passport confiscated.
                       Later he was elected a member of Parliament for the SzDSz (Alli-
                       ance of Free Democrats) political party. In 2000 he was a research
                       professor at the Institute of Philosophy, Hungarian Academy of Sci-
                       ences, Budapest.

1974–89   After the approval of an urban and rural systematization law, an
                       official policy of systematic destruction of monuments and sites in

dozens of towns, including large areas of old Bucharest, and an unknown number of villages, was carried out, thus threatening the Romanian historical patrimony. In November 1977 the Directorate for Historic Monuments was dissolved (reestablished February 1990). In late 1989, when the National Salvation Front (on 23 December) ended the program, twenty-nine towns had been "restructured" almost totally and another thirty-seven were in the process of being "restructured", while 7,000–8,000 of the 13,000 villages were scheduled to disappear in a rural resettlement plan. Likewise, up to 300 medieval Transylvanian walled churches were scheduled to be destroyed within the next two years.

Between 1984 and (at least) 1986, several letters and one anonymous article by prominent intellectuals protested the massive demolition of Romanian historical monuments, including churches, monasteries, and synagogues. One of the signatories of an October 1985 appeal was historian Virgil Candea (1927–), secretary of the Romania Association, a cultural association aiming at "recuperating the emigration" and said to be tightly controlled by the political police. In August 1986 historian Andrei Pippidi (1948–), a researcher at the Institute for Southeast European Studies in Bucharest and grandson of Iorga [q.v. 1948–], sent a letter to several Romanian journals in which he denounced the demolition of Iorga's house.

In April 1988 **Dinu Giurescu** (1927–), son of Constantin Giurescu [q.v. pre-1954], historian and curator, professor of the history of European civilization at the Nicolae Grigorescu Institute of Fine Arts, Bucharest (?1968–87), and member of the Romanian Central Commission of the National Patrimony (1975–85), went into exile in the United States. He lived in New York and Texas. From 1980 to 1985, he had joined in the protests against the destruction of historic monuments.

In June 1988 a meeting at the Nicolae Iorga History Institute discussed Ceauşescu's plans (orthography) for the "systematization" of two-thirds of Romania's villages. Eight historians criticized the plans, describing them as an attack on the nation's historical heritage; others spoke in favor. Among the eight, **Nicolae Stoicescu**, of pensionable age, was instructed not to return to the institute, while the others, including the future institute director **Şerban Papacostea** and **Ştefan Andreescu**, received verbal reprimands.

1977–   In March 1977 historian **Vlad Georgescu** (1937–88), senior researcher at the Institute of Southeast European Studies in Bucharest (1963–79), specialized in the Romanian Enlightenment, secretly (through the American embassy) sent four manuscripts to Eliade [q.v. 1945–] for publication abroad. Three of them, dealing with successive distortions of the Romanian historical record to fit Marxist ideological schemes, would be collected in *Politics and History: The Case of the Romanian Communists, 1944–77* (Munich 1981, 1983; Romanian edition: 1991). The fourth, *History of Romanian Political Ideas, 1369–1878*, was published in Munich in 1987. Georgescu was arrested in April 1977 and briefly detained. In the spring of 1979, he was among a group of people who were arrested or had "disappeared". He was forced into exile because of his dissident activities (which included plans to start a "free university"). He became the director of the Romanian Service of Radio Free Europe in Munich.

After years of isolation, historian **Alexandru Zub** (1937–) earned a traineeship for Freiburg im Breisgau and went into exile in the Federal Republic of Germany. Later he taught at Iasi University.

1980–97   Since at least 1980 history and geography teachers in Transylvania had to be Romanian by government decree. This was deemed provocative because Romanians and Hungarians gave conflicting accounts of Transylvanian history. In at least [1991–94], another decree (called the Education Bill in 1993) made Romanian the mandatory language for these subjects, despite protests from the Hungarian Democratic Union of Romania. In July 1997 the decrees were reportedly abolished.

1985   Two Transylvanian archivists, **Erzsébet Muckenhaupt** and **Pál János**, secretly rescued the works concealed by the Franciscans of Csiksomlyó (Şumuleu) in their monastery's walls in the early 1950s and attempted to transfer them to a safer place. The operation, however, was detected by the security police and both archivists were prosecuted for stealing state property.

Károly Borbáth was found murdered in unexplained circumstances. A scholar who voluntarily worked over several years to sort out the collection of the Reformed Church archdeaconry at Aiud devoted to the religious life of the Hungarian minority, he was harassed by the secret police because any attention to the archives' contents was unwelcome to the atheistic and nationalist government.

1986   A three-volume *History of Transylvania* did not treat the post-1918 period because its editor, **Béla Köpeczi**, working for the Hungarian Academy of Sciences, was afraid of aggravating the lot of the Hungarian minority in Transylvania. Nevertheless, the Romanian government called it a "conscious forgery of history under the aegis of the Hungarian Academy of Sciences" and banned it.

1989   Art historian, philosopher, and writer **Andrei Plesu** (1948–), who
            had signed a letter of support for poet Mircea Dinescu, was dis-
            missed and banned from publishing. He was told that the nearest
            job available was 150 miles away from his home. After the Ceau-
            şescu era, he became minister of culture (1989–91) and foreign af-
            fairs (1998–99).

pre-1990   Access to "restricted" material in the Bucharest University central
            library, such as prewar historical texts, was reportedly carefully con-
            trolled. As this state control was seen as a symbol of Ceauşescu's
            rule, the library was set on fire during the December 1989 revolt.
            Over half a million volumes were lost, including rare and valuable
            manuscripts and archives.

1991   In January writer and physician **Banu Rădulescu** (1924–), chief
            editor of *Memoria*, a journal devoted to the history of political de-
            tention and persecution in communist Romania, was knocked to the
            ground in Bucharest's center. This followed a series of unofficial
            threats before the release of the first issue. In the 1950s Rădulescu
            had been a political prisoner.

pre-1991   On 21 May 1991, **Ioan Culianu** (1950–91), historian of religion,
            myths, magic, and the occult, who collaborated with Eliade [q.v.
            1945–] and wrote his biography, was murdered while working as a
            lecturer at the University of Chicago Divinity School. In July 1972
            he had fled Romania after almost three years of Securitate harass-
            ment and censorship. He was convicted in absentia and sentenced
            to seven years' imprisonment for "denigrating the state". His name
            or work could not be quoted. He became a critic of the Ceauşescu
            and post-Ceauşescu regimes and worked in Italy (1972–75), the
            Netherlands (1976–85), and the United States (1986–91). From 1989
            he began receiving threats by letter and telephone. He considered
            the December 1989 events as a coup d'état that allowed the com-
            munists to remain in power, suggesting links between them and the
            extreme right. Although unsolved, the murder is connected with sur-
            viving Securitate agents by many.

1992–   In January 1992 the Romanian Parliament decided to keep the ar-
            chives of the Securitate closed for forty years. Only victims of the
            Securitate could apply for access to information about their own
            cases. In October 1997, however, the government agreed to make
            the archives accessible to the public. In June 1998 the vice president
            of the Romanian Intelligence Service (RSI; successor to the Secur-
            itate under the authority of the Ministry of Defense, which in early
            1990 took over at least part of the Securitate archives and many
            important historical archives from the 1930–89 period) declared that

around 350,000 Securitate files had been burned in 1971–79 and after the 1989 revolt. Stories about alleged RSI attempts to destroy classified Securitate documents that incriminated former RCP members were corroborated by the discovery of at least four caches in remote places in 1989–90. There were also reports about a massive purge of archival and library repositories; for example, the RCP archives in Arad, western Romania, had disappeared.

In November 1992 police removed demonstrating Hungarian students from Liberty Square in Cluj after they had tried to prevent the erection of a plaque on the statue of Hungarian King Matthias Corvinus (1458–90), bearing a quotation from the work of Iorga [q.v. 1948], to the effect that Matthias had been defeated by Moldavia's invincible army. The following days other demonstrations were disrupted or banned. In December the mayor of Cluj banned a rally to commemorate the 1989 revolution. In 1994 he sought to remove the statue of King Matthias, and in April 1995 he announced that he would place a Romanian and English inscription at King Matthias's birthplace, explaining that the Hungarian king was a Romanian. During 1995 local authorities of various Transylvanian towns attempted to remove all traces of Hungarian history and culture.

1994   In January television director-general **Paul Everac** resigned after criticism of a television documentary on the 1946 execution of wartime military dictator General Ion Antonescu, in which the deposed King Michael's involvement was suggested.

2000   Historian and philosopher **Horea-Roman Patapievici** (?1957–) was threatened with death by far-right political leader Corneliu Vadim Tudor, former chief propagandist of Ceauşescu.

Also see Hungary (1944–45: archives; 1945–: Balanyí, Bíró).

SOURCES

Allen, D., & D. Doeing, *Mircea Eliade: An Annotated Bibliography* (New York/London 1980) xiii–xxiii.
Amnesty International, *Report 1977* (London 1977) 268.
Annual Obituary 1986 (Chicago/London) 246–50 (Eliade).
Anton, T., *Eros, Magic and the Murder of Professor Culianu* (Evanston 1996) 23–25, 43–44, 51–52, 54–56, 58, 61–62, 67, 74, 78–80, 89, 91, 94–95, 98, 111, 114, 117, 122, 135, 157, 173, 179–80, 189, 194, 202, 206, 208, 236–37, 262.
"Archieven Securitate blijven gesloten", *Mensenrechtenmagazine*, March 1992: 43.
Article 19, *Information, Freedom and Censorship: World Report 1988* (London 1988) 206.
Beer, K.P., "Die Interdependenz von Geschichtswissenschaft und Politik in Rumänien

von 1945 bis 1980", *Jahrbücher für Geschichte Osteuropas*, 1984: 241–45, 248, 255–57, 260, 269, 271.

Bernath, M., & F. von Schroeder eds., *Biographisches Lexikon zur Geschichte Südosteuropas* (Munich) vol.1 (1974): 252–53; vol.2 (1976): 6–7, 52–53.

Boia, L. ed., *Great Historians of the Modern Age: An International Dictionary* (Westport 1991) 514–22, 524–26.

Boyd, K. ed., *Encyclopedia of Historians and Historical Writing* (London/Chicago 1999) 112–13.

Calvocoressi, P., *World Politics since 1945* (London/New York 1991) 235.

Cannon, J. ed., *The Blackwell Dictionary of Historians* (Oxford 1988) 208.

Deák, I., "Historiography of the Countries of Eastern Europe: Hungary", *American Historical Review*, 1992: 1060.

Deletant, D., "Rewriting the Past: Trends in Contemporary Romanian Historiography", *Ethnic and Racial Studies*, 1991: 64, 68, 72–86.

Detrez, M., "Geschiedschrijving en maatschappij op de Balkan", *Vlaamse gids*, 1993, no.6: 14.

Devine, E., M. Held, J. Vinson, & G. Walsh eds., *Thinkers of the Twentieth Century: A Biographical, Bibliographical and Critical Dictionary* (London 1983) 150–51.

Eco, U., "Murder in Chicago", *New York Review of Books*, 10 April 1997: 4–7.

Erdmann, K.D., *Die Ökumene der Historiker: Geschichte der internationalen Historikerkongresse und des Comité international des sciences historiques* (Göttingen 1987) 242.

Georgescu, V., *The Romanians: A History* (originally Romanian 1984; London/New York 1991) 238–40, 243, 251, 357.

Giurescu, D.C., *The Razing of Romania's Past* (London 1990) x–xiv, 67–70.

Held, J., *Dictionary of East European History since 1945* (Westport 1994) 417–18.

Hitchins, K., "Historiography of the Countries of Eastern Europe: Romania", *American Historical Review*, 1992: 1081–82.

Hoeven, H. van der, *Lost Memory: Libraries and Archives Destroyed in the Twentieth Century* part 1, *Libraries* (WWW-text 1996) 14–15, 17–18.

Human Rights Watch, *World Report* (Washington) 1992: 512–13; 1996: 226.

Index on Censorship, 4/79: 68; 2/83: 41; 2/84: 33; 5/84: 46; 1/85: 62; 5/85: 29; 1/86: 39, 40; 6–7/89: 79; 8/89: 33, 39; 2/92: 38; 9/92: 37–38, 46; 3/93: 39; 7/93: 39; 1–2/94: 245; 4–5/94: 247; 5/97: 179; 1/01: 74–79.

Ionescu, D., "More Protests against Demolitions in Bucharest", *RFE Research*, 2 October 1986, IV: 33–36.

———, "An Underground Essay on Urban and Rural Redevelopment", *RFE Research*, 14 February 1986, I: 9–13.

Ionescu, S.N., *Who Was Who in Twentieth-Century Romania* (New York 1994) 247.

Keesings historisch archief, 1988: 264; 1990: 135, 442; 1998: 31, 658.

Keesing's Record of World Events, 1985: 33414, 33813; 1990: 37194.

Love, J.L., *Crafting the Third World: Theorizing Underdevelopment in Rumania and Brazil* (Stanford 1996) 51–52.

Manea, N., "Happy Guilt: Mircea Eliade, Fascism, and the Unhappy Fate of Romania", *New Republic*, 5 August 1991: 27–36.

Marès, A. ed., *Histoire et pouvoir en Europe médiane* (Paris 1996).

NRC-Handelsblad, 30 May 1996: 4 (Transylvania), 9 December 2000: 5 (Patapievici).

Pearton, M., "Nicolae Iorga as Historian and Politician", in: D. Deletant & H. Hanak eds., *Historians As Nation-Builders: Central and South-East Europe* (London 1988) 157–73.

Péter, L., "The National Community and Its Past: Reflections on the *History of Transylvania*", *New Hungarian Quarterly*, Spring 1992: 7–10.

Petre, Z., "Past Imperfect", *UNESCO Courier*, May 1994: 17–18.

Pippidi, A., "Une Histoire en reconstruction: La Culture historique roumaine de 1989 à 1992", in: Marès ed. 1996: 241–47, 251, 259.

Pippidi, D.M. ed., *Nicolas Iorga: L'Homme et l'oeuvre* (Bucharest 1972).

Rady, M., "Transylvanian Libraries and Archives in Contemporary Romania", *Journal of the Society of Archivists*, 1991: 123–26.

Shafir, M., "Political Culture, Intellectual Dissent, and Intellectual Consent: The Case of Romania", *Orbis*, 1983: 413.

Stone, N., "History of a Troubled Region" *Hungarian Quarterly*, 1997: 119.

Sturdza, M., "The Files of the State Security Police", *RFE/RL Research Institute Report on Eastern Europe*, 13 September 1991: 22–27, 31.

Tamás, G.M., "On Memory and Horror: A Response to Tzvetan Todorov", *Common Knowledge*, 1996, no. 1: 31.

————, "The Position of Hungarian Minorities in the Neighboring Countries", in: U.S. Helsinki Watch Committee, *Violations of the Helsinki Accords: Report from Hungary* (New York 1983) 25–36.

Tamse, C., personal communication, September 1999.

Tismăneanu, V., "Miron Constantinescu, or the Impossible Heresy", *Survey: A Journal of Soviet and East European Studies* 1984: 175–87.

Tucker, M. ed., *Literary Exile in the Twentieth Century: An Analysis and Biographical Dictionary* (Westport 1991) 225–28.

Veres, E., "The Mixed Towns of Transylvania", *Transitions: Changes in Post-Communist Societies*, December 1997: 87.

Woolf, D.R. ed., *A Global Encyclopedia of Historical Writing* (New York/London 1998) 104–5, 265–66, 470–71, 785.

World University Service, *Academic Freedom 1990* (London 1990) 180.

Zub, A., "Horizon clos: L'Historiographie roumaine des années 80", in: Marès ed. 1996: 106–9, 114.

————, "Sur le Discours historique en Roumanie sous régime communiste", in: F. Glatz & A. Pók eds., *The Soviet System and Historiography, 1917–89: The Influence of Marxism-Leninism on the Historical Sciences* (unpublished papers; Budapest 1995) 90–92.

RUSSIA

pre-1991   *See* Union of Soviet Socialist Republics (USSR) (1975–: Grigoryants).

1993   Two archivists, **R. Usikov**, director of TsKhSD (Center for the Preservation of Contemporary Documentation; the post-1952 archive of the Communist Party of the Soviet Union Central Committee), and **Vladimir Chernous**, from Rosarkhiv (State Archival Service of Russia), were dismissed. Among the reasons reported were their liberal approach to archival access and charges of illegal financial dealings (including, for the former, the sale of documents).

1996   In December it was announced that the Academy of Sciences and the Center for Gender Studies were seeking damages for the publication in Moscow's *Playboy* edition of provocative portraits of famous women from Russian history, such as Catherine the Great, seventeenth-century religious dissident Feodosiya Morozova, and nineteenth-century mathematician Sofia Korvalevskaya.

1997   In October the Voronezh Oblast Duma (parliament) adopted a non-binding recommendation, urging teachers not to use an allegedly "anti-Russian" textbook on twentieth-century European history. Deputies claimed that the book, written by professor **Aleksandr Kreder** of Saratov University, was "unpatriotic and tendentious", belittling and distorting Russian history, although these claims were not supported by the federal Ministry of Education.

1999–   In October **Mayerbek Vachagayev**, historian and representative of the Chechen Republic to the Russian Federation, was arrested and charged for possession of arms. It was believed that evidence supporting the charge was fabricated in order to punish him for assisting international media in obtaining safe access to the conflict areas in Chechnya, thus evading the prohibition imposed by the Russian authorities on foreign journalists visiting the conflict.

In late 1999 customs in Moscow seized the print run (2,000 copies) of a history book, *Famous Chechens*, by **Musa Geshayev**, chairman of the League of Vainakh Peoples, when it arrived from a Belgian printer, because of its alleged anti-Russian content. It contained descriptions of Chechen traditions and heroes. The Press Ministry had to decide whether the book's presence in Russia was lawful.

SOURCES

Amnesty International, *Russian Federation: Chechnya; For the Motherland: Reported Grave Breaches of International Humanitarian Law; Persecution of Ethnic Chechens in Moscow* (WWW-text of EUR 46/046/1999; London December 1999).

Davies, R.W., *Soviet History in the Yeltsin Era* (Basingstoke 1997) 104, 237.

Index on Censorship, 2/97: 95; 1/98: 97.

Moscow News, 1–7 December 1999 (Geshayev).

Onwijn, K., "Rusland Neemt Tsjetsjeens geschiedenisboek in beslag", *Historisch nieuwsblad*, July 2000: 10–11.

RWANDA

Belgian Ruanda-Urundi

1947–   From May 1947 to late 1949, Tutsi Catholic priest and historian **Alexis Kagame** (1912–81) was virtually confined to the mission station near Astrida (Butare) by his bishop because of his political columns in the Catholic newspaper *Kinyamateka* and the journal *Aequatoria* in a time of tension between the Catholic Church and the Belgian administration of Trust Territory Ruanda-Urundi. His 1945 article in *Aequatoria* about the Rwandese king created a great stir and brought him ecclesiastical censorship until September 1949. His stay at the Pontifical Gregorian University, Rome (1952–55), to write his doctoral study of philosophy (published as *Philosophie bantu-rwandaise de l'être*, 1956) was in practice a measure of temporary expulsion because the Belgian authorities found his work which glorified Tutsi traditions (e.g., his 1952 work *Code des institutions politiques du Rwanda précolonial*) disturbing. As early as 1945, Kagame had been coopted among the biru (court ritualists; the guardians of the secret ritual code of the Rwandese monarchy) and he had written down the text of their esoteric sacred liturgies (published in 1947). During the violent ethnic clashes of October–November 1959 and June–July 1960 between Hutu and Tutsi, he stayed home and remained unaffected by the bloodbath despite his identification with the former ruling class. In 1963 he became professor of Rwandese literature, history, and language at the National University, Butare, and later also professor at the Grand Séminaire of Nyakibanda.

Rwanda

1990–   During the war with the invading armed Ugandan-based exiles (October 1990–), archives were reportedly destroyed. During the 1994 genocide, many governmental archives, including those from the Ministry of Justice and the land registry, were destroyed.

1994   Historians **Jean-Népomucène Nkurikiyimfura** (1941–), a Tutsi, and **Jean Rumiya**, a Hutu professor of mixed parentage, were both attacked during the 1994 genocide. The former was probably not killed; the latter was. According to Gérard Prunier, they maintained the integrity and dignity of the historical profession. Although Rumiya had collaborated for a while with some of the extremist Hutu intellectuals of the Mouvement Révolutionnaire National pour le Développement et la Démocratie, he had broken with them and publicly criticized them.

1997–98 In December 1997 **Philomène Mukabarali** (?1943–), a Tutsi director of a catering and tourism training college at Gikondo in the

capital, Kigali, who was threatened several times in 1997, was arrested and held first at Nyamirambo brigade, then at the Crimino-
logie (a detention center of the Gendarmerie) and in January 1998
at Kigali Central Prison. She was reportedly charged with endan-
gering state security for possessing leaflets which expressed support
to the Rwandan monarchy, allegedly found in her home at the time
of her arrest. Mukabarali was a member of Abatangana ("the unanimous" named after the unanimous sons of eighteenth-century King
Cyilima Rujugira), which organized cultural activities, including traditional songs and dances, with the objective of promoting reconciliation. Some of its activities referred to pre-1959 history when
Rwanda was ruled by a monarchy. This monarchism was seen as a
political threat by some members of the republican government. Mukabarali, the wife of a former Hutu diplomat and opposition party
leader himself imprisoned, was released later.

SOURCES

Albada, J. van, " 'Memory of the World': Report on Destroyed and Damaged Archives",
    Archivum, 1996, no.42: 19.
Amnesty International, *Urgent Action 405/97* (22 December 1997; 6 & 14 January 1998).
Auer, L., "Archival Losses and Their Impact on the Work of Archivists and Historians",
    Archivum, 1996, no.42: 4.
Brockman, N.C., *An African Biographical Dictionary* (Santa Barbara 1994) 162.
De Temmerman, E., *De doden zijn niet dood: Rwanda, een ooggetuigenverslag* (Am-
    sterdam/Antwerp 1995) 11, 29, 83–84, 88, 126, 132, 202, 260.
Dorsey, L., *Historical Dictionary of Rwanda* (Lanham 1994) 266–67.
Harroy, J.-P., "Alexis Kagame", *Bulletin des séances de l'Académie royale des sciences
    d'outre-mer*, 28 (1982 no.1) 72–73, 75.
Lemarchand, R., *Rwanda and Burundi* (London 1970) 137.
Prunier, G., *The Rwanda Crisis 1959–1994: History of a Genocide* (London 1995) vi,
    19, 28–29, 137, 172, 224, 239, 362–64.
Radler, R. ed., *Kindlers Neues Literatur Lexikon* vol. 9 (Munich 1990) 57–58.
Vansina, J., *Living with Africa* (Madison 1994) 63–64, 80.
——, personal communication, August 1999.
Vinck, H., "Correspondence Hulstaert-Kagame (1944–1976): Un Débat sur les civilisa-
    tions blanche et noire", *Annales aequatoria*, 1995: 467–72, 499–500, 538, 553,
    581–88.

S

SÃO TOMÉ AND PRÍNCIPE

See Portugal (1968–74: Soares).

SAUDI ARABIA

Among the sensitive historical topics in Saudi Arabia were the House of Saud, the *ikhwan* (Muslim Brotherhood) and tribal autonomy and conflict. Bedouin oral culture, including its historical parts, was sometimes in contradiction with the official Wahhabi doctrines. Burning and destruction of private manuscripts in which this oral culture was recorded allegedly occurred throughout Saudi Arabia.

1977　Between 7 and 10 December, *Sunday Times* foreign correspondent **David Holden** (died 1977) was murdered by unknown persons in Cairo. He was shot in the back and stripped of all means of identification. From late 1976 he had been writing a history of the House of Saud, but his colleague who completed and published the book, *The House of Saud* (1981) declared that he did not believe that the murder had anything to do with this research.

1979　On 17 or 18 December, Saudi national **Nasir al-Said** was kidnapped by the Saudi secret service in Beirut. The leader of a clandestine opposition group called the Union of the People of the Arabian Peninsula (1953–), he "disappeared" after he had informed reporters that his group supported the seizure of the Holy Mosque in Mecca on 20 November 1979. In 1956 Nasir al-Said had gone into exile after the suppression of a

strike of Aramco workers in the Saudi oilfields in which he had participated. He was the author of *History of al-Saud* (1984–85).

1995   The authorities reportedly prohibited, inter alia, the study of evolution.

SOURCES

Amnesty International, *Report 1980* (London 1980) 352.
Article 19, *Information, Freedom and Censorship: World Report 1991* (London 1991)
    389.
Holden, D. & R. Johns, *The House of Saud: The Rise and Fall of the Most Powerful
    Dynasty in the Arab World* (New York 1981) x–xiii, 188, 250, 532.
Index on Censorship, 2/78: 59; 4/96: 79.
Kurpershoek, P.M., *Oral Poetry and Narratives from Central Arabia*, vol. 2, *The Story
    of a Desert Knight: The Legend of Slêwîh al-'Atâwi and Other 'Utaybah Heroes*
    (Leiden 1995) 10, 24.
Peterson, J.E., "The Arabian Peninsula in Modern Times: A Historiographical Survey",
    American Historical Review, 1991: 1441, 1444.

SENEGAL

Several Senegalese historians were active in politics and harassed for that reason.

1961–   **Cheikh Anta Diop** (1923–86), politician, historian, and egyptologist, founder of the Institut Fondamental d'Afrique Noire, in which
he developed Africa's first carbon-14 dating laboratory, was not appointed to a post at Dakar University, apparently for his radical
political views. In December 1961 he was also possibly excluded
from attending a conference on African history in Dakar. Only after
President Léopold Senghor resigned in 1980 was he offered a professorship of ancient history. He was the author of *Nations nègres
et cultures* (Paris 1954), which was initially rejected as a doctoral
thesis (said to be the first by a francophone African historian) at the
Sorbonne because of its controversial theory about the alleged black
origin of ancient Egypt and the consequent cultural unity of Africa
and its equally controversial methods of proof. He eventually obtained his doctorate from the Sorbonne with a different double thesis
in January 1960. He was the cofounder of three political parties, all
declared illegal: the Bloc des Masses Sénégalaises (founded September 1961; banned October 1963; Secretary-General Diop spent a
term in prison in 1962 and was forbidden to make radio speeches
in 1963), the Front National Sénégalais (founded November 1963;
banned October 1964); the Rassemblement National Démocratique
(RND; founded February 1976, banned after appeal in January
1978). As RND's Secretary-General, Diop appeared before the criminal court in December 1980 on charges of illegal political activity

but in April 1981 he was acquitted and the ban was lifted after the decision to outlaw the RND was itself considered illegal and without motivation. A legal party since June 1981, RND never made a major breakthrough. Diop's works were reportedly banned in Cameroon, at least in 1985.

1967   When the sixth Pan-African Congress of Prehistory and Quaternary Studies was held in Dakar, the Senegalese press and some politicians sought to exclude the South African delegates, but Senghor said they were free to attend the Congress.

1976–84   In 1976 the film *Ceddo*, by novelist and filmmaker **Sembène Ousmane** (1923–), was banned. Set in the seventeenth or eighteenth century, the epoch of slavery, it concerned the people's resistance to forcible conversion to Islam. It was shown for the first time in July 1984.

pre-1988   As a student leader, historian **Abdoulaye Bathily** (1947–) was imprisoned several times for opposition activities. At one occasion he was put into the army with a group of student leaders. He was also banned, which implied that he could not go to school in Senegal or get a fellowship from the state. He completed a doctoral dissertation in history at Birmingham University. After his return to Senegal, he became Secretary-General of the Marxist Ligue Démocratique-Mouvement pour le Parti des Travailleurs (Democratic League-Movement for the Labor Party). In April 1988 he was arrested and convicted of participating in an illegal demonstration (a peaceful demonstration in Dakar against the cost of living and in support of the release of opposition leaders). He was given a one-month suspended sentence. Bathily became minister of urban development and housing (1993–) and minister of energy and water (2000–).

[?]   Historian and politician **Iba Der Thiam** (1937–) was a leader of the teachers' union when he obtained his licence (master's degree). He was accused of bombing the French cultural center and imprisoned, but he was allowed to take his exams under police guard. He was eventually cleared and permitted to go to France, where he specialized in political and trade union history. He became history professor and rector at Cheikh Anta Diop University, Dakar, and Senegal's minister of national education (1983–88). He was a member of the International Commission for UNESCO's *History of Humanity*. In the February 2000 presidential elections, he was the candidate for the Convention des Démocrates et des Patriotes political party. He obtained 1.2 percent of the votes.

Also see Burkina Faso (1983–92: Ki-Zerbo).

SOURCES

Amnesty International, *Report 1989* (London 1989) 81.

Awak' Ayom, "Mort de Cheikh Anta Diop (1923–1986) et réactions dans le monde africain et la diaspora africaine", *Zaïre-Afrique*, 1989, no.233: 82, 88–89.

Boyd, K. ed., *Encyclopedia of Historians and Historical Writing* (London/Chicago 1999) 312–14.

Brockman, N.C., *An African Biographical Dictionary* (Santa Barbara 1994) 102–3.

Diouf, M., "Intellectuals and the State in Senegal: The Search for a Paradigm", in: M. Mamdani & M. Diouf eds., *Academic Freedom in Africa* (Dakar 1994) 228–29, 233.

Index on Censorship, 2/80: 72; 4/81: 21, 32–33; 6/84: 47.

Jewsiewicki, B., & D. Newbury eds., *African Historiographies: What History for Which Africa?* (London/Beverly Hills 1986).

Keesings historisch archief, 1993: 341, 648.

Klein, M.A., "The Development of Senegalese Historiography", in: Jewsiewicki & Newbury 1986: 215–17, 220–23.

Mazrui, A.A. ed., *UNESCO General History of Africa*, vol. 8 (Paris 1993) 633–34, 645–46, 670–71.

Mbodj, M., & M. Diouf, "Senegalese Historiography: Present Practices and Future Perspectives", in: Jewsiewicki & Newbury 1986: 211–12, 214.

Middleton, J. ed., *Encyclopedia of Africa South of the Sahara*, vol. 1 (London 1997) 468–69.

Mokhtar, G., ed., "Introduction" & Ch.A Diop, "Origin of the Ancient Egyptians" & "Report of the Symposium on 'The Peopling of Ancient Egypt and the Deciphering of the Meroitic Script' ", all in G. Mokhtar ed., *General History of Africa*, vol. 2 (Paris/London 1981): 13–15, 49–51.

Monteil, V., "The Decolonization of the Writing of History" (originally French 1962), in: I. Wallerstein, *Social Change: The Colonial Situation* (New York 1966) 593–94.

Papa Demba Sy, "Itinéraire politique de Cheikh Anta Diop", *Nomade: Revue culturelle*, 1990: 192–98.

Tobias, P.V., "Prehistory and Political Discrimination" (originally 1985), *Minerva*, 1988: 589.

Vansina, J., *Living with Africa* (Madison 1994) 271.

SERBIA & MONTENEGRO

See Yugoslavia.

SIERRA LEONE

See Malawi (1972–: White), Zimbabwe (pre-1974: Mudenge).

SINGAPORE

1998   In July the Film and Publicity Department announced a review of, inter alia, the long-banned *Year of Living Dangerously*, a 1982 film by Australian director **Peter Weir** (1944–) about the 1965–66 killings in Indonesia.

SOURCES

Index on Censorship, 5/98: 97.

SLOVAKIA

pre-1993   *See* Czechoslovakia.

1996   In May–June 1996 Dušan Kováč, president of the National Committee of Slovak Historians, informed the International Committee of Historical Sciences that the Academy of Sciences History Institute was in danger of being taken over by the nationalist Matica Slovenská (the Slovak Cultural Foundation, established in 1863).

1997   In July the government announced that it would withdraw a controversial primary-school history textbook, *The History of Slovakia and the Slovaks*, by Catholic priest **Milan Durica**, following an outcry from, among others, Slovak historians, that it denied the persecution of Slovak Jews during priest Joseph Tiso's pro-Nazi regime (less than 10,000 of 70,000 Jews survived in 1939–45). The textbook was written and published with funding from the European Union (EU), but its treatment of the wartime fascist Slovak state persuaded EU external relations commissioner Hans van den Broek to press the government to withdraw it from Slovak schools. Prime Minister Vladimir Meciar conceded that parts of the book were historically inaccurate but initially refused to ban it from the bookstores. Deputies from the ultra-right Slovak National Party, a partner in the ruling coalition, condemned the EU's "censorship order".

SOURCES

Bulletin d'information du Comité international des sciences historiques, no. 23 (Paris 1997) 47, 55.
Human Rights Watch, *World Report 1998* (Washington 1997) 278–79.
Index on Censorship, 5/97: 181.
Jablonický, J., personal communication, June 1996.

SLOVENIA

See Yugoslavia (1948: Hauptmann; 1971: play; 1976–77: Blažič; Miklavčić; 1980s: archives; 1990–91: archives).

SOUTH AFRICA

Topics liable to be censored in apartheid South Africa (1948–90) included contemporary history; the emergence of African nationalism (including the history of the various political organizations involved) in South Africa, South West Africa (Namibia), and elsewhere in sub-Saharan Africa; the development of Black Power organizations in the United States; and the history of communism and communist parties in Europe. Due to the absence of many historical documents, academic research on South Africa's history could often be more successfully pursued outside than inside the country.

1950   In 1950 history student **Mangosuthu Buthelezi** (1928–), a descendant of Cetshwayo (last king of independent Zululand, ruled 1872–79, 1883–84), was expelled from Fort Hare University for his role in the protest against a visit by the governor-general of South Africa. In 1951 Buthelezi received a degree in history from the University of Natal, Durban. He was officially appointed chief of the Buthelezi in 1957. In 1976 he became chief minister of the KwaZulu homeland with the approval of the African National Congress (ANC), but he refused to accept independence for KwaZulu. Heading the cultural and political Inkatha movement (1975–), he increasingly followed his own political strategy.

1952–   The two-volume *Three Hundred Years: A History of South Africa* (Cape Town 1952), written by the white left-wing author **Hosea Jaffe** (1921–), appeared under the pen name **Mnguni**. The book, banned until [1984], was published as part of an opposition campaign against the celebration of three hundred years' white settlement in South Africa and looked at South Africa's history as a struggle between oppressors and oppressed. The author, who had asserted as early as the 1940s that segregation was connected with the capitalist system, went into exile in Europe. In 1980 a new and expanded Italian edition of the book was published. Another, Marxist-inspired, book, *The Role of the Missionaries in Conquest* (Johannesburg ?1952), by **Dora Taylor** (died in the late 1970s), was published under the pen name **Nosipho Majeke**. The book presented the missionaries as agents of British imperialism. Taylor went to London in the early 1960s. Both books anticipated the work of the radical historians of the 1970s.

1953–   In 1953 British socialist historian of Africa **Basil Davidson** (1914–), then a foreign correspondent for the *New Statesman and Nation* (1950–54), became a "prohibited immigrant" (1953–?94) because in 1951–52 he had written articles and a book against apartheid. Trying to return in 1953, he was allowed only transit rights to

Swaziland. In 1954 he was dismissed from the *New Statesman and Nation* because of his strong criticism of the then-controversial policy of German rearmament. The prohibited immigrant order in South Africa also prompted Davidson's banning by the Central African Federation (the two Rhodesias and Nyasaland) and from East Africa (Tanganyika, Uganda, Kenya). After a 1954 visit to Angola, he criticized forced labor and racial discrimination in the Portuguese colonies, which earned him a banning order there too. In 1967–74 Davidson undertook several trips to those areas of the Portuguese colonies under control of liberation movements.

1953   The South African government banned **Silas Molema** (1891–1965), ANC treasurer (1949–53), inter alia, because he had condemned the apartheid view of history in a speech during the 1952 celebrations. His *Bantu Past and Present: An Ethnographical and Historical Study of the Native Races of South Africa* (Edinburgh 1920) had reportedly been scarcely distinguishable from the accounts of his white contemporaries, but gradually he had changed his views.

1959–   Several critical and radical historians left South Africa, often as exiles, and lived in the United Kingdom, where much of the new work on South African history first appeared: **Shula Marks** (1936–), lecturer (1963–76), reader (1976–84), and director (1983–93) at the Institute of Commonwealth Studies and professor in Commonwealth History and Southern African history (1993–) at the School of Oriental and African Studies, London University, cofounder of the *Journal of Southern African Studies*. Marks left in late 1959 but was always able to go back to South Africa to do research. She was subjected to constant scrutiny in the archives, however, especially after 1976 when archivists were reportedly warned to watch her research; **Harold Wolpe** (1926–), tutor at Oxford University (1965–66), lecturer at Bradford University (1966–69), principal lecturer and head of sociology at the Polytechnic of North London (1969–73), lecturer (1973–76), senior lecturer (1976–87), and reader (1987–) at the sociology department of the University of Essex; **Stanley Trapido** (1933–), lecturer in politics at Durham University (1966–70), lecturer in the government of new states (1970–) and senior research fellow in African Studies, Lincoln College, Oxford University (1987–); historian **Frederick Johnstone** (1944–), who became a lecturer in sociology; Marxist historian **Martin Legassick** (1940–), exiled in [1974], became a lecturer in sociology at Warwick University. In 1979 he was one of those suspended from the ANC for advocating stronger links with the proletariat. In 1996 he worked at the University of the Western Cape.

1960– In August or September 1960, two South African security officials reportedly attended a lecture on South African historiography given by historian **Leonard Thompson** (1916–), history professor at Cape Town University (1946–61), at a conference on African history organized by the University College of the Rhodesias and Nyasaland in Salisbury. In 1961 Thompson emigrated and worked as a professor of African history at the University of California, Los Angeles (1961–68), and as a history professor and founder-director of the Southern Africa Research Program at Yale University, New Haven, Conn. (1968–85).

1960–90 Among the banned historical works were **Leo Kuper** (1908–), *An African Bourgeoisie: Race, Class and Politics in South Africa* (Princeton 1965); **Hans Kohn** (1891–1971) and **Wallace Sokolsky**, *African Nationalism in the Twentieth Century* (1965); *History and Class Consciousness* (originally German 1923; Cambridge Mass., 1971), by Hungarian cultural philosopher **György Lukács** (1885–1971); Marks [q.v. 1959–] and Trapido [q.v. 1959] eds., *The Politics of Race, Class and Nationalism in Twentieth-Century South Africa* (1988); Mzala [q.v. 1984–91], *Gatsha Buthelezi: Chief with a Double Agenda* (1988); Wolpe [q.v. 1963–], *Race, Class and the Apartheid State* (1988); all paperback editions of the novels *I, Claudius* and *King Jesus* by **Robert Graves** (1895–1985). Among the works on a list of banned books, compiled by the United Nations Center Against Apartheid in [1973], and not already mentioned, were the following: *Chapters in the History of the March to Freedom* (Cape Town 1959) by **Lionel Forman** (1927–59); *Marxism in the Twentieth Century* (originally French 1966; London 1970) by French communist philosopher **Roger Garaudy** (1913–); *A History of Post-war Africa* (London 1965) by **John Hatch**; *South Africa: A Political and Economic History* (London [1966]) by **Alex Hepple**; *The Idea of Racialism: Its Meaning and History* (Princeton 1962) by **Louis Snyder** (1907–); and *History of the Twentieth Century: Race and Colour*. In 1990 many publications were unbanned, including *South Africa Belongs to Us: History of the ANC* (Harare 1988) by **Francis Meli** (1942–90), an exile working for the ANC (1963–); and *Unity in Action: A Photographic History of the African National Congress*. In 1991 the works of Simons [q.v. 1965–90] and Wolpe [q.v. 1959–] could be quoted and disseminated again.

1963–79 In 1963 **Neville Alexander** (1936–), educator and political activist with an M.A. in history and German (1957) and a doctorate in

German literature (1961), was arrested. In 1961 he had formed the Yu Chi Chan Club to study guerrilla warfare and founded the National Liberation Front, which advocated the violent overthrow of the state. In 1964 he was convicted of conspiracy to commit sabotage and sentenced to ten years' imprisonment at the penal Robben Island. After his release in 1974, he was banned and put under house arrest for five years.

1963–85   Late in 1963 **Kwedi Mkalipi** (1934–), member of the banned Pan-African Congress, was arrested and charged with unlawful activities. Released in April 1964, he was rearrested in November under the ninety-days detention law. Charged with sabotage in March 1965, he was sentenced in February 1966 to twenty years' imprisonment. On Robben Island, he obtained a B.A. in history and Xhosa. He was released in December 1985.

1964–90   In 1964 Trotskyist **Baruch Hirson** (1921–99) was convicted of sabotage and sentenced to nine years' imprisonment for his part in the activities of the armed African Resistance Movement. In prison he became a historian. An exile in the United Kingdom after his release in 1973, he wrote several books about the history of the South African black working class.

1965–90   In January 1965 antiapartheid activist **Edward [= Eddie] Roux** (1903–66) was forced to resign as professor of botany at the University of the Witwatersrand, Johannesburg (1946–64), after which he was allowed neither to teach nor to publish. Almost all his works, including *Time Longer Than Rope: A History of the Black Man's Struggle for Freedom in South Africa* (London 1948, 1964) were banned until 1990 because he had been a prewar member of the Communist Party of South Africa (CPSA). At the time, he spent several terms in prison (1930, 1934, 1936).

In May 1965 **Jack Simons** (1907–95), a Marxist lecturer in African governmental law at Cape Town University (1937–), and Latvian-born **Ray Alexander Simons** (1914–), trade-union organizer, both CPSA members, left South Africa. In 1954 Alexander had been elected as a member of Parliament but was prevented from taking her seat because she was listed as a communist. In December 1964 Simons had been barred from teaching and conducting research under the 1950 Suppression of Communism Act. In the United Kingdom, where Simons got a fellowship at Manchester University, Simons and Alexander completed *Class and Colour in South Africa 1850–1950* (1969), a book banned but read clandestinely in South Africa. They finally settled in Lusaka, where Simons became professor of sociology at the University of Zambia (until 1975) and

Alexander worked for the International Labor Office. Later Simons became a member of the ANC's constitutional committee. In 1990 both returned from exile.

1971–72   In February 1972 **Benjamin Pogrund** (1933–), assistant editor at the Johannesburg Rand Daily Mail, was found guilty of possessing written notes and copies of the banned publications *New Age, Guardian*, and *Fighting Talk*, which he needed for doctoral research on the history of African nationalism in South Africa. Many of the documents were twenty years old and had only just been banned. The materials apparently included information dealing with the ANC in the 1940s (before the 1950 Suppression of Communism Act proscribed the ANC). At the trial (started November 1971 but adjourned), Pogrund received nine months' imprisonment suspended for three years, reduced on appeal to one month suspended for three years on the grounds that the material had been acquired for study purposes only. In an earlier case (1965–69), he had been intimidated and harassed because of his involvement in a three-part *Rand Daily Mail* series on prison conditions.

1975   In September **Jenny Curtis**, archivist at the South African Institute of Race Relations, was arrested and detained under the 1967 Terrorism Act. She was released in November.

[1975–91]   In May 1985 **John Pampallis** started writing a history textbook for the last two years of the secondary Solomon Mahlangu Freedom College, near Morogoro, Tanzania, an ANC school for young South African exiles. The textbook's emphasis was on the history of national liberation and labor movements. In 1991 a revised version, *Foundations of the New South Africa*, was also distributed within South Africa. After fifteen years' exile, eight of which he had spent as a history teacher, Pampallis returned to South Africa to become director of the Center for Educational Policy Development, University of Natal.

[1978]   A lawsuit was initiated against distribution of a pamphlet entitled *Heroes of Yesterday, Martyrs of the Struggle*, published by the Black People's Convention, for "fomenting feelings of hostility between different population groups". The pamphlet called upon people to observe a week of mourning in commemoration of the victims of the 21 March 1960 Sharpeville uprising and other incidents, including the 1976 events in Soweto. The appellants were acquitted on appeal.

1978–96   From 1978 to 1996, many state records, especially on the inner workings of the security apparatus, were destroyed in an attempt to remove incriminating evidence and, in the words of the Truth and Reconciliation Commission (TRC), "to sanitize the history of the apartheid era", particularly in 1990–94 when deliberate destruction occurred systematically and massively. In June 1993 the destruction was explicitly sanctioned by the cabinet and designed, according to the TRC, "to deny a new government access to apartheid secrets through a systematic purging of official memory". In mid-1993 archivist Verne Harris disclosed the destruction to the press. The National Intelligence Agency destroyed records as late as November 1996, in defiance of two government moratoria on the destruction of state records. Before 1990 "sensitive" records were routinely destroyed by state bodies, particularly those within the security services. Records confiscated from the antiapartheid resistance were apparently completely destroyed.

1979–87   During his imprisonment (1964–87), **Govan Mbeki** (1910–), teacher, journalist, former CPSA member, former national ANC chairman, and one of the founders of the ANC military wing Umkhonto we Sizwe, established a program of political education at Robben Island. In the years following 1979, he wrote two syllabi: a detailed history of the ANC and a materialist history of the development of human society. Both were based on material drawn from newspapers and texts he received as part of correspondence courses in economics from the University of South Africa, Pretoria. In December 1987, after his release, Mbeki was formally banned and restricted to Port Elizabeth. Having been arrested in July 1963 and then tried with other ANC leaders in 1964 on charges of conspiracy to overthrow the South African government, Mbeki had originally been sentenced to life imprisonment.

1979   In March, during a conference lecture at the University of South Africa, **Floris [= Floors] van Jaarsveld** (1922–95), history professor at the Afrikaner University of Pretoria, attempted to demythologize the Battle of the Blood River, where the Boers defeated the Zulus on 16 December 1838, an event annually commemorated. After about five minutes of reading, a thirty-person contingent of the far-right Afrikaner Weerstands Beweging (AWB; Afrikaner Resistance Movement) burst into the hall and poured tar and feathers over van Jaarsveld. AWB leader Eugene Terre'Blanche was quoted as saying: "As young Afrikaners we have reached the end of our tether. Our spiritual heritage and everything we consider holy to the Afrikaner are being trampled underfoot and desecrated by . . . stray academics and false prophets who hide under the cloak of learning and false religion like Professor Floors van Jaarsveld. In this symposium they defile the holiest of holies of the Afrikaner being. This attitude is blasphemous and annuls the meaning of Afrikaner history." Around the same time, van Jaarsveld's house was shot at. In 1991 van Jaarsveld publicly apologized for the distorted way in which he had for four decades depicted South African history.

1984–91   After 1984 Buthelezi [q.v. 1950] publicly attacked historians who did not share his view of history. In a September 1984 speech, he attacked **Thomas Karis** (1919–), professor of political science at City College, City University of New York, and **Tom Lodge**, lecturer and later professor of politics at the University of the Witwatersrand, for their "histories of the ANC". In 1987 he allegedly threatened with prosecution **Gerhard Maré** and **Georgina Hamilton** for their book *An Appetite for Power: Buthelezi's Inkatha and South Africa* (Braamfontein/Bloomington 1987). In 1988 he threatened with prosecution distributors and libraries selling or lending *Gatsha Buthelezi: Chief with a Double Agenda*, by **Mzala**, a member of the ANC Research Department in Lusaka. On 21 September 1991, Shaka Day, he attacked Marks [q.v. 1959–] in his speech.

1984–85   **John Laband** wrote the manuscript of a study commissioned by the KwaZulu government, *Fight Us in the Open: The Anglo-Zulu War through Zulu Eyes* (Pietermaritzburg 1985). After historian Oscar Dhlomo (1943–), minister of education and culture of KwaZulu (1978–) and Inkatha secretary-general (1978–90), had read it, Laband had to excise evidence that Mnyamana, grandfather of Buthelezi [q.v. 1950], had displayed poor generalship in the 1879 war.

1986–   In mid-1986 **Annica van Gylswyk**, archivist at the Documentation Center for African Studies at the University of South Africa and activist for the women's organization Black Sash, was detained. As she was closely involved with the antiapartheid movement, security police interrogations focused on her travels as a collector of archival material. She was put under severe pressure for some weeks and her employers placed her on unpaid leave. Imprisoned without trial, she elected to be deported to Sweden. She was a Swedish citizen, although she had lived in South Africa for thirty years.

1986   In December **Philip Bonner**, British historian at the history department, University of the Witwatersrand, expert on labor history and History Workshop coorganizer, was served with a deportation order. He had been a trade union adviser and editor of a labor magazine. He was later allowed to stay after giving an "unequivocal undertaking that he would employ only lawful means in the pursuit of bona fide academic activities".

1989   An author writing on the artificial historical legitimation of President Lennox Sebe's Ciskei government preferred to remain anonymous.

On 1 May **David Webster** (1945–89), lecturer in social anthropology at the University of the Witwatersrand, editor of *Essays in South African Labour History* (1978), and History Workshop member, was shot dead in Johannesburg by three unidentified gunmen believed to belong to a hit squad of the Civil Co-operation Bureau, a secret wing of the South African Defence Force. As an anthropologist, Webster conducted research into the culture of the Thembe-Tonga people of the Kosi Bay region, Natal. As a human-rights activist, he opposed population removals as a result of conservation policies in the region; he was also interested in the covert South African aid to Mozambican Renamo rebels based in northern Zululand. As a member of the Detainees' Parents Support Committee (an organization publicizing the plight of thousands of detainees held without charge or trial, itself banned in 1988), he was engaged in research into death squads. Because his killing was condemned by the minister of law and order, a high-level police inquiry was opened. In May 1996 his partner Maggie Friedman, testifying to the TRC, denounced the fact that the numerous investigations and inquiries into Webster's death had remained without results and also denounced the destruction or disappearance of some of the documentation. In June 1998 a former Civil Co-operation Bureau agent was sentenced to life imprisonment for the murder.

1991   On 21 March Cape Town police fired tear gas and rubber bullets at crowds commemorating Sharpeville Day. A similar incident took place at Uitenhage.

1997   In 1997 writer **Gertrude Fester**, who spent two years in prison for ANC activities before 1990, was writing a history of the ANC women's movement.

1998   The release of the TRC report in October provoked strong reactions. Former President F.W. de Klerk challenged the report in court and was successful in having a short section removed (namely that he had been an accessory after the fact to two bombings in the late 1980s). The ANC claimed that its own abuses were justified because it was fighting a national liberation war against an abusive regime. The ANC's court injunction, intended to delay the disclosure of some of the TRC's findings on ANC human rights violations, such as the targeting of civilians and indiscriminate use of landmines, failed.

Also see Senegal (1967: congress), Turkey (1960–90: Garaudy), United Kingdom (1968–71: Kuper; 1986: World Archaeological Congress).

SOURCES

Africa Watch, *Academic Freedom and Human Rights Abuses in Africa* (New York 1991) 77, 81–82.

Amnesty International, *Academics Imprisoned in African Countries Who Are Prisoners of Conscience* (AFR 01/02/89; London 1989) 2.

———, *Report* (London) 1990: 215; 1993: 261; 1998: 308; 1999: 307.

Anonymous, "Ethnicity and Pseudo-ethnicity in the Ciskei", in: L. Vail ed., *The Creation of Tribalism in Southern Africa* (London 1989) 395–413.

Article 19, *Information, Freedom and Censorship: World Report 1991* (London 1991) 48.

Blussé, L., F.-P. van der Putten, & H. Vogel eds., *Pilgrims to the Past: Private Conversations with Historians of European Expansion* (Leiden 1996) 267–69.

Boraine, A., J. Levy, & R. Scheffer eds., *Dealing with the Past: Truth and Reconciliation in South Africa* (Cape Town 1997) 155.

Boyd, K. ed., *Encyclopedia of Historians and Historical Writing* (London/Chicago 1999) 286–87, 765–66, 1117, 1190–92.

Bozzoli, B., "Les Intellectuels et leurs publics face à l'histoire: L'Expérience sud-africaine du 'History Workshop' (1978–1988)", *Politique africaine*, June 1992: 15, 17–18.

Bunting, B., *The Rise of the South African Reich* (Harmondsworth 1969) 294, 308.

Cornevin, M., *L'Apartheid: Pouvoir et falsification historique* (Paris 1979) 140, 142.

Denis, P., "Quand la dictature s'effondre . . . , les tâches de l'histoire après l'apartheid: Réinventer l'histoire", *Clio*, 1996, nos.108–9: 41.

Duffy, J., M. Frey, & M. Sins eds., *International Directory of Scholars and Specialists in African Studies* (Waltham, Mass. 1978) 131, 136, 172, 226, 288, 309, 319.

Forsyth, P., "The Past in the Service of the Present: The Political Use of History by Chief A.N.M.G. Buthelezi 1951–1991", *South African Historical Journal*, 1992: 89–90.

Garson, N.G., "Censorship and the Historian", *South African Historical Journal*, 1973, no.5: 6.

Harries, P., "Imagery, Symbolism and Tradition in a South African Bantustan: Mangosuthu Buthelezi, Inkatha, and Zulu History", *History and Theory*, 1993, Beiheft 32: 114.

Harris, V., "The Archive and Secrecy in South Africa: A Personal Perspective", and "Knowing Right from Wrong: The Archivist and the Protection of People's Rights", both in: *Janus*, 1999, no.1: 8–9, 36–37.

Hodder-Williams, R. ed., *A Directory of Africanists in Britain* (Bristol 1990) 81, 121–22, 132.

Human Rights Watch, *Ifex Alert*, 7 July 1997: 3.

———, *World Report* (Washington) 1998: 454; 1999: xix, 70, 304; 2000: 73.

Holland, H., *The Struggle: A History of the African National Congress* (London 1989) 102.

Index on Censorship, 1/72: 86; 2/73: viii–ix; 3/73: 42–43; 4/73: 99–102; 4/74: 101; 1/76: 86; 3/76: 12–13, 96; 4/82: 9; 2/86: 17; 2/87: 39; 2/88: 22, 24, 39; 7/90: 39; 7/91: 39; 6/92: 31; 5–6/93: 21–22; 6/95: 184; 5/96: 43, 47, 58–60; 2/99: 86.

International Journal of African Historical Studies, 1992: 439–41 (Mbeki).

Keesings historisch archief, 1999: 382–83, 2001: 256.

Lodge, T., B. Nasson, et al. eds., *All, Here and Now: Black Politics in South Africa in the 1980s* (London 1991) 292–93, 301, 315–16.

Marcus, G.J., "Racial Hostility: The South African Experience", in: S. Coliver ed., *Striking a Balance: Hate Speech, Freedom of Expression and Non-discrimination* (London 1992) 212, 218.

Maré, G., *Ethnicity and Politics in South Africa* (London 1993) 82, 98–99.

Marks, S., "The Historiography of South Africa: Recent Developments", in: B. Jewsiewicki & D. Newbury eds., *African Historiographies: What History for Which Africa?* (London/Beverly Hills 1986) 165, 167.

———, personal communication, February 2001.

Martin, C., "Après l'apartheid, réécrire l'histoire", in: *Le Monde diplomatique, Manière de voir 40* (July–August 1998) 37–38.

Mbeki, G., *Learning from Robben Island: The Prison Writings of Govan Mbeki* (London 1991) ix–xxx.

———, *South Africa: The Peasants' Revolt* (Harmondsworth 1964) 11–14.

"Of Memory and Forgiveness", *Economist*, 1 November 1997: 22.

Merrett, C., *A Culture of Censorship: Secrecy and Intellectual Repression in South Africa* (Claremont/Pietermaritzburg 1995) 13, 15–16, 25, 37, 44, 52, 62, 68–69, 126, 134, 170, 188, 191, 194, 198–99, 234, 236, 240, 245–46, 263–64, 266, 275, 281.

———, "In a State of Emergency: Libraries and Government Control in South Africa", *Library Quarterly*, 1990: 16–17, 20.

Munslow, B., "Basil Davidson and Africa: A Biographical Essay", *Race and Class*, October–December 1994: 1–6, 9, 16.

Pampallis, J., *Foundations of the New South Africa* (Cape Town 1997) viii, back cover.

Potgieter, D.J. ed., *Standard Encyclopaedia of Southern Africa*, vol. 9 (Cape Town 1973) 413.

Ray Alexander, Jack Simons (WWW–text 2001).

Saunders, C., "Historians & Apartheid", in: J. Lonsdale ed., *South Africa in Question* (London/Cambridge 1988) 20.

———, *Historical Dictionary of South Africa* (Metuchen 1983) 98–99, 105, 169.

——— ed., *The Making of the South-African Past: Major Historians on Race and Class* (Totowa 1988) 165–67.

Schutte, G., "Afrikaner Historiography and the Decline of Apartheid: Ethnic Self-Reconstruction in Times of Crises", in: E. Tonkin, M. McDonald, & M. Chapman eds., *History and Ethnicity* (London 1989) 217–18 (quote van Jaarsveld).

Smith, K., *The Changing Past: Trends in South African Historical Writing* (Johannesburg 1988) 75–76, 99, 157–59, 164, 177–78.

Smith, P. ed., *Africa Confidential: Who's Who of Southern Africa* (Oxford 1998) 75–76.

Thompson, L.M., *The Political Mythology of Apartheid* (New Haven 1985) 65–66, 68.

———, "South Africa", in: R.W. Winks ed., *The Historiography of the British Empire-*

Commonwealth: Trends, Interpretations, and Resources (Durham 1966) xii–xiii, 217, 227, 234–35.

Truth and Reconciliation Commission of South Africa, *Interim Report* (WWW-text; Cape Town 1996) chapter 15: 13.

————, *Report* (London 1998) vol. 1: 201–43; vol. 5: 225–27.

Truth Commissions: A Comparative Assessment (Cambridge 1997) 47.

Vansina, J., *Living with Africa* (Madison 1994) 87.

Vrij Nederland, 4 January 1997: 13.

Woolf, D.R. ed., *A Global Encyclopedia of Historical Writing* (New York/London 1998) 887.

Zuid-Afrika, 1995, no.2: 39 (van Jaarsveld).

SOUTH KOREA

See Korea.

SOUTHERN RHODESIA

See Zimbabwe.

SPAIN

The Spanish civil war (1936–39) resulted in the total or partial destruction of over 1,700 repositories. In addition, scores of private archives were destroyed. Under the military government of General Francisco Franco (1939–75), any informed research into twentieth-century political themes was suppressed. Only right-wing, Catholic historiography was tolerated. Particularly sensitive were the histories of the nationalists, the falange (the Spanish fascist political party), and the political parties before the Spanish civil war. Access to archives and libraries was very difficult (due to slow cataloging and tight control of source material). For example, the Spanish diplomatic archives for 1870 were still closed to historians in 1957. Official permission was required to consult sensitive materials such as those relating to the civil war.

Among the historians and others concerned with the past who emigrated before 1945 (and living in exile after 1944) were

1936	**Américo Castro** (1885–1972) and **Salvador de Madariaga** (1886–1978).
1937	**José Miguel de Barandiarán** (1889–1991), **José Moreno Villa** (1887–1955), **Luis Recaséns Siches** (1903–77), and **Claudio Sánchez Albornoz** (1893–1984).
1938	**Juan María Aguilar y Calvo, Jesús Bal y Gay** (1905–93), **Juan de la Encina** (1890–1963), and **José Gaos** (1900–69).

1939   **Rafael Altamira** (1866–1951), **Genaro Artiles Rodriguez, Modesto Bargalló Ardevol** (1894–1981), **Francisco Barnés** (1877–1947), **Carlos Bosch García** (1919–), **Pedro Bosch Gimpera** (1891–1974), **Pere Calders i Rossinyol** (1912–94), **Luis Carretero y Nieva** (died 1950), **Anselmo Carretero y Jiménez** (1908–), **Luis Castillo Iglesias** (1904–81), **Manuel Castillo Quijada** (1870–1964), **Juan Comas Camps** (1900–79), **José María Gallegos Rocafull** (?1899–1963), **Juan Pablo García Álvarez** (1908–), **Juan David García Bacca** (1901–92), **Francisco Guerra, Jorge Hernández Millares** (1911–), **Ramón Iglesia** (1905–48), **Vicente Lloréns Castillo** (1906–79), **Julio Luelmo y Luelmo, Javier Malagón Barceló** (1911–), **José Ignacio Mantecón Navasal** (1902–), **Leonardo Martín Echeverría** (1894–1958), **Ana Matilde Martínez Iborra, Otto Mayer Serra** (died 1968), **Agustín Millares Carlo** (1893–1978), **José María Miquel y Vergés** (1904–64), **José Miranda González** (1903–67), **Lluís Nicolau D'Olwer** (1888–1961), **Juan Antonio Ortega y Medina** (1913–92), **José María Ots Capdequí** (1893–1975), **Pedro Pagés** (pseudonym: Víctor Alba; 1916–), **Ceferino Palencia** (1882–1963), **Antonio Ramos Oliveira** (1907–73), **Víctor Rico González** (1900–?), **Wenceslao Roces** (1897–1992), **Adolfo Salazar** (1890–1958), **Manuel Sánchez Sarto** (1897–1980), **Rafael Sánchez Ventura** (1897–1984), and **Germán Somolinos D'Ardois** (1911–73).

[?]   Year of emigration unknown: **Amaro del Rosal** (1904–).

[1939]–   Among the young refugees who became historians in their new country were **Pedro Armillas García** (1914–84), **Carlos Blanco Aguinaga** (1927–), **Margarita Carbó Daramaculleta** (1940–), **Pedro Carrasco Pizana** (1921–), **Emilio García Riera** (1929–), **Santiago Genovés Tarazaga** (1923–), **Manuel Jiménez Martín** (1924–), **José Luis Lorenzo** (1921–), **Juan Marichal** (1922–), **Margarita Martínez Leal, Dolores Masip Echafarreta** (1925–), **Angel Palerm Vich** (1917–80), and **Carmen Viqueira de Palerm** (?1919/23–), **Manuel Pérez Vila** (1922–), **Rafael Segovia Canosa** (1928–), **Juan Somolinos Palencia** (?1937–), and **María Teresa Vidal Hernández**.

[1939]–   Historian **Jaime Vicens Vives** (1910–60) was purged from Barcelona University at the end of the civil war and sent into internal exile in Andalusia until his appointment as professor of modern European history at the universities of Zaragoza (1946–) and Barcelona (1948–). His work is said to have suffered much from censorship, although it concentrated more on social-economic than on political history. He was called "a symbol of historiographical renewal in Spain".

1946–83   In 1946 journalist and historian **Manuel Tuñón de Lara** (1917–97) was imprisoned for his underground activities in the communist-inspired Juventudes Socialistas Unificadas during the civil war. He went into exile in France (1946–80), where he specialized in the history of nineteenth- and twentieth-century Spain and the Spanish labor movement. He was a professor of Spanish history and literature at Pau University, France (until 1981), and director of its Centro de Investigaciones Hispánicas. From 1970 he organized scholarly meetings of historians of the opposition, called the Pau colloquia. From 1973 he regularly traveled to Spain, but at one point he was refused a position at a university [identity unknown]. In 1983 he became professor of contemporary history at the Universidad del País Vasco, Bilbao, and director of its journal *Historia contemporánea*.

1948   In September history student **Nicolás Sánchez Albornoz** (1926–), son of Claudio Sánchez Albornoz [q.v. 1937], was imprisoned for his activities as a leader of the liberal Federación Universitaria Escolar, Madrid, but he escaped from detention and fled to France. He went into exile in Argentina, where he became an economic historian of nineteenth- and twentieth-century Spain at various universities. In [1966] he fled from the Argentinian military junta to the United States, where he became a professor of Latin American history at the University of New York.

1955–69   Among the articles censored in the bimonthly *Índice* (a review of political, literary, and intellectual affairs), were the following: "Comments on the Book 'On the Spanish Monarchy of the Baroque Period' " by **Álvaro Fernández Suárez** (1955; although several paragraphs and sentences were to be censored, it was published intact); "The European Scene: On [historian Marcelino] Menéndez Pelayo [1856–1912]" by socialist writer and journalist **Luis Araquistaín**, who was exiled in Switzerland (1956; censored and not published); "A Questionnaire on Spain and America" (1958; answers by Mexican historian Leopoldo Zea (1912–); one paragraph to be censored was published nevertheless); "The Dead Sea Scrolls" by **Rafael Pérez Delgado** (1958); "Some Information on My Manuscript of Don Quijote" by **A.M. Ortíz Alfau** (1959; a paragraph mentioning historian Ramón Menéndez Pidal [1869–1968]; to be censored but published nevertheless); "The Spaniards and Posterity" by Fernández Suárez (1959; comments on a book by Claudio Sánchez Albornoz [q.v. 1937–]; to be censored entirely but published nevertheless); "Ortega, or the Passion for Spain" by historian **José Luis Abellán** (1933–) (1959; to be censored entirely but published nevertheless); "Trade Unionism and Economic Development in

Spain" by **José Luis Rubio** (1965; on the history of Spanish trade unionism; not published); "Madariaga and 'The Business of Spain' " by **Luis Espina Cepeda** (1967; interview with diplomat and historian de Madariaga [q.v. 1936–] about Spain's past, present and future; not published); "Life during the War" by **Salvador Bueno** (1917–) (1969; chapters of a history of Cuba's independence war; not published); "On 'X-Day': An Interview with Sánchez Albornoz on the Future of Spain" by **Carlos Briones** (1969; not published).

1961   **Miquel Coll i Alentorn** (?1904–?90), historian and leader of the Catalan Christian Democratic Movement, was reportedly in prison.

1961–   Among the books on the Falange banned but circulating clandestinely were *Falange: A History of Spanish Fascism* (Stanford 1961) by **Stanley Payne** (1934–); *Die verbotene Revolution: Aufstieg und Niedergang der Falange* (Hamburg 1963) by **Bernd Nellessen**; *La falange en la guerra de España: La unificación y Hedilla* (Paris 1967) by **Maximiano García Venero**; *Antifalange: Estudio crítico de la falange en la guerra de España* (Paris 1967) by **Herbert Southworth**.

pre-1966   At least until 1966, when the Ley Fraga abolished preventive censorship, most works published by exiled historians since 1939 were not found in Spanish libraries.

pre-1970   In the late 1960s, historian **Ricardo de la Cierva** (1926–) anonymously published a chronicle of the civil war.

1972   In May **Manuel Gruells Piferré**, a historian specialized in Catalan history of the 1920s and 1930s, was arrested in Barcelona by the secret police, together with eight others. He had previously delivered occasional talks on Catalan history to members of the Catalan Liberation Front but, contrary to official claims, he was not a member of the organization.

1973–   In October **Martín de Ugalde** (1921–), novelist and author of *Síntesis de la historia del País Vasco* (Barcelona, fourth edition 1977; Synthesis of the History of the Basque Lands), was expelled from Spain. He had already lived in exile from 1936 to 1969, mainly in Venezuela, where he had been a journalist and lecturer at the Universidad Andrés Bello, Caracas.

1979   In December **Pilar Miró**, director of the film *El crimen de Cuenca* (The Crime at Cuenca), was arrested and charged with the dissemination of ideas that were disrespectful of the armed forces. Her trial (before a military court) was suspended and later (before a civil court) annulled. The film, dealing with events in 1913 and containing twelve minutes of torture scenes involving the Guardia Civil (Civil Guard), was banned and the negative and copies confiscated.

1981   In July Galician priest and historian **Francisco Carballo** was sentenced to six months' imprisonment and a fine for slandering the police because in his book *History of Galicia* he had referred to a "wave of terror" in Galicia in August 1975 culminating in a political leader's killing, which he had attributed to the police.

1982   In April the award-winning drama-documentary *Rocío* (Dew) by **Fernando Ruiz** was impounded. It dealt with the influence of religion in Andalusia in the 1930s and with the killing of Republican sympathizers by local landowners. The sons of a landowner implicated in the events took Ruiz to court for injury to their dead father and for insult to religion. Pending the trial, the film was banned nationally, and after the second charge had been upheld, it was prohibited in three southern provinces.

1996   On 14 February **Francisco Tomás y Valiente** (1932–96), former judge and president of the Constitutional Court (1986–92), professor of legal history at the Universidad Autónoma de Madrid (1992–96) and specialist in constitutional history, was murdered by an alleged member of the Basque separatist movement Euzkadi Ta Askastasana (ETA).

1997   In March the Supreme Court ruled that secret military intelligence documents detailing the operation of covert government anti-ETA actions (1983–87), when twenty-eight suspected militants died, should be declassified.

1998   Spain's public television channel withdrew a 1997 drama series on Philip II (1527–98) because "it made more sense to combine it with a series on his father Charles V, which was scheduled to be completed in 2000". The original script included critical material on Philip's anti-Semitism and his role in inquisition trials and the 1572 Paris Massacre. The Spanish State Memorial Society for the Philip II and Charles V Anniversaries rejected the passages and issued guidelines mandating that Philip be portrayed as a family man of high moral standing. Academics were disturbed by what was seen as an "an attempt to brush up the darkest sides of a ruler who always preferred the brute suppression of dissidents over diplomacy or negotiations, whether it involved the Protestants in the Netherlands or the Conversos [Jews converted to Christianity] in Spain."

2000   In June the Real Academia de la Historia (Royal Academy of History) published a report in which it criticized the systematic omission of Spanish and noncontemporary history and the nationalistic bias in some high school history textbooks of the Galician, Basque, and other regions. The report sparked a controversy.

Contemporary historian **Txema** (=**José María) Portillo** (?1962–)
and social anthropologist **Mikel Azurmendi** (?1943–), both working
on the history of Basque nationalism at the Universidad del País
Vasco, Vitoria, and involved in protests against terrorism, went into
voluntary temporary exile in the United States after three years of
ETA harassment and threats. Azurmendi had been an ETA member
until 1970, but after ETA's violent attacks on the Franco regime, he
left to join the Basque pro-democracy movement.

Also see Dominican Republic (1956–: Galíndez), France (1991: Basque book),
Mexico (1967–68: Palerm), Morocco (1986: Bouissef).

SOURCES

Albada, J. van, " 'Memory of the World': Report on Destroyed and Damaged Archives",
    Archivum, 1996, no.42: 15, 19.
Algemeen dagblad, 14 October 1998: 26 (quote Philip II).
Amnesty International, *Amnesty International "Firsts"* (WWW-version of ACT 30/004/
    2001; London 5 April 2001).
Amnesty International, *Report* (London) 1980: 299; 1982: 291; 1997: 290.
Boia, L. ed., *Great Historians of the Modern Age: An International Dictionary* (Westport
    1991) 638–39.
Boyd, K. ed., *Encyclopedia of Historians and Historical Writing* (London/Chicago 1999)
    1133–34.
Bruch, R. vom, & R.A. Müller eds., *Historikerlexikon: Von der Antike bis zum 20.
    Jahrhundert* (Munich 1991) 330–31.
Burguière, A. ed., *Dictionnaire des sciences historiques* (Paris 1986) 261, 263, 266, 683.
Cannon, J. ed., *The Blackwell Dictionary of Historians* (Oxford 1988) 190, 431–32.
Conde Villaverde, M.L., & R. de Andrés Díaz, "Destrucción de Documentos en España:
    Historia, Prevención, Reconstrucción", *Archivum*, 1996, no.42: 119–29.
El exilio español de 1939 (Madrid) vol. 2 (1976): 237; vol. 6 (1978): 361.
El exilio español en México 1939–1982 (México 1982) 728, 751–52, 779–81, 794, 800,
    805–6, 809, 830, 859, 875.
Index on Censorship, 2/72: 98; 3–4/72: 197–210; 3/80: 69; 4/81: 25; 3/82: 4–5; 6/85:
    17, 27–29; 3/97: 132; 2/99: 10.
Instituto Panamericano de Geografía e Historia, *Guía de personas que cultivan la historia
    de América* (México 1967) 11, 47, 92–93, 224.
Lorente, M., "Historia como compromiso: F. Tomás y Valiente y el oficio de historiador",
    Jueces para la democracia: Información y debate, 1996, no.25: 3–8.
Malagón, J., "Los Historiadores y la Historia", in: *El exilio español de 1939*, vol. 5
    (Madrid 1978) 279–80, 300, 303–7, 345.
Muilekom, J. van, "Censuur op geschiedschrijving onder Franco: Het beeld van de Fa-
    lange", *Theoretische geschiedenis*, 1986: 295, 297, 305.
Ortega y Medina, J.A., "Historia", in: *El exilio español en México 1939–1982* (México
    1982) 278, 283, 345–61.
El País (WWW-text) 25, 28, 30 June, & 1 to 7 July 2000 (Report); 15 June 1998; 18
    August 2000; 13 July 2001.
Powers, J.F., "Claudio Sánchez-Albornoz y Menduiña (1893–1984)", in: H. Damico &

J.B. Zavadil eds., *Medieval Scholarship: Biographical Studies on the Formation of a Discipline*, vol. 1 *History* (New York/London 1995) 237.

Romero-Maura, J., "Spain: The Civil War and After", in: W. Laqueur & G.L. Mosse eds., *The New History: Trends in Historical Research and Writing since World War II* (New York 1967) 150–51, 160–61.

Society for Spanish and Portuguese Historical Studies Bulletin, 1997, no.2: 7-9 (Tuñón).

Storm, E., personal communication, 1997.

Tuñón de Lara, M., "Historia", in: *La cultura bajo el franquismo* (Barcelona 1977) 23, 29–36.

———— ed., *Historia de España* (Barcelona) vol. 10 (1980) 6, 242; vol. 10–3 (1991) 334.

Wilson, K., "Introduction: Governments, Historians, and Historical Engineering' ", in K. Wilson ed., *Forging the Collective Memory: Government and International Historians through Two World Wars* (Oxford/Providence 1996) 5.

Woolf, D.R. ed., *A Global Encyclopedia of Historical Writing* (New York/London 1998) 921.

SRI LANKA

1981   The 95,000 volumes of the public library of Jaffna that were destroyed by fire during an attack of the police on the Tamils in June included many irreplaceable manuscripts.

1994   In May Tamil exile **Sabarotnam Sabalingham** was shot dead in Paris by two Tamil youths. He had been working on a history of the Tamil militant movements which exposed assassinations among rival groups.

Also see Iran (1989–: Rushdie).

SOURCES

Index on Censorship, 3/94: 184.

Satyendra, N., "Tamils of Sri Lanka: 'Legitimate Expectations' ", in: *Ethnic Violence, Development and Human Rights* (SIM Special 5; Utrecht 1985) 108, 114.

SUDAN

1970s–   In the 1970s one of the songs by **Mohamed Wardi** (1931–) was banned by the government of President Gaafar Nimeiri (1969–85). It commemorated the October 1964 uprising that overthrew Lieutenant General Ibrahim Abboud (ruled 1958–64), independent Sudan's first military ruler. The singer was imprisoned in the 1970s and 1980s. In the 1990s he went into self-imposed exile.

1979   In August or September, six lecturers working at the Institute of Music and Drama in the capital Khartoum, including lecturer in drama and art history **Fatah el Rahman Abdel Aziz**, were dismissed after they refused to organize a special concert for Nimeiri during the busy examination period.

1979–85   In [November] 1979, history lecturer at Khartoum University **Mo-hamed Murad el-Hag** was detained during antigovernment demonstrations and riots. In May 1980 he and four others were tried before a security court on charges of membership in the illegal Sudan Communist Party, found guilty, and sentenced to six months' imprisonment. Although due for release because the sentence began at the time of their arrest, they were immediately rearrested. In April 1982 el-Hag was transported from Kober Prison to Port Sudan prison. He was released after 6 April 1985, when Nimeiri's government was overthrown.

[1985]–   In [1985] schoolteacher **Suleiman Mohamed Soail** had opened a kiosk to sell newspapers and magazines while doing research in social history. He presented a paper entitled *The Ideological Origins of the Mahdist Revolution* to the centenary conference of the Mahdist Revolution (1885) organized by the Khartoum University history department. He was dismissed and detained. While in detention, he reportedly taught history to his fellow prisoners. He was allegedly tortured under President Omar Hassan al-Bashir's rule (1989–).

1988–   In 1988 the minister of culture and information, Abdallah Mohamed Ahmed, ordered the pharaonic statues in the National Museum to be clothed because he considered their nudity to be offensive. He required the removal of all Christian relics from the museum on the grounds that only the Islamic heritage counted as authentic history. In 1990, serving as the education minister, he dismissed the National Museum's senior staff, who reportedly had "offended" him in 1988. They included three prominent archeologists: **Osama Abdel Rahman al Nur**, director-general of the Department of Antiquities and National Museums, **Mohamed Hassan Basha**, the museum's assistant director, and **Ali Osman Mohammed Salih**, associate professor of Nubian archeology at Khartoum University. In May 1990 the first and the second were arrested and held at Kober Prison.

1989–   After the 1989 coup by the National Islamic Front, pre-Islamic history was officially regarded as an epoch of ignorance. The National Salvation Revolution (NSR) government reportedly wanted to dismantle pre-Islamic (Nubian) and Christian relics, scriptures, icons, and books, through either confiscation and physical destruction or their dispersion as gifts. Large amounts of studio archive material were deliberately lost: in 1992, for example, the controllers of radio Juba erased its tapes of the southern Sudanese singer Yousif Fataki and used them for Bashir's public addresses.

             Since 1989 a sustained campaign had been waged against historians, among others, by media loyal to the NSR. One of the classic books attacked was a major source for the Mahdist period (1885–98), *History of the Sudan*, by **Naum Bey Shuqayr** (1863–1922), an adviser to the British. It was dubbed "un-Islamic" and deserving of being banned.

In September 1989 **Mohamed Sayyed al-Gadal**, associate history professor at Khartoum University, author of several books on Sudanese history, vice chairman of the Writers' Union executive committee, was arrested. He was held in Port Sudan Prison, later transferred to Kober Prison and released in October 1990. In April 1992 four professors, including al-Gadal, were dismissed by presidential decree, although the vice chancellor had sent letters commending their dedication and service. The decree also banned their employment in other academic institutions and government departments. No reason was given, but they were probably blacklisted as political opponents. Al-Gadal had already been among the 1979 detainees [q.v. 1979–85: el-Hag].

1989   In November **Farouq Mohamed Ibrahim el-Nur**, a biology lecturer at the Khartoum University faculty of science, was arrested, kept in a secret interrogation center for about twelve days, and reportedly tortured before being transferred to Kober Prison. He was questioned about his teaching of the Darwinian theory of evolution, which was considered incompatible with Islam by fundamentalist security officials. The torture was an attempt to force him to recant his views.

1990s   In the early 1990s, students reportedly received a two months' forced training in the Popular Defense Force Camps before entering the university. The curriculum included listening to extensive lectures on Islamic history.

Also see Egypt (1954–: Shalabi).

SOURCES

Africa Watch, *Academic Freedom and Human Rights Abuses in Africa* (New York 1991) 87–91.

Amnesty International, *Report* (London) 1980: 80; 1981: 84; 1982: 82; 1983: 84; 1985: 96; 1986: 96; 1990: 223.

Codesria, *Bulletin*, 1/91: 11.

Fluehr-Lobban, C., R.A. Lobban Jr., & J.O. Voll, *Historical Dictionary of the Sudan* (Metuchen 1992) 194.

Hussain, M.E., "The State of Academic Freedom in Sudan", in: Codesria, *The State of Academic Freedom in Africa 1995* (Dakar 1996) 152.

Index on Censorship, 1/80: 61–62; 6/98: 75, 78.

World University Service, *Academic Freedom* (London) 1993: 130–31, 133; 1995: 82–83.

SURINAME

1993   On 25 October Dutch historian and anthropologist **Bernardus [= Ben] Scholtens** (1954–93), former history lecturer (1983–86) at Anton de Kom University (later: University of Suriname) and coordinator at the Ministry of Education culture department (1986–93), was murdered at his home in Paramaribo. In January 1989 he had belonged to a team of anthropologists studying the funeral of a Bush Negro (Maroon) chief when they were harassed by Ronnie Brunswijk's Jungle Commando. Just before his death, Scholtens had completed a doctoral thesis entitled *Bush Negroes and the Government in Suriname: The Development of the Political Relations 1651–1992* (1994; in Dutch). He was awarded his degree posthumously by Nijmegen Catholic University, the Netherlands. The connection between his scholarly interests and the murder is not clear.

Also see Netherlands (pre-1945: Anton de Kom).

SOURCES

NRC-Handelsblad, 26 May 1994: 7.
Scholtens, B.P.C., *Bosnegers en overheid in Suriname: De ontwikkeling van de politieke verhouding 1651–1992* (Paramaribo 1994).
Volkskrant, 1993 (2 January, 26 October).

SWAZILAND

See South Africa (1953–: Davidson), Zimbabwe (pre-1974: Mudenge).

SWEDEN

1967   A report stated that the secrecy rules surrounding official source material on relations with foreign states (for instance, Nazi Germany or the USSR) were perhaps stricter than elsewhere.

Also see South Africa (1986: Van Gylswyk).

SOURCES

Article 19, *Information, Freedom and Censorship: World Report 1988* (London 1988) 221–23.
Wahlbäck, K., "Sweden: Secrecy and Neutrality", in: W. Laqueur & G.L. Mosse eds., *The New History: Trends in Historical Research and Writing since World War II* (New York 1967) 176–77.

SWITZERLAND

1952–61   When in 1952 Switzerland was allowed to consult records captured from the Germans and Italians by the Allies at the end of World War II, the government was concerned about the intended publication of three documents on the secret Franco-Swiss military cooperation of 1939–40 in a volume of the series *Documents on German Foreign Policy, 1918–1945* (Washington/London, series C 1957–83; series D 1949–64)—*Akten zur deutschen auswärtigen Politik, 1918–1945* (Göttingen, series C 1971–81; series D 1950–70). The French Foreign Ministry, the North Atlantic Treaty Organization, the Central Intelligence Agency, and the United States Army also intervened to prevent the documents' publication, especially in 1955–56, because it could jeopardize relations with Switzerland. Although French series editor Maurice Baumont could not convince his colleagues—the American Paul Sweet and the British Margaret Lambert—to omit the three documents, they were not printed as planned in volume 10 (Series D). Postponed until April 1961, they appeared in volume 11 (Series D).

Between 1953 and 1960, diplomats acting on orders of the government tried to block access of several historians and others to the above-mentioned captured records. Among those denied access were the following:

1953–54   From July 1953 to [October] 1954, **Fritz Steck-Keller**, a history student and radio journalist in Bern who did doctoral research on the Swiss counterintelligence during World War II attempted to gain access. He never completed the dissertation.

1954   In May–July **Rudolf von Albertini** (1923–), then a Privatdozent (lecturer) in modern history at Zürich University who had just completed his postdoctoral dissertation (Habilitation) on French history, was barred from consulting Italian wartime records in Washington. He became a professor specialized in colonial and Third World history.

In July–November 1954, **Carl Ludwig** (1889–1967), a professor at Basel University in charge of an official investigation into the Swiss policy toward refugees in 1933–55, did not receive the government support he requested for consulting a record (a telegram) in London. His report, completed in 1955, was published in 1957 as *Die Flüchtlingspolitik der Schweiz seit 1933 bis zur Gegenwart*. This official edition was distributed in small numbers, but on public demand a commercial reprint appeared in Bern in 1966.

1958–59   From November 1958 to January 1959, a Swiss diplomat (unsuc-
           cessfully) approached the British Foreign Office in order to block
           the archival access of **Johann Wolfgang Brügel** (1905–), a trade
           union official in London and journalist for Swiss social-democrat
           newspapers who published many articles about World War II.

1959–60   From March 1959 to 1960, **Werner Krause**, a German history stu-
           dent, consulted the captured records in London for his doctoral re-
           search about Swiss diplomacy and neutrality in 1917. In reaction,
           the draft of an official version of the events was prepared. In addi-
           tion, National Archivist Leonhard Haas attempted to persuade
           Krause's German supervisor that he, Haas, read and comment upon
           the dissertation before publication. Krause never completed the dis-
           sertation.

Several other historians encountered obstacles surrounding politically sensitive
Swiss issues.

1962–76   When in July 1962 **Edgar Bonjour** (1898–1991), history professor
           at Basel University, was asked to prepare an official internal report
           on Swiss foreign policy during World War II, he was given privi-
           leged and confidential access to the archives. His report was pub-
           lished as the nine-volume *Geschichte der schweizerischen
           Neutralität* (Basel 1967–76; A History of Swiss Neutrality). The
           government, however, reduced by at least one-third the number of
           the records inserted in the first complementary volume of sources
           (volume 7). After a public outcry in the summer of 1974, most of
           the documents were inserted in the next volumes, although those too
           were censored. Only in 1973–75, when a thirty-five-year term of
           embargo was introduced, did access to Swiss archives gradually be-
           come more liberal.

1983–99   In 1983 **Walther Hofer** (1920–), history professor at Bern Univer-
           sity and member of Parliament, was sued for libel by the son of
           lawyer Wilhelm Frick (died 1961) for writing in the newspaper *Neue
           Zürcher Zeitung* that Frick had had connections with the Gestapo
           during World War II. In 1986 the court ruled that Hofer's statements
           were libelous because, instead of checking the primary sources him-
           self, he had based them on a dissertation. Frick's son also threatened
           to sue the many historians who publicly protested the decision. The
           case was reopened in 1998–99 when Hofer submitted new research
           data by historian Klaus Urner to the Supreme Court (Bundesgericht),
           but the judgment remained unaltered and Hofer had to pay damages.

1984–   In April a Zürich court ruled that journalist **Jürg Frischknecht** in
           his *Unheimlichen Patrioten: Politische Reaktion in der Schweiz; ein*

aktuelles Handbuch (Zürich 1979; a historical work on right-wing activists and movements in Switzerland), did not have the right to publish true but generally forgotten historical-biographical details. After the Allgemeine Geschichtforschende Gesellschaft der Schweiz protested the decision, it was revised by the Swiss Supreme Court.

1996–   In December 1996, amid a large-scale controversy over dormant accounts of Holocaust victims, **Christoph Meili** (1968–), a night watchman of the Union Bank of Switzerland (UBS), Zürich, discovered documents related to property sold by Jews in Nazi Germany in the shredder room and handed them over to a Jewish organization. He was dismissed for disclosing confidential material and sued for breaking the banking secrecy rules. In April 1997, after death threats and police interrogations, he went into exile with his wife and children in the United States. They were given permanent resident status there. Meili found work as a porter. UBS first denied the destruction of documents but confirmed it in July. In November the prosecution was canceled.

1997–   In October 1997, after a complaint was lodged, the *Autorité indépendante d'examen des plaintes en matière de radio-télévision* (AIEP) ruled that *L'Honneur perdue de la Suisse*, a documentary by **Daniel Monnat** about the importance of German–Swiss wartime economic collaboration shown on French-speaking Swiss television in March 1997, was biased. The film, in which nine historians participated, was judged to illustrate theses and opinions, not facts, without acknowledging that it had done so. The Schweizerische Radio- und Fernsehgesellschaft (SRG) complained that it had not been consulted by the AIEP and that it had had no access to two expert reports about the documentary written by historians Jean-Claude Favez and Georg Kreis for the AIEP. A court order enabled the SRG to organize a hearing with the two historians in June 1999. In November the AIEP confirmed its earlier decision on the documentary, but in December the SRG appealed the decision and the court ordered AIEP to consult the SRG and to reevaluate the film.

SOURCES

Der Bund, 10 November 1999: 15 (Hofer); 9 January 2000: 11 (AIEP).

Dubois, A., "Zur Urteilsbegründung im Prozess Eibel contra 'Unheimliche Patrioten': Sollen Gerichte Geschichte machen? Eine Erklärung der Allgemeinen Geschichtforschenden Gesellschaft der Schweiz", *Neue Zürcher Zeitung*, 15–16 December 1984: 38.

Gross, R., "Mächtiger als die Gerichte? Geschichte und historische Gerechtigkeit", in: N. Frei, D. van Laak, & M. Stolleis eds., *Geschichte vor Gericht: Historiker, Richter und die Suche nach Gerechtigkeit* (Munich 2000) 168–69.

Hug, P., & B. Studer, " 'Historische Wahrheit' contra 'Thesen' zur Zeitgeschichte", *Traverse*, 1998, no. 3: 128–39.

Index on Censorship, 4/97: 126.

International Herald Tribune, 29 July 1997: 6 (Meili).

Keesings historisch archief, 1997: 243.

Kreis, G., " 'Wahrheitsfindung': Zweite Runde; Wieviel Spielraum für zeitgeschichtliche Dokumentarfilme?", *Traverse*, 2000, no.1: 150–54.

Le Monde, 6 October 1997: 5 (AIEP).

New York Times, 6 May 1997: B3 (Meili).

"Pour sauver le mythe de la neutralité, la Suisse a saboté le travail des historiens", *Nouveau quotidien: Journal suisse et européen*, 19–21 September 1997: 1, 20.

Weber, W., *Biographisches Lexicon zur Geschichtswissenschaft in Deutschland, Österreich und der Schweiz: Die Lehrstuhlinhaber für Geschichte von den Anfängen des Faches bis 1970* (Frankfurt/Main 1987) 1–2, 52–53, 250–51.

Zala, S., "Das amtliche Malaise mit der Historie: Vom Weissbuch zum Bonjour-Bericht", *Schweizerische Zeitschrift für Geschichte*, 1997: 759–60, 765–80.

———, *Gebändigte Geschichte: Amtliche Historiographie und ihr Malaise mit der Geschichte der Neutralität, 1945–1961* (Bern 1998) 60–62, 69–71, 73–97, 100–101, 103–10, 113, 125.

———, *Geschichte under der Schere politischer Zensur: Amtliche Aktensammlungen im internationalen Vergleich* (Munich 2001) 250–326.

———, personal communication, November–December 1998; March–June 2000.

SYRIA

From 1963, but increasingly from 1970, censorship of history was stepped up at all levels. Taboo subjects could be found in the realm of contemporary history, especially the history of ethnic and religious groups. Many books about the politics and contemporary history of Syria and the Middle East were banned, at least before 1991. For example, a seven-volume collection of early Baath documents *Struggle of the Baath*, published in Beirut, was banned because it contradicted the official party history. However, the censorship system in Syria was not absolute and indirect criticism via historical parallels was tolerated. Some historians reportedly left Syria, voluntarily or unvoluntarily, for political reasons or because of their Islamic or Marxist convictions.

1952   Historian **Constantine Zurayq** (1909–) resigned as vice chancellor (1949–52) of the Syrian University in Damascus after the military had invaded the university campus following student demonstrations against the military rule of President Adib Shishakli (1951–54). Zurayq was a history professor (1930–45, 1956–77), vice president (1947–49, 1952–54), and acting president (1954–57) at the American University of Beirut and an intellectual leader of the Arab cause. As a diplomat he served as Syria's delegate to the United Nations General Assembly and alternate delegate to the Security Council (1945–47). He was also active in the International Association of Universities, of which he was president (1965–70). He was a member of the UNESCO International Commission for a Scientific and Cultural History of Mankind (1950–69).

1966   In March 1966 philosopher of pan-Arab nationalism **Michel Aflaq** (1910–89) was expelled from the Baath Party (Arab Resurrection Party), which he had cofounded, and went into exile in France. In the months before his exile, he had tried to oust the Baath Party's Syrian Regional Command, but in February 1966 the military elements associated with the Regional Command seized power. The Baath Party split over the event and in February 1968 Aflaq accepted the (largely honorary) post of Secretary-General in the Baghdad-based Baath Party wing. In 1971 he was sentenced to death in absentia in Syria. Around 1980 he took up residence in Iraq. Aflaq had been a history student at the Sorbonne, Paris (1928–34), and secondary school history teacher in Damascus (1934–42). In 1949 he was briefly minister of education. In the period before February 1954 (when parliamentary life was restored), he had been imprisoned twice and, from January to October 1953, he had lived in exile in Beirut. During and after the United Arab Republic (the Egyptian–Syrian union) of 1958–61, Aflaq's policies had met with increasing resistance within the Baath Party.

1970– In a year after 1970, a doctoral student (name unknown) who had written a thesis about Ottoman Libya based on Libyan archives and given a positive opinion of that era had to recant his views during his defense, as Ottoman history tended to be seen as an instance of imperialism.

1975– In mid-1975 **Ahmed Roummo** (?1936–), a history teacher and supporter of the Baath Party's Iraqi wing, was arrested with many others after a sharp deterioration in Syria's relations with Iraq. As late as 1978, he was reportedly still detained.

In September 1975 **Abd al-Massih Kiryakos** (1941–), historian and headmaster of a secondary school in al-Qamishli, was arrested as an alleged member of the Baath Party National Command's pro-Iraqi wing. He has been imprisoned since then, without charge or trial, at al-Mezze military prison, Damascus. His daughter was born after his arrest. Only in 1980 did his wife obtain permission to see him for thirty minutes every other week.

Publications on Ebla, an ancient Syrian metropolis which dominated the present territories of Syria and Palestine (2400–1650 BCE) and was excavated in 1975, became almost taboo for a decade. Rumors that some of the thousands of archival clay tablets found at the site mentioned persons and events from the Old Testament, thus implying possible proof for these events having taken place on Syrian territory and strengthening possible Israeli claims, had reportedly upset the authorities.

1985–   *Die Bibel kam aus dem Lande Asir* (Hamburg 1985; *The Bible Came from Arabia*, London 1985), a book by Lebanese historian **Kamal Salibi** (1929–), history professor at the American University of Beirut, was banned in Syria and most other Arab countries.

1987   The multiauthor, five-volume *"History of the Peasants"* was already printed, bound, and ready for distribution when a final check of the censors revealed a problem. Although the authors were not told what problem, distribution was postponed. The stock was put in a warehouse and finally destroyed. A new abridged and revised edition was planned.

[?]   Marxist historian **Abdallah Hanna** (1932–) could reportedly not occupy an academic position because of his scholarly approach. He tried to write history from the viewpoint of workers and peasants with the help of oral history techniques. In the 1990s he had censorship problems with several of his historical publications. In September 2000 he was among the 99 signatories of a statement in the Lebanese newspaper *al-Safir* calling for the lifting of martial law and the release of political prisoners.

Also see France (1947: Rodinson), United Arab Emirates (1979: Aqil).

SOURCES

Amnesty International, *Report* (London) 1978: 271; 2001: 233.
———, *Wordt vervolgd*, March 1986: 16 (Kiryakos).
Benewick, R., & P. Green eds., *The Routledge Dictionary of Twentieth-Century Political Thinkers* (London/New York 1992) 4–5.
Choueiri, Y.M., *Arab History and the Nation-State: A Study in Modern Arab Historiography 1820–1980* (London 1989) 118–19.
Faris, H.A., "Constantine K. Zurayk: Advocate of Rationalism in Modern Arab Thought", in: G.N. Atiyeh & I.M. Oweiss eds., *Arab Civilization: Challenges and Responses; Studies in Honor of Constantine K. Zurayk* (Albany 1988) 1–3.
Freitag, U., "Die Entwicklung der Syrischen Geschichtswissenschaft", *Periplus*, 1993: 87, 90–92.
———, "Entwicklung und Probleme nationaler arabischer Geschichtsschreibung am Beispiel syrischer Historiker", *Saeculum*, 1994: 191–93.
———, *Geschichtsschreibung in Syrien 1920–1990: Zwischen Wissenschaft und Ideologie* (Hamburg 1991) 313, 390–91.
———, personal communication, October 1999.
Gallagher, N.E. ed., *Approaches to the History of the Middle East: Interviews with Leading Middle East Historians* (Reading, UK 1994) 173.
Gordon, D.C., *Self-determination and History in the Third World* (Princeton 1971) 23, 71.
Human Rights Watch, *World Report 2001* (Washington 2000) 409–10.

Index on Censorship, 6/00: 189.

Middle East Watch, *Syria Unmasked: The Suppression of Human Rights by the Asad Regime* (New Haven 1991) 110, 124, 127, 193.

Reich, B. ed., *Political Leaders of the Contemporary Middle East and North Africa: A Biographical Dictionary* (New York 1990) 32–39.

Simon, R.S., P. Mattar, & R.W. Bulliet eds., *Encyclopedia of the Modern Middle East* (New York 1996) 51–53, 1960–61.

T

TAIWAN

1966–88   In 1966 historian and journalist **Chang Hua-min** (?1926–) was sentenced to eight years' imprisonment on charges of making procommunist propaganda. Upon his release in 1974, he continued to write political essays, mostly banned, and actively supported an opposition candidate during the December 1978 election campaign. In September 1979 he was arrested on suspicion of sedition in connection with his writings, held incommunicado for at least two months, and tried *in camera*. He was sentenced by a military court to ten years' imprisonment in January 1980, again for sedition and alleged pro-communist propaganda. In April 1988 he was released during an amnesty commemorating President Chiang Ching-kuo's January 1988 death.

1966–76   In January 1966 the security agency Taiwan Garrison Command banned the sociohistorical study *Sun Yat-sen and the Westernization of Medicine in China* published by satirist and historian **Lee Ao (Li Ao)** (1935–). It also revoked the license of the monthly magazine *Wen Hsing*, which he edited. In July six other books of Lee's were banned, including *Monologues against Tradition* (1963) and *History and Portraits* (1963). In 1970 he was placed under house arrest after the escape from Taiwan of Peng Ming-min, the leader of the Taiwanese Independence Movement. On 23 February 1971, he was arrested for a few hours after rumors of a demonstration to be held on 28 February in commemoration of the 1947 uprising (this uprising against the rule of Nationalist Chinese Governor-General Chen Yi was crushed). In March he was rearrested and held for months without bail or legal counsel and with little or no contacts with friends or family. In August he was charged with sedition and in April 1972 sentenced by a secret military tribunal to ten years' imprisonment with a further six years' loss of civil liberties for handing materials on political prisoners to foreigners for publication, for keeping copies of "rebel publications which were plans to overthrow the government" at his home, and for allegedly accepting an invitation to serve as a member of "the Taiwan headquarters of the rebel organization" (possibly the World Formosans for Independence). It was believed that his critical writings were the real reason for his imprisonment. In September 1975 his sentence was reduced after a retrial and he was released in December 1976. In 1948 Lee had moved with his family from mainland China to Taiwan. He was Hu Shi's student, about whom he wrote two books. He graduated in history in 1959.

1968–   In June **Ch'iu Yen-liang** (?1952–), student at the National Taiwan University archeology department, was arrested, probably by the Taiwan Garrison Command of Kuangtung, and sentenced to six years' imprisonment for alleged membership in a Marxist study group.

pre-1987   In July the government lifted the ban on books, including history works written by Chinese authors before the communist takeover in 1949, on the condition that they delete or change all references to the communist ideology. Works written by mainland Chinese after 1949 were not allowed.

Also see China (1948–50: exiles; 1954–: Hu Shi), Japan (1945: Yanai), United Kingdom (1995–97: textbooks), United States (1953–63: *FRUS*).

SOURCES

Amnesty International, *Report* (London) 1973–74: 57; 1974–75: 88; 1977: 221; 1980: 236; 1983: 235; 1988: 184; 1989: 202.
Barmé, G., & L. Jaivin eds., *New Ghosts, Old Dreams: Chinese Rebel Voices* (New York 1992) 202–3.
Index on Censorship, 2/72: 99; 3/73: 45–49, 103; 3/74: 83; 9/87: 39.

TAJIKISTAN

pre-1991   *See* Union of Soviet Socialist Republics (USSR).

1993   In September **Kodir Kholikov**, associate professor at the history department of the State University of Tajikistan and active member of the popular movement Rastokhez, was under serious threat of losing his job. Over the summer newspaper articles had alleged that he was unfit to teach because he did not adhere to communist ideals and because of his political activism. He was not permitted to teach his history courses. His courses on Tajikistan's twentieth-century political history were assigned to another instructor.

SOURCES

Human Rights Watch, Letter, Committee for International Academic Freedom to Rector of the State University of Tajikistan (14 September 1993).

TANGANYIKA/TANZANIA

See Congo (1981–: Wamba-dia-Wamba), Guyana (1974–96: Rodney), Jamaica (1968: Rodney), Kenya (1981–89: Mukaru Nganga), South Africa (1953–: Davidson; [1975–91]: Pampallis).

THAILAND

Among the sensitive subjects was the history of Thailand's monarchy. Marxist historians were frequent targets of persecution.

1957–66   From 1957 to 1964, **Jit Phumisak** (?1930–66), musician, poet, essayist, and historian, was imprisoned by Field Marshal Sarit Thanarat's military government because of his antiimperialist and Marxist writings. In prison he wrote many songs and essays, most of which were smuggled out of prison and published under various pen names. Upon his release, he joined the guerrilla opposition in the northeast. Two years later, in May 1966, he was shot dead by border patrol police. His writings became very popular and controversial after the 1973 students' uprising. Until then, and again between October 1976 and 1979, his Marxist book *The Real Face of Thai Feudalism Today* (1957, reprinted 1974) was banned. So was a study of his writings (Suchart Sawasdisri ed., *Jit Phumisak*, 1974). In his book, Jit depicted the king as a "committee chairman" who safeguarded the profits of the feudalist ruling class. In 1953, when still a history student, he had had a conflict with university authorities over his leftist writings, which led to a temporary interruption of his study at Chulalongkorn University, Bangkok. When graduating in 1957, he had refused to accept his diploma from the king.

1950s–   In the late 1950s, journalist and literary critic **Udom Sisuwan** (?1920–), author of the Marxist historical work *"Thailand, a Semicolony"* (1950), was arrested and imprisoned by the Sarit government. Upon his release in the mid-1960s, he joined the Communist Party of Thailand in the jungle and became one of its leaders until his resignation in September 1982. From 1958 to 1973 and from October 1976 to (at least) 1978, his book was banned.

1974   **Gularb Saipradit** (1905–74), a Marxist who had studied Buddhist philosophy and meditation in prison (1952–56) and was living in exile in China (1957–74), published *History of Thai Women* (Bangkok 1974).

1976–78   After the October 1976 coup, **Thongchai Winichakul**, a Sino-Thai history student at Thammasat University, Bangkok, was one of eighteen student activists tried and convicted on charges of lèse majesté (defamation of the monarchy). He was released in September 1978. He became known for his study of nineteenth-century maps, a 1988 doctoral research at Sidney University. In 1995 he worked at the University of Wisconsin–Madison, United States.

1983–86   In July 1983 **Saman Kongsuphol** (possibly: **Samaan Khongsuphon**), a campaigner for civilian democracy, was arrested on a charge of lèse majesté because he had allegedly published a critical history of the Thai monarchy. Without bail, he was held incommunicado for six days. In December he was sentenced to eight years' imprisonment by a martial law court. **Thawan Saengkaanjanaanon** and **Phongtheep Manuuphiphatphong** were sentenced to four years' imprisonment for helping him to publish the booklet. In January 1986 all were pardoned by King Bhumibol Adulyadej Rama IX. Two students were arrested in Chiang Mai in July 1984 after having been accused of possessing the booklet.

1984–   In August 1984 social critic and lay Buddhist author **Sulak Sivaraksa** (1933–) was arrested and his book *Interviews with Sulak Sivaraksa: Unmasking Thai Society* was confiscated and banned. Thousands of copies of the book were seized by the police. The arrest centred on an article on Thai education history in which he criticized kings and princes of the last two centuries for their ignorance of Buddhist teaching and tradition. After a four-month public trial, the king intervened in November to have the charge of lèse majesté withdrawn. In September 1991 he was forced to go into hiding, and he fled to Sweden after an arrest warrant had been issued. The reason was his speech at Thammasat University in which he criticized the logging trade and the close relationship between the National Peace Keeping Council military government (which had seized power in February) and the Burmese junta. Upon his return from exile in December 1992 after the junta was replaced by a civilian regime, he was arrested. Formally charged in March 1993, his trial continued intermittently from June 1993 until his acquittal in April 1995. One source described him as a critic loyal [in the 1970s] to the viewpoints of historian Prince Damrong Rajanubhab (1862–1943), "the Father of Thai History", a son of King Mongkut Rama IV (reigned 1851–68) and half-brother of King Chulalongkorn. In 1976 Sivaraksa had fled abroad from an arrest warrant during the coup. He founded the International Network of Engaged Buddhists. In 1994 he was a Nobel Peace Prize nominee. He organized the so-called Jungle University for fleeing Burmese students. In 1996 he was awarded the Right Livelihood Award, an alternative Nobel Peace Prize.

1998–   In [November] the film board rejected two revised scripts for *Anna and the King* (1999; Twentieth-Century-Fox), a new version of the musical *The King and I* (1956) about Rama IV, on the grounds that the king was depicted as a tyrant rather than a scholar. In December 1999 the film, made in Malaysia by **Andy Tennant**, was banned immediately upon release.

Also see Indonesia (1994: Spielberg).

SOURCES

Amnesty International, *Report* (London) 1984: 265; 1985: 248–49; 1986: 263; 1987: 272; 1992: 251; 1993: 282; 1994: 286; 1995: 283; 1996: 295.

Anderson, B., "Radicalism after Communism in Thailand and Indonesia", *New Left Review*, November–December 1993: 13.

Article 19, *State of Fear: Censorship in Burma (Myanmar)* (London 1991) 13.

Boia, L. ed., *Great Historians of the Modern Age: An International Dictionary* (Westport 1991) 600–602, 604–5.

Gorman, R.A. ed., *Biographical Dictionary of Marxism* (Westport 1986) 274–75.

———, *Biographical Dictionary of Neo-Marxism* (Westport 1985) 368–69.

Human Rights Watch, *World Report 1999* (Washington 1998) 213.

Index on Censorship, 6/84: 43, 48; 1/85: 65; 2/85: 36; 4/85: 4; 10/91: 56; 3/93: 40; 3/95: 187; 1/99: 100–101.

Kasetsiri, C., "Thai Historiography from Ancient Times to the Modern Period", in: A. Reid & D. Marr eds., *Perceptions of the Past in Southeast Asia* (Singapore 1979) 168–69.

Legge, J.D., "The Historiography of Southeast Asia", in: *The Cambridge History of Southeast Asia*, vol. 1 (Cambridge 1992) 22, 42.

Reynolds, C.J., & Hong L., "Marxism in Thai Historical Studies", *Journal of Asian Studies*, 1983, no.1: 81–85, 87, 90.

Sulak Sivaraksa (Thailand) (WWW-text 1995).

Thongchai Winichakul, "The Changing Landscape of the Past: New Histories in Thailand since 1973", *Journal of Southeast Asian Studies*, 1995: 103.

Woolf, D.R. ed., *A Global Encyclopedia of Historical Writing* (New York/London 1998) 881–82.

TIBET

See China.

TOGO

1985   In December, thirty people, including **Adimado Adamayom**, history lecturer at the University of Bénin, Lomé, were arrested and detained for possessing literature of an allegedly subversive or offensive nature. The arrested academics were not allowed to return to their university posts.

1989   In September **Nyaledome Kodjo** was arrested by security police because, during a seminar, he had asked government officials to explain their decision not to celebrate 27 April as a national day and why they avoided talking about Togo's history between 1960 and 1967 (the year that President Gnassingbe Eyadéma took power following a military coup). He was reportedly released later following pressure from the National Commission for Human Rights.

SOURCES

Africa Watch, *Academic Freedom and Human Rights Abuses in Africa* (New York 1991) 116.
Article 19, *Information, Freedom and Censorship: World Report 1991* (London 1991) 52.

TRINIDAD AND TOBAGO

1953–   In 1953 Trotskyist historian, writer, and activist **C.L.R. [= Cyril Lionel Robert] James** (1901–89), author of *The Black Jacobins: Toussaint L'Ouverture and the San Domingo Revolution* (London 1938; about the 1791 San Domingo slave revolution which eventually established Haiti as an independent nation), was deported from the United States where he had been living since November 1938. James had been forced to operate largely underground there after 1940, when his United States visa expired. He was involved in the Trotskyist movement in the country. He failed in his application to obtain United States citizenship, although in 1948 he married an American citizen. Before his deportation he had been interned for some time on Ellis Island (1953). In 1958 he accepted an invitation from Williams [q.v. 1955–], his former pupil and collaborator, to return to Trinidad as the editor of *The Nation*, the newspaper of the leading political party, People's National Movement (PNM). He served as its editor until July 1960, when a conflict with Williams over United States control of the naval base at Chaguaramas forced him to resign and to break with the PNM. He was briefly detained because he openly campaigned in favor of a broader West Indian Federation. In 1959 he went to the United Kingdom, where he had already lived (1932–38, 1953–58). In 1965 he returned to Trinidad, but he was put under house arrest. As a result he formed the Workers and Farmers Party, which challenged Williams's rule, but he was defeated in the 1966 elections. He returned to the United Kingdom and in 1968 to the United States, where he eventually worked at the history department of Federal City College, Washington, D.C. (1972–80) and the political science department of Howard University, Washington, D.C.

1955–   In May 1955 historian **Eric Williams** (1911–81), assistant (1939–46), and associate professor (1946–55) of social and political science at Howard University, Washington, D.C., was dismissed from the Anglo-American Caribbean Commission (a body initially formed to encourage social and economic cooperation between the United States and the United Kingdom in the Caribbean and to further the welfare of the Caribbean people). Working for the commission since 1943, he had been the deputy chairman of the commission's Research Council since 1948. Many tensions preceded the dismissal, especially after the 1945 publication of his *Negro in the Caribbean*, which was sharply critical of Caribbean sugar planters. The reason for the dismissal reportedly lay in the conflict between Williams's outspoken defense of the interests of the Caribbean workers over those of foreign businessmen and the viewpoints of other commission members. Soon afterward he started giving public lectures at Woodford Square, Port of Spain (July 1955–January 1956), became PNM founder and leader (January 1956), first chief minister (1956–59) and prime minister (1959–81) of Trinidad and Tobago. On 31 August 1962, when the country achieved independence, Williams published *History of the People of Trinidad and Tobago*, said to be the first national history. He was the author of *Capitalism and Slavery* (1944), in which he maintained that slavery was a causal factor in the making of the Industrial Revolution and was abolished only because it was no longer useful for British capitalism. Although completed as a doctoral thesis and successfully defended at Oxford University in 1938 and published in the United States in 1944, a British edition did not appear until 1964.

SOURCES

Abelove, H., et al. eds., *Visions of History* (Manchester 1984) 265.
Annual Obituary 1981 (Chicago/London) 218–20 (Williams).
Boyd, K. ed., *Encyclopedia of Historians and Historical Writing* (London/Chicago 1999) 611–12, 1303–4.
Brereton, B., *A History of Modern Trinidad 1783–1962* (Port of Spain 1981) 241–43.
Button, J., *The Radicalism Handbook* (London 1995) 192–93.
Cannon, J. ed., *The Blackwell Dictionary of Historians* (Oxford 1988) 453.
Farred, G. ed., *Rethinking C.L.R. James* (Cambridge 1996) 2, 176.

Glaberman, M., "Introduction", *Radical America*, 1970, no.4: iii–vi.

Gorman, R.A. ed., *Biographical Dictionary of Neo-Marxism* (Westport 1985) 214–16.

Grimshaw, A. ed., *The C.L.R. James Reader* (Oxford 1992) 11, 15, 21, 423–25.

Hennessy, A., "Intellectuals: The General and the Particular", in: Hennessy ed. 1992: 14–15.

———, ed., *Intellectuals in the Twentieth-Century Caribbean*, vol. 1 (London/Basingstoke 1992).

Palmer, C.A., "Introduction", in: E. Williams, *Capitalism & Slavery* (originally 1944; Chapel Hill/London 1994) xi–xxiii.

Sheridan, R.B., "Eric Williams and *Capitalism and Slavery*: A Biographical and Historiographical Essay", in: B.L. Solow & S.L. Engerman eds., *British Capitalism and Caribbean Slavery: The Legacy of Eric Williams* (Cambridge 1987) 317–19, 325.

Sutton, P., ed., *Forged from the Love of Liberty: Selected Speeches of Dr. Eric Williams* (Port of Spain 1981) xxi–xxii, xxvi, 269–80, 461–62.

———, "The Historian As Politician: Eric Williams and Walter Rodney", in: Hennessy ed. 1992: 101–3.

Tenenbaum, B.A. ed., *Encyclopedia of Latin American History and Culture*, vol. 3 (New York 1996) 312.

Tucker, M. ed., *Literary Exile in the Twentieth Century: An Analysis and Biographical Dictionary* (Westport 1991) 343–44.

Woolf, D.R. ed., *A Global Encyclopedia of Historical Writing* (New York/London 1998) 480.

TUNISIA

French Tunisia

pre-1956   Due to political sensibilities, research in contemporary history at the Institut des Hautes Études at Tunis was ignored during the colonial period.

Tunisia

1986   **Mohamed Ben Salah**'s book *The Village's Hundred Years*, an account of the history of his native village, Zamardine, from the days of French colonial rule to independence, was banned. It described the villagers' resistance and the way in which the freedom they gained was curtailed by independent Tunisia's rulers.

1988   In December **Hichem Djaït** (1935–), a historian specialized in medieval Islamic history at the Tunis University history department, was prosecuted for an article published that month in the weekly magazine *Réalités*. In it, he had criticized the continuing pattern of human-rights violations, observing that, as in the past, improvements relied on the president's goodwill. The magazine was seized and he was charged with "defamation of justice". After a campaign in support of Djaït, the charge was dropped.

1989   In July and August, the weekly *Le Maghreb* published a series of articles about the history of sexuality in Islam, written by journalists **Slim Daoula** and **Ziad Krichen**. Some weeks later, both journalists and their director were prosecuted and charged under the Press Code with "undermining Islam and public morals". Later the charges were dropped and the cases dismissed.

2000   On 23 October, a double issue of the French weekly *Jeune Afrique— L'Intelligent* was impounded, presumably because President Zine al-Abidine Ben Ali took umbrage at a lengthy profile, *The Tunisian Sakharov*, of historian and human-rights activist **Mohamed Talbi** (?1920–), specialist in medieval Islamic history, former dean of Tunis University, and author or works on medieval historian Ibn Khaldun.

Also see Argentina (1976–83: Memmi), France (1951: Raymond; 1952: Julien).

SOURCES

Article 19, *Information, Freedom and Censorship: World Report 1991* (London 1991) 397–98.
Index on Censorship, 1/89: 23; 10/90: 22; 1/01: 124.
Miège, J.L., "Historiography of the Maghrib", in P.C. Emmer & H.L. Wesseling eds., *Reappraisals in Overseas History* (Leiden 1979) 72.

TURKEY

The 1960 and 1982 coups severely limited the autonomy of Turkish historians, especially those with a left-wing orientation. Among the sensitive areas was the history of minorities such as Armenians and Kurds.

1946–   In 1946–48 Cypriot-born philosopher and historical sociologist **Niyazi Berkes** (1908–88), a senior lecturer at the faculty of language, history, and geography, Ankara University (1939–48), and three others were suspended, then reinstated, and finally, in January 1948, dismissed for expressing left-wing views in their journalistic writings and lectures. These viewpoints were labeled communist. After the Inter-University Board overturned the university's decision, Education Minister Şemseddin Sirer turned to the legislative assembly and had it pass a law cutting the funds for the courses taught by the four. In February 1950 three of the four, including Berkes, were sentenced to three months' imprisonment. In June the sentence was overturned and the three were acquitted. Berkes emigrated to Canada, where he became a visiting (1952–56) and associate (1956–75) professor at the Institute of Islamic Studies, McGill University, Montréal. Until 1960 his writing was unofficially boycotted in Turkey. Although able after 1960 to visit Turkey, he was not allowed to return. His main work was *Development of Secularism in Turkey* (originally Turkish 1964; London 1998). One of the others dismissed and tried was folklorist **Pertev Boratav** (1907–), who went into exile in Paris, where he worked at the Centre National de Recherche Scientifique (1952–74), interpreting folkloric material in its historical context.

1948–52 At least four orientalists, hired at Ankara University in a program to westernize Turkish education, were dismissed because young Turkish scholars thought they were occupying posts that by rights belonged to them: assyriologist **Benno Landsberger** (1890–1968), hittitologist **Hans Güterbock** (1908–2000), sinologist **Wolfram Eberhard** (1909–89), and **Tibor Halasi-Kun** (1914–91). The three Germans were exiles from Nazi Germany (1935, 1936, 1937, respectively); they went to the United States, where Landsberger and Güterbock became professors at the University of Chicago Oriental Institute (1948–68 and 1949–71) and Eberhard professor at the University of California, Berkeley (1948–76). In 1952 the Hungarian Halasi-Kun, professor of Turkic Studies (1942–52), went to Columbia University, New York, where he cofounded the Department of Near and Middle East Studies and established Turkic Studies.

1949–56 Although between 1949 and 1956 the Turkish government opened the Ottoman archives, and scholars such as Ömer Lütfi Barkan (1903–79) and Bernard Lewis (1916–) could use them, British historian of the Arab world **Albert Hourani** (1915–93) was refused permission to work in them.

1960– After the 27 May 1960 coup, **Fuad Köprülü** (1890–1966), descendant of the Ottoman Grand Viziers, literary and cultural historian, professor at the Ottoman University (later reorganized as Istanbul University; 1913–43), founder-director of the Institute of Turkology (1924–?), president of the Institute of Turkish History (1927–?), member of the Turkish Grand National Assembly (1935–57), cofounder of the Democratic Party, minister of foreign affairs (1950–56), and minister of state and deputy prime minister (1955) in various Adnan Menderes governments, was arrested on charges of treason but acquitted. In 1961 he cofounded a new political party, which was banned by the public prosecutor's office. A specialist in early Ottoman history, he was a firm opponent of the nationalist ideology, officially supported by the government in the late 1920s and 1930s, that postulated (in the "sun-language theory") that Turks were the first people to inhabit the earth and that Turkish was the original language spoken by humankind, from which all Semitic and Indo-European languages descended. His publication that refuted such theories, *Les Origines de l'empire ottoman* (1935; *The Origins of the Ottoman Empire*, 1992), was not published in Turkey until 1959.

1962–   In 1962 British archeologist **James Mellaart** (1925–), assistant director at the British Institute of Archaeology in Ankara and discoverer of the neolithic site of Çatal Hüyük (one of man's earliest urban settlements) was barred from fieldwork in Turkey and had to leave his digs unfinished. A few years later, he was declared persona non grata. The dismissal occurred after the newspaper *Milliyet* had published a series accusing him of smuggling out the so-called Royal Treasure of Dorak. In 1958 Mellaart had seen this clandestinely excavated treasure after coincidental contact with its owners in Izmir. At that occasion he had been allowed to make many detailed drawings of the items. He had reported the treasure's existence to the Turkish authorities and to the British institute director and published an article about it in 1959, after written authorization from the owners. A 1962 police investigation could not trace the treasure or its owners. One theory holds that the treasure's owners needed a scholar's opinion to authenticate the trove in order to sell it. Mellaart became a professor at the London University Archaeology Institute.

1971–   Among the books banned after the proclamation of martial law on 12 March 1971 were *National Liberation Movements in Africa* by British socialist historian of Africa **Basil Davidson** (1914–); and *Marxism in the Twentieth Century* (originally French 1966; New York 1970) by French communist philosopher **Roger Garaudy** (1913–).

1972   In July the Third Military Court of the Ankara Martial Law Headquarters decided to confiscate 138 "leftist" books, including *Sharafnamah* (1597–98; Book of Honor) by **Sharafkhan Bidlisi** (1543–?1603/4), called the "father of Kurdish historiography".

1973   Early in 1973 historian and political scientist **Mete Tunçay**, specialist in Ottoman "socialism", was arrested. In 1983 he was dismissed from his post as a university lecturer on the faculty of political science, Ankara University. In 1984 he was among fifty-six intellectuals charged with "acting against the orders of the martial law authorities" and faced a sentence of three to six months after signing a petition to President Kenan Evren, asking for more democracy. In 1986 his translation of *On Religion*, by historian and philosopher David Hume (1711–76), was banned.

1976–   In 1976 **Server Tanilli**, law faculty member at Istanbul University and part-time teacher at the Sigli School of Political Science in Istanbul, became a target for criticism by the paramilitary Hearths of Idealism, the youth movement of the Pan-Turkish Nationalist Action Party (NAP; a coalition partner in the government). In March he had been denounced to the police for being the author of the textbook

A History of Civilization. He was charged with subversion but acquitted on 3 April 1978. On 7 April a group believed to be NAP militants attempted to murder him. Four bullets left him paralyzed from the chest down.

1978–85   Between September 1978 and at least 1985, the government defended its denial of the 1915 Armenian genocide by conducting lobby campaigns at a United Nations Human Rights Subcommittee (removal of a paragraph on the Armenian case in September 1978), at the United States State Department (its denial of the 1915 genocide in November 1981), at the United States Congress (January 1985 letter of the Turkish ambassador designed to prevent passage of a resolution to mark the Armenian genocide), and at the Israeli government (Israel's withdrawal of sponsorship for an International Conference on the Holocaust and Genocide, Tel Aviv, 1982). American historians studying the genocide reportedly received letters from Turkish embassies. **Roger Smith**, professor at the department of government, College of William and Mary, Williamsburg, Va., specialized in the comparative study of genocide, was the object of complaints by the Turkish embassy, which criticized his position on the genocide. The Russell Tribunal eliminated the 1915 genocide from its list of genocides in history in order to satisfy the Turkish judge. The Turkish government also allegedly attempted to efface traces of the civilization of the Armenians in their historical homeland, for example, by changing the names of towns and villages in the eastern provinces in the late 1950s or by destroying Armenian churches and other historical monuments.

pre-1978   A 1978 report stated that the authorities systematically purged works on Kurdish history from libraries and destroyed Kurdish historical monuments. Research on Kurdish history was forbidden.

1978   In July **Bedrettin Comert** (died 1978), art historian, writer, translator, and critic teaching at Hacettepe University, Ankara, was shot dead in a residential suburb of the city.

1979–   In September 1979 sociologist and political scientist **Ismail Beşikçi** (1939–) was sentenced to thirty-months' imprisonment for "making propaganda for communism and separatism" and for violating the "law protecting the legacy of [Mustafa Kemal] Atatürk" (Turkey's first president, 1923–38) because of his book *The Turkish Thesis on History, the Theory of Sun and Language, and the Kurdish Question*, published and immediately confiscated in December 1977 while its author was on trial for another book on the Kurds. He was also given an additional forty months because of his defense speech during the trial. He was released in April 1981 but a decade later sentenced

once again for the second edition (1991). In 1991 several of Beşikçi's other books were banned and confiscated: *The Republican
People's Party Program (1927) and the Kurdish Problem* (1979,
1991); *The Tunceli Laws (1935) and the Dersim Genocide* (1991)
about the suppression of a Kurdish revolt in the Dersim (renamed
Tunceli) area (1937–38); *The Conditions of Resistance* (1991), in
which a 1936 assimilation plan was analyzed; and *The General Muğ-
lali Incident: 33 Bullets* (1991), about the 1943 arbitrary execution
of thirty-three Kurds in Özalp. The 1992 second edition of the last
title was banned in 1994. In 1993 Beşikçi was on trial for *The Imperialist Partition Struggle-in Kurdistan 1915–25* (1992). Beşikçi
had been dismissed at Ankara University and often imprisoned for
his writings, seminars, and lectures about the Kurds since 1971
(1971–74, 1979–81, 1981–87, 1990, 1991, 1993–99). All his works,
about thirty-five, were banned.

1980s   In the early 1980s, the second edition of *History of Nicodemia* (1966,
             1981), by historian **Avni Öztüre**, was withdrawn from circulation
             by the Turkish government, probably because of its sympathetic ac-
             count of the Armenians.

1982   In January Armenian extremists broke up a Turkish history class in
             the United States conducted by **Stanford Shaw** (1930–), professor
             of Ottoman Studies at the University of California, Los Angeles
             (1968–). He was threatened, his house was bombed, and his office
             was ransacked. He was forced to cancel his regularly scheduled clas-
             ses and go into hiding. The apparent reason for the harassment was
             the pro-Turkish views he expressed in his two-volume *History of
             the Ottoman Empire and Modern Turkey* (1977–78).

[1980s]–   In the [first half of the 1980s], a journalist [name unknown] who
             wrote a book on the history of human rights and torture in Turkey
             and the book's publisher were indicted and convicted. About a dec-
             ade later, in August 1996, a trial against writer and Human Rights
             Association deputy secretary **Erol Anar** (1965–), author of *The His-
             tory of Human Rights* began. He was charged with "separatist prop-
             aganda" under the Anti-Terror Law for a four-page chapter in the
             book *The Kurdish Question*, which discussed state relations with the
             Kurds in both the Ottoman and the Republican periods.

1982   In 1982 **Riza Olgun**, author of *The Socialist Movement from the
             Communist Party to the Present*, was reportedly serving a sentence
             of seven-and-a-half years' imprisonment.

1985–   In September newspaper columnist and historian **Ilhan Bardakçi**
             was convicted of treason and sentenced to seventeen years' impris-

onment. He and a Turkish translator at the Libyan diplomatic mission were found guilty of espionage for Libya, Syria, and Iraq. His sentence was reduced to fifteen years after a retrial by a military court in Ankara.

1986–87　In November 1986 historian **Halil Berktay** (1947–), a specialist in the history of Turkish nationalism, was arrested on charges of "communist propaganda" after having participated in a panel discussion on "Intra-Party Democracy in a Socialist Party" organized by the monthly *Saçak* in July. In February 1987 he was released following a protest campaign abroad. An assistant at the political science faculty (Ankara), later an associate professor and assistant-director of the Atatürk Institute at Boğaziçi University, Istanbul, he had already been detained and arrested in May–June 1972. On that occasion he had been tortured at the headquarters of the National Intelligence Organization and awaited trial for at least two years. In 2000 he worked at Sabanci University, Istanbul.

In December thirty-nine tons of books, periodicals, and newspapers were pulped, including *The Penguin Map of the World, National Geographic Atlas of the World*, the Turkish editions of the *Encyclopaedia Britannica*, and of the *Nouveau, petit Larousse illustré*. The editor of the Turkish *Encyclopaedia Britannica* was arrested because of the encyclopedia's references to the Armenian people. In March 1987 twenty similar foreign publications were declared "means of separatist propaganda" by the Turkish authorities for containing articles or maps related to Armenian or Kurdish history.

1988　In November the *Encyclopedia of Modern Times* was confiscated for "containing articles insulting Atatürk".

1989　On 12 May the Turkish government opened parts of the Ottoman archives (the so-called prime minister's archives) for scholarly research, including documents related to the 1915 genocide against the Armenians. In January historian Tunçay [q.v. 1973] of Istanbul had declared in a newspaper interview that he was concerned that the archives might have been searched and any documents detrimental to Turkey's official view on the genocide removed. The archives of prohibited or dissolved organizations, for example the Republican People's Party, had been destroyed. Before 1985 access to the archives had been very difficult and prior to 1989 all archival material of the post–May 1915 period had been closed to scholars.

1989–99　There were several cases of censorship in which conflicting interpretations of Kurdish history played a major role. Writer and television journalist **Günay Arslan**, a Turk of Kurdish origin, wrote the book *History in Mourning, 33 Bullets* (first edition December 1989;

second edition July 1991), about the 1943 extrajudicial execution on
the orders of a Turkish general of thirty-three Kurdish peasants suspected of stealing horses and about contemporary events in southeastern Turkey against this historical background. The first edition
won a prize, but it was confiscated and its author was prosecuted.
In March 1991 Arslan was sentenced to six years and three months'
imprisonment for disseminating separatist propaganda. The sentence
was based on a Criminal Code article that was repealed in April
1991. Subsequently the conviction was annulled and the return of
the confiscated copies of the book was ordered. The book's reprint,
however, led to a new prosecution. In January 1993 Arslan was
sentenced under the new Prevention of Terrorism Act to twenty
months' imprisonment and fined for disseminating separatist propaganda. In October 1993, after having attempted to leave Turkey, he
began serving the sentence. In January 1995 he was released. Lawyer
Ahmet Zeki Okçuoglu (1950–), a Turk of Kurdish origin, had spoken in a round-table debate about which the magazine *Demokrat*
published an article entitled "The Past and the Present of the Kurdish
Problem" in May 1991. In March 1993 Okçuoglu was sentenced to
twenty months' imprisonment and fined for disseminating separatist
propaganda. The magazine was confiscated. A book by writer **Edip
Polat** (1962–), entitled *We Made Each Dawn a Newroz* (first edition
May 1991; second edition November 1991), in which he related,
inter alia, historical episodes marked by Kurdish rebel movements
in Turkey (including the 1925 rebellion of Sheikh Said), was confiscated in December 1991. In December 1992 Polat was sentenced
to two years' imprisonment and fined for disseminating separatist
propaganda. In December 1991 *The Song of a Rebellion: Dersim*,
an anthology of poems by psychologist **Hüseyin Karatas** (1963–),
a Turk of Kurdish origin, was confiscated. In Dersim (renamed Tunceli), fifteen violent riots involving clashes between Kurdish clans
and government forces had taken place between 1847 and 1938. In
February 1993 Karatas was sentenced to twenty months' imprisonment and fined for disseminating separatist propaganda. Journalist
and economics professor **Fikret Baskaya** (1940–) wrote a book
*Westernization, Modernization, Development—Collapse of a Para-
digm; An Introduction to the Critique of the Official Ideology* (Istanbul April 1991) which described the socio-economic evolution of
Turkey since 1919 and criticized Turkey's policy of "colonizing
Kurdistan". In August 1993, Baskaya was sentenced to two years'
imprisonment (later reduced to twenty months) and fined for disseminating separatist propaganda, after the Court of Cassation had annulled an earlier acquittal. His publisher **Mehemet Selim Okçuoglu**
(1964–) was sentenced to six months' imprisonment and fined. In
March 1994, Baskaya was dismissed from his lectureship at the Uni-

versity of Ankara. The book was confiscated when the sixth edition appeared in October 1997. In July 1999 the European Court of Human Rights judged that the freedom of expression of Arslan, Okçuoglu, Polat, Karatas, and Baskaya had been violated.

1991–   In August 1991 **Sinami Orhan**, editor of the Islamic political magazine *Ak-Dogus* (Bright Dawn), was prosecuted and sentenced to four months' imprisonment for publishing controversial historical documents concerning Atatürk. Orhan began the sentence in May 1992.

1992   In November the Kurdish Institute in Istanbul was raided by the police, who arrested five people and confiscated books and magazines on Kurdish language, literature, and history.

1994–   In April 1994 journalist **Ragip Duran** (?1954–) wrote an article for the journal *Özgür Gündem* (Free Agenda), "Apo 91/Öcalan 94", in which he analyzed two interviews he had conducted with Workers Party of Kurdistan leader Abdullah Öcalan, also known as Apo. In the article he made a casual comparison between Öcalan and the Italian hero of independence Giuseppe Garibaldi (1807–82). On the basis of this comparison, he was accused of separatist propaganda and sentenced to ten months' imprisonment in December 1995. In October 1997 the Supreme Court confirmed the sentence, which he began in June 1998.

1995–   German historian **Hilmar Kaiser** (1962–) was forbidden access to the Turkish archives, where he had done research on the Armenian genocide since 1991.

In the spring of 1995, the book *Genocide As a Question of National and International Law: The 1915 Armenian Event and Its Consequences* written by **Vahakn Dadrian**, former professor of sociology at State University College, Geneseo, N.Y., United States (1970–91), was banned. The publisher of the book's Turkish translation, **Ayşe Nur Zarakolu** (1947–), director of Belge publishers, known for her books on minority rights and Turkey's military history and already serving thirty months' imprisonment for publishing *The Armenian Taboo* (originally: *Les Arméniens, histoire d'une génocide*), by French historian **Yves Ternon** (1932–), faced prosecution for separatist propaganda. In December 1995 she was acquitted for this book (but charges for other books were upheld). Zarakolu had served prison terms in 1982 (for publishing documents from the Turkish Communist Party's founding congress), 1984, 1994 (for publishing one of the 1991 books of Beşikçi [q.v. 1979–]), and 1996. A new trial was to start against her in connection with the seizure in January 1997 of *Disaster of Dersim* by **Haydar Isik** (1937–).

In April writer and journalist **Ahmet Altan** (1950–) was dismissed, charged with "inciting racial hatred", and given a twenty-month suspended sentence because in a satirical article he had suggested that the Turkish independence war following World War I (1920–22) had been led by Kurds rather than Turks.

1996   In June the Islamist-run town council of Kayseri in central Turkey banned *Istanbul beneath My Wings*, a popular Turkish film portraying Murad IV (ruled 1622–40) as bisexual. The mayor declared that the film "approaches our history from a distorted viewpoint".

1997   In February the second Turkish-language edition of *Gladio, das Erbe des kalten Krieges: Der Nato-Geheimbund und sein deutscher Vorläufer* (Reinbek 1991; Gladio: The Legacy of the Cold War), a book by **Leo Müller** (1959–), was confiscated and both the publisher and the translator were tried for, inter alia, "inciting racial hatred". In September they were given a suspended sentence and a fine. Both sentences were under appeal.

In February the center-left daily *Radikal* was seized because it reprinted an article from the French weekly *Figaro Magazine*, "Turkey: Army against the Islamists", written by Islamist intellectual **Abdurrahman Dilipak** (1949–). The article described Atatürk as an "authoritarian military ruler".

[1997] The University of California at Los Angeles refused to allow the Turkish government to fund a chair in Ottoman studies because the government attached conditions to their $1 million offer that would have forced scholars to ignore the 1915 genocide of Armenians.

2000   In February *The Chronological Album of the Kurds: 1900 to 2000*, a book distributed by the pro-Kurdish daily *Özgür Bakis* (Free Perspective), was banned on the grounds that it was "separatist propaganda".

Officials put pressure on the Microsoft company to modify an article in its digital encyclopedia *Encarta* that called the 1915 murder of thousands of Armenians "the first genocide of the twentieth century". The authors, including professor of political science and Armenian history **Ronald Grigor Suny**, were asked to "tone down" the article and remove the word *genocide*.

In October officials warned the United States that it risked losing the use of a military base for launching air patrols over northern Iraq if the House of Representatives approved a resolution accusing Turkey of genocide against Armenians in 1915–23. The resolution was not put to the vote.

Reporter **Julide Kalic** was beaten and interrogated after photographing a police attack on a remembrance day meeting for Haci Bektâs Veli (?1248–?1337), a dervish and scholar who founded a Sufi order.

On 23 October Istanbul State Security Court charged **Akin Birdal**, vice president of the International Federation for Human Rights and former president of the Turkish Association for Human Rights, with "incitement to hatred" for his criticism of Turkey's stance on the 1915 Armenian genocide.

Also see France (1995: Lewis), Germany (1985–: Engelberg), Greece (1978–81: Koundouros), USSR (1964–: Ovannisian).

SOURCES

American Association for the Advancement of Science, *Directory of Persecuted Scientists, Engineers, and Health Professionals* (Washington 1997–98) 33.

Amnesty International, *Human Rights Are Women's Right* (London 1995) 74–75.

———, *Newsletter*, August 1994: 2.

———, *Report* (London) 1980: 300; 1982: 295; 1983: 281; 1984: 307; 1987: 317; 1991: 229; 1992: 258; 1993: 290; 1995: 291; 1996: 20; 1999: 337.

———, *Turkey: No Security without Human Rights* (London 1996) 13–14.

Article 19, *Information, Freedom and Censorship: World Report* (London) 1988: 227, 228; 1991: 328–30, 437.

Bacon, E. ed., *The Great Archaeologists and Their Discoveries As Originally Reported in the Pages of the Illustrated London News* (Indianapolis/New York 1976) 356, 421.

Berkes, N., *The Development of Secularism in Turkey* (originally Turkish 1964; London 1998) xv–xxxii.

Berktay, H., "Der Aufstieg und die gegenwärtige Krise der nationalistischen Geschichtsschreibung in der Türkei", *Periplus*, 1991: 122.

Bernath, M., & F. von Schroeder eds., *Biographisches Lexikon zur Geschichte Südosteuropas*, vol. 2 (Munich 1976) 471–72.

Beşikçi, I., H. Alderkamp, & Y. Yeşilgöz, *Ismail Beşikçi: Kemalisme, Turkese wetenschapsbeoefening en de Koerdische kwestie* (Amsterdam 1998) 59–73.

Boyd, K. ed., *Encyclopedia of Historians and Historical Writing* (London/Chicago 1999) 73–74, 339–40, 560–62, 657–59.

Chaliand, G. ed., *Les Kurdes et le Kurdistan: La Question nationale kurde au Proche-Orient* (Paris 1978) 128.

Charny, I.W. ed., *Genocide: A Critical Bibliographic Review* (London) vol. 1 (1988): 8, 11, 18–19; vol. 2 (1991): xii–xiv, xx–xxii, 12–13.

A Crime of Silence: The Armenian Genocide, ed. the Permanent Peoples' Tribunal (originally French 1984; London 1985).

Dyer, G., "Turkish 'Falsifiers' and Armenian 'Deceivers': Historiography and the Armenian Massacres", *Middle Eastern Studies*, January 1976: 99–107.

European Court of Human Rights, *Case of Arslan versus Turkey: Judgment* (WWW-text; Strasbourg, 8 July 1999).

————, *Case of Baskaya and Okçuoglu versus Turkey: Judgment* (WWW-text; Strasbourg, 8 July 1999).

————, *Case of Karatas versus Turkey: Judgment* (WWW-text; Strasbourg, 8 July 1999).

————, *Case of Okçuoglu versus Turkey: Judgment* (WWW-text; Strasbourg, 8 July 1999).

————, *Case of Polat versus Turkey: Judgment* (WWW-text; Strasbourg, 8 July 1999).

Fermi, L., *Illustrious Immigrants: The Intellectual Migration from Europe 1930–41* (Chicago/London 1968) 66–70, 253, 359–63.

Foss, C., "The Turkish View of Armenian History: A Vanishing Nation", in: R.G. Hovannisian ed., *The Armenian Genocide: History, Politics, Ethics* (Houndmills 1992) viii, 263–64, 273–74.

Freitag, U., "A Turkish Vision of History and a Greek Answer", *Storia della storiografia*, 1994, no.26: 132–35.

Gallagher, N.E. ed., *Approaches to the History of the Middle East: Interviews with Leading Middle East Historians* (Reading, UK 1994) 7, 29, 154, 161.

Gunter, M.M., *"Pursuing the Just Cause of Their People": A Study of Contemporary Armenian Terrorism* (New York/London 1986) 3, 5–6, 17–18, 129–31, 139–40.

Heper, M., *Historical Dictionary of Turkey* (Metuchen 1994) 99–101, 207–8.

Heyd, U., "The Later Ottoman Empire in Rumelia and Anatolia", *Cambridge History of Islam*, vol. 1 (Cambridge 1970) 373.

Human Rights Watch, *Ifex Alert*, 23 August 1996; 7 July 1997.

————, *World Report* (New York) 1997: 244–45, 326; 1998: xxxix, 286, 375, 449, 454–55; 1999: 235, 295.

Index on Censorship, 1/73: 8, 17–18, 20; 2/73: xiii; 2/74: 41–43, 47; 6/78: 52, 67; 1/82: 13; 1/83: 49; 3/83: 47; 5/84: 5–6; 7/86: 46; 4/87: 39; 5/87: 41; 8/87: 40; 2/89: 40; 6/90: 42; 3/93: 40; 3/94: 185; 1/95: 251; 4/95: 188; 6/95: 186; 2/96: 104; 4/96: 113; 2/97: 100; 4/97: 127; 1/98: 34; 2/98: 104; 3/99: 117; 5/99: 145; 6/99: 102, 254; 1/00: 106; 2/00: 128–29; 3/00: 109, 6/00: 191–2, 1/01: 125; 3/01: 119–20.

International PEN Writers in Prison Committee, *Half-Yearly Caselist* (London) 1997: 51, 53–55; 1998: 49, 52.

Israel Exploration Journal, 1968: 133 (Landsberger).

Karpat, K.H., "An Update on Turkish Archives", *Middle East Studies Association Bulletin*, 1989: 181–87.

Keesing's Record of World Events (CD-rom version) (Bardakçi).

Kohl, P.L., & G.R. Tsetskhladze, "Nationalism, Politics, and the Practice of Archaeology in the Caucasus", in: P.L. Kohl & C. Fawcett eds., *Nationalism, Politics, and the Practice of Archaeology* (Cambridge 1995) 170.

Kouymjian, D., "The Destruction of Armenian Historical Monuments As a Continuation of the Turkish Policy of Genocide", in: *A Crime of Silence* 1985: 173–76.

Kuper, L., "The Turkish Genocide against the Armenians and the United Nations Memory Hole", in: Kuper, *Genocide* (Harmondsworth 1982) 219–20.

Kurdistan Informations-Zentrum, *Ismail Beşikçi: A Life in the Service of Truth* (WWW-text 1994).

Mellaart, J., "Western Asia during the Neolithic and the Chalcolithic (about 12,000–5,000 years ago)", in: S.J. De Laet ed., *History of Humanity*, vol. 1 (Paris/London 1994) 425–40.

MESA Bulletin, 1991: 311–12 (Halasi-Kun).

Meyer, K.E., *The Plundered Past* (London 1974) 70–73.

NRC Handelsblad, 31 October 1998: 49 (Mellaart); 27 May 2000: 51 (Kaiser).

Peleg, I., "Freedom of Expression in the Third World: The Human Rights of Writers in Developing Countries", in: I. Peleg ed., *Patterns of Censorship around the World* (Boulder 1993) 115.

"Reforming the Archive System in Turkey and Making Its Use by Researchers Easier", *Studies on Turkish–Arab Relations*, 1989: 109–16.

Simon, R.S., P. Mattar, & R.W. Bulliet eds., *Encyclopedia of the Modern Middle East* (New York 1996) 1040–41.

Strauss, H.A., & W. Röder eds., *International Biographical Dictionary of Central European Émigrés 1933–1945*, vol. 2 (New York 1983) 232–33, 433–34, 688.

Strauss, J., "Neue Bestimmungen über die Benutzung der Archive in der Türkei", *Die Welt des Islams*, 1990: 219–25.

Suny, R.G., *Looking toward Ararat: Armenia in Modern History* (Bloomington/Indianapolis 1993) 96.

Vidal-Naquet, P., *Assassins of Memory: Essays on the Denial of the Holocaust* (originally French 1987; New York 1992) 120–21.

―――, By Way of a Preface and by Power of One Word", in: *A Crime of Silence* 1985: 3–5.

Vryonis, S. Jr., *The Turkish State and History: Clio Meets the Grey Wolf* (Thessaloniki 1991) 116–17.

Woolf, D.R. ed., *A Global Encyclopedia of Historical Writing* (New York/London 1998) 255–56, 426–27.

Yapp, M.E., *The Near East since the First World War* (London/New York 1991) 156.

Zürcher, E.J., *Political Opposition in the Early Turkish Republic: The Progressive Republican Party 1924–1925* (Leiden 1991) 5–6.

TURKMENISTAN

pre-1991 *See* Union of Soviet Socialist Republics (USSR).

1996– In October 1996 **Marat Durdyev**, a prominent journalist, Academy of Sciences member, and author of more than twenty books on Turkmen historical and cultural issues, was reportedly incarcerated in a psychiatric hospital in Ashgabat for more than a month after he had published a critical article about Turkmenistan in the Russian newspaper *Pravda*. Released in November, he was in poor condition. He was dismissed from the editorial boards of the publications with which he was associated as well as from his teaching positions. His academy membership was reportedly revoked.

2000 President Saparmurad Niyazov ordered that the entire printing of a new Turkmen history textbook be burned.

SOURCES

Committee to Protect Journalists, *Ifex Alert*, 23 December 1996: 1.

Human Right Watch, *World Report 2001* (Washington 2000) 331.

U

UGANDA

1971–79   Among the thousands of refugees under President Idi Amin's rule (January 1971–April 1979) was **Semakula Kiwanuka** (1939–), history professor at the Makerere University history department, Kampala.

In the same period, British historian and school director **Graham Heddle** was sent to a school in a remote area, reportedly because he was white. Later he went to Gambia, where he worked for another six years. He then returned to the United Kingdom.

1972   Historian **James Bertin Webster** (1927–), former lecturer at Ibadan University, Nigeria, (until 1967) and professor at the Makerere University history department (1967–72), left Uganda after Idi Amin's coup. He went to Chancellor College, University of Malawi, where he became full professor and head of the department of history and government.

1973–   In April 1973 Kenyan scholar **Ali Mazrui** (1933–), professor and head of the department of political science and public administration at Makerere University (1963–73), left Uganda because of "restrictions on academic freedom and the insecurity of faculty members and students". Under the previous government, he had been publicly denounced by President Milton Obote for his support of an imprisoned editor. A specialist in the contemporary history of Africa and editor of volume 8 (*Africa since 1935*) of the *UNESCO General History of Africa* (1993), he became professor of political science at the University of Michigan, Ann Arbor, United States (1974–91),

Albert Luthuli Professor-at-Large at Jos University, Nigeria (1981–87), Andrew White Professor-at-Large at Cornell University, Ithaca, N.Y. (1986–92), Albert Schweitzer Professor in the Humanities and director of the Institute of Global Cultural Studies at the State University of New York, Binghamton (1991–), Ibn Khaldun Professor-at-Large at the School of Islamic and Social Sciences, Leesburg, Va., and Walter Rodney Professor at the University of Guyana, Georgetown, Guyana (1997–98). He was a member of the Group of Eminent Persons appointed in 1992 by the Organization of African Unity to explore issues of African Reparations for Enslavement and Colonization.

SOURCES

Boyd, K. ed., *Encyclopedia of Historians and Historical Writing* (London/Chicago 1999) 787–88.

Duffy, J., M. Frey, & M. Sins eds., *International Directory of Scholars and Specialists in African Studies* (Waltham, Mass. 1978) 309.

Knoppert, R., personal communication, December 1996.

Kyemba, H., *A State of Blood: The Inside Story of Idi Amin* (New York 1977) 283.

Mazrui, A.A., *Soldiers and Kinsmen: The Making of a Military Ethnocracy* (London 1975) 3.

Mutunga, W., & M. Kiai, "The State of Academic Freedom in Kenya 1992–94", in: Codesria, *The State of Academic Freedom in Africa 1995* (Dakar 1996) 81.

NRC-Handelsblad, 30 November 1996: 49 (Heddle).

Nyeko, B. ed., *Uganda* (Oxford 1996) 42–43.

Vansina, J., *Living with Africa* (Madison 1994) 116, 273–74.

Woolf, D.R. ed., *A Global Encyclopedia of Historical Writing* (New York/London 1998) 606.

UKRAINE

pre-1991   *See* Union of Soviet Socialist Republics (USSR).

1996   In August the Hungarian community was refused permission to erect a monument and hold a religious service in the Verecke pass. The monument and service were intended to mark the 1,100th anniversary of the crossing of Magyar tribes through the Verecke pass into the Carpathian basin in the year 896.

1997   In June the reconstruction of a cemetery in Lviv was the subject of a controversy between Poles and Ukrainians. In the cemetery, destroyed by the Soviets after the war, many members of the Polish youth unit "Eaglets" (who died in the Polish–Ukrainian conflict of 1918–19) were interred. The controversy concerned the inscriptions on the graves.

SOURCES

De Baets, A., *Navchal'ni programi z istorïï ta tsenzura pidruchnikiv—Khronologiia tsenzuri istorichnoï dumki v Ukraïni (1945–2000)* (Educational Programs on History and Censorship of Textbooks—Chronology of the Censorship of Historical Thought in the Ukraine [1945–2000]) in: M. Telus & Y. Shapoval eds., *Ukraïnc'ka Istorichna Didaktika: Mizhnarodnij dialog (History Didactics in the Ukraine: International Dialogue on Textbook Problems)* (Kiev 2000) 174–210. *Index on Censorship*; 5/96: 105; 6/97: 164–65.

UNION OF SOVIET SOCIALIST REPUBLICS (USSR)

Almost from the beginning, Soviet historiography was guided by Marxism-Leninism, the laws of historical materialism (histomat), and partiinost (party-mindedness or party spirit). It was characterized by frequent retroactive rewriting imposed by the guidelines of the Communist Party of the Soviet Union (CPSU). Themes outside the Marxist-Leninist canon were likely to be ostracized; themes within the canon had to be handled according to orthodoxy. Contemporary history was an especially dangerous field. Among the *belye piatna* (blank spots) were the following: the origins of the early Russian state, especially the Normanist theory; the Mongols (1240–1380); the Tsars, especially Ivan IV the Terrible (1533–84) and Peter the Great (1694–1725); Russian expansion and imperialism; the partitions of Poland (1772, 1793, 1795); Napoleon's 1812 Russian campaign; non-Bolshevik revolutionaries; CPSU history (especially, the inner-party struggles), its leaders (especially Vladimir Lenin, Joseph Stalin, Leon Trotsky, Lev Kamenev, Grigory Zinoviev, Nikolai Bukharin, Sergei Kirov, Aleksei Rykov, Lavrenty Beria, and Nikita Khrushchev) and its secret police; foreign relations; the nationalities policy, including nationalism, the incorporation of non-Russian nations into the USSR (especially in 1917–21, 1940, and during national uprisings), and the mass deportations of Baltic citizens, Volga Germans, Crimean Tatars, Meskhetian Turks, Karachai, Kalmyks, Balkars, Chechens, Ingush, Caucasian Greeks, Kurds, and others during World War II; religion and ecclesiastical history; pogroms and Jewry; nobility; and such specific contemporary events as the 1917 February and October revolutions, the 1918 murder of the last tsar, Nikolai II, and his family, the civil war (1918–21), the dictatorial nature of the Soviet state under Lenin, the New Economic Policy (1921–29) and its accompanying political repression, the suppression of the church, the forced mass collectivization of agriculture, the dekulakization (1929–33) and the ensuing famine (1932–33), the repression, purge trials, and mass executions of the 1930s (including the 1936–39 "Great Purge"), the secret protocols of the 23 August 1939 Molotov–Ribbentrop nonaggression pact (which led to the 1939 occupation of Poland and to the 1940 forced incorporation of Estonia, Latvia, and Lithuania into the USSR), the 1940 Katyń massacre, the invasion of the USSR by the German Army on 22 June 1941 and Soviet military strategy on the eve of and during World War II, the number of

Soviet losses in the war, the suppression of the June 1953 uprising in the German Democratic Republic (GDR), of the 1956 Hungarian Revolution, and of the 1968 Prague Spring, the dissident movement and Jewish emigration under Leonid Brezhnev, and the 1979–89 war in Afghanistan. A permanent complaint during the whole period was the severely restricted and unequal access to the archives, with huge quantities of classified documents. The Chief Archival Administration, *Glavarkhiv*, was under the control of the Komitet gosudarstvennoi bezopasnosti (KGB; Committee of State Security) and its predecessors from 1938 to 1960–61. Many documents on CPSU history were destroyed. Genuine historical photos were subjected to retouching so that inconvenient people would disappear; some figures were even removed from the negatives. Most Western historical works were either banned or only available in the special sections (*spetskhran*) of archives or libraries. After a period of relaxation from 1953 to 1964 (the Khruschev era), control was again tightened. For two decades (1964–85), suppression of research into the Stalinist period was the most serious obstacle in the field of history. Until the late 1970s, no foreigner was allowed to use any archives of the post-1920 period. From 1986–87, however, the continuing calls for *glasnost* (openness) eased or lifted restrictions from many formerly proscribed subjects. Several aspects of USSR history began to be publicly reexamined. Many victims of the repression were rehabilitated. Archival access improved during the last years of the USSR and the first of her successor states, especially in Russia in 1986–93, but the KGB Archives and the Presidential Archive (APRF, containing, inter alia, documents of the CPSU Politburo and General-Secretaries) in particular retained a privileged status.

Among the historians and others concerned with the past who emigrated after 1917 (and were living in exile after 1944) were the following:

1917–23 **Mark Aldanov** (?1886–1957), **Grigori Adamovich** (1894–1971), **Lev Bagrov** (1881–1957), **Nikolai Beliaev** (?1883–1955), **Nina Berberova** (1901–93), **Elias Bickerman** (1897–1981), **Pavel Buryshkin** (1887–1959), **Vladimir Golenischev** (1856–1947), **Mikhail Karpovich** (1888–1959), **Anton Kartashov** (1875–1960), **Georgy Katkov** (1903–85), **Pyotr Kovalevsky** (1901–), **Alexandre Koyré** (1892–1964), **Viktor Leontovich** (1902–59), **Sergei Melgunov** (1879–1956), **Vladimir Minorsky** (1877–1966), **Boris Nikolaevsky** (1887–1966), **Boris Nolde** (1876–1948), **Aleksandr Pogodin** (1872–1947), **Sergei Pushkarev** (1888–1984), **Mikhail Rostovtzeff** (1870–1952), **Leonid Savelov** (1868–1947), **Pitirim Sorokin** (1889–1968), **Fedor Stepun** (1884–1965), **George Vernadsky** (1887–1973), **Vladimir Vikentiev** (1882–1960), and **Nikolai Zernov** (1898–1980).

1924–44 **Abdurachman Avtorkhanov** (1908–), **Sergei Lesnoi** (1909–68), **August Mälk** (1900–1987), **Nikolai Pervushin** (1899–?), **Boris Sa-**

pir (1902–89), **Konstantin Shteppa** (1896–1958), **Arveds Svabe** (1888–1959), **Aleksandr Vasiliev** (1867–1953), and **Max Weinreich** (1894–1969).

Edgars Dunsdorfs (1904–), **Vasily Eliashevich** (1875–1957), **Antony Florovsky** (1890–1968), **Georgy Florovsky** (1893–1979), **Joseph Klausner** (1874–1958), **Mikhail Kutuzov-Tolstoi** (1896–1980), **Georgy Lukomsky** (1884–1952), **Vladimir Riabushinsky** (1872–1955), **Pyotr Savitsky** (1895–1968), **Aleksandr Soloviev** (1890–1971), **Arnold Soom** (1900–1977), and **Nikolai Talberg** (1886–1977).

Among the young refugees who became historians in their new country were:

S.P. Andolenko, Nikolai Andreev (1908–82), **N.S. Eliseev, V.S. Eliseev, S.S. Obolensky, George Ostrogorski** (1902–76), **Léon Poliakov** (1910–97), **Michael Postan** (1899–1981), **Marc Raeff** (1923–), and **Aleksandr Shmeman.**

1927–47 From 1927 to 1947, *Vizantiysky Vremennik* (Byzantine Journal) was suspended. In 1948 it was criticized for attempting to cooperate with Byzantine scholars outside the USSR.

1935–53 In 1935 art historian **Nikolai Punin** (1888–1953), third husband of poetess Anna Akhmatova, was arrested. In 1953 he died while in internal exile.

1937–45 **Stasik Liudkiewicz,** Jewish history student at Moscow State University, was arrested soon after his father, a Polish revolutionary who had emigrated to the USSR. He spent five years in the camps and another three in exile. After his release he went to Poland, where he eventually became head of Polish television. After the 1956 events there, he advocated greater democratization and in 1957 he was dismissed. He became a secretary on the editorial staff of a Warsaw evening newspaper. After the 1968 anti-Semitic campaign, he went into exile in Israel, and later in Sweden.

1937–55 **Yevgenya Ginzburg** (1906–77), history professor at Kazan University, Russia, and journalist, was imprisoned, interned, and exiled as the wife of an "enemy of the people" (an important Bolshevik mayor). In 1955 she was released and in 1956 rehabilitated, but her memoirs were banned. They circulated in samizdat (self-publishing) and were published abroad (*Journey into the Whirlwind*, London/ New York 1967).

1938– Two historical films by director **Sergei Eisenstein** (1898–1948), *Aleksandr Nevsky* (1938) and *Ivan the Terrible* (part 1: 1944, part

2: 1946), were severely hampered by political restrictions. In France distribution of his 1925–26 film *Battleship Potemkin*, depicting a successful rebellion against political authority, was forbidden outside specialized cinema clubs until 1952. The French police burned every copy that they could find. From September 1926 to 1954, the British Board of Film Censors refused it a certificate, in case it should foment mutiny in the Royal Navy. It was the second-longest running ban in British cinema. In Brazil after 1964, Plínio Sussekind da Rocha, director of the film library of the University of Rio de Janeiro, spent three weeks in prison for possessing copies of *Battleship Potemkin*. The copies were confiscated.

1938–53   In 1938 **Aleksandr Todorsky** (1894–1965), corps commander, head of the Air Force Academy, director of the higher educational system of the Commissariat of Defense, was arrested and spent fifteen years in prison camps. Released in 1953, he was eventually promoted to Lieutenant General. As a military historian, he compiled official statistics showing that Stalin's terror had destroyed virtually the entire Soviet officer corps.

History student **Anton Antonov-Ovseyenko** (1920–) was the son of the executed V.A. Antonov-Ovseyenko, an Old Bolshevik (a prominent CPSU member who survived the Lenin era) who led the seizure of the Winter Palace in October 1917. In 1938, the son was expelled from a Moscow institute for refusing to renounce his father as an "enemy of the people". He was reinstated on appeal and received his diploma in 1939. Arrested in 1940, released and rearrested on 23 June 1941, one day after the German invasion, he was imprisoned from 1941 to 1953 on charges of "terrorism" and "anti-Soviet agitation", except for a brief period at liberty in 1943. He was released from the Arctic camps in late 1953 and judicially exonerated in 1957. In 1960 he received permission to return to Moscow, where he began publishing historical studies of the revolution and collecting materials for his father's biography. In September 1967 he signed a letter of forty-three children of CPSU victims of the Stalinist terror that warned against neo-Stalinism. His 1980 book *The Time of Stalin: Portrait of a Tyranny*, unpublishable in the USSR, appeared in New York.

1939–58   From 1939 to 1958, historian **Mikhail Frenkin** (1910–86) was imprisoned in labor camps. After his release he worked at the Moscow Historical Archives Institute. In the early 1930s, he had already been arrested and imprisoned for one year.

1939–   During and after World War II, **Mikhail Miller** (1882–1968), historian and archeologist, specialist in the ancient history of the Don and Azov regions, was a prisoner in a German camp and a camp for displaced persons in West Germany. He became an émigré and died in Munich.

1944–   History student **Dora Shturman** (born **Shtok**; 1923–) was arrested and sentenced to five years in a labor camp. She worked as a journalist, critic, and sociologist but left the USSR in 1977 and settled in Israel.

Literary historian **Arkady Belinkov** (1921–70) was arrested for his unpublished novel *A Notebook of Feelings*, dealing with the 1939 nonaggression pact, and sentenced to death (later commuted to eight years in a labor camp). Although sentenced to an additional twenty-five years for his writings in 1950, he was released in late 1956. In 1958 he was dismissed from his lectureship at the Gorky Literary Institute. He remained active as a dissident until his immigration to the United States in 1968.

1945–55 In 1945 literary historian **Pavel Negretov** (1923–), who had lived under German occupation during the war, was repatriated and imprisoned in a labor camp in Vorkuta (1945–55). In 1966 he graduated from Leningrad University by correspondence.

1945–89 The official interpretation of Dagestani leader Shamil (who in 1834–59 had led the struggle against the Russian conquest) as a progressive figure was challenged for years, coinciding with the deportation and repression of the Chechens by Stalin. From 1945 Shamil was branded as an agent of British and Ottoman imperialism; his resistance movement was called reactionary. In 1945 **Anna Zaks** could not defend her doctoral thesis, "Tashev Khadzhi, Comrade-in-Arms of Shamil, and the Chechen Uprising of 1840". It was accepted in 1950 only, during a brief relaxation in Shamil's official condemnation. Despite repeated attempts, the thesis remained unpublished until at least 1989 [q.v. Azerbaijan 1950–56: Guseinov, Magomedov].

[?]   Soon after completing his doctorate, philosopher **Mikhail Petrov** (1923–87) was dismissed from the CPSU for his liberal views. He then became a historian of science, but most of his works were banned.

1945   In June the *Istorichesky zhurnal* (Historical Journal), successor of *Borba klassov* (Class Struggle) since January 1937, was liquidated, reportedly because it was edited in the spirit of the alliance between the USSR and the United States. It was succeeded by the monthly *Voprosy istorii* (Problems of History).

1946–47 In 1946 historian of Muscovy **Pavel Smirnov** (1882–1947) was criticized by *Voprosy istorii* and others because of an article the monthly had asked him to write "for discussion" on the problem of the formation of the Russian centralized state. He was charged with "Pokrovskyism" (Pokrovsky [q.v. 1980] was the leading Soviet historian fallen into disgrace after his death in 1932) and lack of patriotism for failing to understand the role of national consciousness developed during the struggle against the Mongols. The wave of criticism undermined his health and may have caused his death. No obituaries were published. An account of the memorial service held in his honor at the Historical Archives Institute (where he had worked in 1938–47) in May 1947 was not published until 1981. From 1912 to 1923, Smirnov taught at Kiev University; from 1927 to 1934, he "involuntarily" taught at the Central Asian University in Tashkent: he was dismissed from both positions, presumably for political reasons. His work at the time, defending the Normanist origin of the Russian state, was denounced as attributing too much influence to the Varangians (the Normans headed by Rurik). In 1943 he was awarded the Stalin Prize for his work on the townsmen and their class struggle up to the mid-seventeenth century. It was published posthumously in two volumes in 1947–48, but only volume 1 was reviewed twice.

1947–53   In December 1947 **Nina Gagen-Torn [Hagen-Thorn]** (1900–86), poet, historian, and ethnographer of northern Russia and the Volga region, was arrested at the USSR Academy of Sciences library. She was imprisoned until 1953 and rehabilitated afterward. She had already been imprisoned from 1937 to 1942. In one of the camps, she reportedly taught Russian literature and history to a group of ill Ukrainian girls.

1947–   **Solomon Lurye** (1891–1964), historian of ancient Greek thought and Cretan history, used the script of ancient Cyprus to criticize the Soviet totalitarian system in his notebooks. He kept his notes even at the height of the anticosmopolitan campaign, when they could have been seized and deciphered.

1947–   Among the victims of the (anti-Semitic) campaign against cosmopolitanism (1947–49; defined as "a reactionary bourgeois ideology" indifferent to patriotism and advocating a "world government") were the following:

Isaak Mints (1896–1991), academician (1946–) and historian of the October Revolution and civil war, came under attack. Together with other historians such as his pupil I.M. Razgon, he was accused of monopolizing the history of Soviet society. His book *The History of the USSR* (Moscow 1946) was criticized. He was removed from the *Voprosy istorii* editorial board and forced to leave the USSR

Academy of Sciences History Institute for several years. He retained, however, his chair in Soviet history at the Lenin Pedagogical Institute, Moscow.

From 1947 to 1953, **Grigory Pomerants** (1918–), Jewish philosopher and bibliographer, was imprisoned on a political charge. Later he became the author of many samizdat articles on, inter alia, history, including "On the Role of Individual Moral Outlook in the Life of a Historical Group" (1965, published in the collection *Feniks-66*, revised 1969).

Essay on the History of Modern Turkey, a book by **Anatoly Miller** (1901–73), historian and orientalist, senior research associate at the USSR Academy of Sciences History Institute (1941–65) and later at the Institute of the Peoples of Asia (1966–1973?), adviser at the Teheran (1943) and Yalta (1945) conferences, was condemned. After three years of persecution, Miller preferred not to publish anymore. He devoted himself to the ten-volume collective work *World History*.

The 1947 doctoral dissertation of **Yioganson Zilberfarb** (died 1968), historian of socialist ideas at the USSR Academy of Sciences History Institute, entitled *The Socialist Philosophy of Charles Fourier and His Place in the History of Socialist Thought in the First Half of the Nineteenth Century*, was not approved by the Higher Qualifications Commission until 1964 because academician Pyotr Pospelov (1898–1979), teacher of Lenin's wife, director of the Institute of Marxism-Leninism, editor of *Pravda*, and member of the CPSU Central Committee (CC), rejected it and called it "bourgeois-objectivist" (which meant "neglecting the class struggle and revering the facts"). Throughout this period and also after he had eventually become a doctor of historical sciences, Zilberfarb remained unemployed. His monograph "The Ideological Preparation of German Imperialism for World War II" was never published.

In the late 1940s, the doctoral dissertation of **Aaron Gurevich** (1924–), a case study of thirteenth-century English feudalism supervised by Kosminsky [q.v. 1947–], was not published, probably because its author was Jewish. Despite Kosminsky's advice, Gurevich, a medievalist specialized in English and Norwegian history and a historical anthropologist, refused to change specialties and become a Byzantinist, nor did he join the CPSU. After great difficulties of finding a job, he was eventually employed at the Pedagogical Institute, Kalinin. Later Gurevich became a professor at the Russian Academy of Sciences Institute of General History, Moscow. His *Questions of the Rise of Feudalism in Western Europe*, a work that described feudalism as a Western phenomenon nonexistent in Russia, sparked much controversy in the late 1970s. When Gurevich refused to make a self-criticism, the book was banned and he was expelled from the Academy of Sciences for some time. Not until 1988 was he able to visit colleagues abroad.

In January and June 1947, *A History of Western European Philosophy* (1946; English 1949) by **Georgy Aleksandrov** (1908–61), philosopher and director at the CPSU-CC propaganda department (1940–47), was attacked by Politburo member and cultural ideologue Andrei Zhdanov for its insufficient partisanship and militancy. Aleksandrov had to leave his post and was transferred to the USSR Academy of Sciences Philosophy Institute, where he served as director (1947–54). He eventually became USSR minister of culture (1954–55). In 1955, however, after another controversy involving the 1954 book *Dialectical Materialism* which he had edited, he went to work at the Belorussian Academy of Sciences Philosophy Institute (1955–61).

On 15–20 March 1948, **Nikolai Rubinshtein** (1897–1963), Jewish historian and deputy director for scholarly activities at the State Historical Museum (1943–49), was forced to criticize his own book *Russian Historiography* (Moscow 1941) at a meeting of the All-Union Conference of Heads of History Departments because he had overemphasized the foreign influence upon Russian historiography and defended the Normanist theory. An exhibit under his supervision on nineteenth-century Russian history was criticized for downplaying Russian in favor of European achievements. Many of his colleagues called his book "antipatriotic", "cosmopolite" (for mentioning foreign historians), and "objectivist" (for mentioning native "bourgeois" historians). The attacks, including those from Zhdanov, continued until late in 1949. The book was banned; Rubinshtein was dismissed from the museum in 1949. In March 1949 the book *Historiography of the Middle Ages*, by **O. Veinshtein** from Leningrad, was criticized. Veinshtein's 1942 review of Rubinshtein's book had been criticized before, which in 1948 had led him to recant the views expounded in it. He was harassed for many years.

In 1948 **Sergei Bakhrushin** (1882–1950), lecturer (1909–27) and professor (1927–50) at Moscow University, member of the USSR Academy of Sciences History Institute (1937–50), specialist in the colonization of Siberia and Central Asia, was attacked for his "bourgeois" interpretations in a keynote report on periodization that he provided at a conference held at his institute. His report had ignored the existence of a Russian prefeudal state. He denied the official theory of the presence of a strong and unified ancient Russian state in Kievan Rus in the ninth and tenth centuries (Kievan Rus was a state ruled in the ninth–thirteenth centuries by princes of the House of Rurik). As early as 1931, his writings had been singled out as "deviationist" and "reactionary" by Pokrovsky [q.v. 1980] in an address delivered on behalf of the Society of Marxist Historians. Bakhrushin had been arrested and briefly incarcerated. Released after Pokrovsky's fall, he was able to continue his work.

Konstantin Bazilevich (1892–1950), historian and collector of sources at the USSR Academy of Sciences History Institute (1936–50), was attacked for "cosmopolitanism" for his work on the feudal monarchy in sixteenth- and seventeenth-century Russia and for his textbooks on USSR history. In 1949 he was also attacked (at the same time as Bakhrushin [q.v. 1947–]) for "economic materialism" and for following too closely the ideas of historian Vassili Klyuchevsky (1841–1911) concerning the nature of the Muscovite autocracy.

In October **Aleksandr Andreev** (1887–1959), historian at the USSR Academy of Sciences History Institute (1929–), specialist in seventeenth-century Siberian historiography, and editor of Peter the Great's letters and papers, was severely criticized during a meeting at the History Institute Academic Council because his 1942 article "The Trip of Peter the Great to England" was deemed too pro-English. He defended his article by saying that he had emphasized England's role in the reform work of Peter the Great because wartime relations with England were different from those in 1948.

When in late 1948 the Jewish Anti-Fascist Committee was shut down, the printing plates of a book about the murder of Jews on German-occupied Soviet territory during World War II, compiled by writers **Vasily Grossman** (1905–64) and **Ilya Ehrenburg** (1891–1967) in 1944–46, were destroyed. A Russian-language edition of the manuscript was later published by Yad Vashem, the Martyrs' and Heroes Remembrance Authority in Jerusalem. Stalin ordered the dissolution of the Extraordinary Commission to Ascertain and Investigate the War Crimes of the Fascist-German Invaders and Their Accomplices. As part of the affair, Polish-born **Iosif Yuzefovich** (1890–1952), working at the Soviet Information Bureau and at the USSR Academy of Sciences History Institute, was arrested, accused of Jewish nationalism, imprisoned, and executed. He was rehabilitated posthumously. In 1912–16 Yuzefovich had been arrested for his radical activities. After 1917, he was a trade unionist until the 1930s.

In 1949 and 1952, archeologist **Vladislav Ravdonikas** (1894–) an alternate member of the Academy of Sciences from Leningrad, was accused of cosmopolitanism.

In 1949 **Abram Deborin** (pseudonym of Abram Ioffe) (1881–1963), Jewish expert on Marxist philosophy, head of the Section of Modern History and Current Events at the USSR Academy of Sciences History Institute, and academician (1929–), was dismissed but later reinstated as a senior researcher. Adhering in his youth to illegal Marxist circles, he was persecuted by the tsarist police and went into exile in Switzerland (1903–8). Upon his return, he struggled against tsarism with Menshevik political views (1907–17). (Menshevism was the moderate faction of Marxist socialists in those years.) He joined the CPSU in 1928. Refusing in 1930 to proclaim Stalin as the foremost Marxist philosopher, he was denounced in January 1931 as a "Menshevik idealist" and barred from philosophy. His entire work was banned and his manuscripts on the history of Nazi ideology were not published anymore. In [1958] the ban was lifted, and his works were republished, one of them posthumously.

In 1949 **Lev Zubok** (1894–1967), specialist in United States history, was criticized, but he refused to repent. He was forced to leave the USSR Academy of Sciences History Institute (1938–49) and the Moscow University history department (1942–49) but was able to remain at the Foreign Ministry Institute of International Relations (1948–61). In 1957 he was reinstated as a senior research associate at the History Institute.

In 1949–55 **Ivan Maisky** (1884–1975), academician (1946–) and specialist in the history of international relations, was persecuted. His book *Mongolia Today* (1920) was criticized and he promised to revise it (a new edition appeared in 1959). A revolutionary in his youth, Maisky was arrested by the tsarist police (1906) and lived in exile in Germany and the United Kingdom (1908–17). Upon his return, he joined the Mensheviks and later the Bolsheviks. He was a diplomat, an ambassador to London (1932–43), a participant in the Yalta and Potsdam conferences (1945), and the USSR deputy minister of foreign affairs (until 1946) before his dismissal from the ministry. In September 1952 he was criticized by the USSR Academy of Sciences presidium for having approved a 1951 book by diplomat and historian Boris Shtein, *Bourgeois Falsifiers of History*, which, while exposing the falsification of history by bourgeois sources, had alleged that the United States had attempted to avert the outbreak of World War II. In late February 1953, Maisky was arrested and charged with treason and espionage for the United

Kingdom. After thirty months' solitary confinement, he was pardoned in the summer of 1955, released, and later entirely rehabilitated.

In 1949 **Yevgeny Kosminsky** (1886–1959), historian and academician (1946–), specialist in the medieval agrarian history of Western Europe, particularly England, was criticized for his "cosmopolitan errors" and "economic materialism" and accused of belittling the importance of Russians and Slavs in European history. He was dismissed from his chair of medieval history at Moscow University (1934–49). In 1950 he made a self-criticism and revised his medieval history textbooks. In 1952 he was dismissed from the Medieval History Section of the USSR Academy of Sciences History Institute (1936–52).

In 1950 **Abram Guralsky** (died 1955?), historian of France at the USSR Academy of Sciences History Institute, was arrested. He was released in 1955 but died soon afterward. His major works were never published. After the civil war, he had become a functionary of the Comintern (the third Communist International, 1918–43) and worked abroad. Having supported the antiparty opposition for a while, he had come under suspicion. In 1937 he was arrested but soon released.

1948–54 In 1948 **Vadim Shavrov** (1924–83), a church historian who had studied, inter alia, at the Moscow State University history department, was arrested in connection with the arrest of his father, an Old Bolshevik, and sentenced to ten years in a labor camp. In 1954 he was released. He became a theologian. In the 1960s he was the coauthor (with Levitin [q.v. 1974–]) of the three-volume samizdat *Essays on the History of Church Sedition: The Renovationist Movement in the Russian Orthodox Church*. In 1982 he was interned in a special psychiatric hospital. He was released shortly before his death.

1949–54 In 1949 Austrian historian **Arnold Reisberg** (1904–80) was imprisoned for "counterrevolutionary Trotskyist activities" and sentenced to life imprisonment in eastern Siberia. In 1954 he was entirely rehabilitated. He then worked as a teacher in Kaluga, western Russia (1955–59). Refused entry into Austria, he immigrated to the GDR in 1959, became a member of the Marxism-Leninism Institute, and co-edited Lenin's works. An active member of the Kommunistische Partei Österreichs from 1924, Reisberg had been imprisoned and expelled from Austria in 1934. Active in émigré circles in Czechoslovakia, he had gone to the USSR, where he taught history at the Komintern Lenin School, Moscow. In [1937] he had been sentenced to five years' imprisonment on the same charge as in 1949 and sent to a Siberian camp. He was released from that imprisonment in 1946.

1949–56   In 1949 historian and orientalist **Lev Gumilev** (1912–), specialist in Central Asian nomadic Mongol and Turkic-speaking peoples, son of poets Nikolai Gumilev and Anna Akhmatova, was arrested and sent to a camp in Siberia. He was released in 1956. Previously, he had been arrested after the 1934 Kirov murder and sent to a camp. In 1937 his second arrest followed. During World War II, he was sent to the front until 1945. In the 1990s Gumilev was accused of anti-Semitism in his 1993 writings about the Khazar khanate. (In the seventh century many Khazars had converted to Judaism.)

1950–90   Over the years 1950–78, *A History of Soviet Russia* (London) by British historian **Edward Carr** (1892–1982), journalist, inter alia, for the (London) *Times*, diplomat for twenty years and senior fellow at Trinity College, Cambridge University (1953–82), was published. All ten volumes (fourteen books), covering USSR history from 1917 to 1929, were banned but translated into Russian and published in a secret edition of which every copy was numbered. In 1990 the first two volumes were published in Russian and circulated freely. Other works banned until the late 1980s included *Stalin: A Political Biography* (Oxford 1949) by **Isaac Deutscher** (1907–67), and *Bukharin and the Bolshevik Revolution: A Political Biography, 1888–1938* (New York 1980) by historian **Stephen Cohen** (1938–).

1952–   In early 1952 **Sergei Kan** (1896–1960), professor of modern European history, particularly the 1848–49 revolutions and the 1871 Paris Commune, was dismissed from his post as senior research associate at the USSR Academy of Sciences History Institute (1944–52) and, "politically and scientifically compromised", forced to teach in a provincial town, where he worked at the Municipal Potemkin Pedagogical Institute (1955–59).

1952–53   The July 1952 issue of *Voprosy istorii* was impounded and the journal attacked in the magazine *Bolshevik*. In October the USSR Academy of Sciences presidium judged *Voprosy istorii*'s work unsatisfactory and planned to purge it of "alien views". Stalin's death in March 1953 prevented the plan from being executed.

1952   On 3 October, **George Kennan** (1904–), historian and diplomat and United States ambassador to the USSR (1952), was declared persona non grata and expelled from the USSR, officially for a remark at Tempelhof airport, Berlin, on 19 September, in which he had compared his five-months' internment as a prisoner of the Germans in 1941–42 with the regime of isolation applied to him as a diplomat in Moscow. According to Kennan, the real reasons were that he had addressed a Soviet crowd on Victory Day in 1945 and that, as an ambassador, he had resisted Soviet provocations and discovered an eavesdropping device in his house.

Late in the year the Higher Qualifications Commission stripped **G. Basharin**, who had written a work on the history of Yakutia, of his doctoral credentials.

1952–   Among the editorial board members of the *Diplomatic Dictionary* who were dismissed in late 1952 was **Aleksandr Belenky**, historian and specialist in eastern studies. In April 1953 he was given a severe reprimand with a warning.

1953–55   On 5 March 1953, the day of Stalin's death, historian and bibliographer **Sergei Pisarev** (1902–) was arrested because he had written a letter to Stalin with the request to review the "doctors' plot" case (an alleged January plot of mostly Jewish doctors to kill Soviet leaders, manufactured by the secret police). He was sent to a psychiatric hospital until he was declared sane in February 1955 and released. After his release he became an active dissident and campaigner against psychiatric abuse.

1953   Immediately after Stalin's death, some documents disappeared from the CPSU-CC archives and from Stalin's personal archives.

1953–   After Stalin's death several texts were withdrawn from circulation: the consecutive versions of a CPSU history, the protocols of the CPSU congresses from 1917 to 1934, and the early editions of Lenin's works. The *History of the Communist Party of the Soviet Union (Bolsheviks): Short Course* (1938), attributed to Stalin himself, which in many revised editions had dominated history teaching for fifteen years, was not reprinted. It was criticized and disappeared.

1954–   The publishers of the *Great Soviet Encyclopedia* advised their subscribers to cut out the pages about Lavrenty Beria—the head of the NKVD (People's Commissariat of Internal Affairs; predecessor of the KGB) purged in December 1953 and the author of the 1935 *On the History of the Bolshevik Organizations in Transcaucasia*, alternatively titled *Stalin's Early Writings and Activities*, well-known for its falsifications—and to replace the pages with a newly supplied article on the Bering Strait. In 1957 the second edition of the *Great Soviet Encyclopedia* devoted five pages to Stalin. The first (1947) had fifty-eight, the third (1976) two.

In 1954 historian, philosopher, and expert on international relations **Mikhail Voslensky** (1920–) had to delete a "bourgeois" description of the 1919 Versailles Peace Conference from his book *The History of the USA in the German Question*. In 1965–72 he served as academic secretary of the Commission on Scientific Problems of Disarmament. In 1972 he emigrated to the Federal Republic of Germany (FRG) and Austria. In March 1981 he became the director of the Institute of Contemporary Soviet Research, Munich.

1950s–   In the mid-1950s critic and historian **Mikhail Geller (Heller)** (1922–97) went into exile in Poland, where he became an editor at the Polish press agency. In 1969 he moved to France and became a historian of modern Russian literature at the Sorbonne, Paris.

1955–88   In 1955 the historical novel *Doctor Zhivago*, situated in 1905–29 and written in 1948–55 by poet **Boris Pasternak** (1890–1960), was rejected by Soviet publishers as anticommunist because it opposed violence as a revolutionary means and expressed a negative attitude toward the 1917 Revolution. The manuscript was smuggled abroad in 1956 and published in Italy in 1957. It was then published in several other languages, became a best-seller, and in 1958 earned Pasternak the Nobel Prize in Literature. Pasternak was expelled from the Writers' Union, threatened with exile, and forced to renounce the prize. He spent the rest of his life in isolation. Only excerpts from the novel were allowed to appear in the USSR until it was finally published in 1988.

1956   When confronted with a French delegation asking in May for historical research into the political persecutions under Stalin, his successor Nikita Khruschev declared (in the words of the delegation): "Mais les historiens aussi ont besoin d'être dirigés." ("Historians too must be directed")

1956–57   On 30 June 1956, a CPSU-CC resolution criticized *Voprosy istorii* (the organ of the Academy of Sciences History Institute) for not applying CPSU principles in assessing historical phenomena. The resolution came after mounting criticism expressed in memorials (*zapiska*) since 1955. From 1953, and particularly from the February 1956 20th CPSU Congress, *Voprosy istorii* had been publishing revisionist articles, especially about the critical 1890–1922 period, the role of the Mensheviks and Socialist Revolutionaries (an agrarian party), the tactics of the Bolsheviks during 1917, and the role of the United States in the Russian Civil War, criticizing in the process Stalinist distortions of history. After the Polish revolt and the Hungarian Revolution in October 1956, the attacks became more frequent. On 9 March 1957, the CC issued a decree "On the journal *Voprosy istorii*" in which it was severely criticized. The chief editor since June 1953, **Anna Pankratova** (1897–1957), specialist in the history of the proletariat, CPSU-CC and Supreme Soviet member, and academician (1953-), was reprimanded but was allowed to remain at her post (until her sudden death on 25 May 1957). Eight out of eleven editorial board members—including **Eduard Burdzhalov** (1906–85), formerly a director at the department of USSR history of the CPSU-CC Higher Party School, a teacher at the CPSU Academy for Social Sciences, an assistant editor of the journal (1953–56)—were removed. Burdzhalov had taken the lead with two revisionist articles on the events between the February revolution and Lenin's return to Russia in April 1917, stating that the revolution had occurred spontaneously and challenging the leading position of the Bolsheviks in these events. He refused to admit any wrongdoing and received a severe reprimand. He was sent to work at the USSR Academy of Sciences History Institute, where in 1959 he was dismissed. Unemployed for six months, he secured a position at the Moscow Pedagogical Institute, where he taught until his retirement in 1976. Volume 1 of his book on the February revolution appeared in 1967 (no Soviet historical journal reviewed it), volume 2 in 1971; both were translated into English in 1987. The editorial worker responsible for preparing Burdzhalov's articles for publication, **S. Keshin** was dismissed, but after two years' unemployment he was hired at the History Institute.

1957– In 1957 **Sergei Bernadsky** (1932–), son of a history professor who belonged to the Socialist Revolutionaries, and graduate from the Leningrad State University history department (1956), was arrested and convicted of sympathizing with the Yugoslav system. In [1962] he was released before the end of his term and rehabilitated. After new proceedings in 1970, his case was dismissed.

1957–63 In 1957 **Viktor Trofimov**, a student at the Herzen Pedagogical Institute history department in Leningrad, was arrested and sentenced for anti-Soviet propaganda and participation in a counterrevolutionary organization (the Union of Communists). In the fall of 1963, he was granted a pardon and released.

1957– In August 1957 **Lev Krasnopevtsev** (1929–), history teacher at Moscow State University, **Leonid Rendel**, historian, **Marat Cheshkov** (1932–), graduate from the Moscow State University history department (1955) and research officer at the Institute of the Peoples of Asia (1956–57), **N. Obushenkov**, candidate in history, and five others were arrested for membership of the illegal Marxist group League of Patriots of Russia (founded in May by seven graduates of the Moscow University history department with the aim of achieving consistent de-Stalinization and liberalization in politics and economics). In February 1958 they were tried on the charge of "participating in an organization with the purpose of subverting Soviet power" and sentenced to ten (Krasnopevtsev, Rendel), eight (Cheshkov), and six (Obushenkov) years in a strict-regime camp. They were released in [1964] (Cheshkov) and August 1967 (Krasnopevtsev, Rendel). Cheshkov became an expert in Vietnamese affairs. Rendel wrote many samizdat pieces, including *The Specific Character of the History of Russia* (1970) and *Thirty Years Ago* (1972; dealing with the 1941 military activities at the Soviet-German front), for which he was threatened with criminal prosecution.

1959–64   Many cultural and historical monuments, mostly churches, were closed and destroyed during an official campaign in this period.

1959–   In February 1959 **Vladimir Osipov** (1938–), a poet and publicist who studied history at Moscow State University, was expelled from the university after he had publicly defended a classmate. After KGB harassment he was arrested in October 1961 and in February 1962 tried on the charge of "planning a terrorist attack against Soviet leaders" and "making anti-Soviet remarks". He was sentenced to seven years in a hard-regime camp. Released in October 1968, he became an active samizdat writer, particularly as chief editor of the Slavophile samizdat journal *Veche* (1971–74). He protested, inter alia, the demolition of historical monuments in Moscow. In November 1974 he was again arrested and in September 1975 tried on the charge of "anti-Soviet agitation and propaganda" for publishing *Veche*. He was sentenced to eight years in a strict-regime camp.

1960–72   Around 1960 **Yuri Galanskov** (1939–72), a worker and poet who studied at the Moscow State University history department and at the Moscow Historical Archives Institute, was expelled from the university because of the independence of his views. He was an active dissident and served as the editor of the samizdat anthology *Feniks* (1961), for which he was confined to a psychiatric hospital for several months (1961–62). In January 1967 he was arrested for distributing the samizdat magazine *Feniks-66* and interned. In January 1968 he was tried (together with, among others, Ginzburg [q.v. 1966–67]) on the charge of "anti-Soviet agitation and propaganda" and sentenced to seven years in a strict-regime camp. On 4 November 1972, he died in a camp hospital after a forced but unsuccessful operation.

1961   Literary historian **Liudmila Kleiman** (1936–) immigrated to Israel.

           Vladimir Turok-Popov (original name: **Popov**) (1904–), historian of the Austro-Hungarian monarchy and specialist in the international workers' movement and in international relations, was forced to leave the USSR Academy of Sciences History Institute and to transfer to the Institute of Slavic and Balkan Studies after he wrote the article "The Historian and the Reader" in *Literaturnaya gazeta* (4 February 1961), in which he had criticized political obstacles to historical scholarship.

1961–   In September 1961 **Pyotr [= Petrol] Grigorenko** (1907–87), major general, cybernetician, and historian, was dismissed from the Frunze Military Academy, Moscow, and demoted after he had warned against the revival of the personality cult and demanded more democratic procedures in the CPSU. Two decades earlier, in 1941, he had already been reprimanded after criticizing Stalin's purge of the Red Army leadership. In February 1964 he was arrested after having demanded the return to pure Leninism in November 1963. His activities were connected with the covert organization "Alliance for the Rebirth of Leninism". In April 1964 he was declared insane and in August interned in a special psychiatric hospital. In the same month, he was demoted to the rank of common soldier and expelled from the CPSU. In May 1965 he was released. He subsequently worked as a construction laborer and porter. In December he was declared sane. In 1967 a historical work of his appeared in samizdat (published in France as *Staline et la deuxième guerre mondiale*, 1969). In October 1967 he wrote a letter, "The Concealment of Historical Truth—A Crime before the People", to *Voprosy istorii* in defense of the book by Nekrich [q.v. 1967–]. Despite frequent harassment, Grigorenko remained active in the dissident movement, inter alia, as a supporter of the national rights of Crimean Tatars, Volga Germans, and Meskhetian Turks, until his arrest in May 1969 for "anti-Soviet activities". While awaiting trial in a prison in Tashkent in June, he began a hunger strike in protest against his treatment. In November he was again declared insane at the Serbsky Institute, Moscow. In February 1970 he was tried in absentia and sentenced to compulsory confinement in a psychiatric hospital. In 1971 he was declared sane but his psychiatric term was twice prolonged. In June 1974 he was released. In May 1976 he and Ginzburg [q.v. 1966–67] were among the eleven signatories of the initial proclamation of the first Moscow Helsinki Group. He also became a member of the Ukrainian Helsinki Group. In December 1977 he left for the United States. In March 1978 his Soviet citizenship was revoked.

In October 1961 poet, historian, and publicist **Anatoly Ivanov** (1935–) was arrested in connection with the samizdat collection *Feniks*. In February 1962 he was tried and sentenced to seven years in a hard-regime camp, part of which he spent in a psychiatric hospital. In October 1968 he was released. From 1971 he wrote many samizdat pieces on the 1914–18 period and the Russian national traditions.

1962–64   A limited and abridged edition of the protocols of the December 1962 All-Union Conference of Historians (the first such conference since 1928), documenting sharp confrontations between revisionist historians and the CPSU apparatus, was not published until the summer of 1964. Many examples of historical falsification under Stalin were edited out.

pre-1963   Around 1963 **Viktor Dalin**, historian of France and of socialist thought, and **Sergei Dubrovsky**, historian of the USSR, arrested during the terror of the 1930s, and imprisoned in a work camp for about twenty years, returned to the USSR Academy of Sciences History Institute as senior staff members.

1963–   In February 1963 **Aleksandr Zimin** (1920–80), historian of medieval and early modern Russian history and specialist in the formation and development of the Muscovite state in the fifteenth–sixteenth centuries (especially Ivan the Terrible's reign), researcher (1948–51), and senior research associate (1951–) at the USSR Academy of Sciences History Institute, lecturer (1947–71) and professor (1971–73) at the Moscow State Historical Archives Institute, attempted to prove that *Slovo o polku Igoreve* (The Song of Igor's Campaign) was not written in 1187 as most believed but fabricated as late as the 1770s. During a three-hour conference at the Institute of Russian Literature in Leningrad, he outlined his conclusions, questioning the tale's authenticity, destroying it as a source of Russian and Soviet pride in the process. His conclusions aroused much controversy and hostility. In May 1964 they were discussed at a three-day symposium of the USSR Academy of Sciences History Institute on the basis of copies of the first draft of his book. Although his work could not appear, Zimin succeeded in publishing his argument in a dozen journal articles. Until the 1990s, almost nothing from what Zimin wrote was published—his manuscripts totaled many thousands of typed pages. The controversy reportedly contributed to his early death. From a book in his honor on the theme of centralization (1982), the official Festschrift designation was removed prior to publication. Three articles in the book explicitly about Zimin had all notice of that fact removed from their titles.

In 1963 **Mustafa Dzhemilev** (1943–), who was to become the leading spokesman for the Crimean Tatars, wrote *Brief Historical Outline of Turkish Culture in the Crimea from the Thirteenth to the Eighteenth Century*. In April 1962 he had already been interrogated for three days by the Uzbek KGB, which had led to his dismissal from a Tashkent aircraft factory. He spent fifteen years in Soviet camps, including a two-week imprisonment in May 1974, at that occasion apparently to prevent him from publicly commemorating the thirtieth anniversary of the 1944 deportation of the Crimean Tatars for alleged collaboration with the Nazi occupation forces.

In 1963 history student **Andrei Amalrik** (1938–80) was expelled from Moscow State University for defending the officially rejected theory of the Normanist origins of the Russian state in his paper *The Normans and Kievan Rus*. In March 1965 he was threatened with criminal prosecution by the police on the charge of lack of permanent employment (he had held jobs as a construction worker, proofreader, film technician, and postman). In May he had his home searched and he was arrested for writing anti-Soviet plays. He was tried under the antiparasite law and sentenced to thirty months' internal exile and forced labor on a collective farm near Tomsk, Siberia (about his stay there, he wrote *Involuntary Journey to Siberia* in 1966–67, published in New York in 1970). In June 1966 the Supreme Court annulled the sentence. He obtained work as a journalist for the Novosti news agency. In October 1968 he was dismissed from this job, apparently because he protested arms deliveries in the Biafra war, and subsequently worked as a postman. In 1969 and 1970, he refuted his alleged collaboration with the KGB (who had often intimidated him). In May 1970 he was arrested and in November tried on the charge of "anti-Soviet fabrication" for, inter alia, writing (April–June 1969) and circulating his essay *Will the Soviet Union Survive until 1984?* (Russian, Amsterdam 1969; published in twenty languages). He was sentenced to three years in a hard-regime corrective-labor camp. In June 1971 he was transferred to Kolyma camp, Magadan, Siberia. At the end of his term, in May 1973, he was rearrested, tried in July on the charge of imparting information which damaged the Soviet system in the camp, and sentenced to another three years in a strict-regime camp. Subsequently he held a hunger strike for 117 days. In November the Supreme Court reviewed his case, following public protests at home and abroad, and his sentence was commuted to three years of internal exile in Magadan, where he obtained work as an assistant researcher. In May 1975 he was allowed to return to Moscow but urged by the authorities to apply to immigrate to Israel. In September he was detained by the police and threatened with criminal prosecution for staying in Moscow without a residence permit. He subsequently settled in Kaluga. In July 1976 he was released as a result of international protests and went into exile in the Netherlands and France, where in 1980 his diary *Journal d'un provocateur* (*Notes of a Revolutionary*) was published. His essay on *1984* circulated widely in samizdat in the USSR. He died in a car accident near Guadalajara, Spain, while traveling to Madrid to take part in a conference organized by dissident groups.

1964– In 1964 **Vladimir Dremliuga** (1940–) was expelled from Leningrad State University, where he was a history student (1962–), because he had made a joke at the expense of a former KGB member. He was active as a dissident and in 1968–74 spent a term in prison. In December 1974 he emigrated.

After his downfall on 14 October 1964, Nikita Khrushchev's name was completely eliminated from newspapers, textbooks, and historical monographs for almost two decades.

1964–91 In the fall of 1964, the proofs of a book on the collectivization of agriculture in 1927–37, approved prior to Kruschchev's fall and edited by **Viktor Danilov** (?1930–), were completed but the argument about publishing the book continued as late as 1969. Criticism of Danilov's approach to collectivization appeared in 1966. The book was banned for political reasons (it would not be rescheduled for publication until 1990–91), and almost all its authors (probably **Vyltsan, [Ilya] Zelenin**, and **Moshkov**) were transferred to work on other periods of history. Danilov himself was removed from his positions as head of the Soviet peasantry sector of the USSR Academy of Sciences History Institute and as secretary of its CPSU committee. In the late 1970s, he could publish a multivolume book on the Soviet peasantry before collectivization. He was reinstated to his former post in the fall of 1987.

1965–66 In 1965–66 the report *On the Status of Historical Study*, which indicated "blank spots" in history, was prepared by the CPSU Committee of the Academy of Sciences History Institute under the supervision of its secretary Danilov [q.v. 1964–91]. Unanimously approved after two discussions by a general CPSU assembly at the institute (about 300 people) and already typeset, it was nevertheless, censored and never published.

1965 In the spring a short study of the Soviet elite from a Leninist point of view, written by **Oleg Puzyrev**, historian at the USSR Academy of Sciences History Institute, was criticized. Puzyrev was expelled from the institute and transferred to the Mendeleev Chemical Institute library.

In June a letter about the duty to search for the historical truth from a group of prominent historians to the newspaper *Izvestia*, which refused to publish it, was published in the samizdat journal *Political Diary* [q.v. 1969–89: Medvedev].

1966–   In 1966 or before, electrician **Basyr Gafarov** and engineer **Yusuf Osmanov** (1941–), both Crimean Tatar activists, wrote a survey of Soviet falsification of Crimean history. It was addressed to the USSR Academy of Sciences History Institute, to the newspapers, and to the CPSU-CC. Osmanov had written several articles and letters on Crimean Tatar history and the Crimean Tatar movement, addressed to the higher CPSU and state officials. In January 1968 he was arrested in Tashkent, tried on the charge of writing and disseminating anti-Soviet articles and letters, and sentenced to thirty months in a hard-regime camp.

1966–71 *Andrei Rublev*, a 1966 film by **Andrei Tarkovski** (1932–86) about the most important icon painter (?1370–?1430) of medieval Russia and his fate as an artist in times of war and repression, was not released until December 1971 because of its "negative" view of history (including a shot of Christ's face).

1966   Historian **V. Dunaevsky** was forced to recant because in *Europe in Modern and Contemporary Times*, (Moscow 1966), a collection of articles he helped write and edited, he had used the memoirs of historian **A.G. Slutsky**, a coauthor. In October 1931 Slutsky's article on the degree of criticism in Lenin's views on the pre-1914 internal party struggle among German Social Democrats within the context of the Second International had been attacked by Stalin himself. In an article in *Proletarskaya revoliutsiia* and *Bolshevik* written in the form of a letter to the editor, "Some Questions Concerning the History of Bolshevism", Stalin had branded Slutsky as a "semi-Trotskyist" and had also written: "Who, except archive rats, does not understand that a party and its leaders must be tested primarily by their deeds and not merely by their declarations?" Dunaevsky's article was a refutation of Stalin's letter.

The transcript of a discussion concerning a draft version of the third volume of the *History of the CPSU* held at the Institute of Marxism-Leninism in 1966 was published in the samizdat journal *Phoenix 1966*. The discussion developed in a conflict over the presentation of evidence on the position of leading Bolsheviks on the eve of the October 1917 revolution.

1966–   In April 1966 administrative measures were taken against the Methodological Sector (an interdisciplinary seminar on methodology) at the Academy of Sciences History Institute apparently because of its discussions about the capitalist nature of pre-1917 Russia and, consequently, about the socialist nature of the October 1917 revolution and the validity of the histomat stages theory. The seminar was suspended in 1970, and the responsible leader since 1964, **Mikhail Gefter** (1918–95), war veteran and specialist in prerevolutionary Russian economic history, was dismissed from his directorship and barred from publishing. His unpublished speech at the April meeting, criticizing Stalinist historiography, was reproduced by Medvedev [q.v. 1969–89]. The volume *Historical Science and Contemporary Problems: Articles and Discussions* (Moscow 1969), a book on the relationship between sociology ("laws") and history ("facts") in the USSR, edited by Gefter, was censured at a February 1971 bureau meeting of the Academy of Sciences History Institute. His *Lenin and Problems of the History of Classes and Class Struggle* was never published. A book with a methodological contribution by Gefter, written in 1969 and inadvertently published in Sverdlovsk in 1972, was immediately withdrawn from the bookshops. After 1970 Gefter joined the sector on modern and contemporary history of the West but retired early in 1974. He started writing in such samizdat journals as *Pamyat* [q.v. 1978–]. In April 1982 his house was searched, his archives were confiscated, and he was interrogated, but he refused to talk as long as he was impeded from attending the trial of the younger *Pamyat* historians. In the same year, he resigned from the CPSU. He was able to publish again in the late 1980s. In February 1993 he became a member of the Russian Presidential Council.

1966   Historian **Natan Eidelman** (?1929/30–1989) wrote a samizdat article about the nineteenth-century populist N. Serno-Solovevich. He would later be one of the first Soviet historians to use the glasnost period (1985–) for research on the nineteenth century.

1966–   In 1966 **Mikhail Meerson-Aksenov** (1944–), history student at Moscow State University, was expelled from the university for nonconformism after he converted to Christianity and became an activist in the Russian Orthodox movement. He was a samizdat writer on historical, philosophical, and religious themes. In 1967 he published abroad *Reactions to the Anthology 'From the Depths'*, a collection of articles on the Russian Revolution. From 1968, when he graduated in history, to 1971, he was employed at the Academy of Sciences Institute of General History, but he resigned because he refused to cooperate in a project on communism. He left the USSR.

1966   In February **Sergei Skazkin** (1890–1973), a medievalist specializing in the history of feudalism and absolutism in Western Europe, professor (1935–) and head of the department of medieval history at Moscow State University (1949–), academician (1958–) and head of the Section of Medieval History at the USSR Academy of Sciences History Institute (1962–), signed a letter from twenty-five cultural figures to CPSU-CC Secretary-General Leonid Brezhnev warning against the rehabilitation of Stalin.

1966–67   While a student at the Moscow Historical Archives Institute and after having written *Outline of the History of Russian Literature in the Twenties* (1965), journalist **Aleksandr Ginzburg** (born **Chizov**) (1936–) compiled a samizdat *White Book* on the trial of Andrei Sinyavsky and Yuli Daniel, which was published abroad. In January 1967 he was arrested for the third time (after prison terms in 1960–62 and 1964), in January 1968 tried (together with Galanskov [q.v. 1960–72] and two others) on the charge of "anti-Soviet agitation and propaganda" and sentenced to five years in a strict-regime camp. In August 1970 he was tried in the camp and sentenced to strict-regime imprisonment until the end of his term. In January 1972 he was released. Despite persistent persecution he assisted Solzhenitsyn [q.v. 1973–94] in organizing regular aid for political prisoners and their families in the USSR. After Solzhenitsyn was deported and had founded the Russian Fund for Aid to Persecuted Persons and Their Families in exile, Ginzburg acted as the chief manager of the fund in the USSR. In 1976 he was a founding member of the Moscow Helsinki Group. Arrested in February 1977 and held incommunicado, sentenced to eight years in a camp in July 1978 on charges of "anti-Soviet agitation and propaganda", he and others (Moroz [q.v. Ukraine 1965–]) were exchanged for two Soviet spies in April 1979. He went into exile in France.

1967–73   In 1967 and later, **Pyotr Zaionchkovsky** (1904–83), history professor at Moscow University (1948–83), leading specialist in the history of the state and of the domestic politics of late imperial Russia (1855–1917), was not permitted to travel abroad to attend his election as an honorary member of the American Historical Association (1967), to receive a prize at Harvard University (1972), or to attend his election as an honorary member of the British Academy (1973). His views on the reform efforts of the last Tsars and their bureaucrats were criticized in various polemics.

1967   In 1967 historian **Aleksandr Kan** (1925–), specialist in Scandinavian history, encountered difficulties during the defense of his doctoral dissertation because of his past as deputy head of the section for universal history at the *Voprosy istorii* editorial staff (1954–58). For the same reason his appointment as a Scandinavia expert at the Academy of Sciences History Institute in 1960 had already drawn objections. (Son of Sergei Kan [q.v. 1952–], he had been denied a place at the same institute in 1952.) Later he immigrated to Sweden.

1967–68   In 1967 or 1968, **Aleksandr Tvardovsky** (1910–71), leading writer and editor of *Novy Mir* (1958–70), completed his last epic poem, *By Right of Memory*, a long reflection on Stalinism and its legacy, but he was denied permission to publish two of its three parts.

1967–87   In February 1967 several activists of the underground organization All-Russian Social-Christian Union for the Liberation of the People (VSKhSON; founded 1964)—including **Georgy Bochevarov** (1935–), orientalist, engineer, writer of several essays on historical topics for VSKhSON use in 1965–66, **Nikolai Ivanov** (1937–), historian, lecturer in art history at Leningrad University and expert on religion, **Leonid Borodin** (1938–), son of a Lithuanian shot during Stalin's purges, historian, poet, and secondary-school director, **Viacheslav Platonov** (1941–), orientalist with a dissertation on Ethiopian history—were arrested. In March–April 1968 they were tried on the charge of membership in an illegal anti-Soviet organization, and sentenced to two-and-a-half (Bochevarov), six (Ivanov, Borodin), and seven (Platonov) years in a strict-regime camp. After their release in respectively [1970], March 1973, and March 1974, they remained active as dissidents. Borodin, for example, worked as a laborer and churchwarden and co-edited the samizdat journals *Veche* [q.v. 1959–: Osipov] and *Moskovsky sbornik* (Moscow Anthology). In May 1983 he was tried on the charge of "anti-Soviet agitation and propaganda" for his literary work and sentenced to another ten years in a special-regime camp and five years of internal exile. He was released in [June] 1987.

1967   Historian **Y. Borisov** had to leave the USSR Academy of Sciences History Institute after his chapters on the history of collectivization in volume eight of *A History of the USSR* were criticized.

1967–   In June 1967 **Aleksandr Nekrich** (1920–93), Jewish contemporary historian and senior research fellow at the USSR Academy of Sciences History Institute (1950–76), was expelled from the CPSU for his refusal to admit his "errors". He had published *1941, 22 June* (Moscow: Nauka publishers, September 1965), a book about the first days of the German army's invasion of the USSR and the handling of the military situation by the Soviets, which contained criticism of Stalin and the government. It was reviewed by five censors before it was published. When it was launched in October 1965, 50,000 copies were sold in three days. There were, however, almost no reviews and it was attacked by official historians. In February 1966 it was discussed by an audience of between 130 and 250 at a meeting of the Division of History of the Great Patriotic War of the CPSU-CC Institute of Marxism-Leninism. On 20 March 1967 the German journal *Der Spiegel* published an article on the book which, when shown to Brezhnev, enraged him because of a statement that he, Brezhnev, had supposedly wished to rehabilitate Stalin. Brezhnev reportedly ordered the CPSU-CC Control Committee to investigate the book and the use being made of it abroad. The investigation led to Nekrich's expulsion in June, his being barred from publishing, traveling abroad, and attending academic meetings. In August Glavlit (Central Board for the Protection of State Secrets in the Press) ordered all libraries without special collections to remove the book, register it, and destroy it. The book was torn up and burned in many libraries. In the meantime it was translated abroad and published in eight languages. In 1969 Nekrich was almost deprived of his academic degree of doctor of historical science, granted to him in 1963.

Historian **Aleksandr Samsonov** (1908–), Nauka director and author of war books, was given a reprimand and dismissed (but he was later appointed senior editor of *Istoricheskie zapiski*), **Viktor Zuyev**, head of Nauka's history publications, was transferred to the journal *Novaya i noveishaya istoriya*. In the wake of the affair, the director (1961–67) of the Institute of Marxism-Leninism, academician Pyotr Pospelov [q.v. 1986], and the director (1959–67) of the USSR Academy of Sciences History Institute, **Vladimir Khvostov** (1905–72), had to resign in June 1967. When in 1968 the institute was divided into the Institute of World History and the Institute of USSR History, Khvostov became director of the former.

In the spring of 1975, Nekrich completed the manuscript *The Punished Peoples: The Deportation and Fate of Soviet Minorities at the End of the Second World War*, a copy of which was sent to the West and published in New York in 1978. In May 1976 he went into "voluntary" exile in the United States (where he worked at the Russian Research Center of Harvard University) and in France. Upon his departure, he had to destroy all the sources he had gathered on the Warsaw Pact invasion of Czechoslovakia. Of his autobiography *Forsake Fear: Memoirs of an Historian* (Russian 1979; English 1991), written in 1972–79, only isolated copies reached the USSR. Nekrich had first encountered difficulties in 1949 when the defense of his doctoral dissertation "British Policy on the Eve of World War II" had to be postponed from May to September for political reasons. In July 1952, while his revised and typeset candidate dissertation was screened for publication, he was attacked and ordered to revise it once more. It was published in March 1955.

In 1966–67 **Leonid Petrovsky**, historian at the Lenin Museum,

Moscow, grandson of an Old Bolshevik and son of a CPSU official, spoke out in defense of Nekrich. He was the author of the summary record of the February 1966 discussion of the latter's book. Later Petrovsky cosigned the September 1967 letter of forty-three children of communist victims of the Stalinist terror that warned against neo-Stalinism.

1967–71   In June 1967 pensioner **Victor Grebenshikov** (1907) was arrested while attempting to smuggle his manuscript "A History of the Collectivization in the USSR" into the American Embassy in Moscow and sentenced to [seven] years in a camp. In June 1971 he was released.

1968   **Marina Gromyko**, history professor at Novosibirsk University, Siberia (Russia), specialist in eighteenth- and nineteenth-century Siberian history, was dismissed after she signed a letter requesting a review of the Ginzburg [q.v. 1966–67] and Galanskov [q.v. 1960–72] trials.

1968   **Militsa Nechkina** (1901–85), academician (1958–), leading specialist in Soviet historiography and nineteenth-century revolutionary movements, particularly the Decembrists, at the USSR Academy of Sciences Institute of USSR History, was forced to give up her post as head of the historiography section. She had already been attacked in 1952 for defending the struggle of the border peoples of Central Asia and the Caucasus against tsarism in a university textbook. The textbook's 1954 revised edition was criticized in 1959 for omitting tsarist aggression.

1968–   In 1968 poet and songwriter **Aleksandr Petrov** was arrested and in January 1969 tried on the charge of "anti-Soviet agitation and propaganda" because he had written poetry which criticized the repressions under Beria. He was sentenced to seventy-seven years of imprisonment. Before 1968 he had already spent more than twenty years in labor camps.

1968–73   In March 1968 **Ilya Gabay** (1935–73), teacher of literature and history and Tatar leader, active as a dissident and friend of Pyotr Yakir [q.v. 1972–82], was dismissed as an editor at the Institute of the Peoples of Asia and in May 1969 arrested and imprisoned. In January 1970 he was tried on the charge of preparing and circulating samizdat materials and sentenced to three years in a general-regime camp. After his release in May 1972, he remained unemployed and was subjected to KGB harassment. He commited suicide on 20 October 1973.

1968–   In the spring of 1968, **Ludmilla Alexeyeva** (1927–), historian and Nauka editor, was dismissed and expelled from the CPSU after she had protested the unfair trial of Ginzburg [q.v. 1966–67] and Galanskov [q.v. 1960–72]. She was frequently interrogated by the KGB and had to undergo several home searches. Alexeyeva became president of the International Helsinki Federation for Human Rights.

In April 1968 **Vladlen Pavlenkov** (1929–) was dismissed as a history lecturer at a technical college in Gorky after leaflets calling "to follow the Czech example" were discovered. In October 1969 he was arrested, subjected to psychiatric examination, and declared sane. In March–April 1970 he, **Mikhail Kapranov** (1944–), a secondary-school history teacher arrested in August 1969, **Sergei Ponomarev** (1945–), a graduate at the faculty of history and philology of Gorky State University arrested in June 1969, and **Vladimir Zhiltsov** (1946–), a student at the same faculty arrested in June 1969, were tried in a closed session on charges of planning to found an anti-Soviet organization and writing and circulating samizdat writings and anti-Soviet works. They were sentenced to seven (Pavlenkov, Kapranov), five (Ponomarev), and four (Zhiltsov) years in a strict-regime camp. In July 1974 Ponomarev was released.

1968   In August or September, **Tatiana Baeva**, an employee simultaneously studying at the Moscow Historical Archives Institute, was detained, interrogated, released, had her home searched, and was denied further access to the institute after she had witnessed a demonstration against the Warsaw Pact invasion of Czechoslovakia at the Red Square on 25 August. She was active in the dissident movement.

In December 1968 writer **Pyotr Dudochkin** (1915–) criticized General Shtemenko's book *The Supreme Command during the War* at a readers' conference at the Kalinin Military Science Society and afterward distributed a samizdat version of his speech. Before, Dudochkin had published, inter alia, historical sketches about Kalinin Oblast and in March 1968 had proposed to give Kalinin back its former name Tver at the Second Kalinin Oblast Conference of the All-Union Society for the Protection of Historical and Cultural Monuments.

1968–89   *The Great Terror: Stalin's Purge of the Thirties* (London 1968, 1990), a book by **Robert Conquest** (1908–), historian at Stanford University, Calif., was published in Russian in Florence (1972) and circulated as a samizdat publication in the USSR. It was serialized in the Soviet periodical *Neva* in 1989–90.

1969–   In 1969 **Iosif Meshener** (1936–), a Jewish secondary-school history teacher, was expelled from the CPSU and dismissed because he had written letters to the CPSU-CC and the United Nations protesting, inter alia, the invasion of Czechoslovakia. In February 1970 he was arrested and in October tried on charges of writing anti-Soviet letters and preparing and distributing samizdat writings. He was sentenced to six years in a strict-regime camp. In November 1974 he tried to commit suicide while in prison.

1969–89   In 1969 philosopher and historian **Roy Medvedev** (1925–), whose father (a Marxist philosopher) had perished in a labor camp in 1941, published in samizdat a three-volume study *Before the Court of History* which exposed Stalin and Stalinism from a Marxist point of view and took him six years of research (1962–68). It was published abroad as *Let History Judge: The Origins and Consequences of Stalinism* (Russian and English, 1971). A request for official publication had been rejected in 1968. Around the same time, Medvedev protested the attempts of the official CPSU journal *Kommunist* to rehabilitate Stalin. In October 1969 he was expelled from the CPSU. In 1971 he resigned his position as research officer and department head at the Academy of Pedagogical Sciences Institute of Vocational Education, Moscow (1961–71), to become a freelance writer. Despite frequent harassment (including a KGB house search in October 1971, in which his manuscripts and notes were confiscated), he was active in the dissident movement. Threatened with arrest, he disappeared from Moscow for several months in 1971–72. He was sometimes called a leader of the Leninist opposition in the USSR. In 1975 he and his brother Zhores published in samizdat and abroad their study *N.S. Khrushchev: Ten Years in Power*. In March 1975 Medvedev began publishing the samizdat journal *Dvadtsatiy vek* (Twentieth Century) as the successor of *Politicheskii dnevnik* (Political Diary), of which he had edited eighty monthly issues between October 1964 and March 1971. He was warned by the KGB to stop its publication. In 1979 his *On Stalin and Stalinism*, a sequel of *Let History Judge*, was published in Oxford. In June 1988 he made his first official appearance for decades at a conference on the Stalinist terror. In April 1989 he was rehabilitated as a CPSU member. In March 1992 he was elected to the Presidium of the USSR Congress of People's Deputies, which attempted to hold a sixth extraordinary session.

1969–75   In August 1969 **Aleksandr Romanov** (1949–), a student in the Saratov State University history department, was arrested and in January 1970 tried on charges of anti-Soviet propaganda and cofounding a "Party of True Communists". He was sentenced to six years in a strict-regime camp and (possibly) two years of internal exile. He was released in August 1975.

1970   Around 1970 historian **Vadim Borisov** (1945–) was refused permission to defend his thesis on the history of the Russian Orthodox Church in the fourteenth–fifteenth centuries for political reasons. He was an active dissident.

Around 1970 **Mikhail Zand** (1927–), Jewish philologist, journalist, specialist in the history of Persian and Tajik literature, and research associate at the USSR Academy of Sciences Institute for the Peoples of Asia, was dismissed and expelled from the Journalists' Union for his public statements in defense of civil rights. In June 1974 he immigrated to Israel. He had already been imprisoned from 1951 to 1954.

The papers of two 1967 conferences edited by Mints [q.v. 1947–55] and others—one on the overthrow of the autocracy and the other on the Russian proletariat (addressing, inter alia, the role of spontaneity in the revolutionary process)—were published but severely criticized.

The Higher Qualifications Commission refused to validate a doctoral dissertation on the Soviet historiography of Russian imperialism by **Konstantin Tarnovsky** (1921–87), associate at the USSR Academy of Sciences History Institute (1959–), because he was accused of Trotskyism in the press. This came after a period in which he had collaborated with Danilov [q.v. 1964–90] on the report "On the Status of Historical Study" [q.v. 1965–66] and with Volobuev [q.v. 1972–]. In 1981 he was awarded the doctorate for a thesis on Lenin.

1970–   In 1970 **Boris Orlov** (1930–), historian and activist in the Jewish emigration movement, was dismissed after having applied in vain for an exit visa to Israel. Despite frequent harassment, he continued his activities for the Soviet Jews until his emigration in late 1973.

1971–74   In June 1971 **Aishe Seitmuratova** (1937–), Crimean Tatar activist and graduate in history, was arrested, tried on the charge of preparing and disseminating anti-Soviet literature (a copybook with her own verse had been confiscated) and sentenced to three years' deprivation of freedom. In 1967 she had already been sentenced to three years' probation. After her release in December 1974, she requested in vain her readmission to the Academy of Sciences History Institute to complete a postgraduate course.

In August 1971 **Enver Odabashev** (1917–), history teacher and Meskhetian Turk leader, was arrested, tried, and sentenced to two years' deprivation of freedom for his activities as elected chairman of VOKO (Provisional Organization Committee for the Liberation from Exile and for the Restoration of Leninist Norms of Law for the Illegally Deported and Forcibly Held Turkish People). In April 1974 he was released.

1972   A samizdat author published *Russian History before the Great Court* under the pseudonym **L.O.**

1972–   Art historian and critic **Igor Golomstock** (1929–), who wrote several books on the history and theory of Western European art, emigrated to the United Kingdom, where he became a lecturer at Oxford University (1975–). There he published, inter alia, about art under totalitarianism.

1972–   In March the interpretations of the 1905 and February 1917 revolutions advanced by historian **Pavel Volobuev**, director of the USSR Academy of Sciences Institute of USSR History and specialist in twentieth-century history, in two collections of articles on the preconditions of the October revolution edited under his supervision, *Sverzhenie samoderzhaviia* (Moscow 1970) and *Rossiiskii proletariat: oblik, borba, gegemoniia* (Moscow 1970), were rejected at a joint session of the sectors for the pre-October and Soviet periods of the Academic Council of the Academy of Sciences History Institute. This was confirmed by a resolution of the bureau of the Historical Division in July. Volobuev had emphasized, inter alia, the role of monopoly capital in pre-1917 Russia, Russia's backwardness in 1917, and the spontaneous character of the February revolution. Historian **Y. Kiryanov**, research specialist at the History Institute, was also censured. In January 1973 Volobuev apologized but in March 1974 he was eventually dismissed and transferred as a senior researcher to the Academy of Sciences Institute of the History of Natural Sciences and Technology. In 1987 he was a corresponding member of the USSR Academy of Sciences. In 1955, then an instructor at the historical section of the CPSU-CC Department of Science and Educational Establishments, he had been a critic of *Voprosy istorii*.

In February 1972 Jewish sinologist, candidate in history, and specialist in ancient China **Vitaly Rubin** (1923–81), temporary senior researcher (1969–72) at the Academy of Sciences Institute of Oriental Studies, Moscow, was deprived of his titles and forced to resign after he had applied for a visa to Israel. His emigration application was refused on the grounds that he was an important specialist. He remained unemployed, his works were withdrawn from printing, orders for reviews of his book *Ideology and Culture in Ancient*

China (1970) canceled, and citations and mentions of his previous works removed. Despite frequent harassment and short-term detentions, he continued his activities.

1972   In [March], **Aleksandr Nemirovsky**, historian of antiquity, professor at Voronezh State University, Voronezh, was severely reprimanded in connection with the samizdat journal *Seksual-demokrat*. The journal, advocating democratic reforms and open discussion of sexual problems, was published by three second-year history students, among them **Semenov** and **Vysotsky**, who were expelled from the university in March. Nemirovsky's book *The Thread of Ariadne* was not published because its cover photograph of the King Minos labyrinth reminded the Voronezh Oblast Party Committee of the fascist symbol.

1972–   In June 1972 writer and publicist **Boris Evdokimov**, author of the book *Young People in Russian History* (published abroad in Russian), was sentenced in his absence to indefinite internment in a prison hospital, on the charge of publishing articles abroad under pseudonyms.

1972–82   In June 1972 historian and leading human-rights activist **Pyotr Yakir** (1923–82) was arrested and charged with "anti-Soviet agitation and propaganda" after six years of dissident activities. As the son of military commander Iona Yakir, executed in 1937, he spent his youth in prisons and camps as a "son of an enemy of the people" and a "socially dangerous element" (1937–54), with only a brief interruption in 1942. He attempted to escape several times. In 1956 he returned to Moscow and studied history at the Moscow Historical Archives Institute. In a speech during the 22nd CPSU Congress in 1961, Khrushchev personally referred to him in a friendly way. He was given a post at the USSR Academy of Sciences History Institute (until 1972). In 1963 he co-edited a memorial volume for his father. He spoke and wrote in support of many dissidents, including Nekrich [q.v. 1967–] in 1966, Ginzburg [q.v. 1966–67] in 1968, Solzhenitsyn [q.v. 1973–94] in 1969–70, and Amalrik [q.v. 1963–] in 1970. He repeatedly warned against the revival of Stalinism, for example in a cowritten piece, *Appeal to Public Figures in Science, Culture, and the Arts* (January 1968). In March 1969 he wrote an open letter to *Kommunist*, detailing Stalin's crimes and calling for his posthumous indictment. In May he cofounded with fourteen others the Action Group for the Defense of Civil Rights in the USSR. In August 1970 he wrote a letter to the secretariat of the 13th International Congress of Historical Sciences (held in Moscow), regarding the second anniversary of the Warsaw Pact occupation of Czechoslovakia and proposing the addition of several topics for historical research to the congress's agenda, including a comparative study of Stalin's and Hitler's roles in history.

He and his wife had frequently been harassed before his arrest in June 1972. In 1971 he published the first part of his memoirs, *A Childhood in Prison* (Russian 1971; English 1972—about the years 1937–42) in samizdat. His house was twice searched and many of his books and papers were removed.

After his arrest in June 1972, sixty prominent European intellectuals launched a call for his release. He broke under physical threat during the pretrial investigation. He "confessed" and repented the errors of his previous actions, cooperated with the KGB, and gave information about his own and other people's activities. As a consequence, more than two hundred persons were interrogated during the preliminary investigation. In April 1973 he wrote a letter from prison to Andrei Sakharov, urging him to cease his dissident activity. From 27 August to 1 September, he was tried (together with economist Viktor Krasin) and charged with compiling, signing, keeping, and distributing numerous letters of protest, leaflets, and the *Khronika tekushchikh sobytiy* (*Chronicle of Current Events*; appearing from 1968 to 1983), with passing on these documents to foreign correspondents, and with cooperating with émigré organizations. He pleaded guilty and was sentenced to three years' imprisonment and three years of internal exile. On 5 September 1973, he was presented to the Soviet and foreign public at a press conference, at which he showed remorse and admitted that he had plotted against the Soviet state and had furthered the hostile activities of anti-Soviet organizations abroad. On 28 September the Supreme Court reviewed his case and his sentence was commuted to sixteen months' imprisonment (the term he had served already) and three years of internal exile at Ryazan. In October 1973 he and his wife went into exile in Ryazan. In September 1974 he was granted pardon by the USSR Supreme Soviet Presidium. After his release Yakir was ostracized by dissident circles. He died in Moscow, completely isolated. **Andrei Dubrov**, author of the appeal in Yakir's defense, was deprived of his permission to immigrate to Israel and subjected to intensive interrogations.

1972–74   In August or September 1972, **Aleksandr Zheleznov**, historian, sociologist, and orientalist, was arrested, tried on charges of hooliganism, speculation in religious ritual objects, belonging to a Buddhist group, and having links with Zionism and was prescribed compulsory treatment in a special psychiatric hospital. In late 1974 he was released.

1973–86   A 1987 journal wrote that the replies of historians who were attacked between 1973 and 1986 were never published.

1973–   In 1973 historian and orientalist **Mikhail Bernshtam** (?1940–) was arrested for writing a book on Soviet history and allegedly forming an anti-Soviet group among students. He was declared insane and committed to a psychiatric hospital. In 1974 he was released. In April 1976 he was interrogated about a samizdat collection that he was allegedly preparing for publication.

1973–83   From 1973 to 1983, **Aleksandr Yakovlev** (1923–), historian and specialist in American history, acting head of the CPSU-CC propaganda department (1965–73), was the Soviet ambassador in Canada. He was "exiled" to Canada because in 1972 he had criticized Russian nationalism under the Brezhnev administration. From 1983 to 1985, he was director at the Institute of World Economy and International Relations of the USSR Academy of Sciences. In 1985 he returned to his old post as CPSU-CC Secretary for Propaganda and Agitation and in June 1987 he became a CPSU-CC Politburo member. He was called "the father of glasnost and perestroika". As the chairman of the Politburo Commission on the Further Study of the Repressions of the 1930s, 1940s, and Early 1950s (1988–90), he admitted that documents indicating Stalin's connection with the 1934 Kirov murder were deliberately destroyed. As the chairman of the Commission on the Legal and Political Evaluation of the German-Soviet Treaties of August 1939, he confirmed the existence of the secret protocols. In December 1992 he was appointed chairman of the Commission for the Rehabilitation of the Victims of Political Repression.

1973–   In March and early April 1973, **Irina Yakir** (1948–99), daughter of Pyotr Yakir [q.v. 1972–82] and a former history student (1966–69), was interrogated for three weeks about her dissident activities. From 1967 she had signed many appeals for persecuted dissidents and against state repression. In 1968 she had been expelled from Komsomol (Communist Youth League). In June 1969, while watching a Crimean Tatar demonstration, she was detained, interrogated and expelled from the Moscow Historical Archives Institute. During her 1973 interrogation, Yakir was confronted with her imprisoned father and she admitted her involvement in producing sixteen *Khronika* issues between 1969 and 1972. When summoned by the KGB in October 1973, she refused to write a statement in which she would agree to desist from dissident activity. Yakir was married to Yuly Kim (1937–), a composer who in 1960 had graduated from the history and philology faculty of the Moscow Pedagogical Institute and was also engaged in dissident activity.

In July 1973 literary archivist and critic **Gabriel Superfin** (1944–), editor of the memoirs of Mikoyan [q.v. Ukraine 1956], was arrested after repeated interrogations about the *Khronika* archives' location. His literary work and notebooks were confiscated and he was transferred to an investigation prison. In May 1974 he was charged with "anti-Soviet agitation and propaganda" for, inter alia, his involvement in publishing the *Khronika* and sentenced to five years in a strict-regime forced-labor camp and two years of internal exile. In September he was sent to a camp in Perm, where in January 1975 he was placed in a punishment cell for five days. He was transferred to the camp prison (March) and then to prison (September). In January 1976 he went on hunger strike there because the prison guards had confiscated his Bible, prayer book, and other religious literature. In May he was put on strict regime for three months. He was in poor health. The first volume of *Pamyat* [q.v. 1978–] was dedicated to him and Sergei Kovalev.

1973   In July the house of **G. Shapiro**, a Jewish retiree, was searched and his personal papers were confiscated in connection with a book he was preparing on the history of Jewish participation in Soviet politics and society from 1917 to 1945.

1973–   In August 1973 the house of Moscow art historian and Orthodox Christian writer **Yevgeny Barabanov** (1943–) was searched. He was interrogated for three weeks in connection with the Superfin [q.v. 1973–] case. In September he admitted his involvement in systematically transmitting the *Khronika* and other samizdat works to the West in an open letter to foreign correspondents, arguing that it was the only sure way of saving valuable parts of Russian literature and culture from loss or destruction. The interrogation ceased and he was not arrested. He was dismissed in October and not allowed to emigrate, despite several invitations to lecture abroad. In the fall of 1976, he was threatened with internment.

1973–94 On 6 September 1973, writer **Aleksandr Solzhenitsyn** (1918–), 1970 Nobel Prize winner in Literature, declared that he would publish *The Gulag Archipelago 1918–1956: An Experiment in Literary Investigation* (Russian: 1973–74; English: London/New York 1973–78), a historical account of life in the labor camps based on personal testimonies and reports, memoirs, and letters by 227 witnesses and written secretly in 1958–68. The decision was triggered by the suicide of typist Elizaveta Voronyanskaya (?1903–73) in Leningrad in August 1973. She had hidden part of the manuscript but revealed its whereabouts after the KGB had interrogated her for five days, enabling the KGB to seize it.

Solzhenitsyn's harassment had begun in February 1945 when, as a commander of the reconnaissance artillery battery, he was arrested for anti-Stalinist statements in some of his intercepted letters, tried, and sentenced to eight years' imprisonment (1945–53) and three years of internal exile (1953–56). He was rehabilitated in March 1957. He wrote many literary works about his camp experiences and, despite constant threats, harassment, confiscation of many of his papers, and censorship by the KGB, the press, and the Writers' Union (from which he was expelled in 1969), he was a leading dissident emphasizing traditional cultural values and freedom of expression and religion, until his arrest on 12 February 1974 and deportation the next day, to the FRG, Switzerland, and the United States, where he settled in Vermont (1976–90). It was reportedly the first deportation of a dissident since Leon Trotsky's in 1929. In exile, Solzhenitsyn continued writing a multivolume historical work, *The Red Wheel* (started in 1968), on life in Russia in 1914–18. The first volume, *August 1914*, had already appeared abroad (Russian; Paris 1971).

Many Soviet citizens ran into trouble for possessing or circulating copies of *The Gulag Archipelago* or other works of Solzhenitsyn. In March 1974 the Finnish publisher decided not to issue a Finnish translation of *The Gulag Archipelago*, allegedly out of fear that it might harm the ruling Social Democratic Party and possibly diminish Soviet confidence in it. A Finnish translation was eventually published in Sweden in the fall of 1974. In June 1989 *Novy Mir* (New World) began publishing *The Gulag Archipelago* (under the supervision of historian and editor Vadim Borisov [q.v. 1970]). In August 1990 Solzhenitsyn's citizenship, lost at the time of his expulsion, was restored. In May 1994 he returned to Russia. In February 1972 **Anatoly Reshetnik**, lecturer in history and social studies, had been sentenced in Sverdlovsk to two years in a labor camp for making critical statements and writing an open letter in Solzhenitsyn's defense.

1974–   In 1974 **Anatoly Levitin** (1915–) (pseudonym: Anatoly Krasnov), a religious writer, teacher, activist in the Russian Orthodox movement and member of the Action Group for the Defense of Civil Rights in the USSR, went into exile. He had often been imprisoned and written numerous samizdat essays, including a historical one with Shavrov [q.v. 1948–54]. He spoke or wrote in defense of, among others, Ginzburg [q.v. 1966–67], Galanskov [q.v. 1960–72], Grigorenko [q.v. 1961–], Solzhenitsyn [q.v. 1973–94], Pyotr Yakir [q.v. 1972–82], and Dzhemilev [q.v. 1963–].

[1974]   Activists among the USSR's German minority started to issue a samizdat almanac called *Repatria*, about the history, culture, and problems of the Soviet Germans.

1974–   **Yuri Bregel** (1925–), research fellow at the USSR Academy of Sciences Institute of Oriental Studies (1962–73), emigrated to Israel,
where he became the Eliahu Eilath history professor at Hebrew University, Jerusalem. Later he worked at the department of Uralic and
Altaic studies, Indiana University, Bloomington, United States
(1981–).

In March **Boris Shragin** (1926–), research officer at the Institute of
Art History, Moscow, who published many pseudonymous samizdat
essays, including *Andrei Amalrik* [q.v. 1963–] *As a Publicist* and
Anguish for History, emigrated.

In April 1974 writer and historian **Mikhail Kheifets** (1934–), who
wrote several historical-documentary essays, film and television sce-
narios, and novels about the nineteenth century, was arrested by the
KGB. In September he was tried on charges of "preparing and disseminating samizdat writings" for writing the introduction to an unpublished five-volume collection of poems by the banned poet
Joseph Brodsky and for possessing and distributing excerpts from
Khronika; Smolensk under Soviet Rule (Cambridge, Mass., 1958) by
historian **Merle Fainsod** (1907–72); and *Will the USSR Survive until
1984?* by Amalrik [q.v. 1963–]. Kheifets was sentenced to four years
in a strict-regime camp and two years of internal exile. Upon his
release in 1980, he went into exile in Israel, where he became a
member of the editorial board of the magazine *22* in Tel Aviv.

1974–   In October 1974 historian, philosopher, and journalist **Aleksandr
Yanov** (1930–) emigrated to the United States and wrote *The Ori-
gins of Autocracy: Ivan the Terrible in Russian History* (Berkeley/
London 1981).

pre-1975 Historians and others concerned with the past engaged in dissident
activities in the pre-1975 decade were literary historian **Aleksandr
Anikst** (1910–); art historian **Liudmila Belova**; writer **Valentin Be-
restov** (1929–), a graduate from the Moscow State University history
department; **I. Denisov**, who wrote a samizdat essay on the history
of the Russian Orthodox Church; writer **Gennady Fish** (1903–71),
graduate in art history (1924); art historian and critic **Yury Gerchuk**;
literary historian **Emma Gershtein** (1903–); **Vitaly Kireiko** (1926–),
composer and candidate of art history; **Andry Nimenko** (1925–),
sculptor and art historian; **Lev Ospovat** (1922–), a graduate from
the Moscow State University history department; writer **Konstantin**

Paustovsky (1892–1968), who had studied art history at Kiev University; **Konstantin Rudnicky** (1920–), employed by the Institute of Art History; **Igor Shafarevich** (1923–), academician, mathematician, and human-rights campaigner, who in [1974] (the year of his dismissal) wrote a samizdat study, *Socialism As a Phenomenon in World History* (published in France in 1977), which treated socialism as an aspect of the human urge to self-destruction; **Fedor Shakhmagonov** (1923–), who in the 1960s wrote a samizdat historical novel about the purge of Marshal Mikhail Tukhachevsky; **Viktor Shklovsky** (1893–1984), literary historian and critic amnestied in 1923 after he had fought against the Bolsheviks in 1918; **S. Sukhaltuev** [possibly a pseudonym], who in 1973 published a samizdat essay on nineteenth-century intellectuals; **I. Tropinin** [possibly a pseudonym], who in 1972 published a samizdat essay on Russian historical consciousness; art historian and composer **Leopold Yashchenko**; and **Neia Zorkaia** (1924–), historian of Soviet theater and cinema, who for her dissident activity was demoted from senior to junior officer at the Institute of Art History, Moscow, for one year.

1975   In 1975 philologist and cultural historian **Dmitry Likhachev** (1906–99), academician of the USSR Academy of Sciences (1970–) and expert on ancient Russian literature, was attacked by KGB thugs because he refused to condemn leading dissident Andrei Sakharov. During the 1970s Likhachev experienced difficulties as a historian and took no part in public life. Calling for the return of artifacts and archives taken out of Russia during and after the 1917 revolution and participating in the movement for the protection of ancient monuments, he became Mikhail Gorbachev's adviser on cultural and historical heritage matters in early 1985 and was one of the most influential cultural figures of the glasnost period. From 1989 to January 1992, he was a member of Parliament. In 1991 he became chairman of Russia's International Cultural Foundation. From October 1928 to August 1932, Likhachev, a graduate from Leningrad State University, had been imprisoned, mostly in Solovki concentration camp. He had been a literary editor (1932–38), researcher (1938–54), and head (1954–?) of the ancient Russian literature department at the USSR Academy of Sciences Institute of Russian Literature (Pushkin House). From 1946 to 1953, he was professor at Leningrad State University.

1975–   Art historian **Vladimir Teteriatnikov** (1938–), who had worked as an icon specialist at the Rublev Museum, immigrated to the United States.

In March 1975 historian and literary critic **Sergei Grigoryants** (1947–) was arrested, tried in September and sentenced to five years in a hard-regime camp. In 1980 he was released. In February 1983 he and Viktor Beskrovnykh were arrested in the Kaluga region in connection with the publication of a samizdat human-rights bulletin, *Express Information Bulletin V*. In February 1984 Grigoryants was sentenced to seven years' imprisonment and three years of internal exile for issuing *Bulletin V* (which closed down in May). In February 1987 he was released. Shortly afterward, he led a group of ex-prisoners asking permission to publish an unofficial current affairs journal, *Glasnost*, which was launched in June 1987 but never officially registered. The threat of confiscation was permanent and the journal's staff was regularly harassed. In May 1988 Grigoryants was detained at the journal's headquarters, where the third session of the founding conference of a new political party, the Democratic Union, was due to take place. He was put under administrative arrest for seven days for allegedly "resisting the police". As the chief informant of the Western press on the situation in Armenia and Karabakh, he came under attack in the official press because of his regular contact with Western correspondents. While he was in prison, the journal's equipment was confiscated and its archives destroyed. In February 1990 he was refused permission to travel to Paris for a UNESCO conference on the press in Eastern Europe. In November 1991 the newly founded Independent Trade Union of Journalists, headed by Grigoryants, held its first congress. In December 1995 at Moscow airport he was detained as the chairman of the organizing committee of the International Public Tribunal on Chechnya as he was about to leave for the tribunal's hearings in Stockholm. His books, computer disks, videotapes, and documents were confiscated. In August 2000, masked police commandos stormed the office of *Glasnost Foundation*, a human-rights organization that he headed, without any apparent reason. The police carrying out the raid taunted him with the knowledge that he was a former dissident.

1975   In May journalism student **Eduard Samoilov** (1950–) was arrested for attempting to convey to the West his heterodox work on Soviet political history. He was committed to a psychiatric hospital.

In May KGB agents searched the houses of several persons involved in the publication of the samizdat journal *Jews in the USSR*. Published since October 1972, it carried articles on the history and present situation of the Jewish community in the USSR.

1976   The Russian translation of *History of the Second World War* (originally 1944; London 1970) by **Liddell Hart** (1895–1970) showed many cuts in the text, the maps, and the bibliography in the following areas: Stalin, his generals, and their wartime policy mistakes and failures; Soviet treatment of neighboring states invaded or occupied by the USSR during the war and affected by postwar territorial changes; remarks criticizing the USSR and Red Army actions or praising other countries, including their assistance to the USSR and their role in defeating Nazi Germany. Another British work, the six-volume *Second World War* (London 1948–53), which earned its author, former British Prime Minister **Winston Churchill** (1874–1965), the 1953 Nobel Prize for Literature, was translated without deletions but was made available only in limited editions to professional scholars and held in reserved libraries.

In March **Ilya Serman** (1913–), literary historian and coauthor of the nineteenth-century portions of *History of Russian Literature I*, was dismissed from his position at a publishing house in Leningrad, presumably as a retaliation for his daughter's emigration to Israel in December 1975.

In September Siberian museum worker **Pavel Bashkirov** was tried and sentenced to eighteen months' imprisonment, inter alia, because he distributed *1984*, a novel about the falsification of history in totalitarian regimes by **George Orwell** (1903–50), and various samizdat works by and about Solzhenitsyn [q.v. 1973–94].

1978   History student **Yury Felshtinsky** (1956–) immigrated to the United States, where he continued his studies and wrote about the fate of the socialist parties after the 1917 October revolution.

In the months after the samizdat journal *Poiski* (Searches) was founded, its editorial board, including historian **Pyotr Pryshov**, came under increasing KGB pressure.

1978–   Around 1978–80 the historian(s) (name[s] unknown) writing under pseudonym(s) and allegedly responsible for the publication of the journal *Pamyat* (Memory) was/were reportedly sentenced to four years in a labor camp [q.v. 1966–: Gefter]. In the spring of 1979, the homes of Roginsky [q.v. 1981–], **Sergei Dedyulin**, and **Valery Sazhin** in Leningrad were searched in connection with the case. In 1976 the *Pamyat* group had prepared her first anthology (*Pamyat: Istoricheskii sbornik I*: Moscow, samzidat, 1976; New York 1978). It was followed by five volumes (published in Paris and edited by Natalya Gorbanevskaya) with memoirs, diaries, correspondence, essays, and annotated reprints of small-edition works about tsarist and Soviet repression during 1906–77, the official documents of which were kept in restricted-access archives or were possibly partially destroyed. In the 1980s *Pamyat* evolved into a right-wing and anti-Semitic group.

Art historian **Yevgenya [= Gena] Gutkina** (?1922–) was reportedly fined and sentenced to ten years of hard labor in a prison camp near Gorky on the charge of "smuggling antiques and works of art out of Russia". It was widely believed that the real reason was that she protected and encouraged living artists and unearthed the works of some deceased artists. Her art collection and her manuscripts were confiscated. Despite her bad health, she was given fifteen days' solitary confinement in December 1981.

Aleksandr Kazhdan (1922–97), historian of Byzantium and senior researcher in Byzantine studies at the USSR Academy of Sciences History Institute (1956–78), was forced to emigrate to the United States because his son had emigrated in 1976. He became a senior researcher at Dumbarton Oaks, Washington, D.C. (1979–97). In 1947–56 he had reportedly been a victim of anti-Semitism, finding and then losing positions at small institutions far from Moscow. He is the editor of the three-volume *Oxford Dictionary of Byzantium* (1991).

1979   Samizdat writer **Yuri Galperin** (1947–), who studied history at Leningrad University, immigrated to Switzerland.

In September the Soviet authorities confiscated more than forty books at the Moscow International Book Fair, including books by Orwell [q.v. 1976] and Solzhenitsyn [q.v. 1973–94]; *A Cartoon History of Foreign Policy 1776–1976*, by **David Levine** (1926–); and a biography of Nikolai Bukharin (the leading intellectual in the "right-wing" opposition to Stalin in 1928–29, executed in 1938 and rehabilitated in 1988) by Cohen [q.v. 1950–90].

1980   According to a 1980 report, the use of works written by historians who (for very different reasons) had fallen in disgrace, such as **Sergei Platonov** (1860–1933) or **Michael Pokrovsky** (1868–1932), had been forbidden for a long time (although Pokrovsky had been referred to favorably in 1955 and rehabilitated in 1961). The KGB confiscated materials for a biography of Russian scholar Vladimir Khavkin (1860–1930) in the possession of a historian from the United States [name unknown] at the border. Attempts to send copies of the archive documents by mail failed.

With the onset of the Solidarity period in Poland, a number of books on Polish history were taken out of circulation, partly because they cited Polish historians who supported Solidarity. Among them was **Stefan Kieniewicz** (1907–), who had lectured at Moscow University in the 1970s and was the coeditor of a joint Soviet–Polish publication of documents related to the 1863 Polish uprising.

1981   In June the exhibition of paintings "Moscow-Paris 1900–1930" opened in Moscow, but some Soviet works had been dropped from the catalog by the organizers.

1981–   In August 1981 **Arseny Roginsky** (?1947–), a specialist in early-nineteenth-century social history, was arrested in Leningrad and accused of "forgery and the production and sale of forged documents". The documents were letters that he needed to obtain permission to use the Leningrad archives for research into his father's imprisonment and execution in a labor camp. Previous efforts to research his father's history had led the KGB to block his acceptance as a history student to Leningrad University. Roginsky graduated from Tartu University instead. Subsequently, as a Jew and son of a political prisoner, he was barred from work in any Soviet research institution. From 1977 his apartment was regularly searched. During one of those searches in the spring of 1979, the KGB confiscated some books and, as a result, Roginsky was dismissed as a teacher. Arrested then in 1981, he was presented with the choice of emigration or detention. In his final defense speech, Roginsky pleaded not guilty. He maintained that he had only wished to consult material which should normally have been available. He complained about the obstacles Soviet historians met when they tried to access archival materials. In December 1981 he was sentenced to four years in a labor camp. A decade later, he became secretary of the Scientific Council of Memorial [q.v. 1987–] In that capacity, he was able to examine the KGB archives concerning the Stalinist past.

1981   In October **Viktor Kholodkovsky**, historian of the USSR Academy of Sciences History Institute and specialist in modern Finnish history, argued that Stalin deviated from the Leninist policy during the 1939–40 Russo-Finnish war. He was forced into retirement. Aleksandr Kan [q.v. 1967] was reprimanded for not criticizing Cholodkovski enough.

1982   In January a play about Lenin, *This Is How We Conquer*, by **Mikhail Shatrov** (real name: **Marshak**), was banned on the grounds that it idealized the New Economic Policy. Another of his plays, *Strokes in the Portrait of Lenin*, written in the early 1970s, was broadcast on television for the first time in January 1987.

In [August] **Sergei Batrovin** (?1957–), artist and spokesman for an independent disarmament and peace group, was forced into a psychiatric hospital for one month after authorities broke up an antiwar exhibit commemorating the anniversary of Hiroshima. He was released as an outpatient after international protests.

1983   In March historian and archivist **Dmitry Markov**, who worked as a photographer in Kaluga, was arrested for his involvement in *Bulletin V* [q.v. 1975–: Grigoryants]. More than two hundred rolls of film of samizdat and tamizdat ("published over there"; banned works published abroad) works were confiscated from his apartment. In the early 1970s, the KGB had already interrogated him when Pyotr Yakir [q.v. 1972–82] testified against him in connection with his involvement in the distribution of the *Khronika*.

[1983]–   In [March] historian **Viktor Artsimovich**, translator at the Tomsk Institute of Geophysics and member of a group that circulated samizdat and tamizdat writings and literature published abroad, was arrested. A large number of books, including books on history, and the manuscript *Contradiction upon Contradiction* (a critical analysis of Karl Marx's works allegedly written by Artsimovich), were seized. In September he was charged with "slander of the Soviet state and social system" and "writing samizdat", judged unaccountable for his actions and suffering from schizophrenia and "philosophical intoxication", and committed to a special psychiatric hospital.

1986   In April **Vladimir Rusak**, a former deacon of the Orthodox Church, was arrested in Moscow and charged with "anti-Soviet agitation and propaganda". He was the author of a book on the history of the Russian Orthodox Church (extracts of which were published abroad under a pseudonym). In 1982 he had been exiled to a monastery after he had spoken in a sermon of the sufferings of the church since the revolution. In 1983 he was forced to seek employment as a manual laborer. His personal archive and manuscripts were confiscated.

In mid-1986 the ninth edition of the 1959 one-volume CPSU history, prepared under the supervision of **Boris Ponomarev** (1905–) and most of the multivolume CPSU history supervised by academician **Pyotr Pospelov** [q.v. 1947–] were rejected because they were too positive about Stalinism and withdrawn from use in Soviet schools.

1986–89   In September 1986 liberal historian **Yuri Afanasiev** (1934–), specialist in French historiography and Stalinism, section head at the Academy of Sciences Institute of World History, was dismissed because of staff reductions. The real reason for his dismissal was reportedly his September 1985 essay for *Kommunist*, "The Past and Ourselves", which advocated a thorough review of the prevailing representation of history. This was considered the initial major assault on official history. In December 1986 he was appointed history professor and rector of the Moscow State Historical Archives Institute (later the Russian State University of the Humanities), responsible for the training of archivists. As late as [July] 1988, a lecture of his at the Moscow Physical-Technical Institute was banned. In October 1989 he was personally attacked by President Mikhail Gorbachev (who suggested that he should return his CPSU card) and the press. The CPSU and the Department of Education sent investigators to the institute to examine his and his staff's ideological loyalty. He was the first prominent personality to leave the CPSU (April 1990). As a member of Parliament for the Inter-Regional Group of Deputies, he was active in the opposition (March 1989–1992).

pre-1987   *Children of the Arbat*, a novel by Gulag (the Soviet penal system under Stalin) victim and writer **Anatoly Rybakov** (pseudonym of **Anatoly Aronov**, 1911–98) about the Stalinist terror, was published. Written around 1966, it was offered in vain for publication at the time.

1987–91   In April 1987 **Dmitry Yurasov** (1964–), a student who carried out detailed research on the Stalinist purges and the subsequent rehabilitation under Khrushchev, was summoned for questioning by the KGB after he had given a speech about his work at a discussion meeting of the Moscow Writers' Union. From the age of twelve, Yurasov had been compiling a file of victims of the Stalinist repression from archival and published sources (containing, by November 1990, a quarter of a million index cards). Between July 1981 and November 1982, and again between January 1985 and November 1986 (while studying at the Moscow Historical Archives Institute in the evenings), he worked in several archives. There he secretly recorded information and smuggled it out. In November 1986 his activities were discovered and he was dismissed. The April 1987 speech was his first public appearance. After an article for *Glasnost* [q.v. 1987], he was again interrogated by the KGB. In September 150 notebooks and 15,000 to 20,000 index cards were confiscated at his apartment. Although frequently harassed, and at one time (September 1988) detained and interrogated for three days, he started lecturing on Stalinism all over the USSR after a television appearance in the fall of 1988, acting as a liaison officer for Memorial [q.v. 1987–]. In 1991 he accepted a post at the CPSU archives.

1987   In July Grigoryants [q.v. 1975–] and Yurasov [q.v. 1987–91] reported in the underground publication *Glasnost* that the documentary evidence of the arrests, expulsions, and trials under Stalin was being systematically destroyed. They declared that only a few hundred thousand files remained in the Combined Special Archive of the Military Collegium and the Supreme Court of the USSR. The rest, millions of investigation files and records of conviction, had been burned in the archives of regional and territorial courts, the Procuracy, the Ministry of Justice, and the KGB in the 1960s and 1970s. In 1985–87 parts of the Special Archive, referring to the years 1940 and 1948–49, were also destroyed on the pretext that there was insufficient space.

1987–   In November 1987 local authorities detained and fined signature gatherers (who had formed a group since August 1987) for a petition that led to the establishment of Memorial, the All-Union Historical-Enlightenment Society. In the first years of existence, Memorial's work to investigate the history of Stalinist repression met with official disapproval. Its collaborators, who established chapters everywhere in the USSR, were obstructed and sometimes detained (including **M.Y. Kovalenko, V.A. Kuzin, Dmitry Leonov, Vladimir Lysenko, Lev Ponomarev, Yuri Samodurov, Y.P. Shubko, Nikolai Starkov, Aleksandr Vaisberg**, and **Elena Zhemkova** in November 1987 and **Sivert Zoldin** in February 1988), when they tried to find disappeared Gulag victims, gather and investigate archives, interview survivors, or collect funds. On 30 October (Political Prisoners Day since 1974) 1988, riot police detained scores of demonstrators in various cities during rallies organized by Memorial in support of political prisoners. On 28–29 January 1989, Memorial held its constituent assembly: among the founders were Andrei Sakharov, Afanasiev [q.v. 1986–89], Medvedev [q.v. 1969–89], and Yevtushenko [q.v. Ukraine 1985]; the members of the Scientific Council also included Gefter [q.v. 1966–] and Roginsky [q.v. 1981–]. On 30 October 1990, a stone memorial "in honor of the millions of victims of the totalitarian regime" was unveiled in a park opposite the KGB headquarters at Lubyanka. Memorial's official registration—repeatedly denied—took place in the fall of 1991. Until then Memorial had not been allowed officially to use archival materials. In 1992 Memorial was transformed from an All-Union into an Inter-Republic Society. From that year microfilmed copies of its archives have been deposited at the International Institute of Social History, Amsterdam, and at Columbia University, New York, for security reasons. In March 1992 the chairman of the Russian branch of Memorial, Boris Pustyntsev, was beaten up in St. Petersburg, possibly in connection with Memorial's earlier attempts to dissolve the KGB. In 1995 Memorial united about one hundred independent organizations in Russia, the Ukraine, Kazakhstan, Armenia, Georgia, and

Poland. Called "Memorial, International Historical and Educational Human Rights and Charity Society", it concentrated on the history of political repression, on contemporary human-rights violations (such as during the war in Chechnya), and on charity.

1988   When historian **Igor Bestuzhev-Lada** (?1932–) began publishing about Stalinist atrocities in April and tried to file an official court case against Stalin in August, he was threatened with death by alleged "World War II veterans".

In May the State Committee for Education canceled the June final exit examination in history and social science (for sixteen- and seventeen-year-olds), and the annual examinations in the history of the Soviet period for other age groups because the old history textbooks had been found full of lies: their credibility had disappeared. New textbooks appeared in 1989 and 1990.

[1989]   In [1989] **Oleg Zakirov**, a KGB major assigned to Smolensk and conducting research into the 1940 Katyń massacre, was harassed and pressured to resign, especially when he produced names of NKVD officers who participated in the massacre.

1989   In February 1989 the first report of an atrocity committed by Soviet troops in Afghanistan was published. In April the full text of Khrushchev's secret speech at the 1956 20th CPSU Congress, in which he condemned Stalin, was published for the first time.

pre-1990   Before 1990 the existence of the so-called Central State Special Archive, containing millions of documents seized from Germany and German-occupied Europe after World War II, could not be mentioned in the press.

1990–91   In 1990 **V. Tsaplin**, the director of TsGANKh (Central State Archive of National Economy, after 1991 RGAE), who in 1989 had published a pioneering article about the mass repressions based on secret material from his archive, addressed a detailed report on the failings of the state archives to the CPSU-CC. The report was forwarded to Glavarkhiv director Fedor Vaganov (died 1993), who reportedly regarded it as extremely disloyal. Tsaplin had to take early retirement. He was replaced by E. Kuzmina. In December 1991, when the USSR ceased to exist, all Glavarkhiv activities were transferred to Roskomarkhiv (Russian Committee for Archival Affairs, in December 1992 reorganized as Rosarkhiv), under the directorship of Rudolf Pikhoya. The main archivists Vaganov, I. Kitaev (director of TsPA, the Central CPSU Archive, after 1991 RTsKhIDNI), and Kuzmina were removed from their posts.

1990   In September twenty-nine people were detained after a meeting in Moscow to commemorate victims of the "Red Terror". Five were subsequently put under administrative arrest.

In late 1990 large quantities of operational files and files on informants and agents in the KGB archives were reportedly ordered to be destroyed. This was partially prevented, however, and after the August 1991 coup attempt some KGB archives were sealed.

1991   In June General, philosopher, and historian **Dmitri Volkogonov** (1928–95), biographer of Lenin, Stalin, and Trotsky, was dismissed from his position as director (1988–91) of the USSR Defense Ministry's Institute of Military History after he had accused the military leadership of trying to "control history". Later he became chairman of the parliamentary Commission for the Transfer and Acceptance of the Archives of the CPSU and the KGB (end of 1991–September 1993) and a close adviser to President Boris Yeltsin. For his biographies he had been granted privileged—often monopolistic—access to many secret archives.

A November 1991 report stated that about 4,000 documents by Lenin were being kept hidden in former CPSU archives because they did not fit his "idealized image".

Non-Russian Republics (general)

1940–   In the Baltic area, the forced annexation of Estonia, Latvia, and Lithuania by the USSR (1940), the Sovietization of 1940–41, the German military occupation of 1941–44, and the Soviet reannexation in 1944–45 prevented any serious historical research. In Latvia, for example, the Soviet authorities banned more than 4,000 books, many of those on Latvian history. Many subjects remained taboo until 1989, especially the interwar independence era and the Stalinist period. A number of historians of the interwar period were reportedly deported to Siberia. Most Baltic exiles went to Sweden, Australia, Germany, and North America.

pre-1951   A 1951 report stated that, in the reassessment during 1945–50 of the national liberation struggles by non-Russian nationalities within the tsarist empire, an entire group of historians and literary critics in Kazakhstan, Azerbaijan, Kirgizia, Yakutia, and Dagestan were expelled from the CPSU, dismissed, and stripped of their academic degrees. Some were arrested.

1952–   Between February and June, old national epics such as *Alpamish* (Uzbek), *Keroghly* (Azeri Turk), *Korkut-Ata* (Turkmen), *Manas* (Kirgiz), and *Pesno Nabegakh* (Dagestani) were attacked as "feudal" and "fanatic-religious" and censored. They disappeared from libraries, and exhibits on their heroes were removed from museums. Scores of museums in Central Asia and also in Lithuania were purged because they failed to show the influence of the Russian culture. Historians were criticized for their idealization of the epics and called "bourgeois-nationalist". In 1954 some of these national epics were restored to favor.

Armenia

1937–[54]   From 1937 to [1954], Armenian historian **Ashot Hovhannisian** (1887–1972) was imprisoned. In 1954 he resumed his historical studies and was appointed director of the Armenian Academy of Sciences Historical Section in 1961. In 1927 he had been dismissed as the leader (1925–27) of the Armenian Communist Party (CP) for his underestimation of the dangers of Trotskyism and specifism (independent Marxism).

1947   In August the CPSU-CC passed a resolution on ideological shortcomings in Armenia, in which "bourgeois-nationalist distortions" in historical writing such as the "idealization" of the pre-Russian past were mentioned.

1948   In November the Armenian CP Congress condemned scholars and writers for "idealizing the historical past of Armenia", for "ignoring the class struggle" in Armenian history, and for being too attracted to the "reactionary culture of the bourgeois West."

1953–54   *The Narodnik Organizations of the Trans-Caucasus between 1870 and 1880* (1940), *The Armenian Liberation Movement between 1850 and 1880* ([1943]), and another [1945] work by Armenian historian and academician **Mkrtich Nersesian** (1910–99), director of the Armenian Academy of Sciences History Institute (1939–47), head of the subdepartment of history of the Armenian people, Yerevan University (1947–50), and academy vice president (1950–60), were severely criticized by the Armenian Academy of Sciences social science department for not being Marxist-Leninist enough. Nersesian was accused, inter alia, of labeling the Armenian Liberation Movement "democratic" instead of "bourgeois" and praising nineteenth-century figures like Raffi (1835–88). He confessed his "shortcomings" in the press. He was absolved at the 1954 Seventeenth Party Congress of Soviet Armenia. His colleague **Vardan Parsamian** was criticized for not recognizing that the Russian annexation of Armenia in the 1820s had had "progressive significance" for the Armenians.

1964–   In November 1964 **E. Ovannisian** wrote a letter to *Pravda* request-
            ing the erection of a memorial to the Armenian victims of Turkish
            mass murders. Around 1965 he protested *Pravda*'s alleged efforts to
            disregard the mass murders of Armenians in order not to disturb
            good relations with Turkey.

1988–94   During the 1988–94 conflict on the disputed region of Nagorno-
            Karabakh (an Armenian-populated enclave in Azerbaijan), many cul-
            tural monuments were destroyed. A 1988 publication of the
            Armenian Academy of Sciences claimed that dozens of ancient Ar-
            menian settlements, cemeteries, khachkar (carved stones), and in-
            scriptions had been destroyed during the last decades in the enclave.
            At least thirty such monuments, including churches, had been de-
            stroyed in Nakhichevan (a detached area of Azerbaijan).

1988–89   In December 1988 **Levon Ter-Petrossian** (1945–), an Armenian or-
            ientalist and academic secretary at the Matenadaran (the library of
            ancient manuscripts), Yerevan (1978–), was arrested along with the
            rest of the Karabagh Committee (a group leading a mass movement
            to unify Armenia with Nagorno-Karabagh) and imprisoned. In May
            1989 he was released. He became a leader of the Armenian National
            Movement and in 1991–96 the first president of the newly inde-
            pendent Armenia.

Azerbaijan

1950–56   In May 1950 *Pravda* and *Izvestiia* attacked Azerbaijani historian and
            philosopher **Geidar Guseinov** (**Haydar Huseynov**) (1908–50), vice
            president of the Azerbaijani Academy of Sciences (1945–), for
            having glorified "imperialist agent" Shamil [q.v. USSR 1945–89].
            Although Guseinov had received the Stalin Prize for his book *On
            the History of Social and Philosophical Thought in Azerbaijan in
            the Nineteenth Century* (Baku 1949) the previous March, he was
            condemned by dozens of historians and writers. One of them, Mir
            Bagirov, first secretary of the Azerbaijani CP-CC and author of *On
            the History of Bolshevik Organizations in Baku and Azerbaijan*
            (Moscow 1946), allegedly had tried to inscribe his name upon Gus-
            einov's work. The USSR Council of Ministers decided to withdraw
            the award. Guseinov was dismissed and committed suicide. In Sep-
            tember 1950 Dagestani historian **Rasul Magomedov** (?1910–), au-
            thor of three books on Shamil, was also criticized and dismissed as
            director of the Dagestan History Institute and vice chairman of the
            academy's Dagestan branch. He was restored to his positions after
            1956.

1958   Azerbaijani poet **Bakhtiar Bakhabzade** published *Gulistan*, a poem
            in which he condemned the north–south partition of Azerbaijan at
            the 1813 Gulistan Treaty, in the newspaper of Sheki, but the issue
            was removed from circulation and the poet harassed.

1975–77   In 1975 **Abulfaz Elchibey** (1938–2000), history lecturer at Azer-
            baijan State University, Baku (1969–74), was arrested by the KGB
            and sentenced "for slandering the Soviet state". He was sent to a
            labor camp until 1977. He became a collaborator of the Azeri Acad-
            emy of Sciences Institute of Manuscripts (1977–92). A Popular Front
            Party cofounder and chairman (1989–), he was president of Azer-
            baijan (June 1992–June 1993). After disagreement over his policy
            on Nagorno-Karabakh, he failed to disarm a disobedient military
            garrison and fled into exile in his native Nakhichevan. Later he be-
            came an opposition leader.

[1988]   The first Azerbaijani samizdat book, *Vatan* (Motherland), appeared.
            It contained many historical documents and eyewitness accounts.

Belorussia

1930–   In 1930 **Iosif Dyla** (1880–?), Belorussian literary figure, economist,
            and historian, involved from his student days in radical and revo-
            lutionary activities, senior scholar of the Belorussian Academy of
            Sciences (1928–), was arrested by the secret police because of his
            Belorussian nationalism and sent into exile. He was rehabilitated
            after 1956 but he remained in Saratov, southern Russia, writing nov-
            els on historical themes.

1930–46   Historian **Vladimir Picheta** (1878–1947), specialist in the medieval
            social-economic history of Belorussia, first rector of the Belorussian
            State University (1921–30), Minsk, was a victim of political repres-
            sion from the early 1930s until his death. In the summer of 1930 he
            was arrested for "Belorussian nationalism", expelled from the Belo-
            russian Academy of Sciences (1928–30, readmitted in 1946), and
            internally exiled for five years. In the mid-1930s he was released.
            He worked for a time as a secondary school teacher. From 1939 he
            was a corresponding member at the USSR Academy of Sciences and
            history professor at Moscow State University. In 1946 he became
            an academician and deputy director of the USSR Academy of Sci-
            ences Institute of Slavic Studies. His major works on Belorussian
            history, which had been banned or remained in manuscript, appeared
            in two volumes in Moscow (1958, 1961).

1971–86   **Bolha Ipatava** was unable to publish anything for fifteen years be-
          cause in 1971 she had written a small book on twelfth-century Cath-
          olic saint Euphrosyne of Polatsak.

Estonia

1950–55   In 1950 **Hans Kruus** (1891–1976), leading Estonian historian after
          1930, professor of USSR history (1931–41), and rector (1940–41)
          of Tartu University, deputy prime minister of the Estonian People's
          Government (1940–41), active as an anti-German propagandist
          (1941–44), minister of foreign affairs of the Estonian SSR (1944–
          50), and Estonian Academy of Sciences president (1946–50), fell
          victim to the so-called Cult of Personality. In 1955 he was rehabil-
          itated and became a research professor at the USSR (1955–58) and
          Estonian (1958–76) academies of sciences.

1953   **Aleksis Rannit** (1914–85), an Estonian poet who studied, inter alia,
          art history and classical archeology, went into exile in the United
          States, where he became a curator of Russian and East European
          studies at Yale University (1960–).

1957   The editor of the Estonian monthly *Looming* (Creativity) was dis-
          missed after he had published a conference report by Estonian his-
          torian **V. Miller**, in which the 1952 edition of the *History of the
          Estonian SSR* and a new 1956 draft were severely criticized.

1975–88   Estonian historian **Tunne Kelam** (1936–), graduate from Tartu State
          University, senior research fellow at the history archives (1959–65)
          and member of the editorial staff of the *Estonian Encyclopedia*
          (1965–75), spent thirteen years in internal exile as a night watchman
          at a chicken farm for his dissident ideas. He became one of the
          leaders of the Estonian independence movement, and after inde-
          pendence in August 1991, he became vice chairman of the Estonian
          Parliament (1992–).

1979–   In 1979 Estonian, Latvian, and Lithuanian dissidents signed joint
          appeals for Baltic independence, calling for the withdrawal of Soviet
          troops and denouncing the 1939 nonaggression pact. In January 1980
          one of them, Estonian dissident **Mart Niklus** (1934–), biologist and
          language teacher, was arrested and charged with "anti-Soviet agita-
          tion and propaganda", inter alia, for signing the appeal. In January
          1981 he was sentenced to ten years in a strict-regime labor camp
          and five years of internal exile. He had already served eight years
          in prison in the early 1960s for circulating photographs showing the
          poor social conditions in and around Tartu.

1981–   In March Estonian construction engineer and dissident **Veljo Kalep** (?1935–) was sentenced to four years in a labor camp on charges of "anti-Soviet agitation and propaganda" and of possessing banned literature. He had been collecting material on the missing Swedish diplomat Raoul Wallenberg (1912–?), who had rescued thousands of Hungarian Jews from the Nazis and "disappeared" (probably arrested by Soviet forces and deceased in the USSR) in Budapest in January 1945.

1989   In March historian **Mart Laar** (1960–), cofounder of the Estonian Heritage Society (1987), specialist in the history of the Soviet takeover of Estonia, was attacked and threatened with prosecution by the Estonian CP newspaper *Voice of the People* because of his article "Time of Horrors", about the atrocities committed by the retreating Red Army in 1941 published in the review *Vikerkaar* (Rainbow) in November 1988. Laar was prime minister of Estonia twice (1992–94, 1999–), nominated by president (1992–) Lennart Meri, also a historian.

1990   In April Estonian journalists reported the murder of Protestant minister **Harold Meri** (?1920–90) and linked it with his research into the deportation of Estonians to Stalin's prison camps.

Georgia

1948   In February a CC resolution condemned *The Great Friendship*, an opera by **V. Muradeli** dealing with the relations among Caucasian peoples during the Russian Revolution and civil war, for "erroneously" suggesting that Georgians and Ossetians were, at that time, hostile to the Russians. According to Politburo member and cultural ideologue Andrei Zhdanov, only the Chechen and Ingush peoples had been hostile to the Russians.

1975–   In July **Teimuraz Dzhvarsheishvili**, a historian who in 1974 wrote *Testimony Concerning Crimes Committed in the Patriarchate of Georgia since the Death of Efrem II in Spring 1972*, about the involvement of high KGB officials in corruption and robbery, was arrested in Sukhumi, Abkhazian ASSR, tried in August on the (unsubstantiated) charge of rape, and sentenced to four years in a hard-regime camp.

1977–   In April **Viktor Rtskhiladze** (?1939–), historian, chief inspector of ancient monuments at the Georgian Ministry of Culture, member of the Georgian Helsinki Group, author of an article on the fate of the Meskhetian Turks, was arrested. This was preceded by a campaign in the Georgian press. In September he recanted at his trial in the capital Tbilisi and was conditionally released, but he still had to serve two years of internal exile.

pre-1981   In March 1981 a demonstration in Tbilisi demanded, inter alia, greater emphasis on the teaching of Georgian history in schools and universities. In October hundreds of people staged a demonstration in Mtskheta in protest against the reduction of the study of Georgian language and history in the republic's schools and universities. In at least the 1970s and 1980s, everything that contradicted the "tradition" of Russo-Georgian friendship, such as the period of Georgian independence (1918–21) or the Georgian anti-Soviet revolt (1924), was obliterated. Most Georgian historians were not allowed to consult *spetskhran* that covered the "unacceptable" periods in Georgian history.

1984   In 1984 Georgian film director **Tengiz Abuladze** (1924–) completed *Repentance*, a film about Stalinism and its excesses. It was shown in Georgia only. Abuladze reportedly concealed the film until its release in January 1987. Seventeen million people saw it in three weeks.

pre-1985   Until 1985 no historical works on Abkhazia were printed.

1991–92   In January 1991 South Ossetian leader **Torez Kulumbekov** was imprisoned in Georgia for the dissemination of "distorted historical facts". In January 1992 he was released after a military council took over power from President Zviad Gamsakhurdia and wanted to negotiate a solution for the South Ossetian problem.

Kazakhstan

1934–   In 1934 attempts by Pankratova [q.v. USSR 1956–57] and others to compile history textbooks were condemned by party leaders Stalin, Sergei Kirov, and Andrei Zhdanov for allegedly failing to demonstrate the colonial nature of tsarist rule. After 1944 emphasis on the progressive nature of Kazakh and other anti-tsarist resistance movements led to harsh reviews of later editions of Pankratova's three-volume *History of the USSR* (1939–40) and of her *History of Kazakhstan* (Alma-Ata 1943). The latter was condemned by the Kazakh CP in 1945, as was its revised 1949 edition. In the late 1940s, Pankratova lost her position at the Lenin State Pedagogical Institute and at the Academy of Pedagogical Sciences and had difficulties at the Academy of Sciences History Institute, but by the early 1950s she had recovered her status.

1941–55   History student **Wolfgang Ruge** (1917–) was deported to Kazakhstan because of his German nationality. There he worked in a labor camp and lived in internal exile during this period. A communist youth member who in 1933 had immigrated to the USSR, he had lived in Moscow as a cartographer and history student. Upon his release he returned to the GDR, where he became a historian at the Academy of Sciences Zentralinstitut für Geschichte (1956–83) and specialized in the history of the Weimar Republic.

1950–56   In December 1950 *Kazakhstan from the 1820s through the 1840s* (Alma-Ata 1947), a book originally written as a doctoral dissertation by Kazakh historian **Ermukhan Bekmakhanov** (1915–66), professor at Kazakh State University, Alma-Ata, and director of the Kazakh Academy of Sciences Institute of History, Archeology, and Ethnography, and the second edition of *History of the Soviet Socialist Republic of Kazakhstan* inspired by it, were attacked in *Pravda* because they called Kazakh Sultan Kasimov Kenesary's anti-Russian insurrection (1836–47) progressive. The successful 1947 book had already been denounced by some Kazakh historians in July 1948. During a meeting of the Academic Council of the USSR Academy of Sciences History Institute in February 1951, Bekmakhanov was denounced as a "bourgeois-nationalist". In October he was deprived of his doctoral title, as was Kazakh historian **E. Dilmukhamedov**, author of a 1940 dissertation on Kenesary and favorable reviewer of Bekmakhanov's work. Bekmakhanov was dismissed and arrested. He went into "intellectual exile" and was possibly imprisoned for six years. Rehabilitated in 1956, he had his academic title restored. Journalist **Kasym Sharipov**, who had reviewed Bekmakhanov's work in *Voprosy istorii* in 1949, was dismissed.

Kirgizia

1951–52   In 1951 the book *Outline of the Culture of the Kirgiz People* (Frunze 1946) by **Saul Abramzon** was criticized for "falsely" representing the Kirgiz annexation by Russia as a "conquest", idealizing "reactionary Kirgiz historical figures", and belittling Russian cultural influences. In February 1952 **A.N. Bernshtam's** *Great Heritage of the Kirgiz People* (Frunze 1945) was similarly criticized.

Latvia

1969   In November the Latvian militia detained ten persons who were present at a meeting near the grave of former Latvian president (1922–27) **Janis Cakste** (1859–1927) at Riga cemetery to commemorate independent Latvia. They were released eight days later.

1978   Latvian art historian and painter **Yurgis Skulme**, senior member of the art history department at the Latvian Academy of Art, was sentenced to thirty months in a labor camp for "anti-Soviet agitation and propaganda", although he reportedly had no links with any dissident groups.

1983–88   In December 1983 Latvian technician and translator **Gunnars Astra** (1932–88) was sentenced to seven years' imprisonment and five years of internal exile on charges of "anti-Soviet agitation and propaganda" for allegedly having circulated a Latvian samizdat translation of *1984*, the novel by Orwell [q.v. USSR 1976], which was banned. In February 1988 he was released. He spent almost two decades in prison for his pacifist defense of the Latvian cause.

1987   In June 1987, at a large demonstration organized by the Riga Helsinki Group to commemorate the mass deportation of Latvians to Siberia in 1941, about ten people were arrested. Leading Soviet academic Nikolai Shmelev (1936–) publicly declared that some seventeen million Soviet citizens had spent terms in the labor camps in 1937–53. It was reportedly the first time that some statistics of the terror were publicly mentioned by a figure in authority. On 23 August several organizers of another mass demonstration there to commemorate the 1939 nonaggression pact were put under house arrest, and police surrounding the Monument to Freedom eventually resorted to force in attempting to disperse the demonstrators. In August 1988 an Estonian newspaper published the text of the pact, including the secret protocols, for the first time in the USSR.

1990   In January customs in Riga, Latvia, returned seized materials brought in by two Latvian activists from Sweden in December 1989. They confiscated, however, two books, deemed anti-Soviet, by exiled Latvian historian **Uldis Germanis**. One of the books, *For Your Information*, was a collection of essays on Latvian history and Soviet diplomacy and a survey of the disinformation campaigns waged against the Latvian émigré society.

Lithuania

1948–52   In 1948 **Lev Karsavin** (1882–1952), mystic philosopher, and expert on medieval history and history professor at Kaunas and Vilnius universities, was arrested and imprisoned. He died in a labor camp. In 1922 he had been expelled from the USSR for his opposition to the government and exiled to Germany, where he wrote *Philosophy of History* (1923).

pre-1975   **Vaclav Sevruk**, philosopher at the Lithuanian Academy of Sciences History Institute, was engaged in dissident activities in the decade before 1975.

1978–   **Viktoras Petkus [Viktor Piatkus]** (1928), imprisoned during 1947–53 and 1957–65, taught Lithuanian history to a group of young people. Also a Bible translator and cofounder of the Lithuanian Helsinki Group, he was sentenced in July 1978 to fifteen years' imprisonment and labor.

1979   In 1979 the samizdat journal *Lietuviu archyvas* (Lithuanian Archives) was started. It was intended to preserve in the national memory the history of the struggle in Lithuania against the German and Soviet occupations of the 1940s.

[1986]   **Petras Grazulis** was arrested and sentenced to ten months' imprisonment because he campaigned to fill in the blank spots of Lithuanian history.

Tajikistan

1949   Tajik CP secretary and historian **Bobodzan Gafurov** (1908–) was severely criticized for failing to note the progressive consequences of the annexation of the Tajiks to Russia and for suggesting in his *History of the Tajik People* (Moscow 1949) that capitalism would have developed faster without the annexation. In 1951 Gafurov recanted his views and published revised editions.

1971   **Anatoly Nazarov** (1946–), a correspondent course student at the Tajik State University history department, Dushanbe, was arrested in Dushanbe, charged with slandering the USSR, and sentenced to three years in a hard-regime camp.

[1986]   **Slava Denisov**, archeologist from Dushanbe, was arrested and confined to a psychiatric hospital for collecting signatures in protest against the war in Afghanistan.

Turkmenistan

1948   A three-volume documentary series on Russian–Turkmen relations (Ashkhabad 1946) was severely criticized for "bourgeois-nationalist" distortions which failed to show the positive significance of Turkmenia's annexation by Russia.

1951–52   In December 1951 the Turkmen CP-CC accused several Turkmen historians of idealizing epic heroes as well as reactionary groups at the time of the Russian Revolution. In late 1952 historian **Baimuchamed Karryev** was severely reprimanded for his articles refuting the friendly relations between Turkmens and Russians.

Ukraine

1929–52   In 1929 Ukrainian historian **Mykhailo Slabchenko** (1882–1952), founder of a center of historical studies at Odessa, was arrested. He died in obscurity.

1944–   In October 1944 poet **Mikhail Lucik** (1921–), son of a historian who was exiled in Krasnoyarsk, graduate of the history and geography faculty of Lemberg [Lvov in 1945–91; Lviv after 1991] University (1943), was arrested by the security service NKVD on the charge of belonging to the Organization of Ukrainian Nationalists (OUN). He was sentenced to fifteen years in a camp and five years of internal exile. In August 1943 he had organized a fighting unit of Ukrainian monarchists which freed the inmates of a German concentration camp. Previously he had been arrested in 1939 (by the Polish police) and in November 1940 (by the Gestapo on German-occupied territory). In June 1956 he was released. From November 1957 to November 1972, he was again in prison and strict-regime camps. From July 1973 he spent terms in strict-regime camps and a psychiatric hospital.

1947   In August the Ukrainian CP-CC passed a resolution, "Concerning Political Mistakes and Inadequate Work of the Historical Institute of the Academy of Sciences, Ukrainian SSR", condemning three wartime books on Ukrainian history as survivals of the prewar "bourgeois" school of historian Mihailo Hrushevsky (1866–1934).

[1950s]–   From the 1950s, the Ukrainian diaspora produced miniature versions of banned religious and history books to smuggle them into the Ukraine.

1956   At the 20th CPSU. Congress in February, party and government official Anastas Mikoyan spoke out against the book *The Victory of the October Revolution in the Ukraine 1917–22* (Moscow 1954) by historian **A. Likholat**, head of the CPSU-CC History Section. The controversial book was known to contain many lacunae and falsifications. Likholat had to leave his CC post. He went to work at the Ukrainian History Institute, Kiev.

1963–   In July 1963 **Ivan Dzyuba** (1931–), a Ukrainian literary critic and historian who had written numerous samizdat essays on literary themes, was to preside over an evening dedicated to poet Lesja Ukrainka (1871–1913) which was banned by the authorities. In August he wrote a memorandum about the ban. After a speech at an unofficial meeting in a Kiev cinema in September 1965, in which he protested the arrest of Ukrainian intellectuals, he was dismissed at Molod publishers. In December 1965 he sent his samizdat essay

Internationalism or Russification? (London 1968), denouncing the Soviet nationalities policy as anti-Leninist, to Ukrainian party and government leaders. After intense samizdat and protest activities, he was expelled from the Writers' Union Kiev branch in December 1969. The expulsion was revoked in January 1970 after Dzyuba had written a letter to the union, dissociating himself from the Western editions of his work. Although Moroz [q.v. 1965–] condemned Dzyuba's letter, the latter protested the arrest, closed trial, and sentence of the former in 1970. In March 1972 he was again expelled from the Writers' Union for "contravening the statutes of the union, preparing and disseminating anti-Soviet and anticommunist materials, and slandering the Soviet nationalities policy". In April he was arrested. In March 1973 he was tried on the charge of writing and distributing *Internationalism or Russification?* and sentenced to five years in a hard labor camp. When translator Mykola Lukash offered to serve Dzyuba's sentence in his place in view of his poor health, he was dismissed from the editorial board of a Kiev monthly. On 6 November Dzyuba wrote and signed a letter of recantation to *Literaturna Ukraïna*, which was published on 9 November. He was subsequently released from prison. In the summer of 1975, he reaffirmed his recantation, to refute the widespread belief abroad that it was made under duress. He started work in the editorial offices of the Kiev Aviation Factory house journal. Many people were reportedly prosecuted specifically for reading his *Internationalism or Russification?*

1965–   In August 1965 historian **Ihor Hereta** (Igor Gereta) (1938–), assistant director at the Ternopol Museum of Local Lore, was arrested in Odessa and in February 1966 sentenced to five years' probation. After some time he was reinstated at the museum as a senior research officer.

In September 1965 **Valentin Moroz** (1936–), a Ukrainian poet, history teacher (1958–64), and historian specialized in the prewar Ukrainian nationalist movement, was arrested. In January 1966 he was tried on the charge of possessing anti-Soviet literature in which he allegedly advocated Ukraine's secession from the USSR. Sentenced to four years in a strict-regime camp, he was confined in the camp prison for six months in December. After his *Report from the Beria Reservation* (Toronto 1974) (which included a passage on the suppression of Ukrainian historical scholarship by the KGB) was published in samizdat in April 1967 while he was in the camp, he was sentenced to prison in July for the remainder of his term. In September 1969 he was released but unable to obtain work because of his "criminal record". In January 1970 he published the samizdat essay *A Chronicle of Resistance* on the demolition of Ukrainian traditions and resistance to assimilation. In February he published a samizdat essay criticizing Dzyuba [q.v. 1963–] for his lack of principle. In April three men attempted to arrest him in a church near Ivano-Frankovsk, but this was prevented by local churchgoers. Rearrested in June, he was tried in camera in November on charges of writing and disseminating articles defaming Soviet society and sentenced to six years' imprisonment, three years in a labor camp with special regime and five years of internal exile.

In January 1971 he was sent to prison, but he suffered from bad health. In July 1972 he was severely injured by criminal prisoners. From August [1973], he was kept in solitary confinement and had his food allegedly mixed with drugs in order to produce mental deterioration. In July 1974 he went on hunger strike to support his request to transfer him to a camp. Subsequently, he was force-fed. In November he ceased his hunger strike after his solitary confinement was lifted. He returned to prison and was under psychiatric observation. In May 1976 (three weeks before his prison term was due to end), he was transported to the Serbsky Institute of Forensic Psychiatry in Moscow and in June declared sane and brought to a Mordovian camp. In the spring of 1978, he went on hunger strike to protest the refusal to allow family visits. In April 1979 Moroz was released as part of a Soviet–American exchange of political prisoners for Soviet spies. He went into exile in the United States, where his extreme, integral-nationalist (ethnic-based) ideas were criticized.

1966–   In 1966 historian **Mikhail Braychevsky** (1924–), author of numerous works on Ukrainian and Slavic history and archeology, published his samizdat historical study *"Annexation or Reunification"*, in which he challenged the official theory that Ukraine was "reunited" with Russia after the 1654 Treaty of Pereyaslav. In May 1968 he was dismissed as a senior research officer at the Ukrainian Academy of Sciences History Institute, but he obtained a position at the Institute of Archeology. In 1971 or 1972, his 1966 study was published in Canada, apparently against his will. In September 1972 he was again dismissed for his "nationalist and anti-Soviet moods".

1966   **Bohdan Horyn (Bogdan Goryn)**, a literary and art critic who worked on the history of Western Ukrainian art, and **Myroslava Zvarychevska** (1936–), editor at the Publication Department of the Lvov Oblast Archive, were both sentenced for distributing samizdat literature.

1967–   In March history teacher **Dmitry Kvetsko** (1935–) was arrested and in November tried on the charge of distributing *The Motherland*

and Liberty (the samizdat journal of the Ukrainian National Front of which he was the principal publicist and theoretician) and circulating OUN pamphlets dating from 1947–49. He was sentenced to five years' imprisonment, ten years in a strict-regime camp, and five years of internal exile.

1968–   In June 1968 **Aleksandr Nazarenko** (1930–), an electrician who followed an evening course at the Kiev University history department, was arrested and in January 1969 tried on the charge of distributing nationalist leaflets, Ukrainian samizdat, and books published in Western Ukraine in the 1920s and 1930s. He was sentenced to five years in a strict-regime camp.

1969–   In the fall of 1969, Ukrainian writer and translator **Sviatoslav Karavansky** (1920–), who was serving a term in prison, was charged with anti-Soviet propaganda. In April 1970 he was tried for writing an article in prison on the reconciliation of East and West and the history of the 1940 Katyń massacre. He was sentenced to five years' imprisonment and three years in camp in addition to the remainder of his former sentence. Arrested in 1944, he had been sentenced for high treason in February 1945 to twenty-five years' imprisonment, of which he served sixteen. In November 1965 he had been rearrested on the grounds that he had not served his full sentence.

1972   Historian **Nikolai Dashkevich**, previously imprisoned for several years on political charges, was dismissed from his job at the Lvov Museum of Ethnography and Handicrafts "because of staff reductions".

1972   In October the chairman of the Kiev branch of the Writer's Union criticized *Arey's Sword* ([1972]), a historical novel by **Ivan Bilyk**, for its "serious ideological and artistic defects" and urged more preliminary censorship.

1973–   In June journalist and literary critic **Valery Marchenko** (born **Umrilov**) (1947–) was arrested. In December he was tried on the charge of disseminating views defaming the Soviet system for publishing several samizdat articles, including several ones on Ukrainian cultural history, and sentenced to six years in a strict-regime camp and two years of internal exile. As a prisoner he wrote *Letter to My Grandfather* (1975), about the loyal and submissive attitude toward the Soviet government of his grandfather, Ukrainian historian M.I. Marchenko (1902–).

In October engineer **Alexander Feldman** (1947–) was arrested in Kiev. During a search of his flat the following day, many items were confiscated, including a *History of the Jewish People*, vol. 3. He was charged with hooliganism, but the real reason for his arrest was reportedly his activities for the Jewish emigration movement. In November he was tried and sentenced to forty months in an intensified-regime camp.

pre-1975   **Ivan Honchar (Gonchar)** (1911–), a sculptor who was also a candidate in art history, **Ivan Hel (Gel)** (1937–), a worker and evening history student at Lvov University, and **Igor Kalynets** (1939–), poet and employee at the Lvov Oblast archives, were all engaged in dissident activities in the pre-1975 decade.

1976–   After 1976 historian and sociologist **Vladimir Lityinov** (1930–85) prepared a lengthy manuscript on Nestor Makhno (1889–1935) and his Ukrainian anarchist movement, but no established historian read it because of Litvinov's reputation as a dissident.

1977–   In March 1977 art historian **Vasyl Barladianu**, a Ukrainian Helsinki Group member, was arrested in Odessa on charges of "Ukrainian, Romanian, and Old-Bulgarian nationalism". In June he was tried in camera and sentenced to three years' imprisonment for distributing materials of the group. In 1980 a new charge was brought against him in order to prolong his detention. In August he was sentenced to three further years' imprisonment for "anti-Soviet slander".

1977–88   In April 1977 **Mikola Matusevich**, historian and member of the Ukrainian Helsinki Group, was arrested in Kiev. In March 1978 he was sentenced on charges of "anti-Soviet agitation and propaganda" to seven years in a labor camp and five years of internal exile. In late 1988 he was released.

pre-1979   A spring 1978 report stated that Ukrainian historian **Mykola [= Nikolai] Melnyk** (died 1979), a Ukrainian Helsinki Group member, had been persecuted for many years because of his devotion to Ukrainian nationalist poet Taras Shevchenko (1814–61). On 6 March 1979, he died in mysterious circumstances, having apparently poisoned himself after a twelve-hour KGB search of his apartment.

1979–88   In April 1979 Ukrainian historian and philologist **Georgy Badzyo** (pseudonym: Yuri Badzyo) (1936–) was arrested and imprisoned. Shortly before his arrest, he wrote *The Elimination and Russification of Ukrainian Historiography in the Soviet Ukraine: An Open Letter to Russian and Ukrainian Historians*, in which he accused the official Soviet historiography of falsifying the early past of the Ukrainian and Belorussian peoples. In 1965 he had been expelled from the CPSU and dismissed at the Ukrainian Academy of Sciences Institute of Literature for helping to organize a Shevchenko evening. In 1968 he had been dismissed as an editor at Molod publishers. From 1971 he had worked as a bread-loader or a porter. His 1979 arrest followed a search of his flat by the KGB, who confiscated a 400-page critical study of the Soviet nationalities policy in the Ukraine. In December 1979 he was sentenced to seven years' imprisonment and five years of internal exile for "anti-Soviet agitation and propaganda". In late 1988 he was released.

1979   Late in the year **Yaroslav Dashkevich**, Ukrainian history professor and Armenian studies specialist, was dismissed from his post at the Ukrainian Central State Archive in Lvov. Thereafter he sought permission to take up a position offered to him by Harvard University. He and his wife were frequently harassed.

1981–87   In August 1981 **Yevgeny Antsupov** (?1930–), a historian from Kharkov, arrested for distributing leaflets with pictures of himself and two others demanding exit visas, was convicted of "anti-Soviet agitation and propaganda" and sentenced to six years' imprisonment and five years of internal exile. In 1987 he was released on the grounds of serious illness and given permission to emigrate.

1985   At the December congress of the Soviet Writers' Union, poet **Yevgeny Yevtushenko** (1933–), author of the epic poem *Babi Yar* (1961), condemned the "blank spots" in USSR history and its periodic rewriting. According to an account of the speech in the *New York Times*, several of his remarks were censored from the published version of his speech. In 1989 he became one of the founders of Memorial [q.v. USSR 1987–].

pre-1987   In early 1987 historian and Pentecostalist **Galina Barats-Kokhan** was released from prison in Rostovna-Donu.

1991   The September 1991 commemoration of the fiftieth anniversary of the massacre at Babi Yar, near Kiev, was the first official recognition of the event. On 29 and 30 September 1941, more than 33,000 Jews were murdered by a German Einsatzkommando unit assisted by Ukrainian militiamen. A further 70,000 bodies were added between 1941 and 1943.

Uzbekistan

1952   In late 1952 the Higher Qualifications Commission stripped **Z. Radzhabov**, a former doctoral candidate who had written a dissertation on the history of social thought in colonial Uzbekistan, of his doctoral credentials.

pre-1970s   In the 1970s archives on the Jadids (political and social modernizers of the early twentieth century in tsarist Turkestan) were opened. Access to them had long been forbidden.

1981–   After publication of his historical novel *Immortal Cliffs* (1981),
         writer **Mamadali Makhmudov** (?1943–) was forced to repudiate it.
         Within Uzbek literary tradition, Makhmudov was an *ozan* (poet)
         who had written a *dastan* (epic verse) with an *alp* (hero), Buranbek,
         who became inspired by the spirit of his ancestors, sought to unite
         the Turkic peoples, and fought the invading Russians of the late
         1800s. The dastan genre was labeled "impregnated with the poison
         of feudalism". After independence Makhmudov's book won a prize.
         Because of his association with the exiled writer Muhammad Salih,
         leader of the banned opposition political party Erk, Makhmudov was
         imprisoned in 1994–95 and from 1999.

For incidents after 1991, *see* Armenia, Azerbaijan, Belarus, Estonia, Georgia,
Kazakhstan, Latvia, Moldova, Russia, Tajikistan, Turkmenistan, Ukraine, Uzbekistan.
   Also see Canada (1981: Ustinov), Czechoslovakia (1949–50: Kalandra; 1973:
Solzhenitsyn), Greece (1972: Trotsky), Israel (1989: Solzhenitsyn), Latvia (pre-
1945: Laserson), Malawi (1975–: Trotsky), Poland (pre-1945: Deutscher; 1940–
90: Eidelman; 1968: Kieniewicz; 1987: Solzhenitsyn), United Kingdom (1989–
90: Tolstoy), United States (1950–: Lattimore, Kennan; 1951–52: Karpovich).

SOURCES

Abdurazakova, D.B., "Black Holes of Central Asian History: An Overview", *Central
   Asian Survey*, 1992, no.4: 85–92.
Academic Freedom under the Soviet Regime (New York 1954).
Adler, N., *Victims of Soviet Terror: The Story of the Memorial Movement* (Westport
   1993) ix–xviii, 1–3, 5, 46, 52–55, 60, 63, 65, 70–72, 77–78, 87, 90–91, 97, 114–
   17, 129, 136–37, 141–50.
Afanasiev, Y., "Memorial Adopts Its Charter", *Moscow News*, 1989, no.6: 1.
———, "Rusland Zoekt Naar Zijn Ware Geschiedenis", *Parool*, 27 April 1996: 7.
Alexeyeva, L., *Soviet Dissent: Contemporary Movements for National, Religious and
   Human Rights* (originally Russian 1984; Middletown 1987) 13–15, 36, 40, 42,
   42, 98, 279–81, 284, 291, 310, 312–16, 320–22, 326, 353, 360, 362, 373, 375,
   377–79, 416–21.
Alho, O., *Finland: A Cultural Encyclopedia* (Helsinki 1997) 47.
Amalrik, A., *Dagboek van een provocateur* (originally Russian 1980; Utrecht/Antwerp
   1983) 137–40.
———, *Haalt de Sovjetunie 1984?* (Amsterdam 1984) 7, 13, 38, 43, 83–84, 101–2, 114–
   18.
Amnesty International, *Report* (London) 1967–68: 7; 1970–71: 71; 1971–72: 44; 1972–
   73: 70; 1973–74: 68; 1974–75: 119–20; 1975–76: 174; 1977: 277–80; 1978: 240;
   1979: 145, 148, 162; 1980: 307–9; 1981: 329; 1982: 300; 1983: 286; 1984: 313;
   1985: 295; 1996: 318; 1997: 331; 2001: 200, 263.
———, *Voices for Freedom* (London 1986) 65, 83.
Annual Obituary 1980 (Chicago/London) 130–32 (Zimin).

Antonov-Ovseyenko, A., *The Time of Stalin: Portrait of a Tyranny* (originally Russian 1980; New York 1981) vii–xi.

Article 19, *Information, Freedom and Censorship: World Report* (London) 1988: 212, 214–15; 1991: 310–11, 313.

Barber, J., *Soviet Historians in Crisis, 1928–1932* (London 1981) 176.

Barghoorn, F.C., "The Post-Khrushchev Campaign to Suppress Dissent: Perspectives, Strategies, and Techniques of Repression", in: Tőkés ed. 1975: 69, 74–76.

Baron, S.H., & N.W. Heer eds., *Windows on the Russian Past: Essays on Soviet Historiography since Stalin* (Columbus 1977) ix–x, xiii–xiv.

Baumgartner, G., & D. Hebig eds. *Biographisches Handbuch der SBZ/DDR 1945–1990* (Munich 1996) 700–701.

Bentley, M. ed., *Companion to Historiography* (London/New York 1997).

Berelowitch, A., "Des Romans contre les tabous de l'histoire", in: Brossat et al. eds. 1990: 430–43.

––––––, "Russia: An Unfinished Job", *UNESCO Courier*, December 1999: 28–30.

Berelowitch, W., "De geschiedenis opnieuw overdacht: Nieuwe trends in de sovjetgeschiedschrijving", in: Van Goudoever & Naarden eds. 1989: 51–60.

Besteman, T., "Terreur op microfilm", *De Groene Amsterdammer*, 25 January 1995: 8–9.

Biller, P., "Popular Religion in the Central and Later Middle Ages", in: Bentley ed. 1997: 230–31.

Black, C.E. ed., *Rewriting Russian History* (Princeton 1962) xiii, 18–19, 25–26, 29–30.

Boer, S.P. de, E.J. Driessen, & H.L. Verhaar eds., *Biographical Dictionary of Dissidents in the Soviet Union 1956–1975* (The Hague 1982) 12–13, 16–18, 21, 24, 34–35, 39, 45, 48–49, 51, 54–55, 63–65, 67, 89–90, 100, 105, 112, 116–24, 137, 140, 144–47, 153–54, 156, 158, 160–61, 168–69, 174–76, 178–81, 183, 188, 196–98, 204–6, 210–11, 221, 227–28, 244, 253–56, 288, 305–6, 321–24, 332, 338, 348–49, 358–61, 367, 379–80, 389, 392–93, 397, 400–401, 404–5, 409–12, 418–19, 421–22, 429–30, 434–35, 437, 435, 446–47, 466–67, 474, 478, 480, 488, 496, 499, 501, 505–6, 509–10, 518, 525, 542–45, 549–50, 561, 564, 586, 631, 636–37, 640, 643, 647, 649, 660.

Boia, L. ed., *Great Historians of the Modern Age: An International Dictionary* (Westport 1991) 59–60, 62–64, 191–92, 530–31, 550–51, 553–54, 562–63, 566–68, 573–74, 591–92, 789–91.

Bolkhovitinov, N.N., "Power, Liberty and the Work of the Historian (Based on the Example of Russia in the XXth Century)", (paper presented at the 18th International Congress of Historical Sciences; Montréal 1995).

Boris, P., *Die sich lossagten: Stichworte zu Leben und Werk von 461 Exkommunisten und Dissidenten* (Cologne 1983) 24, 41, 90, 92–93, 96, 100, 122, 185–86, 194, 201, 244, 266–68, 286–87.

Boyd, K. ed., *Encyclopedia of Historians and Historical Writing* (London/Chicago 1999) 180–81, 500–501, 636–37, 794–95, 890–91, 939–41, 950–51, 976–77, 1033–35, 1349–50.

Bregel, Y., *Notes on the Study of Central Asia* (Bloomington 1996) 8.

Bronkhorst, D., *Truth and Reconciliation: Obstacles and Opportunities for Human Rights* (Amsterdam 1995) 61–62.

Brossat, A., S. Combe, J.–Y. Potel, & J.–C. Szurek eds., *A l'Est, la mémoire retrouvée* (Paris 1990).

Brown, A. ed., *The Soviet Union: A Biographical Dictionary* (London 1990) 2–3.

Brown, S., D. Collinson, & R. Wilkinson eds., *Biographical Dictionary of Twentieth-Century Philosophers* (London/New York 1996) 14, 174–75.

Burdzhalov, E.N., *Russia's Second Revolution: The February 1917 Uprising in Petrograd* (originally Russian 1967–71; Bloomington 1987) ix–xxii, 1–5.

Button, J., *The Radicalism Handbook* (London 1995) 313–15.

Canadian Slavonic Papers 1982: 182–83 (Yanov).

Cannon, J. ed., *The Blackwell Dictionary of Historians* (Oxford 1988) 63–64, 70–71.

Charachidze, G., "The Historian's Responsibility", *UNESCO Courier*, May 1994: 20–22.

Chentalinski, V., *La Parole ressuscitée: Dans les archives littéraires du K.G.B.* (Paris 1993) 198–204.

Chernykh, E.N., "Postscript: Russian Archaeology after the Collapse of the USSR—Infrastructural Crisis and the Resurgence of Old and New Nationalisms", in: Kohl & Fawcett eds. 1995: 145–47.

Chronicle of Current Events (London) nos.28–30 (1975) 32, 36–37, 89–90; nos.32–33 (1976) 144–45; nos.34–36 (1978) 32–33, 58, 72, 83, 85, 167, 179; no.46 (1978) 29, 32–33, 66, 89–91; no.50 (1979) 25, 69–77.

Cohen, S.F. ed., *An End to Silence: Uncensored Opinion in the Soviet Union; From Roy Medvedvev's Underground Magazine Political Diary* (New York/London 1982) 7–14, 56–69, 117, 137.

Conquest, R., *The Great Terror: A Reassessment* (New York/Oxford 1990) vii–viii, 484.

Dance, E.H., *History the Betrayer: A Study in Bias* (London 1964) 69.

Davies, R.W., *Soviet History in the Gorbachev Revolution* (Basingstoke 1989) viii, 1–5, 8–10, 129–84, 188, 220, 222.

———, *Soviet History in the Yeltsin Era* (Basingstoke 1997) 7, 17–19, 81–114, 117, 119–26.

Dawidowicz, L.S., *The Holocaust and the Historians* (Cambridge/London 1981) 72.

Der Spiegel, 1989, no.7: 164–66 (Afanasiev).

Devroey-Zoller, C., & J.P. Devroey, "Historiographie et droits de l'homme", in: R. Bruyer ed., *Les Sciences humaines et les droits de l'homme* (Brussels 1984) 41.

"Discussion of Nekrich's Book", *Survey: A Journal of Soviet and East European Studies*, 1967, no.63: 173–80.

Dornan, P., "Andrei Sakharov: The Conscience of a Liberal Scientist", in: Tökés ed. 1975: 396–98, 401–3.

Dowd, S., "Life Imitating Art: Mamadali Makhmudov", *Literary Review* (WWW-text; November 1999).

Eastern Europe and the Commonwealth of Independent States 1997 (London 1997) 897.

Eckert, R., W. Küttler, & G. Seeber eds., *Krise-Umbruch-Neubeginn: Eine kritische und selbstkritische Dokumentation der DDR-Geschichtswissenschaft 1989/90* (Stuttgart 1992) 489.

Ehrenburg, I., & V. Grossman, *The Black Book: The Ruthless Murder of Jews by German-Fascist Invaders throughout the Temporarily-Occupied Regions of the Soviet Union and in the Death Camps of Poland during the War of 1941–1945* (New York 1981) xii, xxiii–xxiv.

Enteen, G.M., "A Recent Trend on the Historical Front", *Survey: A Journal of Soviet and East European Studies*, 1974, no.4: 122–31.

Erdmann, K.D., *Die Ökumene der Historiker: Geschichte der internationalen Histori-*

kerkongresse und des Comité international des sciences historiques (Göttingen 1987) 319–20.

Fainsod, M., "Soviet Russian Historians, or: The Lesson of Burdzhalov", *Encounter*, 1962, no.3: 82–89.

Fennell, J.L.I., "The Recent Controversy in the Soviet Union over the Authenticity of the *Slovo*", in: L.H. Legters ed., *Russia: Essays in History and Literature* (Leiden 1972) 1–9.

——, "The Tale of Igor's Campaign", in: Fennell & A. Stokes, *Early Russian Literature* (London 1974) 194–95.

Ferretti, M., "Les Archives Entrouvertes", in: Brossat et al. eds. 1990: 444–64.

Ferro, M., *Comment on raconte l'histoire aux enfants à travers le monde entier* (Paris 1981) 153.

——, *L'Histoire sous surveillance: Science et conscience de l'histoire* (Paris 1985) 67, 147–48.

"Filling in the Blank Spots in Soviet History", *History Today*, February 1989: 12–18.

Glatz, F., "Politics and Historical Science in the Countries of the Soviet System", in: Glatz & Pók eds. 1995: 7–24.

Glatz, F., & A. Pók eds., *The Soviet System and Historiography, 1917–1989: The Influence of Marxism-Leninism on the Historical Sciences* (unpublished papers; Budapest 1995).

Gorman, R.A. ed., *Biographical Dictionary of Neo-Marxism* (Westport 1985) 52–53, 129–30, 157–58, 184–85, 292–93.

Goudoever, A.P. van, & B. Naarden eds., *Gorbatsjov en Stalins erfenis: Witte plekken in de sovjetgeschiedenis* (Utrecht 1989).

Great Soviet Encyclopedia (New York/London) vol. 11 (1976): 387; vol. 14 (1977): 496; vol. 17 (1978): 467.

Guefter, M.I., "Staline est mort hier . . .", *L'Homme et la société*, 1988, no.2: 35–36, 43.

Gurevich, A.I., "The Double Responsibility of the Historian", *Diogenes*, 1994, no.168: 68, 103.

Heller, M., "History As Contraband" (originally French 1982), *Survey: A Journal of Soviet and East European Studies*, 1982: 186, 188–89, 192, 196, 200.

Heller, M., & A. Nekrich, *Utopia in Power: The History of the Soviet Union from 1917 to the Present* (originally Russian 1982; New York 1986) 490–91, 582–83, 663.

Historical Abstracts (CD-rom version) (Badzyo, Hovhannisian, Kruus, Litvinov, Lurye, M. Petrov, Rubinshtein, Zaks).

Historisch nieuwsblad, 1993, no.4: 20–22 (Gurevich).

Hoeven, H. van der, *Lost Memory: Libraries and Archives Destroyed in the Twentieth Century*, part 1, *Libraries* (WWW-text 1996) 3–4, 11–12.

Hosking, G.A., "Memory in a Totalitarian Society: The Case of the Soviet Union", in: T. Butler ed., *Memory: History, Culture and the Mind* (Oxford 1989) 125–26.

Hovian, S.H., "The History of Armenian Literature and Its Study in Soviet Armenia", in: *Academic Freedom* 1954: 98–99.

Human Rights Watch, *World Report 2001* (Washington 2000) 318, 526.

Husband, W.B., "History Education and Historiography in Soviet and Post-Soviet Russia", in: Jones ed. 1994: 125, 127–39.

Iggers, G.G., *Historiography in the Twentieth Century: From Scientific Objectivity to the Postmodern Challenge* (London 1997) 81–82.

Index on Censorship, 1/72: 78–80, 86–87; 2/72: 96–97; 3–4/72: 120–22, 161–62, 215;

1/73: ix–xii; 2/73: ix–x; 3/73: viii–x; 4/73: ix, 12, 31–45; 1/74: ix–x; 2/74: viii–xi, xii, 65–74; 3/74: xii–xv, xvi, 85; 1/75: 19–20, 91–93; 2/75: 93–95; 3/75: 88–90, 161–62; 4/75: 78; 1/76: 85, 87, 90–91; 2/76: 87–88; 3/76: 84–85; 4/76: 84; 1/77: 63–64; 2/77: 69; 4/77: 73; 5/77: 70–71; 6/77: 44–47, 54–55, 68; 1/78: 77–78; 2/78: 63; 3/78: 68–69; 4/78: 29, 70; 5/78: 71; 6/78: 66; 1/79: 64; 2/79: 25–31, 69; 3/79: 3–11, 33–37; 4/79: 38, 68; 5/79: 43, 45, 49, 70–71, 76–78; 6/79: 78–79; 1/80: 73–74, 78–79; 3/80: 68; 4/80: 4–7, 16, 18; 5/80: 68; 6/80: 73; 1/81: 77; 3/81: 52, 78; 4/81: 12, 15, 47; 5/81: 47; 6/81: 110; 1/82: 47; 2/82: 47; 3/82: 40; 6/82: 47; 1/83: 47; 3/83: 2, 48–50; 4/83: 43; 2/84: 49; 3/84: 14–16, 49; 4/84: 15–16, 47; 6/85: 15–17; 4/86: 28–30; 7/86: 45; 1/87: 6; 2/87: 8, 40; 3/87: 40–41; 4/87: 5, 40; 5/87: 4–5, 41; 7/87: 14–20, 40; 8/87: 40; 9/87: 39; 10/87: 40; 1/88: 6, 28; 2/88: 4–5; 5/88: 13–14, 132; 6/88: 40–41; 7/88: 39–40; 9/88: 40; 10/88: 40; 1/89: 5, 39; 2/89: 34–35, 41; 3/89: 40–41; 4/89: 41; 5/89: 26, 33–34, 41; 9/89: 41; 2/90: 41; 3/90: 41; 4/90: 30–31, 41; 5/90: 41; 6/90: 43; 8/90: 41; 9/90: 41; 10/90: 41; 1/91: 14, 16, 40–41; 2/91: 6–7; 3/91: 41; 8/91: 3–5, 12–17; 9/91: 41; 1/92: 2–3; 3/92: 40; 4/92: 36; 6/92: 39; 3/93: 21; 5–6/93: 49; 4–5/94: 75–81; 2/95: 142; 3/95: 53–60, 64–67; 6/95: 29; 1/96: 115, 119–27, 140; 2/96: 99; 4/97: 91; 5/97: 165; 3/98: 93; 6/98: 45–46; 1/99: 79, 157, 162; 6/99: 256.

Ingerflom, C.S., "Moscou: Le procès des Annales", *Annales E.S.C.*, 1982: 68, 71.

International Helsinki Human Rights Committee, *Violations of the Helsinki Accords: A Report to the Helsinki Review Conference, Madrid, November 1982* (Oslo/New York 1982) 19–20.

Jansen, M., "Sovjethistoriografie en Russische dissidenten", *Groniek*, 1983, no.83: 27.

——— (various articles on history textbooks) *Kleio* 1983/1: 15–18; 1989/2: 10–13; 1990/1: 10–13; 1991/7: 3–7.

Jaubert, A., *Le Commissariat aux archives: Les Photos qui falsifient l'histoire* (Paris 1986) 15–50, 77–96, 165–74.

Jeffery, K., & C. Lennon, "Historians, Politics, and Ideology: Report", in: *17th International Congress of Historical Sciences*, vol. 2, *Chronological Section/Methodology* (Madrid 1992) 1067–68.

Jones, A. ed., *Education and Society in the New Russia* (Armonk/London 1994).

Jones, S.F., "Old Ghosts and New Chains: Ethnicity and Memory in the Georgian Republic", in: R.S. Watson ed., *Memory, History, and Opposition under State Socialism* (Santa Fe 1994) 155, 162, 164.

Kan, A., "Anna Pankratova and *Voprosy Istorii*: An Innovatory and Critical Historical Journal of the Soviet 1950s", *Storia della storiografia*, 1996, no.29: 71–97.

———, "Neue theoretische Ansätze der sowjetischen Historiker (Eine Skizze)", in Glatz & Pók eds. 1995: 70–78.

Keenan, E.L., "A.A. Zimin 1920–1980", *Kritika: A Review of Current Soviet Books on Russian History*, Winter 1980: 1–4.

Keep, J., "The Current Scene in Soviet Historiography", *Survey: A Journal of Soviet and East European Studies* 1973, no.1: 14–17.

Keep, J., & L. Brisby eds., *Contemporary History in the Soviet Mirror* (London 1964) 9–18, 43.

Keesings historisch archief, 1991: 378; 1992: 386; 1998: 340.

Kennan, G.F., *Memoirs 1950–1963* (New York 1972) 145–67.

Kleimola, A.M., "In Memory of A.A. Zimin (1920–1980)", *Soviet Studies in History*, Fall 1981: 2–7.

Kohl, P.L., & C. Fawcett eds., *Nationalism, Politics, and the Practice of Archaeology* (Cambridge 1995).

Kohl, P.L., & G.R. Tsetskhladze, "Nationalism, Politics, and the Practice of Archaeology in the Caucasus", in: Kohl & Fawcett eds. 1995: 155.

Kopossov, N., "Wanted: A New Language", *UNESCO Courier*, May 1994: 12–15.

Kotkin, S., "Terror, Rehabilitation, and Historical Memory: An Interview with Dmitrii Iurasov, *Russian Review*, 1992: 238–62.

Krekic, B., "George Ostrogorsky (1902–1976)", in: H. Damico & J.B. Zavadil eds., *Medieval Scholarship: Biographical Studies on the Formation of a Discipline*, vol. 1, *History* (New York/London 1995) 301–11.

Kuper, L., *Genocide* (Harmondsworth 1982) 142–46.

Laqueur, W.Z., *The Fate of the Revolution: Interpretations of Soviet History* (London 1967) 134–56.

Larin, M., & W. Banasjukevich, "Ausnahmesituationen und Erhaltung von Archiven: Die Lage in Russland", *Archivum*, 1996, no.42: 197–205.

Lewis, B.E., "Soviet Taboo", *Soviet Studies*, 1977: 603–6.

Lewytzkyj, B., & J. Stroynowski eds., *Who's Who in the Socialist Countries* (New York/Munich 1978) 373.

Leys, S., *Ombres chinoises* (Paris 1974) 264.

Marko, K., "History and the Historians", *Survey: A Journal of Soviet and East European Studies*, July 1965: 73, 76.

Mathews, T.D., *Censored* (London 1994) 40–44.

Mazour, A.G., *Modern Russian Historiography* (Princeton 1958) 234–45.

———, *The Writing of History in the Soviet Union* (Stanford 1971) xiii–xiv, 25–30, 362.

Mazour, A.G., & H.E. Bateman, "Recent Conflicts in Soviet Historiography", *Journal of Modern History*, 1952: 60–63, 65–66, 68.

McCauley, M., *Who's Who in Russia since 1900* (London/New York 1997) 229–30.

——— ed., *Longman Biographical Directory of Decision-Makers in Russia and the Successor States* (London 1993) 147, 189–91, 341, 667–69.

Medvedev, R.A., *Let History Judge: The Origins and Consequences of Stalinism* (New York 1972) xxxi–xxxii, 223, 501, 515–18.

"Memorial: Eine Gesellschaft zur Aufklärung von Verbrechen und Repressionen", *Osteuropa*, 1989: A230–37.

Mendel, A.P., "Current Soviet Theory of History: New Trends or Old?", *American Historical Review*, 1966–67: 54–56, 59–63, 68.

Merridale, C., "The Soviet Revolution", in: Bentley ed. 1997: 528–29.

" 'Mit Lagern machst du uns nicht bange!' Sowjetische Historiker und Offiziere diskutieren über Stalins Verbrechen", *Der Spiegel*, 20 March 1967: 132–38.

Monteil, V., "The Decolonization of the Writing of History" (originally French 1962), in: I. Wallerstein, *Social Change: The Colonial Situation* (New York 1966) 598–600.

Musterd, C., *De waarheid in pacht: Studies over de geschiedschrijving in de Sovjet Unie* (Bergen 1985) 13–14, 31–35.

Nekrich, A.M., *Forsake Fear: Memoirs of an Historian* (originally Russian 1979; Boston 1991) vii, 5–7, 22–23, 26–35, 37–46, 49–58, 62–67, 69–73, 80–91, 93–96, 100–102, 109–21, 130–36, 141–62, 164, 166–74, 179–211, 224–33, 235–44, 260–62, 264, 268–81.

————, "Perestroika in History: The First Stage", *Survey: A Journal of Soviet and East European Studies* 1989, no.4 22–43.

New Left Review, September–October 1979: 26 (Medvedev).

Nove, A., "In a Hostile Country", *Times Literary Supplement*, 3 September 1982: 950.

NRC-Handelsblad, 19 September 1996: 6; 29 April 1999: 6 (Kelam).

Ohloblyn, A.P., "Soviet Historiography", in: *Academic Freedom* 1954: 69–76.

Orlovski, E., "Notities over 'glasnost', 'witte plekken' in de geschiedenis en de informatiebronnen in de Sovjetunie", in: Van Goudoever & Naarden eds. 1989: 30–50.

Paillard, D., "Figures de la mémoire: *Mémorial* et *Pamiat*", in: Brossat et al. eds. 1990: 368–72, 375.

Paxton, J., *Companion to Russian History* (London 1983) 17, 27–28, 103, 127, 148, 196, 346, 372–73, 467.

Perlina, N.M., "A New Russian Free Press?" *Survey: A Journal of Soviet and East European Studies*, 1982: 177, 179, 184.

Petersen, K., "History in the Remaking: Jadidist Thought in Post-Soviet Uzbekistan", *Central Asia Monitor*, 1996, no.4 (WWW-text).

Petrov, N., & M. Jansen, "De archieven van de KGB", *De nieuwste tijd*, 1996, no.6: 35.

Phelps, G., *Film Censorship* (London 1975) 145–46.

Pivert, M., "Problèmes du socialisme: Quelques aspects théoriques des entretiens du Kremlin", *Revue socialiste*, 1956: 289.

Pork, A., "History, Lying and Moral Responsibility", *History and Theory*, 1990: 321–30.

Renner, H., "Roj A. Medvedev (geb. 1925)", in: A.H. Huussen, E.H. Kossmann, & H. Renner eds., *Historici van de twintigste eeuw* (Utrecht/Antwerp 1981) 347–63.

Röder, W., & H.A. Strauss eds., *Biographisches Handbuch der deutschsprachigen Emigration nach 1933*, vol. 1 (Munich 1980) 596.

Roht-Arriaza, N. ed., *Impunity and Human Rights in International Law and Practice* (Oxford 1995) 118–23.

Roskis, E., "Ces archives qu'on manipule", in: *Le Monde diplomatique, manière de voir 40* (July–August 1998) 25.

Rudnytsky, I.L., "The Political Thought of Soviet Ukrainian Dissidents", in: P.L. Rudnytsky ed., *Essays in Modern Ukrainian History by Ivan L. Rudnytsky* (Cambridge 1987) 478–80.

Russia, 1981, no.3: 45, 49–50 (Kazhdan).

Shahrani, N., "The Lessons and Uses of History", *Central Asia Monitor*, 1993, no.1 (WWW-text).

Schmidt, Y., & T. Smith, "Sources of Inter-Ethnic Discord throughout the Former Soviet Union", in: S. Coliver ed., *Striking a Balance: Hate Speech, Freedom of Expression and Non-discrimination* (London 1992) 133–34.

Schulz, H.E., P.K. Urban, & A.I. Lebed eds., *Who Was Who in the USSR* (Metuchen 1972) 44, 302, 435–36, 446–47.

Schulz-Torge, U.-J. ed., *Who's Who in Russia Today* (Munich 1994) 105, 234.

Sherlock, T., "Politics and History under Gorbachev", *Problems of Communism*, May–August 1988: 16–18, 29, 32, 34, 36–37, 39–40.

Shteppa, K.F., *Russian Historians and the Soviet State* (New Brunswick 1962) 88–90, 212, 221–30, 232–33, 247, 374–80.

Simon, R.S., P. Mattar, & R.W. Bulliet eds., *Encyclopedia of the Modern Middle East* (New York 1996) 1755–56.

Sirotkin, V., "USSR: Filling in the Blank Spaces", *UNESCO Courier*, March 1990: 43–44.

Slater, T.J. ed., *Handbook of Soviet and East European Films and Filmmakers* (New York/London 1992) 36, 45.

Slusser, R.M., "History and the Democratic Opposition", in: Tőkés ed. 1975: 329–37, 339, 343–53.

Smith, T., R. Perks, & G. Smith, *Ukraine's Forbidden History* (Stockport 1998) 21–22, 35.

Solzhenitsyn, A., *The Gulag Archipelago 1918–1956: An Experiment in Literary Investigation* (originally Russian 1973; Glasgow 1974) iv–xii, 625.

Stalin, J.V., *Works*, vol. 13, *July 1930–January 1934* (Moscow 1955) 99 (quote).

Starr, S.F., "You Can't Murder History", *New York Times Book Review*, 19 July 1992: 1, 26–27.

Stieg, M.F., *The Origin and Development of Scholarly Historical Periodicals* (Alabama 1986) 172–75.

Storia della storiografia, 1997, no.32: 171–72 (Kan).

Suny, R.G., *Looking toward Ararat: Armenia in Modern History* (Bloomington/Indianapolis 1993) 147, 156, 159–60.

Szayna, T.S., "Addressing 'Blank Spots' in Polish–Soviet Relations", *Problems of Communism*, 1988: 57–58.

Thompson, K.W., *Masters of International Thought: Major Twentieth-Century Theorists and the World Crisis* (Baton Rouge/London 1980) 67–69.

Tijn, T. van, "Zwarte tragedie", *Vrij Nederland*, 21 April 1990: 12.

Tikhvinsky, S.L., "L'Historien soviétique aujourd'hui", in: R. Rémond ed., *Être historien aujourd'hui* (Paris 1988) 221, 227–34.

Tillett, L., *The Great Friendship: Soviet Historians on the Non-Russian Nationalities* (Chapel Hill 1969) 70–76, 80–81, 83, 88–89, 92–93, 95–97, 101–70, 194–221, 225, 228–36, 240–49, 260–61, 364.

Tőkés, L. ed., *Dissent in the USSR: Politics, Ideology, and People* (Baltimore/London 1975).

Tolz, V., " 'Blank Spots' in Soviet History", *Radio Liberty Research*, 21 March 1988: 1–12.

———, " 'Glasnost' and the Rewriting of Soviet History", *Radio Liberty Research*, 18 May 1987: 1–10.

Trigger, B.G., *A History of Archaeological Thought* (Cambridge 1989) 218.

Tucker, M. ed., *Literary Exile in the Twentieth Century: An Analysis and Biographical Dictionary* (Westport 1991) 68–69, 308–10, 563–65, 632–40.

Vaillant, J.G., "Reform in History and Social Studies Education in Russian Secondary Schools", in: Jones ed. 1994: 141–68.

Valkenier, E.K., "Glasnost and Filling in the 'Blank Spots' in the History of Polish–Soviet Relations, 1987–1990", *Polish Review*, 1991: 259.

Voerman, G., "Mogelijkheden en moeilijkheden in Moskou: Over de archieven van de voormalige Sovjet-Unie", *Contactblad VGTE*, July 1994: 7–9.

Voren, R. van, *Gorbatsjov: Tussen hoop en illusie* (Amsterdam 1988) 81–83.

Vronskaya, J., & V. Chuguev, *The Biographical Dictionary of the Former Soviet Union* (London 1992) 4, 17, 19–20, 55, 67, 116, 119, 134, 140, 149, 153, 171–72, 178,

184–85, 187, 198, 236, 254, 298, 330, 342, 358–59, 370, 379, 411, 422, 463–64, 469, 480, 485, 507–8, 537, 603.

Weber, H., "Die Aufarbeitung der DDR-Geschichte und die Rolle der Archive", in: B. Faulenbach, M. Meckel, & H. Weber eds., *Die Partei hatte immer Recht: Aufarbeitung von Geschichte und Folgen der SED-Diktatur* (Essen 1994) 52–53.

Wheatcroft, S., "Unleashing the Energy of History, Mentioning the Unmentionable and Reconstructing Soviet Historical Awareness: Moscow 1987", *Australian Slavonic and East European Studies*, 1987, no.1: 97–102, 105–7, 110–25, 127–29.

Wieczynski, J.L. ed., *The Modern Encyclopedia of Russian and Soviet History* (Gulf Breeze) vol. 1 (1976) 216; vol. 3 (1977) 11–14, 179–81; vol. 8 (1978) 221–22; vol. 13 (1979) 206–8; vol. 15 (1980) 225–26; vol. 16 (1980) 41–42; vol. 17 (1980) 224–25; vol. 20 (1981) 198–99; vol. 22 (1981) 127; vol. 26 (1982) 224–29; vol. 27 (1982) 50–53; vol. 28 (1982) 76–77; vol. 31 (1983) 227–28; vol. 35 (1983) 161–62; vol. 36 (1984): 37–42; vol. 45 (1987) 94–95; vol. 46 (1987) 76–82, 136–37; vol. 48 (1988) 43–44; vol. 49 (1988) 173–74; vol. 50 (1989) 211–13; vol. 51 (1989) 237; vol. 54 (1990) 12–13; vol. 55 (1993) 185–89, 252–55.

Wishnevsky, J., "Conflict between State and 'Memorial' Society", *Report on the USSR*, 20 January 1989: 8–9.

Wolfe, B.D., "Leon Trotsky As Historian", *Slavic Review*, 1961: 495–502.

———, "Operation Rewrite", *Problems of Communism*, 1953, nos. 3–4: 26–34.

———, "Totalitarianism and History", in: C.J. Friedrich ed., *Totalitarianism* (New York 1964) 262–77.

Woolf, D.R. ed., *A Global Encyclopedia of Historical Writing* (New York/London 1998) 66, 143, 295, 545–46, 565, 652, 680, 693, 854–56, 906.

Yakir, P., *A Childhood in Prison* (London 1972) 11–20.

Zaprudnik, J., *Historical Dictionary of Belarus* (Lanham/London 1998) 171–72.

Ziman, J., P. Sieghart, & J. Humphrey, *The World of Science and the Rule of Law* (Oxford 1986) 98.

Zwart, A. de, "Glasnost en de Baltische geschiedenis", in: Van Goudoever & Naarden eds. 1989: 193.

UNITED ARAB EMIRATES

[1979] In early [1979] an unsigned leaflet—ostensibly originating from students at al-Ayn University in Abu Dhabi—was sent to the authorities in the United Arab Emirates (UAE). It condemned a book, *The Umayyad Caliphate*, and its author, the Syrian historian **Nabih Aqil**, dean of the College of Education at al-Ayn. The book was used as a first-year course text in history at their university and also at Qatar University. The students' complaint was explicitly tied to charges made previously in the National Assembly that Aqil was a communist and had attacked Islam. Although on that occasion the minister of education had replied that the accusation was "street gossip", the pamphlet challenged the minister's reply. In February and March 1979, the weekly *Akhbar Dubai* published five articles on the affair. Aqil was defended by, among others, the university authorities, but condemnations were more frequent. They came from an imam in a local mosque, Shaik Muhammad Mutawalli al-Sadawi (presumably the pamphlet's author), the UAE chief prosecutor, the Association for Social Reform and Orientation, and from a researcher on religious affairs in the Ministry of Justice and Islamic Affairs. After the latter published the judgment that the book was written in a spirit alien to Islam and to Muslims, Qatar reportedly withdrew the book from the university library and from class use. Aqil had also invited German historian Werner Ende (1937–) to talk about his book *Arabische Nation und islamische Geschichte: Die Umayyaden im Urteil arabischer Autoren des 20. Jahrhunderts* (Beirut 1977; Arab Nation and Islamic History: The Umayyads according to Twentieth-Century Arab Authors), but upon his arrival he could not deliver the lecture.

Also see Indonesia (1994: Spielberg).

SOURCES

Donohue, J.J., "Rewriting Arab History", in: *Arab Society 1978–79: Reflections and Realities; Cemam Reports*, no.6 (Beirut 1981) 189–202.
Freitag, U., personal communication, October 1999.

UNITED KINGDOM

Four categories of historians found it difficult to work in the United Kingdom or its colonies: communist-inspired historians, historians working on the history of intelligence services, historians studying the colonial empire, and historians dealing with Northern Ireland. Also noteworthy was the relatively high incidence of British historians censored in other countries (see "also see" section).

1946–56   From at least 1946 to 1956, the Communist Party of Great Britain (CPGB) constrained the work of its Historians' Group concerning the history of the Communist Party of the USSR and of the twentieth-century British labor movement. Despite several preparatory steps, the group was not allowed to write an official CPGB history.

1948–60   In the late spring of 1948, blacklisting of communist historians looking for an academic position allegedly began in the context of the Cold War and would last until about 1960, after which those already in academic positions were gradually promoted or received offers.

[1950s]   In the [1950s] Marxist historian **Christopher Hill** (1912–), specialist in seventeenth-century England (1560–1660), fellow, tutor, and master in modern history at Balliol College, Oxford University (1938–78), member of the CPGB Historians' Group, was

passed over for a chair and rejected by some publishers because of his CPGB membership (1936–56). In World War II Hill had worked at the Foreign Office and written *The Two Commonwealths* (London 1945) under the pseudonym of K.E. Holme.

1950s

The Cold War climate of the 1950s reportedly made it impossible for **George Rudé** (1910–93), Marxist social historian specialized in the history of revolutionary crowds, CPGB member (1935–59), teacher of modern languages and history in public schools (1931–59), to find a position in a British university. He became a history professor at Adelaide University (1960–67), Australia, Stirling University (1968), Flinders University of South Australia (1968–70), and Sir George Williams University, Montréal (1970–87).

1953

In December **Elie Kedourie** (1926–92), Iraqi-born historian of the Middle East working at St. Antony's College, Oxford University (1951–53), was orally examined about his doctoral dissertation. He refused to make a number of modifications in the dissertation, requested by orientalist Sir Hamilton Gibb (a Foreign Research and Press Service member servicing the Foreign Office in 1939–45). The dissertation was a critical appraisal of British Middle East policy and questioned Britain's indulgence of Arab nationalism in 1914–21. Although Gibb's request was endorsed by Kedourie's supervisor in February 1954, Kedourie did not make the changes, withdrew the dissertation, and never received his degree. The work was published unchanged as *England and the Middle East: The Destruction of the Ottoman Empire, 1914–1921* (April 1956). Kedourie became professor of politics at the London School of Economics and Political Science (1953–90) and founder-editor of the journal *Middle Eastern Studies* (1964–92).

1950s

In the mid-1950s the publisher Hutchinsons turned down a book on the working class they had commissioned to **Eric Hobsbawm** (1917–), a historian and refugee from Nazi Germany (1933), on the grounds that it was "too biased". The book, which would have been the author's first, was never published, but the material was eventually used in other books. A fellow at King's College, Cambridge University (1949–55), Hobsbawm was turned down three times for a lectureship in economic history in Cambridge's Economics Faculty and at least once for a chair because economic historian Sir Michael Postan (1899–1981), himself a refugee from the USSR (1919), reportedly opposed Hobsbawm's communism. After many years, Hobsbawm was finally appointed as a professor of economic and social history at Birkbeck College, London University.

1956   **Frank Donnison**, former chief secretary to the British Govern-
                ment of Burma and member of the team of historians producing
                official war histories under the direction of J.R.M. Butler, pub-
                lished the official history *British Military Administration in the
                Far East 1943–46* (London), for which he had access to confi-
                dential government documents.

1957–   In 1957 socialist historian **Alan J.P. Taylor** (1906–90), fellow
                and tutor at Magdalen College, Oxford University (1938–76), spe-
                cial lecturer in international history at the same university (1953–
                63), cofounder of the Campaign for Nuclear Disarmament (1958),
                was passed over for the regius chair of history at Oxford Univer-
                sity, reportedly because he wrote for the *Sunday Express* and re-
                fused to finish his collaboration. As a result of the storm over his
                book *The Origins of the Second World War* (1961), his lectureship
                at Oxford University was not renewed in 1963, in spite of his
                record of publications and his skills as a lecturer. He was report-
                edly also passed over for a chair at the London School of Eco-
                nomics. He was a freelance journalist from 1963. Elected to the
                British Academy in 1956, he resigned, amid much publicity, in
                1980 during the controversy over the membership of Soviet spy
                (and art historian) Anthony Blunt (1907–83).

1968–71   Clarendon Press and the editors of the *Oxford History of South
                Africa*, Monica Wilson and Leonard Thompson, excluded a chap-
                ter written by South-African-born **Leo Kuper** (1908–94), profes-
                sor of sociology at the University of California, Los Angeles
                (1961–), and director of its African Studies Center (1968–72), on
                "African Nationalism in South Africa 1910–64" from the first
                South African edition of volume 2 (pages 424–76), in order to
                comply in advance with the political censorship laws of South
                Africa (which proscribed quoting banned persons and unlawful
                organizations). This South African edition appeared with fifty-two
                blank pages; it included a note of regret by the publishers and
                editors but not a statement by Kuper. Kuper called it an instance
                of "surrogate censorship" because the chapter did appear in the
                second edition (1975) with permission of the South African min-
                ister of justice. Kuper also suggested that South African contrib-
                utors to the volume had refrained from citing proscribed sources
                for their own safety. South African editor Wilson replied that it
                was preferable to publish a reliable and broadly liberal history of
                South Africa in the country itself, even if it was incomplete. Later
                Kuper became a pioneer of genocide studies.

[1976]   In [1976] some cabinet records from 1946 were at first kept back,
                whereas others were made public under the thirty-year rule, and
                then disclosed.

1980–90   In 1980 the study *Strategic Deception: British Intelligence in the Second World War*, on British wartime counterintelligence operations, was not published. Commissioned in the early 1970s by the Edward Heath government and written by military historian **Michael Howard** (1922–), professor at Oxford University (1968–89), it was completed in 1980 and submitted to the cabinet office. Prime Minister Margaret Thatcher personally decided against publication. It was eventually published on 5 April 1990.

1981   In July **Edward Palmer Thompson** (1924–93), social historian and political activist, member of the CPGB (until 1956) and its Historians' Group (1946–56), author of *The Making of the English Working Class* (New York 1963), figure of the British New Left, reader in social history at the Center for the Study of Social History, Warwick University (1965–71), cofounder and leader of the European Nuclear Disarmament movement, had an invitation to deliver the Dimbleby lecture over British Broadcasting Corporation (BBC) television in November vetoed by the director-general, after it had been endorsed by BBC staff involved in the selection. In 1956 Thompson had been suspended from CPGB membership after he had cofounded a journal, *Reasoner*, to serve as a discussion forum within the CPGB. Subsequently he had resigned the CPGB. The *Reasoner* became the *New Reasoner*, a forerunner of the *New Left Review*. In 1971 Thompson had resigned his Warwick chair on the grounds that students were being trained to become good capitalists.

1982–   The government obtained an injunction against the second volume of an account of domestic security service operations, *A Matter of Trust: MI5 1945–1972* (London 1982), written by **Nigel West** (pseudonym of **Rupert Allason**) (1951–), having ignored the first volume, *MI5: British Security Operations 1909–1945* (London 1981). Faced with imminent publication in the United States and an offer by the *Sunday Times* to meet West's legal expenses, publication was permitted after the removal of the names of some agents. In the 1980s, the government also tried to stop publication of memoirs by former intelligence agents such as Peter Wright and Anthony Cavendish. In August 1997 former journalist and MI5 staff member David Shayler alleged that MI5 had kept thousands of secret files on individuals. An injunction was placed on the *Mail on Sunday*, preventing it from publishing any further allegations. In September the injunction was extended. In July 1998 Home Secretary Jack Straw revealed that MI5 had amassed files on nearly 500,000 people since its inception in 1909. The files would not be made available to the public.

1982   Files with discussions on the United Kingdom's claim to the Falk-
              land Islands/Islas Malvinas reportedly disappeared from the Public
              Records Office (PRO; the national archives in London), where
              they had previously been available for public inspection.

1984–92   In July 1984 **Clive Ponting** (1946–), historian and Defence Min-
              istry civil servant (1970–), sent two documents to Labour member
              of Parliament Tam Dalyell. The documents gave a version of the
              sinking of the Argentinian cruiser *General Belgrano* by British
              forces in the Falklands/Islas Malvinas war on 2 May 1982 that
              was different from the version given by the Defence Secretary. In
              August Ponting was charged with unauthorized disclosure under
              Section 2(i)(a) of the 1911 Official Secrets Act (OSA). In Janu-
              ary–February 1985, he was tried and acquitted. Channel 4 Tele-
              vision was prevented from broadcasting the trial. After the trial
              Ponting began to study official secrecy and published the result
              in such books as *The Right to Know: The Inside Story of the
              Belgrano Affair* (London 1985) and *Secrecy in Britain* (1990). In
              1992, when writing Winston Churchill's unofficial biography, he
              complained that official documents (dating from 1919 and first
              released in 1969) describing how British forces were ordered to
              use gas on Iraqi dissidents, including Kurds, after World War I,
              had been removed from the PRO without explanation. He sug-
              gested that the Defence Ministry was increasingly reluctant to re-
              lease sensitive archive material. In 1992 Ponting published *A
              Green History of the World*, in 2000 *World History: A New Per-
              spective.*

1986   In September 1986 twenty-seven South African and Namibian
              participants were refused entry visas to attend the 11th Congress
              of the International Union of Prehistoric and Protohistoric Sci-
              ences (IUPPS)—entitled the World Archaeological Congress—in
              Southampton. The banned scholars included **David Lewis-
              Williams**, senior lecturer at the archaeology department of the
              University of the Witwatersrand, Johannesburg, and appointed as
              coorganizer of a congress theme; **Philip Tobias**, professor at the
              University of the Witwatersrand, member of the IUPPS Permanent
              Council and vice president of its Commission on the earliest hom-
              inids; at least one black archeologist; and at least six British-born
              scientists and one American national who were working
              temporarily or permanently in South Africa. The decision by the
              British congress organizers to ban them, made in September 1985,
              was inspired by a variety of reasons: to avoid withdrawal of fi-
              nancial support, to avoid disruption of the congress by antiapart-
              heid groups, to maximize the number of participants from those

countries (especially from Africa) who would not attend if South Africans and Namibians were present, and to demonstrate solidarity with the black majority of South Africa who, through the African National Congress, had called for the boycott. In January 1986 the IUPSS withdrew recognition from the World Archaeological Congress. Among the banned South Africans, several strongly opposed apartheid.

1987   In the autumn the Association of Polish Combatants instructed all its bookstalls to withdraw an issue of *Słowo ojczyste* (The Voice of the Motherland), the periodical of the Macierz Szkolna (an institution supervising Polish educational and cultural transmission in the Polish diaspora) from sale because of an article by its editor, **Jerzy Samborski**. He had written a positive appraisal of a nine-part television series on Polish twentieth-century history, *The Struggles for Poland*, transmitted in June and July on Channel 4, but some Polish émigré circles criticized it because of the alleged slanderous portrayal of interwar Poland.

1988   In January government papers released under the thirty-year rule revealed that in 1957 Prime Minister Harold Macmillan had ordered the suppression of information about an accident at the Windscale (renamed Sellafield) nuclear plant, considered the worst known nuclear accident before Chernobyl. This reportedly boosted the campaign for reduction of secrecy, widely regarded as far too extensive. In 1989 a new OSA replaced the 1911 OSA, but it was also criticized.

1989–95   In October–November 1989 Conservative peer Lord Aldington brought a libel action over a pamphlet entitled *War Crimes and the Wardenship of Winchester College*, written by historian Count **Nikolai Tolstoy Miloslavsky** (1935–) and alleging that in May 1945 Aldington (then Brigadier Toby Low in the Eighth Army V Corps in Carinthia, Austria) "issued every order and arranged every detail of the lying and brutality which resulted in" the massacres of 70,000 Cossack and anti-Titoist Yugoslav prisoners of war and refugees who were handed over by the British to Soviet and Titoist communist forces. Tolstoy, author of several books on the subject, including *Victims of Yalta* (London 1977), was found guilty of libel and ordered to pay £1.5 million in damages. In addition, an injunction prevented him from making any future comment on Aldington's role. The judge said that there was a difference between the viewpoint of the military man on the ground and the historian exercising hindsight. Tolstoy criticized the manner in which the judge drew attention to the relevant documents and issues and the disparaging way in which he, Tolstoy, was referred to as a "so-called historian". In July 1990 he dropped his appeal because of excessive costs. In July 1995 the European Court of Human Rights unanimously decided that Tolstoy's right to freedom of expression was violated regarding the award of damages but not regarding the injunction.

1994–   *Occupation: Nazi-Hunter; The Continuing Search for the Perpetrators of the Holocaust* (Hoboken 1994), a book about a Nazi war criminal living in Britain, written by historian **Efraim Zuroff**, head of the Simon Wiesenthal Center in Jerusalem, reportedly could not be sold in the United Kingdom because of its libel laws.

1995   Among the subjects surrounded by secrecy according to historian, former minister, and Conservative member of Parliament Alan Clark (1928–99), were the following: the cabinet discussion of peace terms with Adolf Hitler; the full degree of pressure applied by the Americans over Suez (1956); and the text of the consultations during the Cuban missile crisis (1962).

1995–97 In mid-November 1995 a delegation of Hong Kong educationalists visited Beijing and learned of forthcoming revisions of history and geography textbooks. In June 1996 the Hong Kong Educational Publisher's Association announced that school textbooks would be revised after 1 July 1997 (Hong Kong's return to China after 150 years of British rule) to reflect the official Chinese view of history. More emphasis would be placed on Hong Kong's shared past within China. References to the Opium War (1840–42) were to be purged of "Western bias", the cooperation between Sun Yat-sen and the warlords would be questioned, Taiwan would no longer be referred to as a "country", and there would be a ban on the expression "mainland China" with its implication that there is more than one China. Details of the 1989 Tiananmen massacre would be left to the discretion of individual editors, but fears were expressed by the Teachers' Union Resource Center that schools were already dropping the use of teaching materials on the massacre in anticipation of a possible ban. In March 1997 Chinese Foreign Minister Qian Qichen suggested that Hong Kong schoolbooks that "do not accord with history or reality" and "contradict the spirit of 'one country, two systems' and the Basic Law" should be revised after 1 July. In July Joseph Wong, the new secretary for education and manpower in Hong Kong, announced some "fair and routine changes" in history teaching, especially concerning the Cultural Revolution and the Tiananmen massacre.

1995–96 In December 1995 Cambridge University Press (CUP) decided not to publish *Fields of Wheat, Hills of Blood: Passages to Nation-*

hood in Greek Macedonia 1870–1970, a manuscript written by Greek-born social anthropologist **Anastasia Karakasidou**—then a lecturer at the State University of New York, Stonybrook, later assistant professor at Wellesley College, Mass.—following advice from the Secret Intelligence Service MI6 and the Foreign Office that publication could provoke a terrorist attack by nationalist extremists against CUP staff in Greece. The manuscript, endorsed for publication by the panel of experts to which CUP had submitted it, contained a historical ethnography that contradicted the official Greek view that there is no Slavic Macedonian minority in Greece. In February 1996 two American anthropologists, Michael Herzfeld and Stephen Gudeman, resigned CUP's anthropology series editorial board in protest against CUP's decision. Among the others who protested were Jack Goody, the series founder, Mark Mazower, Anniversary professor of history at Birkbeck College, London, and Ali Mazrui. The book was published in 1997 by the University of Chicago Press. In May 1994 Karakasidou's number plate and address in Thessaloniki had been published in a right-wing newspaper after she had received several rape and death threats. She was, however, given unrestricted access to state-supported archives and did freely speak at state-supported symposia in Greece. By 2001, Karakasidou's book had been translated into Greek.

1996   Protestors clashed with the police in Hong Kong as they met to commemorate the twentieth anniversary of China's prodemocracy 5 April 1976 Movement.

1996–2000   In the autumn of 1996, **Deborah Lipstadt** (1947–), Dorot professor of modern Jewish and Holocaust studies, Emory University, Atlanta, Georgia, and Penguin Books were sued for libel by the extreme-right historian David Irving (1938–) because in her book *Denying the Holocaust: The Growing Assault on Truth and Memory* (1993) she had characterized him as a Holocaust denier. During the trial (January–April 2000), Irving rejected Lipstadt's accusation, although he did question the number of Jewish dead in the Holocaust and denied the systematic extermination of Jews in the concentration camps. He charged that the book had irrevocably damaged his reputation. He was forced to subpoena two witnesses, historians John Keegan and Donald C. Watt, who would not give evidence voluntarily. In April 2000 the judge ruled that Irving had "for his own ideological reasons persistently and deliberately misrepresented and manipulated historical evidence" and that he was "an active Holocaust denier". He also said "that no objective, fair-minded historian would . . . doubt that there were gas chambers at Auschwitz and that they were operated on a substantial scale to kill hundreds of thousands of Jews." Overall, Irving had "treated the historical evidence in a manner which fell far short of the standard to be expected of a conscientious historian". Under British libel laws, the burden of proof falls on the defendant. Among the evidence submitted by the defense were the testimony by Holocaust historian Robert Jan van Pelt and a 700-page report on Irving's historical methods written by Richard Evans, professor of modern history at Cambridge University. In 1996 Irving had also sued *The Observer* and writer **Gitta Sereny** because, in a review of his Goebbels biography, she had accused him of deliberately falsifying history.

1998   In June the third edition of *Lord Elgin and the Marbles* (first edition 1967), a book about Lord Elgin, who removed the Parthenon sculptures from the Acropolis of Athens in the late eighteenth century, was published. Its author, **William St Clair**, claimed that in the late 1930s the marbles were irreparably damaged when scrubbed with metal scrapers. Although the British Museum denied suppressing the facts surrounding this incident, St Clair was not given access to its records in 1994.

Northern Ireland

1970s   In the mid-1970s several historians were denied access to documents in the Public Record Office of Northern Ireland (PRONI), Belfast. Among them were **John Ditch**, lecturer in social policy at the University of Ulster; **Michael Farrell**, a Republican socialist activist, former internee, Marxist historian and author of *Northern Ireland, the Orange State* (London 1976, 1980) and *Arming the Protestants* (1982); **Paul Bew**, Marxist historian, lecturer (later professor) of Irish politics at the department of political science, Queen's University, Belfast, coauthor of *The State in Northern Ireland 1921–1972: Political Forces and Social Classes* (Manchester 1979, 1995); **Deirdre McMahon**, then at the Institute of Historical Research in London, later author of *Republicans and Imperialists: Anglo-Irish Relations in the 1930s* (New Haven 1984). In some cases, others had already been given access to the documents before; in other cases, files on certain security matters could be freely consulted at the PRO but not at the PRONI. Some complained about the removal of political material from PRONI files. The PRONI also withdrew from publishing their own collection *Northern Ireland and the Second World War* (Belfast 1976), edited by archivist **Patrick Ratcliffe** (died 1985). Some documents relating to pre-1921 British rule in Ireland had to be kept secret until 2021.

1988–94 From October 1988 to September 1994, broadcasting voices of spokesmen for eleven "terrorist organizations" such as Sinn Féin (a legal political party in Northern Ireland and political wing of the Irish Republican Army [IRA]), Republican Sinn Féin, and the Ulster Defense Association, was banned. The ban also applied to historical and archive material. In November 1988 the first television program to fall victim to the ban was a Channel 4 52-minute video *Mother Ireland*, on contemporary Ireland, including contributions from elderly participants in the Irish Civil War (1922–23). The channel's legal office stated that the ban apparently also "cover[ed] any such material recorded at any time in the past—for example newsreel footage shot before the creation of the Republic of Ireland". Also in November, a song by the Dubliners about the United Irishmen Rebellion of May–June 1798, *Kelly the Boy from Killanne*, was banned from a London radio station. Another forbidden ballad was *Streets of Sorrow/Birmingham Six*, by the Pogues, because it supported the claims of miscarriage of justice over the convictions of ten Irish defendants for pub bombings in 1974. In September 1990 the Home Office decided not to allow the words of Eamon de Valera (1882–1975)—the Irish Republic's first prime minister (1932–48) and Sinn Féin president—and of Seán MacBride (1904–88)—IRA member and leader (1916–37), minister of foreign affairs (1948–51), former chairman of the International Commission of Jurists and Amnesty International, and Nobel (1974) and Lenin (1977) Peace Prize laureate—to be broadcast as part of an Ulster television six-part history for schools entitled *Understanding Northern Ireland*, insisting that their voices be replaced by a commentator's paraphrases or be dubbed by actors. The decision was condemned by, among others, the Historical Association, representing most of the United Kingdom's history teachers.

Also see Afghanistan (1982: Pinder-Wilson), Bahamas, Bulgaria (1995: Bailey), Cambodia (1978: Caldwell), China (Hong Kong), Ethiopia (1972: Gilkes), France (1995: Lewis), Germany (1979–89: Garton Ash), Hungary (1949: Cushing; 1984–: Krassó; 1981: Lomax; 1981–82: E.P. Thompson), India (British India; 1984: documentary), Iran (1989–: Rushdie), Ireland, Japan (1989: BBC documentary, Behr), Kenya (British Kenya), Korea (1981–88: Dobb; Hill), Malawi (1975–: Toynbee; 1984–85: Ross), Malaysia (British Malaya), Myanmar (1964: Luce), Pakistan (British India), Saudi Arabia (1977: Holden), South Africa (1953–: Davidson; 1986: Bonner), Trinidad & Tobago (1953–: James; 1955–: Williams), Turkey (1971–: Davidson; 1949–56: Hourani; 1962–: Mellaart), Uganda (1971–79: Heddle), United States (1950–: Lattimore; 1951–: Finley; 1975: Needham; 1977: BBC), USSR (1938–: Eisenstein; 1950–90: Carr; 1976: Hart), Zimbabwe (1961–63: Ranger; 1976: Ziegler).

SOURCES

Abelove, H. et al. eds., *Visions of History* (Manchester 1984) 5–6.

Amnesty International, *Report 1986* (London 1986) 316.

Annan, N., *Our Age: Portrait of a Generation* (London 1990) 266–67.

Article 19, *Information, Freedom and Censorship: World Report* (London) 1988: 231, 233–35, 238–39; 1991: 333–37, 340–41.

———, *No Comment: Censorship, Secrecy and the Irish Troubles* (London 1989) 65, 86.

Birmingham, D., "History in Africa", in: M. Bentley ed., *Companion to Historiography* (London/New York 1997) 701–2.

Boyd, K. ed., *Encyclopedia of Historians and Historical Writing* (London/Chicago 1999) 531–33, 637–38, 1022–23, 1173–75, 1188–89.

Cannon, J. ed., *The Blackwell Dictionary of Historians* (Oxford 1988) 41, 188–89, 361, 406–8.

Cantor, N.F., *Inventing the Middle Ages: The Lives, Works and Ideas of the Great Medievalists of the Twentieth Century* (New York 1991) 432.

———, *Perspectives on the European Past: Conversations with Historians*, vol. 2 (New York/London 1971) 41, 268.

Charny, I.W. ed., *Encyclopedia of Genocide* (Santa Barbara 1999) lxxxvii, 373-83.

Connolly, S.J. ed., *The Oxford Companion to Irish History* (Oxford 1998) 81.

Duffy, J., M. Frey, & M. Sins eds., *International Directory of Scholars and Specialists in African Studies* (Waltham, Mass. 1978) 351.

European Court of Human Rights, *Case of Tolstoy Miloslavsky versus the United Kingdom: Judgment* (WWW-text; Strasbourg, 13 July 1995).

Gargan, E.A., "Hong Kong's History: An Open Book", *International Herald Tribune*, 4 April 1997: 4.

Garson, N.G., "Censorship and the Historian", *South African Historical Journal*, 1973, no.5: 5, 8.

Gorman, R.A. ed., *Biographical Dictionary of Neo-Marxism* (Westport 1985) 409–11.

Guardian, 1990 (12 July: 2; 20 July: 4; 25 July: 39), 1996 (2 February); 2000 (8 January: 3; 16 March; 12 April) (Karakasidou, Lipstadt, Tolstoy, Zuroff).

Hall, M., "Archaeology under Apartheid", *Archaeology*, November/December 1988: 62, 64.

Herrup, C., "Christopher Hill and the People of Stuart England", in: W.L. Arnstein ed., *Recent Historians of Great Britain: Essays on the Post-1945 Generation* (Ames 1990) 57–58, 61.

Hobsbawm, E., "The Historians' Group of the Communist Party", in: M. Cornforth ed., *Rebels and Their Causes: Essays in Honour of A.L. Morton* (London 1978) 25, 28–34, 41, 44.

———, personal communication, July 1999.

Index on Censorship, 3/75: 48–50; 1/78: 12; 6/81: 107; 2/84: 44; 6/84: 44; 2/85: 52; 3/85: 48; 6/85: 23–25; 8/86: 37; 7/87: 36; 1/88: 2, 27; 2/89: 7–8 (quote Channel 4: 8), 32; 9/89: 36; 6/90: 36; 10/90: 34; 1/91: 34; 2/91: 2–3; 6/92: 34; 8–9/93: 4; 3/94: 173; 6/94: 251; 2/95: 27, 32; 1/96: 178; 2/96: 105; 3/96: 109; 4/96: 103; 1/97: 114; 3/97: 121; 4/97: 7, 114; 6/97: 127; 4/98: 132; 5/98: 103; 4/99: 19–23; 2/00: 5, 32, 120, 128–29; 3/00: 98, 111; 2/01: 128.

International Herald Tribune, 2000 (1 March, 12 April) (Lipstadt).

Internationale samenwerking, November 1998: 22–25 (Karakasidou).

Kaufman, P.T. ed., *The Best in General Reference Literature, the Social Sciences, History and the Arts* (New York/London 1986) 393, 477–78.

Kaye, H.J., *The British Marxist Historians: An Introductory Analysis* (Cambridge 1984) 12, 15, 17–18, 101–3, 134, 169–71.

————, *"Why Do Ruling Classes Fear History?" and Other Questions* (Houndmills/ London 1996) 203–4.

Kedourie, E., *England and the Middle East: The Destruction of the Ottoman Empire 1914–1921* (originally 1956; London/Boulder 1987) 1–8a.

Keesing's Record of World Events, 1986: 34115A.

Keuneman, P., "Eric Hobsbawm: A Cambridge Profile 1939" (originally 1939), in: R. Samuel & G. Stedman Jones, *Culture, Ideology and Politics: Essays for Eric Hobsbawm* (London 1982) 366–68.

Kuiken, K., "Hong Kong and Macau" (manuscript for D. Jones ed., *Censorship: A World Encyclopedia* [London/Chicago 2001]) 7.

Kuper, A., "Anthropology and Apartheid", in: J. Lonsdale ed., *South Africa in Question* (London/Cambridge 1988): 47–48.

Kuper L., "A Matter of Surrogate Censorship", in: Kuper, *Race, Class and Power: Ideology and Revolutionary Change in Plural Societies* (Chicago 1975) 289–314.

Lipstadt, D., *Denying the Holocaust: The Growing Assault on Truth and Memory* (originally 1993; Harmondsworth 1994) 8, 111, 161–62, 179–81, 234.

Merrett, C.E., *A Culture of Censorship: Secrecy and Intellectual Repression in South Africa* (Claremont/Pietermaritzburg 1995) 62–63.

Parool, 6 June 1996 (Sereny).

Ponting, C., *Secrecy in Britain* (Oxford 1990) 23–24, 40, 49, 54, 64–66, 78–81.

Salibi, K., "Elie Kedourie: A Tribute", in: S. Kedourie ed., *Elie Kedourie 1926–1992: History, Philosophy, Politics* (London/Portland 1998) 1.

Shaw, T., "The Academic Profession and Contemporary Politics; The World Archaeological Congress: Politics and Learning", *Minerva*, 1989: 64–86.

Shermer, M., & A. Grobman, *Denying History: Who Says the Holocaust Never Happened and Why Do They Say it?* (Berkeley 2000) xv, 48–58, 258–59.

Tinker, H., "Burma", in: Winks ed. 1966: 456–57.

Tobias, P.V., "Prehistory and Political Discrimination" (originally 1985), *Minerva*, 1988: 588–97.

Turnbull, C.M., "Malaysia", in: Winks 1966: 475–76.

Ucko, P., *Academic Freedom and Apartheid: The Story of the World Archaeological Congress* (London 1987) vii–xiii, 1–5, 252–56.

Walker, B., *Dancing to History's Tune: History, Myth and Politics in Ireland* (Belfast 1996) 136.

Washington Post, 3 February 1996 (Karakasidou).

Williams, H.R., "A.J.P. Taylor", in: H.A. Schmitt ed., *Historians of Modern Europe* (Baton Rouge 1971) 78–80.

Wilson, J., "Defending Eighth Army's Reputation: Military Problem, Legal Outcome", *Army Quarterly and Defence Journal*, 1998: 5–9.

Wilson, M., & L. Thompson eds., *The Oxford History of South Africa*, vol. 2 (Oxford 1971) v, 424–76.

Winks, R.W. ed., *The Historiography of the British Empire-Commonwealth: Trends, Interpretations, and Resources* (Durham 1966).

Woolf, D.R. ed., *A Global Encyclopedia of Historical Writing* (New York/London 1998) 410–11, 427, 791, 877–78, 886–87.

UNITED STATES

The handling of current and archival official information was a major focus of attention in the United States. From 1945 to 1972, access to the archives was regulated by a series of restrictive executive orders issued by presidents Franklin Roosevelt (1940), Harry Truman (1950, 1951), and Dwight Eisenhower (1953). According to Steven Mitchel, "Heavy overclassification and neglect of declassification in the 1950s and 1960s could not be considered abuses of the security classification system because the regulations, by their vagueness, were so permissive". Only a 1959 executive order by President Eisenhower provided for unofficial historical research into classified materials. Executive orders issued by presidents Richard Nixon (1972) and Jimmy Carter (1978) brought substantial relaxation. However, the period between 1982 and 1995 was critical. In April 1982 Executive Order 12356 on National Security Information, issued by President Ronald Reagan, almost entirely reversed the government's overall attitude toward access to its documentary records. The order advised that, when there was doubt about whether to classify, documents should be classified, and it allowed documents to be classified for "as long as required". Two new provisions permitted reclassification of information previously released, and classification of unclassified documents after they had been requested under the Freedom of Information Act (FOIA; went into effect on 4 July 1967). The order eliminated the earlier 1978 requirement to balance the government's interest in secrecy against the public's interest in disclosure of the requested documents. At the same time, severe budget cuts at the National Archives and Records Service were said to paralyze its systematic review program. In April 1995, Executive Order 12958, issued by President Bill Clinton, revoked the 1982 order.

Within the historical profession, McCarthyism left the most important traces of censorship. It was directed against real or alleged communist historians and against many historians whose subject was the USSR or China. Some left-wing historians were also attacked in the 1960s. Another issue arousing major debate over most of the period was the contents of history textbooks.

1940/41–   During the Rapp-Coudert investigations, historians **Philip Foner** (1910–94), specialist in labor and Afro-American history, and **Herbert Aptheker** (1915–), specialist in Afro-American history and contemporary American thought, were denied tenure because of their membership in the Communist Party of the United States of America (CPUSA). During the 1941 loyalty probe, Foner was dismissed as a history instructor at City College of New York (1933–41), together with others, including his twin brother **Jack Foner** (1910–99), also a historian at the same college and pioneer in black studies. Philip Foner became the educational director of the Fur and Leather Workers Union (1941–45), chief editor of Citadel Press, New York (1945–67) and professor of Pennsylvanian History (1967–79) and Independence Foundation Professor (1980s) at Lincoln University, Penn. He wrote the ten-volume *History of the Labor Movement in the United States* (1947–92). Jack Foner became a freelance lecturer on current events until his appointment at Colby College, Waterville, Maine (1969–76). In 1981 the City University of New York Board of Trustees passed a resolution apologizing to the Foners and their colleagues, and terming the 1941 events a violation of their academic freedom. Aptheker taught history at the Jefferson School of Social Science for several years. He was the biographer of Du Bois [q.v. 1951–63] and chief editor of the progressive magazine *Political Affairs* (1957–63). He was barred from speaking at most campuses. He had no passport until the Supreme Court reversed the decision in 1964. He became director of the American Institute of Marxist Research (1964–). Concurrently, he was a staff member at the history department of Bryn Mawr College, Pa. (1969–73). In [1976] he was prevented from teaching at Yale University, New Haven, Conn.

1948–56   On several occasions the brief involvement of historian **Henry Stuart Hughes** (1916–99), Europe researcher at the State Department (1946–48), in the 1948 Henry Wallace presidential campaign made him a target for repression. In the same year, when serving as an assistant director of the Russian Research Center at Harvard University, he was informed by his superior that the Carnegie Corporation, which supported the center, found his presence an embarrassment and that his continuation in office might endanger future grants. He resigned but was paid his salary by the Carnegie Corporation for the remaining four years of his assistant professorship (1948–52). In late 1951 or early 1952, his appointment at Stanford University (1952–56) was held up until he could be questioned on his political beliefs. In 1956 there was opposition to his permanent appointment at Harvard University (1957–75) because of his lack of "political sagacity". From 1975 to 1986 he was a history professor at the University of California, San Diego.

1949   In January the University of Pennsylvania history department decided to offer an assistant professorship in East Asian history to **Lawrence Rosinger** (1915–), sinologist and staff member at the Institute of Pacific Relations (IPR). Less than two months later, the offer was withdrawn, apparently after an attack on the IPR and on Rosinger made by a visiting congressman. Later, during the IPR hearings in connection with the Lattimore [q.v. 1950–] case, Rosinger would invoke the Fifth Amendment (a constitutional privilege against self-recrimination) when questioned about his past political activities. He reportedly left the profession, worked in a hardware establishment, and taught English in a junior college in or around Ann Arbor, Mich.

In September a Boston Federal Bureau of Investigation (FBI) report stated that the American Committee for Democracy and Intellectual Freedom [q.v. 1951– Finley] had been cited by the House Un-American Activities Committee (HUAC) as "subversive and un-American". Members of the committee were **Henry Steele Commager** (1902–98), professor of American and constitutional history at New York University (1926–38), Columbia University (1938–56), and Amherst College (1956–72); **Allan Nevins** (1890–1971), journalist, history professor at Columbia University (1928–58), leading scholar of the American Civil War, oral history, and business history, and author of the eight-volume *Ordeal of the Union* (1947–71); and **George Sarton** (1884–1956), historian of science, founder-editor of the journals *Isis* (1913–) and *Osiris* (1936–), author of the three-volume *Introduction to the History of Science* (1927–48), research associate at the Carnegie Institution (1918–49), and professor at Harvard University (1916–51). In 1914 Sarton had left Belgium after the German invasion and gone to the United States in 1915.

The appointment of historian **Armin Rappaport** at the University of California, Berkeley, was postponed until historian John Hicks, who was worried about Rappaport's "ultra left-wing tendencies", received a guarantee that he was not an opponent of American foreign policy.

1950s   Before she studied history and became a history professor at Rutgers University specialized in the slave societies of colonial American history, **Gwendolyn Hall** (1929–) was active in the civil-rights movement in New Orleans during the 1940s and did political work during the 1950s and 1960s. She initiated medical treatment for heroin addicts in Detroit and Ann Arbor but worked as a temporary legal secretary during the McCarthy era to avoid dismissal due to FBI harassment.

1950–   In 1950 political scientist **Stuart Schram** (1924–) went to France to work on his Columbia University dissertation (completed in 1954) and stayed there after the State Department revoked his passport because he had interviewed some European communists and written some articles about European politics critical of American policy in a French weekly newspaper. According to the State Department, he "assisted in the development of various anti-American propaganda

campaigns which are communist-controlled and directed." He became director of the Soviet and Chinese section at the Centre
d'Études des Relations Internationales of the Foundation Nationale
des Sciences Politiques, Paris (1954–67), professor of politics with
reference to China at the School of Oriental and African studies,
London University (1968–89), and a research associate at Harvard
University (1989–). He became famous for his analysis of Mao Zedong's thoughts.

In April 1950 historian and leading sinologist **Owen Lattimore**
(1900–89), editor of the Institute of Pacific Relations journal *Pacific
Affairs* (1934–41), President Franklin Roosevelt's personal wartime
adviser to Jiang Jieshi (Chiang Kaishek) (1941–42), and professor
at Johns Hopkins University, Baltimore, Md. (1938–63), where he
directed the Page School of International Relations (1939–53), was
called the "top Russian espionage agent" by Senator Joseph McCarthy at a Senate hearing and accused of having led the State Department along communist lines when he was the principal adviser on
China. In July he was interrogated by a Senate committee, which
concluded that the charges against him were "groundless". In the
spring of 1952, he became the main target of the Senate Internal
Security Subcommittee's investigation led by Senator Pat McCarran.
He was interrogated for eleven days. In December 1952 he was
indicted for perjury on the basis of some inconsistencies in his testimony; but the judge dismissed the charge against him and the government eventually abandoned the prosecution in mid-1955. The
representatives of the American Historical Association (AHA) to the
10th International Congress of Historical Sciences in Rome (1955)
did not cancel his nomination to give a paper at the Congress. Lattimore had to curtail his public speaking engagements and encountered problems in getting published. In 1963 he moved to the United
Kingdom, where he occupied a chair of Chinese studies at Leeds
University until his retirement (1963–70). In 1970 he returned to the
United States. In 1973, while on a visit to China, the official Chinese
press accused him of being a spy, reportedly because he had mentioned Confucius with approval, a taboo topic at the time. In 1949–
50 Soviet historians had classified Lattimore as a "falsifier of history" because he had declared that Jiang Jieshi was the bearer of the
revolutionary tradition of the Chinese people.

1950   The appointment of China historian **Joseph Levenson** (1920–69) at
the University of California, Berkeley, was postponed until Raymond Sontag (1897–1972), a historian with longstanding connections with the Central Intelligence Agency (CIA), could be
convinced that Levenson was not a Marxist.

Historian and diplomat **George Kennan** (1904–), author of the 1947 "Mr. X" article in *Foreign Affairs* in which he introduced the foreign policy concept of "containment" and coarchitect of the Marshall Plan, wrote a report to the State Department about a journey in February–March 1950 to several Latin American countries, including Brazil, where students vehemently protested his presence. Secretary of State Dean Acheson did not accept it, blocked its distribution within the department, and locked away all copies, probably because Kennan expressed despair about the region and his conclusions were sharply at variance with the American foreign policy of the time. In 1953 Kennan became a professor at the Institute for Advanced Study, Princeton (1953–74), of which he had already been a member in 1950–52. He also taught at the universities of Chicago and Oxford. He was the United States ambassador to Yugoslavia in 1961–63.

In May Russian-born historian, physician, and psychologist **Immanuel Velikovsky** (1895–1979) was informed by Macmillan Company's president that a number of scientists threatened to boycott the company's textbook division because of his best-selling but highly controversial book *Worlds in Collision: Earth in Upheaval* (1950). With the author's permission, the book's rights were subsequently transferred to Doubleday & Company, which had no textbook department and was thus less vulnerable to such pressure. In his book Velikovsky had challenged orthodox views of the earth and solar system's history by suggesting planetary near-collisions. He argued that a great catastrophe (the near-collision of Venus and the Earth) had taken place at the time of the Exodus of the Israelites from Egypt (1500 BCE) and that this event was recorded in many mythical traditions. Although given some credit, his theories in this and later books were rejected by most scientists.

In August historians **John Caughey** (1902–95), **Ludwig Edelstein** (1902–65), **Ernst Kantorowicz** (1895–1963), and **Charles Mowat** refused, on grounds of conscience, to sign the text of a loyalty oath circulated at the University of California, Berkeley, and, as a result, were dismissed. In 1949 the regents of the University of California had demanded that all faculty members swear that they did not believe in overthrowing the United States government and that they were not communists. They dismissed thirty-one nonsigners. A collective lawsuit resulted in an order for reinstatement in April 1951, but some of the nonsigners had already found employment elsewhere.

Kantorowicz, German medievalist, biographer (1927) of the Hohenstaufen emperor Frederick II, and specialist in rites of power, had a past as a right-wing nationalist fighting the Spartacist and communist groups in Berlin and Munich in 1918–19, but he had retired from his professorship (1930–34) at Frankfurt University in August 1934 rather than having to sign, as a Jew, an oath of loyalty to Adolf Hitler. After some uncertain years as a private scholar, he went into hiding in November 1938 and emigrated in December 1938 from Germany to Oxford University. His family business was confiscated by the Nazis. In September 1939 he went to Berkeley, where he became a member of the University of California history department (1939–50). Concurrently, he had become a professor emeritus at Frankfurt University (1945–). After leaving Berkeley, he became a visiting scholar at the Dumbarton Oaks Foundation (1951) and a professor at the Institute for Advanced Study School for Historical Studies at Princeton (1951–63).

Mowat was a historian of interwar Britain. Edelstein, a student of philosopher Karl Jaspers in Germany and historian of science and medicine in antiquity, was dismissed from the Institut für Geschichte der Medizin und Naturwissenschaften in 1933 and went into exile in Italy (1933–34) and the United States. There he worked at the Institute of the History of Medicine, Johns Hopkins University (1934–47). Due to the oath controversy, he left his position as a professor of Greek at Berkeley (1948–51), and went back to Johns Hopkins (1951–65). He did research on, inter alia, the Hippocratic oath. Caughey was active in the American Association of University Professors. He was reinstated in [1953] and specialized in the history of California.

During the loyalty oath controversy, both the American Historical Association and the Mississippi Valley Historical Association passed resolutions deploring the oath. In 1950 historian **Henry May** turned down a job at Berkeley in protest against the oath. In 1950 psychoanalyst **Erik Erikson** (until 1939: Erik Homburger) (1902–94), an exile from Nazi Germany who went to the United States in 1933, resigned from the University of California Institute of Child Welfare, Berkeley (1939–50), in protest against the oath. Reinstated by court order, he nevertheless went to the Austen Riggs Center, Stockbridge, Mass. (1951–60), and Harvard University (1960–70). A pioneer of psychohistory, Erikson wrote biographies of Martin Luther (1958) and Mahatma Gandhi (1969).

1951–52   **Robert Lee Wolff**, wartime director of the Balkan Section of the Research and Analysis Branch of the Office of Strategic Services (OSS) and in 1951–52 associate history professor and director of the Russian Research Center at Harvard University, was the object of rigorous FBI scrutiny. The result was that he was considered "loyal".

The FBI reportedly also had a file on **Michael Karpovich** (1888–
1959), professor of Russian history at Harvard University (1927–?)
and member of the Russian Research Center executive committee.
A leading Russian anticommunist emigrant, Karpovich had been a
secretary at the embassy of the Russian Provisional Government in
the United States and remained in the United States after the 1917
revolution.

1951   During the Institute of Pacific Relations hearings, Harvard sinologist
            and historian **John Fairbank** (1907–91), special assistant to the
            United States ambassador (1942–43) in Chongqing, Sichuan, the cap-
            ital of the Chinese Nationalist government, working at the Office of
            War Information and OSS (1942–45), director of the United States In-
            formation Service in China (1945–46), professor at Harvard Univer-
            sity (1936–40, 1946–77) and director of its East Asian Research
            Center (1959–73), was falsely accused of having been a communist.
            He was refused a visa to Japan. He felt obliged to circulate a long list
            of extracts from his writings to document his anticommunism.

1951–63   In February 1951 **W.E.B. [William Edward Burghardt] Du Bois**
            (1868–1963), historian of Afro-American history and former profes-
            sor of sociology at Atlanta University (1897–1910, 1934–44), was
            indicted by a federal grand jury for his chairmanship of the Peace
            Information Center (an organization disbanded in October 1950) and
            accused of being an "unregistered foreign agent". At age eighty-three
            he was arrested, faced a sentence of five years' imprisonment, a fine
            of $10,000, and loss of his civil and political rights. He and four
            codefendants were acquitted in November after a three-week trial.
            The judge ruled that the government had failed to corroborate its
            allegations. In April 1953 the Council of African Affairs, an organ-
            ization of which Du Bois was vice chairman, was put on the list of
            "communist-front groups". It was closed in 1955. In the same year
            complimentary copies of a Czech translation of his book *In Battle
            for Peace* (New York 1951) sent to him were confiscated. (In 1958
            Du Bois received a honorary doctorate in historical sciences from
            Charles University, Prague). From 1952 to 1958, he was forbidden
            the use of his passport on political grounds and was unable to travel
            to other countries. In the following years, he visited the USSR and
            China, but his passport was temporarily sequestered upon his return.
            In 1959 he was awarded the Lenin Peace Prize. Increasingly alien-
            ated from American life, he joined the CPUSA in October 1961 and
            immigrated to Ghana at the invitation of President Kwame Nkrumah,
            as director of an *Encyclopedia Africana* project.
                Du Bois's career had begun seventy-five years before. His doctoral
            thesis, *The Suppression of the African Slave Trade to the United
            States of America, 1638–1870*, was the first volume to be published

in the Harvard Historical Series (1896; reprinted 1954). In 1900 he drafted "To the Nations of the World", a statement issued by the first Pan-African Conference in London. In 1910 he resigned from Atlanta University under political pressure because his opposition to the policy of Booker T. Washington—president of the Tuskegee Institute in Alabama and symbol of a gradualist solution to the problems of blacks in the United States—increasingly deprived him and the university of research funds. From 1919 to 1945, he coorganized five pan-African congresses. In [1929] he withdrew his contribution on the history of the American Negro, to appear in the fourteenth edition of the *Encyclopaedia Britannica*, because the editors, he claimed, had deleted all references to Reconstruction (the 1865–77 period following the civil war) and refused even to include a short positive statement on the black contribution to the nation during that period. In 1934 he resigned from the National Association for the Advancement of Colored People (NAACP), which he had cofounded in 1909, over differences on the desirable degree of black integration and moved to Atlanta University again, until his forced resignation there in 1944. In 1944 he returned to the NAACP as its director of special research until his dismissal in 1948. The Marxist-inspired *Black Reconstruction: An Essay toward a History of the Part which Black Folk Played in the Attempt to Reconstruct Democracy in America, 1860–1880* (New York), his most influential book, appearing in May 1935, was ignored by many (though not all) white historians until its 1964 reprint.

1951–   In August 1951 **Moses Finley** (born Moses Finkelstein) (1912–86), former researcher and editorial assistant for the *Encyclopedia of the Social Sciences* (1930–33), instructor at the City College of New York (1934–42), historian of ancient Greece teaching at Rutgers University, Newark campus (1948–52), was accused of having run a communist study group while a graduate student at Columbia University during the 1930s. The accusation came from historians William Canning and Karl Wittfogel. Both were testifying before the Senate Internal Security Subcommittee and had already accused Finley on earlier occasions. As early as 1938–41, Finley had been the executive secretary of the American Committee for Democracy and Intellectual Freedom, a group headed by anthropologist Franz Boas (1858–1942). Wittfogel had labeled this committee an "academic front organization". In March 1941 Canning named Finley as a communist during the Rapp-Coudert investigations; Finley's appointment at City College of New York was not renewed in 1942. In March 1952 Finley testified before the Senate Subcommittee that he was not a CPUSA member but invoked the Fifth Amendment when asked if he had ever been one, thus avoiding a possible indictment for perjury (as the Lattimore [q.v. 1950–] case two weeks later would confirm). Initially, Rutgers University supported Finley, but in December 1952 its board of trustees unanimously declared that invoking the Fifth Amendment was a cause for immediate dismissal, thus overruling the conclusions of two special advisory committees. Finley was dismissed from his assistant professorship and blacklisted at American universities. He founded the American Committee for the Defense of International Freedom in response to the rise of McCarthyism. From 1954 he pursued his career at Cambridge University, United Kingdom (1954–82), where he was knighted in 1979. A nomination to the history department of Cornell University, Ithaca, N.Y., in May 1958 was rejected by the university president. The history department's efforts to appeal the decision to the faculty's committee on academic freedom and tenure were fruitless.

1952–53   Historians **William Langer** (1896–1977), CIA research director and wartime head of the OSS research and analysis branch, and **S. Everett Gleason** (1905–), deputy executive secretary of the National Security Council (NSC), wrote a two-volume history of the American entry into World War II (*The Challenge to Isolation, 1937–1940* and *The Undeclared War, 1940–41*). They received privileged access to material denied to other historians. Other scholars given privileged access to classified documents included Admiral **Samuel Eliot Morison** (1887–1976), professor at Harvard University (1925–55), Christopher Columbus's biographer, and historian of naval operations appointed by the navy in 1942, for his fifteen-volume *History of United States Naval Operations in World War II* (1947–62); historian **James Field** for his *History of United States Naval Operations: Korea* (1962); and **Herbert Feis** (1893–1972), State Department official and diplomatic historian, for his *China Tangle: The American Effort in China from Pearl Harbor to the Marshall Mission* (1953). The allegation, made in the late 1940s and 1950s, that historians taking a revisionist stand regarding the origins of, and responsibility for, World War II (especially regarding President Franklin Roosevelt's role) were more restricted in their access to archives and publishers than others, proved unsubstantiated. The main spokesman of the revisionists was **Harry Elmer Barnes** (1889–1968), also a historiographer and revisionist of World War I, who wrote about a "historical blackout" on the part of "powerful pressure groups". As to the specific point of exclusion of revisionists from archives, he received selective support from historian **Charles Beard** (1874–1948). In later years Barnes supported theses of Holocaust deniers.

1952–57   From 1952 to 1957, **William Appleman Williams** (1921–90), who had left the navy to study history, particularly the history of foreign relations, in which he took a revisionist stand, was a target for HUAC at the University of Oregon. In 1957 he moved to the University of Wisconsin (1957–68). In the same year George Braziller, Inc., however, refused to publish his new book, *The Tragedy of American Diplomacy* (eventually published by World Publishing Company in 1959). In 1960–61 HUAC subpoenaed him in connection with the manuscript of his *Contours of American History* (1961), some articles he had written, and a grant he had received. After a hearing, the case was dropped. He later worked at Oregon State University (1968–85).

1952–   In 1952 the State Department confiscated the passport of historian of early modern Europe **Natalie Zemon Davis** (1928–) and her husband, mathematician Chandler Davis, probably in connection with a pamphlet she and Elizabeth Douvan wrote, *Operation Mind*, published anonymously before the 1952 HUAC visit to Michigan and attributed to Chandler Davis. The pamphlet reviewed HUAC history and tried to show with excerpts from testimonies that HUAC attacked specific ideas about peace, trade unions, and equality, rather than efforts to overthrow the government. They did not protest because they thought that they would have to swear a loyalty oath, which they refused to do. Davis was without a passport for many years and could no longer travel to France to work in the archives. As a result, her doctoral research (eventually completed in 1959) was hampered. She had to raise three children while her husband was imprisoned (for six months in 1960 on charges brought against him by HUAC) and blacklisted at United States universities. After her term as a history professor at Brown University, Providence, R.I. (1959–63), both went to work at Toronto University (1963–71). Later she became a professor at the University of California, Berkeley (1971–77) and Princeton University (1977–96).

In March 1952 **Daniel Thorner** (1915–74), economic historian of India and assistant professor of economics at the University of Pennsylvania, invoked the Fifth Amendment before the HUAC McCarran subcommittee during the Institute of Pacific Relations hearings because he had been named during the Rapp-Coudert investigations. In May–October 1953, the university administration refused the economics department's request to give him tenure while he was in Bombay on a one-year research grant. Thorner stayed in India, where he could teach part-time at Delhi University and do some paid research. When in 1957 he tried to get an academic position in the United States, he received only one reply. In 1960 he became a member of the Sixième Section of the École Pratique des Hautes Études, Paris.

1953–57   **Daniel Cosío Villegas** (1898–1976), a leading Mexican historian, specialist in the Porfiriato (1876–1911; an epoch when President Porfirio Díaz attempted Mexico's modernization at great human cost), editor and coauthor of the ten-volume *Historia moderna de México* (1955–74), cofounder of La Casa de España (the refuge of numerous intellectuals from Spain, which later became El Colegio de México, of which he was president in 1958–63), founder-editor of *Historia mexicana* (1951–61), and publisher and political columnist, was to deliver a lecture on *El comunismo en América latina* at Columbia University. Interrogated by the FBI, he took the first flight back and was not allowed into the United States until [1957].

1953–59   In 1953 **Nikki Keddie** (1930–), a historian who wrote a dissertation on Iranian history at the University of California, Berkeley, and taught (1957–61) at Scripps College, Claremont, Calif., could not get a passport because of her left-wing political views. After a Supreme Court ruling in 1958, she received a passport and in 1959 went to Iran. Later she taught Middle Eastern and Iranian history at the University of California, Los Angeles (1961–).

1953   In 1953 **Samella Lewis** (1924–), historian of African American art and professor and chair of fine arts at Florida Agricultural and Mechanical University (1953–58), was accused by the state of Florida of having communist sympathies because she had designed a greeting card for the NAACP. She was followed by the government and then by the Ku Klux Klan, who shot out the rear windows of her home.

1953–63   In 1953 the State Department Historical Office (and with it, the various State Department agencies responsible for the clearance of documents) was accused by Republican politicians of hiding evidence that would contradict an official white paper, *United States Relations with China: With Special Reference to the Period 1944–49* (a response to criticism of the Far East policies of the Truman administration—especially its refusal to support the Chinese Nationalists in 1948–49—which contained, inter alia, a history of American policy in China since 1844). The Historical Office was also accused of postponing the publication of the papers of the wartime summit conferences in order to protect Democratic administrations. In response, the Historical Office began to prepare a special series of *Foreign Relations of the United States (FRUS)*, the official history of United States foreign policy published since 1861. In December 1956 the first volume, covering the events of 1942, was published, but the Taiwanese nationalists resented the revival of the criticisms of Jiang

Jieshi's regime. Publication of the remaining fourteen volumes of the China series was postponed indefinitely, to be resumed only in 1963 with the *FRUS* volume covering the events of 1943 still bearing its 1957 imprint.

1953–55   In 1953 left-wing labor historian **Herbert Gutman** (1928–85), at that time a history student at the University of Wisconsin, Madison, was subpoenaed by HUAC and questioned about his CPUSA membership and his participation in the 1948 Henry Wallace campaign. He reportedly denounced the committee and refused to answer its questions. As late as 1955, a witness before HUAC reported about Gutman's communist activities. Gutman directed the American working-class history project at the Graduate Center of City University, New York (1975–85).

1953   In February 1953 **Daniel Boorstin** (1914–), lawyer and intellectual historian at the University of Chicago (1944–69), director of the National Museum of History and Technology, Smithsonian Institution (1969–75), librarian of Congress (1975–87), and known as a proponent of the consensus school of American history, was subpoenaed by HUAC. He reported on his and his associates' activities when he belonged to a Marxist study group at Oxford University and during his brief CPUSA membership in 1938–39 (until the August 1939 Nazi–Soviet pact). He was the author of, inter alia, the three-volume work *The Americans* (1958–73).

Historian **Richard Schlatter** (1912–87), a lecturer in American history at Rutgers University named by Boorstin [q.v. 1953] as his CPUSA associate from 1936 (the Spanish Civil War) to 1939 (the year of the Nazi–Soviet pact), was subpoenaed by HUAC. With the Finley [q.v. 1951–] case in mind, he did not want to be an informer or invoke the Fifth Amendment. He told HUAC in a private session that he had contacted all the persons he was planning to name and that he had their permission to name them. He then was not asked by HUAC to testify publicly. In 1975 he supervised the organization of the 14th International Congress of Historical Sciences in San Francisco.

1953–54   In the fall of 1953 and the spring of 1954, historian **Sydney James**, CPUSA member while an undergraduate at Harvard University in the late 1940s, reluctantly cooperated with the FBI, but when finally asked to serve as a prosecution witness in a contempt trial, he refused. Although he believed that the FBI watched him until the late 1960s, he reportedly did not encounter any difficulties.

1954   Historian **Oscar Handlin** (1915–), son of Jewish immigrants, spe-
            cialist in the history of immigration and acculturation, refused to
            delete specific criticism of senators McCarran and McCarthy from
            his contribution to a series of books sponsored by the Library of
            Congress. He worked at Harvard University for many years (1939–
            78) and became director of its Center for the Study of Liberty in
            America (1958–66), its Charles Warren Center for Studies in Amer-
            ican History (1965–72), and its University Library (1979–85).

            In the preface of his privately printed collection of essays *On the
            Nature of History: Essays about History and Dissidence* (Lawrence
            1954), **James Malin** (1893–1979), history professor at the Univer-
            sity of Kansas (1921–63) and environmental historian specialized in
            Great Plains history, claimed that six of the eight essays had been
            previously denied publication through conventional channels be-
            cause in them he had attacked historical relativism.

            The school board in El Paso, Tex., banned the use of a history
            textbook which printed the United Nations Declaration of Human
            Rights and the U.S. Declaration of Independence without comment.
            The State Board of Education, however, rejected a demand to drop
            the book from its list.

1954–   In 1954 historian **Lee Benson** was named as a former communist
            before HUAC. He described himself as "intellectually terrified" in
            the 1950s. As late as 1960, he did not want to make explicit his
            "Marxian standpoint" in his historiographical work *Turner and
            Beard* (Glencoe 1960), out of fear of never getting tenured. In 1967
            historian **Edward Saveth** (1915–), who was involved in the 1940
            Rapp-Coudert investigations because of his brief association with the
            communist milieu in the 1930s, expressed the same fear. He re-
            mained without permanent employment for many years. He became
            a member of the New School for Social Research, New York (1959–
            67), and history professor at the State University of New York Col-
            lege, Fredonia (1968–[86]).

[1954]   In [January] historian **Val Lorwin** (1907–) was indicted for perjury
            in a loyalty investigation. American Historical Association executive
            secretary Boyd Shafer refused Lorwin's offer to withdraw for that
            reason from a program at the AHA annual meeting.

1954   In the spring the Harvard University administration investigated the
            historian of science **Everett Mendelsohn** because as a radical un-
            dergraduate at Antioch he had been active in the 1948 Wallace cam-
            paign and the peace movement. He was wrongfully suspected of
            being a CPUSA member and asked to clear himself before his ap-

pointment as a teaching fellow for 1955 could be approved. Mendelsohn consulted a lawyer and gave explanations to the faculty dean, which were accepted.

In [April] an offer to historian **Sigmund Diamond** (?1920–99), an adviser to faculty fellows and research fellow in entrepreneurial history at Harvard University, for a five-year administrative position with some teaching duties at Harvard was canceled. The dean of the faculty of arts and sciences had learned of Diamond's past CPUSA affiliation (1941–50) when he was a student and of his refusal to inform the FBI on his former political associates; the dean withdrew his recommendation. When he was on the verge of moving to the United Kingdom, Diamond was offered a position in the sociology department at Columbia University. There he became Giddings professor of sociology and history (1955–86).

1954– In June 1954 labor historian **Ray Ginger** (1924–75), assistant professor of research in business history at Harvard Business School with a three-year contract and author of a biography of socialist leader Eugene Debs (1855–1926), was forced to resign for alleged communist sympathies "and flee to New York". After several years, he was employed at Calgary University, Alberta, Canada.

In the summer of 1954, **Leonard Marsak**, European history instructor at the history department of Reed College, Portland, Ore., invoked the Fifth Amendment before a HUAC hearing. Although he was not dismissed, his contract was not renewed in late 1955. He was told that he was unemployable at state universities. He said that he was later denied several academic positions at first offered to him when he told about his "Reed experience". Later Marsak worked at the University of California, Santa Barbara.

[1955] HUAC investigated the case of machinist and communist trade-union activist **David Montgomery** (1927–) in Newark, N.J. Montgomery was dismissed and blacklisted by employers for his union activity and in 1960 he decided to become a labor historian. He worked at, inter alia, the University of Pittsburgh (1963–77) and Yale (1979–) and edited the journal *International Labor and Working-Class History*.

1955 In the spring an opinion survey was conducted among 2,451 social scientists, including 681 historians. One historian declared that he was a suspected communist, only because he had given a reading assignment to his students on the USSR constitution. Another historian said that he had concealed his support for the recognition of Red China and stressed the opposing view instead. A third historian felt uneasy when two strangers appeared in his lecture on Marxism in the United States in the 1930s. A fourth, who was completing a book, decided to "stop with 1945 when the Cold War began". A fifth preferred not to start work on a history of China after all.

In December an internal State Department memorandum reported that Polish-born **Richard Pipes** (1923–), history professor at Harvard University (1950–), specialist in the 1917. Russian Revolution, had had a series of contacts with Soviet historians (among others, A.L. Sidorov of the Soviet Academy of Sciences) at the 10th International Congress of Historical Sciences in Rome in September 1955. The memo recommended that his contacts be made a matter of record in the State Department. Pipes became director of the Russian Research Center at Harvard University (1968–73), and served as director of East European Studies and Soviet Affairs for the NSC (1981–82).

Sociologist **Norman Birnbaum** submitted for consideration by the *American Historical Review* a critique of *The Social Sciences in Historical Study: A Report of the Committee on Historiography* (New York 1954), a report of the Social Science Research Council with business historian Thomas Cochran (1902–99) as the committee's chairman. It was rejected because one referee allegedly found it Marxist.

1957–   In March 1957 clergyman and historian **Clennon King** (1921–), head of the history department at Alcorn College, Mississippi, was dismissed as of June 1958—after students had demonstrated against him because he had written several letters to the *Jackson State Times* denouncing the NAACP for arousing the antagonism of white people. In the same month, he was momentarily arrested for trying to enroll in the all-white University of Mississippi and then allowed to return to his hometown.

[1950s]   The appointment of historian **Richard Reichard** to the faculty of George Washington University, Washington, D.C., was canceled because he invoked the Fifth Amendment before HUAC.

1961   The right-wing group Texans for America (TFA) reportedly intimidated the Texas State Textbook Committee and pressed several publishers to make substantial changes in their books on American history and geography. Macmillan deleted a passage saying that World War II might have been averted if the United States had joined the League of Nations, and the Silver-Burdett Company took out two passages on the need for the United States to maintain friendly relations with other countries and the possibility that some countries would occasionally disagree with the United States. The substituted passages simply stated that some countries were less free than the United States.

1961–62 The TFA took action against the use in Texas of the history textbook *This Is Our Nation* (St. Louis 1961) by **Paul Boller**, then a historian at Southern Methodist University, Dallas, and **Jean Tilford**, a Cincinnati high school teacher. Boller was accused, inter alia, of being soft on communism, of omitting vital facts about American history, of giving too much space to the Indians and to the subject of slavery, and of providing a too favorable view of President Franklin Roosevelt and the New Deal. He received hate calls in the middle of the night. Notwithstanding the pressure, the book was approved by the Texas State Board of Education in November 1961. In 1962, however, the TFA sent out a four-page circular throughout Texas denouncing the book and threatening "indignation meetings" if it was selected anywhere. The book was successfully boycotted in all school districts but one. Boller became a historian specializing in the American presidency.

1962 The FBI looked into the case of radical historian **Howard Zinn** (1922–), chairman of the history department at the black Spelman College in Atlanta, Ga. (1956–63), because he had published a article critical of police conduct during the civil-rights campaigns in the South. Later Zinn also protested the American presence in Vietnam. He was arrested several times, inter alia, because he participated in the blockade of an army base near Boston (May 1970), where he was a professor of political science (1964–88), and in an occupation of Congress in Washington, D.C. In his books Zinn discussed civil disobedience, civil rights, and American militarism. He was the author of *A People's History of the United States* (1980).

[1963] The TFA wanted fifty textbooks to be banned from the classrooms, including **Gertrude Hartman**, *America: Land of Freedom* (Boston 1946, 1955); *A History of the United States*; **Willis West** and **Ruth West**, *The Story of Our Country* (Boston 1948); *American History; Living World History*; *The Rise of the American Nation* (New York 1950, 1961), by **Lewis Todd** (1906–) and **Merle Curti** (1897–); **Ralph Harlow** and **Ruth Miller**, *The Story of America* (New York 1953); Boller [q.v. 1961–62] & Tilford [q.v. 1961–62], *This is Our Nation*; *The Record of Mankind*; *The Adventure of the American People* (New York 1959), by **Henry Graff** (1921–) and **John Krout** (1896–); and *United States History*.

1963–71 In 1963 **Francis Russell** (1910–), a historian specializing in the American history of the 1920s and biographer of President (1921–

23) Warren Harding, discovered 250 love letters, written between 1909 and 1920 by Harding to Carrie Phillips, the wife of an Ohio department-store owner, in two shoeboxes in the possession of Phillips's guardian, lawyer Don Williamson. The letters came into the temporary official custody of the Ohio Historical Society, where they were microfilmed by its curator of documents **Kenneth Duckett**; they were also, at several moments, in danger of being destroyed by others. Several parties claimed legal ownership of the letters. In 1964 the president's heirs sued Duckett, Russell, Russell's publisher McGraw-Hill, and the magazine *American Heritage* (which planned to publish an article by Russell on the letters), asking for the impounding of the letters and for $1 million in damages, claiming that they had been "irreparably damaged" by publication of some extracts. The Court of Common Pleas in Columbus, Ohio, issued an order enjoining the defendants from "publishing, producing, copying, exhibiting, or making any use whatsoever" of the letters pending a final hearing and a decision on the suit. Duckett sent the microfilms to *American Heritage* magazine in New York for safekeeping, received an official reprimand from the society, resigned in the spring of 1965, and became an archivist at Southern Illinois University. Russell was forced to excise all direct quotations of the letters (some 800 words) from his biography, of Harding, eventually published in 1968. The letters' originals were bought by the Harding family. In December 1971 the heirs agreed to donate the letters to the Library of Congress, restricting access until 2014.

1965   Richard Nixon, then a Republican gubernatorial candidate for New Jersey and future president (1969–74), called for the dismissal of **Eugene Genovese** (1930–), associate history professor at Rutgers University (1963–67) and neo-Marxist historian of black slavery and the antebellum South, because of his anti–Vietnam War activities. At a Vietnam teach-in in April, Genovese had said: "I do not fear or regret the impending Vietcong victory in Vietnam: I welcome it". Although the governor and the university administration publicly defended his right to teach and although he was not dismissed, Genovese resigned to avoid further embarrassment and went to Sir George Williams University, Canada (1967–69); the University of Rochester, N.Y. (1969–86), where he headed the history department; and the University Center of Georgia, where he was a Distinguished Scholar (1986–). While an undergraduate, he had been expelled from the CPUSA for "failing to conform with party discipline". He had also been discharged from the United States army after ten months because of his previous CPUSA membership.

1965–   From 1965 Mexican philosopher and historian **Leopoldo Zea Aguilar** (1912–), director-general of cultural relations at the Mexican Ministry of Foreign Relations (1960–66), professor emeritus at the School of Philosophy and Letters, Universidad Nacional Autónoma de México (1971–), was repeatedly denied a visa to enter the United States, probably because he had written an article condemning the 1965 occupation of Santo Domingo by the Marines. In [1980] he was detained at San Antonio airport on his way to Washington to participate as a guest lecturer in a program sponsored by the Organization of American States at Georgetown University, Washington, D.C. He was questioned about how he had acquired his visa and about his political teachings. He was released only after a group of Mexican officials on the same flight had protested.

In August 1965 New Left historian **Staughton Lynd** (1929–), an assistant professor at Yale University, was arrested during the first demonstration he coorganized against the American intervention in Vietnam. He also traveled to North Vietnam, among others, with Aptheker [q.v. 1940–41], in defiance of a State Department ban. In May 1968 his most influential book, *Intellectual Origins of American Radicalism* (New York), appeared. In the same year, he was dismissed by Yale University and blacklisted, at least partly for his political activities. Although he was recommended for appointment by the history departments of four universities in 1967–68, at each institution the administration rejected him. The Chicago State College Board of Governors stated that his trip to Hanoi was the reason for their action; the other institutions gave no reason. At the 1969 American Historical Association business meeting, he was the first opposition candidate for the AHA presidency in its history; he got 30 percent of the vote. He left the historical profession, became a community organizer in Chicago, and enrolled in law school. He practiced labor law in a Youngstown, Ohio, firm and worked as a legal representative of steelworkers. He continued to write about working-class history.

1966   Immediately after the 1966 election of governor Ronald Reagan in California, school inspector Max Rafferty opposed any revision of textbooks aimed at giving a larger share to ethnic and racial minorities. One of the textbooks he reportedly condemned was the eighth-grade-level *Land of the Free: A History of the United States* (New York 1966), written by historians Caughey [q.v. 1950], **John Hope Franklin** (1915–), an Afro-American historian of the South at Brooklyn College, Brooklyn, N.Y. (1956–64), and the University of Chicago (1964–82), and editorial board member of the *Journal of Negro History*, and **Ernest May** (1918–), history professor at Harvard University. Before breaking the "color line" by accepting tenure at Brooklyn College in 1956, Franklin reportedly could teach only at black colleges despite his Harvard doctorate. Until the 1960s, he reportedly faced discrimination and racism within the Mississippi Valley Historical Association, the AHA, and the Southern Historical Association.

[1967]   Radical historian **Jesse Lemisch** (1936–) was dismissed at the University of Chicago because of his left-wing political activities.

1968–74   On 16 March 1968, United States Army troops of the America-1 Division massacred more than 400 Vietnamese noncombatants in My Lai, Vietnam. Efforts to suppress and withhold information about this war crime were made at every command level within the division. Most files and records of documents relating to the crime and its investigation were removed or destroyed. A March 1970 four-volume report by General William Peers to the Secretary of the Army and the Chief of Staff denouncing the "incident" and its cover-up was itself kept secret for more than four years until publication was partially authorized in November 1974.

1968–   In May 1968 **Julius Epstein** (1901–75), a Vienna-born Jewish refugee from Nazi Germany who fled in 1933 to Czechoslovakia, in 1938 to Switzerland, and in 1939 to the United States, journalist, Office of War Information collaborator, research associate at the Hoover Institution on War, Revolution and Peace, Stanford University (1963–66), and professor of international politics at Lincoln University, San Francisco (1966–), sued the secretary of the army for refusing to release the top secret *Operation Keelhaul* file. *Operation Keelhaul* was the code name given by the United States Army to its own documentary record of the forced repatriation of more than one million Russian, Ukrainian, Polish, Hungarian, and Baltic prisoners of war and displaced persons by several Allied countries to USSR-controlled countries, mainly between 1944 and 1947. Many of them were anticommunist and had fought in the German army. Epstein, who accidentally discovered the file's existence in April 1954, argued that, according to the 1953 executive order, the records should have been declassified. In his attempts since 1954 to get the file declassified, he received some congressional backing between 1955 and 1959 (when Dwight Eisenhower, commander-in-chief during World War II, was president). In 1968 it became the first case in which an exemption to the FOIA, applying to matters of national defense or foreign policy, faced judicial review. The district court and later the court of appeals in San Francisco both refused to examine the classified documents in camera to judge the reasonableness of the claimed exemption and ruled, on the basis of the description of the documents alone, that classification was "not arbitrary". The Supreme Court denied Epstein's petition to revise this verdict. Epstein published his book on the forced repatriation (written in 1963–66) in 1973. Later criticism of FOIA requests included long delays, large deletions, and lack of generosity concerning fee waivers for research "in the public interest".

1968   Historian **Francis Loewenheim**, professor at Rice University, Houston, Tex., accused the Roosevelt Library of concealing six letters from historian and U.S. ambassador to Germany William Dodd (1869–1940) to President Franklin Roosevelt, which he needed for his edition of the Dodd-Roosevelt letters. He charged that he had been the victim of unfair and discriminatory treatment because the letters were subsequently used by library archivist Edgar Nixon (1902–) in his 1969 compilation, *Franklin D. Roosevelt and Foreign Affairs, 1933–37*. The charges were investigated by a joint committee of the AHA and the Organization of American Historians (OAH), which rejected them in its final report of August 1970. The committee found no deliberate and systematic withholding of documents. The affair, however, sparked a debate among archivists about professional ethics.

1969–70   **Robert Starobin** (died 1970), left-wing historian and supporter of the Black Panthers, delivered a conference paper on slavery at Wayne State University, Detroit. Severe criticism by two black commentators reportedly devastated him and contributed to his suicide in 1970.

1970–72   Political activist and historian **Eqbal Ahmed** (1933–99) was among those ("the Harrisburg Seven") arrested and tried on the charge of plotting to kidnap Secretary of State (and historian) Henry Kissinger. It was believed that Ahmed's activity in the civil-rights movement and his outspoken opposition to the Vietnam War had led to his arrest. In the spring of 1972, he was acquitted of all charges. After temporary positions at several universities, he became a tenured professor at Hampshire College, Amherst, Mass. (1982–97), and an analyst of the postimperial world. Born in Bihar, British India, and immigrated to Pakistan in 1947–48, Ahmed had come to the United States as a Rotary Fellow in American history at Occidental College, Calif., in the mid-1950s. As a student of political science and Middle Eastern studies, he went to Algeria, joined the Front de Libération Nationale (1958–?), became an associate of Martinique-born Algerian revolutionary theorist Frantz Fanon, and was arrested in France. Later he was a member of the Algerian delegation to the Évian peace talks (1961–62). Regularly returning to Pakistan after 1988, he attempted to create an alternative university, Khalduniyah (named after historian Ibn Khaldun).

1970   In November historian **Theodore Draper** (1912–) sought access to the classified and uncited State Department documents to which historian Jerome Slater had referred in the preface of his 1970 book, *Intervention and Negotiation: The United States and the Dominican Revolution*. The State Department denied that Slater had been given any classified material. In 1971 Draper, who had written about the 1965 Dominican Revolt himself, denounced the use of not-for-citation sources and the government policy of unequal access and "favoritism".

1971–   On 13 June 1971, the *New York Times* began publishing a nine-part series of articles based on the so-called *Pentagon Papers* (original title: *History of United States Decision-Making Process on Vietnam Policy*, totaling thirty-seven studies and fifteen collections of documents), a study commissioned by Secretary of Defense Robert McNamara in June 1967 (and completed January 1969) as a top-secret history of United States involvement in Indo-China from 1945 to 1968, and to be used in further policy decisions. A Vietnam History Task Force (thirty-six researchers headed by Morton Halperin and supervised by Leslie Gelb at the International Security Affairs division of the Pentagon [Department of Defense]) carried out the study and had access to most files of the secretary of defense; limited access to the files of the State Department, CIA, and the Joint Chiefs of Staff; and no access to White House papers. Among the revelations were the American involvement in the 1963 ousting of Prime Minister Ngo Dinh Diem and the drafts of the 1964 Tonkin Gulf Resolution. In February 1971 the photocopied papers (with the exception of the so-called negotiating volumes) were given to reporter Neil Sheehan by coauthor **Daniel Ellsberg** (1931–), economist, former marine officer, and Pentagon policy analyst. Ellsberg had tried to publicize the document for almost two years. On 15 June 1971, the Justice Department obtained a temporary restraining order against further publication on the grounds of national security. The *New York Times* and the *Washington Post*, which had also begun publishing the series, appealed, and on 30 June the Supreme Court decided 6–3 that prior restraint on publication violated the First Amendment (a constitutional privilege protecting freedom of speech and religion). In July a paperback edition of the *New York Times* articles and of selected documents appeared. In 1972 the near-full report (consisting of 3,000 pages of narrative and more than 4,000 pages of documents) was published (the five-volume Senator Gravel edition). Although the Supreme Court ruled that publication of the full report was not protected under the First Amendment, sale of the volumes continued. After a trial that lasted from June 1971 to May 1973, all charges against Ellsberg and his codefendant Anthony Russo, Jr. (1936–), indicted under the espionage statutes, were dismissed because of "improper government conduct" (including illegal wiretapping of telephone conversations and a break-in at the offices of Ellsberg's psychiatrist to steal his confidential medical records). The *Pentagon Papers* were considered an indispensable source for research into subjects ranging from the political history of Southeast Asia to the internal workings of the executive branch. Along with a number of other foreign policy leaks at the time, the affair inspired the 1972 Executive Order 11652 concerning security classification. The extent of secret historical research in executive departments was unknown.

1974– Late in 1974 the Mississippi State Textbook Purchasing Board refused to approve *Mississippi: Conflict and Change* (1974), written by **James W. Loewen** and **Charles Sallis**, for use as a textbook in state schools. The board did not give any reasons for the ban. The book was the product of a collaboration between students and staff of Tougaloo and Millsaps colleges, Mississippi. It discussed racial conflict, pointed out contributions of black people and other ethnic minorities to the state, and gave much attention to the recent past. It also featured a photograph of a lynching. The book's manuscript had reportedly been turned down by eleven textbook houses before Pantheon published it. In 1975 it won an award for the best work of southern nonfiction. In late 1975 the authors and three school districts sued the state school authorities in a First Amendment challenge in order to obtain classroom authorization for the book. They argued that the only authorized history book championed white supremacy. In April 1980 the court ruled that the textbook "was not rejected for any justifiable reason" and that the ban was "motivated and influenced by racial issues". It ordered the book to be placed on the approved list for a period of six years. In March 1981, the *New York Times* reported that in some schools pressure (including threats of dismissal) was applied against teachers interested in adopting the textbook. In 1995 Loewen, then a professor of sociology at the University of Vermont, wrote *Lies My Teacher Told Me: Everything Your American History Textbook Got Wrong* (New York).

[1975]– In or around 1975, the FBI began destroying many of its documents, but a January 1980 court order stopped the destruction and instructed the FBI to provide the court with plans and schedules for file retention. Historical associations supported the court order. FBI appeals were rejected in mid-1980 and in the fall of 1983.

[1975]   Twenty-two state legislators in Arkansas sought to compel the University of Arkansas to dismiss associate history professor **Grant Cooper** because he was a member of the Marxist Progressive Party by appealing to a state law that prohibited state agencies and institutions from employing communists and fascists. The Arkansas Supreme Court, however, unanimously ruled that the law was unconstitutional.

1975   **Joseph Needham** (1900–95), British historian of Chinese science, fellow, reader in biochemistry, and master of Gonville and Caius College, Cambridge University (1924–76), director of its Needham Research Institute (1976–90), and a foreign associate of the United States National Academy of Sciences, was refused a visa to travel to the United States to give a series of lectures at Washington University and to visit the Massachusetts Institute of Technology. Several months later it was reportedly informally acknowledged that the basis for the denial were Needham's alleged Marxist beliefs. Later Needham traveled several times to the United States without apparent difficulties. He spent 1942–46 in Guomindang-held parts of China as head of the Sino-British Science Cooperation Office. His participation in the International Commission for the Investigation of Charges of Bacteriological Warfare in North China and Korea in the 1940s had been criticized because he had reported evidence unfavorable to the United States. His major work was the multivolume *Science and Civilisation in China* (1954–95).

1977   The Boston educational television station WGBM deleted several scenes from the BBC series *I, Claudius*—based on the historical novel by **Robert Graves** (1895—1985)—before screening it for American audiences because they showed "tasteless sex and violence".

1978   The *American Heritage Dictionary* (1969) was banned in Eldon library, Missouri, because of thirty-nine "objectionable" words.

1979   **Stuart Gibbs**, a history teacher in Mathews County, Virginia, assigned Aldous Huxley's *Brave New World* to his eleventh-grade students in United States history. The principal requested that he withdraw the assignment, but he refused to comply and was dismissed for "insubordination". Gibbs sued the school, and the case was settled out of court. He was, however, not reinstated.

1981   In the summer **Richard Curry**, historian of nineteenth-century American political and intellectual history and coeditor of the book

Conspiracy: The Fear of Subversion in American History (1972), was allegedly intimidated in telephone calls and conversations with officials of the United States Information Agency (USIA, formerly USICA) when he was lecturing in Australia. USIA apparently feared that he might criticize President Ronald Reagan's foreign and domestic policies.

1982–83   In March 1982 the United States Immigration and Naturalization Service (INS) denied a request for permanent resident status to Uruguayan critic and literary historian **Angel Rama** (1926–83), who lived as an exile (?1974–83) in Venezuela and the United States, where he had become a tenured professor of literature at the University of Maryland (1980–83). In July a visa request to allow him to teach at that university was also denied. The grounds given were his supposed links with communist and anarchist organizations, but the evidence against him was kept secret. Rama believed that the denial was based on a series of articles he had contributed to the Uruguayan magazine *Marcha* before 1973, in which he wrote about CIA attempts to infiltrate Latin American intelligence organizations and to intervene in intellectual life. The evidence against him reportedly rested on distorted information supplied by the Uruguayan intelligence services. Ever since the late 1960s, Rama's requests for a United States visa had met with difficulties because he was branded as a communist subversive. The denial paralyzed his work on a book on Latin American cultural history from 1810 to 1910, as he needed to do research in Europe but would be refused reentry to the United States if he left. In 1983 he died in an airplane crash near Madrid.

1982–85   From 1982 to 1985, *The Collapse of the Weimar Republic: Political Economy and Crisis* (Princeton 1981), a book by historian **David Abraham** (1946–) written from a Marxist viewpoint, was attacked by historians Henry Turner (1932–) and Gerald Feldman (1937–) because it contained many errors and because it was allegedly fraudulent. Abraham apologized for the many errors but denied the fraud charges. The campaign against Abraham included an unfavorable book review, the distribution of circular letters to historians in the United States and Germany, pressure on Princeton University Press to withdraw the book from circulation (the press canceled plans for a revised edition, which was eventually published by Holmes & Meier in 1986), a recommendation against his tenure at Princeton history department (he was not hired), involvement in blocking his appointment at four universities (he was not hired), and support to an (unsuccessful) attempt to get the University of Chicago to rescind his 1977 doctoral degree. Although there were various protests against the denunciation campaign, Abraham eventually left the profession. As of 1988, he was enrolled in law school.

1983   The Texas Board of Education was considering world history books and ordered publishers to make several changes in the portrayal of prehistory and evolution, religion, capitalism, communism, and the New Deal, in accordance with the views of a conservative group led by Mel and Norma Gabler, a couple from Texas active in textbook selection since 1961 and operating as Educational Research Analysts, Inc. A few years before, in [1981], an Alabama State Board had removed *Unfinished Journey: A World History* from the approved list of school texts because it defended the evolutionary position.

The National Security Agency (NSA) ordered the George Marshall Research Library in Virginia to reclassify letters from the private papers of former collaborator **William Friedman**. The letters had previously been accessible to researchers such as James Bamford, who cited them in his book on the NSA, *The Puzzled Palace: A Report on America's Most Secret Agency* (Boston 1982). In February 1984 the AHA and OAH filed a suit in federal district court in Washington seeking to deny NSA's authority to classify or close private papers deposited by individuals in libraries or archives.

1983–   In March 1983 the Reagan administration proposed lifelong review of books and speeches written by former government officials who had access to classified information, and lie detector tests for those suspected of leaking sensitive government information (National Security Decision Directive 84). After protests, the prepublication review provision was suspended in September 1984. Even so, more than 290,000 government employees had already signed a lifetime prepublication agreement. In 1983 alone, government censors reviewed 28,364 books, articles, speeches, and other writings for clearance (1984: 21,718 items; 1985: 22,820 items). In August 1986, Standard Form (SF) 189 required all government employees with security clearance not to divulge classified and "non-classified but classifiable" information. In 1987 the enforcement of SF 189 was temporarily suspended because two government employee unions filed suit challenging its constitutionality.

1984   Congress exempted CIA operational files from the 1966 FOIA; this law was considered a serious obstacle to historical research.

1984–92   In [1984] **David McCalden**, the former director of the Holocaust-denying Institute for Historical Review, sued the Simon Wiesenthal Center (SWC) and the American Jewish Committee (AJC), arguing that they had conspired to deprive him of his constitutional rights to free speech. McCalden had rented space for an exhibit about the Holocaust "hoax" at the California Library Association's annual conference but after protests from the SWC and the AJC, the association had canceled his contract. The court dismissed his complaint, but the United States Circuit Court of Appeals reversed the decision in 1992.

1985–89   In October 1985 the INS denied the permanent residency application of American-born Mexican citizen **Margaret Randall** (1936–), a writer and historian specialized in oral history who in early 1984 had returned to the United States. After she had given up her American citizenship in 1961, she had lived in various Latin American countries (1961–84), including one year in hiding in Mexico (1969) because she had feared assassination for her support of the Mexican 1968 student uprising. The INS tried to deport her under the so-called ideological exclusion clauses of the 1952 Immigration, Naturalization and Nationality Act (or McCarran-Walter Act) on the charge that her writings about American foreign policy and left-wing revolutions went "beyond mere dissent" and advocated "doctrines of world communism". She appealed the INS decision. In December 1987 the clauses of the law were temporarily suspended and in October 1988 the act was revised. In July 1989 the Immigration Board of Appeals ruled that Randall had always been an American citizen.

1987   In March a federal district court ordered the removal of forty-four previously approved history, social studies, and home economics textbooks from Alabama public school classrooms on the grounds that they violated the First Amendment by promoting the "religion of secular humanism". The ruling was a victory for conservative Christians, who claimed that secular humanism was essentially a religion, based on human instead of divine values. In August the decision was reversed by the Eleventh Circuit Court of Appeals.

1988   In February four members of *The Dartmouth Review*, a conservative weekly newspaper, confronted **William Cole**, a black professor of music history. The newspaper had published a highly critical review of his course and during the confrontation both sides shouted and pushed. Black students charged that the article and the incident were racially motivated, but the newspaper said that they were fair criticism. A university panel found three staff members guilty of disorderly conduct, harassment, and invasion of privacy because they had initiated and secretly recorded the confrontation. In an ensuing heated exchange, Dartmouth president James Freedman criticized the newspaper for "poisoning . . . the intellectual environment", but the newspaper accused him of censorship and reverse discrimination.

Freedman described the conflict not as a matter of expression but as one of protecting academic diversity.

In June a historian (name unknown) researching the 1985 strike of a meatpackers' union in Austin, Minn., submitted a FOIA request to the FBI seeking documents concerning the FBI's monitoring of the strike. The FBI first said that it had found 1,400 documents relevant to the request and that the cost of processing the request would be $130. The historian waited a full year and was then informed that he had been reclassified as a commercial user (for unspecified reasons) and would have to pay $3,500 for the same material.

1989   In 1989 the private group National Security Archive (NSAr), the American Library Association, the AHA, and the Center for National Security Studies filed a lawsuit against the White House to order it to retain its computer records and backup tapes, arguing that they were official records which had to be preserved. The George Bush administration disagreed, but in November 1992 a federal judge ordered the White House to retain the information. In a similar case early in [1991], the NSAr won a legal challenge to the Bush administration over NSC regulations that would have allowed the destruction of electronic messages from top national security advisers to President Reagan during the Iran-Contra affair (1985–86). An appeals court had prevented the Reagan administration from destroying the computer tapes. In January 1993 a federal appeals court modified the rulings and allowed departing White House officials and the NSC to erase material stored in their personal computers, as long as they preserved the information elsewhere. The decision came amid concern that erasing the records could interfere with investigations such as those into the Iran-Contra cases. In February the Justice Department said it was reviewing a decision by former federal archivist Don Wilson to grant legal control to President Bush over government computer tapes, which contained millions of electronic messages between the White House and the NSC. As early as 1985, a committee of historians and archivists chaired by historian Ernest May [q.v. 1966] had called upon Reagan to issue an order to safeguard government records, especially the drafts of policy statements or memoranda.

In November the FBI agreed to purge its files of thousands of names of persons and organizations collected during its surveillance activities, as a result of a lawsuit in which it admitted its program of surveillance and harassment of opponents of the government's Central American policy.

[1990]   Eight black families sued the New York State education authority for failing to teach their children about black achievements in the history lessons.

1990   At its April convention, the OAH adopted a resolution condemning excessive secrecy and gaps in *FRUS*. The OAH claimed that recent *FRUS* volumes showed "significant increases in deletions and omissions".

1992–95   In late August 1992, a Los Angeles district judge gave the FBI until 11 September to provide detailed reasons for refusing to release files on the murdered former Beatle John Lennon. The order came after a decade-long legal conflict stemming from a FOIA request made by **Jonathan Wiener**, history professor at the University of California, Irvine. A 1988 ruling in favor of the FBI had been overturned in 1989, and in June 1992 the Supreme Court had refused to accept the FBI's challenge to that decision. The files were reportedly released in 1995.

1994–   In September the government transferred 160,000 pages of documents and other materials seized from Haitian army headquarters and from the offices of the paramilitary organization Front Pour l'Avancement et le Progrès d'Haïti (FRAPH; Front for the Advancement and Progress of Haiti) to the U.S. embassy in Haiti. They reportedly contained information relating to human rights violations committed by both the military and FRAPH under the Haitian military government (1991–94). The United States authorities declared that the documents would be returned only after United States citizens' names had been excised, apparently for the purpose of covering up complicity of CIA agents in political murders and other abuses. The Haitian government of President René Préval (1996–) continued to reject this condition. FRAPH was reportedly founded with CIA assistance.

[1995]   Warner Brothers, which encouraged popular magazines and tabloids to make free use of its film stills, denied permission to use them on a paying basis for the book *Past Imperfect: History According to the Movies*, edited by **Marc Carnes** (1950–), historian of Barnard College, Columbia University.

pre-[1995] Photographs of the destruction of Hiroshima after the dropping of the atom bomb on 6 August 1945 were not released until almost fifty years after the event.

1995   On 30 January the Smithsonian Institution's National Air and Space Museum decided to eliminate text and pictures of Japanese atomic bomb victims from the exhibition "The Last Act: The Atomic Bomb

and the End of World War II", planned for June 1995. Only the
fuselage of the Enola Gay (the airplane that dropped the bomb), a
plaque, and a film of the plane's crew would be displayed. The
change came after criticism from the Congress and World War II
veterans in September 1994. Some had found the portrayal of the
Japanese in the aftermath of the war too sympathetic. Subsequently,
a heavily revised exhibition draft was released in October 1994 but
in January 1995 eighty-one members of the United States Congress
sent a letter to the Smithsonian Institution demanding that the display
be canceled, that the National Air and Space Museum's director
Martin Harwit be dismissed, and threatening to curtail future funding
for the Smithsonian. The secretary of the Smithsonian Institution,
Michael Heyman, and the exhibit's curator, Michael Neufeld (1951–),
reportedly apologized because they had erred in attempting to combine historical analysis with the commemoration of the closing of
the war. In May Harwit resigned his position under pressure. A
group of sixty-two historians, organized as the Historians' Committee for Open Debate on Hiroshima, however, protested in 1994–95
what they called a one-sided presentation. The OAH also issued a
statement of protest in October 1994. In January 1995 three OAH
presidents wrote the Smithsonian a letter that focused on censorship
and urged the museum not to cancel the exhibit.

On 6 December a Library of Congress exhibition, *Sigmund Freud:
Conflict and Culture*, was indefinitely postponed after protests from
academics who believed that Freud's theories were widely discredited. On 19 December the Library of Congress closed *Back of the
Big House: The Cultural Landscape of the Plantation*, an exhibition
about slavery and plantation life, after complaints from black staff
members and officials that the display lacked a proper historical context.

1997   **George Herring** (1936–), historian at the University of Kentucky,
former editor of *Diplomatic History*, former president of the Society
for Historians of American Foreign Relations (1990) and former
member of the official CIA Historical Review Panel (1990–96), accused the CIA of not releasing records on its covert operations (including the 1953 Iranian coup, the 1954 Guatemalan coup, and the
1961 invasion of Cuba), despite the policy of openness promised in
1984. CIA officials replied to this accusation that various files concerning the operations in the 1950s had been destroyed in the early
1960s, among them nearly all files concerning the Iranian coup. In
May 1997 the Bill Clinton administration declassified 1,400 pages
of CIA documents about the Guatemalan coup that overthrew the
elected government of President Jacobo Arbenz in 1954 (less than

1 percent of the CIA files on the incident). The documents revealed the CIA's encouragement of political assassination and murder. When in August 1996 the CIA had removed Herring and two other historians from the panel, he had suggested that their criticism of the low declassification levels of CIA materials had played a role in the removal.

1998   In October the Clinton administration released heavily edited excerpts from a 1995 CIA investigation into death squad activities in Honduras in the 1980s. The investigation was ordered after allegations of CIA complicity in atrocities committed by a secret Honduran military intelligence unit.

Also see Argentina (1950–: Blanksten), Brazil (1964–: Frank), Burundi (1980s: Nsabimana), Canada (1970: Kolko), Cuba (1996: Meyers), Dominican Republic (1956–: Galíndez), Egypt (1954–66: Qutb, 1981–: Gran), Ethiopia (1982: Clarke, White, Johanson), Germany (1965–89: Heym; [1990–]: Rosmus), Grenada (1983–85), Guatemala (1995–), Haiti (1982–: Hurbon), Indonesia (1994: Spielberg; 1997: Fredriksson), Israel (1992: Glock), Italy (1981: Katz), Poland (1993: Spielberg), Romania (pre-1991: Culianu), South Africa (1960–90: Kuper), Trinidad & Tobago (1953–: James; 1955–: Williams), Turkey (1978–85: Armenian genocide; 1982: Shaw; 1995–: Dadrian; 1997: University of California; 2000: Suny, military base), United Kingdom (1968–71: Kuper), USSR (1950: Kennan; 1974–80: Fainsod).

SOURCES

Abelove, H., et al. eds., *Visions of History* (Manchester 1984) 104–5, 132–35, 149–51, 169, 175, 187–88, 241–42.
Al Ahram Weekly, 13–19 May 1999 (Ahmad).
Amherst, Spring 1998: 2–5; Spring 1999: 29–30, 36 (Commager).
Amnesty International, *Report* (London) 1972–73: 52; 1997: 171–72.
Annual Obituary (Chicago/London) 1986: 357–60 (Finley); 1989: 307–10 (Lattimore).
Aptheker, H., ed., *The Correspondence of W.E.B. Du Bois*, vol. 3, *Selections 1944–1963* (Amherst 1978) 84, 166, 255, 303, 306, 310, 318, 332, 334–35, 346–48, 388, 390, 421, 433, 435, 438–39, 443.
————, "Du Bois As Historian", *Negro History Bulletin*, 1969, no.32: 6–16.
Article 19, *Information, Freedom and Censorship: World Report* (London) 1988: 120, 125; 1991: 134–35, 137.
Barendt, E., *Freedom of Speech* (Oxford 1985) 132, 136–37.
Barker, C.M., & M.H. Fox, *Classified Files: The Yellowing Pages; A Report on Scholars' Access to Government Documents* (New York 1972): 16–18, 22, 27–33, 36, 46, 54, 61–62, 66–71, 77–83, 87.
Benedict, M.L., "Historians and the Continuing Controversy over Fair Use of Unpublished Manuscript Materials", *American Historical Review*, 1986: 864.
Bentley, E. ed., *Thirty Years of Treason: Excerpts from Hearings before the House Committee on Un-American Activities, 1938–1968* (London 1972) 296, 601–12.

Bird, K., "Silencing History", *Nation*, 20 February 1995 (WWW-text).
————, & M. Sherwin (Historians' Committee for Open Debate), Letter on Hiroshima to Secretary of the Smithsonian Michael Heyman, 20 July 1995.
Boia, L. ed., *Great Historians of the Modern Age: An International Dictionary* (Westport 1991) 195–97, 654–55, 720–22, 730–31, 734–36, 746–48, 751–52, 770–71.
Boller, P.F. Jr., "High School History: Memoirs of a Texas Textbook Writer", *Teachers College Record*, 1980: 317–18, 322–25.
Boyd, K. ed., *Encyclopedia of Historians and Historical Writing* (London/Chicago 1999) 106–7, 240–41, 255–56, 290–91, 325–27, 362–63, 375–77, 385–86, 391–92, 415–16, 443–44, 514–15, 631–32, 757–58, 832–34, 838–39, 867–70, 922–23, 1052–53, 1241, 1305–6, 1353–54.
Braeman, J., "Charles A. Beard", in: C.N. Wilson ed., *Dictionary of Literary Biography*, vol. 17, *Twentieth-Century American Historians* (Detroit 1983) 39–55.
Bruch, R. vom, & R.A. Müller eds., *Historikerlexikon: Von der Antike bis zum 20. Jahrhundert* (Munich 1991) 91, 163.
Camp, R.A., *Who's Who in Mexico Today* (Boulder 1993) 193–94.
Cannon, J. ed., *The Blackwell Dictionary of Historians* (Oxford 1988) 48–49, 112, 127, 131–32, 154, 222–23, 301.
Cantor, N.F., *Inventing the Middle Ages: The Lives, Works and Ideas of the Great Medievalists of the Twentieth Century* (New York 1991) 80, 95–101.
Carnes, M.C., et al. eds., *Past Imperfect: History According to the Movies* (New York 1995) 10.
Christ, K., *Neue Profile der Alten Geschichte* (Darmstadt 1990) 295–99.
Craven, J., "Managing Community Controversy: New Mexico As a Case Study", *Social Education*, 1982: 254, 273–76.
Current Biography Yearbook (New York) 1957: 564–66; 1980: 467 (Velikovsky).
Curry, R.O., "Introduction", in: Curry ed. 1988: 10–13.
————, "Paranoia—Reagan Style: Encounters with the USIA", in: Curry ed. 1988: 178–85.
————, ed., *Freedom at Risk: Secrecy, Censorship, and Repression in the 1980s* (Philadelphia 1988).
Davis, C., "The Purge", in: P. Duren et al. eds., *A Century of Mathematics in America* (Providence 1988–89) 422–23.
Dawn, 12 May 1999 (Ahmad).
Degler, C.N., "Modern American Historiography", in: M. Bentley ed., *Companion to Historiography* (London/New York 1997) 718.
DelFattore, J., *What Johnny Shouldn't Read: Textbook Censorship in America* (New Haven/London 1992) 2, 76–89, 134–35, 147–53.
Delgado, R., "Campus Antiracism Rules: Constitutional Narratives in Collision", in: S. Coliver ed., *Striking a Balance: Hate Speech, Freedom of Expression and Non-discrimination* (London 1992) 285, 287.
Devine, E., M. Held, J. Vinson, & G. Walsh eds., *Thinkers of the Twentieth Century: A Biographical, Bibliographical and Critical Dictionary* (London 1983) 39–42, 233–34, 398–401.
Diamond, S., *Compromised Campus: The Collaboration of Universities with the Intelligence Community, 1945–1955* (New York/Oxford 1992) 3–19, 37, 57–62, 69, 74–79, 125, 131, 293, 299, 301, 308.

Directory of American Scholars, vol. 1, *History* (New York/London 1982) 18, 261, 356, 830.

Draper, T., "The Dominican Intervention Reconsidered", *Political Science Quarterly*, 1971: 1–3, 34–36.

Du Bois, W.E.B., *Black Reconstruction in America: An Essay toward a History of the Part Which Black Folk Played in the Attempt to Reconstruct Democracy in America, 1860–1880* (originally 1935; Cleveland/New York 1964) 713.

Encyclopaedia Britannica: Micropaedia, vol. 12 (Chicago 1994) 297–98 (Velikovsky).

Epstein, C., *A Past Renewed: A Catalog of German-Speaking Refugee Historians in the United States after 1933* (Cambridge 1993) 62–64, 145–47.

Epstein, J., "The Search for the Truth in the United States", in: Epstein, *Operation Keelhaul: The Story of Forced Repatriation from 1944 to the Present* (Old Greenwich 1973) 195–206.

Erdmann, K.D., *Die Ökumene der Historiker: Geschichte der internationalen Historikerkongresse und des Comité international des sciences historiques* (Göttingen 1987) 311–12.

Fermi, L., *Illustrious Immigrants: The Intellectual Migration from Europe 1930–41* (Chicago/London 1968) 356.

Fitzgerald, F., *America Revised: History Schoolbooks in the Twentieth Century* (originally 1979; New York 1980) 29–30, 34, 38.

Frankel, B. ed., *The Cold War 1945–1991*, vol. 1, *Leaders and Other Important Figures in the US and Western Europe* (Detroit 1992) 160–62, 187–88.

Gallagher, N.E. ed., *Approaches to the History of the Middle East: Interviews with Leading Middle East Historians* (Reading, UK 1994) 134–36.

Ginger F.A., & D. Christiano eds., *The Cold War against Labor: An Anthology* (Berkeley 1987) 164, 504–8, 573–76, 710.

Goldstein, J., Marshall B., & J. Schwartz, *The My Lai Massacre and Its Cover-up: Beyond the Reach of Law? The Peers Commission Report with a Supplement and Introductory Essay on the Limits of Law* (New York/London 1976) 1–17, 52–56, 299–313, 316–17, 368–70.

Gorman, R.A. ed., *Biographical Dictionary of Neo-Marxism* (Westport 1985) 123–26, 159–60, 270–72.

Great Soviet Encyclopedia (New York/London) vol. 2 (1973): 209; vol. 27 (1981): 292.

Green, J. ed., *Workers' Struggles, Past and Present: A "Radical America" Reader* (Philadelphia 1983) 409.

Haight, A.L., & C.B. Grannis, *Banned Books, 387 B.C. to 1978 A.D.* (New York/London 1978) 102, 116–18.

Hein, L., "Introduction: The Bomb As Public History and Transnational Memory", *Bulletin of Concerned Asian Scholars*, 1995, no.2: 3–7, 10.

Herring, G.C. ed., *The Secret Diplomacy of the Vietnam War: The Negotiating Volumes of the Pentagon Papers* (Austin 1983) vii–xi.

Higman, J., "Changing Paradigms: The Collapse of Consensus History", *Journal of American History*, 1989: 461.

Hoff-Wilson, J., "The Pluralistic Society", in: W. Zeisel ed., *Censorship: 500 Hundred Years of Conflict* (New York/Oxford 1984) 113–14.

Honan, W.H., *Jack D. Foner, Historian and Pioneer in Black Studies, Dies at 88* (WWW-text 1999).

Human Rights Watch, *World Report* (Washington) 1998: xxxii, 90, 120–22, 124; 1999: 131; 2001: 134.

Index on Censorship, 1/72: 90; 3–4/72: 126; 1/73: xiv–xv; 2/73: xiv; 3/73: xi, 86; 4/75: 79; 1/76: 55; 1/78: 10, 72; 2/78: 52; 2/79: 41; 1/80: 52; 5/80 9; 1/81: 40–41; 1/82: 21; 2/83: 48; 3/83: 15; 4/83: 7–10, 48; 6/83: 35, 48; 6/85: 24, 45; 5/87: 41; 2/88: 3; 5/88: 131; 7/88: 29–31; 3/89: 40; 5/89: 41; 10/89: 41; 1/90: 5, 10–11; 9/90: 40; 4–5/91: 56–57; 10/92: 49; 2/93: 41; 5–6/93: 49; 6/94: 252; 1/95: 253; 2/95: 190; 3/95: 190; 2/96: 105; 4/97: 15; 4/99: 18; 6/99: 131.

Instituto Panamericano de Geografía e Historia, *Guía de Personas que Cultivan la Historia de América* (México 1967) 232–33.

Kahin, G.M., "*The Pentagon Papers*: A Critical Evaluation", *American Political Science Review*, 1975: 675–84.

Kaufman, P.T. ed. *The Reader's Adviser: A Layman's Guide to Literature*, vol. 3 (New York/London 1986) 314–15, 319–20, 330, 463–64, 466–67.

Kennan, G.F., *Memoirs 1925–1950* (London 1968) 476–83.

Krauze, E., "Daniel Cosío Villegas", in: E. Florescano & R. Pérez Montfort eds., *Historiadores de México en el siglo XX* (Mexico 1995) 99.

Lazarsfeld, P.F., & W. Thielens Jr., *The Academic Mind: Social Scientists in a Time of Crisis* (Glencoe 1958) 197, 199, 208, 219.

Lerner, R.E., "Ernst H. Kantorowicz", in H. Damico & J.B. Zavadil eds., *Medieval Scholarship: Biographical Studies on the Formation of a Discipline*, vol. 1, *History* (New York/London 1995) 263–68.

Linden, A.A.M. van der, *Opstand onder historici: De Amerikaanse radicale historiografie 1959–1976* (Utrecht 1994) 311–12, 320.

Lipstadt, D., *Denying the Holocaust: The Growing Assault on Truth and Memory* (originally 1993; Harmondsworth 1994) 67–83, 220–1.

Loewen, J.W., *Lies My Teacher Told Me: Everything Your American History Textbook Got Wrong* (New York 1995) 6, 160, 274.

Lynd, S., "Intellectuals, the University, and the Movement" (originally 1968), *Journal of American History*, 1989: 479–85.

Malin, J., *On the Nature of History* (Lawrence 1954) iii.

Mazour, A.G., & H.E. Bateman, "Recent Conflicts in Soviet Historiography", *Journal of Modern History*, 1952: 67.

McAulay, R., "Velikovsky and the Infrastructure of Science: The Metaphysics of a Close Encounter", *Theory and Society*, November 1978: 315–23.

Mitchel, S., "Classified Information and Historical Research", *Government Publications Review*, 1983: 428 (quote), 429–31, 434–36.

Nelkin, D., "Science, Rationality, and the Creation/Evolution Dispute", *Social Education*, 1982: 265.

New York Times, 1995 (6 December: A18; 21 December: A21).

"Nixon off the Record", *Newsweek*, 3 November 1997: 46–48.

Novick, P., *That Noble Dream: The "Objectivity Question" and the American Historical Profession* (Cambridge 1988) 225, 245, 304–5, 327–32, 401, 418–19, 422–23, 428, 431, 446, 447 (quote Genovese), 458, 463–64, 475–76, 479, 612–21.

O'Brien, J. et al., "New Left Historians of the 1960s", *Radical America*, 1970, nos. 8–9: 83.

Olson, J.S. ed., *Dictionary of the Vietnam War* (Westport 1988) 133–35, 171, 360–62, 400–401.

Parry, M. ed., *Chambers Biographical Dictionary* (Edinburgh/New York 1997) 1353–54.

Paterson, T.G., "Thought Control and the Writing of History", in: Curry ed. 1988: 61–67.

Paxton, J., *Companion to Russian History* (London 1983) 195.

Preiswerk, R., & D. Perrot, *Ethnocentrisme et histoire: L'Afrique, l'Amérique indienne et l'Asie dans les manuels occidentaux* (Paris 1975) 23.

Randall, M., "When the Imagination of the Writer Is Confronted by the Imagination of the State", in: Curry ed. 1988: 169–77.

Röder, W., & H.A. Strauss eds., *Biographisches Handbuch der deutschsprachigen Emigration nach 1933*, vol. 1 (Munich 1980) 160.

Rosenzweig, L.W., "Vision, Revision, and History Education" (unpublished paper, 18th International Congress of Historical Sciences, Montréal 1995) 1–3, 14.

Roth, C. ed., *Encyclopaedia Judaica*, vol. 7 (Jerusalem 1971) 1260–61.

Ruetten, R.T., "Harry Elmer Barnes and the 'Historical Blackout' ", *Historian*, 1970–71: 202–14.

Russell, F., *The Shadow of Blooming Groove: Warren G. Harding in His Times* (New York/Toronto 1968) ix, 650–66, 693.

Saveth, E., personal communication, May 1996.

Scanlon, J., & S. Cosner, *American Women Historians, 1700s–1990s* (Westport/London 1996) 53–56, 98–99, 125–27, 146–48.

Schrecker, E.W., *The Age of McCarthyism: A Brief History with Documents* (Boston 1994) 26–27, 67–69, 189.

———, *No Ivory Tower: McCarthyism and the Universities* (New York/Oxford 1986) 54, 82, 118, 130, 162, 165–67, 171–79, 182–83, 185, 195–96, 238, 249, 255, 260–62, 267, 269–70, 272–73, 275–77, 282, 287, 293–94, 297, 299, 301, 303–4, 314, 322, 324, 331–32, 336, 390.

———, personal communication, May 2000.

Schwendinger, H., & J.R. Schwendinger, *The Sociologists of the Chair: A Radical Analysis of the Formative Years of North American Sociology (1883–1922)* (New York 1974) 503–7.

Scott, J.A., "Book Banning in the High Schools, 1975–81", *Social Education*, 1982: 258–60.

Shapiro, H., " 'Political Correctness' and the American Historical Profession" (unpublished paper, 18th International Congress of Historical Sciences, Montréal 1995) 5.

Shattuck, J., "Federal Restrictions on the Free Flow of Academic Information and Ideas", in: Curry ed. 1988: 48–49, 51–53, 59.

Shils, E., "Academic Freedom", in: P.G. Altbach ed., *International Higher Education: An Encyclopedia*, vol. 1 (New York/London 1991) 12, 15.

Schlatter, R., "On Being a Communist at Harvard", *Partisan Review*, 1977: 605–15.

Shteppa, K.F., *Russian Historians and the Soviet State* (New Brunswick 1962) 348, 429.

"Snowed by the CIA", *Harper's*, September 1997: 17–21 (taken from the May 1997 *Organization of American Historians Newsletter*).

Strauss, H.A., & W. Röder eds., *International Biographical Dictionary of Central European Émigrés 1933–1945*, vol. 1 (Munich 1983) 235, 268–69, 593–94.

Tenenbaum, B.A. ed., *Encyclopedia of Latin American History and Culture* (New York 1996) vol. 2: 279; vol. 4: 532; vol. 5: 498.

Thelen, D., "A Round Table: What Has Changed and Not Changed in American Historical Practice?", *Journal of American History*, 1989: 395.

Thomas, J.R., *Biographical Dictionary of Latin American Historians and Historiography* (Westport 1984) 141–43.

Thompson, K.W., *Masters of International Thought: Major Twentieth-Century Theorists and the World Crisis* (Baton Rouge/London 1980) 144–47.

The Times (London), 22 October 1990: 12 (1990 black families).

Tucker, M. ed., *Literary Exile in the Twentieth Century: An Analysis and Biographical Dictionary* (Westport 1991) 216–17, 560–63.

Turnbaugh, R., "The FBI and Harry Elmer Barnes: 1936–44", *Historian*, 1980: 385–98.

Ullman, R.H., "The Pentagon's History As 'History' ", *Foreign Policy*, Fall 1971: 150–56.

Vidal-Naquet, P., *Assassins of Memory: Essays on the Denial of the Holocaust* (New York 1992) 80–82.

Werner, M.S. ed., *Encyclopedia of Mexico: History, Society and Culture*, vol. 1 (Chicago/London 1997) 355–56.

Who's Who 1998 (London 1998) 1769.

Wieczynski, J.L. ed., *The Modern Encyclopedia of Russian and Soviet History*, vol. 16 (Gulf Breeze 1980) 40.

Wiener, J.M., "Radical Historians and the Crisis in American History, 1959–1980", *Journal of American History*, 1989: 4; 392, 401, 403–5, 407, 409–12, 416–18, 422, 430–31.

————, "Rejoinder", *Journal of American History*, 1989: 475.

Woolf, D.R. ed., *A Global Encyclopedia of Historical Writing* (New York/London 1998) 27, 71–72, 78–79, 101–2, 224, 245, 292, 306, 317, 327, 354, 389, 470, 501–2, 545, 633, 652–53, 656, 746, 797, 809–10, 946.

World News (Inter Press Service), 12 May 1999 (Ahmad).

The Writers Directory 1988–90 (Chicago/London 1988) 317.

Zinn, H., *Academic Freedom: Collaboration and Resistance* (23rd T.B. Davie Memorial Lecture; Cape Town 1982).

UPPER VOLTA

See Burkina Faso.

URUGUAY

Under the military dictatorship (June 1973–1985), historical research at the official level practically disappeared, although the situation slightly ameliorated after 1983. The Department of the History of Ideas at Montevideo University was closed down. All copies of the English historical journal *Past and Present* were reportedly destroyed because of its Marxist "connections". Certain major historical events—like the 1789 French Revolution—remained in the study programs, but teachers were advised not to cover them in any depth because this would "exalt the fruit of Jewish-Masonic conspiracies". Periods deemed worthy of study by the military included the Spanish Conquest, the Catholic Counter-

Reformation, and the reign of Philip II in Spain, during which Western Christendom, in their view, was saved. In art history courses for the B.A. degree, the use of slides was forbidden because nude Renaissance art offended morality.

1968   In October *La battaglia di Algeri* (The Battle of Algiers), a film by **Gillo Pontecorvo** on the Algerian war of independence (1954–62), was banned because it was seen as indirectly condoning the Tupamaro guerrilleros, who were very active at the time.

1969–   **Eleuterio Fernández Huidobro** (1942–), cofounder of the Movimiento de Liberación Nacional–Tupamaros in 1965, imprisoned in 1969–71 and 1972–85, became the historiographer of the Tupamaros after his release. In October 1998 he became a senator.

1971–85   Journalist and academic publisher **Eduardo Galeano** (1940–), member of the left-wing Frente Amplio, went into exile in Buenos Aires after the occupation of Montevideo University by the police in March 1973. In April he was arrested during a short visit to Montevideo and held incommunicado for ten days because he had allegedly received press communiqués related to guerrilla movements in Venezuela. The same year he founded and directed the cultural magazine *Crisis* in Buenos Aires. It was considered subversive and Galeano closed it in July 1976 because his staff was being persecuted. He declared that he did not want it to be used by the junta (ruling since March 1976) as an example of press freedom. *Las Venas Abiertas de América Latina* (1971; *Open Veins of Latin America*), his dependency analysis of post-1500 Latin American history, had been banned in Uruguay in 1971, and later it was also in Chile and Argentina. Its inclusion in a reading list at the National University of the South, Bahía Blanca, Argentina, was used as evidence against some lecturers who were arrested in July 1976. The authorities denounced the book on television and in the press as a "corrupter of youth". From August 1976 to 1985, Galeano lived in exile in Barcelona, Spain. In 1983 he unsuccessfully applied for the renewal of his Uruguayan passport. In early 1985 he returned to Uruguay, assumed editorial responsibilities for the new periodical *Brecha*, and became one of the organizers of the 1989 referendum about the 1986 Expiry Law (a law that had ended state powers to prosecute military and police personnel for human-rights violations committed under the military government). Galeano wrote profusely on history. He was also the author of the three-volume *Memoria del fuego* (1982–86; *Memory of Fire*, 1989).

1973–   In March 1973 **Raúl Cariboni da Silva** (?1931–), history professor, educational planner, and founding member of the Federación Nacional de Profesores, was arrested by the army and severely tortured (which resulted in a heart attack). In the Penal de Libertad he was again tortured in 1975 and 1976. In 1977 he was tried by a military court and sentenced to thirteen years' imprisonment on charges of subversive association and conspiracy. In 1979 the punishment was increased to fifteen years. In spite of his health problems, he was not released on parole in September 1980, although he fulfilled all the conditions.

After the 1973 coup d'état, the work of **Carlos Real de Azúa** (1916–77), literary critic, intellectual historian, and political scientist, anti-imperialist and nationalist, who during the 1960s had denounced the failure of Uruguay's oligarchy to devise a sound political and social system, was reportedly banned. Many of his writings of the time remained unpublished. His death was not mentioned in the Montevideo press.

1976–   In September 1976 **Alfonso Fernández Cabrelli** (?1919–), municipal lawyer, historian, and journalist, was arrested and held without trial. He was accused of "an attempt to subconsciously influence the reader of his book *Los orientales* (1971)" by distorting Uruguayan history and drawing parallels between hero of independence General José Artigas (1764–1850), and the revolutionaries Camilo Torres (1929–67) and Ernesto "Che" Guevara (1928–67). The book was called excessively critical of "the measures taken by the authorities to preserve the values of our nationality against the penetration of Marxism". Fernández was director of, inter alia, *Grito de Asencio*, a series of political and historical publications. In 1980 he was reportedly still in prison.

Also see United States (1982–83: Rama).

SOURCES

AIDA, *Argentine: Une Culture interdite; Pièces à conviction 1976–1981* (Paris 1981) 44, 59–61.
Amnesty International, *Boletín Informativo*, February 1979: 6 (quote Fernández), March 1982: 3.
——, *Report 1980* (London 1980) 165.
Boia, L. ed., *Great Historians of the Modern Age: An International Dictionary* (Westport 1991) 679.
Flores, A., *Spanish American Authors: The Twentieth Century* (New York 1992) 328–31.
Galeano, E., "Aantekeningen over het geheugen en het vuur", in: *Het collectieve geheugen: Over literatuur en geschiedenis* (Amsterdam 1990) 25–37.
——, *Open Veins of Latin America: Five Centuries of the Pillage of a Continent* (New York 1974) 287–88.
Hispanic American Historical Review, 1978: 697–99 (Real de Azúa).

Index on Censorship, 2/73: xiv; 4/74: 77–78; 3/77: 9–14; 2/78: 3–5; 3/78: 19–21, 24–28; 1/79: 50–51; 2/79: 41; 6/79: 73–74; 4/81: 24; 6/81: 20–21; 3/95: 33–36.

Lovell, W.G., "Ninety-two Not Out: Eduardo Galeano and the Columbus Quincentenary", *Journal of Historical Geography*, 1993: 196–204.

Publishers Weekly, 3 June 1988: 64–65 (Galeano).

Rial, J., & J. Klaczko, "Historiography and Historical Studies in Uruguay", *Latin American Research Review*, 1982, no. 3: 233–34.

Rosencof, M., & E. Fernández Huidobro, *Schipbreukelingen: Een dialoog uit de kelders van de dictatuur* (originally Spanish 1987–88; Amsterdam 1993) 428–29.

Saz, S.M., " 'Breath, Liberty, and the Word': Eduardo Galeano's Interpretation of History", *Secolas Annals*, 1990: 59–70.

Steenhuis, A., *In de cakewalk: Schrijvers over de twintigste eeuw* (Amsterdam 1990) 144–61 (Galeano).

Tenenbaum, B.A. ed., *Encyclopedia of Latin American History and Culture*, vol. 3 (New York 1996) 6.

Thomas, J.R., *Biographical Dictionary of Latin American Historians and Historiography* (Westport 1984) 299–300.

Tucker, M. ed., *Literary Exile in the Twentieth Century: An Analysis and Biographical Dictionary* (Westport 1991) 258–59.

The Writer and Human Rights: Proceedings of a Conference Held in Toronto in October 1981 (Toronto 1983) 13–17, 121–23, 226.

UZBEKISTAN

pre-1991   *See* Union of Soviet Socialist Republics (USSR).

1990s   The version of the life of the Samarkand-based Mongol conqueror Timur (Tamerlane; 1336–1405) as shown in a play by **Alim Salimov** at the Khamza Theater apparently deviated from the official version, in which Timur was a national hero. The play was banned. In the two decades before independence, the cult of Timur had been suppressed.

1992   Few days after his summer arrival for a first visit back to his homeland in fifty years, émigré historian **Baymirza Hayit** (1917–), a strong critic of Soviet rule, was asked by the authorities to leave Uzbekistan. Although his works began to appear in Uzbek periodicals, plans to publish his latest book on the Basmachi (guerrilleros who had resisted incorporation of the Uzbek region into the USSR) were canceled.

SOURCES

Bregel, Y., *Notes on the Study of Central Asia* (Bloomington 1996) 23.

Cavanaugh, C., "Historiography in Independent Uzbekistan: The Search for National Identity", *Central Asia Monitor*, 1994, no.1 (WWW-text).

Index on Censorship, 2/98: 159, 161.

Nettleton, S., "Teaching National History—Selective Change in Uzbekistan's Schools", *East/West Education*, 1994: 165–70.

V

VATICAN

pre-1996– According to a 1996 report, access to the Vatican Archives records was very limited: about two hundred research permits were issued every year. Records produced after 1922 (Pope Benedict XV's death) were closed for research. A special eleven-volume collection of documents on World War II, however, was published by a special team (Pierre Blet et al., *Actes et documents du Saint–Siège relatifs à la seconde guerre mondiale* [Vatican City 1965–81]). In 1999 a scholarly commission of Jewish and Roman Catholic historians would take the collection as the basis for a study of the role of Pope Pius XII (1876–1958) during World War II, in particular his silence during the Holocaust. For their October 2000 study, they were not allowed to consult Pope Pius XII's diaries and memos.

Also see Germany (1996: the Pope), Poland (1978 & 1997: the Pope).

SOURCES

Cantor, N.F., *Inventing the Middle Ages: The Lives, Works, and Ideas of the Great Medievalists of the Twentieth Century* (New York 1991) 31.
Fryskén, A., "Archives for Millennia", *Archivum*, 1996, no.42: 330.
Index on Censorship, 2/99: 79; 1/00: 113.
Keesings Historisch Archief, 2000: 677.

VENEZUELA

pre-1945 Among the historians and others concerned with the past who emigrated before 1945 (and living in exile after 1944) was **Miguel Acosta Saignes** (1908–89).

1945–64   In October 1945, when the Isaías Medina Angarita government was overthrown by a military coup, **Caracciolo Parra Pérez** (1888–1964), historian, diplomat, politician, and minister of foreign affairs (1941–45), was forced into a short exile and settled in Paris. He decided to spend the rest of his life there. He headed delegations into the League of Nations (1923–39), the United Nations (1945), and UNESCO (1951–58). In 1962 he was elected a member of the Institut de France.

1952–58   In 1952–58, during the Marcos Pérez Jiménez dictatorship, **Mario Briceño Iragorry** (1897–1958), a writer, historian, teacher, politician, and diplomat, went into exile in Madrid. He returned to Venezuela after Pérez Jiménez's overthrow but died a few months later.

1983   On 10 March editor and presidential candidate **Jorge Olavarria** was arrested on charges of insulting the memory of Simón Bolívar (1783–1830), the liberator of Latin America, by printing his image as if he had been beaten on the cover of *Resumen* (a magazine dealing with the state of the national economy). He was released on 21 March after the detention order was declared unconstitutional.

Also see El Salvador (1981: Arrieti).

SOURCES

Boia, L. ed., *Great Historians of the Modern Age: An International Dictionary* (Westport 1991) 648–49, 675–76.
Index on Censorship, 4/83: 48.
Instituto Panamericano de Geografía e Historia, *Guía de personas que cultivan la historia de América* (México 1967) 163–64.
Thomas, J.R., *Biographical Dictionary of Latin American Historians and Historiography* (Westport 1984) 118.

VIETNAM

During the war in Vietnam (1945–75), many archives, including the former Imperial Archives of Annam at Hue, were ravaged or destroyed. After 1975 the Communist Party of Vietnam (CPV) exercised tight control over the whole sector of historical research. Certain areas were obliterated, for example the existence of the Associated State of Vietnam (1949–54) and the Republic of South Vietnam (1954–75).

French Vietnam

pre-1945   Several leading revolutionaries organized schools of political education while they were imprisoned by the French. Some also did extensive historical research to prepare the Marxist historiography of the Vietnamese Revolution. Among those imprisoned in 1943 was historian **Tran Huy Lieu**, in August 1945 the minister of propaganda in the Provisional Republican Government and head of the delegation to Hue which accepted the abdication of Emperor Bao Dai. After 1954 Tran Huy Lieu became a leading historian of North Vietnam, writing histories of the anti-French resistance movement.

1945–   Due to the conflict between the French and the Vietminh (League for the Independence of Vietnam), the excavations at Oc Eo (a port city considered the earliest town in Southeast Asia and the center of the first kingdom of present Cambodia known as Funan [second century CE]) led by **Louis Malleret** (1901–70), museum director, archeologist, and historian, became increasingly difficult. Abruptly halted in March 1945, when the Japanese began their direct rule of French Indochina, the excavations were discontinued after 1949. Malleret, administrator at the École Française d'Extrême-Orient (1950–56), returned to France in 1957.

1945   During the August 1945 revolution, the prime minister of the Japanese-endorsed government (March–August 1945) and conservative historian **Tran Trong Kim** (1882–1953) had to resign. His two-volume *Outline History of Vietnam* (Saigon 1920) remained a standard text in the Republic of South Vietnam until 1975. It was often republished and used in thousands of classrooms.

Vietnam

1977–   In April 1977 **Dang Phuc Tue** (religious name: **Thich Quang Do**) (1927–), a Buddhist scholar and poet, author of several novels and studies of Buddhist history, lecturer at the Buddhist Van Hanh University, Saigon (until 1975), and secretary-general of the unofficial Unified Buddhist Church of Vietnam (UBCV), was arrested (together with six other monks) and tried in December 1978 on charges of, inter alia, exploiting religion and undermining national security, but he was acquitted and released. From 1982 to 1992, he was placed under house arrest in his native village in north Vietnam because of his protests against government persecution, human-rights violations, and the 1981 creation of the state-controlled Vietnam Buddhist Church. His presence in Ho Chi Minh City (formerly Saigon) was deemed "dangerous for the well-being of the people". When he returned to the Thanh Minh Thien Vien Pagoda in Ho Chi Minh City, he was confined to its immediate surroundings. In January 1995 he was rearrested and in August tried in camera and sentenced to five years' imprisonment on charges of "undermining national security" and "misuse of democratic rights to encroach on the rights of citizens and of the State". In a November 1994 letter, he had denounced the arrests of UBCV monks and lay Buddhists who had distributed relief to flood victims without government approval. He was in very poor health. In September 1998 he benefited from a presidential amnesty. In March 1999 he was summoned for questioning and ordered to return to Ho Chi Minh City after he had traveled to central Vietnam to visit UBCV's supreme patriarch. In August he was interrogated about his letter to European Union ambassadors in Hanoi calling for human rights and religious freedoms. He has frequently been harassed since.

1984–98   In April 1984 **Le Manh That** (religious name: **Thich Tri Sieu**) (1943–), UBCV monk and professor of Vietnamese Buddhist history and literature at Van Hanh University, author of, inter alia, *A Short History of Vietnamese Buddhism*, was arrested with many others. Held without charge for four years, he was sentenced to death at a closed trial in September 1988 for his membership in an illegal organization (the National Front for Human Rights) and for attempting to overthrow the government. The sentence was commuted to twenty years' imprisonment. In 1989 he was transferred to a "reeducation" camp. In 1995, at a political indoctrination session, he spoke out for democracy and human rights and was put into solitary confinement. In September 1998 he was released.

In 1987, **Pham Que Dong** (?1933–), colonel, military historian, and chief editor of *Military History Journal* (1982–87) was dismissed because he refused to obey orders not to mention exploits of dismissed officers. Investigated and accused of supporting advocates of pluralism in 1990, he resigned from the CPV in solidarity with a dissident in 1999 and became an (often harassed) democracy activist. In September 2001, he was arrested while campaigning for reform.

1987–   In January 1987 novelist **Nguyen Huy Thiep** (1950–) challenged conventional wisdom about two prominent Vietnamese historical figures (names unknown) in a series of short stories in the weekly *Van Nghe*. This prompted an uproar in literary circles. In December 1988 the weekly's chief editor was dismissed, a fact that led to a widely publicized controversy. In May 1991 Nguyen Huy Thiep and a filmmaker were arrested and accused of treason for making an unauthorized film with French journalist Bernard Gesbert.

[1988–89] A historical work on religions and beliefs, *Spirits, Man and Vietnamese Land*, written by historian **Ta Chi Dai Truong** in difficult conditions, was smuggled abroad and published in Westminster, Calif., United States, in 1989. An earlier prize-winning work of his, *History of the Civil War in Vietnam from 1771 to 1802* (Saigon 1973), about the Tay Son rebellion, was vehemently criticized by Hanoi historians because it did not emphasize the role of the peasant leaders in the rebellion.

1989–   In December a new press law was adopted, article 22 of which strictly prohibited, inter alia, any publication which "distorts history, negates the revolutionary accomplishments of the Communist Party, denigrates national heroes, or slanders national organizations". In August 2000 the Ministry of Culture proposed new regulations (not yet officially adopted as of October), which would impose fines for the production or possession of "culturally inappropriate" materials, including those which "distorted Vietnam's history or defamed its national heroes".

1991   From January to August, the works of official historian **Nguyen Khac Vien** (1913–97), former director of Hanoi's Foreign Languages Publishers, were banned because he had submitted a petition to a CPV meeting, criticizing its leadership and calling for democracy, political pluralism, and respect for human rights.

1993   A 1993 report stated that a young historian [name unknown] conducted research on the Chinese presence in Vietnam in 1945–46 while an expatriate in France.

1993–   In November 1993 **Nguyen Dinh Huy** (1932–), a high school teacher of history and English, journalist, and editor of *The Progressive* and *Human Rights*, was arrested with eight others for planning to hold an "illegal" international conference on economic development and democracy in Ho Chi Minh City. After an unfair trial in August 1995, he was found guilty of "acting to overthrow the people's government" and sentenced to fifteen years' imprisonment for his leadership of the "Movement to Unite the People and Build Democracy", a nonviolent political group which advocated political change and organized the conference. He was permitted only brief, infrequent family visits and his health was deteriorating rapidly. Nguyen Dinh Huy had previously been imprisoned in 1957–59 (under the Ngo Dinh Diem government) and in 1975–92 (under the communist government) for his allegedly "counterrevolutionary" political beliefs.

1997–   In December writer **Pham Van Viem** was kidnapped by the Vietnamese secret police in Bulgaria and returned to Hanoi after he had translated the book *Fascism* (1982) by Zhelyu Zhelev. He has not been seen or heard from since.

Also see Bulgaria (1967: Zhelev), France (1991–93: Boudarel), United States (1968–74: My Lai; 1971: *Pentagon Papers*).

SOURCES

Albada J. van, " 'Memory of the World': Report on Destroyed and Damaged Archives", *Archivum*, 1996, no.42: 19.

Amnesty International, *News*, January 1993: 4; August 1995: 7; January 1999: 2.

———, *Report* (London) 1979: 117; 1985: 252; 1986: 267; 1987: 275–76; 1988: 189; 1989: 206–7; 1990: 257–58; 1991: 247; 1992: 275; 1993: 309; 1996: 323; 1998: 359; 1999: 360–61; 2000: 261; 2001: 266.

Anh Nguyen The, "Historical Research in Vietnam: A Tentative Survey", *Journal of Southeast Asian Studies*, 1995: 122–23, 131–32.

Article 19, *Information, Freedom and Censorship: World Report 1991* (London 1991) 237–39.

Auer, L., "Archival Losses and Their Impact on the Work of Archivists and Historians", *Archivum*, 1996, no.42: 4.

Boia, L. ed., *Great Historians of the Modern Age: An International Dictionary* (Westport 1991) 619–20.

Duiker, W.J., *Historical Dictionary of Vietnam* (Metuchen 1989) 179–80, 245.

"Free Vietnam Alliance, PEN Canada, and CCPJ Appeal for Support of Freedom of Expression in Vietnam", *Ifex Alert*, 27 May 1998: 2 (quote press law).

Hall, D.G.E. ed., *Historians of South-East Asia* (London 1961).

Hodgkin, T., *Vietnam: The Revolutionary Path* (London/Basingstoke 1981) 3, 314–15, 332.

Honey, P.J., "Modern Vietnamese Historiography", in: Hall ed. 1961: 95.

Human Rights Watch, *Ifex Alert*, 7 July 1997: 1, 5.

———, *World Report* (Washington) 1990: 336–37; 1992: 470, 475; 1996: 182–83; 1999: 214, 493; 2000: 216–17; 2001: 227, 229.

Index on Censorship, 4/84: 44; 7/90: 24; 8/91: 57; 1/92: 48; 6/99: 257.

International PEN Writers in Prison Committee, *Half-Yearly Caselist* (London 1997) 41–42.

Jameson, N.L., *Understanding Vietnam* (Berkeley 1993) 80–81, 190–93.

Keesing's Record of World Events, 1991: 38149C.

Limqueco, P., "Interview with Nguyen Khac Vien", *Journal of Contemporary Asia*, 1977: 213–19.

Malleret, L., "The Position of Historical Studies in the Countries of Former French Indo-China in 1956", in: Hall ed. 1961: 304–5.

Military Historian Turns in Party Card to Protest Gen. Tran Do's Expulsion (WWW-text 1999).

Nguyen Khac Vien, "Historical Research in Vietnam since Independence", *Journal of Contemporary Asia*, 1980: 241–48.

"Nguyen Khac Vien: The Party's Over", *Indochina Digest*, 8 March 1991 (WWW-text 1995).

Tertrais, H., "Un État des recherches sur l'histoire du Vietnam", *Vingtième siècle*, October–December 1993: 98, 104.

Tran Huy Lieu, "Tradition und Gegenwart in der Vietnamesischen Geschichtswissenschaft", *Zeitschrift für Geschichtswissenschaft*, 1969: 12.

Tsvetov, P., "History Studies in Vietnam Today", *Far Eastern Affairs*, 1980, no.4: 139.

Winters, C. ed., *International Dictionary of Anthropologists* (New York/London 1991) 447–48.

Woolf, D.R. ed., *A Global Encyclopedia of Historical Writing* (New York/London 1998) 896, 924.

Y

YEMEN

1967–92   In 1992 President Ali Abdullah Saleh rehabilitated eighteen journalists who had been dismissed from their jobs under the slogan of
"cleaning the public sector of the remnants of [British] colonialism"
when South Yemen went under Marxist rule in November 1967.

2000   From 16 to 19 June, Italian archeologist **Alberto Alessio** (1967–)
and seven Yemeni collaborators were held hostage by tribesmen who
demanded the release of two tribal members imprisoned on theft
charges.

SOURCES

Index on Censorship, 5/92: 40.
International Herald Tribune, 21 June 2000 (Alessio).

YUGOSLAVIA

During the communist period (1944–90), historiographic disputes about nationalism were discouraged and prevented. For example, the third volume of the
History of the Peoples of Yugoslavia (vol. 1: 1953; vol. 2: 1959), about
nineteenth- and twentieth-century national integration and state-building, never
appeared. The historical establishment was mainly preoccupied with the pre-
1918 period. The work of twentieth-century historians, especially those belonging to the interwar period, was dismissed as negative for having ignored the
class struggle. Among the "untouchable" subjects were nationalism; the events
of 1940–48, including the wartime massacres by partisans and the breach with
the USSR and the Cominform in 1948. Many archives were inaccessible and

statistics about the number of persons killed during the war remained under lock and key at the Institute of Military History in Belgrade. Discussion of methodology or epistemology was avoided so as not to clash with official viewpoints, resulting in a disinclination to theoretical and methodological reflection. From 1991 to 1999, many historic urban structures, historical monuments, castles, churches, mosques, monasteries, museums, libraries, archives, mansions, and graveyards were destroyed or damaged by all sides in the conflict in the former Yugoslavia, frequently in a deliberate effort that has been termed by some a "denial of the enemy's history" and by the Council of Europe as "cultural cleansing". For example, when the Institute for Oriental Studies in Sarajevo was burned down by the Serbs, the collections containing thousands of Ottoman documents—sultans' edicts, governors' reports, and land records going back to the sixteenth century—were destroyed. In the National and University Library of Sarajevo, tens of thousands of archival documents were burned.

1941–   Yugoslav archives suffered grave damage during the two world wars. For example, in 1941 the National Library in Belgrade was entirely burned.

1941–90   In 1941 Serbian historian, constitutional jurist, and liberal statesman **Slobodan Jovanović** (1869–1958), specialist in nineteenth-century Serbian history, member and president of the Royal Serbian Academy of Sciences (1928–31), and vice prime minister in General Dušan Simović's government after the anti-Nazi putsch in Belgrade on 27 March 1941, was forced to leave Yugoslavia after the German invasion on 6 April 1941. From January 1942 to June 1943, he was prime minister of the Royal Yugoslav government-in-exile in London and supported General Draža Mihajlović's Chetniks (Serbian royalists who fought the Axis invaders and opposed the communist-led partisans in World War II). He was opposed to philosophical and historical materialism. In June–July 1946 a revolutionary Yugoslav court charged him with being "a co-performer in acts of collaboration with the occupier and war crimes committed by the Chetnik organization" and "a representative of reactionary, capitalist, and fascist regimes". He was sentenced in absentia to twenty years' imprisonment, with the loss of his civil rights for an additional ten years, and the confiscation of all his property. During the first postwar years, his writings, including an eight-volume history of Serbia from 1838 to 1903, were banned. Jovanović spent the rest of his life in London, where he presided over the émigré Yugoslav National Committee (founded August 1945), criticized the postwar Yugoslav regime, and continued writing historical essays. In 1963, a publishing house succeeded in publishing a volume of Jovanović's selected *Portraits from History and Literature*, which was denounced by

Marxist historian Nikola Petrović. From late 1983 to February 1985, two Belgrade publishers competed to reissue his complete works (first published in 1932–40), but after strong protests from the League of Communists (Communist Party) in Belgrade, the project was given up on the grounds of copyright difficulties. The works were eventually published in Belgrade in 1990.

1941–49   In 1941 **Momčilo Ninčić** (1876–1949), another Serbian jurist and historian in the 1941 Simović government, went into exile after the German invasion and became the minister of foreign affairs in the government-in-exile (1941–43). In 1915–26 he had been a minister in various governments. As the minister of foreign affairs (1921–26), he had worked for détente with Italy.

1942–   In October 1942 Serbian historian **Dimitrije Djordjević** (1922–), then a student and member of the Chetnik resistance, was arrested by the Gestapo and deported, first to Banjica camp outside Belgrade, in late December to Mauthausen concentration camp, Austria, and later to several other prisons. In February 1943 he was released for medical treatment. In September he rejoined the Chetniks until August 1944. In late 1944 he organized the anticommunist resistance in Belgrade. In November 1945 he and many others of his group were arrested, imprisoned, and interrogated for months. In May 1946 Djordjević was tried and sentenced to four years' imprisonment for "illegal" activities. He was released in the general amnesty of May 1947. He was then banned from all Yugoslav universities for several years. In 1956, after his studies (1950–54), he went to work at the Serbian State Archives, but he was dismissed after three months when his secret police file was reviewed. From 1958 to 1969, he worked as a history professor at the Serbian Academy of Sciences and Arts (SANU), Belgrade. Given a passport and travel opportunities after 1965, he emigrated and became a professor of Balkan history at the University of California, Santa Barbara, in 1970. His work was published in Yugoslavia and in 1985 he was elected a SANU member. He was a specialist of nineteenth-century Serbian history.

1944–   In the communist period, the statue of nineteenth-century General Josip Jelačić (1801–59), Ban of Croatia (1848–59), was removed in Zagreb because Karl Marx had called him a counter-revolutionary. It was reinstated in October 1990.

1945–   After the war historian **Ivo Omrčanin**, a former representative in Berlin of the Ustasha Independent State of Croatia (Nezavisna Država Hrvatska or NDH; 1941–45), went into exile and became a history professor at the University of Pennsylvania, United States.

1948   Slovenian medievalist **Ljudmil Hauptmann** (1884–1968), professor at Zagreb University (1926–48), was dismissed on political grounds, probably in connection with his "Gotha-Iranian" theory (or "Croat theory"), which attributed Iranian origins to the Croats and was reportedly the basis of Ustasha ideology.

1949   Three annual calendars—*Prosveta* (Civilization; Serb), *Napredak* (Progress; Croat), and *Preporod* (Rebirth; Muslim)—published by cultural societies and carrying many short articles on pre- and postwar regional history and occasionally on general Yugoslav history, were suspended and their properties transferred to the Union of Cultural and Educational Societies.

1954–   In 1954 historian, politician, and writer **Vladimir Dedijer** (1914–90), director of the federal government's information and propaganda department, was expelled from the Central Committee (CC) of the League of Communists of Yugoslavia (LCY; Yugoslav communist party) and other LCY positions in connection with his defense of free speech for former vice president Milovan Djilas. In 1955 Dedijer was sentenced to six months on probation. A professor of modern history at Belgrade University, he was not reappointed after his expulsion. A close wartime collaborator of Djilas, chronicler of the partisan struggle, and delegate to United Nations General Assemblies (1945–52), Dedijer wrote the first volume of the biography of President Josip Tito (1892–1980) (*Tito Speaks*, 1953), published in almost thirty languages. Around 1959–60 he was allowed to go abroad; he lectured and did research at Scandinavian, English, and American universities (1960–71). In 1964 he completed his manuscript on the 1914 assassination of Archduke Franz Ferdinand in Sarajevo (*The Road to Sarajevo*, 1966). In the same year, he was appointed as a researcher at the Academy of Sciences History Institute, Belgrade. In 1966–67 he served as president of sessions of the Russell International War Crimes Tribunal on the American intervention in Vietnam. (He also attended sessions about the USSR and Vietnam in later years.) He was rehabilitated in progressive stages and elected to the SANU in 1968. He and others joined Ćirković [q.v. 1970s] in writing a *History of Yugoslavia* (1972; English 1974), which aroused controversy in 1972–73. In 1980–81 he published two volumes of the three-volume *New Contributions to a Biography of Josip Broz Tito* (vol. 1: 1980; vol. 2: 1981) which, being very critical of the late Tito (and of Djilas), provoked a storm of protest. Several groups, including some military historians and partisan veterans, launched a campaign against Dedijer which lasted until April 1982. The Defense Ministry decided that the book should be excluded from army libraries. A roundtable of conformist historians, organized by

Borba, harshly criticized Dedijer but only in general terms. In November 1983 Dedijer complained that he, his family, and his research team were being threatened and blackmailed and that he had had to send his wife and sons to live with friends in Italy. He said that the manuscript of the third volume was being heavily censored by the authorities and that a fire was started outside his home in Istria and at the home of one of his sources on LCY history in the summer of 1983. The third volume appeared in print in June 1984, though not with the original publisher, who had refused to publish it.

1959–76   On a list of publications, films, and plays banned between 1959 and 1976 were the following: *Feljton*, a Belgrade weekly, banned in June 1968 because of "historical falsehoods"; *Književne novine*, a Belgrade literary paper banned in August 1971 because of an article on "past relations between Serbs and Croats"; *Vidici*, a Belgrade student paper, banned in November 1971 for comparing "Nazism with the growth of nationalism in Yogoslavia"; *Whither and till When?* a book by **Ljubomir Momčilović**, banned in August 1972 for "presenting certain World War II events in a way that could provoke public unrest"; *Serbia in the Wars 1912–1914*, a book banned in December 1972.

1964   In December Tito criticized "nationalist manifestations in historiography" by denouncing "instances of indirect claims that averred some kind of primacy of one national history over the others". He referred to a monograph of partisan General **Velimir Terzić**, Tito's Serbian acting chief of staff during World War II, *Yugoslavia during the April War of 1941* (1963), which blamed the Croats for collaboration with the Axis powers and provoked recriminations from Zagreb. Terzić was also director of the Institute of Military History, Belgrade. The 1983 expanded reedition of the work contributed to the growth of Serbian nationalism and again provoked many reactions from Croatian historians.

1960s   In the late 1960s, **Jovan Marjanović**, former partisan, LCY-CC history department director and director of the National Archives, was expelled from the LCY for raising the Serbian national question.

1970s   In the early 1970s, a high school textbook, *History of Philosophy*, was banned because one of its authors was **Miladin Životić**. With others at the Belgrade University faculty of philosophy, Životić was a member of the dissident Marxist Praxis group and editorial board member of the international edition of *Praxis*. All were suspended indefinitely from their posts in January 1975. In 1975 or 1976, Životić was dismissed from the Institute for the Study of the International Labor Movement, where he had been offered a job. Anticipating the suspension of the eight in January 1975, **Sima Cir-ković** (1929–), faculty dean, medievalist, and member of the History Institute, resigned earlier that month. He was succeeded by Samard-žić [q.v. 1985–] in September 1976. In 1992 Ćirković wrote *A History of the Serbian People*.

1971–   In 1971 a play was taken off after a short run in Belgrade and in 1972 a novel was banned without explanation because both had the Goli Otok concentration camp (1948–56) as their subject. In March 1980 a theater director in Belgrade decided to take a play on the same subject off a few days before its first performance. It was later staged in Slovenia.

1971   In [December] the brief synthesis *History of the Croatian People* (Zagreb 1971), by historian **Trpimir Macan**, was banned and destroyed. The book's offense had reportedly more to do with the author's known political viewpoints and his reviewer Tudjman [q.v. 1972–] than with its bias or omission of postwar history.

1972–   In January 1972 the Croatian cultural organization Matica Hrvatska (founded in 1842) was raided and its archives confiscated. Eleven board members were arrested on charges of plotting to overthrow the social and political system, setting up a counterrevolutionary organization, and advocating the secession of Croatia. They were sentenced in the fall. One of them was historian **Franjo Tudjman** (1922–99), who served in the wartime communist underground army under Tito. He became general (1960), director of the Institute of Military History (1961–67), director (1961–67) of the Institute for the History of the Labor Movement of Croatia, Zagreb, and professor of contemporary history at the School of Political Science, Zagreb University (1963–67). In 1967 he was dismissed from all his posts because of his support for the 1967 *Declaration on the Name and the Position of the Croatian Language*. His writings were condemned as being anti-Marxist and supportive of Croatian nationalism. In 1972 he was expelled from the LCY and served nine months of a two-year sentence for "distributing enemy propaganda and cooperating with extremist political émigrés". He was charged with, inter alia, belonging to a "counterrevolutionary nationalist group" and "calling for a reexamination of the historical circumstances that contributed to the never-ending Croat struggle for survival". In February 1981 he was indicted again, this time for "hostile propaganda with aid from abroad". The charges were based on his statements about discrimination against Croats in four interviews with Western European journalists from 1977 to 1980 (one of which was even-

tually shown on Swedish television) and in a discussion with a Serbian graduate in journalism, Marković [q.v. 1979]. In November
1980 Tudjman also signed a petition to the Yugoslav State Presidency calling for a general amnesty of political prisoners; the petition
was rejected as "legally and politically unacceptable" on the eve of
his trial. At the trial Tudjman was sentenced to three years' imprisonment and a five-year ban on public activity, including public appearance, publication, and travel abroad. In his defense Tudjman
declared that his work as a historian on the atrocities in World War
II was the strongest reason for his prosecution. He said that the
official figures (much higher than his own estimates) were exaggerated and utilized to discredit the Croats in order to keep them in a
subordinate position in Yugoslavia. In September [1984] Tudjman
was conditionally released on health grounds. As the chairman of
the Croatian Democratic Union (HDZ) (1989–99) and president of
Croatia (1990–99), he made many statements about history, including some controversial opinions on the NDH, Jasenovac concentration camp (the "Auschwitz of the Balkans"), and the Holocaust, as
in his book *The Wasteland of Historical Reality* (Zagreb 1990). He
was also the probable author of *Authentic Fundamentals of the Constitution of the Republic of Croatia*, a December 1990 text containing
a synthesis of Croatian history.

Another Matica Hrvatska board member arrested in January 1972
was **Zvonimir Komarica** (1920–), historian, ex-military, ex-
politician, and retired director at the Institute for Migrations and
Nationalities (1967–71). In October 1972 he was tried on the charges
of having established a counterrevolutionary group within the Matica
Hrvatska and having organized a student strike in Zagreb in November 1971 in order to create a political crisis and start a revolution.
In November 1972 he was sentenced to two years' imprisonment.

1972 Historian and political scientist **Latinka Perović** (1933–) was forced
to resign as a secretary of the League of Communists of Serbia CC
and expelled from the party because of "liberal deviation". She went
to work at the Institute of Modern History, Belgrade, and specialized
in nineteenth-century Russian and Serbian socialism and in the history of pan-Slavism. In 2001 she became a member of the official
truth commission but she resigned after two months reportedly because she questioned the commission's mandate and independence.

1974–80 In July 1974 **Davor Aras**, university professor, archivist, and secretary of the Yugoslav Academy of Sciences History Institute in
Zadar, was arrested and later sentenced to six-and-a-half years' imprisonment on charges of antistate propaganda, of collaborating with

foreigners for the overthrow of the government, and of expressing views on the Croatian national question (which, however, did not involve the use of violence). He and historian Zelimir Mestrović were reportedly members of an extreme-right Ustasha-inspired organization. He was allegedly in solitary confinement for about a year and had to paint pieces of furniture in Lepoglava prison. As a result he contracted inflammation of the lungs. In March 1979 his sentence was suspended on health grounds and, after a heart operation in March 1980, he was exempted from serving the remainder of the sentence.

1974–   In 1974 writer **Djuro Djurović** (?1900–), a prewar member of Parliament and wartime adviser to Mihajlović and the Chetniks, was arrested and sentenced to five years' imprisonment because of his alleged connections with émigré organizations, for declaring that he wanted to change the constitution, and for reading *Tito, Mihajlović and the Allies 1941–1945* (New Brunswick 1973), a book by American historian Walter Roberts (1916–) which gave a version of the activities of Tito's partisans deviating from official accounts. Djurović, already ill before his imprisonment, appealed the sentence. The book was allegedly given to him by someone from the Udba security police with the intention of incriminating him. In 1945 Djurović had been sentenced to death for his wartime activities, but the sentence was commuted to hard labor for life. He had been released in [1962].

1975   In the spring, after having defended dissident writer Mihajlo Mihajlov in a trial, lawyer **[Bozo] Kovačević** was threatened with suspension and possible persecution. Neither threat was carried out. In his final plea for Mihajlov, Kovačević had referred to Tito's February speech, made while the trial was in progress and which attacked Mihajlov. He recalled the first Serbian Codex in which Tsar Stefan Dušan (reigned 1331–55) had admonished judges not to fear the tsar but to judge only in accordance with the law.

1976–77   In May 1976 **Franc Miklavčič**, a Ljubljana district judge, and **Viktor Blažič**, a Slovenian Catholic intellectual, were arrested. In September Blažič was convicted of "hostile propaganda" and sentenced to two years' imprisonment (reduced on appeal to fifteen months) for an article in the monthly journal *Zaliv* (printed in Italy) written under the pseudonym Zorko Prelog. In it Blažič had alleged restriction of religious and political freedom in Slovenia, called for the right "to free settlement in the areas of our memory", and compared the situation in Slovenia to the "cultural pogrom" of the Slovenian counterreformation after the 1555 Treaty of Augsburg. In October Miklavčič was sentenced to five years and eight months' imprisonment, later reduced to thirty months, for "hostile propaganda" because of his *Zaliv* article "Political Lie and Historical Truth", written under the pseudonym Joze Galicic. Miklavčič challenged the official account of the role played by Slovenian Catholic intellectuals in the wartime communist-led Liberation Front. He cited historical sources to defend Edvard Kocbek, a poet and wartime leader of the Slovene Christian Socialists who participated in the front. Kocbek had claimed in *Zaliv* that front members had executed many war prisoners handed over to Yugoslav partisans by British and United States forces in 1945. Miklavčič and Blažič were released in November 1977 under an amnesty to mark the Day of the Republic.

1979   **Vladimir Marković** (?1953–) was confined by court order to a psychiatric hospital because in mid-1978 he had sent a circular letter to a number of individuals and institutions in Yugoslavia and abroad which included an interview with historian Tudjman [q.v. 1972–], who had condemned war crimes committed under the NDH regime but who had also claimed that official Yugoslav statistics exaggerated their number.

In June **Nikodije Minić** (?1919–), a Yugoslav citizen living in Belgium, was arrested in Yugoslavia. In December he was sentenced in Serbia to five years' imprisonment on charges of "hostile propaganda", inter alia, because in 1974 he had expressed concern about Serbia's future after Tito's death and because in May 1979 he had referred to past events in Balkan history concerning Serbia and Bulgaria.

1980s   In Slovenia no historical work was banned in the 1980s, but some archives were inaccessible and some subjects sensitive (e.g., the resistance during World War II).

1980   One author and the chief editor of the *Encyclopedia of Croatian History and Culture* (1980) suffered attacks by party forums because the author had stated that "tens of thousands of people passed through [the NDH] Jasenovac camp, most of whom were executed in the many massacres carried out there".

In April lawyer **Žarko Aleksić** was sentenced to seven years' imprisonment for "hostile propaganda" in Bosnia-Herzegovina. He was charged, inter alia, with having eulogized the Chetniks.

1980s   Serbian statistician **Bogoljub Kočović** was one of the historians living in exile in Western Europe in the 1980s. In a 1985 work, he challenged the official estimates of the war losses of 1941–45 (which he considered too high). In the 1990s he was a proponent of dialogue between all the peoples of Yugoslavia.

1981   In a wave of purges after demonstrations in Kosovo in the spring, one of the persons dismissed was the History Institute director (name unknown).

1981–   In August 1981 Franciscan friar **Jozo Zovko** was arrested. In October he was sentenced in Bosnia-Herzegovina to three-and-a-half years' imprisonment on charges of "hostile propaganda" because in a sermon in July he had allegedly referred to Yugoslavia's postwar history as "forty years' imprisonment".

1983   In August heavy prison sentences were passed on twelve Muslim intellectuals, including **Alija Izetbegović**, in Sarajevo, in connection with the publication by one of them of the book *Red Cancer*, which alleged that the Yugoslav communists massacred some 50,000 Muslims on taking power in 1944.

1983–   In August–September a book by social scientists **Vojislav Koštunica** (1944–), research fellow at the Institute of Sociology, Belgrade, and former Praxis member, and **Kosta Cavośki**, research fellow at the Institute of Comparative Law, Belgrade, *Party Pluralism or Monism: Social Movements and Political Systems in Yugoslavia, 1944–1949* (originally Belgrade 1983; Boulder/New York 1985), about the elimination of independent political groups after 1944, was attacked and banned. The authors were obliged to declare that they were not in favor of a multiparty system. Both became members of the unofficial Committee for the Defense of Freedom of Thought and Expression (established November 1984) in Belgrade. Later Koštunica became a professor of constitutional law, a cofounder and leader of the Democratic Party of Serbia, and, in October 2000, president of Yugoslavia.

1984   On 20 April 1984, police interrupted one of the seminars about recent history which were regularly held in the private apartments of Belgrade intellectuals during the early 1980s, as part of the so-called Open University. Twenty-eight participants were detained, including Milovan Djilas, who talked about the nationalities problem that evening. The police seized a manuscript, "The Making of Tito's Despotism", by one of the participants, scriptwriter and amateur historian **Miodrag Milić** (?1929–). He was arrested, tried (November 1984–February 1985), and charged—first with conspiracy, later with hostile propaganda—for expressing views that "maliciously and untruthfully portrayed the heritage of our liberation struggle, the building of socialism, and the character and deeds of Tito" and sentenced to two years' imprisonment, later reduced to eighteen months. In July 1986 Milić was arrested at his home and imprisoned after failing to respond to a summons to serve his sentence despite the fact that he had lodged a new appeal in the meantime. His manuscript was published in Serbo-Croat in London in 1985.

In June a thousand copies of a 237-page "white book" of quotations on Yugoslav historiography, compiled by Croatian LCY ideologue **Stipe Šuvar** and attacking historians (the majority of whom were Serbian) who doubted LCY legitimacy, were confiscated in Belgrade. The book was banned in Serbia.

The first volume of the *Croatian Biographical Lexicon*, a work by 270 authors which appeared in Zagreb in January, came under attack. According to one critic, it contained examples of "insufficient Marxist critical evaluation of the contributions of individual personalities to national history". In June the ideological commission of Zagreb's League of Communists of Croatia City Committee organized a discussion on the suspect publication.

In December Croat hardliners attacked a book by **Ivo Škrabalo**, *Between Public and State: A History of Croatian Cinematography, 1896–1980* (1984). It was denounced as an anticommunist "pamphlet". In 1996 Škrabalo was a member of the oppositional Croat Social Liberal Party.

1985   In October history teacher **Hamza Asllani** was sentenced to two years' imprisonment for "hostile propaganda" because he had described the situation in Yugoslavia in a "malicious and untruthful" way in a petition filed with the Constitutional Court.

1985–   In November 1985 Serbian historian **Veselin Djuretić** (1933–), former collaborator at the Institute of Contemporary History, Belgrade, researcher at the SANU Institute of Balkan Studies, was expelled from the LCY after high-level LCY criticism of his controversial book *The Allies and the Yugoslav War Drama* (June 1985), copublished by the SANU. The two reviewers whose reports led to the publication of the book, military historian **Savo Skoko** and member of a commission of veterans Zoran Lakić, were also expelled from the LCY. The book, publicly supported by many Serbian historians, had already run into two editions before criticism started in October–November, from Serbian Communist Party leader Ivan Stambolić among others. The first edition of 400 copies had sold out the day of its presentation at SANU in September. The second edition of 2,000 copies was sold out before the bookshops outside Belgrade were served. The LCY theoretical journal *Kommunist* and other journals condemned the book as a "defense of the Chetnik movement" and suggested that there was some kind of historians' plot behind it. *Kommunist* called for an end to the "silence surrounding the publishing of some works of historiography". Djuretić was accused of portraying Tito as a Machiavellian figure, of claiming that there had also been a noncommunist resistance during the war, and, generally, of depicting the Serbs too much as victims. When the third edition was postponed, the book was reprinted by Serbian émigrés in January 1986. In February 1987 Serbia's Supreme Court reversed the ban. In April Djuretić lodged a further appeal with the Supreme Court after his book was banned for a second time, but this time the appeal was rejected. The court insisted instead that all copies should be destroyed. A fourth expanded edition appeared in Belgrade in 1992 (in the Federal Republic of Yugoslavia).

In December 1985 **Dragoljub Petrović**, professor at Novi Sad University, Vojvodina, was sentenced to sixty days' imprisonment for saying in two recent articles that the communists had treated their opponents brutally after assuming power in March 1945. In January 1986 an appeals court in Novi Sad upheld Petrović's sentence. In February the imprisonment was protested during a series of weekly literary meetings at the Serbian Writers' Union.

Nationalist historiography increased in Serbia in the 1980s and included an incomplete and controversial 1986 memorandum—itself banned and written by a SANU committee (of which two historians, **Radovan Samardžić**, SANU Institute of Balkan Studies director and secretary of the SANU history department, and **Vasilije Krestić** [in 1995 member of the SANU presidency], were members) between June 1985 and October 1986. Serbian historiography increasingly aligned itself with Slobodan Milošević's movement. The "late and inadequate" non-Serb reaction to this phenomenon was attributed by one source to "the tight control of party censorship . . . almost everywhere outside Serbia proper except in Slovenia". This allegedly resulted in silence by most non-Serb historians, who avoided political history in favor of noncontroversial social studies. The few Serb historians who reacted were reportedly isolated.

1986   In June history professor **R. Hazin** was sentenced to eleven years' imprisonment in Kosovo on charges of "antistate activities".

1989–   In March 1989 the autonomy of Kosovo was forcibly withdrawn. The region was claimed by the Serbian government as Serbian territory, notably on the occasion of the 600th anniversary of the battle against the Ottoman Turks on Kosovo Polje (1389) in June 1989. From 1990 the teaching of history in Kosovo was reportedly "serbianized" and Albanian history replaced with Serbian history. School textbooks were heavily censored. The National Archives of Kosovo, the National and University libraries, and the Kosovo History Institute were closed. Files documenting Kosovo's twentieth-century history, dealing with land reform in the period 1918–41 as well as with criminal and court-martial cases, were removed from the National Archives of Kosovo and sent to an unknown destination. In one town at least, the "unsuitable" names of streets and squares were replaced with names from Serbian and Montenegrin history and culture. In August 1992 Radio Tirana reported that Albanian historical and archeological monuments in Kosovo were being destroyed by the Serbian authorities.

1990–   After the December 1990 presidential elections in Serbia won by Milošević, one of the losing candidates, Serbian historian **Ivan Djurić**, author of theoretical-historical works and proponent of a democratic federal Yugoslavia, went into exile in France.

1990–91   During the events leading to the independence of Slovenia in June 1991, most of the confidential archives were destroyed or hidden by officials of the former regime. The archives in Belgrade were not accessible for "non-Yugoslav" researchers.

1991–   *See* Bosnia-Herzegovina, Croatia, Macedonia.

Yugoslavia (Serbia and Montenegro)

1998–   Government officials intended to disband the Belgrade University fac-
2000   ulty of philosophy and move its component departments (including its history department) to other faculties because more than seventy professors (nearly one-third of the staff) refused to sign contracts under the May 198 University Act. The act, rescinded under the new government in October 2000, was widely thought to remove basic protections for academic freedom and university autonomy.

1999   In April **Branka Prpa**, historian at the Institute of Modern History, Belgrade, was knocked unconscious when her companion, Slavko Čuruvija, publisher and chief editor of *Dnevni telegraf* (a daily critical of the Milošević government) was assassinated in Belgrade.

Also see Germany (1949–: Leonhard; 1951: Markov), Romania (1944–54: Pătrăşcanu), United Kingdom (1989–96: Tolstoy), USSR (1957–: Bernadsky).

SOURCES

Albada, J. van, " 'Memory of the World': Report on Destroyed and Damaged Archives", *Archivum*, 1996, no.42: 11, 19, 26, 67–78.
Amnesty International, *Report* (London) 1971–72: 44–45; 1972–73: 71–72; 1974–75: 122–23; 1975–76: 177; 1977: 286–87; 1978: 247; 1979: 151; 1980: 313–17; 1981: 342, 345; 1982: 307, 309–10; 1984: 321; 1986: 318–19.

Andrejevich, M., "Concern in Yugoslavia over Anti-Semitism", *RFE/RL Research Report*, 13 November 1991: 59.

Anzulovic, B., *Heavenly Serbia: From Myth to Genocide* (London 1999) 114–18.

Auer, L., "Archival Losses and Their Impact on the Work of Archivists and Historians", *Archivum*, 1996, no. 42: 4.

Banac, I., "The Fearful Asymmetry of War: The Causes and Consequences of Yugoslavia's Demise", *Daedalus*, 1992: 149–51, 155–57, 169–70, 172–73.

———, "Historiography of the Countries of Eastern Europe: Yugoslavia", *American Historical Review*, 1992: 1086–87, 1089–94, 1096–1103 (quote, party censorship: 1103).

Baudet, F., personal communication, October 1996 & October 1999.

——— & A. De Baets, "Kosovo: Het geheugen op spitsroeden", *Feit en Fictie*, 1999, no. 3: 99–111.

Bernath, M., & F. von Schroeder eds., *Biographisches Lexicon zur Geschichte Südeuropas* (Munich) vol. 2 (1976): 130–31, 307–8; vol. 3 (1979): 331–32.

Blodgett, S.W., "The Role of Microfilming in the Preservation and Reconstitution of Documents", *Archivum*, 1996, no. 42: 308–9.

Boia, L. ed., *Great Historians of the Modern Age: An International Dictionary* (Westport 1991) 784–86.

Boris, P., *Die sich lossagten: Stichworte zu Leben und Werk von 461 Exkommunisten und Dissidenten* (Cologne 1983) 65–66, 282.

Bruch, R. vom, & R. A. Müller eds., *Historikerlexikon: Von der Antike bis zum 20. Jahrhundert* (Munich 1991) 128.

Calvocoressi, P., *Freedom to Publish* (Stockholm 1980) 43–44.

Ćirković, S., "Historiography in Isolation: Serbian Historiography Today", *Helsinki Monitor*, 1994, special issue: 37.

Dedijer, V. ed., *Tribunal Russell: Le jugement de Stockholm* (Paris 1967) 19–20.

Djordjević, D., "Historians in Politics: Slobodan Jovanović" (originally 1973), in: W. Laqeur & G.L. Mosse eds., *Historians in Politics* (London/Beverly Hills 1974) 253–56, 259, 262, 266–71.

———, "Yugoslavia: Work in Progress", in: W. Laqueur & G.L. Mosse eds., *The New History: Trends in Historical Research and Writing since World War II* (New York 1967) 254.

Drachkovitch, M.M., "The Shaping of a Balkan Scholar: The Background, Youth, and Education of D.V. Djordjević", in: R.B. Spence & L.L. Nelson eds., *Scholar, Patriot, Mentor: Historical Essays in Honor of Dimitrije Djordjević* (New York 1992) 1–5.

Goldstein, I., "The Use of History: Croatian Historiography and Politics", *Helsinki Monitor*, 1994, special issue: 88–94, 96.

The Guardian, 8 September 2000: 16 (Koštunica).

Hayden, R.M., "Recounting the Dead: The Rediscovery and Redefinition of Wartime Massacres in Late- and Post-Communist Yugoslavia", in: R.S. Watson ed., *Memory, History, and Opposition under State Socialism* (Santa Fe 1994) 173–78, 181–82.

———, "The Use of National Stereotypes in the Wars in Yugoslavia", in: A. Gerrits & N. Adler eds., *Vampires Unstaked: National Images, Stereotypes and Myths in East Central Europe* (Amsterdam 1995) 213–14, 221.

Held, J., *Dictionary of East European History since 1945* (Westport 1994) 454–55, 495.

Hoeven, H. van der, *Lost Memory: Libraries and Archives Destroyed in the Twentieth Century*, part 1, *Libraries* (WWW-text 1996) i, 18.

Holland, G., "War Damage to Art Works and Monuments in Bosnia-Herzegovina and Croatia", *Common Knowledge*, 1995, Fall: 9–23.

Human Rights Watch, *Deepening Authoritarianism in Serbia: The Purge of the Universities* (New York 1999) 14.

––––––, Letter, Committee for International Academic Freedom to President Slobodan Milosevic, 16 February 1993.

Ifex Communiqué, 13 April 1999: 1.

Index on Censorship, 1/72: 91; 2/72: 144–46; 3–4/72: 127; 1/73: xv–xvi; 2/73: 62; 3/74: 76; 4/74: [no page]; 2/75: 97; 4/76: 59–60, 62, 65; 1/77: 66; 5/77: 49–52; 2/78: 65; 5/78: 79; 4/79: 70; 2/80: 75; 3/81: 20–22, 80; 2/82: 23; 6/83: 48; 3/84: 49; 4/84: 24–25, 37–38; 6/84: 49; 1/85: 64–65; 2/85: 57; 3/85: 24–26; 6/85: 51, 1/86: 3–4, 36; 7/86: 46; 9/86: 52; 1/87: 41, 51; 4/87: 40; 6/87: 41; 7/87: 41; 5/88: 35–36; 2/92: 19; 6/92: 41; 10/92: 48; 3/96: 116; 3/98: 54–58; 3/99: 95, 114.

International Who's Who 1996–97 (London 1996) 1565.

Kaiser, T., "Archaeology and Ideology in Southeast Europe", in: P.L. Kohl & C. Fawcett eds., *Nationalism, Politics, and the Practice of Archaeology* (Cambridge 1995) 114, 116–17.

Keesings historisch archief, 2000: 276.

Kolanović, J., "Archives en temps de guerre: L'Expérience de la Croatie", *Archivum*, 1996, no. 42: 173–80.

Kovačević, M., "War Damage Suffered by the State Archive of Bosnia and Herzegovina", *Archivum*, 1996, no. 42: 181–86.

Kozar, A., "War Destruction of Archival Materials", *Janus*, 1999, no. 1: 92–95.

Limqueco, P., P. Weiss, & K. Coates eds., *Prevent the Crime of Silence: Reports from the Sessions of the International War Crimes Tribunal Founded by Bertrand Russell* (London 1971) 369.

Lipstadt, D., *Denying the Holocaust: The Growing Assault on Truth and Memory* (originally 1993; Harmondsworth 1994) 7.

Maletić, F. ed., *Who Is Who in Croatia* (Zagreb 1993) 351, 771.

Marès, A. ed., *Histoire et pouvoir en Europe médiane* (Paris 1996).

Marjanović, V., "L'Historiographie contemporaine serbe des années 80: De la démystification idéologique à la mystification nationaliste", and "L'Histoire politisée: L'Historiographie serbe depuis 1989", both in: Marès ed. 1996: 144, 147–59, 161, 165–66, 168, 285–86, 290, 293–96, 298, 300–304, 306–7.

Marlowe, L., "Destroying Souls", *Time*, 8 August 1994: 38–43.

Mihailović, K., & V. Krestić eds., *Memorandum of the Serbian Academy of Sciences and Arts: Answers to Criticisms* (Belgrade 1995).

NRC-Handelsblad, 4 December 1996: 5 (Koštunica).

Pavlowitch, S.K., "Dedijer As a Historian of the Yugoslav Civil War", *Survey: A Journal of Soviet and East European Studies*, 1984, no. 3: 97–99.

––––––, "L'Histoire en Yougoslavie depuis 1945", *Vingtième siècle*, 1988, no.17: 84, 86–90.

––––––, *The Improbable Survivor: Yugoslavia and Its Problems 1918–1988* (London 1988) 129–42.

––––––, personal communication, July 1999.

Petrov, K.V., "Memory and Oral Tradition", in: T. Butler ed., *Memory: History, Culture and the Mind* (Oxford 1989) 81–84.

Petrovich, M.B., "Slobodan Jovanović (1869–1958): The Career and Fate of a Serbian Historian", *Serbian Studies*, 1984–85, nos. 1–2: 14–22.

Phillips, J., "How to Invent a Nation", *Living Marxism*, March 1992: 33.

Ramet, S.P., *Nationalism and Federalism in Yugoslavia, 1962–91* (Bloomington/Indianapolis 1992) 202–3.

Roksandić, D., "L'Historiographie croate après 1989", in: Mareš ed. 1996; 274, 280–81.

Schöpflin, G. ed., *Censorship and Political Communication in Eastern Europe: A Collection of Documents* (London 1983) 170–72.

Shelah, M., "Croatia", in: I. Gutman ed., *Encyclopedia of the Holocaust*, vol. 1 (New York 1990) 325–26.

Skilling, H.G., *Samizdat and an Independent Society in Central and Eastern Europe* (Oxford 1989) 199.

Smrekar, A., & S. Bernik, "The Endangered Monuments of Croatia", *New York Review of Books*, 21 November 1991: 23.

Stallaerts, R., & J. Laurens, *Historical Dictionary of the Republic of Croatia* (Metuchen 1995) 217–18.

Stanković, S., "Article Condemns Persecution of Intellectuals", *RFE Research*, 21 February 1986, 1: 7–9.

———, "The Serbian Academy's Memorandum", *RFE Research*, 28 November 1986, II: 7–11.

Stroynowski, J. ed., *Who's Who in the Socialist Countries of Europe* (Munich 1989) 228.

Šuster, Z.E., *Historical Dictionary of the Federal Republic of Yugoslavia* (Lanham/London 1999) 103–6, 239, 312–13.

Tanner, M., *Croatia: A Nation Forged in War* (New Haven/London 1997) 191.

Vodopivec, P., "L'Historiographie en Slovénie dans les années 80", and "L'Historiographie slovène 1989–1994", both in: Mareš ed. 1996: 129, 133, 269.

Vucinich, W.S., "Postwar Yugoslav Historiography", *Journal of Modern History*, 1951: 41–42, 44–46, 50, 52, 56–57.

Woolf, D.R. ed., *A Global Encyclopedia of Historical Writing* (New York/London 1998) 210, 496–97, 825–26.

World University Service, *Academic Freedom 3* (London 1995) 182, 184.

Zukin, S., "Sources of Dissent and Nondissent in Yugoslavia", in: J.L. Curry ed., *Dissent in Eastern Europe* (New York 1983) 134–35.

Z

ZAIRE

See Congo.

ZAMBIA

1980–   In December 1980 **Robert Papstein**, lecturer in African history at the Free University of Amsterdam and former lecturer at the University of Zambia, was not allowed to do fieldwork in Chavuma. In 1979 he had coedited a book by Luvale author **Mose Sangambo**, *The History of the Luvale People and Their Chieftainship* (Los Angeles 1979), which challenged the historical views of the Lunda on the authenticity and antiquity of their senior chief, Ishinde. The book's publication led to an increase of tension between Luvale and Lunda, resulting in blocked roads, suspension of government services, house burnings, beatings, and a resurrection of ethnic animosity unknown in the district since the 1950s. The Lunda saw the book as a dangerous Luvale attempt to control Chavuma and sought to have the book banned, confiscated, and burned. Part of Papstein's research was directed toward preparing a new, expanded edition of Sangambo's book. After long deliberations between the district governor, the Luvale and Lunda delegations, and Papstein, his research was permitted on a limited scale and in a restricted part of Chavuma.

1982   In April **Susan Heuman** (1941–), former lecturer at Brooklyn College, City University of New York (until 1974), visiting fellow at the Russian Institute of Columbia University, New York, expert in Russian and Soviet history at the University of Zambia, Lusaka, was picked up from the press gallery of the high court and questioned after she had greeted two defendants in a long-running treason trial. She was released after a few hours.

In late October the Thames Television series based on **Elspeth Huxley**'s novel, *The Flame Trees of Thika*, was withdrawn by Zambian state television after five of the seven episodes had been shown. The head of Zambian Broadcasting reportedly said that the series had a colonial bias and portrayed the Africans in a bad light.

SOURCES

Index on Censorship, 4/82: 48; 1/83: 22–23, 48.
Papstein, R., "From Ethnic Identity to Tribalism: The Upper Zambezi Region of Zambia, 1830–1981", in: L. Vail ed., *The Creation of Tribalism in Southern Africa* (London 1989) xiv, 372, 388–89.

ZIMBABWE

Southern Rhodesia

After the emergence of the Rhodesia Front government in 1962, several historians went into exile and others were deported or imprisoned. A federal project to write the history of Southern Rhodesia, Zambia, and Nyasaland (Malawi) collapsed. The publications of the Central African Historical Association were exposed to censorship and history books from abroad were banned. Much material relating to African history and to the activities of Africans was removed from the files open to the public at the National Archives, an interference glossed over by recataloging. Fieldwork became nearly impossible. Archeologists who supported the thesis of the African origin of the Great Zimbabwe ruins ran a risk.

1960s   **(John) Richard Gray** (1929–), historian, research fellow (1961–63), reader (1963–72), and professor (1972–89) at the School of Oriental and African Studies, London, attempted to follow up Donald Abraham's work on Shona oral history but was prevented from entering the African areas and eventually from revisiting Southern Rhodesia. In 1957 he had not been appointed as history lecturer at the newly established University College of the Rhodesias and Nyasaland because of his nationalist sympathies; Ranger [q.v. 1961–63] was appointed in his stead. Later Gray became the editor of *The Cambridge History of Africa*, vol. 4, *1600–1790* (Cambridge 1975).

1961–63   In September 1961 some lay members of the Council of the University College of the Rhodesias and Nyasaland insisted on taking action against British historian **Terence Ranger** (1929–), who was history lecturer there (1957–63), after he had been involved in sit-in campaigns against the color bar in the capital, Salisbury. As a National Democratic Party member, Ranger actively supported African nationalism. According to Ranger, the government began to censor his publications and sent spies to his classes. In [September] 1962 he was served with a restriction order. He was barred from entering the African rural areas (which partly prevented his historical research). In March 1963 he was deported. He pursued his career at University College, Dar-es-Salaam, in the newly independent Tanganyika/Tanzania (1963–69), at the University of California, Los Angeles (1969–74), and at the universities of Manchester (1974–87) and Oxford (1987–97). His 1967 history of the ChiMurenga (the Shona name for the 1896–97 uprisings), *Revolt in Southern Rhodesia 1896–97: A Study in African Resistance*, reportedly inspired the blacks to compare the revolt with their own uprising against the Rhodesian regime after its 1965 Unilateral Declaration of Independence. Consequently, the book could not be reprinted until after 1980, when a black government came to rule the country, renamed Zimbabwe, and Ranger was again allowed to visit there. In addition, the book was reportedly used as a textbook in counterinsurgency by the Rhodesian army. Some of the files at the National Archives of Southern Rhodesia that Ranger used were removed from open access.

1962– Among the group of historians who either could not or did not wish to return after 1962 were **Lewis Gann** (1924–), in 1978 senior fellow at the Hoover Institution, Stanford University; **Ian Henderson** (1934–), in 1978 principal lecturer in history and politics, Lancaster Polytechnic, United Kingdom; **Robin Palmer** (1940–), in 1978 senior history lecturer, University of Zambia; Ranger [q.v. 1961–63]; **David Kwidini**; and Samkange [q.v. Rhodesia 1968–].

Rhodesia

1968– In 1968 historian **Stanlake Samkange** (1922–88), journalist, novelist, publisher, politician, and Secretary-General of the African National Congress for many years, who obtained a doctoral degree at Indiana University, Bloomington, United States, had his book *Origins of Rhodesia* banned. While in exile he taught African history at various American universities. In 1978 he was professor of African-American Studies at Northeastern University, Boston.

1970– Two archeologists, **Roger Summers**, employed by the National Museum (1947–70), and **Peter Garlake** (1934–), senior inspector of monuments for Rhodesia (1964–70), resigned and left Rhodesia because they could reportedly no longer work under the Rhodesian

Rasmussen, R.K., & S.C. Rubert, *Historical Dictionary of Zimbabwe* (Metuchen 1990) 293, 318.

Ross, R., "The Politics of Tradition in Africa", *Groniek*, September 1993: 51.

Slater, H., "Dar es Salaam and the Postnationalist Historiography of Africa", in: B. Jewsiewicki & D. Newbury eds., *African Historiographies: What History for Which Africa?* (London/Beverly Hills 1986) 253, 260.

Trigger, B.G., "Alternative Archaeologies: Nationalist, Colonialist, Imperialist", *Man*, 1984: 362–63.

———, *A History of Archaeological Thought* (Cambridge 1989) 3, 134–35.

Ucko, P., *Academic Freedom and Apartheid: The Story of the World Archaeological Congress* (London 1987) 3.

Vansina, J., *Living with Africa* (Madison 1994) 115–16, 124.

Woolf, D.R. ed., *A Global Encyclopedia of Historical Writing* (New York/London 1998) 760–61.

Person Index

Subject Index

About the Author

ANTOON DE BAETS is Professor of Contemporary History at the University of Groningen in the Netherlands and was employed by Amnesty International's Publications Bureau in Costa Rica. He has published in seven languages, mainly on historical popularization and censorship of history. He is on the International Advisory Committee for a forthcoming three-volume work, *Censorship: A World Encyclopedia* (2001), and he coordinates the Network of Concerned Historians.